An Agenda for Economic Reform in Korea

Kenneth L. Judd and Young Ki Lee, Editors

An Agenda for Economic Reform in Korea

International Perspectives

Hoover Institution Press Stanford University Stanford, California

Korea Development Institute Seoul, Korea

The Hoover Institution on War, Revolution and Peace, founded at Stanford University in 1919 by Herbert Hoover, who went on to become the thirty-first president of the United States, is an interdisciplinary research center for advanced study on domestic and international affairs. The views expressed in its publications are entirely those of the authors and do not necessarily reflect the views of the staff, officers, or Board of Overseers of the Hoover Institution.

http://www.hoover.org

The Korea Development Institute (KDI) is a policy-oriented research organization founded in 1971 by the Korean government to provide comprehensive analyses and recommendations on government policy in areas ranging from domestic economic affairs to international economic cooperation.

http://kdiux.kdi.re.kr

Hoover Institution Press Publication No. 465

First printing, 2000

Manufactured in the United States of America

06 05 04 03 02 01 00 9 8 7 6 5 4 3 2 1

The paper used in this publication meets the minimum requirements of American National Standard for Information Sciences—Permanence of Paper for Printed Library Materials, ANSI Z39.48-1984.

Library of Congress Cataloging-in-Publication Data
An agenda for economic reform in Korea : international perspectives
Kenneth L. Judd and Young Ki Lee, editors.
p. cm.
Includes bibliographical references and index.
ISBN 0-8179-9732-6
1. Korea—Economic policy. 2. Korea—Economic conditions—1945–
I. Judd, Kenneth L. II. Lee, Young Ki.

HC467 .A627 2000
338.95195—dc21 00-037001

Contents

Contributors

DONG-SE CHA, President LG Academy; Former President, Korea Development Institute

ROBERT E. HALL, Professor of Economics, Stanford University; Senior Fellow, Hoover Institution

KENNETH L. JUDD, Senior Fellow, Hoover Institution

SUNG HEE JWA, President, Korea Economic Research Institute; Former Senior Fellow, Korea Development Institute

DAE IL KIM, Professor of Economics, Seoul National University; Former Research Fellow, Korea Development Institute

EDWARD P. LAZEAR, Professor, Graduate School of Business, Stanford University; Senior Fellow, Hoover Institution

HYEHOON LEE, Research Fellow, Korea Development Institute

JOUNG-WOO LEE, Professor of Economics, Kyungpook National University

JU-HO LEE, Associate Professor, KDI School of International Policy and Management; Former Research Fellow, Korea Development Institute

KYE-SIK LEE, Head, Government Reform Office, Ministry of Planning and Budget; Former Senior Fellow, Korea Development Institute

YOUNG KI LEE, Senior Fellow, Korea Development Institute

PHILLIP WONHYUK LIM, Research Fellow, Korea Development Institute

YOUNGJAE LIM, Research Fellow, Korea Development Institute

THOMAS MACURDY, Professor of Economics, Stanford University; Senior Fellow, Hoover Institution

THOMAS GALE MOORE, Senior Fellow, Hoover Institution

SANG-WOO NAM, Professor, KDI School of International Policy and Management; Former Senior Fellow, Korea Development Institute

JOHN V. C. NYE, Professor of Economics, Washington University in St. Louis

SHERWIN ROSEN, Professor of Economics, University of Chicago; Senior Fellow, Hoover Institution

HENRY S. ROWEN, Senior Fellow, Hoover Institution

KENNETH SCOTT, Senior Fellow, Hoover Institution; Professor of Law Emeritus, Stanford University

SEONG-HYEON WHANG, Professor of Economics, Inchon University; Former Research Fellow, Korea Development Institute

SUSAN E. WOODWARD, Former chief economist, United States Securities and Exchange Commission; consultant, Cornerstone Research

SEONG MIN YOO, President, Youido Institute; Former Senior Fellow, Korea Development Institute

Acknowledgments

The editors would like to thank the authors of the chapters for their hard work. They have more than fulfilled our requests to consider serious issues of economic reform in Korea and the United States. We are also grateful to the Korea Development Institute and the Hoover Institution for their generous financial support of this project. The Hoover Press, led by Pat Baker and Ann Wood, has done an excellent job in putting the authors' work into a book. Finally, we thank John Raisian and the Hoover Institution staff for their hospitality in hosting the conference "An Agenda for Economic Reform in Korea: International Perspectives," where these papers were presented and discussed.

Kenneth L. Judd and Young Ki Lee

Introduction

The papers in this volume were presented at "An Agenda for Economic Reform in Korea: International Perspectives," a conference cosponsored by the Korea Development Institute and the Hoover Institution. It was held January 15–16, 1997, at the Hoover Institution, in Stanford, California, USA. As the title of the conference suggests, the experience of the United States with economic reform provided a much needed international perspective for the Korean participants at the conference. Similarly, the conference gave American participants an opportunity to examine their ideas of economic reform in a different context.

Less than a year after the conference, Korea was hit by a currency crisis, and the world's eleventh largest economy had to apply for the stewardship of the International Monetary Fund. Hence the publication of this volume at this time may appear to be a case of crying over spilt milk. However, many of the reforms recommended in this volume have been implemented in the financial, corporate, public, and labor sectors to restructure the nation's economic system into a full-fledged market economy compatible with global standards. So the main theme of this volume remains valid. Ironically, however, no one would deny that were it not for the crisis, Korea's comprehensive reforms might not have been possible due to the resistance of vested interest groups.

It is hoped that this volume will show how the Korean model of economic development has led to impressive economic performance but has also generated a moral hazard problem of gigantic proportions. Emphasizing that the cozy tripartite relationship linking the government with big business and banks needs to be broken up, this volume offers a new vision for the Korean economy.

The volume is divided into eight topics, each of which is examined from both the Korean and the American perspective. The first topic is a general overview of the two economies. Dong-Se Cha and Sang-Woo Nam provide an overview of Korea's past economic performance and offer a new vision for the Korean economy in the twenty-first century. The authors note that although Korea's state-led development strategy has made compressed economic growth possible, it has also left unfortunate legacies such as undue concentration of economic power, inadequate social services, and strained industrial relations. The authors suggest that Korea should strive to create a mature civil society fundamentally based on a full-fledged market economy but complemented by effective social safety nets.

Robert E. Hall and Susan E. Woodward present an overview of the American economy. They document the high level of output in the U.S. economy and discuss the features of the U.S. economy that have contributed to American economic performance. A critical feature of the American economy is that many transactions that in other economies occur within firms, or among closely related firms, occur between firms in the U.S. For example, many Korean firms receive loans from closely related banks whereas American firms rely more on a competitive and open capital market to raise capital. In general, disputes that occur within firms or chaebols would be handled within such organizations. Hall and Woodward argue that the more disconnected nature of the American economy makes the American legal system important in resolving disputes among firms. Any economic reform that breaks up close relationships among firms will need to consider the burden it may put on the legal system.

Our second topic is the problem of economic concentration and economic regulation. Seong Min Yoo and Youngjae Lim critically review the debate on the so-called "chaebol problem" and make policy recommendations in light of new empirical findings. They note that chaebols are expected to play a major role in industrial restructuring and to continue to be the engines of growth for the Korean economy in the foreseeable future, and caution that drastic policies such as artificially breaking up chaebols are neither feasible nor desirable. Instead, they argue, chaebol policy should be directed toward strengthening competition and enhancing efficiency through market liberalization.

Economic concentration has also been a concern of American economic policy makers during much of the twentieth century. In "Issues in Regulatory Policy," Thomas Gale Moore reviews efforts to regulate business activity. Government regulation was initially aimed at preventing monopoly power, but it has grown to concern itself with safety, health, and environmental concerns. Moore documents the tendency of many regulatory agencies to go too far, often producing regulations that impose economic costs far in excess of any possible benefits.

Our third topic concerns problems in corporate governance, the rules by which corporations govern themselves. Young Ki Lee and Youngjae Lim observe that distortions in the Korean corporate governance system have resulted from a cozy tripartite relationship between the government, big business, and banks. The government's control of banks, its intervention in the exit market for conglomerates (perpetuating the "too big to fail" myth), moral hazard by conglomerates and banks, and serious agency problems between controlling shareholder-managers and outside shareholders all reduce economic efficiency. Lee and Lim argue that an overhaul of this tripartite relationship is essential to economic reform. In particular, they recommend the reform of the corporate governance system, including enhanced transparency, liberalization of the market for corporate control, strengthening shareholders' rights, normalization of the role of the board of directors, and strengthening the role of institutional investors in monitoring and disciplining corporate management.

Kenneth Scott presents an outline of the basic issues behind problems of corporate governance. He also reviews the great variety of corporate governance structures across countries, showing how, in particular, the American, German, and Japanese systems, though they differ greatly, all appear to be successful. He argues that the focus should be on creating mechanisms that encourage corporate officers to put resources where they have the most economic value, and that remove those officers if others can better manage the corporation.

Any modern economy needs to develop social welfare policies. In "A Korean Model of Social Welfare Policy: Issues and Strategies" (Part IV), Hyehoon Lee and Kye-sik Lee propose a new model of social welfare policy for Korea. They take into account the lessons learned from the experience of developed countries as well as social changes and challenges faced by Korea at the moment. As basic principles for constructing the Korean model of social welfare, the authors suggest balancing growth and welfare, balancing the private- and public-sector roles, preventing the need for welfare, and making the best use of traditional Korean culture.

Thomas MaCurdy's paper, "What Programs Make Up the U.S. Welfare System?" describes social welfare policy in the United States and shows how recent reforms have helped to improve what has long been a patchwork of confusing and poorly coordinated programs. MaCurdy's description of past and current welfare policy illuminates the many problems in creating an effective welfare system that addresses policy goals.

Many are concerned with the distribution of income and the challenges income inequality presents for economic policies. In Part V, "Distribution of Income," Seong-Hyeon Whang and Joung-Woo Lee provide an empirical analysis of changes in income and wealth distribution in Korea since the 1980s. They note that significant inequality in wealth distribution and frequent lack of transparency in the resource allocation process have led to a generally negative view on distributive issues in Korea. They argue that the reinforcement of a property-related tax system, including strengthened inheritance and gift taxation, and the institution of checks and balances to increase the transparency of corporate governance are crucial to resolving distributive problems in Korea.

Kenneth L. Judd offers a general perspective about economic change and income inequality. He points out that there is no clear way to view income inequality. Some income inequality is natural, arising from freely made personal decisions. If one individual decides to earn more income by working more hours but his neighbor prefers to enjoy more leisure, it is unclear why we should be unhappy about the resulting income inequality. On the other hand, we have a very different view if income inequality arises because the government provides educational opportunities for members of one race but not for another. Also, economic change often involves changes in the distribution in income. Economic policy makers often try to undo these changes, but they need to worry about the impact of such policies on technological changes and economic growth. Judd outlines the general issues involved in economic policy making, the forces of economic change and growth, and the likely trends in income inequality.

A key ingredient to any healthy economy is a well-operating labor market (Part VI). "Changes in the Korean Labor Market and Future Prospects" presents an empirical analysis of the Korean labor market. The authors, Dae Il Kim and Ju-Ho Lee, show that market forces, rather than union power, have been the main determinant of labor market outcomes in Korea. Although there is some evidence that industrial relations have had some impact, Kim and Lee show that this has been limited to a few large firms whose near-monopoly rents have been targeted by labor unions. They emphasize that in addition to labor market reforms, product market liberalization and deregulation are crucial for enhanced flexibility of the economy.

Edward P. Lazear and Sherwin Rosen provide a broad perspective of labor issues in "Labor in a Global Economy." They discuss recent trends such as the increasingly important role of women and international trade in labor markets. They also analyze the importance of various government regulations on unemployment and wages.

The last two topics of our volume touch on broad institutional and cultural issues. The most important institution in capitalist economies is property. In "Property Rights and Economic Behavior: Lessons for Korea's Economic Reform," Sung Hee Jwa provides a neoinstitutional analysis of Korea's economic development, focusing on the relationship between property rights and transactions costs. He suggests that Korea is a relatively high transaction cost country with relatively insecure property rights, where legally defined rights are often weakly enforced. From this observation, he develops an interesting argument regarding the behavior of the chaebols. A number of notorious practices associated with the chaebol, such as closed and family-controlled management, excessive diversification, and overexpansion, may be partly or wholly the result of defensive measures taken against the government stemming from the insecurity of property rights.

John V. C. Nye's "Economic Growth and Institutions: What We Think We Know vs. What We Pretend to Measure" examines the difficulties of studying institutional issues. Economic data are often imprecise, and there are many aspects of an economy for which we have no measurements. Nye contrasts the conclusions of institutional perspectives about economic growth and what statistical analyses say.

The final two papers (Part VIII) deal with broad cultural issues. Dong-Se Cha and Phillip Wonhyuk Lim's "In Search of a New Capitalist Spirit for the Korean Economy" provides a historical analysis of the origin and development of the capitalist spirit in Korea. The authors examine the interaction between cultural and institutional factors that have served as a driving force behind Korea's economic development and have created the problem of so-called pariah capitalism in Korea. As they note, strong political leadership committed to economic development has successfully established capitalist institutions in Korea and has remolded the traditional values of loyalty to the nation and devotion to the family into Korea's equivalent of the Protestant ethic in the West. But they also point out that Korea's state-led model of economic development has created a legitimacy problem for Korean capitalists owing to lack of transparency in the resource allocation process, and they emphasize that in order for the Korean economy to escape from the trap of pariah capitalism, transparency and legitimacy in the acquisition and disposal of wealth should be enhanced and all economic players should assume responsibility commensurate with their freedom.

Henry S. Rowen surveys recent economic history in "Societies, Politics, and the Rise of East Asia." He describes the critical ingredients in economic growth and discusses how they apply to the rapid growth of East Asia. He also contrasts their success with the less successful experiences elsewhere in the developing world.

It is our hope that this collection of articles will help to illuminate the similar problems of economic reform that face all economies, even economies as different as those of Korea and the United States. As the world becomes more and more a global marketplace, and as Korea continues its rapid economic growth, the differences between these two economic powerhouses will shrink. This convergence will allow each to learn from the experience of the other. This volume aims to contribute to that learning process.

Part I

Overview

Dong-Se Cha and Sang-Woo Nam 1

The Korean Economy in Transition

Legacies and Vision for the 21st Century

The Korean economy has achieved an unprecedented growth in the last three decades or so. Between 1965 and 1995, the per capita GNP increased from US$105 to over US$10,000. The share of agriculture in GDP decreased from 38 percent to less than 7 percent during this period, while exports recorded a substantial increase, from US$0.2 billion to US$123 billion with 70 percent accounted for by heavy and chemical products. And life expectancy rose from 57 years to 71 years.

Many different elements have contributed to Korea's rapid economic growth. The first is a literate population capable of learning skills quickly—which played a key role in export-oriented (labor-intensive) industrialization during the earlier phases of development. Korea achieved universal primary education as early as the mid-1950s; later, in response to the steady upgrading of the industrial structure, vocational and technical education and training were strengthened, and college student quotas were greatly increased. In the Confucian tradition, Korean parents are willing to make sacrifices for the education of their children, and workers have been industrious and disciplined in their drive to improve their socioeconomic status.

Second, Korea has had a strong leadership commitment to economic development and capable, devoted bureaucrats. The number one promise of the military government of General Chung Hee Park, which came into power by a coup in 1961, was, "We will liberate people from poverty." Delivering this promise was the only way to justify and consolidate the legitimacy of the regime. Civil servants were and are generally well respected (again, a Confucian characteristic), and the bureaucracy was able to attract people who were not only capable and devoted, but also relatively scrupulous. With the success of government-initiated economic progress, public confidence in the government has been strong in Korea.

A third element has been the ambitious entrepreneurs. Though not well respected by people in general, who tend to believe that they accumulated their wealth by means of government favors such as exclusive import licenses and preferential loans, Korean entrepreneurs have proved themselves to be very dynamic and forward looking. They have aggressively exploited overseas markets for trading, local construction, and, more recently, investment. Domestically, Korean business groups have diversified extensively into a number of industries and have dominated in many markets, particularly manufacturing. In spite of high market concentration, the groups have maintained a competitiveness that has been favorable to consumers. With the diversification of business risk, entrepreneurs have been bold and effective in technology and manpower development, thereby generating positive externalities for the society.

Finally, and perhaps most important, Korea's economic performance owes much to government policies. The takeoff of the Korean economy began with the export-oriented industrialization strategy in the early 1960s. This strategy enabled Korea to make the best use of its available resources, mainly labor, and overcome the limitation of the small domestic market. In the 1970s, the emphasis on heavy and chemical industries, although it had some not altogether happy side effects, significantly contributed to upgrading Korea's industrial and export structure. Policy emphasis after the 1980s shifted to promoting the role of the market in resource allocation by reducing direct government intervention and fostering competition (see Table 1).

This strategy of export-oriented industrialization enabled the Korean economy to have an admirable takeoff in the early 1960s. Entering the 1970s, an unfavorable external environment led Korea to undertake heavy and chemical investment projects in order to upgrade the export structure and strengthen defense capabilities. Credit, tax, trade, and exchange rate policies were heavily distorted by the government to favor some sectors against others. At the same time, government intervention proved to be very costly to the economy, particularly because of the worldwide recession caused by the second oil price shock. Many favored projects continued to decline, the financial sector remained weak and inefficient, and rapid increases in bank loans accelerated in-

TABLE 1 Performance of the Korean Economy, 1965–1995

	1965	*1975*	*1985*	*1995*
GNP ($ billion)	3.0	20.9	91.1	451.7
Per capita GNP ($)	105.0	594.0	2,242.0	10,076.0
GNP growth (real, %)		9.1	7.4	8.9
Industrial structure (%)				
Agr., forestry, & fishery	38.0	24.9	12.5	6.6
Manufacturing	18.0	25.9	29.3	26.9
Services	41.9	47.6	57.1	66.2
Commodity exports ($ billion)	0.2	5.0	26.4	123.2
Total exports/GNP (%)	9.5	28.0	35.3	33.7
National savings rate (%)	13.2	18.1	29.8	36.2
Foreign savings rate (%)	0.2	−8.9	−0.9	−1.9
Tax burden/GNP (%)	8.6	15.4	17.5	20.6
Consumer price inflation (%)		13.7	12.1	5.8
Exchange rate (won/$, year-end)	273.0	484.0	890.0	775.0

flation. In reaction to these setbacks major policy efforts in the 1980s, including strong antiinflation programs, reform of the industrial incentive system, trade liberalization and financial liberalization, were largely successful in correcting macroeconomic imbalances and strengthening the industries.

During the mid-1980s, a favorable external environment, particularly the strong Japanese yen, resulted in rapid export growth and a sizable surplus in the current account. The surplus, however, invited strong foreign pressure to further open the domestic market and drove up the Korean won. The historic June 29 Declaration of Democratic Reform in 1987 unleashed workers' demand for wage increases and better working conditions. Substantial wage hikes coupled with strong domestic demand and progress in import liberalization have worked together to lower Korea's current balance. A sense of crisis has recently become widespread among Koreans. Many small and medium-sized firms in light manufacturing have gone bankrupt because they could not compete with products from China and other developing countries in either domestic or foreign markets. For their survival, some have moved their factories offshore. With the weakening Japanese yen, as well as a deteriorating world market for semiconductors, steel, and petrochemicals, exports stagnated in 1996 and early 1997. The current account deficits in 1996 reached almost 5 percent of GDP.

Korea's vision for the next few decades is to achieve an advanced economy and a unified nation. In realizing these objectives, it faces some stiff challenges: weakening competitiveness in the midst of global competition, growing burdens to bear for improvements in the quality of life, and the road to reunification with North Korea. Along with these challenges, there will be promising opportunities from new markets, enhanced technological capabilities, and other efficiency improvements.

This paper describes the legacies of Korea's development strategies since the early 1960s. Then, it discusses the challenges and opportunities Korea faces and the strategies being adopted to realize its vision for the twenty-first century.

Legacies of Past Decades

Korea's development strategies, either explicit or implicit, during the last several decades have largely shaped the characteristics of the Korean economy and economic management. Among the characteristics are (1) preoccupation with growth and less concern with social development; (2) concentration of economic power around large business groups, which generally weakens the position of small and medium-sized firms; (3) immature industrial relations; (4) a weak financial sector, the development of which has been constrained in the government drive for industrialization; (5) regional concentration of industries; and (6) government-initiated development with a multitude of regulations that continue to restrict business activities. Among these, the first three seem to be of the greatest consequence in determining the nature of the Korean economy.

CONCENTRATION OF ECONOMIC POWER AND CORPORATE GOVERNANCE

With the extensive diversification of their business interests, large business groups *(chaebols)* in Korea were able to be aggressive in developing new products and markets and undertaking other risky projects. The chaebols have been efficient in overcoming the principal-agent problem, since the chairman (owner-manager of the group) closely monitors the managerial performances of the member corporations. With shared information, know-how, and resources among member firms, chaebols also had a better chance to adjust to changes in the factor markets and expand their economies.

There has, however, been increasing concern over the concentration of economic power in the chaebols. Not only is there fear that the concentration of economic power could lead to increased political power and distort government policies, the failure of chaebols could also be costly in terms of moral hazards and sacrifices of the financial sector. Second, many chaebol-affiliated corporations often have a market-dominating power, which, together with their extensive business diversification, draws them into practices that constrain fair competition and abuse conflicts of interest for the benefit of the entire group. Third, chaebols may infringe on the interests of smaller firms and minor stockholders. With cross-repayment guarantees and shareholding among member corporations, chaebols tend to limit the access of smaller firms to credit and dividend receipts for small stockholders. Finally, many analysts have serious doubts about the internal efficiency of chaebols. Cross-subsidization among member corporations is likely to cause inefficient allocation of resources, and managerial control concentrated in the chairman often leads to rigidity, red tape, and the absence of any countervailing power to check the dogma and authoritarianism of the owner-manager.[1] (Table 2 shows the concentration of ownership in the thirty largest chaebols, 1981–1995.)

On the whole, Korea frowns on the mix of banking and commercial businesses, believing that this mix (for example, chaebols owning banks) would lead to concentration of economic power with undue influence over the political process, conflict of interest abuses, and instability in the financial system. These are valid concerns when entry into financial services is restricted or banking services have any subsidy elements. Even when financial markets are competitive and allow free entry, the mix of banking and commercial products increases the likelihood of conflicts of interest if the firm has market power in the commercial product. It is probable, however, that the opening of the domestic markets and industries, including banking, to the world, will make it increasingly difficult for any firm to have market-dominating power. Thus, the risk of mixing banking and commerce should not be as serious as before.

A related corporate governance issue is the bank-business relationship. Unlike Japanese main banks or German house banks, Korean

1. In June 1994, the five largest chaebols had 42 subsidiary firms on the average operating in 30 different (two-digit Korean Standard Industrial Classification) industries. For the 30 largest chaebols, the subsidiaries averaged 21, operating in 19 industries.

TABLE 2 Industry Concentration and Ownership, 30 Largest Chaebols

Industry concentration (mining & manufacturing, %)			
Year	*Shipments*	*Value-added*	*Employment*
1981	39.7	30.8	19.8
1985	40.2	33.1	17.6
1988	35.7	30.4	16.9
1990	35.0	30.0	16.0
In-group ownership (%)			
Year	*Total in-group*	*Family*	*Member firms*
1987	56.2	15.8	40.4
1990	45.4	13.7	31.7
1993	43.4	10.3	33.1
1995	43.3	10.5	32.8

SOURCE: Fair Trade Commission.

banks do not have an intimate relationship with their corporate clients. Japanese main banks reduce information asymmetry by serving as the leader of loan syndication and as the delegated monitor for other creditor banks. Mutual shareholding between main banks and their corporate clients is an important feature of the Japanese main bank system. When a firm is in financial distress, its main bank, as both creditor and shareholder, may also intervene in corporate management. However, being basically exclusive and secretive, the main bank relationship also has elements of inefficiency and unfairness.

Korea's principal transactions bank system was introduced to correct the skewed allocation of bank credit toward chaebols. The principal transactions banks, implementing the credit control system and other regulations of the government toward large business groups, have functioned as de facto suborganizations of the supervisory authorities. Given that Korean financial markets are still far from being perfect, with large information asymmetries, the role of banks as credit evaluators and monitors of corporate management could be critical. Thus, a closer and more autonomous bank-client relationship may be promoted by eliminating institutional constraints and improving the policy environment that has suppressed the development of such a relationship.

INADEQUATE SOCIAL DEVELOPMENT AND DISTRIBUTIVE INEQUALITY

In spite of significant improvement in the people's standard of living over the last three decades, it is widely perceived that social development has lagged behind economic growth in Korea. This gap between economic growth and social development is primarily due to Korea's development strategy of putting the highest priority on growth and the belief of the leadership that creating jobs is the best welfare. Because limited resources have been allocated with a view to maximizing short-run results, the share of government expenditures for social development, including health, housing, and social security and welfare, is still very low.

Industrial accident insurance and public assistance programs were in existence even in the 1960s, but the expansion of the social security system has been slow. An extensive medical insurance scheme was introduced in 1977, and in 1988 a national pension system and a minimum wage regulation were put into place. Employment insurance was introduced in 1995. All these programs have to be further broadened and integrated to reach the most needy people and to redress the lack of cohesion and harmony among them.

The slow development of the social security system in Korea has been due in part to traditionally strong family ties. Korean parents make great sacrifices to give their children a good education, with the implicit expectation that the children will take care of them later on. This strong sense of solidarity based upon an extended family concept has acted in the stead of public social security programs. Mutual aid is also provided among brothers and sisters, who are often ready to help each other in times of hardship or emergency. But this East Asian Confucian ethic of placing great emphasis on the family rather than on individuals is now on the ebb. With growing industrialization and urbanization, the modern family in Korea is typically a small nuclear family, and many parents can no longer rely on their children for security in their old age. This change calls for a substantially enhanced role for the social security system in Korea.

The experiences of advanced countries show that, once a welfare program has been put into place, it is very difficult to reduce its benefit level. The ambitious pursuit of a welfare state may weaken people's motivation to work and the dynamism of the private sector, and accordingly adversely affect the vitality of the economy. In Korea especially, a greatly expanded social security budget would be not only an exorbitant fiscal burden on the government but also a social wedge—it could deepen intergenerational conflict and weaken family solidarity and the spirit of mutual aid in local communities. Therefore the great challenge is to develop a balanced social security and welfare system that is consistent with social equity and economic efficiency but also preserves desirable long-held family and communal values.

The distribution of income in Korea is relatively equitable compared with that of most developing countries. As Table 3 shows, in the 1960s particularly, the export-oriented development strategy seems to have contributed to equitable income distribution through the rapid absorption of surplus labor from rural areas into labor-intensive urban manufacturing. This favorable trend was interrupted during the period of heavy and chemical industry promotion in the 1970s, when heavily subsidized credit provided mainly to chaebols and other large firms widened wage disparities and led to drastic rises in rents and real estate prices.

The available data for the 1980s are largely inconclusive or show some improvement.[2] In any case, income distribution becomes very unequal when imputed rental values to the ownership of dwellings as well as capital gains on land and equity stocks are included. Most crucial for the moderation of "perceived inequality" by the people, there-

TABLE 3 Distribution of Income and Land Ownership, 1965–1988

	Income distribution (%)		
Year	*Bottom 40%*	*Top 20%*	*Gini coefficient*
1965	19.3	41.8	0.344
1970	19.6	41.6	0.332
1976	16.9	45.3	0.391
1980	16.1	45.4	0.389
1985	17.7	43.7	0.345
1988	19.7	42.2	0.336

		Land ownership (1993, %)		
Top 5% (1%)	*6–10%*	*11–20%*	*21–30%*	*31–100%*
50.6 (27.9)	12.8	15.2	8.9	12.5

SOURCES: Choo (1992); Economic Planning Board; Hyun (1995).

2. Surveys by the Economic Planning Board (EPB) indicate a marked improvement in income distribution between 1980 and the second half of the 1980s. Kim and Ahn (1987), however, find income distribution worsened slightly, with the Gini coefficient increasing modestly from 0.39 in 1980 to 0.41 in 1982 and 1985. The Gini coefficient calculated from the 1988 EPB survey is 0.34; that from the Korea Development Institute (KDI) survey in the same year shows a much more unequal distribution of 0.40.

fore, is the stabilization of real estate prices, preferably by deregulating rigid rules on land use and strengthening property and inheritance taxation. Other steps toward more equitable income distribution might include tackling such problems as inordinate concentrations of corporate ownership, the poor quality of public school education and the disproportionate private spending on education, and inadequate supplies of low-cost housing. Firmly establishing the newly introduced "real name system" for financial and real estate transactions would also go a long way toward reducing corruption and improving distributive equity.

IMMATURE INDUSTRIAL RELATIONS

Following the June 29, 1987, Declaration of Democratic Reform, the government made sweeping reforms in labor laws that strengthened basic labor rights and stressed the autonomous resolution of labor disputes between labor and management. Nevertheless, the transition from the old repressive industrial relations regime to a new framework has not been smooth. Although union organization and labor strikes increased rapidly, the initial response of the government was largely that of laissez-faire, owing in part to ambiguity and inconclusiveness in the interpretation of the new laws.[3]

In early 1990, for the purposes of law and order, the government issued administrative guidelines concerning the legal interpretation of labor matters in frequent dispute. Most of these guidelines were criticized as being biased toward management: unions were forbidden to conduct political strikes, and third-party sympathy strikes and strikes for wage back pay for the strike period were made illegal. In the midst of deteriorating economic conditions, especially for the export sector, public sentiment, however, was generally in favor of these government initiatives. After a peak in 1987, labor disputes have shown a steady decline (Table 4), the result not only of the tougher government stance on enforcing labor laws and regulations but also of accumulated experience in labor negotiations and the generally poor performance of the economy.

Nevertheless, Korea's industrial relations seem to have a long way

3. Between June 1987 and December 1989, the number of organized establishments jumped from 2,735 to 7,861, and the organization rate (the ratio of membership to permanent employees in the nonagricultural sector) rose from 14.7 percent to 23.3 percent. The number of strikes also increased sharply, to over 3,600 in the second half of 1987.

TABLE 4 Union Membership and Labor Disputes, 1982–1995

Year	*Membership (in thousands)*	*Organization rate (%)*	*Number of unions*	*Number of disputes*	*Labor loss (1,000 man days)*
1982	984	19.1	2,194	88	11.5
1985	1,004	15.7	2,534	265	64.3
1987	1,267	17.3	4,068	3,749	6,947
1989	1,932	23.3	7,861	1,616	6,351
1991	1,803	19.7	7,656	234	3,271
1993	1,667	17.2	7,147	144	1,308
1995	1,615	15.3	6,579	88	392

SOURCE: Ministry of Labor.

to go. Although the worst is over, there is still a deterioration of work discipline and morale and a weak sense of participation or attachment to companies, and Korean employers on the whole are viewed as unwilling to allow union constraints on their authority. Some of the roots of the paternalistic and authoritarian nature of Korean management may lie in the Confucian culture: management has often resisted union recognition and dismissed union leaders, inviting violence. Nor is the high concentration of ownership in large business enterprises, whose unions have generally been most militant, a positive factor. The government's heavy-handed intervention is also largely responsible for management's failure to promote cooperation with unions. When the government is ready to intervene to prevent or break up labor disputes, management has no incentive to deal seriously with the union and establish a working relationship.

Since government guidance and control are no longer very effective, the primary sources of future growth must lie in voluntary participation and creative initiatives in the private sector. For Korean firms, which must continually restructure themselves toward more value-added and knowledge-based industries in order to survive, highly motivated, committed, and creative employees are indeed the most essential asset. Obviously, such an environment is antithetical to antagonistic labor relations with frustrated, alienated, uncooperative, and disloyal employees.

No less important than labor peace for Korean firms is labor market flexibility. The tendency of increasing rigidity in the labor market should be checked so as not to constrain smooth restructuring of businesses. Furthermore, because the rural sector is no longer a large source of labor in Korea, it is imperative to rely more on older citizens and women. Currently their participation in the labor market is very low, but could be encouraged by flexible terms of employment. Certainly greater flexibility in the labor market will help stabilize wages and tend to reduce unemployment in the long run.

The revision of labor laws in March 1997 was mainly geared to this policy objective. These changes allow companies to lay off workers if management finds it imperative to do so (from 1999), and to set up flexible work hours or extended work hours. The changes also allow political activities by unions, third-party intervention, and multiple unions at the nationwide federation level as well as at single work sites (from 2002). Also, employers are not allowed to pay for full-time union officials (from 2002).

Another possible solution to labor problems is that of social partnership with the labor community. In an effort to moderate rapid wage increases after the Democratic Reform in 1987, there have been some attempts to establish a tripartite wage council, or round table, representing labor, management, and public interest. So far, these efforts have not been very successful, owing to continuing mistrust, lack of labor leadership at the national level as well as that of individual firms, and complicated wage structures. Given that the government's one-way wage guidelines have largely been ineffective, broad-based policy consultations with laborers at the national level may be worth further efforts. With continued rapid wage increases unlikely, labor unions would also be able to maximize the long-term welfare of workers by actively participating in the decision-making process of macroeconomic management and social policy issues.

Challenges and Opportunities

The major challenge for the Korean economy in the coming decades is how to cope with changing external environments such as borderless global competition and the prospect of reunification on the peninsula. Domestically, challenges include enhancing competitiveness by stabilizing the high costs of doing business and improving the quality of life without placing excessive burdens on the economy. The major opportunities for Korea are emerging markets like China and other transforming economies, and the expected results of such ongoing efforts as enhanced technological capabilities and the reorganization of public and financial sectors for greater efficiency.

CHALLENGES AHEAD

Global competition in an integrated world economy. With the launching of the World Trade Organization (WTO), the world economy is now more closely integrated, and countries face stiffer global competition. As new rounds make progress in the areas of labor, competition, environmental, and research and development policies, the world economy will witness a deep integration through the standardization of domestic policies. In a deeply integrated global economy, though production wings and corporations move across national boundaries with fewer restrictions, there still remain more specialized features, such as sociopolitical systems, public service, social infrastructure, land, and unskilled labor. It is essential for attracting high-quality mobile factors (both domestic and overseas), and improving national competitiveness, to upgrade the quality of these less mobile factors. Excessive regulations will cause high-quality productive factors to shy away from Korea, and the regulations themselves will become increasingly ineffective.

With Korea's acceptance into the Organization for Economic Cooperation and Development (OECD), we need to increase the opening of markets for agriculture and services, including the capital market. Although market opening will eventually help to enhance competitiveness, a critical task is how to manage this process in such a way as to keep damage to domestic industries at a tolerable level. The opening of the capital market, particularly, gives rise to potentially serious complications in macroeconomic management. Korean firms can benefit from mobilizing low-cost overseas capital, but a large capital inflow will bring strong pressures of inflation and exchange rate appreciation.

Weakening competitiveness with high costs. The recent decline in competitiveness among industries is causing concerns about the lessening growth potential of the Korean economy. Wages are high compared to income levels and labor productivity. Small and medium-sized firms are suffering from a severe shortage of labor and capital. The high cost of borrowing is squeezing corporate profits. Another critical disadvantage facing Korean firms is the cost incurred by traffic congestion, as well as exorbitant prices for land and rent. The level of technology is not high enough to compensate for these disadvantages.

Unless these costs and bottlenecks are significantly eased, Korean industries will find it difficult to strengthen their competitiveness internationally. Entering the twenty-first century, we can expect a sharp drop in the growth of the labor force owing to a stagnant population by the year 2020. For that reason, more women and the elderly will have to be brought into the labor market by allowing diversified work patterns, such as part-time, flexible-time, dispatched and home-based work, and temporary positions. Critical for reducing financing costs are steady financial deregulation and deceleration of inflation. Increased investments on social infrastructure and land development are also important.

The growing burden of improving the quality of life. As people's incomes reach a certain level (but do not increase as fast as before), they will be more interested in improving their quality of life. Currently, the housing situation is generally poor, and health care and medical services are inadequate. Recently, there have been rapidly growing concerns about environmental pollution and traffic congestion in large cities, highways, ports, and so on, and it is clear that expenditures, both government and private, in these areas will have to increase quickly, and that public assistance and other welfare programs will have to be expanded. In pursuing these endeavors, however, incentives for active participation in economic activities should not weaken. Efforts should also be made to avoid excessively burdening the government's budget and the economy.

With the arrival of the pluralistic society, substantial progress is anticipated toward the decentralization of economic and social activities. Accordingly, Korean citizens will demand a greater participatory role in political life and democratic practices will be more firmly established. The challenge political parties and other systems will have to face is how to resolve the increasing number of conflicts of interest among different groups more effectively, while being more responsive to the voters' demands.

Reunification with North Korea. Without any prospects for ending its current economic predicament, the North Korean regime may not be able to remain in isolation. If North Korea establishes formal diplomatic relations with the United States and Japan, economic cooperation between North and South Korea will also deepen, and mutual trust is likely to be enhanced. Reformers in North Korea will then be able to secure stronger support within the regime to pursue bolder market-based reforms.

With mutual trust and cooperation firmly in place, North and South Korea may in time achieve a Korean National Community—separate political systems but a united economic system on the Korean peninsula. Yet before reunification can be realized, South Korea must take on the burden of helping the North develop its infrastructure, providing food and health care, financing reforms in education and training, taking on North Korea's foreign debts, and alleviating its many environmental problems. Perhaps a peaceful and gradual approach toward reunification is only an illusion, but certainly continued resistance to improving relations with the South and making market-based reforms will further aggravate socioeconomic problems in the North. It may disrupt the power group, which could lead to the sudden collapse of the North Korean regime. An influx of North Korean refugees across the border could also cause enormous social disorders and economic burdens.

MAJOR OPPORTUNITIES

There remain a number of major opportunities for the Korean economy—new markets for further exploration, and the enhancement of technological capabilities.

New markets. The launching of the WTO and the deepening integration of the global economy represent both a challenge and an opportunity. As long as our industries remain competitive, they will be able to reach overseas markets with fewer restrictions. This will be particularly significant when big neighboring countries like China join the WTO. Trade with China has expanded, making China the third-largest trading partner for Korea in 1996. By 2010, China (combined with Hong Kong) will compete closely with the U.S. for the world's largest trade, with a trade volume three to four times that of Korea.

Though latecomer developing countries will further weaken our competitiveness in light manufacturing, they will provide growing markets for Korean exports. Developing countries already account for a majority of Korea's total exports. In terms of future growth, the markets of Southeast Asian countries and such transforming economies as Russia and East Europe are the most promising, and it is to be expected that, together with accelerated efforts for structural adjustments toward higher value-added and more technology-intensive products, Korean industries will become more aggressive in seeking viable global cooperation strategies with firms in developing economies.

Fostering cooperation with the North should also be an opportunity for South Korean firms. Making the most of human resources and land in the North, Korea will be able to expand its scope of profitable businesses and exploit economies of scale.

Room for efficiency improvement. In spite of much effort directed toward efficiently managing the economy since the 1980s, many sectors remain untouched—notably, the public sector and the financial sector, which share the function of allocating resources among different activities and sectors. The public sector has direct control over 30 percent of the GNP and heavily influences the resource allocation of the private sector by means of various regulations and incentives. Further deregulation leading to lowered entry barriers, together with an appropriate reorganization of the government, will have a large impact on the efficiency of industries. Privatization of public enterprises and reform of their management environments are also essential. Korean financial institutions, particularly banks, have not handled their intermediary role efficiently. The government's industrial policy of using bank credit as a major policy tool has largely replaced the bank's role of credit screening. In order to protect the banking sector, which was burdened with providing subsidized policy loans, vigorous competition between banks and other financial intermediaries has been restricted, and financial liberalization has generally been slow. Regulations on interest rates and the types of services each financial intermediary can provide, fine guidelines on loan portfolios, and the government's de facto appointment of presidents of privately owned commercial banks, all served such a purpose.

Greater efficiency in these important sectors can open up more opportunities. The public sector has ample room for improving its efficiency by renovating its organization and incentives and by accepting capable experts from outside. We shall also see earnest financial restructuring, which cannot be postponed if the sector is to survive the opening and global integration of the market. The recent corporate drive for downsizing and other restructuring efforts indicate that there probably is much room for efficiency improvement in this sector as well. With rapid increases in the average number of years in school, the overall quality of the nation's workforce keeps improving. Also anticipated are improvements in the quality of education resulting from keener competition among schools and more diversified or demand-oriented education services.

Enhancement of technological capabilities. There is no doubt that technology is one of the most critical areas of future growth for Korea as well as for other newly industrialized economies (NIEs). In this respect, Korea has better prospects than the other Asian NIEs. Its major business groups invest heavily to upgrade their technological capability, aggressively pursuing licensing and other arrangements in order to acquire foreign technology and committing themselves to developing their own product models. However, because their competitiveness is still almost exclusively in end products rather than in specialty inputs, core components, and key production machinery, they find it difficult to compete in differentiated industry segments or to keep up with process innovations.

Only recently, owing to various changes at home and abroad, major Korean corporations have begun to make a transition from an imitative to a more aggressive approach. First, with latecomer developing countries chasing Korea, Korean industries have been forced to move to higher value-added and more technology-intensive segments in order to survive. Second, some of Korea's large corporations have accumulated the necessary capacity to expand their technology base through innovations in manpower, capital, and organization. Third, the size of the domestic market and export production have grown enough to allow minimum efficient scales of operation and to make new technology acquisition feasible. Finally, the external environment for technology acquisition has also improved, and it is now easier for Korean firms to enter into strategic alliances, to secure a technology base abroad, and to make an equity investment in foreign firms with advanced technologies. As these efforts pay off, Korean firms will begin to secure core competence, which is essential for enhancing competitiveness.

Vision and Strategies for the 21st Century

Our vision for the twenty-first century is to achieve a unified, advanced economy with an income level and quality of life comparable to those of other advanced nations.

In spite of rapid economic growth during the last thirty-five years, Korea's per capita GDP in 1995 remained at about $10,000. There are more than thirty countries whose per capita income is higher than that of Korea. Per capita income expressed in the U.S. dollar is, of course, not a good measure of people's purchasing power; still, Korea's per capita income is only one-third of the average income level for Japan, the U.S., Germany, and France, and a little over half that for Italy and the United Kingdom. Sustained economic growth is also desired for increased mobilization of national savings, which is essential for enhancing the quality of people's lives and for bearing the financial burden of reunification.

In the course of Korea's rapid economic growth, as limited resources have generally been allocated with a view to maximizing short-run results, quality of life and allocative equity have been relatively neglected. In spite of a relatively fast increase in budgetary commitment to social development, the share of public expenditures for health, housing, and social security and welfare compares unfavorably even with that of many developing countries. It is widely perceived that social development should catch up with economic growth in the coming years. Economic growth and social welfare or broader social development are largely complementary to each other.

Finally, the reunification of the Korean peninsula is perhaps the greatest task ahead. Korea had been a single united nation for twelve centuries until the Korean War divided the country, and there is no doubt that the Korean people yearn for reunification before the two sides become critically heterogeneous. Nevertheless, it was only a few years ago that the unification of North and South Korea seemed a real possibility. Obviously, the critical question is through what process and in what form reunification will come about. Even though the South cannot dictate the process and form, we shall have to make every effort to achieve a peaceful and economical reunification.

With all these challenges and opportunities, one can suggest major strategies for realizing this vision. First, adequate civil orders and socio-economic institutions required for a matured market economy should be firmly established. Most essential for this task are sound social and professional ethics and legal and judicial systems, an institutional environment ensuring fair competition, and sensible policies toward big businesses and smaller firms. Second, the growth potential of the economy should be sustained by enhancing the competitiveness of Korean industries. This will require stepped-up efforts in R&D, human resource development, improved infrastructure, and efficiency enhancement in the public sector. Third, much more attention should be paid to providing adequate social security and improving people's living conditions without overly burdening the economy. Finally, economic cooperation, both multilateral and bilateral, should be strengthened with an open domestic market and strenuous efforts toward reunification on the Korean peninsula.

A MATURED CIVIL SOCIETY

In the past three decades or so, the Korean government and people have been preoccupied with the efforts to emerge from poverty and achieve rapid economic advancement. In the process, Korean society has failed to cultivate social ethics and a proper capitalist spirit. Now that some measure of success has been achieved and incomes are improved, incentives for hard work seem to have declined.

Sound social ethics cannot be fostered without social fairness and justice. The skewed distribution of people's income and wealth, which is widely believed to be the result of government favors and rent seeking, has critically impaired work ethics. If equal opportunity is to be ensured to all economic agents, we must have a thorough review of current government regulations and support for various economic activities. Social justice should also be enhanced as legal protection becomes more adequate and all men become truly equal before the law.

Sustained economic progress will also depend very much on the professionalism and professional ethics of the workforce. Creative workers with technological know-how are the most valuable asset for the economy, and they should be encouraged to constantly improve their capability with a professional attitude. This is becoming increasingly more important as the labor market undergoes structural changes with rising female participation and higher job mobility.

Elite members of society in particular, including politicians, businessmen, academics, and journalists, need to enhance their accountability and professionalism. Journalism is expected to play a much more constructive role in raising public awareness of major social issues and guiding society in the right direction. An established social leadership will facilitate consensus building toward formulating more effective and timely solutions for emerging problems.

A FULL-BLOWN MARKET ECONOMY

A full-blown market economy will depend on changes in both government and the private sector, each relinquishing some power to achieve a common goal.

Promoting competition and the role of the private sector. With further economic progress, the role of the government will change significantly.

As witnessed as early as the 1970s, under the growing size and structural complexity of the economy along with accumulating experiences of businesses, the government lost its informational advantages vis-à-vis the private sector. This tendency seems to be more pronounced as the world economy deepens its global integration. Also, as the mobility of productive factors and economic agents increases, government regulations and controls are generally less effective. Thus, the government's future role will more and more be limited to creating a fair, open, and competitive environment in which the private sector can pursue its interests. In fostering open and fair competition, regulations concerning monopolistic behavior need to be strengthened, and merit should be the basis for competition instead of social, cultural, or educational background. In the democratization process, the government may be tempted to accommodate the demands of various interest groups in a discretionary way. To minimize this risk, emphasis should be put on "rules rather than discretion," and an intermediate to long-term perspective is needed in macroeconomic management.

Remaining restrictions on price and resource allocation will largely be lifted, and domestic regulations will gradually be reformed to meet international standards in such areas as trade, investment, and industrial support. Deregulation is particularly urgent for the financial sector, which has been sacrificed in an effort to support industrialization through subsidized credit.

Remedying the concentration of economic power. There has been a growing concern over the dominance of the chaebols in the Korean economy. Many people believe that the disproportionate economic (often market-dominating) power and extensive business diversification of chaebols could lead to their influencing the policy-making process and to the restriction of competition and conflicts of interest. It is also obvious that resource allocation could be distorted by chaebols both at the national level and within the group.

Chaebols grew rapidly during the heavy and chemical industry drive in the 1970s. Hoping to check further concentration of economic power, the government then introduced policies to limit bank credit to large chaebols, making it difficult for them to invest in other (or nonmajor) firms or to purchase real estate. Financial intermediaries have been obliged to maintain a portfolio with loans to small and medium-sized firms above a specified share. Many industries have been designated and reserved only for small and medium-sized enterprises

(SMEs). More recently, cross-shareholding and cross-repayment guarantees among member firms of a chaebol are regulated in order to protect the interests of small shareholders and other (potential) borrowers.

Most of these direct controls, however, unduly restrict corporate activities and should be phased out as changes in corporate environment work to ease both concentration and diversification. Without interest subsidies, protection from domestic and foreign competition, and bail-out practices for troubled firms, corporate incentives for expansion should weaken. Furthermore, instead of protecting SMEs from competition, government efforts will have to be directed toward helping them to overcome their managerial weaknesses and increase their ability to survive intensified competition. One such effort is to set up SME support centers and provide management consulting and information on technology, marketing, and other business aspects.

Ownership concentration and the management control of the major owner have also been a source of concern. Without clear evidence on how the corporate ownership-management structure affects corporate performance, however, rigid government policies in this area may be counterproductive. Meanwhile, mechanisms for checks and balances within a corporation will have to be established in order to enhance managerial transparency. These include strengthening the roles of external auditing and the board of directors and protecting the rights of small shareholders.

AN INTERNATIONALLY COMPETITIVE ECONOMY

Research and development. The future of Korean industries depends on how they can obtain "core competence" in their system of R&D, production, and marketing. In this effort, they will increasingly be globalized in the labor market, they will frequently form strategic alliances between corporations to share R&D expenses and hedge risks. In R&D activities, the critical task of building an efficient "national innovation system" will require the joint effort of the government, corporations, universities, and research institutes. The government's role would be to provide R&D infrastructures by establishing research facilities, information networks, and core groups of research staffs.

Human resource development and the labor market. Because knowledge-intensive industries are expected to lead future economic growth, human capital is a decisive factor in a nation's comparative advantage. The educational system should be reformed to produce workers better equipped with creative capacity and citizens with global perspectives. To this end, competition among suppliers of education will be encouraged with deregulation, more autonomy, and an incentive system that allocates financial support on the basis of performance evaluation. Rapid changes in technology and comparative advantages will require constant structural adjustments. To facilitate these adjustments and to accommodate changing conditions in labor demand and supply, the labor market should become more flexible. The training system needs to be reformed so that it responds more effectively to changes in the skills demanded. And because the growth of the labor force is expected to slow down substantially, constraints related to the participation of women, youths, and the elderly in the labor market will have to be eased. Dismissal of workers as part of a corporate reorganization effort should not be made overly difficult.

Social infrastructure. In spite of continued investments, the inadequacy of social infrastructure is hampering improvements in the quality of life as well as in the productivity of the industrial sector. Large infrastructure investments are also called for if Korea is to achieve its goal of becoming a hub country that connects the Northeast Asian continent and other Pacific-basin economies. Along with increased government expenditures, private sector participation should be actively pursued, not only because it would supplement the required capital but more importantly because, with its superior human resources and managerial expertise, it could provide better infrastructure services. Participation of foreign corporations and new financial arrangements, like project financing, would facilitate this change. An integral part of alleviating infrastructure bottlenecks includes heavier taxation on gas and efforts for more productive use of the existing infrastructure.

Efficiency of the government sector. The Korean government's low productivity is widely viewed as restricting the improvement of national competitiveness. The provision of public services should be customer oriented, and aimed at results, with specified goals for each ministry. Decentralized decision making on personnel recruitment and management, job assignment, and budget appropriation will also help. Another broad task is organizational restructuring. Pure policy-making units should be separated from the executive units that are responsible for implementing the policies. Some executive units could be transformed into independent business units or public enterprises, competing with the private sector on an equal footing. In budget appropriation, more flexibility will have to be ensured with the introduction of outcome-based budgeting, multi-year budgeting, and capital budgeting.

ADEQUATE SOCIAL SECURITY AND A PLEASANT LIFE

Living conditions in Korea at the present time are generally poor. Traffic congestion is serious, cities are becoming less safe, and the environment is deteriorating overall. Traffic congestion needs to be relieved by constructing more roads, improving traffic-related systems, and discouraging the use of private automobiles. The safety of urban life would improve with an efficient system of emergency management, systematic maintenance of public facilities, and more efforts at crime prevention. Finally, to halt the deterioration of the environment, stepped-up efforts have to be directed toward adjusting environmental standards, expanding sewage and waste-disposal facilities, and developing environment-related industries.

The government has expanded public assistance programs and has introduced social insurance programs such as health insurance, old-age pensions, and employment insurance. These are still inadequate, nor are the various social security schemes fully integrated. A new framework, the Korean welfare model, may be developed on the concept of a balanced welfare state while preserving and furthering traditional family values and neighborhood relationships. The challenge will be to avoid the pitfalls experienced by Western countries while creating a comprehensive welfare system. Incentives would be strengthened for those supporting their parents at home and neighbors providing welfare services under the coordination of the local communities.

Future welfare policies must also consider the well-being of the growing middle class. The most needed government support for middle-class households is reducing their spending on housing, private education, and medical services, all of which currently take up a large portion of their income. Policy priorities in this area should be the continued supply of new housing and reform of the public education system so that less money has to be spent on private education. Also, in response to the growing demand for leisure activities, more cultural centers, low-priced public sports facilities, recreational parks, and various tourist attractions should be created.

AN OPEN ECONOMY FULLY PREPARED FOR REUNIFICATION

Market opening and international economic cooperation. Since the export-based takeoff of the Korean economy in the 1960s, the market has maintained an outward orientation, and the opening of the domestic market to foreign goods and investment has served to promote competition. As a result, the exorbitant diversification and concentration of economic power by chaebols has lessened, and at the same time imports of cheap foreign products have helped to stabilize domestic prices and to increase consumer welfare. Foreign direct investment is an effective way of obtaining advanced technologies and other expertise. Korea should also support unconditional free international trade.

Korea will also actively participate in such international organizations as the WTO and OECD, which play an important role in shaping the world economic order by setting international standards, coordinating domestic policies of member countries, and settling disputes among nations. Multilateral forums should be preferred to bilateral dialogues in order to minimize the disadvantages of a weak bargaining position for a small open economy. Korea will develop stronger ties with less developed countries, particularly in Southeast Asia, whose resource endowment is complementary to Korea's with large market potential for Korean capital and intermediate goods. Such transitional economies as China, Russia, and East Europe also offer great potential for business opportunities.

Preparation for reunification. The greatest challenge for the country is, of course, the reunification of North and South Korea. Reunification is envisaged to come in three steps: the South first builds mutual trust and cooperation with the North, and then enters into a peaceful coexistence, and finally achieves reunification in the form of a Korean National Community. No one anticipates that reunification will come quickly; given the enormous disparities between the North's and South's political, social, and economic systems, as well as culture and values, a gradual approach seems more realistic. Furthermore, the sudden absorption of the North by the South with a large-scale influx of people would cause immense social and financial burdens. Nevertheless, South Korea should also be prepared for reunification if the North Korean regime were suddenly to collapse. How successfully South Korea can absorb the shocks will largely depend on the stability and efficiency of its political, economic, and judicial systems in addition to the maintenance of sound macroeconomic management, cushioned by government budgets and the balance of payments.

Economic cooperation is the best way to build mutual trust between North and South Korea. An agenda for closer economic cooperation includes diversification of projects to those with a larger economic impact (such as the construction of industrial complexes and social infrastructure) and those making the most of their economic complementarity, collaboration in overseas markets, and joint participation in multilateral cooperative organizations. Establishing necessary institutional arrangements is also essential; these may include settlement methods, investment guarantees, personal security, industrial property rights, dispute settlements, and avoidance of double taxation. In the absence of immediate threats to South Korea's security, economic cooperation should be consistently pursued separately from political issues; once destroyed for any reason, mutual trust is hard to rebuild.

REFERENCES

Cha, Dong-Se. 1988. "Korea Approaching a Developed Economy Regime." *Asian Industrialization: Changing Economic Structures,* vol. 1, Research in Asian Economic Studies. Stamford, Conn.: JAI Press.

Choo, Hakchung. 1992. "Income Distribution and Distributive Equity in Korea." Paper presented at UCSD–KDI Joint Seminar, San Diego.

Hyun, J. K. 1995. "Concentration of Land Ownership and Redistributive Effect of Aggregate Land Tax." Paper presented at the annual meeting of the Korea Tax Association.

Kim, D., and K. S. Ahn. 1987. *Korea's Income Distribution, Its Determinants, and People's Consciousness about Distribution Problems* (in Korean). Seoul: Jung Ang University Press.

Krause, L. B., and F. K. Park. 1993. *Social Issues in Korea: Korean and American Perspectives.* Seoul: Korea Development Institute.

Kwon, Soonwon. 1991. "Social Development Policy and Planning in Korea." Working Paper no. 9109. Seoul: Korea Development Institute.

Lee, Young Ki. 1995. "Corporate Governance: The Structure and Issues in Korea." Paper presented at the Conference on "Korea's Choices in Global Competition and Cooperations," East-West Center, University of Hawaii.

Leipziger, Danny M., David Dollar, Anthony F. Shorrocks, and Su-Yong Song. 1992. *The Distribution of Income and Wealth in Korea.* Washington, D.C.: Economic Development Institute, World Bank.

Nam, Sang-Woo. 1996. "The Principal Transactions Bank System in Korea and a Search for a New Bank-Business Relationship." In *Financial Deregulation and Integration in East Asia.* NBER-East Asia Seminar on Economics, T. Ito and A. O. Krueger, eds., 5:299–301. Chicago: University of Chicago Press.

———. 1994. "Institutional Reform of the Korean Financial System." In L. J. Cho and Y. H. Kim, eds., *Korea's Political Economy: An Institutional Perspective,* pp. 321–39. Boulder, Colo.: Westview Press.

Overview of the U.S. Economy

The economy of the United States is large and complex, but it differs from other economies, even large ones, in some important ways. In selecting topics that correspond to our interests in macroeconomics, public finance, law and economics, and financial economics, we have tried to convey both a sense of how economic life is organized in this country and why the United States has an economy that is remarkably successful, at least in comparison with economies in other places and other times.

We begin with a comparison of the U.S. economy with other economies of the world. The United States does well in this comparison—the country leads all others in output per worker, plant and equipment per worker, and education. It also does well in productivity, though a few countries are ahead in this area. We examine some of the general characteristics of the country that contribute to this success. The fact that the United States has an honest and effective government—in comparison with most other countries—emerges as a significant factor.

We describe the role of the government in the economy both in terms of its use of resources and in the way that the tax system and borrowing provide those resources. One primary reason for the success of the U.S. economy is its capital market. The United States relies much more heavily on the public trading of shares in the stock market than do other large, high-income countries.

Finally, we look at the structure of interactions of businesses made possible by the advanced legal system of the United States. The United States has network relations among separate companies, based on legal contracts, whereas other successful economies, especially in Asia, rely more heavily on large families of affiliated companies. In the United States, disputes are resolved with the assistance of lawyers instead of being handled within corporate families as they are in many other countries.

Comparing the U.S. Economy with Others

A good overall measure of the performance of an economy is its output per worker. Robert Summers and Alan Heston have developed data on output for about 150 countries, with careful attention to consistency across countries in measuring output. Figure 1 shows the distribution of output per worker across countries in 1988. To avoid distortion from small oil-producing countries, the measurement of output excludes the oil and mining industries.

The United States ranks first among the 149 countries in output

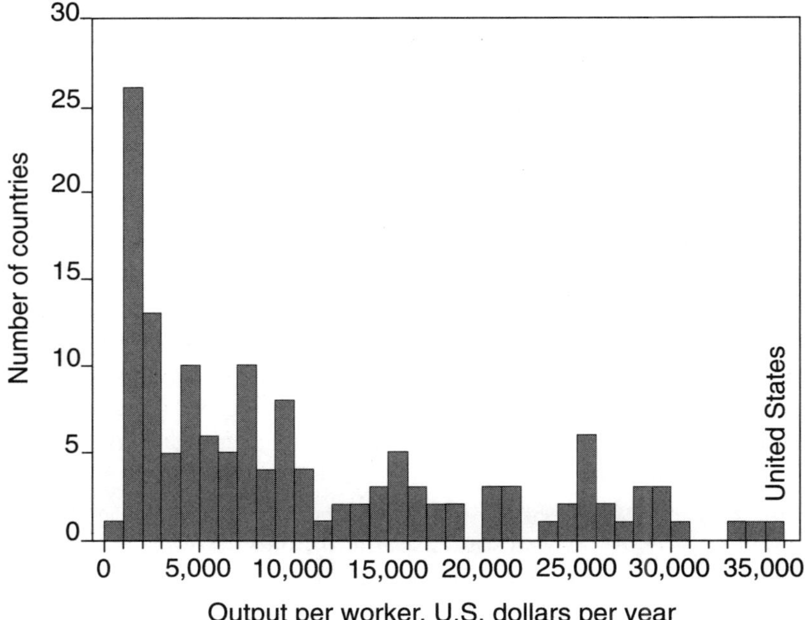

FIGURE 1 Distribution of output per worker across countries. Adapted from Robert E. Hall and Charles I. Jones, "Why Do Some Countries Produce So Much More Output per Worker Than Others?" *Quarterly Journal of Economics*, February 1999, pp. 83–116.

per worker. Not far behind are the advanced countries of northwestern Europe whose economies are similar to the U.S. economy. At the other end of the spectrum are countries such as Burma and Ethiopia, whose output per worker is about 5 percent of the level achieved by the United States and similar economies. In 1988, Korea ranked fortieth in output per worker out of the 149 countries in the study. It produced about 38 percent as much per worker as did the United States. Korea has grown much faster than other countries since 1988 and has moved up in the distribution.

Output per worker can be broken down into three determinants: physical capital (plant and equipment) per worker, human capital (investment in education and training) per worker, and productivity. Although the United States has frequently been criticized for low rates of capital formation, it leads all other countries in the amount of physical capital per worker. Because the United States has such a high level of output, even a modest fraction of output devoted to capital formation results in a high level of capital. Although the United States does not have as high a flow of investment as it did several decades ago, when its advantage in output level was even higher than it is today, it has sustained sufficient flows of investment to retain its position as the country with the highest level of capital per worker. The United States is also the world leader in human capital per worker. New Zealand, Canada, and Hungary are close behind.

The U.S. preeminence in output per worker is due not to production but to the extremely high levels of physical and human capital. A number of other countries, including Italy, Hong Kong, and Mexico, achieve higher levels of output per unit of total factor input; in a sense, they are outdoing the United States in that they get more output from the investments they have made in real and human capital. But because the United States has such a much higher level of both physical and human capital, it remains the country with the highest output per worker even though its productivity levels are not the highest. Table 1 compares data for a number of East Asian countries and United States.

Recent research has explored the relationship between output per worker and various quantitative determinants of output.[1] The determinants are measures of a country's social infrastructures and climates.

1. Robert E. Hall and Charles I. Jones, "Why Do Some Countries Produce So Much More Output per Worker Than Others?" *Quarterly Journal of Economics*, February 1999, pp. 83–116.

TABLE 1 Comparison of East Asian Economies with the United States

Country	*Output per worker*	*Capital per worker*	*Human capital per worker*	*Productivity*
	As a percent of the U.S. level			
Hong Kong	60.8	27.1	79.9	109.0
Singapore	60.6	61.0	58.0	102.7
Japan	58.7	72.5	82.3	74.4
Korea	38.1	27.9	82.0	66.4
Malaysia	26.7	27.2	63.2	56.0
Philippines	12.6	7.2	68.9	38.9
Indonesia	11.0	8.3	50.8	39.8
China	6.0	4.5	62.0	23.2

The measures of infrastructure are (1) an index of government policies that favor productive activities and discourage activities such as corruption that inhibit production, (2) an index of government policies that favor international trade, (3) a measure of the economy's reliance on private rather than government-operated productive enterprises, and (4) a measure of a country's affiliation with certain leading groups of countries through the speaking of a common language, such as Spanish or Arabic. Climate is measured by the distance of a country from the equator.

This research shows dramatic differences in output per worker associated with the measured determinants. An unambiguous finding is that economies with honest and effective governments, with policies favoring production and curbing the activities of organized crime, squatting, lobbying, corruption, and theft, will have much higher levels of output per worker. The difference in output per worker attributed to government effectiveness between the country with the most effective policies, Luxembourg, and the country with the worst policies, Liberia, is 240 percent. This dimension of policy is much more important than is the dimension of government-operated productive units against private enterprise. Although the countries with the very highest levels of output per worker are strongly capitalist, countries with effective governments achieve high levels of output even if many important industries are operated by the government. And countries with completely ineffective or malignant governments have low levels of output even if their economies are capitalist.

Countries that facilitate international trade tend to have much higher levels of output per worker than those with quotas, high tariffs, or other trade barriers. Not only does trade facilitate the acquisition of productive ideas from other countries, but policies favoring trade are a sensitive indicator of many other policies as well. Countries with policies that interfere with trade also tend to interfere with other aspects of production.

Countries with strong ties of language to other countries generally achieve higher levels of output per worker. The ability to engage in subtle commercial relations through a common language is one factor contributing to this advantage. Another is that countries with language ties tend to have common economic institutions, and the institutions associated with major international languages are more fully developed than others. Although the dissemination of successful British legal and other institutions through former colonies is a leading example of this phenomenon, the research finds that the advantages of international languages other than English are just as great.

Finally, a striking finding of the research is the large advantage in output per worker enjoyed by countries that are distant from the equator—countries with temperate climates. A Scandinavian country enjoys a level of output per worker between three- and fourfold (369 percent) higher than an equatorial country, after adjusting for all the other differences between the two countries.

All these factors help explain why the United States has such a high level of output per worker compared with other countries. The United States is not at the very top according to each measure, but it is at the very top in considering all the measures together. The factors that contribute to the advantage are as follows:

The United States scores well on measures of the honesty and effectiveness of government—only a few countries in Western Europe are rated above the United States in this respect.

The United States is in the top category with respect to trade policy. Not only are its trade barriers among the lowest in the world, it has also maintained a policy of relatively free trade throughout its history, so that it has accumulated the benefits of an open economy over a long period.

Thanks to its common language, English, the country participates in the benefits of easy interaction with other countries that are sources of innovation and favorable institutions, notably Great Britain.

And the country's temperate climate, relatively far from the equator, is a substantial advantage.

The Role of Government in the U.S. Economy

Government is an influential and important part of the U.S. economy and every other modern economy. Some functions are widely agreed to be the government's responsibility—national defense and law enforcement, in particular. Other programs, such as agricultural subsidies and national retirement programs, are found in almost every nation but are less widely agreed to be essential responsibilities of government. All around the world, including the United States, governments took on huge responsibilities over the past fifty years, so that government is at least a quarter of the economy in almost every country and in many countries is close to half the economy.

The United States is unique in its assignment of different government responsibilities to different levels of government. The federal level of government assumes responsibility for national defense, the U.S. national retirement program known as Social Security together with the old-age health care program, Medicare, and some income-transfer programs. Nearly all its revenues come from personal and corporate income taxes. State and local governments are responsible for nearly all law enforcement, education, various public welfare programs, and most local infrastructure, such as roads, water, and power. Some state and local revenues come from income taxes, but states and localities also rely heavily on sales and property taxes, with some states choosing greater reliance on sales taxes and others more on income taxes.

During the years since the end of World War II, the federal sector has remained fairly stable in the fraction of GDP that it consumes, but the state and local sectors have grown. Figure 2 shows the size and composition of state-local and federal government spending in the U.S. relative to total output, with federal expenditures broken out into military and nonmilitary spending.

Over the past fifteen years, citizens everywhere have questioned big government and have voted to decrease its size. But voters have been more enthusiastic about lower taxes than about reducing spending. As a result, large government deficits—shortfalls of revenue compared to

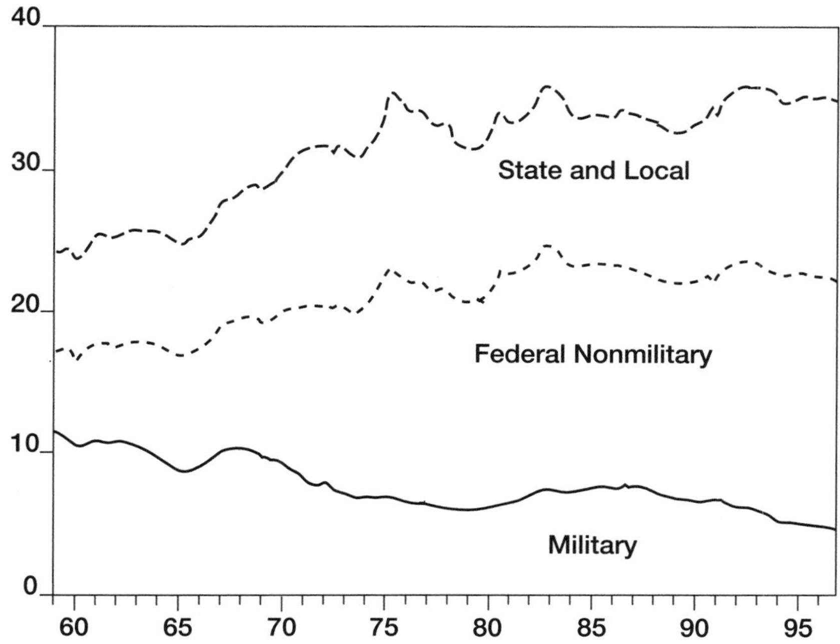

FIGURE 2 Categories of government spending as percents of GDP, 1960–1995.

spending—have been the rule around the world.[2] Until very recently the United States was a leader in this trend. A major tax cut enacted in 1981, plus a rise in defense spending, with little change in other spending, produced big deficits. The total debt owed by the U.S. federal government is now \$3.4 trillion. Citizens and U.S. financial institutions hold 70 percent of this debt; the other 30 percent is held by governments and individuals outside the U.S.

GOVERNMENT PURCHASES

The federal government absorbs resources from the private economy through its purchases of goods and services. To understand purchases, it is essential to divide them into military purchases and other purchases. In Figure 2, which shows the history of federal purchases

2. In the United States, this debt is all at the federal level. State and local governments may borrow (issue bonds) to build particular assets such as schools, dams, and roads, but they cannot borrow to finance current expenditures.

with this breakdown, one fact is immediately apparent: the federal government uses only a tiny fraction of national resources for any purposes other than defense. Nonmilitary purchases—the total payrolls of all federal agencies outside the Defense Department plus their purchases of buildings, equipment, and supplies—account for a stable, low 20 percent of GDP. Concerns about bloated federal bureaucracies and the growth of federal activities cannot be about the nonmilitary use of resources within the federal government.

Military purchases, as shown in the third line in Figure 2, reached a peak of 12 percent of GDP during the Korean War in the 1950s and then fell almost continuously to a level of 4 percent (1995). Two buildups interrupted the decline, one associated with the Vietnam War in the late 1960s and the other during the Reagan administration in the 1980s. Both were transitory. There is a debate today whether military spending can drop much below 4 percent without compromising the United States' position as the primary policeman of the world, but there seems little chance of another buildup rivaling the two shown in the figure.

The decline of military spending freed up resources amounting to 8 percent of GDP over the span shown in Figure 2. The decline in military spending in relation to GDP since the 1950s has made huge amounts of resources available for other purposes. Because military spending is now only 4 percent of GDP and probably cannot drop much further, there cannot be any similar flow of resources in coming decades.

This flow of resources eased many otherwise tough decisions about resource allocation in the economy. In particular, the flow made it easy for the federal government to provide huge increases in resources to some parts of the population, through transfers.

SOCIAL SECURITY AND OTHER TRANSFERS

Transfer programs provide benefits to people whom the federal government designates as needing help. Figure 3 shows the three major categories of transfers; they are roughly equal in size. Retirement benefits are the benefits provided by the social security system to retired people. Although the benefits are related to past contributions to the social security system, workers whose earnings are low receive benefits that are worth far more than their contributions. And after age seventy-two, even someone with no history of contributions will receive the minimum benefit.

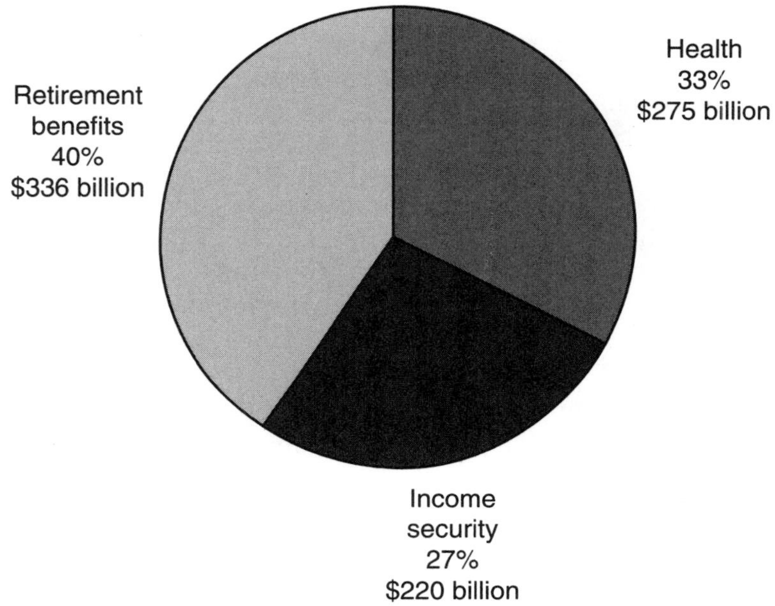

FIGURE 3 Federal transfer programs in 1995.

The second-largest category of transfers occurs in health programs. The social security system provides health benefits to everyone aged sixty-five and over through Medicare. This is a health insurance plan where people can go to any doctor they choose, as often as they want, and Medicare will pay 80 percent of the bills. Most people on Medicare have private supplementary insurance to pay the remaining 20 percent, so that the marginal cost of medical care to them is zero. While virtually all private medical insurance imposes some discipline on the use of doctors and other services, Medicare continues to be completely open ended. Reform of Medicare to reduce its rapidly growing cost has been proposed but little progress has been made so far. In addition to Medicare, the federal government finances state-operated health plans for the poor, often called Medicaid. The cost to the government of these programs, too, has been rising rapidly.

The third and smallest of the three categories of transfers is income security. These programs provide help to poor families. The largest by far is the food stamp program, which gives coupons or special credit cards to qualified families that are good only for buying food. Welfare payments, known as Aid to Families with Dependent Children, are also in this category, but are much smaller than food stamps.

All three categories of transfer programs have grown rapidly in recent decades, and as Figure 4 shows, these total transfer payments as a percentage of GDP have also risen. Growth was most rapid in the 1970s during the Nixon administration. During this period retirement benefits became much more generous, food stamps were introduced, Medicare expanded, and the welfare explosion began. Transfers remained high during the 1980s but did not increase in relation to GDP. Transfers are sensitive to the ups and downs of the economy. Noticeable bulges in transfers relative to GDP occur in recessions, as in 1974, 1981, and 1991, when the number of needy recipients rises and GDP falls.

TOTAL GOVERNMENT SPENDING

Federal spending has three components: purchases of goods and services, transfers, and interest on government debt. Figure 5 shows total spending in relation to GDP. There is a sharp increase in spending in each recession—this is the jump in transfers shown in Figure 4. Also visible are the increases in military spending for the Korean War in the 1950s and the Vietnam War in the late 1960s. Apart from these jumps,

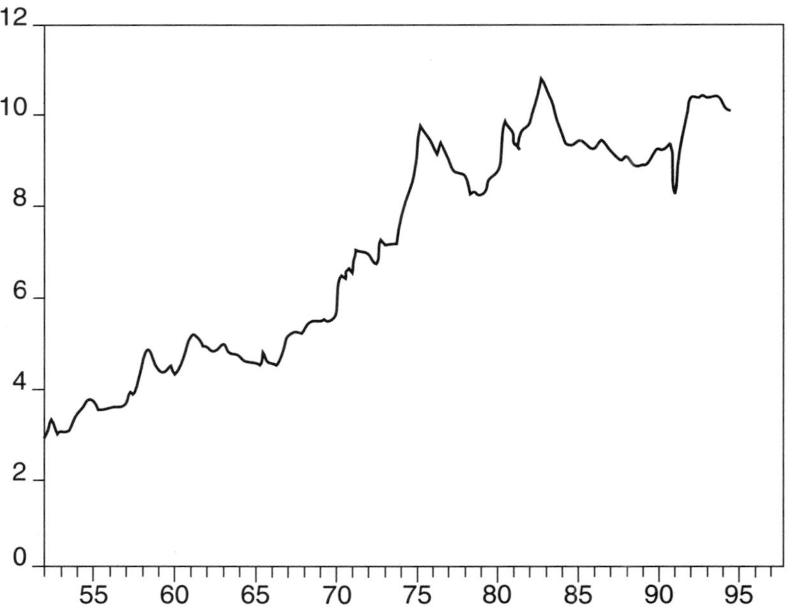

FIGURE 4 Federal transfer payments as a percentage of GDP, 1952–1995.

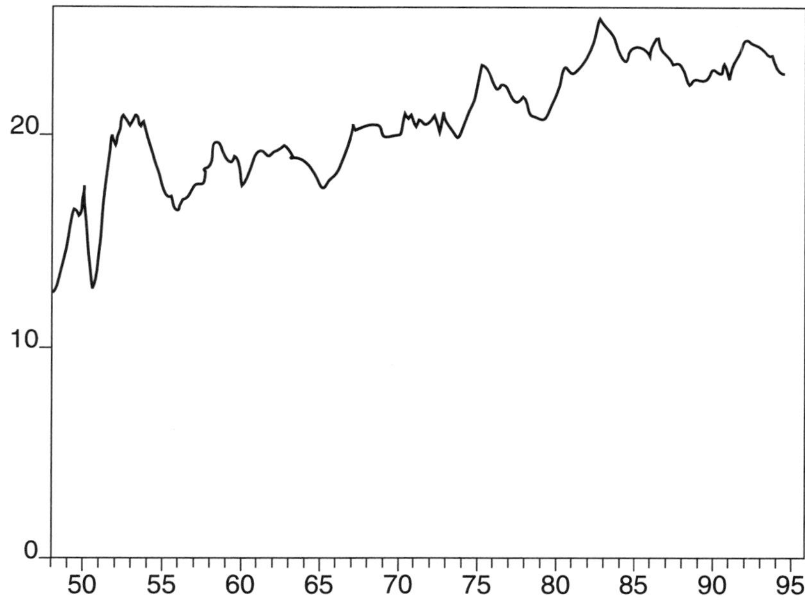

FIGURE 5 Total federal spending as a percentage of GDP, 1948–1995.

another fact stares out of the figure: federal spending as a percentage of GDP has been rising along a trend line. Although there was a large amount of publicity about scaling back the federal government starting in 1994, what shows in the figure is no more than the normal decline in spending when the economy is in good shape.

THE U.S. TAX SYSTEM

The federal government gets most of its revenue from two sources: the personal income tax and the Social Security tax. Table 2 breaks down the revenue from these and the other less important sources.

The personal income tax. Not only is the personal income tax the most important source of revenue for the federal government, it is also the most conspicuous and painful. Almost every adult has to file Form 1040 or one of its shorter cousins. One of the signs of success as an American is seeing your federal tax return swell to the size of a magazine. Proposals to reduce both the amount you have to pay and the complexity of the return are immensely popular.

The personal income tax is designed to be progressive; it seeks most of its revenue from prosperous families and excuses poor families from

TABLE 2 Sources of Federal Revenue, 1996

Source	*Revenue, billions of dollars*
Personal income taxes	652
Corporate income taxes	170
Social Security taxes	508
Excise taxes	54
Other sources	65
Total	1,450

SOURCE: Congressional Budget Office, *The Economic and Budget Outlook, August 1996*, Table 3.

paying any tax at all. Table 3 shows how the tax works on paper, for a family of four taking the standard deduction.[3] It shows the average tax rate, the ratio of the tax payment to the family's income. It also shows the marginal tax rate, that is, the additional tax paid on one more dollar of income. The marginal rate is what matters for incentives. The 40 percent that the federal government takes is a substantial reduction in the incentive that a successful person has to put in more work, to get additional training, or even to remain at work. In addition, someone facing a 40 percent marginal tax on taxable earnings has a strong incentive to seek to be paid in a way that is not taxed—either as untaxed fringe benefits or as under-the-table payments.

TABLE 3 The Personal Income Tax for a Married Couple

Income	*Tax*	*Average tax rate*	*Marginal tax rate*
$10,000	0	0%	0%
20,000	$518	3	15
30,000	2,018	7	15
50,000	5,018	10	15
75,000	11,296	15	28
150,000	33,472	22	31
250,000	68,964	28	36
400,000	127,534	32	40

Calculated from the 1995 Form 1040 Tax Table with the standard deduction of $6,550 and four exemptions.

3. The federal government allows households to deduct certain expenses (like medical care or the costs of moving to a new job) from their income before calculating the tax that they owe, or—alternatively—to deduct a standard amount from their incomes, regardless of their spending patterns.

Table 3 shows that progressivity and high marginal rates are related. If we want to excuse the poor from taxation, to put a low average tax rate on the middle class, and to collect a lot of revenue from those with high incomes, we cannot avoid putting high marginal rates on incomes above the middle-class level. Yet the entrepreneurs, scientists, and executives whose response to incentives may be most important for economic growth are likely to be in the high-income brackets, if they are successful. The tension between progressivity and high-income incentives has made the personal income tax unstable. In 1986, a new set of tax rates went into effect that taxed the highest incomes at only 28 percent, down from 50 percent the year before. By 1993, the desire for more progressivity had pushed the top rate back up to 40 percent.

From Table 3, one might project that the federal personal income tax would collect 15 or even 20 percent of people's incomes. After all, we know that the upper 20 percent of incomes account for over half of all income, and they are taxed at average rates of over 20 percent. But that projection would be wrong. The average rate actually collected from the federal personal income tax is only about 10 percent of total personal income. The tax system shown in the table does not do justice to the ways that people can avoid tax. Many people have deductions far above the standard deduction. And some people earn income that they never report to the government, and on which they avoid paying taxes entirely. People can shelter income in an employer's retirement plan or in a plan of their own. So both the revenue that the tax generates and the adverse effects of high marginal tax rates are less than they might seem from the table. Nonetheless, many economists feel that we would be better off with a tax that had a broader base—fewer opportunities for untaxed income—and lower rates. It could raise the same amount of revenue with fewer bad incentive effects.

The Social Security tax. The Social Security tax applies to wage and salary income only. It was put in place to finance the Social Security system when the system was created in 1936, and it has always been closely associated with the system. Generally, benefits paid to retired workers are about equal to the revenue from the Social Security tax.

Whereas the personal income tax is a nightmare of complex forms and rules, the Social Security tax is remarkably simple. It is currently 15.7 percent of payrolls. The only slight complication is that part of the tax is applied only to earnings below a ceiling of about $70,000 per year. While there is a huge amount of leakage in the income tax, there is amazingly little leakage in the Social Security tax. In 1995, the average rate of the tax—the ratio of revenue to total earnings in the economy—was 15.3 percent, just a hair below its official rate. Because lower-income families are excused completely from the income tax, though they pay the Social Security tax on all their earnings, the Social Security tax is actually the largest tax paid by many Americans. For example, the family with $30,000 of earnings in Table 3 pays $2,018 in federal income tax but $4,710 in Social Security tax.

What are the incentive effects of the Social Security tax? Part of the answer is easy. For people with higher incomes, above the ceiling of about $70,000, the marginal rate is less than 3 percent, so the disincentive to work harder because of added Social Security tax is slight.

For middle-class workers, the incentive effects are more complicated. Social Security has effected substantial income transfers from younger people to older people as the tax rate has risen and eligibility to receive benefits has been broadened. The program also involves some transfer from higher-income workers, who earn a lower implicit "rate of return" on their Social Security contributions, to lower income workers, who earn a higher rate. On the one hand, if earnings are below the ceiling, the taxpayer and employer pay $157 in added taxes for each $1,000 of additional earnings. That by itself would be a significant disincentive. But, unlike the income tax, the Social Security tax has some direct personal value. The government calls it a "contribution for social insurance." The retirement benefits depend, in part, on how much a worker has paid before retirement in Social Security taxes, and partly on how much the worker earns just prior to retirement. For some people, that extra $157 is buying several hundred dollars' worth of later benefits; for them, the effect of the Social Security system—taxes and benefits—may be a subsidy rather than a tax. Generally, workers who are subsidized have lower levels of earnings. Higher-earning workers face a substantial net disincentive from the Social Security system.

There is a growing movement to restructure the Social Security system to bring it closer to the kind of retirement system that more and more employers are offering. This type of retirement plan is called a 401K after the part of the Internal Revenue Code that makes them legal. In a 401K plan, workers are required to contribute a certain amount of their earnings to a personal retirement fund, but they can contribute even more if they want to. They have some choice in deciding how to invest their own funds, and, at retirement age, some choice in how to use the accumulated money to pay for retirement. If Social

Security were more like a 401K, it would solve two incentive problems that we have discussed. First, it would provide a much stronger incentive to save through Social Security, because it would link the benefits that people receive to the amount they saved. The current system pays generous benefits even to those who contributed only a little. Second, a close linkage of Social Security contributions to later benefits would eliminate the disincentive to work and earn income that currently prevails, especially for higher-earning workers. The government's term—contributions to insurance—would become an accurate description, and we would no longer talk about a Social Security tax. If Social Security were more like a 401K retirement plan, it would involve less redistribution of wealth and income. For higher-income workers, this is an advantage, and for lower-income workers, a disadvantage.

Other federal taxes. Table 2 shows that the federal government also collects about $300 billion from other taxes. The most important is the corporate profits tax, which raises $170 billion by taxing the profits earned by corporations at a rate of 35 percent. The tax is widely condemned by economists because of two important distortions. First, the tax applies only to corporations; it can be avoided completely by running a business as a partnership. The tax causes many businesses not to take advantage of the benefits of being corporations because of the extra tax they would have to pay. Second, the corporation tax puts a double layer of taxation on the portion of corporate profits that corporations pay to their owners: they pay once when the corporation is taxed, and again when the profits are included as part of their personal income. The corporation tax is thus a prime target for tax reform. Almost all reform proposals put forward by economists involve integrating the taxation of corporations into the tax system in a way that avoids these two distortions.

The federal government also imposes taxes on certain products such as gasoline, alcohol, tobacco, and air travel. These are called excise taxes. The tax on gasoline is in part a fee on drivers for the use of federal highways, though its revenue is far higher than the amount the government spends on highways. The taxes on alcohol and tobacco are intended to discourage consumption of these harmful products.

Trends in federal revenue. Figure 6 shows total federal revenue, from all the taxes we just discussed, as a percentage of GDP. Over the fifty years shown in the figure, revenue has been remarkably stable at around 20

FIGURE 6 Federal revenue as a percentage of GDP, 1946–1995.

percent. Although, as we shall see, there have been huge changes in the ways that the government collects its revenue and in the ways that it spends the revenue, the government's diversion of resources from private activities by taxation has been held by some invisible law at around 20 percent.

Figure 7 divides total federal revenue into two categories: Social Security taxes and all other taxes. There is a steady upward trend in the flow of resources into the Social Security system, while the other sources of revenue, led by the personal income tax, have declined just enough over the same period to keep total federal revenue at its stable level of 20 percent. Needless to say, there have been corresponding changes in spending and borrowing that lie behind this shrinkage of revenue outside the Social Security system.

It is clear from Figure 6 that federal revenue has hovered just below 20 percent of GDP for forty years, but the last time federal spending was as low as 20 percent of GDP was in the 1960s. Since then, the federal government has spent more than it has taken in. The upward trend in spending means that the shortfall has been worsening over time. This brings us to the critical issue of the deficit—the gap between spending and revenue.

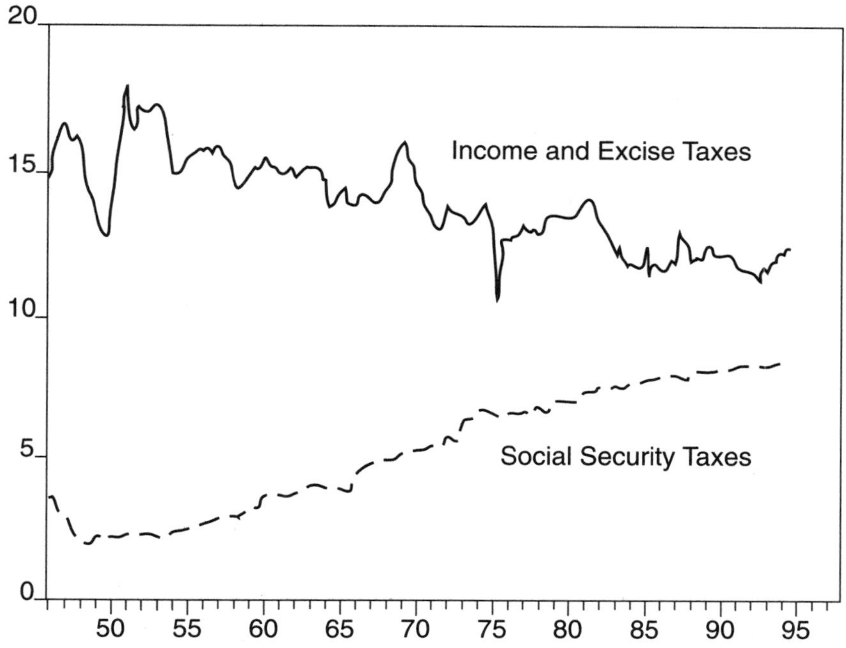

FIGURE 7 Income and excise taxes and Social Security taxes as percentages of GDP, 1946–1995.

THE FEDERAL DEFICIT AND DEBT

The deficit is the difference between the federal government's spending (on purchases, transfers, and interest) and the government's revenue. Figure 8 shows the history of the deficit in recent decades. This figure is actually just the difference between Figure 5, showing spending, and Figure 6, showing revenue, but the deficit looks much choppier because the scale of the diagram is different. Until 1970, the deficit averaged around zero; the budget was balanced on the average and surpluses were as common as deficits. From 1970 on, however, deficits were the strict rule.

The large rise in the deficit in the early 1980s was the combined result of a severe recession, which caused transfers to rise as shown in Figure 4, the rise in military spending shown in Figure 2, and the income tax cut shown in Figure 7. Since 1983, the deficit has generally declined, though it jumped up again in the recession in 1991. With a strong economy, tax increases, and declining military spending, the

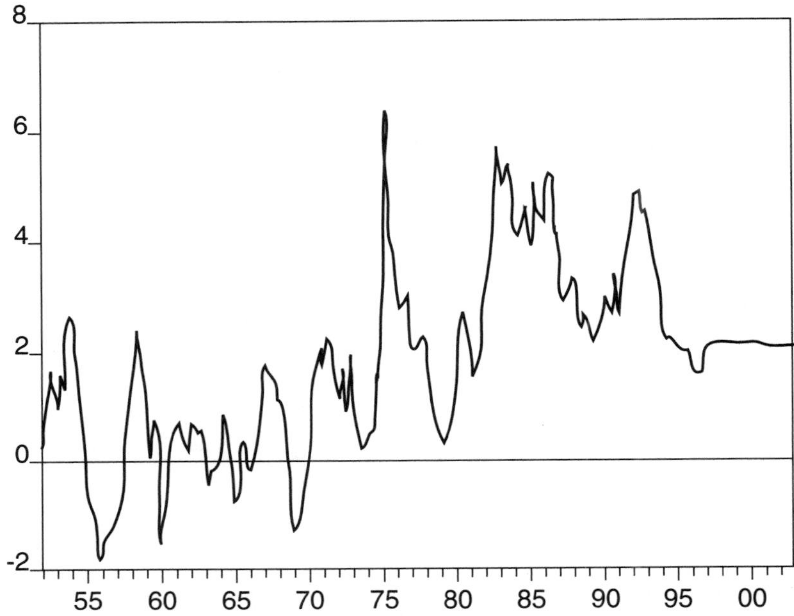

FIGURE 8 The federal deficit as a percentage of GDP, 1953–2000.

deficit fell to around 2 percent by 1994. Figure 8 shows a projection of the deficit made in August 1996 by the Congressional Budget Office, an organization with a reputation for honest analysis of controversial economic matters. The projection shows a continuation of the deficit at 2 percent of GDP.

The federal government can maintain a deficit because it can borrow—that is, it can sell bonds to obtain the funds it needs to cover the gap between spending and tax revenue. When there have been many years of past deficits, the government will be deeply in debt. Figure 9 shows the debt that the government owed investors over the past few decades, in relation to GDP. As of 1996, the debt is about half of annual GDP. It was around a quarter of GDP when it reached bottom in 1974. In 1968 the debt was almost 35 percent of GDP, although the government had not run a deficit in years (the federal debt at that time was mainly the debt remaining from the funding of World War II).

Although the CBO's projection for federal debt until 2002 shows a slight decline, it is likely that when the "baby boomers" (people born from 1949 to 1965) reach retirement age, the U.S. may face some fiscal difficulties due to high Social Security benefits because this cohort is large relative to the rest of the demographic profile.

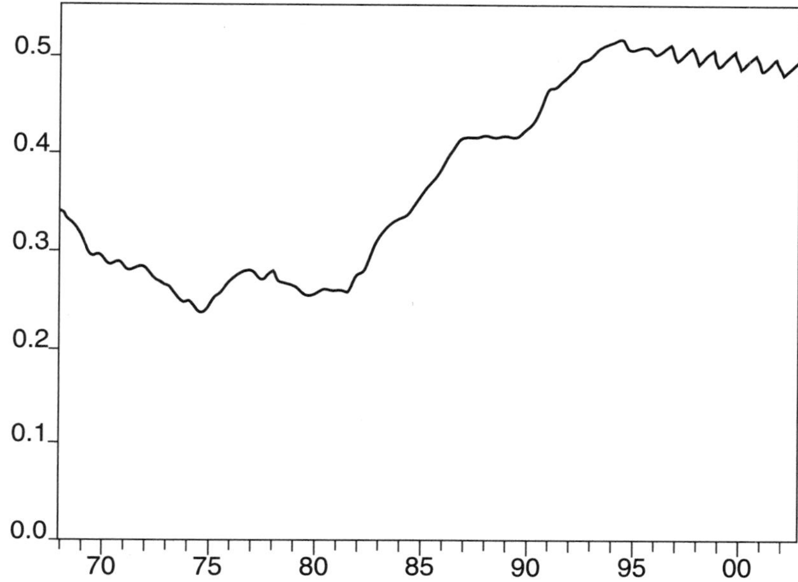

FIGURE 9 Federal debt as a ratio to GDP, 1968–2002.

The U.S. Corporation: Financial Institutions and Capital Markets

In the United States, virtually anyone may establish a business. There are fewer standards for establishing a business than for driving a car (which requires a person to be at least sixteen years of age, to carry insurance, and to pass tests for good vision and knowledge of the rules of the road). Some very special lines of business do have relevant restrictions (for example, a person convicted of securities fraud cannot establish a business in securities), but in general the legal obligations of a business, once established, are mainly limited to the payment of taxes on the income from the business, maintenance of liability insurance (the amount depending on the nature of the business), and compliance with federal and local laws.

There are roughly 25 million corporations in the United States. These 25 million include all the huge companies whose names are household words, plus all the thousands of tiny establishments that are small merchants—dry cleaners, restaurants, hairdressers—and individuals who sell services as diverse as accounting, law, and medicine, and housekeeping and pet care for people away from home.

U.S. companies generally have three features that define the modern corporation: perpetual succession, transferable shares, and limited liability. The transferability of shares was the first feature found to be indispensable by corporations. When the evolution of the modern corporation began, in England, roughly 500 years ago, companies could operate only with a charter obtained from the Crown. The charter limited the duration of the existence of the business, specified the persons who could be shareholders, and restricted the lines of business.

As these early companies and their shareholders' fortunes unfolded, situations arose where some investors needed to sell their investments to obtain funds for other purposes, and other people, sometimes persons who were not already shareholders, wanted to invest in the enterprise. The pressure to buy and sell shares gave rise to many applications to the monarch for approval, and soon a regime of fairly easy transfer of ownership was established. An organized market for company shares was in operation by the late 1600s.

Soon it became clear that transferable ownership would enable a second very useful feature of modern corporations: perpetual succession. It nearly always made more sense to sell shares in a company than to wind up (liquidate) the company, both for individual shareholders and for the shareholders as a group. This is because the company's assets are worth more together as a working unit than they are if sold separately. This organizational capital is the combination of the value of the already assembled assets, plus the human capital that lies in the knowledge and familiarity of the employees in running the business.

Once transferable shares and perpetual succession were in place, limited liability could not be far behind. If company shares are transferable, the company's creditors never know what shareholder assets might lie behind the assets of the company itself. As a result, it is less risky and more straightforward (lower cost, in essence) for those doing business with a firm to base their relationships and prices on just the company's assets (including its insurance policies) rather than to attempt to know, and if necessary, recover from, the individual shareholders. Parties a firm does business with know that companies have limited liability, and they base the terms on which they do business on this knowledge. Limited liability thus does not exploit any customer, supplier, or lender to a company so long as transactions acknowledge and reflect limited liability. The only party who *could* be exploited by limited liability is someone who is injured by a company but has no commercial relationship with it—the unlucky passerby upon whom a brick falls. Hence the requirement for liability insurance.

Most of the 25 million corporations in the United States are financed mainly by an investment provided by their sole proprietors and their families. Varying amounts of capital are supplied to all these businesses by suppliers through "accounts payable." Fewer than half of these corporations have any bank debt. But while these "Mom and Pop" establishments are extremely numerous, the great majority of capital lies in the large corporations whose ownership is not merely transferable but liquid, and traded every day in an organized stock market.

The number of companies with shares that are eligible to be traded in the stock market in the United States is about 12,000, a tiny fraction of the 25 million corporations in the United States. Of these 12,000, about 3,000 are listed on the nation's largest stock market, the New York Stock Exchange. These companies, together with a hundred or so other large companies traded through NASDAQ or on the AMEX rather than through the NYSE, constitute a large fraction of the assets of U.S. business enterprises.

The NYSE limits its membership to large companies. Very few companies start out large: the typical life of a U.S. company begins with a small company started by an individual. If it grows in production and sales, and becomes profitable enough, it can attract investment from a few other individuals and organizations, including perhaps venture capitalists who specialize in making investments in small, growing companies with good prospects.

The next step is to "go public," which means to issue stock to be sold in a public stock market, with hopes that the stock will do well enough and be traded enough to establish a liquid market, enabling further issues of securities and growth in assets. The typical initial public offering is for a company with total assets of under $100 million. Even after the issue, the original owners still hold roughly 70 percent of the interest in the company, on average. As companies' total assets grow, ownership generally becomes more diffuse, and ownership by insiders declines.

In addition to having capital raised through the stock market, the largest among U.S. companies also have capital raised through the bond market. Part of the decision to finance with debt (bonds or bank loans) is driven by the fact that under U.S. tax law, interest on debt is a deductible expense for a business, whereas dividends paid to shareholders are not. Not too surprisingly, the bond market grew tremendously after the introduction of the income tax in 1914. Prior to that time, there were only a few debt issues of note—the railroads built in the United States during the nineteenth century used substantial amounts of debt financing.

But for all its large tax advantages, debt financing is used heavily mainly by companies that are large—large enough to be among the NYSE companies—and in lines of business that enable a contract. Contracts give the bondholders sufficient comfort that they are likely to be repaid and ensure that the managers of the company are not going to take some larger-than-expected risk with their money. Yet at the same time, contracts do not greatly restrict what the owners of the business can do, and therefore they can do a profitable job of running their business. So at one extreme, the United States has regulated public utilities such as local telephones and electricity, which are financed with 90 percent debt and 10 percent equity. Virtually all heavy manufacturing has sufficient economies of scale to be large, and lines of business sufficiently straightforward to be financed with roughly 50 percent debt. On the other extreme, we have the U.S. pharmaceutical companies, which are large ($20 to $50 billion in total assets), old, and highly profitable companies—and have virtually no debt. Companies in the electronic equipment and software businesses also use very little debt. These companies have highly intangible and flexible assets (laboratories and highly educated and skilled employees) and evidently it is very difficult to write a debt contract that can satisfy both the bondholders and the owners.

U.S. regulation of companies that sell stock to the public is at once very liberal and very strict. There are no restrictions on the line of business, or profitability of the business, or who is involved in the business (with some limited exceptions, as noted for firms in the securities business) so long as the business complies with other laws. Even foreign companies may sell stock in the United States. But all companies wishing to sell securities to the public must register their securities with the U.S. Securities and Exchange Commission and must report their results quarterly and annually to their shareholders. The reports must be done in accordance with U.S. GAAP. The single biggest hurdle for foreign companies wishing to sell stock in the United States appears to be compliance with U.S. accounting standards, which evidently require companies to reveal more about their operations than do the standards of any other country. Even so large a company as Daimler Benz had to reveal facts it had not before revealed when it listed on the NYSE.

Besides its success in promoting honesty, another reason that the securities market is so robust in the United States lies in the flaws of U.S. banking institutions. During the nineteenth century, when banking institutions were developing in earnest, the United States was physically very large and a relatively diverse country. The outlying regions of the country, especially the Midwest and Southern farming states, had a great fear of the powerful and large banks of New York City. If the New York banks were allowed to do business in their states, they feared, these banks would suck up all the capital and lend it in New York, leaving little for local borrowers. Whether or not their fears were justified, U.S. banking law, at both state and federal levels, reflects this fear right up into the current era. Restrictions on interstate, and in many cases, even intrastate, banking were formal and restrictive until the deregulations of the 1980s. As a result of these laws, banks in the United States were not as large and their assets were not as diversified as those of other industrialized countries. Evidence that this made the U.S. system more vulnerable lies in a comparison of U.S. vs. Canadian bank failures in the Great Depression. In the United States, one-third of all banks failed; and were closed between 1930 and 1933. In Canada, the country in every other way the most similar to the United States, no banks failed; Canada had five large banks, all of which were nationwide.

Though nearly all these restrictions are gone now, differences in state banking laws still discourage "foreign" banks from entering a new state. In addition, the existing business relationships established under the old regime do not dissolve overnight. As a result, U.S. banking patterns are much more regional than those of other industrialized countries. This is an interesting demonstration of how much institutional choice matters, and how much inertia these choices can have.

With its relatively hobbled banking institutions, it is not so surprising that U.S. businesses turned to the securities markets. The amount of capital raised through securities markets in the United States is an order of magnitude higher in the United States than in any other country. For example, the amount of financing in the form of securities held outside of banks in the United States is, in per capita terms, ten times that of Germany.

Another financial institution of great importance in the United States is the mutual fund, or investment company. Mutual funds did not really exist until the twentieth century, and only experienced substantial growth after World War II. A big stimulus to that growth was the creation, by tax law in the 1980s, of individual retirement programs that could hold securities and mutual funds directly (in contrast to the older style of defined benefit pension plans run by companies for their employees). As of 1980, only 10 percent of U.S. citizens had ever owned a security directly. By 1995, this figure had risen to 37 percent, fueled mainly by the purchase of securities through mutual funds in individual retirement plans. Including the spouses and children of those with retirement plans, well over half the people in the United States are investors in securities, either directly or though mutual funds.

The mutual fund business itself is an astonishing aspect of the U.S. economy. The number of mutual funds now stands at more than 7,000, including the money-market mutual funds, and the number of mutual funds that invest in stocks is larger than the number of companies listed on the NYSE. The securities industry, including mutual funds, is clearly of tremendous importance to the U.S. economy.

The regulation of mutual funds in the United States is very restrictive. The Investment Company Act of 1940 restricts mutual funds to holding mainly only liquid securities. Mutual funds are also restricted in the fraction of their portfolio they may invest in any one security, and are also restricted in the fraction of any particular company that they are allowed to hold. Most important, they are allowed only one model for compensating the fund managers: fund managers can be compensated only as a percentage of the fund's total net asset value. Nonetheless, there is huge variation in the risk of funds offered, from extremely conservative money-market mutual funds to funds with more than five times the risk (on the basis of variance of returns) of the overall stock market. Clearly, the dangers of allowing the legislature to design such an essential institution did not yield disastrous results. The model institution envisioned in the 1940 Act has been a huge success.

U.S. Legal Institutions

Compared with other advanced economies, the United States has a network character. Companies tend to be smaller and to do fewer things, but then to have more interactions with other companies in order to fulfill their productive goals. Functions that are carried out within firms in other countries are done across firms in the United States. An interesting example is the sale of catalog merchandise by telephone. The traditional function of the retail store is replaced by a coalition of specialists. One firm chooses the merchandise and prepares the catalog. Another selects the list of people to receive the catalog. Two separate telephone companies collaborate to provide the toll-free telephone service to the customer. A separate firm operates the facility that takes the orders. Often the merchandise is warehoused, selected, and packed by yet another independent specialist. And two major firms deliver the merchandise to the customer's home.

The network economy rests on a legal system that supports complex contractual relations among firms. The system, inherited from Britain, provides a clear framework for commercial relations. In the event of a breach of a contract, the system prescribes well-understood remedies for the victim—high enough to deter breaches that are harmful to the joint interests of the parties, but not so high as to prevent the termination of a relationship when the termination is in their joint interest.

The United States has courts administered by the states and by the federal government to resolve disputes about contracts. Because the laws governing contracts are well understood by businesses and their attorneys, and because the courts reliably enforce these laws, almost no contract disputes reach the courts for resolution. Rather, the parties make private agreements that approximate the likely outcome in court. As a result, businesses can be reasonably confident as they enter into complex relationships with networks of parties that they will not fall victim to exploitation by their partners, nor are they likely to face a costly trial in court if a dispute arises.

An important implication of the network economy is that the services needed for building complex relationships in the first place and for resolving disputes that inevitably arise in those relationships as they evolve are part of the network economy. In countries where these relationships operate within the boundaries of firms or families of affiliated firms, these services are provided by managers. In the U.S. economy, the same services are provided under contractual relationships by outside law firms. The result is that the United States has vastly more lawyers than any other country. This feature of the U.S. economy is often misunderstood; it is taken to mean that the nation wastes resources in litigation. Instead, it should be seen as just another aspect of the network structure of the economy. It is no more significant that the United States has large numbers of lawyers than that it has so many formatters, that is, firms that specialize in taking orders for catalog merchandise over the telephone.

The U.S. legal system also supports economic activity by deterring harmful conduct that occurs outside of contractual relationships. One important element of the system is antitrust law. The U.S. economy relies on competition among firms to deliver high-quality products at low prices to consumers. Antitrust law helps to preserve the benefits of competition against acts that threaten to decrease competition, lower product quality and variety, and raise prices.

U.S. antitrust law forbids almost all forms of collaboration among firms that compete with each other. Firms may not coordinate their prices or agree to divide markets among themselves. No contractual relationship among rivals is permitted if it has any tendency to raise prices. The victim of a price increase may recover three times the amount of the loss, and the government may seek criminal penalties against violators. The enforcement of laws barring cooperation among rivals is more vigorous in the United States than in other countries; U.S. law also forbids the merger of rival firms if there is a chance of more than a slight diminution of competition—again, more strict than the laws of other countries. Greater reliance on laws to protect competition is the natural counterpart of the low levels of regulation in the U.S. economy.

A second branch of antitrust law forbids predatory acts against rivals if the effect is to reduce competition and raise prices. Vigorous competition inherently involves a healthy form of predation: it is harmful to Ford if Toyota sets a low price, but good for the consumer and for the economy. The trend in U.S. antitrust law since 1980 has been to apply more and more stringent tests to claims of predatory conduct. The government's investigation of complaints about Microsoft is a good illustration. Many of the complaints from Microsoft's rivals were about the firm's policies of selling software at low prices—for example, for bundling new software into operating systems. In spite of intense pressure from the disappointed rivals who were hurt by the low prices, the government did not challenge the low prices; instead, it condemned policies that created an unnecessary barrier to entry into the software business, which Microsoft agreed to discontinue. The Microsoft investigation, along with the government's dismissal of an earlier case against IBM, makes it clear that it is not a violation of antitrust law for a firm to come to dominate a market by developing superior products and selling them at reasonable prices.

Another branch of law protects intellectual property from unauthorized use. The ability to control the use of intellectual property and the resulting ability to charge for its use is the way that the U.S. economic system provides incentives for innovation and development of many kinds. Direct public support for these activities is modest and is concentrated in military applications. Intellectual property is protected by patents, copyrights, trademarks, and by trade-secret laws.

In comparison with other countries, the United States has remarkably little regulation. We mentioned in the previous section that anybody can start a business and sell almost any product. Because there is little prior approval of business activities, there is correspondingly more legal review of situations where harm has occurred. For example, most products do not have to be approved for safety by the government before they are placed on the market. (Pharmaceuticals are a major exception.) But if a product turns out to be unsafe, its maker or seller is held to a strict standard of responsibility. Victims of unsafe products can recover compensation for their injuries even decades after the injury occurs. The anticipation of the possibility of having to pay the compensation provides a strong incentive for designers of new products to pay close attention to safety issues. Consistent with the general principles of the economy, private action to avoid unsafe products occurs as a result of incentives provided by government, but no direct government action is required.

Conclusions

The U.S. economy has the highest output per worker in the world. Part of this achievement is due to extraordinary levels of investment in both physical and human capital (both also the world's highest) and part reflects a set of social institutions that are very successful in supporting production and commerce both in the United States and in other countries. These institutions include a notably honest government and a legal framework that builds confidence in contracts, encourages competition, and discourages interference with competition—along with a great degree of economic freedom to pursue enterprise and engage in transactions.

Besides its role in supporting the legal establishment, government plays a large role in the economy of the United States. Expenditures by the federal plus state and local governments constitute 35 percent of U.S. GDP. The important trends over the postwar years have been slowly growing federal expenditures (as a percent of GDP), with a falling share spent on military goods and services and rising nonmilitary spending, especially transfer payments. State and local expenditures have risen considerably faster than federal expenditures, so that overall, the government plays a larger role now than ever before. Expenditures at the federal level were substantially financed with government debt from 1960 to 1997, with the largest deficits (in relation to GDP) occurring in the 1980s. Presently the federal budget is close to balanced. Whether this will continue to prevail as the cohort born in the baby boom following World War II retires and begins to collect federal pensions through Social Security remains to be seen.

Although some features of the economy of the United States are clear contributors to its prosperity, others are ambiguous. High levels of investment in physical and human capital are clearly contributors to a high level of income. But the United States does not have the highest level of productivity; that is, it does not get as much out of its human and physical capital as some other countries do. Why this is so is not entirely clear. The United States has relatively honest government, but not as honest as those of the Scandinavian countries. Exactly how honest government is achieved is not clear. And though government plays a large role in the U.S. economy, its role is not as large as in many other rich, industrialized countries. Also, though the securities markets in the United States have been extraordinary in their ability to finance business enterprises, their success is partly due to various flaws in the U.S. banking system.

This overview was not intended to reveal all the secrets of U.S. prosperity, simply because we do not know what all the secrets are. Clearly, we believe we understand some of the reasons for the high standard of living in the United States. In that light, we have tried to explain what we believe the key features of prosperity are. But we also believe that some aspects of our economy are the result of our own particular history, not part of any optimal, universal design. Thus, much of what we have covered here was intended simply to explain how the systems work, not to claim that they are the best systems or that everyone should copy them.

Part II

Business Organization and Competition Policy

Seong Min Yoo and Youngjae Lim

3

Big Business in Korea

New Learning and Policy Issues

From an industrial organization perspective, the legacies of Korea's economic development include among others: (1) the state's predominance over the market, (2) the rapid expansion of the industrial base and the emerging forces of market mechanism, and at the same time, (3) monopolistic markets and the concentration of economic power. Of these, the concentration of economic power is perhaps the most intriguing.

The Old Debate, Chaebol Policy, and the Issues

Chaebols, Korea's big business conglomerates, have long been at the heart of any discussion on economic power concentration. Yet in spite of the apparent significance of the chaebol issue, no meaningful discussions about it were undertaken, at least in public, until the mid-1980s, partly because such discussions were taboo under authoritarian governments.[1] During the last decade or so, however, we have witnessed a surge in literature, as well as a lively debate, on various dimensions of the chaebol issue and related topics. These studies include Lee Kyu Uck (1977, 1990, 1994), SaKong Il (1980, 1993), Lee Kyu Uck and Lee Sung Soon (1985), Lee Kyu Uck and Lee Jae Hyung (1990), Kang Myung Hun (1990), Cho Dong Sung (1990), Kang Shin Il (1991), Kang

1. Lee Kyu Uck (1977) and SaKong Il (1980) were among the few exceptions to this observation.

Chul Kyu, Choi Teong Pyo, and Chang Ji Sang (1991), Chung Byung Hyu and Yang Young Sik (1992), Yang Won Keun (1992), Leroy P. Jones (1994), Kim Il Joong (1994), Gong Byeong-Ho (1994), Lee Jae Hyung and Yoo Seong Min (1994), Kwack Man Soon et al. (1995), Yoo Seong Min (1992, 1993, 1996a, 1996b, 1996c), and Sung Soon Lee and Seong Min Yoo (1997).

Although the decade-long effort at studying chaebols contributed to enhancing our understanding of chaebol-related issues, we are still far from reaching any consensus or conclusions on most of the central questions. The difficulties are particularly great because of the so-called anti-chaebol emotion said to exist among the general public in Korea but never clearly defined or proved.

CHAEBOL DEBATE IN KOREA

Various studies of the chaebol have tried to identify in their own terms the merits and defects of the distinctly Korean institution known as the chaebol. In what follows, we try to sum up the merits and defects of the chaebol or the chaebol-dominated economic system in Korea as they have been discussed in the existing literature. It should be noted at the start that so many of the arguments surrounding the chaebol seem to contradict each other (for example, chaebols get credit for their contribution to Korea's rapid economic growth, and at the same time are discredited for their inefficiency and weak competitiveness) that it is hard to discern what is the truth.

Merits

Chaebols have been a growth machine that has made possible the rapid expansion and modernization of the Korean economy

Chaebols have been the main movers behind new products, new markets, and rapid industrial restructuring

Chaebols have been an important source of innovative and risk-taking entrepreneurship

Chaebols have been a driving force behind successful export-led growth, mass production, and realization of scale economies

Chaebols have been an important scheme to overcome the imperfections in such input markets as capital, labor, technology, and managerial talent by internalizing transactions and making the most of synergies within an organization or any economies of scope

Chaebols have contributed to improving the quality of human capital, including both workers and managers

Chaebols have provided the Korean model of corporate ownership, control, governance, and management that proved to have many strengths

Defects

The so-called economic democracy has been retarded or underdeveloped owing to the concentration of economic power in the hands of a small number of chaebols. The chaebol structure is believed to be closely associated with such issues as the inequality of economic opportunities, distributive inequity in terms of income and wealth (sometimes identified as the low contribution of chaebols' growth to people's lives), and the lack of fairness.[2]

The rapid growth of chaebols is not justified owing to the lack of legitimacy. The legitimacy concern is usually based upon the following arguments:

- Chaebols grew at the expense of the "relatively weak" in our society (consumers, taxpayers, small- and medium-sized firms, minority shareholders, etc.).
- The growth of chaebols was made possible by preferential "policy loans" and the repression of the financial sector.
- Chaebols committed many illegal or iniquitous acts that were sometimes connived and overlooked by the state, resulting in social injustice in law enforcement.
- Chaebols could grow through so-called zero-sum entrepreneurial activities such as speculations in land and foreign exchanges, rent seeking in domestic monopolies, etc.

"Chaebol-driven" growth has created distortions in the tripartite relationship among the government, chaebols, and banks, which is now a bottleneck for further development. This "interface concern" is usually based upon the following arguments:[3]

2. As is widely acknowledged, the philosophical notions of equality, equity, and fairness are at best shaky, if they exist at all. Applying these notions to the discussions of Korean chaebols, we encounter many definitional questions that are hard to answer precisely. See Young (1994) and Zajac (1995) for a recent survey, analyses, and applications of equity, fairness, and justice.

3. "Interface concern," which views the distorted tripartite relationship among the government, chaebols, and banks to be a problem, is in fact considered the political economy of big business in Korea. This view presents many interesting aspects to be analyzed by economists as well as political scientists, although the existing literature in both disciplines has explored little on this issue. See Eun Mee Kim (1988), Chung H. Lee (1992), Chung-in Moon (1994) and Haggard (1994) for political scientists' views

"Economic power begets political power,"[4] and chaebols, thanks to their economic as well as political power, could influence government policies to protect their private interests.

The abnormally high debt-equity ratios of most chaebols have resulted in the typical financial structure that is quite vulnerable to economic recessions. However, the widely held perception of "too big to fail" or "too important not to save" made the Korean government insure or underwrite chaebols' investments, especially when the investments had been tailored to the government's industrial policy. It is this insurer's role of the government and actual bailout loans that caused not only a repression of the financial sector but moral hazard on the part of chaebols.[5]

Chaebols, as a party directly involved in the evolutionary process of the government-business relationship, are to some extent responsible for any problems arising from the so-called close intertwining of business and politics.

Because banks act as agents of the government, the bank-industry relationship has been in effect that of regulator and regulatee instead of the normal relationship expected between seller and customer. State control of bank management and the heavy burden of "nonperforming assets" have undermined the competitiveness of the banking industry.

The structure of highly concentrated corporate ownership found in most chaebols has made it easy for chaebols to transfer absolute corporate control within their own family from generation to generation.

The overall concentration of economic power by chaebols, as well as the monopoly power of chaebol subsidiaries in individual markets, may severely restrain competition.

---

on this interface issue; see SaKong Il (1993) and Yoo Seong Min (1996a, 1996b) for economists' views. For journalists' views, see the *Economist* (June 3, 1995, and Nov. 11, 1995) and Clifford (1994).

4. Some institutionalists, including Commons (1937) and Galbraith (1967), argued that economic power begets political power. Marxist theory also provides that economic power is primary in a capitalist economy, and political power is both its offspring and its servant. See Spruill (1982, 88–116)

5. As will be made clear, we try to establish that this aspect of the government-business relationship in Korea, characterized by the government's insurance function and chaebols' moral hazard, is one of the most serious problems associated with chaebols.

Some of the structural and behavioral characteristics of chaebols undermine their efficiency and competitiveness. These include so-called excessive and irrational[6] diversifications (equivalent to the journalistic expression of "octopus expansion of businesses"), loss of flexibility as a result of bureaucratization along with their acceptance of limited competition and protectionism as a source of X-inefficiency, any technological vested interests, lethargy and reluctance to innovate, and the undemocratic nature of their corporate control and governance, which limits the creativity of workers and professional managers.

Finally, chaebols have been criticized for their lack of business ethics and for neglecting their social responsibilities.[7] The criticism is directed toward such matters as chaebols' relations with employees, consumers, the environment, and regional and national economy.

The number of defects listed above may appear to outweigh the merits, but it is by no means clear whether or not this really is the case. Many of the chaebol studies that pointed out these merits and defects suffer from shortcomings in their scope and analysis.

First, these studies were mostly concerned with identifying the causes of the concentration of economic power by the chaebol, and then evaluating this phenomenon. In doing so, the studies relied heavily upon qualitative assessments, subjective value judgments, and hypothetical arguments, most of which were supported by little sound empirical evidence.[8] The results of this unscientific approach to the chaebol issue were both inconclusive and confusing, leading to a subsequent confrontation between "pro-chaebol" and "anti-chaebol" groups of academics, government officials, journalists, and politicians.

A second reason for the unscientific and inconclusive character of

6. The terms excessive and irrational, though never clearly defined, are frequently used to imply by their very meaning the inefficiency of chaebols' diversifications.

7. The terms business ethics and social responsibility have been controversial in Korean discussions of chaebols, but the controversy is an old one in other capitalist economies. The debate on shareholder capitalism vs. stakeholder capitalism in the vast literature on corporate governance of the 1980s and 1990s sheds a new light on this old question; see in particular Allen (1995) and Yoo Seong Min (1996b).

8. The lack of empirical evidence is partly due to the difficulty of gaining access to the relevant data for analysis, or the nonexistence of such data. Lee Jae Hyung (1997), for example, explains what data are available for a chaebol analysis and their limitations.

the chaebol studies was simply their lack of a basic concept as a reference point and an integrated framework. They intermingled equity, fairness, and legitimacy with efficiency, competitiveness, and growth. The lack of an integrated framework for analysis was equally serious because any studies of chaebols could be flawed if they highlighted only a part of the various dimensions of the chaebol issue while leaving other important ones untouched.

A third flaw in these studies was the lack of objectivity. Thus, conjectures, subjective value judgments influenced by political considerations, and conceptually weak and logically inconsistent assertions resulted in biased analyses, usually leading to incorrect diagnoses and inappropriate prescriptions. The Korean government's policies toward the chaebol have not been free from these problems either.

EVOLUTION OF CHAEBOL POLICY

Although there seems to be no consensus on the real problems of chaebols, the so-called chaebol policy, or the policies against the concentration of economic power, have an established tradition in Korea.[9] We note that the chaebol policy has developed into today's "octopus-like policy measures," which have in certain instances been justified on the grounds of equity and fairness, and in other instances by efficiency, competitiveness, and growth, without any plausible explanation of why the rationale could change.[10] Although there is no clear policy objective, the overall direction of chaebol policy has swung as a result of the business cycle and the sociopolitical considerations on the presumed public anti-chaebol attitude. Thus, the ex post empirical trend during the last decade was that Korea's chaebol policy tended to strengthen regulations, but these were eased or became less effective during periods of economic recession. Sociopolitical considerations could be seen in the anti-chaebol slogans of most candidates in the presidential elections of 1987 and 1992.

9. The term chaebol policy is not widely accepted in Korea. Instead, many use the phrase, "the policy to repress (or mitigate) economic power concentration." Chaebol policy can be defined as a set of policy measures either directed in a discriminatory way toward chaebols or having chaebols as their major, if not exclusive, target. Thus defined, chaebol policy has a variety of elements common to other familiar government policies such as industrial policy, corporate policy, competition policy. This definition of chaebol policy remains to be clarified according to how we define "chaebol."

10. Octopus-like policy measures is analogous to the "octopus expansion of chaebols," a popular term in Korean journalism suggesting chaebols' conglomerate nature and ever increasing diversification.

The first policy attempt to regulate big business appeared in 1974, when the concentration of credit supply and corporate ownership and the unhealthy financial status of chaebols were finally recognized as being serious problems. A credit control system was introduced, and public listing in the stock market was encouraged to expedite the breaking up of corporate ownership. These policies were not actively enforced, however, and were neglected during the rest of the 1970s. There were no further chaebol policies during the 1970s, and during the Heavy and Chemical Industries Drive (1973–1979), the government did nothing to check the concentration of economic power. In 1980, another set of chaebol regulations was introduced to discourage chaebols' real estate holdings, to induce the restructuring of chaebols' subsidiaries, to strengthen the credit control system, and so on, but all these regulations were essentially aimed at improving the financial status of chaebols, and after one year of implementation they were abandoned.

The year 1987 marked an important turning point in the history of chaebol policy in Korea. So-called equity investment regulations, introduced through the first amendment of the Monopoly Regulation and Fair Trade Act (MRFTA) in December 1986, were designed to have significant effects on the intragroup shareholding patterns of chaebols. The regulations had several important provisions: (1) direct cross-shareholdings between any two subsidiaries within a big business group[11] are prohibited; (2) total equity investments in other companies (either within the same business group or outside) by any subsidiary of a chaebol are not to exceed the ceiling set by the MRFTA;[12] (3) the establishment of a "pure" holding company is prohibited; (4) voting rights are restricted for the stocks held by other subsidiaries in finance and insurance industries, and so on. Another important shift in chaebol policy in 1987 was the further strengthening of the so-called basket control of credit, introduced in 1984 as one of the regulations in the

11. The MRFTA and the enforcement decree and annual reviews by the Fair Trade Commission will determine what constitutes "big business groups" and who their subsidiaries are.

12. The ceiling was first set at "40% of net assets of the investing company"; the 4th amendment of the MRFTA in December 1994 lowered the ceiling to 25 percent. "Net assets" are defined by the MRFTA as "total assets less the sum of liabilities, equity investments made by other subsidiaries, and any government subsidies." Subtracting the equity investments made by other subsidiaries corrects the otherwise overstated capital.

already complex credit control system. Since 1987 the equity investment regulations and the credit control system have constituted two of the most important chaebol regulations in Korea.

Additional diverse chaebol regulations appeared in the early 1990s. The MRFTA added a new provision in 1992 to regulate an old practice of the so-called mutual loan guarantees.[13] Also in 1992 the Fair Trade Commission announced a new guideline to regulate the anticompetitive behavior of chaebols as a result of "in-group" transactions.[14] Both these regulations invited harsh criticisms from chaebols as well as from economic liberalists, as had been the case with the introduction of equity investment regulations in 1987. The government, however, believed that these regulations were important in dealing with some of the "chaebol problems." In 1996, the 5th amendment of the MRFTA proposed even stronger regulations of mutual loan guarantees and restraints of competition based upon in-group transactions.

The so-called specialization policy announced in 1991 was reinforced in 1993 to induce chaebols to refrain from excessive diversifications and concentrate investment resources on their "core businesses" in order to strengthen their competitiveness. Although this specialization policy sounds like a totally new industrial policy targeting chaebols'

13. Mutual loan guarantees had been a key ingredient in the history of corporate debt financing in Korea. Mutual loan guarantees refer to the practice of subsidiary A guaranteeing or underwriting subsidiary B's liabilities to financial institutions. This practice was widespread among Korean business groups regardless of their size, and the financial institutions on their part regarded this as a prerequisite before they agreed to provide loans. Since mutual loan guarantees are contingent liabilities of the guarantor, they create an important barrier to exit of the guaranteed subsidiary, and in many cases the bankruptcy of a single subsidiary would imply either the bankruptcy of the entire business group or more bailout loans from the financial institutions. Mutual loan guarantees are to be distinguished from the payment guarantees by commercial banks, which are a form of credit supply. The 3d amendment of the MRFTA in December 1992 limited the ceiling of loan guarantees by any single subsidiary of chaebols to 200 percent of its equity capital, and the ceiling was lowered again to 100 percent in the 5th amendment of the MRFTA in December 1996.

14. It is not clear either theoretically or empirically that conglomerate corporations do in fact limit competition by means of transactions with their subsidiaries. The literature of antitrust law and economics reflects conflicting views on the matter. In the case of Korean chaebols, too, the subject is still an open question, although the Korean government strongly believes in the anticompetitive effects of in-group transactions of chaebols. See Adams and Brock (1991, 81–113) for an explanation of this conflict.

core businesses, it was in fact nothing more than exemptions from the existing chaebol regulations such as the credit control system and equity investment regulations. Even though the specialization policy implied more exemptions from chaebol regulations, the business community viewed it as yet another example of government intervention in chaebols' own area of decision making.[15] Many observers question whether the specialization policy has indeed produced its intended effects of discouraging chaebols' diversifications, and more importantly, whether such a policy is desirable.

Deconcentration of corporate ownership appeared as a new chaebol policy issue in 1992 when the 7th Five-Year Plan was announced, and various measures have been introduced since then to encourage the process of breaking up corporate ownership. The original policy of ownership deconcentration soon led to discussions of the problems in chaebols' corporate control and governance, and there has been an upsurge of social interest and academic research in Korea on the subject of corporate governance. In addition to these policy instruments, the privatization of state-owned enterprises, the inducement of private investments in social infrastructure construction, and the deregulation of entry, investment, and ownership in many industries are all closely related to the ups and downs of chaebols in Korea, and thus cannot be discussed independently of the chaebol policy. Indeed, a strong case can be made that, from the point of view of the chaebols themselves, the industrial and competition policy issues, including privatization and deregulation, are no less important than the traditional chaebol regulations.

With all these policy developments, the decade since the mid-1980s was an era of chaebol regulations. Whether or not the chaebol regulations have had the desired effects is not at all clear. Possibly the regulations were ill advised because they were based on incorrect diagnoses of the real problems associated with chaebols. Certainly many of the chaebol regulations were only symptomatic treatments that could not cure the fundamental problems, if there were any; and in many

15. The interventionist character of the specialization policy is highlighted as we look into how the so-called core industries and core companies were determined. According to the revised specialization policy in 1993, the top ten chaebols were allowed three core industries, the eleventh to thirtieth chaebols were allowed two core industries, core companies being defined as any subsidiaries in the core industries satisfying certain requirements. Chaebols complained that they were not free to choose their own core industries and worried about any new regulations of "non-core" businesses.

cases it was not clear at all what the regulations were ultimately pursuing.[16]

LESSONS FROM THE OLD DEBATE AND POLICY EXPERIENCE

Nonetheless, for all these shortcomings, there are some lessons to be drawn from the previous studies and past policy experiences. First, the hot debate has made it clear that economic power concentration was both the driving cause and the consequence of the rapid economic growth in Korea. In a similar context, many people now agree that the centripetal force of capital that can be observed in many market economies around the world must also have worked in concentrating economic power in the hands of a small number of chaebols in Korea, in addition to the fact that the government-led, big business-oriented growth strategy during the 1960s through the 1980s significantly accelerated the concentration process.[17] Thus, the question which factor is a more crucial cause of concentration is still an empirical question difficult to answer. For the moment, the inconclusiveness seems to have ended in a draw.

A second lesson is that as the debate over the causes and evaluations has become exhausted, with no definite evidence and conclusions, we have begun to learn that certain fundamental and conceptual questions need to be zero-based (that is, free from prejudiced judgment) and analyzed, if not answered, as scientifically and logically as possible. We have also learned that we need to identify precisely the meaning of "concentration of economic power," since the term "economic power" has in many cases not been clearly defined. This new learning has led to recent efforts by some researchers to reexamine some of the hypotheses taken for granted in the past and construct a new framework of analysis.

Third, we came to notice certain conditions that change the nature of the chaebol issue. As the Korean economy becomes more open to international competition, we are learning that the rapidly changing economic environment sheds new light on the chaebol issue. The past concentration of economic power in a heavily protected and regulated

16. For a more detailed analysis along this line, see Yoo Seong Min (1996a, 1996b).

17. Berle and Means (1932) suggested that the centripetal force toward market concentration can be balanced against the centrifugal force away from the concentration of corporate ownership. We use the term centripetal force of capital to denote the force of concentration inherent in the evolution of capitalism.

economy is beginning to be interpreted differently in view of the global competition facing the Korean economy and chaebols. In a similar vein, we are learning that elements of the domestic environment such as political democratization can also change the nature of the chaebol issue as the close intertwining of business and politics becomes less justified and sustainable.

Fourth, the government's chaebol policy has come under criticism, raised on the grounds of the policy's desirability and efficiency. The desirability of chaebol policy has been questioned, since certain policy measures were suspected of being based upon incorrect diagnoses of problems, or that their ill effects outweighed the good. It is time to reexamine whether certain policy measures really are desirable for the nation's economic development. The efficiency question about chaebol policy has also been raised when a policy measure did not achieve what it was originally intended to achieve. This mismatch or divergence between policy instruments and policy goals has often been quite serious, and we often experienced only unintended ill effects with no visible benefits.

These lessons have recently prompted a series of studies on the chaebol issue.[18] The studies have certain contributions in common. First, a new framework for breaking the concentration of economic power into three subdimensions has been suggested for a better understanding and analysis of the chaebol issue. These subdimensions are: (1) the size and relative share of chaebols, (2) the extent of diversification, and (3) the ownership, control, governance, and management structure.[19] The three dimensions come from the conventional definition of economic power concentration in Korea, which is "the fact that a small number of business groups, each consisting of a number of companies under a single corporate control, occupy a high portion of the national economy." Although these three dimensions are neither exhaustive nor mutually exclusive, they are believed to constitute a framework for a more meaningful analysis.

Second, for each of the three dimensions thus identified, recent studies have tried to produce "better" explanations of why we are in the present situation. In particular, the studies have tried to base their

18. For example, see Lee Kyu Uck and Lee Jae Hyung (1990), Kim Il Joong (1994), Lee Chul Song (1995), and Yoo Seong Min (1992, 1996a, 1996b).

19. A fourth dimension would be the government-business relationship. Yoo Seong Min (1996a, 1996b) tries to establish that this is another important dimension that should be analyzed in any studies of Korean chaebols.

analyses upon some form of rationality, economic or noneconomic, and have searched for evidence whenever possible. Although these new studies are far from being exhaustive answers to the unsolved questions, they have contributed at least to deepening our understanding. Indeed, the most important achievement of these studies is that they question some of the old beliefs on the chaebol issue and pave the way for more rigorous studies.

Third, as new explanations draw new implications for policy prescriptions, the recent studies have come up with a proposal to revise or reform the old chaebol policy. The lessons drawn from the previous studies are an important clue to these new policy ideas since they stem not only from the new explanations but also from the reflections upon the desirability and efficiency of the old policy instruments and prospects for future competitive conditions.

As of today, the chaebols are recognized as having a complex structure that is best characterized as a unique feature of the industrial organization of the Korean economy. We hardly need to mention how important it is to unveil misconceptions and realities surrounding the chaebol issue in order to arrive at the right chaebol policy, if one is needed at all.

The rest of this paper will deal with certain questions that we believe to be the keys to understanding the chaebol issue.

Who are the chaebols?
Is the concentration of economic power by chaebols "excessive"?
Are chaebols inefficient? Do the "excessive" diversification and the concentrated ownership-control-management structure of chaebols cause inefficiency and undermine competitiveness?
Are chaebols creating inequity and unfairness?
Is the rapid growth of chaebols illegitimate? If so, are chaebols responsible for illegitimacy?
Do chaebols assume any social responsibility?
What is the real threat of chaebols and economic power concentration?
Should chaebols be prohibited from integrating with commercial banks and other financial entities?
What are the problems of the government-chaebol relationship in Korea?
How does the issue of corporate governance reconcile with the chaebol issue? What do the recent discussions of corporate governance imply for chaebol policy?

What is the relationship between chaebol policy, industrial policy, and competition policy?

Facts, Misconceptions, and a New Learning

Who are the chaebols? Do chaebols have any "Korea-peculiar" aspects that cannot be found in big businesses of other capitalist economies? These questions are often raised and answered by many researchers, Korean as well as foreign. Lee Kyo Uck (1994, 471) defines chaebols as: "The conglomerate business groups (in Korea), the majority of whose component firms are monopolistic or oligopolistic in their respective market, owned and controlled by particular individuals or their close family members." Karl J. Fields (1995, 32) offers this definition: "Any group of two or more legally independent firms producing goods and/or services within various product sectors of the Korean economy . . . They typically are: (1) owned and controlled by a single family and managed paternalistically; (2) completely independent from one another, with unambiguous firm membership; (3) diversified across products and industries; (4) (historically, at least) not in control of major financial institutions and thus dependent on external sources of funds; and (5) closely linked to the government."

DEFINING THE CHAEBOL

We can identify points common to any definition of chaebol as follows: concentration of production at the aggregate level, individual market positions of chaebols' subsidiaries, diversified business structure, corporate ownership-control-governance-management structure, chaebol-government relationship. Any attempts to define chaebols tend to result in emphasizing the features that distinguish Korean chaebols from big businesses of other countries.[20] Thus, most of the definitions seem to have led to the widely held belief that there exist "Korea-peculiar" or uniquely Korean characteristics, which are in sharp contrast to those of foreign big businesses. Undeniably, Korean chaebols, especially the leading ones, share certain characteristics such as family domination of corporate ownership and control and highly diver-

20. There have been many other studies that attempted to define chaebol in their own terms. See Cho Dong Sung (1990) for a survey of various definitions of chaebol.

sified businesses under a single control that are rare in today's advanced economies.

When overstated, however, this view may have the danger of justifying "Korea-peculiar" (and possibly irrational) chaebol regulations simply because chaebols *are* Korea-peculiar. We need to have a balanced view on who the chaebols really are. There have been many names for big businesses in the history of capitalism: the trust in the United States around the turn of the century, *Konzerne* in German history, and prewar *zaibatsu* in Japan and business groups (*kigyoshudan* in contemporary Japan).[21] It can be argued that many of these big businesses around the world and throughout the history of capitalism had merits and defects that are more or less similar to those we have described. Although different countries have a different history of industrialization and different names and organizations of big businesses, the very nature of the social, political, and economic problems created by the growth of big business and the concentration of economic power have certain elements in common. Such issues as efficiency, equity, fairness, legitimacy, social responsibility of large corporations, political influence of private corporate power, government-business relationship, and unlawful business conduct were raised with the birth and growth of big business, and the state's response to these issues has become an important determinant of today's capitalism. To the extent that chaebols and the economic power concentration in Korea produce problems similar to those already experienced by advanced capitalist economies, the argument that chaebols are peculiar to Korea is exaggerated.

Another important reason to suspect the Korea-peculiarity of chaebols can be found in the Japanese prewar zaibatsu. Although it could be easily imagined that the origin of Korean chaebols was the Japanese zaibatsu, the tradition of equating chaebols' growth with Korea's rapid industrialization since the 1960s has led to a certain neglect of the period before the 1960s. Like it or not, thirty-five years of Japanese colonial rule must have had a significant influence on Korea's modernization. In particular, many of the first-generation entrepreneurs in Korea, those who started their businesses in the 1930s and 1940s, might

21. Chaebol is a direct translation of the Japanese *zaibatsu*. Both chaebol and zaibatsu are written in the same Chinese ideographs, pronounced in Mandarin Chinese as *caifa*, meaning "financial clique." In Taiwan the big business is called *guanxiqiye*, or related enterprise, which is again to be distinguished from the Japanese *keiretsu*.

have inherited a great deal of intangible assets from their Japanese precedents, including the structure, organization, and management of large corporations, although any tangible assets they inherited were either destroyed during the Korean War or became obsolete after independence. In fact, it is hard to believe that the family dominance of corporate ownership and control, intergenerational transfer of these rights within the family, the endless desire to diversify, and the vertical and authoritative nature of command, control, and communication within the business organization were all invented in Korea. If one looks into the characteristics and criticisms of zaibatsu in the nineteenth century and in the first half of the twentieth, the similarities between the Japanese zaibatsu and Korean chaebol are overwhelming.[22]

Efforts to find the origin of Korean chaebols in the Japanese prewar zaibatsu raise at least two interesting points. The first has to do with the popular prediction in Korea that today's Korean chaebols may very well evolve into business groups similar to contemporary business groups in Japan. The breaking up of the zaibatsu by the United States after the war has, as we know, significantly affected today's big businesses in Japan, but in peacetime a radical breakup of the chaebols might be politically impossible, if indeed it were economically desirable. In any event, it seems unlikely that Korean chaebols will evolve in the near future into the Japanese model of business groups.

A second point relates to the question of how Korean chaebols have differed from Japanese zaibatsu in the course of Korea's economic development for the half century after its liberation from Japanese rule. Most of the chaebol studies emphasizing the government-led, big business–oriented growth strategy and the HCI drive of the 1970s as important causes of the concentration of economic power in Korea will help answer this question.

Curiously, however, the term chaebol is never defined in Korean laws and regulations. The MRFTA defines "big business groups" as the thirty largest business groups in terms of total assets, while the credit control regulations name them *kye-yeol* (Japan's version of the keiretsu, though they differ in meaning). Table 1 reports summary statistics for

22. The study by Lee Kyu Uck and Lee Jae Hyung (1990) is one of the exceptions to the theory that the origin of Korean chaebols lies in Japanese zaibatsu. It is interesting to see foreign observers point to the "colonial origins of Korean capitalism." See Eckert (1991) and Clifford (1994). Morikawa Hideimasa (1978) shows the history of the Japanese zaibatsu and the criticisms in Japan on the problems of the zaibatsu.

TABLE 1 The Thirty Largest Chaebols, April 1995
(bil. won, percents)

Rank and name	*Total assets*	*Equity-assets ratio*	*Paid-in equity capital*	*In-group shareholding ratio*	*Total sales*	*Number of subsidiaries*	*Number of listed subsidiaries*	*Number of KSIC 3-digit industries participated*	*Number of financial subsidiaries*[a]
1. Hyundai	37,221	20.1	3,100	60.4	47,001	48	15	38	5
2. Samung	29,414	18.0	2,667	49.3	51,830	55	15	31	5
3. Daewoo	26,144	27.9	3,883	41.4	20,557	22	9	26	2
4. LG	24,351	24.9	2,872	39.7	29,857	50	13	29	6
5. Sunkyung	12,806	22.7	959	51.2	14,657	32	4	24	5
6. Ssangyong	10,955	26.0	1,191	33.1	11,399	22	10	33	3
7. Hanjin	10,629	12.6	789	40.3	7,653	23	9	27	3
8. Kia	9,814	18.5	783	21.9	7,277	14	5	11	1
9. Hanwha	7,282	13.9	958	36.7	6,240	29	9	22	4
10. Lotte	6,628	21.6	1,556	22.3	6,303	29	5	25	3
11. Kumho	5,374	19.1	835	40.3	2,489	24	4	17	1
12. Doosan	4,808	15.5	283	51.6	3,671	27	9	26	1
13. Daelim	4,638	18.6	363	37.6	3,074	17	5	19	1
14. Dongah Cons.	3,874	12.5	334	40.1	4,203	14	4	15	2

15. Halla	3,430	3.0	201	57.8	3,027	15	3	12	1
16. Dongkuk	3,237	22.1	306	46.6	3,052	16	7	14	2
17. Hyosung	3,040	26.2	241	43.6	4,163	15	2	18	—
18. Hanbo	3,013	16.7	396	88.3	1,306	13	2	13	—
19. Tongyang	2,592	20.4	398	46.1	2,321	19	4	12	5
20. Hanil	2,559	19.2	377	43.1	1,240	13	4	16	3
21. Kolon	2,535	25.9	290	47.6	3,206	20	4	19	—
22. Kohap	2,503	13.5	263	46.7	1,699	10	2	9	—
23. Jinro	2,391	33.3	238	47.2	1,098	12	4	11	2
24. Haitai	2,358	16.0	185	34.0	2,175	13	4	11	—
25. Sammi	2,245	2.9	356	30.9	1,241	8	2	9	—
26. Dongbu	2,128	13.5	268	40.4	3,377	13	6	18	4
27. Woosung Cons.	2,117	10.2	189	62.6	1,209	8	2	10	—
28. Kukdong Cons.	1,966	37.2	409	25.0	838	10	2	9	4
29. Byucksan	1,781	15.7	152	41.3	1,121	18	4	18	2
30. Miwon	1,613	13.6	225	49.8	1,674	14	4	13	2
Total	233,446	18.71[b]	25,067	43.9[b]	248,958	623	172	18.5[b]	67

SOURCE: Fair Trade Commission.
[a] As of April 1993.
[b] Average.

the thirty largest chaebols in Korea as of 1995 (appendix I to the report does not explain why the MRFTA and other chaebol regulations in Korea deal with the thirty largest chaebols). As the table shows, the size distribution of chaebols (in terms of both assets and sales) is highly skewed—note differences between the top two, the top four, the top ten, and the top thirty. The magic number thirty seems hardly justified.

THE EXTENT OF "CHAEBOL CONCENTRATION"

There has existed an old and widespread belief that the level of economic power concentration is "extraordinarily high" in Korea.[23] The matter of extent has sometimes been confused with the speed of concentration that the Korean economy experienced in the past. Unfortunately, we do not have reliable statistics showing the estimates of chaebols' share of the GDP (that is, total value added produced by a certain number of chaebols divided by the GDP). As shown in Table 2, different estimates of chaebols' shares in GDP exhibit wide discrepancies, possibly owing to the differences in the data sources and estimation methods employed. Although the three groups of estimates in Table 2 are inconsistent with each other, they all nevertheless prove clearly that chaebols' value-added share continued to increase from the 1970s until very recently.

The Mining and Manufacturing Census-Survey data allow us to obtain more reliable, if limited, estimates of the chaebol concentration ratios. Figure 1 reports recent estimates of chaebols' shipment share in the mining and manufacturing sector. The empirical regularity found here is that the monotonically increased share reached its peak in 1985, then decreased until 1989, and increased again in the 1990s. The result is somewhat different from what we observed in Table 2. Taken together, Table 2 and Figure 1 show that chaebols' share in the entire national economy has increased considerably over the past two or three decades, and their share in the manufacturing sector has also increased, especially for the largest ones (as in Fig. 1), but less sharply. This would imply that chaebols' share in the service industries must also have increased during the period.

An interesting question is what conditions affect the chaebol concentration ratio. The relative growth performance of chaebols as com-

23. The term chaebol concentration refers to chaebols' share measured in a number of ways, and should be distinguished from the familiar aggregate concentration ratio.

TABLE 2 Chaebols' Value-Added Share of GDP, 1973–1995

	SaKong									*KERI (I)*[a]				*KERI (II)*			
	1973	*1974*	*1975*	*1976*	*1977*	*1978*	*1979*	*1980*	*1981*	*1982*	*1985*	*1990*	*1992*	*1992*	*1993*	*1994*	*1995*
Top[b]	3.5	3.8	4.7	5.1	8.2	8.1	—	—	—	—	—	—	—	7.0	7.2	7.7	9.2
Top 30	—	—	—	—	—	—	—	—	—	7.3	10.6	10.7	11.9	13.5	13.6	14.2	16.2
Top 46	9.8	10.3	12.3	12.3	16.3	17.1	16.6	19.5	24.0	—	—	—	—	—	—	—	—

SOURCES: SaKong II (1980, 1993); Korea Economic Research Institute.

[a] For the year 1989, Chung and Yang (1992) report that the shares of the top 5 and the top 30 chaebols in GNP were 9.2% and 16.3 percent, respectively.

[b] For 1992 to 1995 (KERI II), the estimates are for the top four chaebols.

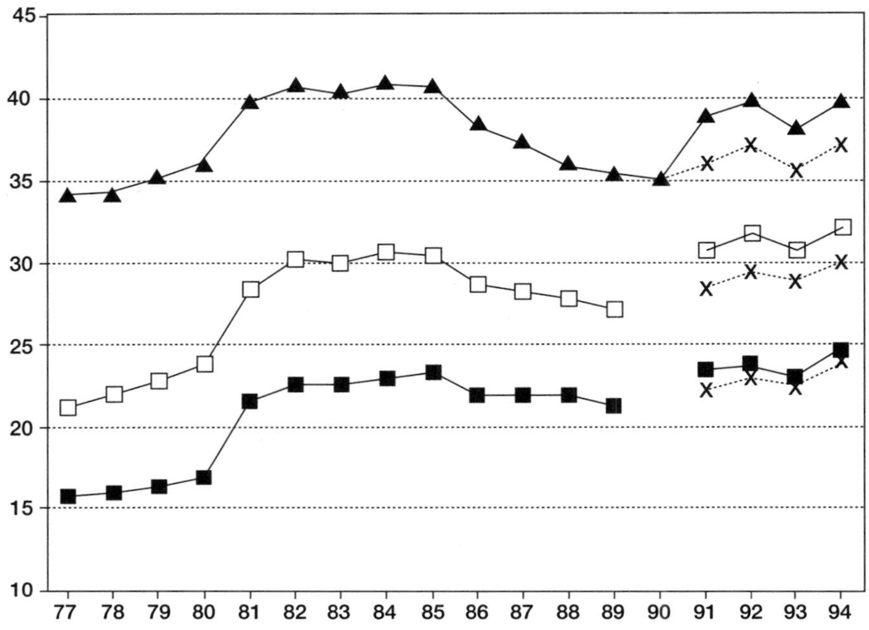

(■ : top 5, : top 10, ▲ : top 30)

FIGURE 1 Chaebol concentration ratios in mining and manufacturing sector, 1974–1994. Estimates are missing for 1990 (top 5 and top 10). The sudden jump in 1981 is partly due to the privatization of the Korea Petroleum Corporation (see note 25). Another jump in 1991 is explained by the new inclusion of POSCO; the dotted line is for the 30 largest excluding POSCO. Adapted from Lee Jae-Hyung (1996); Korea Development Institute; National Statistical Office.

pared with the non-chaebol sector of the economy accounts, by definition, for any changes in the ratio. But there are other important considerations. First, any government policies affecting the growth of chaebols, including credit, tax, trade, and investment policies, could have affected what we observe in Table 2 and Figure 1. An argument can be made along this line that the chaebol regulations that were introduced in 1987 and subsequently strengthened must have slowed down the concentration process, though it is hard to quantify their net effects. Second, because chaebols are by definition a group of firms under a single corporate control, any changes affecting the scope of corporate control must have been reflected in the changes of chaebol concentration ratios. Thus, mergers and acquisitions are an important factor affecting chaebols' share in the economy, and any changes occurring within a chaebol, such as a splitting of corporate ownership and control among the family members and the subsequent establishment of new and legally independent chaebols (the so-called satellite chaebol), can also affect the share accounted for by a given number of chaebols.[24]

A related question is: does economic growth accelerate the concentration of production by chaebols? Many people in the past thought that the answer was yes, since they simply associated Korea's rapid growth with the concentration process. However, this hasty observation has been seriously questioned in view of the decline of the chaebol concentration ratio during the 1985–1989 period (see Figure 1), when the growth rate of the entire manufacturing sector was record-high. A new interpretation with respect to the relationship between economic growth and the concentration of production is that the increase in the share of chaebols, other things being equal, accelerates during economic recession and remains stagnant or can be even reversed during an economic boom. This occurs because high growth implies an enlarged base of industries and a sharp increase in the number of non-chaebol firms, resulting in a decrease or stagnation in the relative share of chaebols. During an economic recession, on the other hand, chaebols are better prepared to keep their businesses and increase their shares. This new hypothesis still remains to be rigorously tested, but it appears to confirm the movement of the chaebol concentration ratio in Figure 1.

Another important question has been how the absolute level of the chaebols' share should be evaluated: are the shares in Table 2 and Figure 1 too high, or are they "tolerable"? Although there cannot be a definite answer to this question, Table 3 gives an indirect reference by comparing the aggregate concentration ratios observed in several market economies. The partial evidence given in Table 4 indicates that the aggregate concentration ratio, which differs considerably across coun-

24. In this context, the privatization of state-owned enterprises, which amounts to M&A between the government and the private sector, could significantly increase the chaebols' share. The sharp increase of the chaebol concentration ratio between 1980 and 1981 (see Fig. 1) can be explained by the privatization of the Korea Petroleum Corporation (acquired by Sunkyung Group in 1980), which occupied 5.6 percent of total value of shipments in the manufacturing sector as of 1980.

TABLE 3 Aggregate Concentration Ratio, 100 Largest Manufacturing Firms, 1970–1994

	1970	*1977*	*1978*	*1979*	*1980*	*1981*	*1985*	*1987*	*1988*	*1989*	*1990*	*1994*
Shipments (%)	28.7	45.0	43.6	43.1	46.3	46.2	43.4	38.5	38.1	37.2	37.7	37.3
Employment (%)	22.8	20.8	20.8	20.6	19.4	19.1	17.5	16.3	16.1	15.5	—	15.7

SOURCES: Fair Trade Commission; Korea Development Institute.

TABLE 4 International Comparison of Aggregate Concentration Ratio, 100 Largest Firms
(in percents)

	Korea (1990)	*Japan (1984)*	*U.S. (1985)*	*W. Germany (1984)*	*Canada (1983)*
Shipments	37.7	27.3[a]	48.0[a]	39.5	—
Value added	34.1	—	33.0[b]	24.8	47.1
Fixed assets	40.8	33.0	49.1	—	52.2

SOURCES: Fair Trade Commission; Marfels (1988).
[a] 1980.
[b] 1982.

tries, is not abnormally high in Korea. In Korea, the aggregate concentration ratio in terms of shipments increased sharply during the 1970s, and then decreased slowly during the 1980s (see Table 3).

A more direct comparison can be made between Japanese business groups and Korean chaebols; in 1987, six business groups accounted for 25.2 percent of the total sales of nonfinancial corporations in Japan,[25] while the five largest chaebols accounted for 21.3 percent of the total value of shipments of the manufacturing sector in Korea. Neither the numbers in Table 3 nor the Korea-Japan comparison yields any definite conclusions on the question of what is a "tolerable or normal level" for the chaebol concentration ratio. We instead note that the share of chaebols may change considerably in the near future owing to the factors we discussed.

EFFICIENCY AND COMPETITIVENESS DEBATE: AN EMPTY BOX

Are the Korean chaebols inefficient, and if so, why? This has been one of the oldest and most confusing questions raised in chaebol debate in Korea. Given that many subsidiaries of chaebols are the leading companies in Korea, the lack of trust in the efficiency and competitiveness of chaebols becomes even stronger whenever economic growth slows down. The so-called competitiveness crisis during the recessionary period of 1989–1993 led many people to find an important cause of recession in the inefficiency and weak competitiveness of the chaebols.

25. This includes not only the 163 member companies of the "President Clubs" but also their 4,960 "subsidiaries" (parent companies' equity shares above 50 percent) and 6,875 "related companies" (equity shares of 10–50 percent). The 163 member companies accounted for 14.7 percent of total sales of nonfinancial corporations.

They argue that because chaebols did not invest their surplus profits realized during 1986–1988 into R&D, upgrading their production facilities, and other productive activities but instead concentrated on diversifying expansion, land speculation, and other rent-seeking activities, the competitiveness crisis after 1989 was a natural outcome. We note that this line of argument is one of the central assertions backing up the recent specialization policy of the Korean government. Such criticisms disappeared as the economy boomed in late 1993, but they resumed in 1995 as the short boom ended. In an economy in which the growth and export performances depend heavily upon such chaebol-dominated industries as semiconductors, electronics, automobiles, shipbuilding, and petrochemicals, it is understandable that chaebols are blamed for occasional economic setbacks.

The critics of chaebols' inefficiency and weak competitiveness tried to find theoretical justifications from the existing literature in economics. Thus, they seem to believe that Korean chaebols are indeed suffering from X-inefficiencies caused by the rigidity, bureaucracy, and wastefulness of large organizations, or monopoly power, and also from technogical lethargy or coolness to innovation. They further go on to argue that the "excessive" diversifications and the concentration of corporate ownership and control in the hands of *chongsu* (the owner-managers of Korean chaebols) are the underlying structural causes of all these problems. This argument, though logically jumpy and theoretically one-sided, has proved to be very popular and powerful; it has been widely supported among government officials, journalists, and even some academics, and it is used as an argument for why the government should regulate chaebols' diversification and encourage the separation of ownership and management.

However, any available evidence does not seem to support the above argument. According to many empirical studies comparing the productivity and profitability between chaebols and non-chaebol corporations, chaebols' subsidiaries are on average more productive and profitable, although the difference is not statistically significant in some cases.[26] A more interesting fact is that, although chaebol firms are in most industries the most productive, there are a few industries in which the reverse is true. Thus, the skewed U-shaped curves in Figure 2 strongly suggest that there does not exist any evidence that would support generalizations about the inefficiency or lack of competitiveness of chaebols.

26. See a survey in Lee Jae Hyung and Yoo Seong Min (1994).

1. Sample of establishments over 500 workers (68 industries)

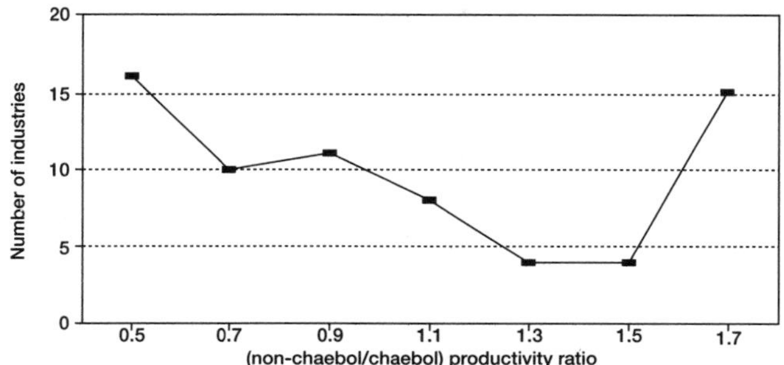

2. Sample of establishments between 300 and 499 workers (34 industries)

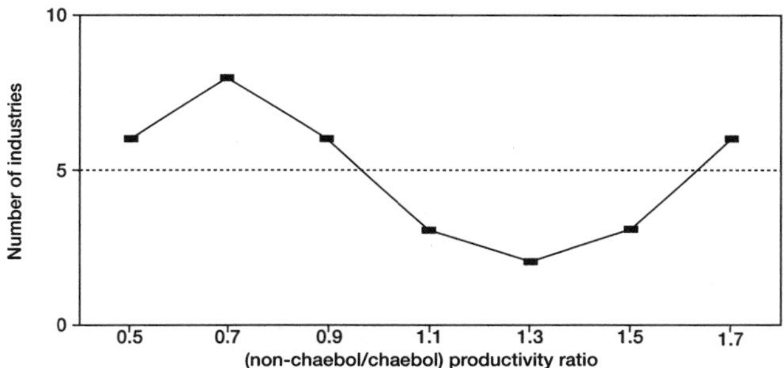

3. Sample of establishments between 200 and 299 workers (31 industries)

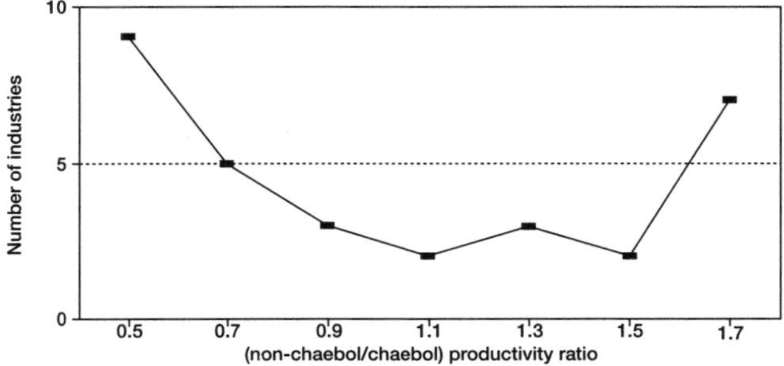

FIGURE 2 Frequency distribution of industries classified by non-chaebol/chaebol productivity ratios. The frequency table is constructed by dividing for each industry the average productivity (value added per worker) of non-chaebol establishments by that of chaebol, both confined to given size category. Adapted from Lee Jae Hyung and Yoo Seong Min (1994), Table 12, p. 113.

In a dynamic context, a reliable ex post criterion of "revealed" efficiency or competitiveness is the changes in market shares. According to this criterion, today's leading chaebols have been expanding their market shares in domestic and/or export markets, which is simply equivalent to their faster growth and increased concentration of production. Fierce competition and different competitive strengths among chaebols themselves resulted in divergent performances and turnovers in chaebols' ranking. Since we interpret changes in market shares as the outcome of dynamic competitiveness, we can say that Korean chaebols do have competitive strengths.

On the other hand, we should be cautious in interpreting the expansion of chaebols as a pure outcome of efficiency and competitiveness, as long as the strengths of chaebols entail organizational and noneconomic advantages. Organizational advantages of chaebols include the ability to overcome any market imperfections through internalization; an example of a noneconomic advantage would be the policy environment of the past that simplified chaebols' access to credit supply. The organizational advantages were an effective tool to overcome the imperfections in such markets as capital, labor, technology, and entrepreneurial talents. It is fair to say, however, that internalization incurs its own costs, which may exceed the benefits if the cross-subsidies to failing subsidiaries impede the restructuring of chaebols by delaying otherwise optimal exit and entry.

Diversification and efficiency: shaky notion and symptomatic treatment. It is no question that Korean chaebols are highly diversified in their business portfolios, which are sometimes described as "excessive," "irrational," or "octopus-like." The terms excessive and irrational may be misapplied, but certainly there is abundant evidence supporting the high extent of diversification by the chaebol. As Table 1 shows, the five largest chaebols in 1995 had, on average, 41.4 subsidiaries (4 financial companies) and did business in 29.6 KSIC 3-digit industries. The number of subsidiaries of the thirty largest chaebols increased dramatically from 126 in 1970 to 623 in 1995, a net increase of 497 firms in twenty-five years. Table 5 shows that the top five and top thirty chaebols are mainly doing business in the largest industries. An international comparison of the diversification by big businesses given in Table 6, along with the evidence given here, suffice to confirm that the extent of Korean chaebols' diversification is really extraordinary.

Koreans differ in their opinions of this diversification. The prevail-

TABLE 5 Size Distribution of Industries and Chaebol's Share (number, bil. won, percents)

Size	*Number of industries*[a]	*Total shipment*[b] *(bil. won, %)*	*Number of industries participated by*		*Chaebols' share of shipments*	
			Top 5	*Top 30*	*Top 5*	*Top 30*
Below 100 bil.	249	8,969 (3.0)	2	20	0.7	5.4
100–500 bil.	227	55,679 (18.7)	22	77	3.6	10.9
500 bil.–1 tril.	64	46,492 (15.6)	25	45	10.4	21.6
1–2 tril.	37	49,241 (16.5)	19	31	15.6	29.0
Over 2 tril.	26	137,463 (46.2)	23	25	42.7	63.3

SOURCES: Lee Jae Hyung (1996); Korea Development Institute.
[a] 5-digit KSIC industries.
[b] The numbers in parentheses are shares of each size class of total manufacturing shipments.

TABLE 6 International Comparison of Diversification by Big Business (in percents)

Types of diversification	*Korea (1989)*	*Japan (1973)*	*U.S. (1969)*	*W. Germany (1973)*	*France (1970)*	*Italy (1970)*
Specialized	8.2	16.9	6.2	22.0	16.0	10.0
Semispecialized	28.6	36.4	29.2	22.0	32.0	33.0
Related	6.1	39.9	45.2	38.0	42.0	52.0
Unrelated	57.1	6.8	19.4	18.0	10.0	5.0

SOURCES: Yang (1992), p. 13; estimates for foreign countries are quoted from Yoshihara (1981).
NOTE: Based on 49 chaebol for Korea, 118 firms for Japan, 100 firms for others. The estimates are obtained by the method suggested in Rummelt (1986).

ing view, as noted earlier, is that chaebols' "excessive" diversification undermines their efficiency and competitiveness, mainly because of the failure to concentrate their investment resources on their core activities. Many opinion leaders in Korea have been obsessed with this idea; in their view, Korean chaebols are large enough as a group when compared with world-class corporations, but the size of their individual member companies is too small to achieve any economies of scale. In fact, they seem to believe that size determines competitiveness.[27] With

27. A simple comparison of leading Korean firms such as Samsung Electronics and Hyundai Motors with their foreign rivals such as Matsushida Tenki, Toyota, and

little regard for its validity, the argument has significantly contributed to the introduction of many direct or indirect regulations of chaebols' diversifying activities and the recent specialization policy that simply equates "specialization" or "vertical integration" (the so-called related diversification in Korea) with competitiveness, and "unrelated" or "conglomerate diversification" with inefficiency. The specialization drive has thus become a vogue.

Unfortunately, economic theory does not provide a clue in resolving the dispute surrounding chaebols' diversification. Economic theory supplies logic for both diversification and specialization. Diversification is desirable to the extent that it reduces risk by means of a well-designed portfolio of businesses, helps overcome market imperfections through organizational advantages and exploits any economies of scope or synergy, and promotes efficient restructuring within an organization. On the other hand, specialization is desirable to the extent that "deepening" economies of scale strengthen competitiveness of business organizations.[28] Thus, *ex ante* theoretical criteria to support either specialization or diversification do not exist. Real world evidence does not yield any definite conclusions on the inefficiency of diversification or the efficiency consequences of specialization. We note that it is meaningless to judge from selected anecdotal evidence whether or not the diversification of chaebols really causes inefficiency. If both theory and empirical evidence do not provide any insights into the competitiveness debate on diversification, it can be concluded that the choice had best be left to private firms.

Amid the specialization vogue, we may need a new explanation of chaebols' diversification.[29] We first start from the factual observation that today's most successful chaebols are those that are highly diversified (see Table 1), whereas many of those specialized chaebols of the 1960s and 1970s went out of business. We also note that the diversify-

General Motors (in terms of sales volume or R&D investments) is frequently cited in arguing that size matters for competitiveness. But this comparison does not explain the success of Samsung Electronics and Hyundai Motors in the past when they were even smaller. We need a better understanding of the dynamics of the changing portfolio of a firm's core competence.

28. Economies of scale do not necessarily justify specialization. Many studies point out significant economies of scale in such activities as advertising, R&D, marketing network, and information gathering. It is not clear whether these economies support specialization.

29. See Jwa Sung Hee (1994) and Yoo Seong Min (1996a) for such efforts.

ing activities continued to expand rapidly during the 1980s and 1990s, in spite of government efforts to discourage diversification by means of various regulations. The traditional association of diversification and inefficiency is now seriously questioned, and logical explanations are needed about why the Korean chaebols have diversified into what they are today.

There is no doubt that the past industrial policy must have played a crucial role in determining today's business structure of chaebols; the big business–oriented, growth-first strategy was implemented for decades via discriminatory industrial policy by which the government selected target industries to promote and the firms to play the role of loyal agents. There have been other fundamentals as well, however, most of which are elementary economics of profit maximization and cost minimization. The essence of this new learning can be summarized briefly.

In a rapidly growing economy, there continue to emerge new markets that guarantee high rates of return for investments, especially when the markets are protected from foreign as well as domestic competition and competitive pressures are weak. Thus, the capital accumulated in the early phase of success combined with preferential loans in the government-controlled credit market can be easily turned into a new activity. In this process, managerial know-how and technological capability grow and often produce synergy effects, and entry regulations, if any, are often *detoured* at some cost. Thus, chaebols' diversification simply reflects the process of rapid industrial restructuring in Korea. The limitations in market size and core technological capacity also make specialization a less viable choice. Even when participating in a new market that is expected to be commercially unprofitable, there still exist other important incentives to diversify: operating a financial company significantly reduces losses when the financial sector suffers from serious market imperfections; owning a newspaper or a broadcasting company sometimes works as a key element in the success of other subsidiaries; the capital gains from holding the real estate of a new subsidiary by far exceed any losses from production when real estate prices soar. All these advantages are in fact the compensating equivalent of the profitability incentive to diversify.[30]

30. There are other noneconomic explanations, an important one being the psychological traits of many owner-managers of the Korean chaebol: for example, they seldom want to shut down one of their businesses because that would indicate total failure of management. This psychology can also be explained in terms of the nonexistence of the exit market in Korea.

In sum, the new learning is that today's structure of diversification is the logical outcome of chaebols' optimal response to changing market fundamentals and government policies. A long list of octopus-like regulations to curb the octopus-like diversification of the chaebol has constituted the core of chaebol policies in Korea, and the new learning raises an important question: with all these policy efforts, why has the extent of chaebols' diversification continued to intensify over several decades? Some would argue that the extent of diversification would have been even higher if such regulations had not existed, though the policy effects are hard to quantify.[31]

It is important to note, however, that the regulations had some serious negative effects, including restraints on competition and the functions of the market mechanism, an intensifying of the close connections between politics and business, and a hampering effect on the creativity of the private sector. Furthermore, the investment regulations of the credit control system have turned banks into regulators of industrial firms, resulting in a distorted relationship between banks and their customers. Another criticism stems from the arbitrariness of these regulations in selecting the winners and losers. These negative effects are especially associated with the microregulations of diversification, while "ceilings" regulations are expected to be less distorted on the market mechanism. Clearly, there is need for reform, but the direction of reform should be based on new knowledge identifying market fundamentals and other factors explaining chaebols' diversification. Important policy implications are that appropriate cures are not a long list of symptomatic treatments but ones that directly address these fundamentals.

With respect to chaebols' diversification, we believe there are two special topics of concern: (1) the diversification of industrial chaebols into the banking sector, and (2) diversification into the media industry. For any country, the relationship between big businesses and financial

31. A brief look at the following list of regulations on chaebols' diversification should explain why these regulations themselves could be termed "octopus": Industrial policy instruments such as entry regulations (including the license and permit system, ownership regulations, etc.), business area regulations, and investment coordination to rationalize industries and curb "excessive and duplicative" investments in many industries; regulations based upon the credit control system, including prior approval requirements for investments, land purchase, and entry into a new line of business; entry regulations to protect small and medium-sized firms; regulations on the total ceiling such as basket control of credit supply and equity investment regulations.

institutions in terms of mutual ownership and control has been the key factor determining its own model of capitalism. Control of the media industry by chaebols is, of course, of great concern in Korea since it can be an important factor in shaping the country's political economy, but this paper will not treat this problem.[32]

Ownership, control, and management: Another puzzle. Like the high degree of diversification, the concentration of corporate ownership of chaebol companies is also extraordinary. The so-called in-group shareholding ratio, a measure of chaebols' ownership concentration, is on average as high as 43.3 percent for the thirty largest chaebols in 1995, although the ratio has been slowly falling over the last decade (see Table 7). The essential feature of the 43.3 percent ownership is that 10.5 percent of the family share combined with 32.8 percent of ownership by the subsidiaries is high enough to consolidate a firm control over all subsidiaries into the hands of the owner-managers (*chongsu*) and their family members. Thus, the ownership structure shown in Table 7 is the root of the subsequent concentration of corporate control and management of chaebol companies.

An interesting point in Table 7 is that the family share continued to decline until 1994, from 17.2 percent in 1983 to 9.7 percent in 1994, but the share of the subsidiaries declined considerably in the 1987–1989 period (by 7.9 percent points), and has remained stable at the level of 32–33 percent since 1989. Although the decline in the family share is no surprise, given the expansion of the capital market in Korea, the increasing reliance of chaebols on equity financing, and the natural limitations on individuals in maintaining their shares, the sharp decline followed by long-lasting stability in the subsidiaries' share needs an explanation.[33] The sharp decline in the 1987–1989 period must be closely

32. Newspaper companies owned and possibly controlled by industrial chaebols are *Choong-Ang Daily, Mun-Hwa Daily, Kyung-Hyang Daily,* and *Korea Economic Daily.* In the broadcasting industry, chaebols have been discouraged from owning and controlling television and radio stations, and the industry has had the tradition of state control since the 1980s. Recently, however, the rapid transformation of the broadcasting industry is likely to allow chaebols' participation.

33. In this respect, the rise in the family share in 1995 is surprising. It is premature to judge whether this upturn in family share has anything to do with the expected liberalization of the M&A market in Korea: Beginning January 1997, one of the most important protections of the incumbent large shareholders in Korea's Stock Exchange Act is to be removed. We predict that regulatory changes and the subsequent liberalization of the capital market in Korea will significantly affect the existing pattern of corporate ownership of chaebols.

TABLE 7 In-Group Ownership Concentration, 1983–1996
(in percents)

	1983	*1987*	*1989*	*1990*	*1991*	*1992*	*1993*	*1994*	*1995*	*1996*
Top 30	57.2	56.2	46.2	45.4	46.9	46.1	43.4	42.7	43.3	44.1
Family	(17.2)	(15.8)	(14.7)	(13.7)	(13.9)	(12.6)	(10.3)	(9.7)	(10.5)	(10.3)
Subsidiaries	(40.0)	(40.4)	(32.5)	(31.7)	(33.0)	(33.5)	(33.1)	(33.0)	(32.8)	(33.8)
Top 5	—	60.3	49.4	49.6	51.6	51.9	49.0	47.5	—	
Family	—	15.6	13.7	13.3	13.2	13.3	11.8	12.5	—	
Subsidiaries	—	44.7	35.7	36.3	38.4	38.6	37.2	35.0	—	
Hyundai	81.4	79.9	—	60.2	67.8	65.7	57.8	61.3	60.4	
Samsung	59.5	56.5	—	51.4	53.2	58.3	52.9	48.9	49.3	
Daewoo	70.6	56.2	—	49.1	50.4	48.8	46.9	42.4	41.4	
LG	30.2	41.5	—	35.2	38.3	39.7	38.8	37.7	39.7	

SOURCE: Fair Trade Commission.

NOTE: "In-group ownership" concentration is a weighted average (where the weight is the size of capital) for each business group of the family ownership shares plus those of subsidiaries. The 1983 figures are for the month of October; all others are for the month of April.

related to the equity investment regulation of the MRFTA. It appears that once the regulatory requirements were met, chaebols wanted to maintain the ownership share of their subsidiaries around the level of 32–33 percent in order to maintain corporate control.[34] Table 8 illustrates the extent of cross-shareholdings in Japanese business groups. A comparison of the figures in this table with those in Table 7 shows the extent of cross-shareholdings in Korea to be slightly greater than in Japan.[35]

In some recent studies, the concentration of ownership and control is recognized as the central feature of the concentration of economic power. Identifying the concentration of corporate ownership and control as the key aspect of the chaebol issue is in itself a new contribution of the recent studies on chaebols, since many of the chaebol organizational characteristics basically come from the ownership and control structure. There still remain, however, a few points to be clarified for a better understanding of the nature of concentration of ownership. First, we note that highly concentrated corporate ownership and control is not simply a chaebol-specific characteristic but is also found in most non-chaebol companies in Korea. A natural question is: why do Korean firms maintain high levels of ownership concentration, and how can they maintain concentrated ownership in the course of rapid

TABLE 8 Cross-Shareholdings of Japanese Business Groups, 1977–1987 (in percents)

	Year			
Group	*1977*	*1981*	*1985*	*1987*
3 ex-zaibatsu groups	28.86	32.18	29.41	28.93
3 bank groups	18.85	18.75	17.39	16.36
Average of 6 groups	23.86	23.86	23.40	22.65

SOURCE: Masuyama (1994), 332.

NOTE: The numbers are obtained by the following formula:

$$\left[\frac{\text{Shares owned by member companies out of total number of existing shares}}{\text{Number of member companies}}\right] \times 100$$

34. The consequences of the amendment of the MRFTA in 1994, which lowered the ceiling of total equity investments from 40 percent to 25 percent of net assets, will be interesting. In Korea, the equity investment regulation of the MRFTA is the government's only tool for controlling the ownership share of chaebols' subsidiaries.

35. It is to be noted that the method of computing the share of chaebol subsidiaries in Table 6 is slightly different from the formula used to compute the extent of cross-shareholdings in Table 7 and 8; see note to Table 8.

growth? The answer lies in the method of corporate financing. It is well known that Korean firms have grown by means of debt financing rather than equity financing: the desire of owner-managers to maintain a large ownership share coupled with debt financing has resulted in ownership concentration.

This observation leads to the second point about the nature of the process of ownership deconcentration. In any capitalist economy, corporate ownership dispersion is achieved when the largest shareholders in the early days of a firm's history are forced into lower levels of ownership share as the firm draws the huge amount of capital necessary for growth in the capital market. An important feature of this change is that the process usually takes a long time, which also depends upon the development of the capital market in the economy.[36] Thus, the nature of ownership dispersion can be interpreted as the dilution of ownership shares in the process of a firm's growth.

The message of these two points is clear: although ownership dispersion may be desirable in many respects, such as the establishment of "property right democracy" and more equitable distribution of income and wealth, it will occur over a long period of time and will require the development of a mature capital market.[37] Since ownership deconcentration is a long-term goal, the role of policies and laws to expedite the deconcentration process is important but has certain limitations. Any misconceptions with respect to the time horizon must be cleared.

Though ownership deconcentration is regarded as a long-term goal, there has nevertheless been some criticism of corporate control and management by the owner-managers, subsequently leading to discussions on the separation of ownership and management and the establishment of professional management in Korea. The criticism points to the fact that the ownership structure in Table 7 resulted in a primitive corporate control structure in which the owner-managers exercise full control over all subsidiaries, and the role of professional managers in individual subsidiaries is quite limited. Indeed, many people favor this

36. Even in the U.S., which today has one of the most advanced and largest stock markets in the world, the dispersion of corporate ownership took nearly a century. According to Herman (1981, 58–62), the proportion of "manager-controlled" companies (in which ownership was widely dispersed) was 23.8 percent in 1990 and 82.5 percent in 1974 in samples of large corporations.

37. In the discussion of equity and fairness that follows, we question the real effects of corporate ownership dispersion on distributive equity.

separation of ownership and control and the introduction of professional management at the earliest time possible.

For our part, although the present form of corporate control and management of chaebol companies obviously suffers from certain problems, we are still not prepared to adopt a definite position the issue.[38] A fundamental question is whether we can choose a priori between owner-management and professional management on the basis of any efficiency criteria. The answer must be negative, because there are pros and cons for both types of management structures. Here again, economic theory and real world evidence offer many important insights, but the choice for Korean chaebols can hardly be made along those lines: for example, the theory of property right based upon a model of principal-agent relationship would tell us that the Korean model of owner-management may suffer less from the inefficiencies in the form of agency costs, but this observation, if valid, is only one of the many merits of the Korean model. In fact, introducing professional management requires ownership dispersion, a market for managers, and the development of a new corporate control–governance mechanism that can replace the present one based upon concentrated ownership. This problem will be discussed in detail in the concluding section, but we note here that these requirements will not be easy to achieve overnight, nor, indeed, did Japanese corporate capitalism, American managerial capitalism, and German financial capitalism become established quickly. Then all came about over a long period of time, and each has its own mechanism of corporate control–governance and management. It is interesting to observe that in Korea, the market for professional managers is itself internalized by chaebols.

It is our tentative conclusion that the separation of ownership and control is neither desirable for efficiency reasons nor supported by practical requirements in the foreseeable future, and the choice should in the meantime be left in the hands of private firms. Therefore, a warning should be given to any attempts by the government to impose a particular type of management structure via coercive policy instruments. Rather, we believe that competitive pressures in the output markets will stimulate chaebols to improve their control and management structure because owner-managers facing the threat of severe competition have a strong incentive to restructure their corporate control and management.

38. See Shin, Yu Kun (1992) for a discussion of the strengths and weaknesses of the owner-management system of the large corporations in Korea.

An emerging related concern having to do with chaebols' ownership, control, and management is the establishment of a holding company. This has been prohibited by the MRFTA (following the postwar Japanese tradition) in an effort to curb the concentration of economic power, but the result has been not the intended effect but rather a variant model of a holding company, in which the corporate ownership is centralized in one or more core companies that are at the top of the pyramid of ownership chain and are owned by the owner-managers and their families (de facto holding company). The functions of top decision making, centralized coordination, and planning are carried out by the so-called chairman's office or planning and coordinating office.[39] In other words, Korean chaebols are structured as if holding companies existed—an important difference from Japan.

EQUITY AND FAIRNESS: REAL OR MISCONCEIVED?

An important message of the new developments relating to the chaebol issue is that chaebols create problems not because they are inefficient but because equity and fairness are structurally undermined and the legitimacy of chaebols' growth is seriously questioned. Although it is often unclear what is meant by equity, fairness,[40] and legitimacy, we believe that the problems of inequity, unfairness, and

39. The structure of intercompany shareholding and the exact status of the chairman's office differ among chaebols. However, for the leading chaebols, there exist one or more core companies at the top of the ownership pyramid, and the role of the chairman's office (different names among chaebols) is quite important. The de facto holding companies of the leading chaebols are: Hyundai Heavy Industries (Hyundai), Samsung Life Insurance and Samsung Electronics (Samsung), LG Chemicals and LG Electronics (LG), Daewoo Heavy Industries and Daewoo Corporation (Daewoo), Sunkyung Corporation (Sunkyung), Ssangyong Cement (Ssangyong), Korean Air (Hanjin), and Kia Motors (Kia).

40. The notions of equity and fairness are at most very shaky and are often condemned as a logic of the weak. Such definitions as "Equity: simply a matter of the length of the judge's ears" (Elbert Hubbard), "Fair: equitably, honestly, impartially, justly; according to rule" (Oxford English Dictionary), show how subjective the notions can be. According to Peyton Young (1994), arguments against the existence of equity take three different forms: first, equity is merely a word that hypocritical people use to cloak self-interest (it has no intrinsic meaning and therefore fails to exist); second, even if equity does exist in some notional sense, it is so hopelessly subjective that it cannot be analyzed scientifically and therefore fails to exist in an objective sense; third, even if granting that equity may not be entirely subjective, there is no sensible theory about it, and certainly none that is compatible with modern welfare economics. In short, it fails to exist in an academic sense.

illegitimacy do exist and that concerns about them are real and reasonable. To the extent that the chaebol-dominated economy creates such problems, the so-called anti-chaebol attitude of the general public is understandable; certainly if such problems exist and are neglected, we may endanger the stability and soundness of our economic system. Further, to the extent that efficiency is rooted in the people's will to participate and their approval of the social system, any instability and unsoundness caused by public fears of inequity, unfairness, and illegitimacy can also undermine efficiency.

It would require an ambitious interdisciplinary research to enhance our knowledge of equity, fairness, and legitimacy in relation to Korean chaebols. Thus, we do not try to question the validity of such concerns or explain what has caused the problems in Korea. Here, we are interested only in trying to highlight some of the misconceptions regarding the issues of equity, fairness, and legitimacy that have appeared in the past and have perhaps led to inappropriate policy responses.

Distributive equity and ownership concentration. The criticism that a chaebol-dominated economy causes distributive inequity relates to the concentration of corporate ownership as seen in Table 7. It has been suggested that if corporate ownership of today's chaebols were widely dispersed among the general public, the public's mistrust of chaebols would have been mitigated. Because the corporate ownership of the leading companies in Korea is highly concentrated in the hands of a small number of chaebol families, criticisms arise that the benefits of rapid economic growth are not shared among many Koreans, and that people's support of the free enterprise system is weakening. As we consider the social demand for people's capitalism and property rights democracy, such criticisms appear valid.

This concern about distributive inequity associated with the concentration of corporate ownership constitutes the basis of many government policies to promote dispersion of ownership in chaebol companies—such as strengthening the administration of inheritance taxes, measures to induce chaebol companies to go public, and so on.

However, one must still ask, does ownership dispersion really tend to equalize distribution? In our opinion, not necessarily. Even if the corporate ownership of chaebol companies should become more dispersed than it is now, distributive equity may not be enhanced unless the stocks are sold below market prices. Stocks and securities are only one of many different kinds of properties, and from the point of view of the chaebol family, selling stocks and purchasing land, for example, though it would change their portfolio, would not change their total wealth. It therefore seems clear that ownership dispersion does not improve distributive equity unless the deconcentration of ownership entails a portion of subsidy to whoever buys the stocks, which is hard to imagine.

There exist, of course, situations in which corporate ownership dispersion leads to enhanced distributive equity. The so-called ESOP (employee stock ownership plan) allows workers to receive shares of the common stock of the company they work for, and in many cases this transaction occurs below the market value of the stock, implying improvement in distributive equity. The company may choose to adopt ESOP if it would give the workers an additional incentive toward greater productivity, or because the company can recover the loss from an investment tax credit. The other shareholders, however, may not be happy with this arrangement because the preferential subsidy to the workers is "not equitable" from their point of view. Another example would be the so-called "people's share," which was introduced in the partial privatization of POSCO and KEPCO in 1988. The policy makers at that time explicitly had in mind selling the stocks of state-owned enterprises below market value to the urban poor and farmers so that distributive equity could be enhanced.[41]

Although the concentration of ownership is often identified with inequity, it is our conclusion that ownership dispersion does not in itself guarantee any improvement in distributive equity. Notwithstanding such exceptional cases as the ESOP or people's share, the traditional association of equity and ownership dispersion is not justified, and it is questioned whether the policies to promote ownership dispersion of chaebol companies have as much effect in enhancing distributive equity as other policies such as tax, utility price regulations, and welfare programs. We note that the traditional criticism of ownership concentration based on distributive equity may originate from people's confusion between distributive inequity and chaebols' illegal practices such as insider trading, misappropriation of the corporate fund by the

41. Ironically, the people's share program in 1988–1989 resulted in a disaster when Korea's stock market collapsed down in 1990. Although the government intended to subsidize the poor by selling those stocks well below the estimated market values, the result was that the poor who bought people's shares incurred serious losses. Many people criticized this program for its naïveté in subsidizing the poor with such a risky asset.

owner-managers as evidenced by the recent political scandal, tax evasion, and other illegal activities of largest shareholders.

Chaebols and fairness in competition. Fairness has also been one of the key concerns in the chaebol debate, albeit its inherent ambiguity. Both equity and fairness seem to be closely related to economic justice, but it is beyond the scope of this paper to explore what these mean in Korea with respect to chaebols. People just like to use the words unfair, inequitable, and injustice when they criticize certain phenomena related to chaebols. A number of provisions in the MRFTA and other economic laws in Korea outline a variety of "unfair" of "undue" practices, but it is never clear what exactly constitutes unfairness or being undue. If fairness implies the equality of economic power or economic opportunity, then the concentration of economic power in the hands of chaebols is by definition "unfair." Fairness in egalitarian terms would condemn any inequalities and therefore is not a useful or operational concept. Admitting that the inequality of power is one of the most palpable facts of human existence, we had better turn to "fairness in the use of power." With respect to the chaebol issue, this concept of fairness raises an old and widely asked question in Korea: Do chaebols abuse their power and restrain competition substantially and unfairly?

A prevailing view in Korea has been that chaebols restrain competition not only because some of their subsidiaries have market power but because their conglomerate structure enables them to deter competition from their independent rivals. The debate in Korea around this issue is essentially the same as the long-standing debate in U.S. antitrust law and economics between the Chicago school and its opponents regarding whether or not vertical and conglomerate integrations restrain competition—and, in the same way, we are not prepared to conclude the issue of chaebols' unfair and undue restraints of competition. It is not clear from theoretical arguments whether chaebols' restraints of competition are based upon the already significant market power of their subsidiaries,[42] or whether the conglomerate nature of chaebols increases the likelihood of abusive practices. In this respect, it is easier to criticize the seemingly unfair practices of chaebols than to establish "a fair rule of the game."

42. In 1994, 83 of the 100 largest manufacturing firms in Korea were the subsidiaries of the top 30 chaebols. Out of the 1,705 commodities produced by the top 30 chaebols (manufacturing sector), they enjoyed the first, second, or third highest market shares in 1,099 (64.5 percent) commodities. See Lee Jae Hyung (1997).

Instead, we point to the fact that some of the chaebol regulations are indeed anticompetitive, since many of these regulations are likely to protect incumbents from important sources of potential competition. Entry regulations intended to prevent so-called excessive competition and duplicative investments are in fact severely limiting competition in such markets as telecommunications, electricity, steel, and automobile manufacturing. These regulations obviously violate the basic premise of competition law, which protects not the competitors but the competition. Entry regulations for small and medium industries also have anticompetitive effects. We have seen in many industries that once these regulations are removed or detoured, Korean chaebols behave more as mutual invaders than the hypothesis of mutual forbearance or marriage agreement suggests.

LEGITIMACY, GOVERNMENT-BUSINESS INTERFACE, AND THE REAL THREAT OF CHAEBOLS

Nothing appears to be more obvious, though not more important, as a defect of chaebols than the illegitimacy of their growth, although the term illegitimate is as unclear as unfair and inequitable. Many Koreans who would disagree on such matters as efficiency, equity, and fairness would agree that chaebols' growth has been possible because of their rent-seeking behavior and the sacrifice of consumers, workers, taxpayers, banks, small- and medium-sized firms, and possibly foreigners. It is interesting to observe that the notion of illegitimacy refers mainly to this repression of the non-chaebol sector and chaebols' rent-seeking, though it seems to include any illegal and unlawful behavior of chaebols.

Illegitimacy: Who is responsible? We acknowledge this criticism of illegitimacy behind chaebols' growth, but we do question how the illegitimate growth was possible or even overlooked in our sociopolitical system. Who is responsible? Answering this question of responsibility is important in understanding what a chaebol policy should do to make the chaebol a legitimate entity. We argue that the government was the "principal offender" while the chaebol was the "accomplice," and also that the uncontrolled growth of chaebols has been possible under the unique government-business relationship rooted in Korea.[43]

43. This view is closely related to the question of the social responsibilities of corporations: that is, whether private corporations are social entities assuming responsi-

In fact, such ingredients of illegitimate growth of chaebols as the repression of the financial sector, consumers, workers, and small and medium industries, and the protection and preferential subsidies extended to chaebols, have been important factors in the growth strategy of the Korean government. To the extent that the Korean government actively sought to employ these strategies, it can be said at the same time that the government neglected their ill effects, and therefore is primarily responsible for the rampant growth of chaebols. The government as planner, entrepreneur, and banker played the role of "gap-filler" or "input-completer," and in many cases picked the winners; the chaebols' share of responsibility for its own illegitimacy was insignificant. Under these circumstances, chaebols can only be accused of having tried to obtain greater access to government-controlled investment resources, of having lobbied for government approval to start or expand their businesses, and of having made speculative investments whenever the expected returns were high.

In sum, it is the government, not the chaebols, that should be criticized for having created the illegitimacy concern. Surprisingly, however, anti-chaebol emotion seems to be far greater than anti-government emotion, justifying any chaebol regulations in the interests of restoring legitimacy. The real danger here is that the past illegitimacy may justify today's irrational chaebol regulations, making chaebols pay for the government's wrongs.

An economist's view of the government-business relationship in Korea. The legitimacy issue discussed in this way calls for a deeper understanding of the government-business relationship in Korea.[44] In terms of government-business relationship the legacies of past economic development appear to be the state's predominance over the market, which has been maintained through government control of vital resources and the government's patriarchal authority and discretionary power. However, underlying this leader-follower or dominance-compliance rela-

---

bilities to their stakeholders or simply profit maximizers accountable only to shareholders. Our view is closer to the property conception of the corporation than to the social entity conception. See Allen (1995).

44. Studies of chaebols and the government-business relationship by political scientists offer similar but slightly different insights. See Chung-in Moon (1994), Haggard (1994), and Eun Mee Kim (1988). Kim views the evolution of the government-business relationship as a transition from dependency to symbiosis. We argue that the nature of symbiosis had existed earlier.

tionship has been a relationship of symbiosis: that is, both the government and chaebols needed each other, though for different reasons.

An essential element of the government-business relationship in Korea is the government's role as the insurer or underwriter and chaebols' opportunism to capitalize on this insurance, which may be termed as chaebols' moral hazard. This insurance and moral hazard aspect of the government-business relationship has been built over decades of government protection, intervention, and support on the one hand, and chaebols' endless expansion through debt financing on the other. Once established, this insurance and moral hazard relationship created its own energy even though the original forces behind the relationship weakened. Knowing that the government was their "risk partner" who feared chaebols' going bankrupt, chaebols were able to expand their businesses much faster and in a riskier manner than they would otherwise have done. On the part of the government, the so-called "too big to fail" (TBTF) argument has quieted any criticism against the insurance function, and in times of economic difficulties the government provided either bailout loans or other rescue measures to chaebols that were on the brink of bankruptcy. The result was even bigger chaebols financially worse off and the government and national economy held hostage by chaebols. Not all chaebols were successful in exploiting the distorted government-business relationship (the bankruptcy of the Kukje Group in 1985, for example), and it is fair to say that chaebols increasingly face the threat of bankruptcy and the challenge of improving their financial status. Nonetheless, the essential nature of this relationship has not yet changed much.

The TBTF argument and distortions in the government-business relationship tell us how important it is to have a properly functioning exit market in Korea. As long as the government manipulates the exit market on an *ad hoc* basis, the moral hazard of chaebols will remain a reality, and the chaebol issue in Korea will not be free of the taint of illegality. If the Korean government wants to escape from the vicious circle of "symbiosis insurance moral hazard illegitimacy," it needs to rethink the validity of the TBTF argument and develop institutions for an exit market whose forces will discipline chaebols. This implies an overhauling of the government-business relationship and Korea's financial sector. The task will not be easy, considering the many obstacles lying ahead.

It is interesting to find a new interpretation of the existing chaebol regulations we criticized earlier. As long as the government continues to play the role of an insurer, it realizes at the same time that it is responsible for improving the financial status of chaebols that are skeptical of maintaining a sound financial status on account of the moral hazard. This explains why the government cannot throw away such symptomatic treatments as the equity investment regulations, the credit control system, and mutual loan guarantees, which are hardly justified when we investigate their rationale independently of the government-business relationship.

What are the real threats? The question whether the Korean government can reduce, if not eliminate, its traditional insurance function either by leaving the exit decisions to market forces or by increasing the "deductible" to be paid by chaebols in order to correct chaebols' questionable validity has a lot to do with political economy. We observe that the TBTF argument is alive even in today's most advanced economies, and that the development of representative democracy in Korea can produce a new form of a government-business relationship where insurance and moral hazard are still maintained.

Although a discussion of the political economy of big business is beyond the scope of this paper, we nevertheless admit that the real threat of chaebols to the Korean economy lies in their social and political power resulting from their economic weight—a danger foreseen by many great economists since Adam Smith. The TBTF argument and the ensuing moral hazard of chaebols are only limited realizations of this sociopolitical power. In general, we are concerned about the power of chaebols being so enormous that it influences the governing body of our nation to adopt laws, institutions, and policies that protect their private interests. As pointed out by Corwin D. Edwards (1955, 345), "By virtue of its size, the large concern also has substantial advantages in activities that lie outside the process of production and sales. These advantages are particularly evident in litigation, politics, public relations, and finance."

As long as economic power seeks political power with which to protect itself, a real threat to our entire system does exist. In Korea, the "bigness" of chaebols, which is the source of political as well as economic power, is increasing at a pace never experienced before. In 1994, total assets and sales of the thirty largest chaebols were 233 trillion won and 248 trillion won, respectively, while the total expenditures of the central government were only 64 trillion won. The total investments in fixed assets of the thirty largest chaebols in 1995 were 35 trillion won, while the total investments were 49 trillion won. Even though we now realize that many of the anti-chaebol criticisms are ill-rooted or misconceived, there exists a blunt but real threat of big business. In this context, we think that the following comments are worth quoting.

> Concentration of economic power in all-embracing corporations represents a kind of private government which is a power unto itself, a regimentation of other people's money and other people's lives. (Franklin D. Roosevelt)

> The myth that holds that the great corporation is a puppet of the market, the powerless servant of the consumer, is, in fact, one of the services by which its power is perpetuated. (John Kenneth Galbraith)

> Capitalist organizers of monopolies constitute one of the two most serious threats to a free society (the other being organized labor). . . . A state which allows such enormous aggregations of power to grow up cannot afford to let this power rest entirely in private control." (Friedrich A. Hayek)

> The great enemy of democracy is monopoly, in all its forms. . . . Effectively organized functional groups—including gigantic corporations—possess tremendous power for exploiting the community at large and even for sabotaging the system." (Henry C. Simons)

Government-Banking-Business Relationship

In the early 1960s the Korean government nationalized all the banks—an act deemed essential to carrying on its policy of export-driven economic development. When the financial market was very much underdeveloped and capital was scarce, the tight control of the financial sector by government was needed for mobilizing capital and channeling it into the strategic target industries. Put another way, the government itself has been playing the role of the Schumpeterian banker: evaluating projects and entrepreneurs, and then channeling scarce capital into the most promising projects and entrepreneurs. Given that, in the early stages of economic development, the financial market was underdeveloped and imperfect, and the government was superior to the existing financial institutions in information and managerial ability, the government's role as the Schumpeterian banker could be justified.

THE GOVERNMENT-BANKING INTERFACE

There seems little question that the government's decisions on preferential policy loans to target industries contributed to the growth of chaebols. In great measure the character of the chaebols today is, indeed, a consequence of their rapid growth through debt financing. We have pointed out the highly concentrated ownership and the high debt-equity ratio. The high concentration of ownership, made possible through the debt financing provided by the government, determined the present corporate governance structure of the chaebols, in which corporate control is concentrated in the owner-managers and their families and allows the transfer of corporate control almost exclusively within the owner's family.

However, as the size of the economy grew and the structure of the economy became more complicated, the government's role as chief banker began to crack. The government was losing its superiority to the market in information and ability, and it often picked the wrong winners and channeled capital into them in an inefficient manner. Furthermore, it brought about distortions in the incentive structure of the chaebols. The chaebols, capitalizing on the insurance provided by the government, increasingly relied on a growth strategy based solely on debt financing, expecting that the government would provide bailout loans to them in the case of bankruptcy risks.

The government's control of the banking sector seriously undermined competitiveness in banks. In the past, the bad loan position of the banks largely resulted from government intervention in the distribution of credit. Another consequence of the government's control of the banking sector is that, to give credence to banks for the mobilization of capital, banks are not allowed to fail, so there was no need for depositors to monitor banks. Thus free to do as they chose, banks could take lending risks, resulting in the heavy burden of nonperforming assets to the banks today in Korea.

The inefficiency of the financial sector, largely brought about by government intervention, has been a deterrent to long-term economic development. Now, as the economy matures, the financial sector itself is better suited to the role of the Schumpeterian banker—better suited to evaluating investment projects and better suited to channeling savings into the most profitable investment projects.

RELAXING THE SEPARATION BETWEEN BANKING AND BUSINESS

From the early 1980s the government started to deregulate the financial market, but the financial system still remains under a number of government controls. In particular, although the commercial banking sector has been privately owned since the mid-1980s, the government still does not allow it to have full managerial autonomy.[45] Related to this government control of the banking sector, the government has pursued the policy of separation between the banks and the chaebols.[46] Relaxing the separation between banks and business offers potential benefits but it also would involve certain costs.

Benefits of managerial efficiency. The separation between the banking sector and the chaebols creates a dichotomy in the capital market that may preserve managerial inefficiencies in the banking sector but at the same time limit the transfer to the banking industry of superior management skills in the chaebols.[47]

Benefits of synergy. Economies of scale might result if, following acquisition by a commercial firm, a bank grows in size and its unit cost of producing banking service declines. To the extent that such cost savings exist, and demand conditions dictate that some of these cost savings are passed on to consumers of bank services, then both banks and con-

45. In 1993, the Office for Bank Supervision set a rule by which bank presidents are selected by committees consisting of representatives of shareholders, corporate clients, general customers, and former bank presidents. But the government's influence on the nomination of commercial bank presidents still continues. More importantly, the five major chaebols are not allowed to participate in this selection committee even if they are shareholders.

46. The government does not, however, have a policy of separating non-bank financial institutions and chaebols. The non-bank financial institutions are somewhat different from the banking industry in that the general public (small depositors) are not much involved in their failure. And the non-bank financial institutions are not so involved as banks are in the creation of money.

47. In a well-developed capital market, if managers operate a firm inefficiently, the firm will eventually become a takeover target for a more efficient group of owners and managers. However, if, because of government regulation, firms are not allowed to acquire banks, this will protect inefficient managers. In an efficient and undichotomized market for corporate control in which firms could acquire banks there would be important incentives for managers to operate their firms efficiently. Takeover and acquisition barriers not only protect inefficient management but could prevent superior management teams from transferring their skills.

sumers could benefit.[48] On the other hand, economies of scope might result if, by producing many products in an optimal or efficient combination, aggregate costs are lowered. The major source of such potential cost savings comes from the efficient sharing of inputs across multiple outputs. For the U.S. banking industry, the empirical finding is that there are insignificant economies of scope in banking.[49] Whereas cost economies of scope analyze banks' savings on costs by utilizing a more efficient combination of input resources, revenue gains may also be generated from an ability to market, distribute, and cross-sell bank and firm products to customers more efficiently.[50] Potential cost-side synergies, such as economies of scope, are best achieved by the fullest form of organizational integration, but a full integration of the organization is not necessary in order to achieve revenue-side synergies.

Benefits of a diversification. The diversification benefit results from the expanded nature of the product scope of a bank-firm conglomerate; that is, if the profits on different bank-firm product lines of a conglomerate are imperfectly correlated, the aggregate profit of the conglomerate will be more stable.[51] It must be noted that any such diversification

48. The extent of economies of scale in banking has long been the subject of dispute in the literature. The empirical results, mostly conducted on U.S. data sets, are consistent with the potential presence of economies of scale in the banking industry for all but the biggest banks. While the average cost function for banks may decline there may be considerable cost deviations from the frontier of the cost function. For instance, Berger and Humphrey (1990) estimate a thick cost function frontier and analyze banks' deviations from that frontier for a U.S. data set. They find that both technical inefficiency (proportionate overuse of inputs) and allocative inefficiency (improper input mix) are so large that the cost function for the lowest cost quartile of banks, for any size group, can differ from the highest cost quartile by up to 30 percent. This is consistent with considerable cost inefficiencies remaining in (U.S.) banking despite the presence of economies of scale.

49. Two interpretations of this finding are possible: (1) there really are no economies of scope to be gained from expanding the range of bank products; (2) economies of scope exist but regulatory restrictions on operational linkages and activity diversification prevent bank management from employing the optimal cost-minimizing mix of financial products. However, as to the second possibility Saunders and Walter (1994) found no evidence of cost economies of scope between banking products and fee-related products for the world's top 200 banks, many of which have universal banking powers.

50. Empirical evidence of its potential size is very scarce.

51. For example, a firm that had big investments in the automobile industry might be better insured against a recession in automobile sales to the extent that the financial services sold by its bank subsidiaries are less sensitive to economic downturns.

gains will only be valued positively by investors in imperfect markets in which they find it impossible to achieve full diversification benefits by their own diversification. Thus the more perfect and frictionless capital markets are, the smaller the private gains to investors from diversification by conglomerates.

The costs of conflicts of interest. It should be noted that the conflicts of interest discussed below are all "potential conflicts" and that a common theme is the existence of either uncompetitive markets or imperfect flows of information. The more one party has monopoly market power or possesses private information, the higher the potential for conflicts of interests. If firms are allowed to own banks, four potential conflicts of interest could arise (Corrigan 1987a): (1) A bank may restrict the supply of credit to the competitors of its affiliated firm while giving preferential credit toward its affiliated firm; for this to be a serious concern, the market for bank loans and bank loan substitutes would have to be uncompetitive. (2) A bank may use its lending powers to tie customers to the products produced by its affiliated firm;[52] this is the fear that a bank might use its consumer finance powers to tie a customer into a specific purchase from its affiliated firm.[53] (3) A bank may make loans to a failing affiliated firm to keep it in business; such practices might ultimately threaten the safety of the bank itself. (4) A bank may disseminate to its affiliated firm valuable private or inside information gathered in the course of its banking business.[54]

On the other hand, the potential losses on the bank's investments that occur when nominal interest rates rise might be significantly offset if real-sector investment returns such as those in the automobile industry are less sensitives to changes in interest rates.

52. For instance, the Hyundai bank could offer special low-priced loans tied to the purchase of Hyundai cars only.

53. It is important to examine the potential market conditions under which such a link would be profitable for a bank-firm conglomerate. Economic theory is very clear in specifying that the market demand conditions under which linking arrangements are profitable are extremely limited (see Posner 1976). In particular, if a firm has monopoly power in one market and attempts to tie a customer to a product sold in another competitive market, its overall profits may well decrease. Thus, if low (below market) interest rates are offered by a car manufacturer for auto financing from its affiliated bank, any attempt by this manufacturer to recoup this cut of interest rate by attempting to tie the customer (in a product package) to a high (over market) priced model is likely to be frustrated because customers will switch to other car manufacturers. At worst, customers might view this arrangement as a package allowing any lower cost of credit to be just offset by a rise in the auto's price.

54. For instance, the Samsung bank could learn of a new investment project of a rival company that could adversely affect Samsung Electronics in the market for consumer durables.

Implicit cost to the safety net. A more indirect cost lies in the possibility that a bank's affiliation with a firm could increase its risk of bank failure and thereby impose costs on the central bank, the deposit insurance system, and the payments system. One can think of several potential directions in which a bank might be weakened by an affiliation with a firm: (1) The bank might be induced to upstream excessive fee payments for the services (for example, management services) provided by the firm-owner, but if the owner charged the bank excessive fees for the services, that could weaken the earnings and capital of the bank at the expense of increasing the owner's profits. (2) The bank might be required to upstream excessive dividend payments to the firm-owner; as in the case of fees, such excessive dividend payments could potentially serve to weaken the capital position of the bank and enhance that of the firm-owner.[55] (3) Bad assets might be transferred from the firm-owner or its affiliates to the bank.[56] (4) Bad news about the firm-owner could have a negative and contagious effect on bank depositors and loan customers.[57] (5) Interlinks between a firm and a bank could lead to doubts about a bank's legal corporate separateness.

As for the implicit cost to the deposit insurance system, the concern is the transfer of explicit and implicit deposit insurance subsidies from the banking sector to its affiliated firms. This concern is about pricing deposit insurance in a correct manner, however, rather than worry about an inherent fault in the concept of deposit insurance as a deterrent to bank runs and illiquidity in the financial system. To the

55. In the U.S. there are a number of existing firewalls that limit such an abuse. For example, the Federal Reserve can restrict the dividend payments of banks whose capital falls below minimum target levels (i.e., 8 percent risk-based capital)

56. If the activities of non-bank affiliates have to be closely related to banking, the transfer of financial assets, say from an insurance affiliate to a bank, may be a real concern. However, it is difficult to conceive of ways in which the firm-owner could transfer bad tangible assets such as plant and equipment to its banking affiliate. As long as banks are largely specialized in purchasing financial assets (either debt or equity) this risk should be a minor concern.

57. To the extent that the parent firm and the bank subsidiary shared the same names and managements, then losses, or bad profit news, relating to the firm-owner would tend to discourage investors from renewing bank deposits, or induce loan customers to seek more stable credit lines elsewhere. It is not clear how relevant such fears are, however—for example, how likely is it that depositors hearing of problems on the Hyundai's production line would jump to the conclusion that the Hyundai's bank was mismanaged? To the extent that the investment and operational decisions at the firm level are very different from those at the bank level, bad news about a firm may have little impact. If the activities of non-bank affiliates are closely related to banking (for instance, insurance), contagion fears might very well be more relevant.

extent that deposit insurance allows banks to raise funds at close to the risk-free rate (rather than the risk-free rate plus an appropriate risk premium), some part of this subsidy net of any deposit-insurance premiums to a bank's cost of funds could be passed on to its affiliated firm via loans at rates tied to the bank's cost of funds.[58]

For the payment system, the major fear is that if a commercial firm used its affiliated bank to transmit its payment messages and was unable to settle its obligations at the end of the day, then a number of other banks might also be unable to settle (since they relied on receiving the affiliated bank's settlement funds). To prevent a systemic crisis, the Central bank would be forced to intervene by providing funds in the place of the defaulting party or opening the discount window to the troubled bank affiliate so that it could meet its parent's settlement commitments. In either case it is argued implicitly that the Central bank would be extending the safety net beyond the banking system to support the parent firm of the bank affiliate.[59]

QUESTIONS ABOUT BANKING-BUSINESS RELATIONSHIPS IN KOREA

Historically, the United States, Germany, and Japan have developed the distinct models of the bank-firm relationship. For example, it is argued that the economic successes of the German and Japanese

58. In the U.S. Section 23A lending firewalls of the Federal Reserve Act limit such loans to an affiliate to 10 percent of a bank's capital; the magnitude of any such subsidy would not be large. One can think of a number of safeguards and reforms that might be used to better insulate the deposit insurance system from the firms that own banks—e.g., consolidated regulation for the firms that own banks. Such a policy would be very difficult, however, because of the nonfinancial nature of a firm's assets production processes, and also because of the extreme heterogeneity of production processes across firms. Enormous examination and monitoring resources might be required for regulators to undertake consolidated regulation of banks and firms. An alternative and possibly more effective method would be to establish strict quality controls on the types of firms that could acquire banks. One of the greatest protections that the deposit insurance system has against abuse of a bank by the firm-owner is to require that the bank itself hold an adequate and transparent level of capital. It is not the size of the capital standard (e.g., 8 percent) that is important but the requirement that regulators closely monitor this ratio and close a bank before capital is fully dissipated. It is crucial to protecting the integrity of the insurance fund and ultimately taxpayers. As long as a bank is closed before its net worth is zero, the insurance fund is protected regardless of who owns the bank.

59. One can think of several safeguards that might be used to avoid such payment system risks. These measures presuppose a sound system of prudential regulation in the economy.

economies are to some extent attributable to the direct equity links and main bank lending relationships developed between banks and firms. Such a proposition is based on the presumption that banks have a unique role in reducing agency costs.[60] On the other hand, out of concerns about the potential growth of large monopolistic banking-commerce conglomerates, the United States has maintained the separation of banking from commerce.

If the Korean government relaxes the historic separation between the commercial banking sector and the chaebols, the relationship between banks and firms would probably develop along lines much different from the German and Japanese cases, and it would also be very much different from the 1991 U.S. Treasury Plan, which advocates that a commercial firm owns the (financial services) holding company to which the bank is affiliated. First of all, commercial banks will be subsidiaries of the chaebols. More specifically, one or more business holding companies in a chaebol conglomerate are likely to be at the top of a commercial bank in the ownership pyramid: if the Samsung group, for instance, is combined with a bank, one or more core companies of the Samsung group (for example, Samsung Life Insurance, Samsung Electronics) would probably be at the top of the Samsung bank in the ownership pyramid.

Corporate separateness of the chaebol's subsidiaries. Although pure holding companies are prohibited by the MRFTA, one or more core companies (businesses holding companies) are usually at the center of the organizational structure of the chaebols. The corporate ownership of the member companies of a chaebol is concentrated in these core companies, and the owner-managers and their families own these core companies. Decision making and coordination among member companies of a chaebol are very centralized and largely the responsibility of the chairman's office or planning and coordinating office, making the organizational structure of the Korean chaebols much more tightly centralized than most conglomerates around the world.

In the early stages of economic development when the markets for inputs such as financial capital or managerial labor are underdeveloped

60. In analyzing Japanese firms with a main bank relationship, Hoshi et al. (1991a, 1991b) found such firms to be less liquidity constrained and more likely to carry on with their investment programs during periods of financial distress than commercial firms without a main bank relationship.

and imperfect, the chaebols could be understood as an organizational response to the market imperfections. The organizational structure of the chaebols is geared to internalize the transactions in such inputs; in other words, the chaebols have the internal markets at work by pooling resources of all their member companies. Presumably, financial assets, human resources, or information are pooled from member companies within the chaebols and applied to the place where marginal productivity is the highest. In general, these interaffiliate transactions are not conducted on the same terms and conditions as the arm's-length transactions with nonaffiliated firms. This implies that for an affiliate the corporate veil could be pierced by the other affiliates in a way not apparent to the outside. Within the chaebols, the assets of member companies are often not easily separated from those of the other member companies. That is, the corporate separateness of a bank affiliate from the other affiliates of a chaebol conglomerate becomes rather ambiguous.

If the corporate separateness between the subsidiaries of the chaebols is maintained, the failure of a separately capitalized affiliate of the chaebols should leave its creditors with only a claim against that firm and not against the bank or other subsidiaries' assets. However, if the separation of companies within a bank-firm conglomerate becomes ambiguous, then uncovered creditors of a failed firm could potentially make claims against a bank subsidiary; they could make a legal claim that the assets of the bank are inseparable from those of the failed firm, thereby "piercing the corporate veil."

Bank regulation and chaebols' governance structure. As discussed above, once the historic separation between the commercial banking sector and the chaebols is relaxed, commercial banks are expected to be subsidiaries of the chaebols; one thinks of the consolidated regulation for the firms that own banks. However, this consolidated regulation of a firm with its affiliated banks would be very difficult because of the nonfinancial nature of a firm's assets and production processes, and because of the extreme heterogeneity of production processes across firms. Furthermore, the present governance structure of the chaebols would make such a consolidated regulation much more difficult.

The governance structure of the chaebols today implies that the corporate separateness of a bank subsidiary would not be clear and transparent. Therefore a serious concern for a bank regulator would be whether the monitoring technologies and firewalls for the public safety net are powerful enough to make clear and transparent the possible relationships between the bank subsidiary and the other firm subsidiaries. Requiring the bank-firm conglomerates to report comprehensive combined financial statements to the regulatory authority would help make such relationships more transparent. But it would not be a sufficient condition for the corporate separateness of the bank subsidiaries, since combined financial statements do not cover all the possible relationships between the bank subsidiary and the other firm subsidiaries that could inflict costs on the public safety net. These could be the transfer of valuable inside information to other affiliates, or, more broadly, the present governance structure of chaebols, which is highly centralized over the affiliates.

To inhibit the transfer of important inside information to other affiliates, Chinese walls within a bank-firm conglomerate might exist, but the real concern here is the possibility that the inside information would be valuable enough for Chinese walls to be breached. Imposing regulatory firewalls over existing internally imposed Chinese walls might have very little effect unless the penalties were so severe (criminal and financial) as to be a real deterrent. In this case, rather than imposing significant regulatory penalties, relying more on external discipline (loss of reputation) as imposed by the competitive markets is regarded as much more effective.

As markets (the market for bank loans and bank loan substitutes, the product market, etc.) become more competitive, concerns about the conflict of interest would be less serious ones. The more the firms owning banks possess private information, the higher the potential for conflicts of interests.

The TBTF concern. We have already pointed out that the TBTF argument and the ensuing moral hazard of chaebols call for the development of the institutions for exit markets whose forces will discipline the chaebols. However, it must be noted that having properly functioning exit markets for financial institutions is not an easy task. Even in countries having relatively well functioning exit markets for nonfinancial firms, the well functioning exit market for financial institutions is still a real challenge. In many countries, because the failure of a very large bank makes it more likely that a major financial disruption will occur, regulatory authorities are reluctant to allow big banks to fail and cause losses to their depositors. In the United States, the TBTF policy has been extended to big banks.[61] When Continental Illinois, one of the ten largest banks in the U.S., became insolvent in May 1984, the U.S. bank regulator guaranteed depositors up to the $100,000 insurance limit, but it also guaranteed accounts exceeding $100,000 and even prevented losses for Continental Illinois bondholders. The consequence of the TBTF policy is that big banks take on even greater risks, thereby making bank failures more likely.

The TBTF subsidy could potentially extend implicit subsidy to liabilities of the firm-owners of the largest banks. This could mean that the creditors and corporate bondholders of the bank's affiliated firms as well as large depositors of the bank would enjoy a similar degree of implicit protection as the explicit protection given to small depositors. That is, the bank's affiliated firms would enjoy a cost of funds subsidy at the expense of the taxpayer.

Toward a Reform in Chaebol Policies

As the Korean economy becomes increasingly open to international competition, the changing economic environment sheds new light on the chaebol issue. What has been a concentration of economic power in a heavily protected and regulated economy is now undergoing a new interpretation from the perspective of the global competition facing the Korean economy and chaebols. If this continues, elements of the domestic environment such as political democratization will also change the nature of the chaebol issue, since the close intertwining of business and politics is becoming less justified and sustainable.

For the Korean economy to continue growing, today's breadwinning industries in Korea need restructuring. In this restructuring the chaebols are expected to play a major role and to continue to be the engines of growth for the Korean economy. Given this, drastic policies such as breaking up the chaebols are neither feasible nor desirable. Korea's future industrial organization is then expected to be one with big businesses of chaebols at the core and small- and medium-sized firms as the fringe surrounding the core.

The future reform of the chaebol policies should be directed toward

61. Though the FDIC Act of 1991 severely limited the scope of TBTF guarantees and required a number of approval screens, including that of the President, it is still in effect.

strengthening competition and enhancing efficiency. To sum up the discussions in this paper, we present the following conclusions.

1. In light of their insufficient deterrence effects and serious negative effects, regulations on chaebols' diversification need to be reformed. The direction of reform could be based on new knowledge identifying market fundamentals and other conditions explaining chaebols' diversification. Appropriate cures are not a long list of symptomatic treatments but ones that directly address these fundamentals.

2. Although ownership dispersion may have many desirable effects, such as the establishment of "property right democracy" and more equitable distribution of income and wealth, dispersion will take a long time and will require the development of a mature capital market. It is a long-term vision, and there are certain limitations on the policies and laws needed. Any misconceptions with respect to the time horizon must be cleared.

3. The separation of ownership and control is neither desirable for efficiency reasons nor supported by practical requirements in the foreseeable future, and the choice should in the meantime be left in the hands of the private firms. Therefore, a warning should be given to any attempts by the government to impose a particular type of management structure via coercive policy instruments. Instead, we argue that competitive pressures in the output markets will stimulate chaebols to improve their control and management structure, since the owner-managers facing the threat of severe competition have a strong incentive to restructure their corporate control and management.

4. Transparent rules of entry and exit into the industries must be established. In fact, some of the chaebol regulations are anticompetitive in that they tend to protect incumbents from the important sources of potential competition. Entry regulations intended to prevent so-called excessive competition and duplicative investments are in fact severely limiting competition in such markets as telecommunications, electricity, steel, and automobiles. These regulations obviously violate the basic premise of competition law, which protects not the competitors but the competition. Entry regulations for small and medium industries also have anticompetitive effects.

5. The TBTF argument and distortions in the government-business relationship tell us how important it is to have a properly functioning exit market in Korea. As long as the government manipulates the exit market on an ad hoc basis, the moral hazard of chaebols will remain a reality, and the chaebol issue in Korea will not be free of the taint of

illegality. If the Korean government wants to escape from the vicious circle of symbiosis, insurance, moral hazard, and illegality, it needs to rethink the validity of the TBTF argument and develop institutions for an exit market whose forces will discipline chaebols. This implies an overhauling of the government-business relationship and Korea's financial sector. There are many obstacles and the task will not be easy.

6. Once the historic separation between the commercial banking sector and the chaebols is relaxed, commercial banks are expected to become subsidiaries of the chaebols. The governance structure of the chaebols today implies that the corporate separateness of a bank subsidiary would not be clear and transparent. A serious concern for a bank regulator is then whether its monitoring technologies and firewalls for the public safety net are powerful enough to make clear and transparent the possible relationships between the bank subsidiary and the other firm subsidiaries. Requiring the firm-bank conglomerates to report comprehensive combined financial statements to the regulatory authority would help make such relationships more transparent. But it would not be a sufficient condition for the corporate separateness of the bank subsidiaries, since combined financial statements do not cover all the possible relationships between the bank subsidiary and the other firm subsidiaries that could inflict costs on the public safety net. They could be the transfer of valuable inside information to other affiliates, or, more broadly, the governance structure of the chaebols today itself, which is very much centralized over the affiliates.

REFERENCES

In Korean

Cho Dong Sung. 1990. *A Study on Korean Chaebol.* Maeil Economic Daily.

Chung Byung Hyu and Yang Young Sik. 1992. *An Economic Analysis of Chaebol in Korea.* Korea Development Institute.

Gong Byeong-Ho. 1994. *Ownership Structure of Japanese and Korean Business Groups.* Korea Economic Research Institute.

Jwa Sung Hee. 1994. *Korean Economy in the Global Age.* Seoul: Korea Development Institute.

Kang Chul Kyu, Choi Jeong Pyo, and Chang Ji Sang. 1991. *Chaebol.* Kyungsilryun Munko 2, Pibong.

Kang Myung Hun. 1990. *Economic Power Concentration and the Korean Economy,* Maeil Economic Daily.

Kang Shin Il. 1991. *Studies on Big Business Groups.* Korea Economic Research Institute.

Kim Il Joong. 1994. *The Logic and Effects of Policies Against Concentration of Economic Power.* Series in Regulation Studies, no.12, Korea Economic Research Institute.

Kwack Man Soon et al. 1995. *The Korean Business Groups.* Korea Economic Research Institute.

Lee Chul Song. 1995. *Criticisms on the Chaebol Policy: A Legal Perspective.* Korea Economic Research Institute.

Lee Jae Hyung. 1997. "Big Business Groups in Korea: Performances, Diversification, and Ownership Structure," *KDI Journal of Economic Policy,* 18, no. 3–4 (January).

Lee Jae Hyung and Yoo Seong Min. 1994. "The Growth and Productivity of Chaebol's Establishments." *Korea Development Review* 16, no. 3.

Lee Kyu Uck. 1977. *Market Structure and Monopoly Regulation.* Seoul: Korea Development Institute.

———. 1990. "Concentration of Economic Power in Korea," *Korea Development Review* 12, no.1 (May).

Lee Kyu Uck and Lee Jae Hyung. 1990. *Business Groups and the Concentration of Economic Power.* Seoul: Korea Development Institute.

Lee Kyu Uck, Lee Jae Hyung, and Kim Joo Hoon. 1984. *Market and Market Structure in Korea.* Seoul: Korea Development Institute.

Lee Kyu Uck and Lee Sung Soon. 1985. *Business Integration and the Concentration of Economic Power.* Seoul: Korea Development Institute.

SaKong Il. 1980. "Economic Growth and Concentration of Economic Power." *Korea Development Review* 2, no.1 (March).

Shin, Yu Kun. 1992. Corporate Management in Korea. Seoul: Pakyoung-sa.

Yang Won Keun. 1992. *An Analysis of Chaebol's Efficiency.* Research Report, Korea Institute for Industrial Economics and Trade.

Yoo Seong Min. 1992. "The Ownership Structure of Korea's Big Business Conglomerates and Its Policy Implications." *Korea Development Review* 14, no.1 (April).

———. 1993. "Specialization Policy: Its Problems and a New Proposal." Mimeo.

———. 1996a. *Chaebol Policy.* Mi-Rae Media.

———. 1996b. "Merits and Demerits of the Chaebol: A Criticism on the Chaebol Debate." In *The Future of Korean Economy and the Chaebol.* Kia Economic Research Institute, Seoul.

———. 1996c. "A Thought on the Debate of Privatization in Korea." *KDI Journal of Economic Policy* 18, no.1 (April).

Yoo Seong Min and Kim Jun Kyung. 1992. *A Policy Proposal to Revise the Credit Control System in Korea.* Policy Report, Korea Development Institute.

In English

Adams, Walter, and James W. Brock. 1991. *Antitrust Economics on Trial: A Dialogue on the New Laissez-Faire*. Princeton, N.J.: Princeton University Press.

Allen, William T. 1995. "Our Schizophrenic Conception of the Business Corporation." Appen. 3 in Robert Monks and Nell Minow, *Corporate Governance*. Oxford: Blackwell.

Amsden, Alice H. 1989. *Asia's Next Giant: South Korea and Late Industrialization*. London: Oxford University Press.

———. 1994. "The Specter of Anglo-Saxonization Is Haunting South Korea." Chap. 4 in Lee-Jay Cho and Yoon Hyung Kim, eds., *Korea's Political Economy*. Boulder, Colo.: Westview Press.

Bartlett, Randall. 1989. *Economics and Power: An Inquiry into Human Relations and Markets*. Cambridge: Cambridge University Press.

Benston, George J. 1980. *Conglomerate Mergers: Causes, Consequences, and Remedies*. Washington, D.C.: American Enterprise Institute.

Berger, A., and D. B. Humphrey. 1990. "The Dominance of Inefficiencies over Scale and Product Mix Economies in Banking," *Journal of Monetary Economics* 28:117–48.

Berle, A. A., and G. C. Means. 1932. *The Modern Corporation and Private Property*. New York: Macmillan.

Blair, Roger D., and Robert F. Lanzillotti, eds. 1981. *The Conglomerate Corporation: An Antitrust Law and Economics Symposium*. Oelgeschlager, Gunn & Hain.

Clifford, Mark L. 1994. *Troubled Tiger: Businessmen, Bureaucrats, and Generals in South Korea*. Armonk, N.Y.: M. E. Sharpe.

Commons, John R. 1937. *Institutional Economics*. New York: Macmillan.

Corrigan, E. G. 1987a. *Financial Market Structure: A Longer View*, Federal Reserve Bank of New York.

———. 1987b. The Separation of Banking and Commerce Statement Before U.S. Senate Committee on Banking, Housing, and Urban Affairs, June 18. (Appears also as Appendix Statement Before the Same Committee, May 3, 1990.)

Eckert, Carter. 1991. *Offspring of Empire: The Koch'ang Kims and the Colonial Origins of Korean Capitalism, 1876–1945*. Seattle: University of Washington Press.

The Economist. June 3, 1995. "A Survey of South Korea."

———. Nov. 11, 1995. "Those Lovely Chaebols and Their Little Local Difficulty."

Edwards, Corwin D. 1955. "Conglomerate Bigness as a Source of Power." In George J. Stigler, ed., *Business Concentration and Price Policy*. NBER.

Fields, Karl J. 1995. *Enterprise and the State in Korea and Taiwan*. Ithaca, N.Y.: Cornell University Press.

Galbraith, John K. 1967. *The New Industrial State*. Boston: Houghton Mifflin.

Haggard, Stephen. 1994. "Business, Politics, and Policy in Northeast and Southeast Asia." Chap. 10 in Andrew MacIntyre, ed., *Business and Government in Industrializing Asia*, Ithaca, N.Y.: Cornell University Press.

Hayek, Friedrich A. 1944. *The Road to Serfdom*. Chicago: University of Chicago Press.

Herman, Edward S. 1981. *Corporate Control, Corporate Power*. Cambridge: Cambridge University Press.

Hoshi, Takeo, Anil Kashyap, and David Scharfstein. 1991a. "Corporate Structure, Liquidity, and Investment: Evidence from Japanese Industrial Groups." *Quarterly Journal of Economics* 106:33–60.

———. 1991b. "The Role of Banks in Reducing the Costs of Financial Distress in Japan." *Journal of Financial Economics* 27:67–88.

Johnson, Chalmers. 1994. "What Is the Best System of National Economic Management for Korea?" Chap. 3 in Lee-Jay Cho and Yoon Hyung Kim, eds., *Korea's Political Economy*. Boulder, Colo.: Westview Press.

Jones, Leroy P. 1994. "Big Business Groups in South Korea: Causation, Growth, and Policies." Chap. 16 in Lee-Jay Cho and Yoon Hyung Kim, eds., *Korea's Political Economy*. Boulder, Colo.: Westview Press.

Kim, Eun Mee. 1988. "From Dominance to Symbiosis: State and Chaebol in Korea." *Pacific Focus* 3(Fall).

———. 1991. "The Industrial Organization and Growth of the Korean Chaebol: Integrating Development and Organizational Theory." In Gary Hamilton, ed., *Business Networks and Economic Development*. Centre of Asian Studies, University of Hong Kong Press.

Lee, Chung H. 1992. "The Government, Financial System, and Large Private Enterprises in the Economic Development of South Korea." *World Development* 20, no. 2: 187–97.

Lee, Kyu Uck. 1994. "Ownership-Management Relations in Korean Business." Chap. 15 in Lee-Jay Cho and Yoon Hyung Kim, eds., *Korea's Political Economy*. Boulder, Colo.: Westview Press.

Lee, Sung Soon, and Seong Min Yoo. 1997. "Evolution of Industrial Organization and Policy Response in Korea: 1945–95." Chap. 10 in Dong-Se Cha, Kwang Suk Kim, and Dwight H. Perkins., eds., *The Korean Economy 1945–95: Performance and Vision for the 21st Century*. Korea Development Institute.

Lee, Young Ki. 1995. "Corporate Governance: The Structure and Issues in Korea." Paper presented at the Conference on "Korea's Choices in Global Competition and Cooperation," East-West Center, University of Hawaii, July.

Marfels, Christian. 1988. "Aggregate Concentration in International Perspective: Canada, Federal Republic of Germany, Japan, and United States." In R. S. Khemani, D. M. Shapiro, and W. T. Stanbury, eds., *Mergers, Corporate Concentration, and Power in Canada*. The Institute for Research on Public Policy, Halifax, N.S., Canada.

Masuyama, Seiichi. 1994. "The Role of the Japanese Capital Markets: The Effect of Cross-Shareholdings on Corporate Accountability." In N. Dimsdale and M. Prevezer, eds., *Capital Markets and Corporate Governance.* Oxford: Clarendon Press.

Moon, Chung-in. 1994. "Changing Patterns of Business-Government Relations in South Korea," Chap. 5 in Andrew MacIntyre, ed., *Business and Government in Industrializing Asia*. Ithaca, N.Y.: Cornell University Press.

Morikawa Hidemasa. 1978. *The History of Japanese Zaibatsu* (in Japanese). Kyoikushya Rekishyo, no. 123. Tokyo: Kyoikushya.

Posner, R. A. 1976. *Antitrust Law: An Economic Perspective.* Chicago: University of Chicago Press.

Rummelt, Richard P. 1986. *Strategy, Structure, and Economic Performance.* Cambridge, Mass.: Harvard Business School Press.

SaKong Il. 1993. *Korea in the World Economy.* Washington D.C.: Institute of International Economics.

Saunders, Anthony. 1994. "Banking and Commerce: An Overview of the Public Policy Issues." *Journal of Banking and Finance* 18: 231–54.

Saunders, Anthony, and I. Walter. 1994. *Universal Banking in the United States: What Could We Gain? What Could We Lose?* New York: Oxford University Press.

Shull, Bernard. 1994. "Banking and Commerce in the United States." *Journal of Banking and Finance* 18: 255–70.

Simons, Henry C. 1948. *Economic Policy for a Free Society.* Chicago: University of Chicago Press.

Spruill, Charles R. 1982. *Conglomerates and the Evolution of Capitalism.* Carbondale: Southern Illinois University Press.

Yoo, Seong Min. 1995. "Chaebol in Korea: Misconceptions, Realities, and Policies." Working Paper no. 9507, Korea Development Institute.

Yoshihara, E. 1981. *The Diversification Strategy of Japanese Firms* (in Japanese). Tokyo: Nihon Keizai Shinbun.

Young, H. Peyton. 1994. *Equity in Theory and Practice.* Princeton, N.J.: Princeton University Press.

Zajac, Edward E. 1995. *Political Economy of Fairness.* Cambridge, Mass.: MIT Press.

Thomas Gale Moore

Issues in Regulatory Policy

Regulations are necessary to specify and protect property rights, to establish rules for enforcement of contracts, and to limit fraud, violence, and theft. These controls are essential for the proper functioning of a market economy. Nevertheless, virtually all governments have gone well beyond the minimum. This paper will sketch the costs and inefficiencies of environmental and safety controls; the origins, misallocations, and losses from industry-specific regulations; and the reasons for and the gains from deregulation.

Government controls are ubiquitous in modern societies. In the United States regulations affect virtually all the private sector: they specify the safety and energy use of consumer products; they mandate labor rules, minimum wages, and working conditions; they control business and competitive practices; they stipulate manufacturing processes, including promulgating rules to reduce workplace risks and to meet environmental concerns; they limit the disposal of wastes by consumers, business, and local governments; they oversee financial dealings to prevent fraud and manipulation; and they restrict the choices of consumers in order to lower their hazards from products and services. Ostensibly these government restrictions on the marketplace were designed to promote the public welfare. Many, however, were crafted to benefit politically influential groups.

The most rapidly growing category of government controls are those crafted to promote a cleaner environment or to protect the safety and financial well-being of the public. Although those objectives arouse little controversy, economists and many commentators have questioned the extent of the regulations, their methods of enforcement, and, in many cases, the need for government intervention. Simply identifying a problem never justifies in and of itself government mandated solutions; the government can and often does make things worse.

The Costs of Regulation

Although the government regulates almost everything, its controls fall into three categories. One set of rules deals with reducing environmental and other risks to people and to our natural world; currently this set is growing the most rapidly and is somewhat more costly to consumers than the other categories. Governments also impose controls that raise or lower prices and restrict entry of firms into the marketplace. Traditionally, those rules have been the most expensive portion of government intervention in the marketplace, but they have recently been exceeded by environmental and risk regulation. Finally, the government requires a huge amount of paperwork; for most individuals, the most time-consuming aspect is preparing documents for the income tax. This paper will concentrate on the first two categories of regulation, but paperwork costs almost equal the costs in the other two categories.

According to Professor Thomas D. Hopkins (1996), compliance costs of meeting environmental and risk-reduction rules in 1996 amounted to $232 billion; price and entry controls totaled $224 billion; and paperwork expenses added up to $221 billion, for a grand total of $677 billion or a little more than 9 percent of GDP.[1] Figure 1 shows how the cost of environmental and risk regulation has escalated from less than 2 percent of GDP to over 3 percent while the cost of price and entry controls has more than halved as a percent of national income. These costs are high, but the total drag on the economy is much greater. The figures reflect the direct cost of meeting the rules established by the government, but they do not include the government's own cost in establishing and monitoring these controls, which in 1996 amounted to $14 billion; nor do they include the much larger effect on economic growth.

1. Entry controls are often used by industry regulators to restrict new competition. Regulation often imposes price controls, and industry usually must seek permission to raise or lower their charges, ostensibly to prevent cutthroat competition or predatory or monopoly pricing.

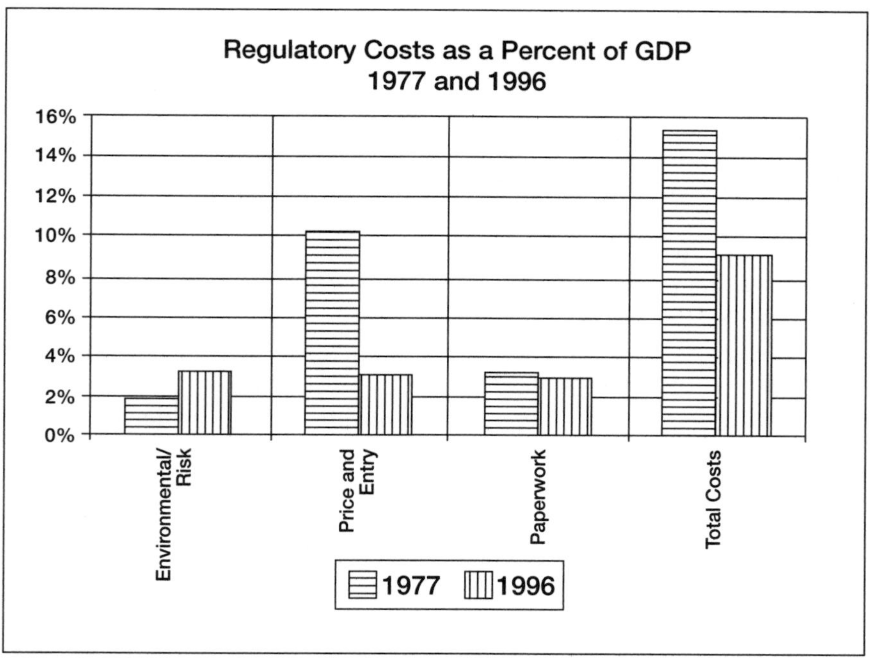

FIGURE 1 Based on Hopkins (1996), Table 2, and author's calculations.

For the major industrial countries—the European Union, Canada, the United States, and Japan—growth depends on three factors: moving resources from less to more productive applications; technological change that allows more goods and services to be produced with existing resources or that provides new ways of satisfying human needs and desires; and additional investment in human and physical capital, often embodying technical change. Regulation can slow or reduce any of these processes. Government controls can slow investment, especially if they force companies to use their scarce capital to invest in pollution-control equipment rather than to increase output.

Economic growth in developing nations, including the so-called Asian tigers, depends on moving resources from less to more productive activities and on investments in human and physical resources. Regulation can slow these advances. The freer the private market and the more investment in human and physical capital, the greater the rate of growth.

Unfortunately, governments often slow or even prevent resources from moving to more productive uses. Agricultural policy within the

EU or the United States, for example, has the specific aim of maintaining incomes and retaining resources in farming that other sectors could utilize more efficiently. Requirements that new investments meet much more stringent air pollution standards than existing plants discourage the construction of new facilities that might lower costs and produce greater output with fewer resources. During the 1970s and 1980s, for instance, the Clean Air Act required electric power companies to install expensive scrubbers on all new power plants. As a result, utilities stretched the lives of existing, less efficient, and ironically more polluting, generating facilitates. Since few new plants were built, compliance costs, that is, the costs of installing scrubbers, looked small; the allocation costs, however, were huge but unmeasured.

Government controls can slow innovations, the principal driving force for long-run improvements in living standards. State-imposed regulations on research hinder inventions and retard technological advance. Biotechnology has been adversely affected almost everywhere, the effect being to slow or stop medical advances for humans and improvements in agricultural productivity needed to feed a growing world population. One study by the National Bureau of Economic Research (Gray and Shadbegian 1993) found that every dollar spent on compliance costs in the paper, oil, and steel industries reduced total factor productivity (that is, growth) by three to four dollars. If this ratio were applicable to the whole economy, then using Hopkins's estimates of compliance cost at $667 billion, the reduction in total factor productivity would be in the neighborhood of $2 trillion dollars.

As is well known, productive growth in the United States and in much of the rest of the world slowed, starting in the late 1960s or early 1970s. It is underappreciated that government controls, mainly to reduce pollution, exploded at the same time. Although measures of regulation are poor, all the evidence—such as pages in the *Federal Register* and spending by regulatory agencies—indicate that overall government controls have mushroomed during the last few decades. Spending by the government on administration and regulatory control as a percent of GDP, a measure of regulation, rose sharply until about 1981, declined, and then escalated again in the late 1980s and early 1990s (Vedder 1966, 13).

In estimating the effect of regulation on productivity growth, Richard Vedder (1996) has found that government controls were negatively correlated with growth over the period 1963–1993. Energy prices were too, while population growth, the share of services in the economy, and taxation and deficit spending showed no significant correlation. Had regulation remained at 1963 levels, Vedder's numbers indicate that productivity growth would be one percentage point higher than it has been. He estimates that if we had enjoyed that much more growth, U.S. GDP in 1993 would have been $1.3 trillion higher or about 20 percent greater than the $6.3 billion actually recorded (p. 16).

Regulations impose other costs on consumers that are harder to measure. Rules that prevent consumers from purchasing or using possible products that they would prefer leave the population less well off. The recent debate over air bags in the United States illustrates this issue. The law requires purchasers of new cars to buy vehicles with air bags whether they want them or not. It is against the law for a dealer or mechanic to disable the devices, even though considerable evidence has accumulated that air bags can kill young children or small-statured adults. Consumers are being forced to purchase a safety device that has the unfortunate effect of increasing mortality for certain vulnerable members of society.

Benefits of Safety and Environmental Regulation

Ostensibly environmental and safety regulation provide benefits to consumers that should be offset against the costs. Cleaner air, water, and land are valuable to everyone. Consumers and workers desire to be safer, live longer, and suffer less from accidents. Environmental regulation has indeed brought benefits, albeit at increasing costs. Safety regulation has reduced accidents and mortality, but at high costs. As may be seen from Tables 1 and 2, the cost to save a year of life varies greatly. Medicine is the most cost effective in saving lives; efforts to clean the environment provide the least benefit for the money. In spite of their

TABLE 1 Median Cost to Save a Year of Life, by Sectors of Society

Sector of society	*Median cost per year of life saved*
Medicine	$19,000
Consumer products	$36,000
Transportation	$56,000
Occupational	$346,000
Environmental	$4,207,000

SOURCE: Tengs (1994), Table 2, p. 14.

TABLE 2 Median Cost to Save a Year of Life, by Regulatory Agency

Regulatory agency	*Median cost per year of life saved*
Federal Aviation Administration (FAA)	$23,000
Consumer Product Safety Commission (CPSC)	$68,000
National Highway Transportation Safety Administration (NHTSA)	$78,000
Occupational Safety and Health Administration (OSHA)	$88,000
Environmental Protection Agency (EPA)	$7,629,000

SOURCE: Tengs (1994), Table 3, p. 15.

costs, environmental controls are necessary and desirable. We have achieved significant improvements in air quality that offer relief to those with respiratory difficulties and furnish aesthetic advantages to others. Nevertheless, these numbers suggest that we should look more closely at environmental controls. A dollar spent on medicine, consumer safety, or transportation can save many more lives than can a dollar allocated to environmental protection.

To put these numbers into context, economists who have examined the value people place on their lives, derived from risk/money tradeoffs, find valuations between $3 million and $7 million (Viscusi 1994, 105). At a discount rate of 3 percent real, one year of life would be worth between $90,000 and $210,000, which implies that the average rule dealing with medicine, consumer products, and transportation would pass a cost-benefit analysis but not occupational or environmental rules. By the same token, typical EPA rules fail any cost-benefit test.

Some government regulations are extraordinarily expensive and some are very cheap. The Harvard Center for Risk Analysis estimates that it would be costless to ban residential growth in tsunami-prone areas, a life-saving control. Measles, mumps, and rubella immunizations cost less than the expense of treating those diseases. On the other hand, the researchers estimate that banning asbestos in diaphragms would cost over $1.4 billion for each year of life saved; benzene emission controls at rubber tire plants would cost over $19.8 billion; and chloroform private well emission standards at forty-eight pulp mills would reduce income by nearly $100 billion for every year of life saved. These numbers are staggering and explain why so much of environmental regulation cannot be cost effective. As these examples show, regulation does provide benefits, but often the costs exceed the gains. Robert

Hahn (1996) has estimated that only 23 of the 54 regulations issued by EPA between 1990 and 1995 would pass a cost-benefit test. If these regulations were repealed, the economy would save $100 billion.

The traditional form of regulation—controls over specific industries—illustrates the inefficiencies of regulation. Many of these rules date back a century or more and were originally instituted in the name of improving the performance of the marketplace. Unregulated industry, especially sectors with large-scale firms that had few competitors, was viewed as a danger to the public. In parts of the world less dedicated to the private sector than the U.S., governments nationalized "essential" industries. In the last few decades there has been a movement both here and abroad to reduce controls or government ownership of many sectors. As shown in Figure 1, the costs of price and entry controls have fallen sharply since 1977 as a proportion of GDP. It is worth exploring the rationale for the origin of state intervention and why the movement toward relaxing controls has gained strength.

Origins of Regulation

Although the institutional details of regulation and deregulation differ greatly around the world, the same political and economic conditions have been involved in both the origins of regulation and its subsequent relaxation. The United States provides much of the institutional detail for this paper, but the same conditions were as a rule operative in other countries.

One difference stands out: in many parts of the world, instead of regulating a privately owned industry, the government chose to own and operate the utility or mode of transportation itself. At an International Monetary Fund seminar, Professor Said El-Naggar, formerly of Cairo University, said, "One of the most distinctive features of the economic situation in developing countries is the predominant role of the public sector in the production structure" (El-Naggar 1989, 1). Though the motivation for nationalizing the industry was often the same as that for regulating it, the results were somewhat different. Moreover, when the deregulation movement began to sweep the world, in sectors where the government owned the operating companies, the movement took the form of privatization.

Privatization and deregulation are alternative approaches to restoring competitive private markets in industries that the government has controlled. In the nineteenth century and early in the twentieth, many governments nationalized or regulated the same set of industries. The forces and considerations that led earlier to the removal of these industries from the market and their more recent return to the unregulated private sector are virtually identical. An earlier loss of faith in the competitive market resulted in government takeovers of specific industries, but government ownership and regulation turned out to have its own set of problems. With a better understanding of government failure as well as market failure, privatization and deregulation have become the dominant paradigm. Both theoretically and empirically, as will be outlined below, unregulated private markets work better than either bureaucratically supervised firms or government-owned monopolies.

The economics of regulation applies across the board to all industries controlled by governments. The government must decide on an appropriate price, on who can offer the service, and often on the quality of the service. At the same time, regulated firms will be attempting to utilize the system to increase their profits.

Transportation is one important sector that governments everywhere have attempted either to own or to control through regulations. Basically a perishable service is offered shippers or passengers. A commercial airplane leaving with empty seats has the same problem as a train leaving with half-filled boxcars or a merchant ship without a full manifest. Some modes such as railroads, subways, and pipelines are capital intensive and inflexible, while other forms of transportation, such as trucks, buses, merchant ships, and airlines, are much more adaptable and have less fixed investment. The services of less-than-truckload motor carriers, most bus operations, and a considerable portion of airline service utilize a hub-and-spoke mechanism, a system pioneered by Federal Express with its introduction of an overnight package network.

Merchant shipping, tankers, truckload carriers, charter buses, and air taxis offer point-to-point transportation, and they can often gain full loads on specific hauls. Carriers operating hub-and-spoke systems must normally provide scheduled service on fixed routes with sufficient capacity to accommodate last-minute shippers or passengers; as a result, they customarily operate at less than capacity. A load factor of 60 percent is now normal in the U.S. airline industry.

Unless a transportation company can differentiate its service from that of other companies, it cannot have an independent pricing policy. Although bus service differs significantly from rail, which is sharply differentiated from air travel, within each of these modes passengers typically see little difference. For example, airlines have tried, with only partial success, to differentiate themselves from other airlines through frequent flyer programs, amenities on the aircraft, and ground facilities. But since all these attractions are easily copied, there can be little sustainable difference between airline fares and service. Moreover, to carry an additional passenger on a flight with empty seats is virtually costless. Carriers are therefore inclined to offer very low fares for standby passengers or others who might fill the plane. To prevent what the industry views as cutthroat competition, the airlines or other carriers are tempted to agree on fares.

Where cartel-type agreements are unenforceable or impractical, carriers have often sought government help to stabilize rates and prevent "excessive" competition. These industries normally claim that such regulation is in the public interest, but the consumer, shipper, or traveler almost always pays more. Cutthroat competition is inherently unstable. One or more firms will either be driven from the market or will learn to control their pricing. This need not result in monopoly, although it may mean that only a few firms offer the transportation service and competition may be less than perfect.

Whether less than perfect competition is acceptable depends on the alternative. We live in an imperfect world. If regulation is instituted either to restrain a less than fully competitive market or to prevent cutthroat competition, will the regulated firm provide a better or less expensive service? Will the benefits of regulation outweigh the costs?

Antitrust

An alternative to industry regulation worth considering is antitrust policy. Even though antitrust cannot turn an industry with only a handful of participants into a perfectly competitive market, it can restrain some of the worst manifestations of oligopoly. Outright collusion can be prohibited and most of the time prevented. Government policy can thwart attempts to block entry of new carriers. Tacit collusion and price leadership, however, may just have to be tolerated.

In 1890, the Congress of the United States passed the Sherman Act, the world's first antitrust law, which prohibited monopolization and efforts to monopolize. Its aim was to prevent big business from dominating the marketplace and exploiting consumers. The Department of Justice moved early against Standard Oil, which in 1898 controlled 88 percent of the market (Brozen 1982). The Department charged the company with attempts to monopolize by purchasing competitors, predatory pricing, and other business practices to achieve and maintain its control. Notwithstanding its huge market share, it proved unable to maintain its dominant position and by 1909 its share had slipped to 67 percent. John McGee (1958) later showed that neither logic nor evidence supported the charge that Standard Oil employed predatory pricing. Nevertheless, the Justice Department succeeded in breaking up Standard Oil into a number of regional petroleum companies, which eventually began to compete among themselves.

Antitrust policy from the Standard Oil case to the most recent cases has required a finding that the offending company engaged in practices that lead to monopoly. If a firm achieves a huge market share by means of efficiency or innovation, the courts have held that it earned its position. As a consequence, antitrust authorities have examined Intel and Microsoft, which control around 90 percent of their markets, only for practices that might maintain or increase their market share. A number of economists, however, contend that market share is almost always the result of efficiency, economies of scale, and market innovation and should not be tampered with (McGee 1958; Telser 1966; Brozen 1982).

In the decades after the Standard Oil case, scholars and antitrust lawyers have been mainly concerned with horizontal issues, such as price fixing and mergers. Collusion on prices has been held to be illegal per se and no showing of public benefit can mitigate the crime. Whether a merger results in a monopoly depends on the definition of the market.

Defining the appropriate market is almost always questionable, however. Certainly General Motors monopolizes Chevrolet cars, Apple is now the only producer of Macintosh computers, Procter and Gamble is the only seller of Crest toothpaste, but all of these firms face active competition within their industry. Even if all the auto companies merged, competition for the consumer's dollar would continue. Every item competes with every other. A family can face the choice of buying a new car or traveling around the world. A teenager can spend her money on the latest pop star's CD, go to a hit movie, or visit the only amusement park in the area. All these entertainment media compete for the girl's money, but is the amusement park a monopoly? Is the record company, which has an exclusive over the star's recordings, a monopolist? If the movie studio buys the amusement park, can that lead to a monopoly?

In practice, scholars and antitrust experts examine concentration ratios, derived from census data, on government-defined industries to measure oligopoly. Until recent decades, when concentration measured by the proportion of the market held by the largest four or eight companies exceeded some level, scholars and antitrust officials considered the industry less than competitive. Leonard Weiss (1974) reported that numerous studies have shown that concentration can be positively correlated with profits of the largest firm, ostensibly confirming collusion. Harold Demsetz challenged that relationship as evidence of collusion or monopoly (1973, 1974). He argues that if a large corporation prices monopolistically, small firms by undercutting that enterprise will be more profitable than the dominant company. Since the evidence shows that the large entities are more profitable than the small, their earnings must reflect efficiency, not monopoly pricing. Policies to deal with concentrated industries are difficult to implement and the evidence that they are collusive is ambiguous, so current U.S. policy is to maintain a careful watch of industries dominated by only a handful of enterprises to prevent overt collusion but otherwise refrain from action.

Periodically the government has turned its attention to vertical problems such as the purchase of suppliers or customers. Academics, especially from the Chicago school, have usually emphasized that mergers with upstream or downstream firms cannot increase monopoly power and therefore are largely benign (Stigler 1966, 237). Others have been concerned that large size in itself may not be in the public interest (e.g., Berle and Means 1932; Galbraith 1967). No credible theory or evidence, however, has been evinced that size, per se, is harmful.

As a general proposition, it is difficult if not impossible for a firm to monopolize a broad industry without government aid in restricting entry. Governments can and have established barriers to new firms, thereby protecting the market of existing businesses. The appropriate policy, therefore, is to open up the market to competition, if need be by dropping foreign trade barriers.

Antitrust policy can play a useful and strong role in preventing would-be competitors from restricting competition. As Adam Smith (1937, 129) put it: "People of the same trade seldom meet together, even for merriment and diversion, but the conversation ends in a conspiracy against the public, or in some contrivance to raise prices." It would seem therefore that a sensible antitrust policy would focus on ensuring that the government did nothing to restrict competition from either domestic or foreign sources and would enforce prohibitions on collusion on price, quality, quantity, or distribution. Worrying excessively about the degree to which the top firms dominate an industry is not worthwhile, provided the market is open to competition.

Theory of Regulation

Good theoretical reasons exist for believing that unregulated private firms will perform better and will enhance consumers' welfare more than either regulated firms or government-owned companies. Competition ensures that prices reflect costs and are driven to the lowest possible levels. It fosters innovation, quality and productivity improvements, and economic growth. In general, competition protects the consumer and makes the economy more efficient. Regulation tends to protect firms from competition. Government monopolies are even worse, since they are not disciplined either by the market or by a regulator. Unregulated private firms are superior to regulated or state-owned because they are subject to the discipline of the market.

Whereas the market forces firms to provide the best service at the lowest costs, regulators have other goals. Regulators are motivated by a desire to please their political superiors, politically influential groups, and the firms they oversee. If the regulators are themselves elected, they must be concerned with raising funds and obtaining support for the next election. If the businesses being controlled oppose a regulator's reelection, the incumbent may not win. Moreover, the regulated industry or its supporters can often be a source of campaign funds.

If the politicians appoint the regulators, they will be concerned with being reappointed or continuing their careers after they leave the commission. Often, since they will have built up considerable human capital in the form of knowledge of the industry, their best job opportunities will lie in working for the businesses that they had supervised. It follows that if they are on good terms with the regulated firms, they are more likely to find good employment once they leave the commission. On the other hand, if they are looking for reappointment, they need the politicians to support their reappointment bid. The politicians who do the reappointing also look to the industries for campaign funds and support in their own reelection bids. Thus the political system is biased toward supporting the businesses' position.

In addition, regulators will often find themselves at industry meetings to explain governmental policies. In the process they will socialize with various industry officials. They will hear the trade's position and its troubles. For reasons that go beyond self-interest, regulators will recognize that they cannot impose rules that would bankrupt enterprises in the industry: bankrupt organizations cannot supply services. Moreover, at least in the United States, the courts will hold that private regulated companies must be allowed to earn a profit.

When the regulators set about fixing rates, the industry will provide the data on costs. Only the regulated companies themselves will have the figures, so almost all information about costs, rates, demand, and service will come from industry officials. Moreover, at rate hearings the regulated firms will employ the best legal and accounting talent available. To counter the industry numbers, regulators must rely on low-paid government employees.

Not only do regulators have to rely on a few civil servants, but most regulatory commissions, especially in the United States at the state level, oversee a large number of firms in different industries. State commissions by and large control the rates and services of telephone companies, electric power utilities, natural gas distributing firms, trucking, intrastate railroads and bus operations, and a variety of industries in other sectors. Before its demise, for instance, the Interstate Commerce Commission oversaw dozens of railroads, both passenger and freight, thousands of trucking firms and bus lines, large numbers of freight forwarders, and pipelines. Like the ICC, commissions have to spread their limited resources over many highly technical topics and are unable to develop the expertise of the regulated. Moreover, a commission will often be subject to intense public scrutiny when deciding on telephone or electricity rates that affect all consumers, whereas its work on motor carriers or railroads will be followed intensely only by the trade. Even in setting telephone, gas, and electric rates and in spite of public opposition to increases, the commission must be concerned with ensuring the viability, that is, the profitability of the operating companies.

At least three studies (Stigler and Friedland 1962; Moore 1970; Denning and Mead 1990) have shown that regulation has little influence on electrical rates charged residential users. Furthermore, since the government normally prohibits new companies from competing with existing regulated firms, regulation strengthens the monopoly position of firms already in the industry. Some research (Nelson and Primeaux 1988) has indicated that even for electric power, often considered the quintessential natural monopoly, competition has worked, producing lower rates.

Regulation also politicizes prices. Each time a change in rates is suggested, political forces are mobilized on both sides of the issue. Economic considerations, such as efficiency, receive little attention. In periods of rapid inflation, opposition to nominal rate increases can often lead to uneconomic charges and financial difficulties for utilities. This may mean that they will be unable to make the appropriate investments in maintaining and expanding their facilities. In other words, during periods of relative stability in prices, regulation fails to prevent monopoly pricing, and during inflationary periods it may actually lead to inadequate revenues for the regulated firms.

Once prices are politicized, increasing them to reflect costs becomes very difficult. The major difficulties being experienced in many East European countries stem directly from state control of prices, especially of daily necessities such as bread. In many other parts of the world, such as Egypt, Colombia, and Peru, riots have broken out when prices of gasoline or bread have been raised to bring them closer to costs. The societal costs of politicizing prices are ultimately high.

Furthermore, if regulation does little to keep rates down and has the side effect of strengthening monopoly, it may be better to suffer from an unregulated single seller that is subject to potential competition than to rely on regulation. Technology and entrepreneurial effort may find ways of eroding the market position of a dominant firm. Additionally, the welfare costs of such a company are never large. The major effect of monopoly is to transfer income from consumers to the stockholders of the corporation. The significance of this transfer depends on the relative incomes of consumers and stockholders and on personal values relative to such income shifts.

As mentioned above, government officials, including regulators, are often tempted to provide benefits for politically influential groups. For example, farmers were influential in securing regulation of the railroads and in opposing regulation of motor carriers transporting agricultural goods. In addition, regulators will frequently provide hidden subsidies for special interest groups. Organized labor has been favored repeatedly by regulators and government agencies. The more workers and the better paid, the more votes for politicians who have supported prolabor policies. Other special interest groups and politically influential consumers, such as the publishers of newspapers and magazines, which typically enjoy subsidized postal rates, are frequently the beneficiaries of such regulation.

Even if regulators were operating solely in the public interest, which would in most cases be contrary to their personal interest, regulation is inherently faulty. Not only is information incomplete and biased, since it comes mainly from the industry, but the regulatory process itself is fundamentally defective. In order to determine appropriate charges in utility rate cases, for example, a regulator must decide on a reasonable profit for the corporation in addition to the allowable expenses of providing the service.[2] Not only are costs unclear, but the utility must be allowed to earn on its investment at least the cost of its capital. If its return is less than the cost of capital, it will not be able to maintain and replace its plant and equipment.

Yet an adequate profit rate is a tricky concept and uncertain at best. Regulators will inevitably allow a return that is sufficient to attract capital to the industry. If this is above the "cost of capital," the firm can increase its profit by increasing its investment: the larger the investment, the higher the rates and profit the utility can justify to the regulator. Since the desire to increase profits motivates business, the firm will have an incentive to "overinvest." This can take the form of having more capital and less labor than would minimize costs. Not only will regulation fail to protect consumers, it will also result in inefficient production. If there is a competitive fringe to the firm's operations, the utility can underprice its competitive business to justify a larger investment (a larger rate base) and higher prices in its monopoly lines, a profit-increasing strategy. Competitors, with good reason, will view this as unfair competition.

To illustrate: consider the current dilemma facing deregulation of telephone service in the United States. Many of the "Baby Bells," that is, local phone companies, want to offer long-distance service. If they were to do so, they would undoubtedly distort the market significantly. A local phone company could offer cheap long-distance rates, leading to an expansion of its investment and rate base; given the size of its investment, it could then request higher charges from its captive local customers in order to preserve its approved rate of return. Naturally the existing long-distance providers, which are not in a position to push some of their investment costs off on captive customers, would con-

2. The analysis in this section is based on the seminal article by Harvey Averch and Leland L. Johnson (1962).

sider this unfair competition. From an economic point of view, it might result in long-distance providers with higher costs capturing the market, resulting in a significant distortion in resource allocation.

To take another instance: suppose a railroad, competing with motor carriers for transporting certain commodities, faces rate regulation. It will be induced to cross-subsidize its competitive traffic by increasing its rates for its noncompetitive traffic. Having low rates in the competitive market allows it to justify investing more in equipment to move that traffic. If it is allowed to make a profit based on a percentage of its investment in transportation equipment, it can justify higher prices on its noncompetitive transport, resulting in increased overall profits.

In some cases allowed rates are based on operating costs rather than an investment. For the motor carrier industry, in which most costs are operating rather than fixed, regulators have traditionally looked at the ratio of operating costs to revenue to determine maximum legal tariffs. In such instances, the industry can profit by agreeing on wages that exceed competitive norms in order to justify higher charges and larger profits.

Although regulators typically use their powers to protect or benefit special interests, the mischief they can perpetrate is at least limited by the desire and needs of the regulated enterprises for profit. Government-owned firms, however, are free from the constraints of profitability. The absence of market discipline frees government agencies to employ more workers than are needed and to be generous in wages and benefits, while accumulating management perquisites. In fact, since any profits will simply be returned to the government treasury without benefit to the enterprise, it is senseless for a government enterprise to do more than cover its costs. Managers of government businesses can always find costly ways to improve working conditions or to further "worthwhile" objectives, precluding realization of positive returns.

Deregulating a government enterprise means privatizing that operation. Regulation limits the freedom and therefore the property rights of firms. Government ownership is the extreme example of limiting property rights. For example, in the United States most public utilities, airlines, and railroads have historically been privately owned but regulated by the government; in other countries for the most part those utilities are government-owned. Hence, to return those activities fully to the marketplace requires deregulation in the United States and privatization elsewhere.

In deregulating or privatizing an activity, the government should foster competition. Structuring the policy correctly can often result in more competition than if a single government monopoly or regulated monopoly were simply privatized or deregulated. The government can break up the monopoly into rival corporations, as the United States did with American Telephone and Telegraph; it can also encourage potential entrants.

In summary, the failure of regulation stems from the lack of accurate and unbiased information available to government officials, from the inherent biases of regulators, from the rate-setting mechanism itself, which leads inevitably to inefficiencies, and from the politicization of price setting. Even though unregulated private monopolies charge excessive prices and produce inefficiencies as well, they are ultimately subject to potential competition by entrepreneurs seeking to earn a portion of the monopolies' profits. Consequently policy makers should weigh carefully proposals to regulate an industry and move wherever possible to deregulate enterprises controlled by the state.

Competition and Regulation

According to one United Nations official, "The absence of a perfect market has especially in the LDCs [Less Developed Countries] necessitated Government intervention to own, control or influence among other things, the pricing system, at the very least for public utilities" (Mwase 1988, 329). For many decades, this attitude was used to justify the regulation of railroads, trucks, and other modes of transportation. The only surprising aspect of this statement by Mr. Mwase of the United Nations Institute for Namibia is that he still believes it. Modern theory and evidence suggest that regulation is not necessarily justified even when the market is "imperfect." We now understand that government regulation is also flawed. In an imperfect world, policy makers must choose which option will achieve a better result—not a perfect result. Consider some of the major industries subject to government supervision in virtually every country.

RAILROAD REGULATION

Almost everywhere in the world, the pattern of regulation or government ownership of railroads originated in the nineteenth century. Many governments, including the U.S. federal government, granted massive subsidies to railroad builders. In rural areas or places with little outside trade, single railroad monopolies were common. As a result, governments often built the railroads themselves, purchased them from the private owners, or regulated them. In Africa, for example, the French government built the few railroads in their colonies; in British territories the private sector, with the encouragement of the government, constructed the railroads. During World War I, however, the British colonial governments took over the roads for national defense reasons, as did the German colonial government in its colonies. After the end of hostilities, the colonial governments retained the roads.

The subsidies provided for construction of the railroads in the United States generated considerable excess capacity in many major markets. This increased competitive pressures that often resulted in rates being bid down to levels that the industry claimed barely covered operating costs with nothing left over for overhead (see MacAvoy 1965). Thus railroad owners were sympathetic to any approach that would stabilize rates at profitable levels.

Where rival railroads did not exist, such as for many short-haul movements, rates were often significantly higher than they were for through traffic that faced competition. In addition, grain shippers, businesses in small communities served by only a single railroad, and various port authorities wanted controls over rates. Moreover, except for a handful of specially chartered corporations, railroad companies became the first large private corporations in history. As such, they appeared threatening to the public, especially since they also exercised monopoly power in some markets. Consequently the railroads supported regulation in order to stabilize and raise rates on competitive routes; grain shippers and small communities did so to obtain protection against monopoly pricing; and port authorities did so to reduce competition among ports for export grain (Kolko 1965). This coalition, given the public unease with the size of the railroads, was able to secure legislation establishing the Interstate Commerce Commission. As a result, rates increased on long haul and declined a little on short haul (MacAvoy 1965).

The same pressures existed in much of the rest of the world, but probably because of stronger central governments than existed in the United States at the time, state ownership was often substituted for regulation. In the nineteenth century, the U.S. government was kept from owning and operating a railroad or almost any major business by the absence of any provision in the Constitution that would explicitly permit it. The Constitution does specifically authorize the government to provide for mail service and for a sound currency, provisions that make government ownership of the post office or a central bank constitutional. The Constitution also provides for the federal government to regulate interstate commerce, hence the name of the commission.

As noted above, government ownership or regulation have always been substitutes. Except for the United States, the more common approach has been government ownership. In the United States, because of constitutional limitations (no longer as binding under current court rulings as they were in the nineteenth century), regulation has been the preferred device for controlling industry. It is far from coincidental that the industries subject to the most extensive regulation in the United States—railroads, airlines, power companies, and water companies—were also those often owned by governments elsewhere. More recently, however, under the less stringent interpretations of the Constitution common in the second half of the twentieth century, the U.S. federal government has acquired ownership of railroad operations (Conrail) and railroad passenger transportation (Amtrak). In both cases, the government took possession of money-losing activities to prevent them from being abandoned or significantly curtailed. Conrail has been successfully privatized; Amtrak, which few believe can operate without subsidies, remains in government hands.

With the recent exception of the Japanese, rail passenger transportation in virtually all major countries has become a government enterprise heavily subsidized by the taxpayer. The almost universal rationale for taxpayer-subsidized rail passenger transportation is that substitution of rail for auto or air travel reduces congestion and pollution: in other words, externalities involved warrant taxpayers' funds to preserve a form of transportation that cannot survive in the free market. Notwithstanding the claims, it is evident that rail transportation may do little for congestion or pollution. In 1988 Amtrak carried less than one percent of all intercity passenger-miles (*Statistical Abstract* 1988, Table 979), and its share has been falling. Under even the most heroic assumptions it cannot be reducing air pollution from travel by more than one-half of one percent. In most other countries, it is true, a somewhat larger percentage of intercity travel is by rail. Nevertheless, railroads can contribute little if anything to the abatement of either congestion or pollution.

For local public transportation, the role of subways or light rail lines is equally negligible. Where new light rail lines or subways have been built in the United States, passenger traffic has never lived up to projections. Those passengers attracted to these systems have often been diverted from bus systems. Mass transit systems have induced few passengers to give up their automobiles. If most passengers were diverted from bus to rail, any environmental benefit must come from that substitution. But because rail systems are costly to construct in terms of energy, the energy savings in operating a rail system must be great enough to repay the energy investment in building the subway or rail line itself.

TRUCKING AND BUS REGULATION

Trucking and bus regulation resulted from competition with railroads. Ironically, one of the main reasons for the regulation of railroads was the monopoly position of many railroads in short-haul markets; the longer routes were usually competitive. With the advent of motor carriers, short-haul transportation was subject to increased competition. One possible policy option, never followed, would have been to abolish controls over railroads. Instead, in the United States, almost from the first horseless carriage, railroads began to agitate for extending regulation to trucking and motor buses. In response, several states imposed limits on motor carriers. In state courts, railroads often successfully brought suits arguing that the legislation establishing controls over railroads should be extended to trucks and buses.

Nevertheless, because the U.S. Supreme Court held that individual states could not regulate interstate trucking or passenger traffic, state controls of motor carriers were largely ineffective.[3] As a result of these court decisions, state regulatory commissions, railroads, and the Interstate Commerce Commission, anxious to limit motor carrier competition, petitioned the Congress to extend federal regulation to trucks and buses. Partly because of opposition by the trucking industry, the Congress failed to act. In 1935, at the depth of the Depression, the American Trucking Associations, speaking for large trucking firms, changed its stance and supported regulation. Thus a naturally very competitive mode of transportation was brought under federal control.

It is unlikely that regulation would have been imposed on the motor carrier industry without at least weak support from voters and the media. Public support for regulation reflected a loss in faith in

3. *Buck v Kuykendall*, 267 US307 (1925), and *Bush and Sons and Company v Maloy*, 267 US 317 (1925).

competition as a regulatory mechanism. The Great Depression contributed significantly to this rejection of the market. The growth of socialist ideas, positive reports from Communist Russia, and a belief that government engineering of the economy could cure instabilities and inequities—all contributed to the belief that regulation was superior to the market. In the case of trucking, many economists and transportation scholars as well as vested interests proclaimed the superiority of regulation. The motor carrier industry was viewed as "excessively" competitive: entry was too easy, firms failed to understand their costs, prices were bid down "too low."

Nonetheless, regulation of motor carriers was a natural extension of regulation or government ownership of railroads. Without the agitation of railroad interests, motor carriers would have remained uncontrolled. To illustrate, the British government under the Road and Rail Traffic Act of 1933 established controls over entry into the trucking industry as a direct result of the Depression and the increased competition with railroads, which found it increasingly difficult to compete with the new mode (Moore 1976). Germany too, imposed controls over its motor carrier industry during the Depression (Moore 1976, chap. 2). Unlike the British but more like the U.S. four years later, the Germans established comprehensive rate controls that tied truck rates to rail rates. The main objective was the protection of rail traffic. As in most countries, the road haulage industry was taking the most profitable traffic, leaving the railroads to transport bulk goods, much of which the government required the railroads to carry at a loss. Bus transport was eating into the lucrative rail passenger market. The reduction in earnings of the German state railroad was most disturbing because, for a hundred years, the profits of this railroad had financed the government. New Zealand, which has recently deregulated its road freight transport industry, introduced controls over road haulage in 1936 "primarily to protect the government owned railways' revenue and to establish price stability in the freight transport industry" (Guria 1988, 169). Prior to the 1983 act deregulating the industry, trucking firms were subject to price controls, route restrictions, and distance limitations.

Virtually everywhere, motor carriers were brought under government supervision, not because they failed to perform satisfactorily but to protect railroad interests. In this process, politicians ignored the interests of passengers, shippers, and ultimately of consumers, who were forced to pay more for goods.

Experience with Regulation

Almost from the start, economists in many countries criticized the regulation of motor carriers. Bus transportation never appeared to be as naturally competitive as trucking, but as long as there was a rival rail passenger network, competition was viewed as adequate. Trucking was generally seen as a highly competitive industry—too competitive in the railroad industry's eyes—that could perform well without government supervision. Regulation, for the reasons given above, would reduce competition and lead to higher tariffs (Nelson 1935; Kaplan 1989). The critics turned out to be right.

In the United States, in Germany, and in New Zealand to take but three instances, regulation over time led to higher rates, monopoly pricing, and less competition (Moore 1976; Guria 1988). In the United States the ICC "grandfathered" existing carriers, which meant granting certificates of public convenience and necessity that limited the truckers' authorities to only routes and goods that they could prove they had hauled before 1935. After the initial grandfathering, new firms found it virtually impossible to enter the trucking industry; an applicant had to show not only that there was a demand for its service but also that the existing carriers would not be able or willing to provide the service.

Eventually the operating rights of regulated carriers became worth hundreds of thousands or millions of dollars, reflecting the monopoly profits inherent in the restrictions. Organized labor shared about half the profits from restricting entry (Moore 1978). The losers were the shippers and, once more, the consumers, who were forced to pay extra for trucking transportation. Under pressure from agricultural interests, however, the Congress exempted the carriage of farm products from regulation. A competitive industry of exempt carriers developed to handle these products.

Worldwide Liberalization

The evidence that unregulated firms perform better than regulated is overpowering. The theoretical justification for believing that a free market works better than regulation is unambiguous. Nonetheless, it took a change in the ideological climate for the political system to change its policies. Partly this change reflected the success of airline deregulation, partly it reflected the success of unregulated trucking elsewhere, and partly it reflected a new appreciation of the market as an allocator of resources.

The worldwide success of domestic liberalization efforts is the result of a shift in intellectual climate. At the end of World War II, the prevailing paradigm was socialistic. Most observers believed that socialism in one form or another would become dominant. Khrushchev's "We will bury you" was only an extreme example.

A growing body of evidence on how poorly government performed, "government failure," and the development of a body of literature that focused attention on the misleading and inappropriate incentives of government bureaucrats helped convince opinion makers, intellectuals, and officials that markets generally work better than the government. Studies of unregulated airline markets, for example, demonstrated their superior performance over regulated markets. The work of James Buchanan and other public choice theorists showed that government administrators have inappropriate incentives and too little information to ensure good outcomes.

Most nations of the world have adopted a policy of privatization and deregulation. Many are simply giving lip service to the concept, but a significant number are actively pursuing liberalization policies. A large number of countries are selling state-owned enterprises and/or reducing government controls over the private sector. Even economists in the Soviet Union are proposing "denationalization" and markets, although they have yet to accept fully the necessity of allowing private property for land. Poland, the Czech Republic, and Hungary have all successfully privatized a good portion of their economy. China has been moving toward deregulation and privatization.

DEREGULATION

Deregulation does not mean abolishing all regulation: antitrust and safety constraints normally continue. In the United States the airline industry, over which all economic controls over entry and prices have been abolished, is still subject to antitrust oversight and FAA supervision of safety. The Federal Highway Administration in the Department of Transportation oversees highway safety.

A number of studies showed that unregulated airlines, trucking, and communication markets were preferable to regulated. Consider the case of the motor carrier industry. During the 1950s a series of court cases deregulated such agricultural products as fresh and frozen poultry and frozen fruits and vegetables. Studies by the U.S. Department of

Agriculture found that, after the courts ruled that these products were exempt from regulation under the law, freight rates fell between 12 to 59 percent (Snitzler and Byrnes 1958). The survey also demonstrated that shippers tended to prefer the unregulated service to the regulated. Other evidence points to the benefits of an unregulated motor carrier industry. In the 1970s, a survey of its members by the National Broiler Council gave further evidence of the effect of regulation on rates and quality of service. In comparing rates for the same routes between the same points, it found that, on average, unregulated rates were some 33 percent less for cooked poultry than the rates charged by regulated carriers (*Transportation Act of 1972*). In the survey the members indicated that they preferred the unregulated carriers to the regulated or found no difference between the two for all aspects of service quality.

Overall, curtailed surface freight regulation has led to significant savings for the American economy. One study indicates that the benefits of surface freight deregulation range between $39 billion and $63 billion annually (*Economic Report of the President* 1989, 188). Those benefits have come largely in the form of reduced inventory costs resulting from "just-in-time" shipping. Trucking and rail firms are now able to offer better service—more off-line and/or guaranteed delivery—than they could under regulation.

Contrary to industry predictions, deregulation has not brought "excessive" competition or instability to transportation markets. A study of Australia, the first major country to deregulate a significant portion of its road haulage industry, found that although there were no data on rates, the industry was reportedly free of any "instability" or "destructive and wasteful competition," and was quite competitive (Joy 1964).

Experience in Europe demonstrates that regulation tends to produce higher rates. In 1970 the United Kingdom, which had never imposed very restrictive regulation on road haulers, removed all economic controls over the trucking industry. After the limits on entry were abolished, rates fell (Moore 1976). In comparison, West Germany, with a more restrictive regime, has sharply limited the number of licensed vehicles. As in the United States, the value of the licenses for each vehicle rose to hundreds of thousands of dollars (ibid.). Since the Federal Republic of Germany has not deregulated its motor carrier industry, these licenses are still very valuable, although the threat of deregulation with the formation of a true common market has undoubtedly tempered their value. A study of rates actually paid during 1973–1974 in West Germany, the United Kingdom, other European countries with light regulation, and the United States showed that costs were highest in heavily regulated Germany, almost as high in the United States, and considerably lower in the unregulated or lightly regulated countries (ibid).

PRIVATIZATION

In country after country, nationalized industries have performed poorly. Often such firms lose money, making large taxpayer subsidies necessary. In many such cases, service is inferior to that provided privately. Moreover, workers, who expected to benefit from government ownership, have frequently found that the government was no better an employer than were capitalists.

Finally and convincingly, the obvious failure of socialistic systems around the world has proved the case for liberalism. West Germany worked better than the communist East. South Korea is more successful than the socialist North. South Vietnam, before it was overrun, was more prosperous than the Marxist North. Hong Kong, with no natural resources, has become the second-richest economy in Asia while China and Shanghai stagnate. Taiwan, although less liberal than Hong Kong, has prospered. Chile, which under Pinochet adopted free market principles, has the most prosperous economy in South America.

This privatization process commenced in the early 1970s when the Chilean military overthrew the former Marxist-socialist government and set out to return land, property, and companies that the state in the previous decade had sequestered. Margaret Thatcher during the 1980s pressed a program that included selling public housing to its tenants, turning public into private utilities, and returning to individual ownership much of the British industry nationalized earlier by the Labour government. Today privatization is sweeping the globe. The old belief that socialism was the road to riches and that the government could manage business as well as greedy capitalists has died a well-deserved death.

To work well, the privatization process should establish a competitive marketplace. Monopoly, whether government owned or private, produces high prices, poor service, and slow technological advance. Although it is probably true that a private monopoly will work harder to satisfy its customers—it cannot depend on the government to bail it out—than a public firm dominating its market, a competitive industry guarantees superior performance.

The solid evidence that unregulated private enterprise works better than either a government-owned firm or a private, regulated one has convinced much of the world to reduce government regulation and to privatize. Unfortunately, opposition forces are strong. The status quo, be it a governmental establishment or a regulated industry, provides benefits for some at the expense of others. Those that benefit naturally oppose privatization or reduction in government supervision of the private enterprises. Even in industries that have been deregulated, those that profited from regulation normally want to restore government's management. Maintaining a liberal economy requires a continuous and often frustrating battle.

For example, in 1989, the Secretary of Transportation of the Philippines supported a limited amount of decontrol of routes of the "Jeepney" business—Jeepneys are small buses that ply fixed routes in Manila. Opposing the Secretary was the Land Transportation Franchising and Regulatory Board, the owners of the Jeepneys, and the Alliance of Drivers Association. The opposition won.

In the United States, some politicians, airline union officials, and a handful of academics have questioned the benefits of airline deregulation. Since organized labor lost benefits under deregulation, the support of unions for re-regulation is understandable In spite of the fact that almost all passengers benefited from decontrol, travelers from a few cities have had to pay higher fares after deregulation than before. Naturally the politicians from those districts advocate re-control. Only one study out of dozens on the effect of airline deregulation has concluded that there were no significant benefits from the liberalization (Dempsey 1990).

Conclusions

A less regulated economy will provide more flexibility and more rapid growth than one that is highly controlled. Between 1982 and 1989, the United States, following a series of important deregulatory measures, enjoyed one of the highest rates of growth among OECD countries. Financial markets, transportation, and communications were given new freedoms. The economy flourished. Although it is impossible to prove that moderating controls on the private sector alone caused the improved market performance of the U.S. economy, it is noteworthy that during the 1960s and 1970s, an era of suffocating regulation, U.S. growth was significantly slower than that in Europe.

The other outstanding performer during the 1980s was the United Kingdom. Between 1985 and 1988, the "sick man of Europe" enjoyed the fastest growing economy in the Common Market. It is plausible that this strong performance stemmed from the British program of privatization, which in turn increased the competitiveness of its economy. As argued above, for an economy heavily government owned, privatization is the equivalent of deregulation.

Even if increased freedoms for private firms fail to improve the growth rate of an economy, they will normally bring benefits to consumers in terms of lower prices, better services, and more innovation. Regulation is inherently biased toward reducing competition and producing benefits for the regulated and other special interests. It rarely if ever helps the consumer. Almost universally, whenever deregulation occurs, prices fall, service improves, and consumers are better off. This is particularly true for transportation. Transportation modes, with the possible exception of railroads and pipelines, are normally quite competitive. Motor carriers and sea transport are potentially fragmented industries with many carriers in which competition can be counted on to provide low rates and good service. Even rail transport, if it faces active trucking and barges industries, is subject to competitive pressures.

Unfortunately for most Third World economies, government control and government ownership are still the norm. Deregulation and privatization would do much to move these economies toward a more efficient system that would eventually produce the growth that is so needed among the poor nations of the world. As Hong Kong proves, an unregulated free market economy performs superlatively well, while, as mainland China demonstrates, government ownership and regulation strangle economic growth.

CONCLUDING THOUGHTS

Regulation has slowed economic growth, lowered real incomes, and cut employment. There is a distinct danger that proposed health, safety, and environmental controls may further limit the possibility of an expanding economy that would reduce unemployment. Virtually all OECD economies are overregulated and desperately in need of restructuring. Unfortunately, vested interests have found that regulation confers gains or protects them against the rigors of competition. Deregulation therefore is difficult, but some countries have succeeded in cutting bureaucratic supervision of economic activity.

Chile and New Zealand have gone from economic sclerosis, stemming from overtaxation, overregulation, and overprotection, to vibrant economies. The economy of Chile has been growing at 7 percent a year for the last decade. New Zealand has enjoyed a 40 percent fall in unemployment with the rate declining from European levels of 10.9 percent to 6.6 percent. If those countries can do it, so can France, Germany, and the other countries in the European Union.

REFERENCES

Averch, Harvey, and Leland L. Johnson, 1962. "Behavior of the Firm under Regulatory Constraint." *American Economic Review* 52 (December): 1052–69.

Berle, Jr., Adolf A., and Gardner C. Means. 1932. *The Modern Corporation and Private Property*. New York: Macmillan.

Brozen, Yale. 1982. *Concentration, Mergers, and Public Policy*. New York: Macmillan.

Council of Economic Advisers. 1989. *Economic Report of the President, 1989*. Washington, D.C.: Government Printing Office.

Dempsey, Paul Stephen. 1990. *Flying Blind: The Failure of Airline Deregulation*. Washington, D.C.: Economic Policy Institute.

Demsetz, Harold. 1973. "Industry Structure, Market Rivalry, and Public Policy." *Journal of Law and Economics* 16 (April): 1–9.

———. 1974. "Two Systems of Belief About Monopoly." In Harvey J. Goldschmid, H. Michael Mann, and J. Fred Weston, eds., *Industrial Concentration: The New Learning*, pp. 164–84. Boston: Little, Brown.

Denning, Mike, and Walter Mead. 1990. "New Evidence on Benefits and Costs of Public Utility Rate Regulation." In James Plummer and Susan Troppmann, eds., *Competition in Electricity: New Markets and New Structures*, pp. 52–73. Palo Alto, Calif.: QED Research.

El-Naggar, Said. 1989. "Privatization and Structural Adjustment: The Basic Issues." In Said El-Naggar, ed., *Privatization and Structural Adjustment in the Arab Countries*, pp. 1–17. International Monetary Fund.

Galbraith, John Kenneth. 1967. *The New Industrial State*. Boston: Houghton Mifflin.

Gilligan, Thomas W., William J. Marshall, and Barry R. Weingast. 1989. "Regulation and the Theory of Legislative Choice: The Interstate Commerce Act of 1887." *Journal of Law and Economics* 32 (April): 35–61.

Gray, Wayne B., and Ronald J. Shadbegian. 1993. *Environmental Regulation and Manufacturing Productivity at the Plant Level*. National Bureau of Economic Research Working Paper no. 4321.

Guria, Jagadish C. 1988. "Effects of the Recent Road Transport Deregulation on Rail

Freight Demands in New Zealand." *International Journal of Transport Economics* 15, no. 2 (June):169–87.

Hahn, Robert. 1996. *Risks, Costs, and Lives Saved: Getting Better Results from Regulation*. Washington, D.C.: American Enterprise Institute.

Hopkins, Thomas D. 1996. *Regulatory Costs in Profile*. Center for the Study of American Business, Washington University in St. Louis, Policy Study no. 132.

Joy, Stuart. 1964. "Unregulated Road Haulage: The Australian Experience." *Oxford Economic Papers*, n.s. 16 (July): 275–85.

Kaplan, Harold. 1989. *Policy and Rationality: The Regulation of Canadian Trucking*. Toronto: University of Toronto Press.

Kolko, Gabriel. 1965. *Railroads and Regulation, 1977–1916*. Princeton, N.J.: Princeton University Press.

MacAvoy, Paul W. 1965. *The Economic Effects of Regulation*. Cambridge, Mass: MIT Press.

McGee, John S. 1958. "Predatory Pricing: The Standard Oil (N.J.) Case." *Journal of Law and Economics* 1 (October): 137–69.

Moore, Thomas Gale. 1970. "The Effectiveness of Regulation of Electric Utility Prices." *Southern Economic Journal* 36, no. 4 (April): 365–75.

———. 1976. *Trucking Regulation: Lessons from Europe*. Washington, D.C.: American Enterprise Institute.

———. 1978. "The Beneficiaries of Trucking Regulation." *Journal of Law and Economics* (October): 327–43.

———. 1988. "Rail and Truck Reform: The Record So Far." *Regulation*, Nov./Dec.: 33–41.

Moving America: New Directions, New Opportunities. 1990. A Statement of National Transportation Policy; Strategies for Action. U.S. Department of Transportation.

Mwase, N. R. L. 1988. "Road Transport Pricing in Developing Countries: The Tanzanian Case." *International Journal of Transport Economics* 15, no. 3 (October): 329–93.

Nelson, James C. 1935. "The Motor Carrier Act of 1935." *Journal of Political Economy* 44 (August): 464–504.

Nelson, Randy A., and Walter J. Primeaux. 1988. "The Effects of Competition on Transmission and Distribution Costs in the Municipal Electric Industry." *Land Economics* 64, no. 4 (November): 338–46.

Smith, Adam. 1937. *The Wealth of Nations*, Reprint. New York: Modern Library.

Snitzler, James R., and Robert J. Byrnes. 1958. *Interstate Trucking of Fresh and Frozen Poultry Under Agricultural Exemption*. U.S. Dept. of Agriculture, Marketing Research Report no. 224.

———. 1959. *Interstate Trucking of Frozen Fruits and Vegetables Under Agricultural Exemption*. U.S. Dept. of Agriculture, Marketing Research Report no. 316.

Stigler, George J. 1966. *The Theory of Price*. New York: Macmillan.

Stigler, George J., and Claire Friedland. 1962. "What Can Regulators Regulate? The Case of Electricity." *Journal of Law and Economics* 5 (October): 1–16.

Telser, Lester. 1966. "Cutthroat Competition and the Long Purse." *Journal of Law and Economics* 9 (October): 259–77.

Tengs, Tammy O. 1994. "Five Hundred Life-Saving Interventions and Their Cost-Effectiveness." Draft ms., Center for Risk Analysis, Harvard School of Public Health, Boston.

Transportation Act of 1972. Hearings on H.R. 11824, H.R. 11826, and H.R. 11207 Before the Subcomm. on Transportation of the House Comm. on Interstate and Foreign Commerce, 92d Cong., 2d Sess., 1434 (pts. 1–3).

Vedder, Richard K. 1996. *Federal Regulation's Impact on the Productivity Slowdown: A Trillion-Dollar Drag*. Center for the Study of American Business, Washington University in St. Louis, Policy Study no. 131.

Viscusi, W. Kip. 1994. "Effects of Regulatory Costs and Policy Evaluation Criteria." *Rand Journal of Economics* 25, no. 1 (spring): 94–109.

Weiss, Leonard W. 1974. "The Concentration-Profits Relationship and Antitrust." In Harvey J. Goldschmid, H. Michael Mann, and J. Fred Weston, eds., *Industrial Concentration: The New Learning*, pp. 184–232. Boston: Little, Brown.

Part III

Corporate Governance

Young Ki Lee and Youngjae Lim 5

In Search of Korea's New Corporate Governance System

Throughout Korea's government-led economic development until the 1980s, the government frequently intervened in the market by setting industrial development programs and allocating financial resources based on corporate performance in investment and exports. The extensive involvement of the government in the monitoring of business performance, frequent bailing out of ailing businesses, and stock market intervention to maintain market stability effectively protected investors from downside risk. With such protection, investors naturally felt little need for corporate transparency or close monitoring of the corporate performance, and the concentration of corporate ownership was furthered by heavy reliance on debt financing.

With less government intervention in the market after financial deregulation and the liberalization of interest rates, investors now have to assume greater investment risks and they therefore have greater incentive to monitor corporate performance closely. Banks and other financial institutions are becoming more concerned about corporate creditworthiness and performance. In the new economic environment, the principal-agent relationship of the past between the government and business is shifting to a relationship between the manager and other corporate stakeholders.

These developments require a new and more sophisticated mechanism of corporate governance to resolve interest conflicts among various corporate shareholders and to minimize agency costs. The role of the government must be replaced by a new means of monitoring the

This chapter is a revised version of Lee (1995).

performance of corporate management and identifying and promoting capable entrepreneurs and managers.

Corporate governance and ownership structure have been a key element in various public policies in Korea. For example, one policy has been aimed at distributing share ownership of private and public corporations widely among a large number of investors. The major objectives of such a policy are both to promote professional management by separating ownership and management and to reduce the concentration of economic power in the hands of a few chaebols, not to mention another major objective of improving corporate capital structures by means of increased equity financing. There is no guarantee, however, that professional managers with the sense of *ju-in* (literally, owner) will be found by simply distributing shares widely among inactive, uninformed, and incapable individual investors, who must then monitor and control corporate performance.

Such a share-distribution policy, therefore, may end up creating management without the necessary *ju-in* responsibility,[1] resulting in greater agency problems unless an effective monitoring and control mechanism is introduced. The limited capacity of the capital market in Korea has worked as a constraint in absorbing a lump-sum supply of equity shares in a rather short period of time, causing government interventions in the capital market to be substantial burdens in supporting the bearish market. Such constraints have worked as impediments to privatization and financial reforms in Korea.

In fact, the government would like to promote large-scale financial institutions or the emergence of financial conglomerates to enhance the managerial efficiency and international competitiveness of the banking sector. In addition, privatization of government-owned enterprises has been a major policy target to enhance efficiency by introducing responsibility or accountability of the *ju-in*. It is not the public intention, however, to allow owners, such as those of the chaebols, to take control of the large-scale privatized corporations.

Perspectives on Corporate Governance

The question of corporate governance arises from problems caused by delegated management and information asymmetry between owner and manager. Market control and organizational control are the two

1. *Ju-in* in this context means managers who will be responsible, or accountable, for the operation of the privatized firms.

main governance mechanisms that attempt to resolve the principal-agent problem or the multiparty contractual problem. The notion of organizational control today has been applied in the analysis of the organizational structure, governance, and monitoring mechanisms of Japanese and German industrial groups.

AGENCY PERSPECTIVE

Berle and Means (1932) observed that as a firm grows in size, ownership and control tend to become separated. In the initial stage, firms are mostly owned by an entrepreneur. An investment opportunity then arises requiring an amount of capital that exceeds the entrepreneur's own capital resources, forcing the entrepreneur to choose between debt and equity as an external financing.[2] Equity financing dilutes the entrepreneur's power of control and weakens his incentive, and as the firm grows, it often results in a diffusion of ownership, in which case the management assumes the effective control of the firm.

This Berle-Means type of firm has benefits. The capital required for large-scale investment becomes easier to mobilize, and portfolio diversification reduces the risks of investment projects and lowers the rates of return required for investors. That is, the capital market not only facilitates the separation of ownership and control but also enhances economic efficiency. The shift of power to the management also leads to the development of professional management. Yet the separation of ownership and management has costs. With diffused ownership, "the stockholders' vote is of diminishing importance as the number of shareholders in each corporation increases, diminishing in fact owing to negligible importance as the corporations become giants. As the number of shareholders increases, the capacity of each to express opinions is extremely limited."[3]

With the separation of ownership and control, the professional managers have the incentive to maximize their own welfare, which may not be in the best interest of the shareholders. They may benefit from the private consumption of corporate wealth or even make investment decisions not to maximize the shareholders' returns but to protect their own job security. Information asymmetry between shareholder and

2. In order to avoid ownership dilution, the entrepreneur may choose to rely on debt financing, but debt financing has limits because of the risk of bankruptcy (Williamson 1988, 577).

3. Berle and Means (1932), as quoted in Roe (1994, 6).

manager leads to this moral hazard problem. Shareholders could set up a monitoring and bonding mechanism to prevent such abuses of corporate resources by the managers, but the monitoring system's incompleteness will have to be borne by the shareholders as agency cost.

Market control is a mechanism of disciplining management and reducing agency cost due to the separation of ownership and control. For instance, corporate takeovers and proxy fighting are effective mechanisms of disciplining management.[4] Stock price movement reflecting corporate performance is another effective mechanism of disciplining management. The agency cost could be mitigated if the competition in the product market, the capital market, and the market for corporate control work to reduce the severity of managerial abuse. If a manager cannot compete effectively in the product market, the firm will not be able to survive.

The agency problem could also be mitigated when the board of directors represents diverse corporate stockholders. Fama and Jensen (1983) distinguish between management decision and control decision and argue that the latter function is appropriately assigned to the board of directors (for example, the German dual board system). Although some are skeptical about the objectivity of management in selecting outside directors, there is little doubt that the board plays an important role in corporate governance (see Rosenstein and Wyatt 1990).

STAKEHOLDER PERSPECTIVE

Stakeholders in the firm include shareholders, managers, employees, creditors, suppliers, customers, the host community, and the government. The contractual governance theory says that a firm could be seen as a governance mechanism for a set of contracts between stakeholders who realize economic gains through participation in these contractual relationships. The aim of creating such a contractual governance structure is to maximize the stakeholders' net gains from the contractual agreements.

Based on this contractual governance framework, Oliver Williamson (1984) argues that stakeholders should be accorded voting rights over how to manage the affairs of the corporation. He also advocates that the voting rights must be strictly limited to those parties who share in the residual risk of the firm and that this group mainly consists of owners, and under special circumstances, managers and suppliers.

4. There are numerous studies on the role and the effects of the M&A market. See Kim, Bradley and Desai (1988) for detailed discussion.

Contrary to this view, Freeman and Evan (1990) and Lazonick and O'Sullivan (1995) argue that shareholders cannot claim the voting right exclusively because they are not the only residual claimants. In fact, for high debt leveraged firms, creditors hold the largest stake in the firm with greater exposure to the business risk of the firm. Their stake could be much larger than that of the shareholders, and their risk exposure is firm-specific, whereas the risk of an equity holder could be diversified. Shareholders usually own only a small fraction of the company and have little incentive to monitor the management's activities, partly because they can always shift their investment to another firm.

This contractual governance framework is useful for analyzing the governance structure of the Japanese keiretsu (also the German industrial arrangements), in which multiple corporate stakeholders participate in the decision making of firms.

DEBT VS. EQUITY AS A DISTINCT GOVERNANCE STRUCTURE

Rather than viewing debt and equity simply as corporate financing instruments, Williamson (1988) argues that it is better to regard them as different governance structures because debt governance functions mainly through strict rules, whereas equity governance allows much greater flexibility and discretion.[5] In the market economy, changes in the financial mix could affect managers' incentives since a higher debt-equity ratio increases bankruptcy risks (Grossman and Hart 1982; Williamson 1988). Given the managers' incentive to avoid bankruptcy, the capital market will equate debt issue with the firm's quality investment projects. Furthermore, the bond covenant restricting the managers' discretionary use of resources could serve as a way of bonding management behavior to the extent that it could signal and control managerial abuse of corporate resources. From this, Williamson (1988) even proposes a new form of governance structure (dequity), which combines the best properties of debt and equity.

In a particular circumstance, creditors could be given voting rights or board representations. With a high debt-equity ratio, for example, creditors are more like shareholders in that they assume a substantial part of the firm's residual risk. The more a firm relies on debt to invest in such intangible assets as long-term high-risk projects, the more exposed creditors are to the residual risk of the firm (compared with in-

5. See also Grossman and Hart (1982) and Jensen (1986) for the discussion of the role of debt in corporate governance.

vestment in such tangible assets as real estate, plant, or equipment). They therefore need to monitor client firms closely, perhaps to remain in a constant consultation. It has a significant implication for the discussion of the bank's role in the governance mechanism especially, as in Korea, when firms rely extensively on debt financing with the stock market underdeveloped. Under such circumstances, the bank's participation in the corporate board might be warranted.

THE INDUSTRIAL GROUP AS A GOVERNANCE MECHANISM

An industrial organization that has close ties among its member firms through cross-ownership has recently been emphasized as a possible corporate governance system. For instance, Gilson and Roe (1993) attempt to understand an industrial group like the Japanese keiretsu as an overlapping structure of corporate governance and industrial organization.

Although industrial groups are viewed in the United States and the United Kingdom as unsound, uncompetitive, or potentially illegal cartels, in some other countries, such as Japan, they are viewed as contributing to economic gains while not necessarily engaging in uncompetitive business practices. The contractual governance system, incorporated into an industrial group, could facilitate the development and maintenance of stable, long-term trading relationships. It could make an industrial group as a whole realize the economic gains that are not usually available to the independent firms transacting on a short-term, arm's-length basis.[6] The economic gains that a successful corporate governance mechanism within industrial groups could realize are: (1) contracting on the basis of long-term trust relationships, and (2) the concentration of ownership to the active and knowledgeable stockholders with long-term interests (Kester 1992, 39).

Governance Structure of the United States, Japan, and Germany

The differences in the corporate governance system across countries can be explained partly by differences in regulations covering bank-industry relationships.[7] Furthermore, the governance system in each

6. For a discussion on the positive contribution of industrial groups, see Kester (1992), Baums (1992, 1994), and Gilson and Roe (1993), among others.

7. For example, the U.S. Glass-Steagal Act and the Sherman Act significantly affected bank-industry relationships (the so-called arm's-length relationship) in that country; the German universal banking system allowed close ties between banks and industrial firms.

country is a product of evolutionary processes under such institutional settings, which are reflections of social and political as well as economic values.[8]

In the United States and the United Kingdom, the governance system relies upon market discipline to reduce the agency cost resulting from the separation of ownership and control; that is, managerial efficiency is forced upon the firm through competition in the product market, the financial market, the market for managerial resources, and the market for corporate control. The Japanese governance system is characterized by organizational control; the keiretsu organization is centered around the main bank and tied into it in long-term relationships through cross-shareholding among member firms. In Germany, through the practice of proxy voting, banks have the power of control over firms. German banks participate directly in corporate control even through a membership in the governing board.

THE U.S. SYSTEM OF MARKET DISCIPLINE

Modern large American enterprises are typically controlled by professional managers. Shareholders are not directly involved in corporate management. Historically, this separation of ownership and control arose in the early 1900s as the ownership of stock in the expanding American corporations became increasingly dispersed. Individual investors now own too few shares to have any influence on corporate decision making. Ownership by institutional investors has grown to the point that by 1990 they controlled over half the total equity holdings on the U.S. stock market.[9] These institutional investors are, however, mostly "silent partners" to the corporate managers, voting consistently for the incumbent management. Also, institutional investors trade their shares frequently for short-term investment returns, which in turn induces managers to maximize short-term business performance. With institutional owners frequently changing, they have little influence over corporate decision making. Thus, American corporate governance is characterized by "strong managers and weak owners" and "short-termism" (Roe 1994).

Today, the structure of corporate governance in the United States

8. See Roe (1993) for rigorous arguments on this point.

9. For the 1,000 largest corporations in the U.S., estimates of percentage of voting shares held by mutual funds, pension funds, and other investment vehicles run as high as two-thirds.

is in upheaval. Debate on the issue is taking place not only in academic circles but also in the public arena. Michael Porter (1992) states that the long-term interests of companies would be better served by having a smaller number of long-term or near-permanent owners, whose goals are better aligned with those of the corporation. Long-term owners must have inside status, full access to information, influence with management, and seats on the board. Under the new structure (of ownership and governance), management will be judged on the basis of its ability to build long-term competitive position and earning power, not current earnings of stock price (Monks and Minnow 1995, 163–64).

In 1992 the U.S. Securities and Exchange Commission (SEC) reduced some restrictions on institutional governance.[10] As ownership becomes more concentrated, and institutions become more active shareholders, they have been doing their best, either by direct contact or by pressure on the board, to apply pressure on managers whose performance is below par. "Shareholder activism" has sparked a new era of activism by boards of directors, with an astonishing series of firings of CEOs in the 1990s.[11]

THE JAPANESE SYSTEM OF ORGANIZATIONAL CONTROL

The structure of large Japanese firms tends to defy the conventional model of corporations (as found in the United States), which focuses on the market-oriented, hierarchical principal-agent contracts (which are conditioned by security market and drawn by the board of directors). Masahiko Aoki (1995, 16–18) defines the Japanese organizational practice as "horizontal hierarchy" in which collective information processing is followed by individual processing, without involving the authority relationship in decision making.

Much discussion concerning the governance structure in Japan is

10. Before 1992, whenever ten or more investors in the same company wished to communicate about an imminent shareholders' meeting or another corporate governance matter, they were required to disclose their intention to the SEC. In October 1992, the SEC made it easier for shareholders to contact each other regarding company performance and other issues requiring shareholders' votes. The SEC also eliminated restrictions on how shareholders can exercise their voting rights and improved disclosure to shareholders regarding proxy solicitations and reporting voting results (USGAO 1993, 68).

11. See Roe (1990, 222); also USGAO (1993). The cases of Sears, American Express, ITT, and Westinghouse are examples of successful shareholder initiatives in firing ill-performing CEOs. See Monks and Minnow (1995).

focused upon the role of the main bank (MB) at the center of the keiretsu group.[12] The main bank system is distinguished from the so-called relational banking where banks and firms are engaged in close, long-term, and often exclusive relationships. In the main bank system, firms are financed not exclusively by their main banks but by other banks, which delegate the monitoring of the borrowing firms to their main banks (Hoshi et al. 1990, 71). The other banks are, however, responsible for the monitoring of firms for which they themselves are the main banks. Thus, an essential aspect of the main bank system is this reciprocity of delegation of monitoring among major banks.[13]

The particular relevance of the main bank system to the corporate governance of Japanese firms derives from the main bank's function of monitoring and control. Since the main bank also holds a stake in the firm's equity, it has an incentive to lessen the inherent agency cost among shareholders, debt holders, and managers. The main bank's screening and monitoring as an insider are particularly important when the market for corporate information is not yet adequately developed owing to the poor accounting and disclosure system. The main bank could have access to the firm's internal decision making, privy even to the firm's business and financial plans—inside information not readily available in the outside capital market. In a good main bank relationship, the firm consults closely with the main bank when drawing up its business plans and provides a regular report on its performance. This process of information exchange is formalized by the main bank's having a direct link with the firm or membership in a "president's club" in which the heads of all group firms participate (Sheard 1989, 403–4).

As a consequence of the main bank's monitoring as an insider, a borrower could obtain credit at a reduced interest rate because of a lower risk premium. The close tie between the bank and the firm could also help reduce the cost of the financial distress of trying to renegotiate financial claims. When there are many creditors and debt is widely diffused, the incentive for creditors to grant financial relief or extend additional credit is reduced because of the free-rider problem.

Equally important is the main bank's ability to intervene in the management of the firm in the case of financial distress. When the financial condition of the firm continues to worsen past a certain

12. See, e.g., Sheard (1989), Hoshi et al. (1990), Horiuchi (1990), Competitiveness Policy Council (1992), and Nakamura (1993).

13. See Sheard (1989); Hoshi et al. (1990); Aoki (1995).

threshold point, the right of control shifts from the firm's management to the main bank, which then can choose either to rescue the distressed firm or to penalize the management either by outright closure or by replacing the managers (Hoshi et al. 1990; Aoki 1995).

These characteristics of the Japanese main bank system are related to the Japanese greater reliance on debt financing. Japanese firms have been able to take on a larger amount of debt because they have a well-established institution to cope with the risks associated with high leverage. The creditor's shareholding in Japan could be regarded as a way of resolving the problem of the debt's agency cost, for which the United States relies on bankruptcy laws. The Japanese mechanism of conflict resolution does, however, require a more on-going close monitoring of debtor firms by banks than is the rule in the United States.[14]

In addition to the main bank system, the Japanese keiretsu system also relies on the practice of cross-shareholding in which firms within a keiretsu organization own a small amount of the shares of other group companies. Although one firm may own only a small amount of the shares of other firms, the total amount of shares owned by the member firms is significant enough to provide mutual interdependence. When taken together as a group, this cross-shareholding amounts to approximately 70 percent of all outstanding shares on the Tokyo Stock Exchange, yet it accounts for only about 10 percent of total transactions in shares.

The primary objective of cross-shareholding is the maintenance and strengthening of business relations. Some of the stock investments by Japanese institutional investors are made to build long-term stable business relationships.[15] Most cross-shareholdings should also be understood as "shareholder stabilization strategies" to reduce the number of floating shares in the market and to maintain high share prices (Nakamura 1993, 14). Cross-shareholding has also developed as a defensive measure against a potential hostile takeover during the early periods of the Japanese capital market's development.

14. Prowse (1990, 65) argues that the negative relationship between leverage and the measure of the agency cost of debt in the U.S. suggests that the expectation of bankruptcy cost might deter U.S. borrowers from risky suboptimal investment policies.

15. Though Japanese shareholders are believed to have been more interested in the growth of the company and the potential capital gains from higher share prices than in higher dividends, there are indications that this tendency is changing; some shareholders such as insurance companies have begun to request higher dividends, and they are more willing to sell poorly performing shares that they have been holding for the long term (USGAO 1993, 89).

It is argued that this cross-shareholding system enables Japanese firms to take a long-term perspective on investment strategies, since they need not be concerned about hostile takeovers.[16] It is also argued that cross-shareholding facilitates the innovation of high technology products and their commercialization by reducing the risk associated with the disproportionate financial burden accruing to a single-group company and that the keiretsu system provides a ready customer base for newly emerging technologies.[17]

THE GERMAN DUAL BOARD SYSTEM

In Germany, corporate governance is characterized by a dual board system, proxy voting, and a close tie between large banks and firms. Under the Joint-Stock Corporation Act, the AG (stock company) consists of three bodies: the board of managing directors, the supervisory board, and the shareholders' general assembly.[18] The strict separation of management and decision making (control) is reflected by the fact that no one may sit on both the board of managing directors and the supervisory board of the same company.

The supervisory board, as the controlling body, supervises the activities of the board of managing directors but it cannot assume any managerial functions. The general shareholders meeting elects representatives to the supervisory board; these are outsiders, that is, they are not employees of the company, and no managers are allowed on the supervisory board. No one may sit on both the board of managing directors and the supervisory board of the same company.[19] The board of managing directors must report regularly to the supervisory board, especially concerning proposed business policy, the profitability of the company, and the course of business.

16. Ibid., p. 91, documents the long-term time horizon of Japanese investments in the semiconductor industry.

17. Ibid., pp. 87–91.

18. The board of managing directors manages the company on its own responsibility and represents it externally. Members are appointed by the supervisory board for a maximum term of five years and may be reappointed for further terms, each lasting a maximum of five years. A member of the board of managing directors may only be dismissed by the supervisory board, and only for a good reason, such as gross neglect of duty (Schneider-Lenne 1992, 14–16).

19. Similarly, a member of the board of managing directors of company A may not be on the supervisory board of company B, if a member of B's board of managing directors is a supervisory board member at A. See: ibid., U.S. Congress (1994), and Roe (1993) for detailed descriptions of the German governance system.

Under the terms of the 1976 Codetermination Act, a company with more than 2,000 employees must have half of its supervisory board chosen by the shareholders and half by the employees; one of the labor representatives must come from middle management or higher. The codetermination system is a process in which employees have a right to take part in entrepreneurial planning and decision making through representation on the supervisory board. In this respect, the German governance system depends upon a mutual sense of intimacy and trust among key stakeholders, including employees. The legal structure does not assume absolute equality between capital and labor, but the chairman will normally come from the shareholder side.[20]

German supervisory boards have often been depicted as passive organs. In fact, the chairman in particular is usually involved in the most important strategic and financial decisions of a company. The boards also play a critical disciplinary role when the company gets into trouble. In such an event, their direct intervention in management serves a function akin to hostile takeovers in the American system of market discipline, but the German method of encouraging corporate restructuring, when required, has the notable advantage of precluding the asset-stripping, short-term planning, and social disruption characteristics of American corporate takeover battles. The capital market in Germany has not played a very important role in corporate control. Although this is changing, it has protected German companies from the ravages of short-termism and excessive M&As (Schneider-Lenne 1992, 21).

The universal banking system in Germany allows German banks to hold equity shares of other non-bank companies.[21] German banks hold about 10 percent of total outstanding shares of all listed companies (Schneider-Lenne 1992). But the power of the big banks (for example,

20. The supervisory board elects a chairman from among its members. If the requisite two-thirds majority is not attained in the poll, the shareholder representatives elect the chairman from among themselves. Because of this structure, the chairman will normally be from among the shareholder side. However, the power of the supervisory board chairman to cast the deciding vote in the event of a deadlock breaks the principle of equality and ultimately the shareholder representatives gain the upper hand. See Scheider-Lenne (1992, 15).

21. There is no specific regulation on the bank's holding of corporate equity shares except the prudential regulation for the soundness of bank portfolio limiting bank holding of equity shares of a single company not to exceed 50 percent of the bank's total equity capital. This limit was recently reduced to 15 percent of a bank's equity capital according to the Second Banking Directive of the Single EU System.

the Deutsche Bank, the Dresdner Bank, and the Commerzbank) over German industries is much more than that. The shares owned by private investors are largely held in the security deposit accounts managed by banks. In 1993 for example, the shares equivalent to more than 15 percent of the total market capitalization were deposited in such bank accounts.

Most private investors themselves do not vote at shareholders' meetings but instead delegate their voting rights to their banks. This is a distinct advantage to the banks at shareholders' meetings, for a bank's own shares and the shares of which it has the voting power make it possible to participate in the corporate supervisory boards.[22]

The role of banks in the German governance systems has been both praised and criticized. For the good side, it is often said that the close ties and long-term relationships between banks and industries in Germany have been very important in the success of the German economy.[23] For instance, Baums and Gruson (1993) assert that the German universal banking system and the German bank-industry relationship are very significant in overcoming the structural change that globalization and financial market innovation demand. On the other hand, Perlitz and Seger (1994) argue that the German firm under bank influence tends to have a higher debt-equity ratio and pay a higher interest rate than firms less influenced by banks. The close tie between big banks and large business firms may also result in discrimination against smaller business firms and financial institutions. By preventing mergers and acquisitions and by frequent insider trading, banks can also affect public confidence in the stock market and the efficiency of the capital market.

GOVERNANCE STRUCTURES COMPARED

As we have outlined, the structure of ownership and control is different from country to country. In the United States the ownership of firms is widely diffused among individual investors. Although in some cases stock ownership is concentrated in the hands of institutional investors, these investors on the whole have little to do with the manage-

22. Bankers hold nearly 10 percent of all nonemployee seats on the supervisory boards of the 100 largest nonfinancial companies in Germany. Moreover, banks often provide the chairman of the supervisory board.

23. See Baums (1992, 1994) and USGAO (1993) among others for discussions of the advantage of organizational control.

ment and control of the firms in which they hold stock. In Germany the practice of proxy voting gives banks the power of control over firms, so they have the double advantage of corporate control either by membership in the governing board or by the delegated voting. In Japan, though the prewar *zaibatsu* (family-owned large conglomerates) were terminated after World War II, some of the old zaibatsu banks still remain as the core members of the industrial keiretsu groups today; no longer family-owned conglomerates but tied together via intricate webs of cross-shareholding, they do not possess the control power over the member firms. In Korea, the control of big business groups remains in the hands of the founder's family through the cross-shareholding within business groups, but cross-shareholding between banks and firms is strictly regulated.

The systems for monitoring and disciplining the corporate management also vary. The United States relies upon stock price and the merger and acquisition market to discipline management. In Japan and Germany, market discipline is relatively insufficient and banks are allowed to participate in corporate governance and to take an active part in monitoring and disciplining corporate management. Korea lacks not only an effective mechanism for market discipline but also a well-established monitoring mechanism by the independent board of directors and an internal audit system.[24]

Both the United States and United Kingdom have better mechanisms for market discipline. In these systems, ownership and control are conferred upon outside investors who do not have stake in the firm and have little incentive to monitor and little ability to control. Takeover, though a response to this structure of ownership and control, is a response to dispersed ownership and weak shareholders. An advantage of this Anglo-Saxon model of corporate governance is a greater degree of portfolio diversification and a greater sharing of risks.

Under the Japanese main bank system, an internal monitoring system replaces the outside monitoring system, which is inefficient owing to the lack of the well-functioning capital market. In a sense, the Japanese insider system relies upon the self-monitoring of the corporate sector. It is a network in which the firms own and monitor one another.

The German supervisory board system might be good at incorporating the diverse interests of stakeholders into the corporate decision-

24. The credit control system has attempted to establish such a bank-firm relationship, but the incentive for banks to monitor their client firms is still relatively weak.

making process. The governance system through the supervisory board is based upon a rather stable and long-term ownership structure. The supervisory board is not only the governing body of the firm but also often provides professional advice to the management. If management fails, the supervisory board intervenes. But the German system is often criticized for allowing banks too much power.

CORPORATE GOVERNANCE, INNOVATION, AND COMPETITIVENESS

In global competition where technological superiority determines the competitiveness of both the enterprise and the nation, the degree of domestic innovation in high-technology industries assumes critical importance.

The question is, how can a nation's economic institutions be structured to ensure that industrial organizations are sources of innovation? In the United States, national debates continue over the organization of American business, the time horizons, and the international competitiveness of the U.S. technology base (U.S. Congress 1994, 159). Policy makers and academic analysts have paid increasing attention to the ways in which different systems of corporate governance affect the long-term planning and investment decisions of corporations. Such corporate decisions are believed to constitute the fundamental building blocks of the national technology base and to have consequences that go far beyond the immediate interests of individual corporations.

It is recognized that core technological competence depends on systems of corporate governance that encourage long-term thinking and further the pursuit of strategies that subordinate immediate returns to the long-term market position (ibid., 40). The corporate governance structure is believed to determine the firm's investment time horizon. Several studies have attributed the lower amount of long-term investment in the United States in part to weaknesses in the U.S. corporate structure and governance system, such as the corporate orientation toward short-term earnings rather than long-term growth; management is all too frequently more concerned with the possibility of a hostile takeover supported by shareholders eager to seize the short-term returns offered by a takeover raider (USGAO 1993, 40).

The U.S. capital markets can affect corporate managers by directing their attention away from long-run considerations of maximizing market shares and toward a short-term focus on quarterly profits (CPC 1992, 24). Management obsession with the short-run objectives can seriously hamper the development of optimal corporate strategies in the longer-term perspectives. The pressure to keep current earnings high and dividend payments stable can force firms to postpone long-term investments in technology or new plants from which new process technologies develop.

Japanese and German companies have been characterized as having a steady base of permanent investors who provide them with a source of dedicated capital or patient capital that is not commonly found in most U.S. firms (USGAO 1993, 40). Japanese and German companies also have distinctive cross-shareholding and corporate banking relationships to help shape business strategies. These institutional arrangements can provide stable foundations for the commercial adaptation, incremental improvement, and optimal diffusion of new technologies.[25]

The Japanese keiretsu structure and the close link between banks and industrial firms are believed to be conducive to long-term, risk-taking investments. This is also the case in the German corporate governance system, which helps to create the climate necessary for long-term investment.

Governance considerations are crucial in competing for capital. As competition for global capital increases, corporations will be forced to make concessions to the providers of capital.[26] This clearly illustrates that corporate governance structures will have to change in order to have access to new and cheaper capital. Transparency, proper disclosure, and good governance can lower the cost of capital, as capital markets increasingly recognize the value of reduced agency costs. In this regard, competition in the globalized business environment is defined as competition of the corporate governance system or competition of the capitalist system because the governance structure influences the investment decisions of corporations, especially long-term investment in plant, equipment, and research and development, the sources of future technological innovation (Kenichi 1992; USGAO 1993; U.S. Congress 1994).

Corporate Governance in Korea: Reform Agenda

The fast economic growth of Korea during the last several decades has been made possible by the Korean government's export-oriented

25. See Competitiveness Policy Council (1992), USGAO (1993), and U.S. Congress (1994) for rigorous discussions on this issue.

26. For example, many Korean companies had to change their long-time accounting and disclosure practices to become eligible to list their securities on the New York Stock Exchange.

growth strategy. The government supressed and tightly controlled the financial sector to channel scarce capital into the strategic export industries. Firms in these strategic industries (mostly firms belonging to chaebols have been given external capital through the loans by the government-controlled financial institutions. During this process, firms in the target industries have grown fast—some, in fact, into chaebols. The Korean corporate governance system today inherits its key characteristics from this growth pattern of firms.

STRUCTURE OF OWNERSHIP AND CONTROL

Many Korean firms, not only chaebols but most non-chaebol firms also, have a highly concentrated structure of ownership and control. In most Korean firms, the ownership concentration is high enough to give the control over all subsidiaries to the hands of the owner-managers and their family members. The control power of the largest shareholder ("owner") of a firm is reinforced by the widespread practice of share-crossholdings among the affiliated companies in a business group.

Table 1 shows the so-called "in-group shareholding ratio," a measure of the ownership concentration, for chaebols. In 1996, for the thirty largest chaebols, the average ratio was as high as 44.1 percent, of which the family share was 10.3 percent and the share-crossholdings among the subsidiaries amounted to 33.8 percent of the total shares outstanding. Table 1 also shows that the ownership is more concentrated for the larger chaebols. Throughout the last decade, the measure of the ownership concentration for the five largest chaebols is higher than in the case of the thirty largest chaebols.

As Table 1 shows the ratio has been declining over the last decade. The family share declined gradually, from 17.2 percent in 1983 to 9.7 percent in 1994; the share of the subsidiaries declined sharply in the 1987–1989 period (by 8.6 percentage points), and stayed at the level of 32–33 percent after 1989. The decline in the family share could be explained by the development of the capital market in Korea, with the chaebols relying more on equity financing owing to the government policy of encouraging firms to improve their excessive reliance on debt financing (Kim and Lee 1990; Lee 1992). The time series pattern of the subsidiaries' share, however, needs a different explanation. The sharp decline in the 1987–1989 period is closely related to the equity investment regulation of the Monopoly Regulation and Fair Trade Act (MRFTA). Once the chaebols had met the regulatory requirements, they presumably tried to keep the share of their subsidiaries around the level of 32–33 percent to maintain their corporate control.

TABLE 1 In-Group Ownership Concentration, 1983–1996
(in percents)

	1983	*1987*	*1989*	*1990*	*1991*	*1992*	*1993*	*1994*	*1995*	*1996*
Top 30 chaebols	57.2	56.2	46.2	45.4	46.9	46.1	43.4	42.7	43.3	44.1
Family	(17.2)	(15.8)	(14.7)	(13.7)	(13.9)	(12.6)	(10.3)	(9.7)	(10.5)	(10.3)
Subsidiaries	(40.0)	(40.4)	(32.5)	(31.7)	(33.0)	(33.5)	(33.1)	(33.0)	(32.8)	(33.8)
Top 5 chaebols	—	60.3	49.4	49.6	51.6	51.9	49.0	47.5	—	
Family	—	15.6	13.7	13.3	13.2	13.3	11.8	12.5	—	
Subsidiaries	—	44.7	35.7	36.3	38.4	38.6	37.2	35.0	—	

SOURCE: Fair Trade Commission.

NOTE: "In-group ownership" concentration is a weighted average (where the weight is the size of capital) for each business group of the family ownership shares plus those of subsidiaries. Figures for 1983 and 1993 are as of the month of April; all others are as of the month of September.

In an effort to curb the concentration of economic power the government prohibited the establishment of a pure holding company, but we now have a variation of pure holding companies, in which a few core companies (de facto holding companies) at the top of the ownership pyramid function more or less like pure holding companies. The corporate ownership of all member companies is concentrated in these core companies, which are in turn owned by owners-cum-managers and their families. This means that control rights are concentrated in the hands of owners-cum-managers. Decision making of business groups is thus very centralized, mostly limited to so called "chairman's office" or "planning and coordinating office."

At the same time, business groups in Korea seem to have tried to pool the resources of all the affiliated companies, developing internal markets for crucial inputs such as financial capital, managerial skills, or information.[27] However, strong linkages among group member firms through cross-shareholding and mutual loan guarantees can easily spread the impact of financial distress or bankruptcy of one firm to other member companies, leading to the financial fragility of the group as a whole.

A frequent criticism of the Korean ownership structure, as shown in Table 1, is that it leads to a distinctive structure of corporate control in which corporate control over all subsidiaries is almost exclusively concentrated in the hands of the owner-managers, leaving little say to professional managers in individual subsidiaries. Furthermore, critics suggest that Korea needs to establish the separation of ownership and management with the professional managers responsible for the management. This shift, establishing a professional management system and separating ownership and control, would probably require certain preconditions, including a new corporate governance mechanism that could minimize the possible agency problems while enhancing managerial efficiency.[28]

In advanced market economies, the growth of firms tends to disperse corporate ownership because firms finance the necessary capital for their growth through the capital market. Since debt financing is not

27. When markets for input are thin and primitive during early stages of economic development, business groups could be understood as an effort to overcome market imperfections.

28. Agency theory points to the fact that the separation of ownership and control does not necessarily enhance economic efficiency.

usually available in limited amounts, and since it increases bankruptcy risks, a proper balance between debt and equity financings results in ownership dilution as the firm grows.

The question of ownership deconcentration is controversial, and it must be seen as a long-term goal, since it depends on the development of an efficient capital market (Lee 1992). Any policy intervention should clearly understand the time horizon involved. Rather than pursuing the separation of ownership and control, public policy should first liberalize the financial market so that the risk-return trade-off becomes part of corporate financing decisions. With the risk of bankruptcy, Korean firms will rely more on equity financing to improve their debt-ridden capital structure.

Compared with the foreign systems we have discussed, the governance system in Korea has many unique features:

1. Most Korean corporations are owned and managed by a principal shareholder, whereas large corporations in the United States, Germany, and Japan show separation of ownership and management.

2. Many Korean corporations belong to a conglomerate business group, forming corporate networks through extensive share crossholdings. These chaebols are predominantly managed by the principal owners, whose control is strengthened by extensive share-crossholdings within group firms.

3. Decisions at the top tend to be made by owners autocratically, especially strategic and financial decisions in the hands of a single individual or family, although decision making in some other tactical areas is decentralized.

4. The owner-manager practice is believed to have an advantage in enhancing "responsible management" and in reducing the agency problem between the owner and management.

5. However, there exists a strong case of serious interest conflict or agency problem between the controlling shareholders and minority outside shareholders. For example, the controlling shareholders (mostly the founding chairmen or their families) have incentives for portfolio diversification through a form of conglomerate business expansion, whereas outside shareholders can diversify more efficiently through the capital market. The controlling shareholders can expropriate corporate assets for the purpose of diversification by cross-subsidy among affiliated firms. They can also take the corporate assets for their personal benefits at the cost of other shareholders' welfare. This possibility in-

creases with the lack of transparency and the proper governance mechanism.

6. The Korean system does not have a well-functioning mechanism to moderate agency problems; there is no mechanism of market discipline such as M&A. The internal control or monitoring system is also deficient. For example, the board of directors in Korea is not independent from the management and the internal auditors are dependent on the principal owner-manager.

REFORMS NEEDED

During the period of government-led development, the principal-agent relationship in Korea was rather simple. The government acted as the principal and monitor, and the corporate sector was the agent who implemented the government's development program. The incentive structure was also rather simple; it was provided through government subsidies to the business sectors based on the investment and export performance. However, as the economic system changed to a market system and as corporations began to rely increasingly upon the capital market, larger numbers of stock and bond holders took a direct interest in a firm's management performance.

As financial deregulation and interest-rate liberalization lessen the government's role in the market, investors have to assume greater investment risks, and accordingly they have a greater incentive to keep close watch on corporate performance. Banks and other financial institutions are becoming more concerned about corporate creditworthiness and performance. In the new economic environment, the principal-agent relationship of the past between the government and corporations is shifting to one between the owner-manager and other corporate shareholders. These developments require a new and more sophisticated means of resolving conflicts of interest among various corporate shareholders and of minimizing costs. The system requires a new mechanism to monitor the performance of corporate management and to identify and promote capable entrepreneurs and managers, which have been mostly the role of government in the past.

First, corporate management needs to be more transparent. It may well be said that this transparency of corporate management is an infrastructure for governance mechanism to work effectively to reduce the agency problem. To make corporate information more credible, more reforms are needed in such areas as corporate accounting, disclosure requirements, and auditing. Measures are needed to enhance the independence and accountability of corporate audit (for example, the requirement of the outside audit by public accountants) and to require consolidated and combined financial statements for business groups. There should be strict rules for the disclosure of corporate information.

Second, related to the transparency of corporate management, against the possibility of expropriation by the largest controlling shareholders, the rights of outside shareholders, creditors, and other stakeholders should be strengthened, and their role as monitors and controlling owners-cum-managers should be enhanced. As noted earlier, in Korea, the excessive concentration of control rights in the hands of owners-cum-managers can result in the largest controlling shareholders' expropriating minority shareholders and other stakeholders. For this purpose, we must strengthen regulations regarding the fiduciary duties of owners-cum-managers, and also ease the cost of stockholder derivative suits.

Third, as one of the most important mechanisms of internal governance, the board of directors needs to be reformed in order to increase its accountability to shareholders. In Korea, members of the corporate board are now formally elected at the shareholders' general meeting, but because owners-cum-managers play a dominant role in the selection process, the board members do not properly represent minority shareholders. To address such problems, the independence of board of directors needs to be enhanced.

Fourth, since internal control mechanisms inevitably have limitations, external control mechanisms like market discipline need to be further developed. Korea should have a sound and vigorous merger and acquisition (M&A) market to act as a disciplinary force to deal with inefficient management. In the absence of an active market for corporate control, the practice of selecting the management from the ranks of permanent employees is all too easily institutionalized, as observed by Aoki (1995, 10).

It is too much to expect that the M&A market will work as efficiently in Korea as in the United States or the United Kingdom, not only owing to its underdeveloped capital market but also because it will not be acceptable, socially and politically, if frequent and massive downswings and restructuring of corporations by M&A activities result in a serious unemployment problem. Furthermore, the major concern with the recent M&A moves has been that the chaebols will become aggressive in expanding business activities by M&A activities, aggravating the issue of concentration of economic power. Therefore, an M&A

market will have to be introduced, provided that it has some safety provisions to minimize its potential drawbacks. For example, certain M&A attempts can be made subject to examination by an independent body.[29]

Recent Developments in Corporate Governance Mechanisms*

Since the mid 1990s when the issue of corporate governance became the topic of heated debate in Korea,[30] various reforms have been implemented in the Korean corporate governance system. Especially with the outbreak of the economic crisis in Korea at the end of 1997, the problems inherent in the corporate governance structure and related practices have been cited as one of the main causes of the failure of the banking and corporate sectors.

The reform measures focus on enhancing the transparency of corporate information in terms of quality and accessibility, strengthening the responsibility of corporate managers and auditors, strengthening the rights of minority shareholders as well as institutional investors, and enhancing the role and function of the board of directors. Furthermore, the M&A market has been liberalized to strengthen market discipline of corporate management and to facilitate corporate restructuring.

ENHANCING THE QUALITY AND TRANSPARENCY OF CORPORATE INFORMATION

To reduce information asymmetry between management and outside investors, major changes have been made in the accounting and disclosure requirements for corporations. In December 1998, Korea's financial accounting practices were revised to meet international standards. Companies listed on the stock exchange and those registered with the over-the-counter market in Korea are now required to file quarterly financial statements. Furthermore, chaebols will have to pro-

29. The independent body can be set up to investigate the effects of such takeovers from the industrial organizations' point of view. Similar to this system is the United Kingdom's Monopolies and Merger Commission (MMC) and the private self-regulatory body, Panel on Takeovers and Mergers.

*To provide readers with recent developments in Korea's governance mechanism, the original paper presented at the KDI-Hoover conference in January 1997 has been substantially revised.

30. See Young Ki-Lee (1995, 1996) for earlier discussions of corporate governance reform in Korea.

duce combined financial statements from year 2000 to provide investors with comprehensive corporate information on their affiliate companies. Once these rules are implemented, the quality and reliability of key financial information provided by banks and corporations will be improved, thus giving regulators, shareholders, and other investors a more credible basis for performance evaluation.

Several measures have also been implemented to strengthen corporate disclosure requirements. Furthermore, effective April 1999, the penalties for unfaithful disclosure will be stiffened.

STRENGTHENING MARKET DISCIPLINES

The government has taken great strides in liberalizing the M&A market. The Commercial Code was amended in 1998 to simplify M&A procedures and to shorten the appeal period for mergers from two months to one month. To this end, the requirement of mandatory tender offers has also been removed. Previously, if anyone intended to purchase more than 20 percent of the shares outstanding of a company, more than 50 percent of the shares outstanding needed to be purchased through tender offer.

In return for liberalized M&A activities, the restriction on corporate share repurchasing was lifted. A corporation may now buy back equity shares equaling the amount of earnings available for the dividend payout. Additionally, measures to allow stock repurchasing through tender offer are also being considered.

Hostile takeovers by foreigners were permitted in 1998 with abolishment of the requirement of approval from the board of directors.

STRENGTHENING THE INTERNAL MONITORING SYSTEM

As a means of strengthening the internal monitoring of corporations, the role of the board of directors has been expanded. As of February 1998, listed firms were required to appoint at least one outside director to promote effective monitoring to reduce conflicts of interests between management and outside investors. Starting in 1999, at least one-quarter of the board members for listed companies must be outside directors. Also under discussion is a proposal to increase the number of outside directors for large publicly traded companies and financial institutions.

To guarantee their independence, outside directors should be unattached to the major controlling shareholders or anyone affiliated with them, and the role and power of outside directors will be strengthened as a check-and-balance mechanism for management. In addition, the cumulative voting system will be introduced to facilitate the election of board members representing minority shareholders.

Another method of increasing the effectiveness of internal monitoring is the enhancement of the independence of auditors. To this end, effective 1998, for all listed companies and the affiliate companies of the top thirty business conglomerates, external auditors must be chosen by an independent selection committee consisting of internal auditors, outside directors, large creditors, and the two largest noncontrolling shareholders.

ENHANCING MANAGEMENT ACCOUNTABILITY

In 1998, the legal liabilities of major shareholders involved in management in any form were strengthened to increase their accountability. In terms of improving the accountability of management, the obligations of de facto directors will be placed in the hands of the controlling shareholders. In the financial sector, there have been recent court rulings against managerial malpractice in financially distressed or exited banks.

STRENGTHENING SHAREHOLDERS' RIGHTS

As of April 1998, legislation was enacted to strengthen the rights of minority shareholders. Specifically, the minimum shareholding requirements to exercise shareholders' rights such as the right to file derivative suits, to request dismissal of directors and internal auditors, to review accounting books, or to call for a general shareholders' meeting (GSM) have been reduced (see Table 2).

As the table indicates, formerly the Securities and Exchange Act stipulated that minority shareholders had to hold at least 1 percent of the total shares outstanding to file a derivative suit against loss caused by mismanagement. This requirement has been lowered to 0.01 percent. Additionally, minority shareholders now have the right to propose the agenda for GSMs. Steps have also been made to enhance the monitoring role of institutional investors. Traditionally, institutional investors in Korea had been banned from exercising their voting power in the general shareholders' meetings.

With the increase in number and sophistication of institutional investors, their role as monitors of corporate management becomes more important. Institutional investors are now, according to 1998 revisions, permitted to exercise their voting rights. In the past, they had

TABLE 2 Minimum Requirement of Shareholdings (percent of the total outstanding voting shares)

	Commercial codes		*Securities and Exchange Act*	
Types of shareholders' rights	*Before*	*Revised*	*Before*	*Revised*
To file derivative suits	5.0	1.0	1.0 (0.5)	0.01
To request dismissal of directors or internal auditors	5.0	3.0	1.0 (0.5)	0.5 (0.25)
To request injunction against directors' illegal actions	5.0	1.0	1.0 (0.5)	0.5 (0.25)
To review accounting books	5.0	3.0	3.0 (1.5)	1.0 (0.5)
To call for GSM	5.0	3.0	3.0 (1.5)	3.0 (1.5)
To propose agenda for GSM	—	3.0	—	1.0 (0.5)

NOTE: The Codes and the Act were revised during 1997–1998.

been allowed only to exercise neutral "shadow voting" rights except in the case of mergers and business transfers. Effective 1998, banks are allowed to exercise voting privileges for the shares in their trust accounts.

It is obvious that significant and important change in shareholders' attitudes is taking place in Korea. In the past, investors used to protest, demanding that the government boost the stock market when it was bearish. Minority shareholders are now becoming more active in monitoring corporate performance and business conduct and in demanding that firms improve their management practices. For example, minority shareholders are becoming active in filing legal suits against and in demanding compensation from firms engaged in business misconduct that means losses for the shareholders. This new phenomenon of shareholder activism was made possible after the drastic reduction in the minimum requirement for shareholder representation.

One distinctive characteristic of shareholder activism in Korea is that it is led by a group of minority shareholders, represented by a coalition people's movement—this in contrast to the United States, where large institutional investors are the leading shareholder activists. However, the institutional investors, foreign as well as domestic, will be more concerned and active in their role of monitoring corporate performance together with improved governance practices in Korea.

LIBERALIZATION OF FOREIGN EQUITY OWNERSHIP

In December 1997, the ceiling on foreign equity ownership was raised from 26 percent to 55 percent of total shares outstanding and then completely eliminated in May 1998. Also, the requirement that foreigners obtain board approval for ownership of more than one-third of shares outstanding was removed. As mentioned earlier, the remaining restrictions on M&As by foreigners were completely lifted in 1998. With their increased equity participation in Korean companies, foreign investors will have a greater voice in demanding improvements in transparency and governance practices and their participation on corporate boards. This will have a great impact on future Korean corporate governance.

OTHER REFORM MEASURES

Other reforms and measures that have been implemented in the corporate and financial sectors include the enhancement of the role of banks in monitoring corporate restructuring. Creditor banks are allowed to send monitoring teams to supervise the progress of firms undergoing restructuring. Another measure currently under consideration is the permissibility of class action suits.

To facilitate the restructuring of the chaebols, the Korean government has permitted under restrictive conditions the establishment of a pure holding company—an institution formerly prohibited for fear of increasing the concentration of economic power by large conglomerates.

Assessing Current Reforms and Future Prospects

We have seen dramatic, indeed, unprecedented changes, in the face of the Korean corporate governance system and practices. Though some business leaders, accustomed to the old tradition of exercising sole control, may consider the new governance system an unnecessary intervention in management, the majority recognize the necessity of such reforms. Although there was strong resistance from the business sector during the initial stages of discussion for reform, criticism against the deficiencies in current Korean business practices and the governance structure intensified after the outbreak and ensuing aftermath of the economic crisis in 1997.

Now there is new phenomena in the realm of corporate governance, as is evidenced by increased recognition of the importance of corporate transparency, enhanced accounting standards, and the introduction of independent outside directors. Domestic as well as foreign investors are becoming aware of the need for an improved governance structure. Most importantly, the business sector has come to realize the significance of corporate governance in gaining investors' confidence, in mobilizing financial capital at lower cost, and in increasing firm value. Unless a company is able to meet the expectations and demand for improved transparency and governance, financing and investments for continued growth will be very limited.

Many concerned parties are not yet accustomed to the new environment. For example, there is a demand for more than 1,000 outside directors with the requirement for 750 listed firms and many financial institutions to select directors from outside their firms. The most difficult challenge facing these firms is the shortage of qualified candidates. Furthermore, outside directors and companies do not fully understand their respective roles and responsibilities.

A period of trial and error will inevitably take place during the initial stages of introducing the new system. Investors and other corporate stakeholders must realize the importance of putting into place a new, suitable governance mechanism that will protect and even maximize their investments. Outside directors are not intended to be simply a burden on management through unnecessary or even excessive intervention in management practices.

Internal control mechanisms inevitably have limitations, and market control mechanisms must be further developed. Korea needs a sound and active M&A market as an effective disciplinary force to deal with inefficient management. It may be naïve to expect that the M&A market will overnight work as efficiently in Korea as such markets do in the United States or the United Kingdom, but once the government completes the introduction of the basic legal structure for a better governance system, resolving conflicts of interest among corporate stakeholders should be left to the market. The relationship between management, outside investors, and controlling owners will differ significantly from that of the past. How it develops in the future will determine a new model for Korea's capitalistic market economy and corporate management.

Concluding Remarks

We have reviewed the theories of corporate governance and their applications in some of the most advanced economies and in Korea. Contrasting the Korean experience vis-à-vis those of the United States, Japan, and Germany, we have discussed current reforms in corporate governance system in Korea.

The previous corporate governance structure in Korea could be characterized by a simple, if not immature, structure of corporate control and management dominated by an owner-cum-manager. This concentration of power is a legacy of Korea's rapid economic development. The framework for Korea's corporate governance was shaped in a very short period of time, and the relationship that developed between the government and big businesses might be likened to a classic principal-agent relationship; the pragmatic and result-driven government took on the role of the principal and monitor, and the big businesses took on the role of the agent executing the government's development programs. The incentive structure was also rather simple, provided through government subsidies to the business sectors based on the investment and export performance.

However, as the economy has grown both in size and complexity, and developed toward a more market-based economic system, the reasoning of government intervention as the principal has waned, and the share of other stakeholders' interest has increased, replacing the government's role of capital provider as firms are forced to draw capital through equity financing rather than debt. Now, there is an acute need for Korea to restructure its corporate governance.

Deregulation of financial markets would provide a fundamental base for the elimination (or at least reduction) of excessive debt financing, which would enhance capital market discipline of corporate management.

Because Korea's corporate governance system lacks both market discipline and organizational control mechanisms, and because the two could be mutually complementary, reforms in the governance system should take a full advantage of both systems. The different models of corporate governance structure prevailing in advanced economies can provide some lessons, but none of these can simply be imitated.

REFERENCES

Aoki, Masahiko. 1995. "Unintended Fit: Organizational Evolution and Government Design of Institutions in Japan." Paper presented at the conference on the role of Government in East Asian Economic Development, Stanford, California, by World Bank.

Baums, Theodor. 1992. "Should Banks Own Industrial Firms? Remarks from the German Perspective." Working Paper, University of Osnabrück.

———. 1994. "The German Banking System and Its Impacts on Corporate Finance and Governance." In Masahiko Aoki and Hugh Patrick, eds., *The Japanese Main Bank System.* New York: Oxford University Press.

Baums, Theodor, and Michael Gruson. 1993. "The German Banking System: System for the Future?" *Brooklyn Journal of International Law* 19.

Berle, Jr., Adolf A., and Gardner C. Means. 1932. *The Modern Corporation and Private Property.* New York: Macmillan.

Chung, Byung Hyu, and Young Sik Yang. 1992. "An Economic Analysis of Chaebol in Korea" (in Korean). Korea Development Institute.

Competitiveness Policy Council. 1992. *Building Competitive America: First Annual Report to the President and Congress.*

Fama, Eugene F., and Michael C. Jensen. 1983. "Separation of Ownership and Control." *Journal of Law and Economics* 41:101–19.

Freeman, R. Edward, and William Evan. 1990. "Corporate Governance: A Stakeholder Interpretation." *Journal of Behavioral Economics* 19:337–59.

Gilson, Ronald J., and Mark J. Roe. 1993. "Understanding the Japanese Keiretsu: Overlaps Between Corporate Governance and Industrial Organization." *Yale Law Journal* 102:871–906.

Grossman, Sanford, and Oliver Hart. 1982. "Corporate Financial Structure and Managerial Incentive." In J. McCall, ed., *The Economics of Information and Uncertainty.* Chicago: University of Chicago Press.

Horiuchi, Toshihiro. 1990. Management Structure of Japanese Banks and Their Optimal Relationship with Firms as 'Main Banks.' Discussion Paper no. 309. Kyoto University Institute for Economic Research.

Hoshi, Takeo, Anil Kashyap, and David Scharfstein. 1990. "The Role of Banks in Reducing the Costs of Financial Distress in Japan." *Journal of Financial Economics* 27:67–88.

———. 1991. "Corporate Structure, Liquidity, and Investment: Evidence from Japanese Industrial Groups." *Quarterly Journal of Economics* 106:33–60.

Jensen, Michael. 1986. "Agency Costs of Free Cash Flow, Corporate Finance, and Takeovers," *American Economic Review* 76:323–29.

Jensen, Michael C., and William Meckling. 1976. "Theory of Firm: Managerial Behavior, Agency Costs, and Capital Structure." *Journal of Financial Economics* 3:305–60.

Kenichi, Imai. 1992. *Shihonsyugi no System Aidakyusou* (Competition between capitalist systems). Chikuma Shobo.

Kester, W. Carl. 1992. "Industrial Groups as Systems of Contractual Governance." *Oxford Review of Economic Policy* 8 (autumn).

Kim, E. Han, M. Bradley, and A. Desai. 1988. "Synergistic Gains from Corporate Acquisitions and Their Division Between the Stockholders of Target and Acquiring Firms." *Journal of Financial Economics* 21:3–40.

Kim, E. Han, and Young Ki-Lee. 1990. "Issuing Stocks in Korea." In S. G. Rhee and R. P. Chang, eds. *Pacific-Basin Capital Market Research.* North-Holland.

La Porta, Rafael, Florencio Lopez-de-Silane, Audrei Shleifer, and Robert Vishny. 1997. "Legal Determinants of External Finance." Working Paper no. 5879, National Bureau of Economic Research, Cambridge, Mass.

Lazonick, William, and Mary O'Sullivan. 1995. "Big Business and Corporate Control." In Malcolm Sawyer, ed., *The International Encyclopedia of Business and Management.* London: Routledge.

Lee, Young Ki. 1990. "Conglomeration and Business Concentration in Korea." In Jene K. Kwou, ed., *Korea Economic Development.* Greenwood Press.

———. 1992. "Korean Capital Market Development: Major Characteristics and Policy Implications." Working Paper no. 9206, Korea Development Agency.

———. 1995. "Corporate Governance: The Structure and Issues in Korea." Paper presented at the Conference on "Korea's Choices in Global Competition and Cooperation," East-West Center, University of Hawaii, July.

———. 1996. *Global Gyoungjeng Sidae Ui Hangook Giup Soyu Jibae Gujo* (Korea's corporate governance system in the era of global competition). Seoul: Korea Development Institute.

Masuyama, Seiichi. 1994. "The Role of the Japanese Capital Markets: The Effect of Cross-Shareholdings on Corporate Accountability." In N. Dimisdale and M. Prevezpp, eds., *Capital Markets and Corporate Governance.* Oxford: Clarendon Press.

Monks, Robert A.G., and Neil Minow. 1995. *Corporate Governance.* Oxford: Blackwell Business.

Nakamura, Tetsu. 1983. *The Japanese Financial System and the Bank's Role.* Working Paper. School of Business Administration, University of Michigan.

Nam, Sang-Woo, and Dong-won Kim. 1994. "The Principal Transactions Bank System in Korea." In Masahiko Aoki and Hugh Patrick, eds., *The Japanese Main Bank System.* New York: Oxford University Press.

Perlitz, Manfred, and Frank Seger. 1994. "Regarding the Particular Role of Universal Banks in German Corporate Governance." Unpublished monograph, School of Business Administration and International Management, University of Mannheim, Germany.

Porter, Michael. 1992. "Capital Choices: Changing the Way America Invests in Industry." Research Report to the Competitiveness Policy Council.

Prowse, Stephen D. 1990. "Institutional Investment Patterns and Corporate Financial Behavior in the United States and Japan." *Journal of Financial Economics* 27:43–66.

Roe, Mark J. 1990. "Political and Legal Restraints on Ownership and Control of Public Companies." *Journal of Financial Economics* 27:7–41.

———. 1993. "Some Differences in Corporate Structure in Germany, Japan, and the United States." *Yale Law Journal* 102:1927–2003.

———. 1994. *Strong Managers, Weak Owners: The Political Roots of American Corporate Finance.* Princeton, N.J.: Princeton University Press.

Rosenstein, Stuart, and Jeffery G. Wyatt. 1990. "Outside Directors, Board Independence, and Shareholder Wealth." *Journal of Financial Economics* 26:175–91.

Schneider-Lenne, Ellen R. 1992. "Corporate Control in Germany," *Oxford Review of Economic Policy* 8 (autumn): 11–23.

Sheard, Paul. 1989. "The Main Bank System and Corporate Monitoring and Control in Japan." *Journal of Economic Behavior and Organization* 11:399–422.

Shleifer, Andrei, and Robert W. Vishny 1997. "A Survey of Corporate Governance." *Journal of Finance* 52:737–82.

U.S. Congress. 1994. "Multinational and the U.S. Technology Base: Final Report of the Multinational Project." Office of Technology Assessment.

USGAO. 1993. *Competitiveness Issues: The Business Environment in the United States, Japan, and Germany.* United States General Accounting Office.

Williamson, Oliver E. 1984. "Perspectives on the Modern Corporation." *Quarterly Review of Economics and Business* 24:64–71.

———. 1988. "Corporate Finance and Corporate Governance." *Journal of Finance* 43:567–91.

Yoo, Seong Min. 1997. "Evolution of Government-Business Interface in Korea: Progress to Date and Reform Agenda Ahead." Korea Development Institute.

Yoo, Seong Min, and Lim, Young Jae. 1997. "Big Business in Korea: New Learnings and Policy Issues." Working Paper, Korea Development Institute.

Kenneth Scott

Institutions of Corporate Governance
Implications for Korea

To make a coherent analysis of a set of corporate governance institutions one has to specify the objective being sought. Modern corporations, to take advantage of technological progress and scale economies, are large organizations requiring heavy capital investment. The amounts of capital required often can be raised only by pooling the savings of a multitude of investors, who must rely on others to manage their investments and run the enterprise. The institutions—the particular set of legal rules and incentives and behaviors—that support and underlie that reliance by investors constitute the system of corporate governance in a given society.

In this paper I shall assume that the objective is the economic efficiency of the firm. Discussions of corporate governance sometimes appear to be addressing other concerns such as monopolistic or oligopolistic power, the welfare of particular constituencies, or macroeconomic stability. Those are all valid issues, but the design of corporate governance is not a very direct or effective way to deal with them. It has a real and important contribution to make to economic efficiency but only a tangential bearing on numerous other matters.

It should be noted that other institutions and forces also come to bear on the operations of the firm, pushing it toward greater efficiency. Foremost among them are the pressures that arise from competition in the product and factor markets. Perfect competition, domestically and internationally, would work to eliminate this and many other problems, but in its absence they continue to be matters worth attention.

In this discussion of economic efficiency my focus will be on the cost of external equity capital to the firm—the price, in the sense of expected returns, that the firm must offer outside investors to get them to buy stock in the enterprise. Why are shareholders willing to turn large sums of money over to other people (managers) to invest in specialized assets on very ill defined terms? The managers of the firm do not tell them when they will get their money returned or what compensation will be paid for its use. Others who furnish inputs to the business are not so vague about arrangements for payment.

Why are shareholders' property rights so poorly defined? The usual answer is that the stockholders' essential function necessitates that condition. They are the bearers of the residual risk of the firm, enabling others to contract with it on more definite terms; their claims come last, after all other various contingencies and claims are satisfied, hence it is impractical to try to spell them out in detail under all states of the world. The status of stockholders provides a paradigm of the (highly) incomplete contract. But it leaves the stockholder potentially quite vulnerable to managers acting incompetently or in their own interests.

If the position of stockholders cannot be well protected by contract, then how is it made viable? There are two principal mechanisms that serve this function. One is law: fiduciary rules that require managers (agents) to act in the best interests of stockholders (principals). The other is governance: a set of provisions that enable the stockholders by exercising voting power to compel those in operating control of the firm to respect their interests. Legal rules can best address relatively clear conflicts of interest; managerial competence, except in egregious cases, falls in the domain of governance.

Obviously, corporate governance is not a problem for someone who is the sole owner-manager of a business, nor is it much of a problem for the majority stockholder (or group) that controls the board of directors and can fire the managers at any time. (Protection for minority interests in such a firm will have to come primarily from fiduciary rules, since their voting power is generally ineffectual.) So corporate governance is an issue mainly for minority stockholders, in a firm controlled by the managers where there are no significant stockholders that can easily work together. In that situation, the stockholders potentially can still exert control through the board to protect their interests, but they face formidable difficulties (in terms of transaction costs and inadequate incentives) in acting together and actually doing so.

In a practical sense, therefore, corporate governance is important as a means of reducing the costs imposed by managers acting in their own interests to the detriment of shareholders—"agency costs"—mainly in firms owned by dispersed stockholders. How large a concern is this? That depends on the prevalence of such firms in the economy, and it will vary across countries: reliance on external equity finance displays a wide range, from firm to firm and nation to nation. The explanations for that range constitute one of the major areas of controversy and investigation in this field.

A starting point is to inquire why a firm would want to rely on external equity finance at all. The usual answer is that it is cheaper to finance through the stock market, because portfolio investors can diversify out the nonsystematic or firm-specific risk and the issuer pays a risk premium only for the systematic or remaining risk, and because it opens up a larger potential supply of capital. A lower cost of capital for the firm (or a nation's economy) in turn affects profitability, economic growth, and international competitiveness.

But recourse to the public capital markets means greater exposure of owners to agency costs, and greater need for corporate governance institutions and rules to limit the extent to which managers can mismanage the firm, divert wealth from shareholders and extract "control rents." If the objective seems desirable enough, then what is controversial? How best to achieve it?

Corporate Governance Worldwide

Since all countries and economic systems face the problem of how to economize on principal-agent costs, one approach to an answer is to look around the world and see how it has been dealt with. The comparative approach has attracted considerable attention over the last decade, focusing on the three largest and most developed economies: the United States, Japan, and Germany. Each has a distinctive set of institutions. A full description would go well beyond the scope of this paper, but each is usually characterized in terms of an "ideal type" (even though it does not reflect the actual diversity and complexity to be found in each nation).

For the United States, the ideal type is the Berle-Means (1932) corporation, with equity ownership diffused among a multitude of small stockholders and a self-perpetuating management firmly in control under most circumstances. A degree of discipline over management is provided by the threat, and occasionally the reality, of proxy contests, hostile takeovers, and leveraged buyouts (LBOs). Legal rules also impose on directors and officers certain fiduciary duties, particularly the duty of loyalty, which "require" them in conflict-of-interest situations to act in the best interest of the stockholders rather than of themselves. That general admonition has received development in a number of recurring patterns and is enforced through civil liability actions brought by attorneys on behalf of shareholders.

Underneath the ideal type lie many questions. How accurate is it for the U.S. economy? Institutional, as opposed to individual, investors now own almost half the total U.S. equity market, but there are thousands of institutional investors, such as pension funds, mutual funds, insurance companies, trust companies, foundations, charities, and endowments (*Institutional Investment Report* 1997, 1: 38). How much less acute is their collective action problem? In the twenty-five largest U.S. corporations, an average 27.5 percent of the common stock is held by the top twenty-five institutional investors (ibid. 2: 36). But as capitalization size decreases, so in general does the institutional share; exact data are lacking. And various financial and securities statutes impose a set of technical legal impediments to significant holdings and coordinated action by institutional investors, although the latter were somewhat eased in 1992.

As for fiduciary duties, just how effective are they? There is a multitude of different rules for different contexts, ranging from criminal penalties for theft and embezzlement to civil liability for "unfair" self-dealing or to amorphous admonitions to treat minority shareholders with inherent fairness in a holding company formation. Enforcement also faces a collective action or free rider problem, handled with the devices of derivative suits and class actions, which have their own agency costs.

In Japan, the ideal type is the *keiretsu*, thought of as a group of companies linked by stable cross-shareholdings and seller-buyer relationships. A parent company or more often a main bank is supposed to act as the administrator for the group, monitoring management performance of the member firms and intervening in cases of sufficient financial distress (Aoki 1994). Nonmember shareholdings constitute a substantial minority of the ownership of most of the member firms, but the public shareholders are inactive investors and discipline through market mechanisms such as hostile takeovers is almost unheard of.

Again, there are questions about the extent to which the keiretsu pattern describes the current Japanese economy. Much of the literature is descriptive and assertive, not numerical or empirical. The role of the main bank (which cannot itself own more than 5 percent in any company) was not much tested before the crash at the end of 1989, and (particularly given the propensity in Japanese accounting and bank supervision to conceal rather than disclose financial losses) has not received much definitive analysis since. It may be about to undergo significant change, under current economic pressures (Sheard 1997).

The cross-shareholdings and transaction relationships are laden with potential conflict-of-interest dangers for outside stockholders, and it is not known how they have fared. The Japanese legal system does not rely on a general fiduciary duty of managers to act in the best interest of stockholders; instead, directors may be liable for gross negligence in performance of their duties, including the duty to supervise. The duty and liability run to the company, however, and enforcement by derivative suits is a relatively new phenomenon.

In Germany, the standard account looks at a few hundred large firms, listed on the stock exchanges and operating under the two-tier (supervisory and management) board system required of companies with more than 2,000 employees (who elect half the supervisory board). Major (over 25 percent) blockholders are common; even more significant is the role of the firm's house bank and other banks in terms of their voting power. German banks, as universal banks, can own corporate stock, unlike U.S. banks. In addition, in a system of bearer shares, German banks are the primary depositaries for public stockholders and vote their proxies; the banks also run investment funds and vote those shares. The result is that banks in 1992 cast on average 84 percent of the votes at the annual shareholder meetings of the twenty-four largest widely held stock corporations (Baums 1996).

Does this mean that in Germany banks act as effective institutional monitors on behalf of shareholders? The answer is far from clear, since the same structure applies to the banks themselves. The five largest universal banks as a group cast between 54 percent and 64 percent of the votes in 1992 at their own shareholder meetings, though no one had an absolute majority at its own meeting. If the banks' managements are relatively unconstrained by other shareholders or the stock market, how is their discretion employed?

The legal system is not thought of as playing much of a role in German corporate governance. The civil law is not congenial to the broad fiduciary concepts of Anglo-American equity law. Supervisory board directors really do not have much decision-making responsibility, and codetermination has been criticized as undermining even its monitoring effectiveness (Pistor 1997). Management board directors could act negligently or commit torts, but the institutions of the derivative suit or class action are unknown. For stockholders to sue management in such a situation, it would take a majority at a general meeting, or at least 10 percent to file a court petition; obviously it is a rare occurrence.

Suppose we leave the world of the most highly developed market economies and go to the world of the less developed countries and emerging market economies. Now the typical pattern (to the extent the economy is not state-run) is one of companies closely held or dominated by a founder, his family, and associates. The role of external equity finance is small; the business is financed by retained earnings and heavily by debt (often on a political or subsidized basis from government-controlled banks). The effective constraints of the legal system on managers may be weak or nonexistent, a condition that Russia at this point seems to exemplify.

What explains all these variations? We do not have convincing explanations, in part because we do not even have a good factual picture of corporate governance variables across the world. For a researcher working in English, there is a fair amount of empirical information on the United States and the United Kingdom, and very recently some on Germany and Japan, but it has not been gathered systematically and contains frustrating gaps. As for the rest of Europe, Asia, Latin America, and Africa, the literature is meager in English (and generally, I suspect, in the national language as well).

Of course, even in the absence of comprehensive information, one can speculate. There is a large political component in the generation of these different institutional structures. Mark Roe (1994) has stressed that the American antipathy to private concentrations of economic power led to statutes that geographically fragmented the banking industry and prohibited banks and insurance companies from owning stock, effectively preventing them from playing the role of their counterparts in Germany and Japan. Germany had developed by the end of the nineteenth century large, nationwide universal banks with close relationships to industrial clients; the banks have both directly and indirectly stymied the growth of the public securities market. In Japan, the government took control of the banking industry in World War II and used it to allocate capital to the industrial sector; after the war, with private capital exceedingly scarce, there was no significant stock market and government policy continued to be to finance industrial growth through bank debt, supporting the power of the main bank over its group of client firms.

Such thumbnail sketches are not intended as explanations, but to suggest that understanding corporate governance systems goes beyond the pressures for economic efficiency to a consideration of historical path-dependency and other factors.

The Best System

So which system is preferable? Is that even an answerable question? I have already mentioned the problem of data that are not available or have not been collected and tabulated. For no country, including the United States, can we paint a picture of the entire corporate governance structure. In comparative terms, no one has even attempted to go beyond a half dozen or so of the largest countries (see Shleifer and Vishny 1997).

But there are difficulties at a deeper level. How would one undertake to measure the effectiveness of corporate governance across nations in any rigorous way? How do you isolate and measure agency costs for an economy? In the 1980s, the tendency was simply to say that if economic growth rates in Japan or Germany had been higher than in the United States, corporate governance was one of the factors at work and their systems might be better. If the pattern reverses in the 1990s, does the conclusion reverse? In the absence of good direct measures of corporate governance efficiency, some studies have resorted to the use of proxies, such as the rates of board turnover or management turnover, the level of discretionary spending or free cash flow, or the likelihood of takeover bids and acquisition. All proxies have their flaws, and methodology remains an issue and concern. At this time, we have more plausible stories than tested hypotheses.

Furthermore, critics of corporate governance systems and proposals argue that they have costs that must be taken into account, as well as benefits from the reduction of control rents and mismanagement. One asserted cost of the U.S. system is that market-based discipline creates an undesirable orientation by management toward short-term stock price performance rather than long-term investment returns and growth. The argument rests on the proposition that the stock market is myopic, that it consistently overdiscounts longer-term expected cash flows and returns in pricing companies. Various models of asymmetric information and accounts of short-term speculative bubbles have been offered, but evidence for consistent discount myopia is weak (Abarbanell and Bernard 1995) and would raise questions going far beyond matters of corporate governance.

Another criticism of corporate governance as analyzed here is that it should not be judged in terms of economic efficiency, the cost of capital, and shareholder wealth but should take into account effects on other "constituencies" such as employees, suppliers, customers, managers, and the community at large (see Williamson 1985, chap. 12). All are characterized as "stakeholders," and the corporate governance system is to be judged by how well all interests are served. Focus on shareholders, it is argued, does not take into account costs for these other stakeholders. What is omitted from the argument is consideration of the extent to which these other interests either can protect themselves by contract or do not make firm-specific investments that are subject to expropriation by management. We are returned to a point with which we began: what is unique about stockholder claims is that they are long-term, residual, and necessarily poorly defined.

Some Common Elements

But perhaps we do not need to be able to arrive at a logical and analytical answer to the question of which set of corporate governance rules is to be preferred. We can employ the test of economic survival: does not competition in the product market force evolution toward the most efficient governance structure? We have noted one qualification on that argument; political forces can impose fundamental constraints on the available economic choices. That makes it hard to assert that the U.S. or German or Japanese system would be best for others. Still, each of those systems has worked well enough to sustain capital accumulation, investment, and economic growth in a leading economy. By looking at their common elements rather than their differences we may be able to draw some tentative conclusions.

First, what can we say about their legal institutions? I do not feel altogether comfortable in going beyond the United States, but I can at least offer some impressions. To begin, a distinction should be made between legal rules defining and protecting shareholder voting rights and ability to assert control, and legal rules substituting for (or supplementing) shareholder control by imposing enforceable duties on managers. There is a fairly well developed set of laws establishing voting and control rights for shareholders in each country, although it is not difficult to suggest improvements. This would seem to be a minimum requirement for any effective corporate governance system, but it is lacking in some countries.

The importance of fiduciary duties, or their equivalent, has been less studied. One can postulate a continuum of situations involving conflicts of interest between managers and owners, with the conflict becoming less sharp (and perhaps the legal rules less essential). At one extreme would be outright theft, embezzlement, and misappropriation; without effective legal sanctions in these cases, only the gullible would part with their money. A somewhat less transparent form of achieving the same end is the self-dealing transaction, between the manager and his firm. By buying too low or selling too high, the controlling party transfers wealth from the firm to himself, but the picture can be confused by intricate transactions in nonstandard assets or subject to varying degrees of price unfairness. Enforcement becomes more difficult, but still seems essential if agency costs are to have any bound. The appropriation of corporate opportunities, excessive compensation, and consumption of managerial perks can be still more judgmental, and probably the legal rules are less effective but the order of magnitude is also less. And when one reaches conflicts highly intertwined with the regular operation of the business, such as excessive diversification or self-retention by less competent managers, the fiduciary duty of loyalty (or the Japanese duty of supervision) probably offers little protection.

The United States has, it is my impression, gone considerably further along this continuum than Japan or Germany. How effectively, is hard to measure; the subject has not received much attention. (Notable very recent exceptions are Shleifer and Vishny 1997 and LaPorta, Lopez-de-Silane, Shleifer, and Vishny 1997.) But it cannot just be ignored by any corporate governance system intended to sustain external finance, particularly for companies in which there is a controlling majority shareholder or group.

Second, all three systems have found methods for combining economic and control rights into large blocks in order to overcome the ineffectualness of fragmented voting power. In Germany it takes the form of large investors, with their voting clout sometimes augmented by proxy control. In Japan it takes the form of coordinated networks, acting through institutions like the presidents' council and the main bank. Both those arrangements are relatively stable, whereas in the United States the aggregation is often ad hoc: voting power is assembled for the occasion, through a proxy contest or tender offer or leveraged buyout. The techniques differ, but they appear to be addressing a common need in an effective corporate governance system. Where the arrangement is stable, it can be turned against outside minority stockholders.

In the last analysis, for many reasons we probably cannot point to an individual system as the best. There is some basis for identifying shortcomings or proposing improvements, but a number of quite distinctive institution arrangements seem to work at least passably and equivalently well (Kaplan 1994a, 1994b). That suggests a strategy of not adopting or entrenching any single system but creating if possible an opportunity for any of them to take root and demonstrate superiority, even if only in a special niche (Roe 1994).

For the United States, that would mean removing the legal impediments for financial institutions to accumulate more significant blocks, and for blockholders to work together in monitoring, and if necessary replacing, management. For Germany it would mean encouraging the deepening of the securities market and the capacity of stockholders to oust management (currently usually protected in office by five-year contracts). For Japan it would mean accepting the role of hostile tender offers and other forms of capital market discipline.

Of course, in each country there are political barriers to such reforms, led by managements and sometimes unions, and they may not be attainable. But there are also those who would benefit from enhanced corporate governance, and this might be a sensible strategy for them to follow. The tactics that would have the best prospect of success depend upon local political institutions and forces, and that analysis lies far beyond my competence.

Applications for Korea

In conclusion, what does this collection of institutions, insights, and uncertainties have to offer Korea? Perhaps more than might at first appear. I shall take my understanding of Korean corporate governance and reform proposals from Lee (1996) and also from the contribution of Lee and Lim to the present volume.

The "ideal type" for Korea seems to be the chaebol, best described as a conglomerate web of firms, linked by indirect cross-shareholdings and a common founding-chairman in the core companies. The founder and his family on average own about 10 percent, and through cross-holdings control another 30+ percent, in the group member firms. In those companies that are listed, financial institutions own about 30 percent of the equity. This is a picture of the family-dominated firm, typical for emerging economies, in which control rents are likely to be high.

Lee (1996) does not describe the extent to which the legal system endeavors to bound those control rents, beyond noting that board members do not represent outside shareholders, who are "overlooked." The role of auditors is described as "atrophied."

In addition, "management right" was protected until this year (1997) by a prohibition of hostile tender offers, and custodians of public shares are prohibited from casting independent votes at the annual meeting (that is, they had to shadow vote).

The government has pursued a number of policies to "achieve wider shareholding." Listing on the first tier of the stock exchange requires that over 40 percent of stock be held by shareholders owning less than one percent, and that the principal owner and his family own not more than 51 percent. Cross-shareholdings by a firm may not exceed 25 percent of its net equity capital. A bank cannot without permission own over 10 percent of a company's shares, and no shareholder can own more than 4 percent of a bank. It is apparent that these rules work mainly to disperse outside shareholder voting power and do not threaten the continuance of dominance by the insider control group.

Lee (1996) reviews a number of proposals to improve Korean corporate governance, as employees and the public become larger shareholders and the government moves toward reliance on financial markets for capital allocation. The suggested reforms would include strengthening the position of internal and outside auditors, allowing mergers and acquisitions approved by a panel, requiring more outside directors on boards, introducing the German supervisory board or two-tier system, and allowing banks to own greater equity shares in companies.

To aid in evaluating these and other reform proposals, there are a number of principles that we can derive, at least tentatively, from the body of experience that is available:

1. Attention should be paid to the state of legal protection from conflict-of-interest transactions. Governance in the narrow sense—the exercise of voting rights—is of little immediate help to minority shareholders confronting a controlling block. This is particularly significant

if one is concerned with start-up technology firms in the Silicon Valley mode; venture capital firms are medium-term investors and need an exit for their investments in the form of an active IPO market.

2. It is not enough to note that someone—a house bank, or main bank, or outside directors, or supervisory board—possesses the power to be an effective monitor of management. One must also examine closely their incentives so to act, and observe their performance in actual practice. Where direct incentives are mixed or weak, as in all those cases, it may be a mistake to have high expectations. There is no real substitute for the possession or acquisition by the outsiders of a major economic stake in the firm's success.

3. Charging management or the board with a legal mandate to "balance" the interests of various constituencies or stakeholders is merely to diminish any legally enforceable responsibility to shareholders, without creating any definable obligation to anyone else. In the United States, such statutes have been used by management to enlarge their discretion to ignore shareholder preferences in hostile takeover situations. The result is to increase the scope of potential control rents and agency costs.

4. Who pays for (such an increase in) agency costs? The existing owners of the firm, not new shareholders buying in the market—the price they pay will reflect the reduction in their share of expected cash flows to the firm (Jensen and Meckling 1976). So the owners of family firms, when they sell shares to the public at a higher price, are the beneficiaries of effective legal rules and corporate governance. If understood, this fact would facilitate the adoption of what are usually described as "shareholder" protections.

5. The largest beneficiary is the nation as a whole, since the improvements in management performance and reductions in cost of capital in the economy aid it in domestic productivity and international competitiveness.

REFERENCES

Abarbanell, Jeffrey, and Victor Bernard. 1995. "Is the U.S. Stock Market Myopic?" Working Paper, Michigan Business School, Ann Arbor.

Aoki, Masahiko. 1994. "Monitoring Characteristics of the Main Bank System: An Analytical and Developmental View." In Masahiko Aoki and Hugh Patrick, eds., *The Japanese Main Bank System*, pp. 109–41. New York: Oxford University Press.

Baums, Theodor. 1996. "Universal Banks and Investment Companies in Germany." In Anthony Saunders and Ingo Walter, eds., *Universal Banking: Financial System Design Reconsidered*, pp. 124–60. Chicago: Irwin.

Berle, Jr., Adolf A., and Gardner C. Means. 1932. *The Modern Corporation and Private Property*. New York: Macmillan.

Institutional Investment Report. 1997. New York: Conference Board.

Jensen, Michael, and William Meckling. 1976. "Theory of the Firm: Managerial Behavior, Agency Costs and Ownership Structure." *Journal of Financial Economics* 3: 305–60.

Kaplan, Steven. 1994a. "Top Executive Rewards and Firm Performance: A Comparison of Japan and the United States." *Journal of Political Economy* 102: 510–46.

———. 1994b. "Top Executives, Turnover, and Firm Performance in Germany." *Journal of Law, Economics, and Organization* 10: 142–59.

LaPorta, Rafael, Florencio Lopez-de-Silane, Andrei Shleifer, and Robert Vishy. 1997. "Legal Determinants of External Finance." Working Paper no. 5879, National Bureau of Economic Research, Cambridge, Mass.

Lee, Young Ki. 1996. "Corporate Governance in Korea: The Structure and Issues." Working Paper, Korea Development Institute.

Lee, Young Ki, and Young Jae Lim. 1997. "In Search of Korea's New Corporate Governance System." Paper presented at the Korea Development Institute–Hoover Institution Conference, Stanford, California, January 15–16.

Pistor, Katharina. 1997. "Codetermination in Germany." Working Paper, Harvard Institute for International Development.

Roe, Mark. 1994. *Strong Managers, Weak Owners: The Political Roots of American Corporate Finance*. Princeton, N.J.: Princeton University Press.

Sheard, Paul. 1997. "Financial System Reform and Japanese Corporate Governance." Working Paper, Baring Asset Management, Ltd., Tokyo.

Shleifer, Andrei, and Robert W. Vishny. 1997. "A Survey of Corporate Governance." *Journal of Finance* 52: 737–83.

Williamson, Oliver E. 1985. *The Economic Institutions of Capitalism*. New York: Free Press.

Part IV

Social Welfare

Hyehoon Lee and Kye-sik Lee

A Korean Model of Social Welfare Policy

Issues and Strategies

Introduction

The Korean economy's primary goal during the era of modernization and industrialization beginning in the 1960s was rapid economic growth to eliminate absolute poverty. During that time, rapid economic growth took priority over social welfare policy. There was a tacit consensus that the creation of employment opportunities was the best way to assure national well-being, and the limited resources available were invested in accelerating economic growth on a sustained basis. Though such a growth-oriented policy may well have been appropriate during the period of rapid population increase and industrialization, this strong emphasis on economic growth over a more equitable national income distribution has tended to keep investment in social welfare at a relatively low level. The growth-oriented policy has left a substantial burden on individual households, and rapid economic growth is frequently cited as having been accomplished at the expense of social welfare.

Since the Korean economy achieved its mid-term goal, a per capita national income of U.S. $10,000, much more emphasis has recently been placed on the quality of life and thus social welfare policy. It is frequently contended that now is the time for social welfare policy to take precedence over economic development. Is it true that one can be attained only at the expense of the other? For a leap toward higher development, it is crucial to reconcile the two seemingly conflicting goals of social welfare and economic growth.

Western developed countries have long been regarded as an ideal model of social welfare policy. Since the 1970s, however, most developed countries have suffered from increasing unemployment, a deep fiscal deficit, and sluggish economic growth. Many efforts to overcome the welfare state crisis resulted in legislative reforms in almost all developed countries. Sweden recently changed its slogan "From the cradle to the grave" to "From welfare to competitiveness." In August 1996, the United States government passed the Personal Responsibility and Work Opportunity Reconciliation Act, which is considered one of the most drastic social welfare reforms since 1935. In January 1996, Germany started a reformed social welfare plan. Such reforms are based on the belief that social welfare can never be sustainable without stable economic growth—that is, social welfare and economic growth are mutually complementary and reinforcing, neither conflicting nor contradictory. It is not true that one can be attained only at the sacrifice of the other.

Korea is undergoing drastic social and economic changes that have been generating demand for social welfare in various dimensions. Popular desires and expectations concerning the quality of life will become much stronger in this era than before. As the level of national income rises, people's interest in and desire for social welfare and well-being will greatly increase and diversify. At the same time, the elderly population continues to increase, female participation in various social and economic activities is expanding, and the trend toward nuclear families is intensifying. Such trends will sharply increase the popular demand for improved well-being of the elderly, women, and children.

The purpose of this paper is to propose a new Korean model of social welfare policy, taking into account lessons from the experience of developed countries and the social changes Korea is facing at the moment. Korea's social welfare system is still in its initial stage and is consequently segmented into competing legislative initiatives. The lack of consistency and coherence such as overlapping or omitted benefits has resulted in considerable inefficiency and inequity. To compensate for the public's reluctance, the benefits offered have been very generous compared to the contributions in hopes of attaining rapid and extensive beneficiaries enrollment. Such an offer entails an actuarial imbalance problem and thus raises the conversion issue of going from the current fully funded system to a pay-as-you-go system.

We suggest four basic principles for constructing the Korean model of social welfare policy. (1) Social welfare policy should be designed to support economic growth, which in turn sustains social welfare itself. (2) The public sector should provide basic social security guaranteeing minimum living standards while the private sector should supply supplementary social security in respect for consumer sovereignty. (3) More emphasis should be placed on preventing the need for social welfare rather than responding to the need. (4) Social welfare policy in Korea should make the best of the strengths of its traditional culture such as strong family ties and neighborly assistance.

We divide the social welfare system into the income security system, health security system, and social welfare service. We discuss more specific issues of each category and suggest appropriate solutions to those issues based on the four stated principles.

For income security, we propose a tripartite system as the first-level safety net: minimum income security through a consolidated public pension with a flat structure, additional income security through a corporate pension proportional to the income level, and supplementary income security through a private pension or savings. As a second-level safety net covering those who are excluded from the first-level safety net, a public assistance program should be developed in tandem with an effective self-help program.

For a health security system, we propose a two-tier health insurance scheme: basic coverage through public insurance and supplementary insurance through private health insurance. For those excluded from the two-tier system, a medical aid program needs to be extended in terms of expenses and covered items such as medication.

For a social welfare service, we propose that incentives to work be given to those who are able to work so that they can become self-supporting. Social welfare service is an area that is not free from market failure, and therefore the private sector needs to be encouraged by government subsidies, tax, or financial incentives to take an active role.

Taking into account that Korea should enhance the quality of life considerably in keeping with sustained economic growth, how to finance the implementation of these suggested policies is a very important issue. The best financing method would be one that supports rather than hinders economic growth and minimizes economic distortions in the labor and savings markets.

Following a discussion of current demographic and social changes in Korea that are generating the demand for a new social welfare policy, we present the principles of social welfare policy that Korea should pursue in its policy design. Subsequent discussions deal with specific proposals for income security, health security, and social welfare service, respectively. In order to shed light on optimal financing methods for the Korean economy, we also analyze the macroeconomic effects of various financing options.

The Changing Environment for Social Welfare Policy

Korea is presently experiencing a noticeable demographic change as the population ages, a result both of a decreasing birthrate and longer life expectancy. The aging population will increase both pensions and medical care costs to a great extent because the elderly use two or three times more health care, on average, than the working age population. Moreover, earlier retirement, both voluntary and involuntary, is becoming more common. Though earlier retirement is aimed at releasing more jobs for younger people, it further adds to the cost of pensions.

According to United Nations criteria, a society is classified as an aging society if the ratio of the aged population, over sixty-five, to the whole population exceeds 7 percent. When the ratio reaches 14 percent, it is considered an aged society. In Korea, the aged population currently accounts for 5.7 percent, and it is expected to reach 6.8 percent of the whole population around the year 2000. Thus Korean society is on the eve of becoming an aging society. In France it took seventy years for the ratio to double, going from 7 percent to 14 percent. In Sweden, the United States, the United Kingdom, and Japan, the period required for the figure to double has been shortened to sixty, thirty, twenty, and fifteen years, respectively. Amazingly, it is expected to take only eleven years in Korea—an unprecedented high speed. A projected demographic structure of Korean society is summarized in Table 1.

As the table shows, the dependency ratio of the aged will increase gradually, which means that the burden imposed on the working population to support their parent's generation is going to grow increasingly heavier. At the same time, the ratio of younger dependents is projected to decline owing to a decreasing birthrate. Provided we convert the

TABLE 1 Demographic Trends of Korea, 1960–2020

Year	Whole population	Over 65[a]	Dependency ratio			Birthrate
			Total	Under 15	Over 65	
1960	25,012	2.9	82.6	77.3	5.3	31.9
1965	28,705 (2.6)[b]	3.1	88.3	82.5	5.8	29.5
1970	32,241 (2.2)	3.1	83.8	78.2	5.6	31.2
1975	35,281 (1.7)	3.4 (8.6)	72.5	66.6	6.0	24.8
1980	38,124 (1.6)	3.8 (3.6)	60.7	54.6	6.1	22.7
1985	40,806 (1.0)	4.3 (4.1)	52.5	46.0	6.5	16.2
1990	42,869 (1.0)	5.0 (4.4)	44.6	37.4	7.2	15.3
1991	43,268 (0.9)	5.1 (3.2)	43.7	36.4	7.3	16.6
1992	43,663 (0.9)	5.2 (3.2)	42.9	35.5	7.5	17.0
1993	44,056 (0.9)	5.4 (3.5)	42.3	34.6	7.6	16.5
1994	44,453 (0.9)	5.5 (3.7)	41.5	33.7	7.8	16.5
1995	44,851 (0.9)	5.7 (3.8)	40.6	32.6	8.0	15.2
1996	45,248 (0.9)	5.8 (3.9)	39.7	31.5	8.2	15.1
2000	46,789 (0.8)	6.8 (4.9)	38.8	29.4	9.4	14.2
2005	48,434 (0.6)	8.2 (4.1)	39.8	28.4	11.4	12.7
2010	49,683 (0.4)	9.4 (2.4)	39.9	26.8	13.1	11.3
2015	50,436 (0.2)	10.7 (2.7)	39.3	24.3	15.0	10.1
2020	50,576 (0.0)	12.5 (4.7)	39.9	22.4	17.5	10.0

SOURCES: A *Projection of Future Demographic Trends,* Korea Statistics Office, 1996; *Annual Statistics of Korea for 1995,* Korea Statistics Office, 1996; *Social Indices of Korea: 1995,* Ministry of Finance and Economy.

[a]The ratio of the aged, over 65, out of the whole population is reported. The growth rates of the old population are in parentheses.

[b]The growth rate of the whole population is in parentheses.

present fully funded system to a pay-as-you-go system, the high dependency ratio of the aged implies that beneficiaries will exceed contributors to the pension system, thereby accelerating the imbalance.[1]

With these demographic trends, changes in the family structure have weakened the sound traditional features of the Korean family. Recently, the younger generation has been increasingly drawn to the

1. Even though Korea started its pension systems on a fully funded basis, all pensions are expected to record a deficit because of overgenerous benefits compared to the contribution schedules. This deficit has raised the issue of converting the fully funded system into pay-as-you-go system. Since there are many other related issues, including that of intergenerational equity, no decision has yet been reached.

idea of nuclear families; living with the grandparents has become less and less popular. This attitude further adds to the problem of how to support the elderly. A related development is the increasing participation of women in the workforce, which means that child care is no longer confined to the family and demands appropriate treatment at the societal level. In thirty years, from 1965 to 1995, the proportion of the female population participating in the labor market rose from 36.5 percent to 48.3 percent. This change is another result of the rapidly decreasing workforce due to an aging population. But if women are encouraged to participate in economic activities, then there is new demand for a social welfare policy to supplant the traditional roles of women in various housekeeping duties, raising children, and taking care of the elderly. Over the past twenty years, separations and divorce have also become more frequent. There are now more one-parent families as well as nuclear families, hence an increased demand for more housing.

It is likely that as the Korean economy develops, the need for social welfare will be diversified as well as augmented. As absolute poverty is almost eliminated, more emphasis will be placed on enhancing the quality of life. As leisure and welfare become increasingly valued, there will be a demand not just for health care and sanitation, but also for facilities and equipment for recreation. As industrialization proceeds, industrial or vocational accidents in physical and psychological dimensions will occur more frequently in wider areas.

Structural changes in disease patterns will also affect the demand for medical care. Now that economic well-being has been accomplished to a fair extent, obesity draws more attention than malnutrition. Medical treatment for cancer, hyperplaesia, and apoplexy will become more important than infectious or parasitic diseases, which have long been major causes of death.

Increasing urbanization has brought pollution, overpopulation, and environmental problems to the cities while rural areas experience a shortage of educational, medical, and cultural facilities. Regional diversification of the demand for social welfare will be accelerated when the local autonomy system becomes more established.

Basic Principles for the Korean Social Welfare Model

Our model for a new social welfare system is designed to balance growth and welfare by means of a balanced participation of the private and public sectors, at the same time looking for ways to prevent the need for welfare.

BALANCING GROWTH AND WELFARE

Social welfare policy should be designed to support economic growth, which in turn can sustain social welfare. During the period of industrialization, Korea achieved rapid economic growth partly by keeping investment in social welfare at a relatively low level. It is now generally agreed that, although the growth-oriented policy may well have been justified during the period of industrialization to eradicate absolute poverty, now that absolute poverty in Korea is rare and the economic growth has been substantial, it is time for a change in policy. A more equitable distribution of the national income should take priority over the enlargement of the absolute magnitude of national income—that is, social welfare policy should take precedence over economic development.

Such an assertion sounds dangerous because economic growth and social welfare must be viewed as mutually complementary and reinforcing, not mutually conflicting. It is not the case that one can be attained only at the sacrifice of the other. Social integration and unity are, of course, crucial in accelerating national development. Limitless competition will broaden the gap between the highly competitive sectors and the less competitive sectors of a society. If and when this gap widens, it will breed conflict and disunion. Economic growth in terms of quantity alone is not enough. Social cohesion can be efficiently maintained only when the quality of life is enhanced equitably to benefit all sectors of society.

On the other hand, economic growth is also crucial in sustaining social welfare policy. As shown in many examples of European countries, social welfare policy without the support of corresponding economic growth constitutes a huge fiscal burden and ends up being incapable of providing proper social welfare. Since the mid-1970s, reforms in social welfare policy have been under way in most developed countries. This implies that a social welfare policy that inherently lacks a self-supporting system for economic growth will not last; therefore the most important goal of a successful social welfare policy is to maintain a balance between growth and welfare, encouraging production rather consumption, promoting incentives to work, and helping the needy become self-supporting.

BALANCING THE PRIVATE AND THE PUBLIC SECTOR

We propose encouraging private investment in social welfare services by means of government subsidies, tax, or financial incentives. For social insurance, we suggest basic coverage by the public sector and supplementary coverage by the private sector as a balanced division of roles.

One of the hottest issues in social welfare policy has to do with the role of the private sector. It is argued that public provision of social services is inefficient because services are not supplied at minimum cost. Public employees are not faced with the same constraints as private ones; even if they provide inefficient service, their "firm" cannot be driven out of business or be taken over. This freedom allows them to engage in practices that serve their own ends at the expense of their clients. Generally, resources can be wasted because the public sector lacks accountability. The public sector usually also lacks competition. Public monopolies seldom respond promptly to changes in quality and quantity of demand for social services. It is highly probable that the public sector oversupplies unnecessary services, undersupplies necessary services, produces social services at an unnecessarily high cost, or pays less attention to innovation and service improvement.

The public sector seems unable to shrug off special interest groups; under pressure from interest groups, politicians representing such groups, and bureaucrats, it can oversupply social services, and it has difficulty curbing unnecessary expansion because these well-organized groups get the benefits while the whole population pays. Individuals perceive the cost as being not so high. Moreover, the unorganized general public seldom manifests its view collectively.

Although we have enumerated various rationales for private provision of social services, there are still many reasons of market failure calling for appropriate government intervention in the provision of social service. Social service is one of the public goods that will be underprovided without government intervention.

Incomplete information is yet another cause of market failure. More often than not, someone in need of medical care services lacks the appropriate information to decide what, how much, and from whom he should get care; more often than not, services are usually induced by physicians, and thus overutilization is a common phenomenon in the medical care market.

Adverse selection combined with moral hazard prevents a market system providing social services at a socially desirable level. For example, private insurance companies cannot very well offer unemployment insurance; someone who for various reasons runs a high risk of unemployment may have more incentive to take out unemployment insurance, and if he does take out insurance, he has less incentive to maintain his employment status. As a consequence, insurance premiums will rise, thus attracting more people at risk of unemployment, thus accelerating the adverse selection problem.

In addition to market-failure arguments, it is also argued that the public sector providing social services on a need basis will better achieve the equity goal than the private sector based on the ability to pay. Commodity egalitarianism says that necessary goods and services such as food and medical care ought to be supplied equally to all members of society through the public sector. Social integration can be better achieved by public social service programs than by private programs available only to those who can afford them. But we have learned from the experience of Western welfare states that it is neither feasible nor desirable for the government to provide social welfare that satisfies the needs of all income groups. Resources for social welfare investment are limited while demand increases rapidly and becomes more diversified. Greater private investment in social welfare might fill the gap between the desirable level and the feasible level of social welfare under the current system. In addition, private provision will enhance consumer satisfaction by giving more choice and better-quality services to consumers through competition.

Taking into account the comparative advantages of the private and public sector, typical market failure occurs in the area of social insurance, thus requiring public provision to some extent, whereas this is not necessarily the case for social welfare service. The public sector should provide basic social insurance assuring minimum living standards while encouraging the private sector to offer supplementary social insurance. At least a minimum living standard should be guaranteed for everyone in a society, but this is intrinsically impossible for the private sector to achieve on its own. The government needs to provide the basic level of income, medical care, education, and housing to those whose living standards are below the national minimum. We propose encouraging the private sector to provide supplementary insurance for income and health security, under the government's watchful eye to ensure the effective and efficient management of these insurance systems.

For social welfare services, we suggest private provision to enhance the efficiency and quality of the services. Nevertheless, there still remain equity, nonmarketable and external issues that draw government intervention, even to a minimal extent, to the social welfare service market. Government subsidies and tax or financial incentives are essential to induce the private sector to provide necessary social welfare services. Corporate tax deductions for companies that furnish child care facilities and subsidies for social welfare institutions will serve as good examples of such strategies.

PREVENTING THE NEED FOR WELFARE

We should place more emphasis on preventing the need for welfare rather than supporting the need. Along with unemployment benefits, there should be job training, and assistance in finding employment. A comprehensive social welfare program should also include disability insurance, investment in developing preventive and rehabilitating medicine and the installation of safety facilities. To help prevent juvenile delinquency, there should be frequent and regular counseling for all students, to be done in the schools.

MAKING THE BEST OF THE KOREAN TRADITIONAL CULTURE

The Korean model of social welfare policy should play on the strengths of the nation's traditional culture as well as on the lessons from the experience of other developed countries. Traditions of strong family ties and neighborly assistance have helped retain a solid basis for social coherence and integration, but traditions are weakening under the trend toward nuclear families and increasing participation by women in the labor market. We must create various social and economic incentives to revitalize the sound features of our family system, encouraging familial relations between employer and employee and mutual assistance among relatives.

New Proposals

Based on the four basic principles that we have outlined, we offer several new proposals for a broadened social welfare policy: an income security system, a health security system, and welfare services for three specific groups in Korean society—the elderly, women, and the disabled.

INCOME SECURITY SYSTEM

In Korea, income security is provided through social insurance and public assistance. Social insurance consists of four pension schemes for different types of occupations, industrial accident insurance, and employment insurance. Details for the social insurance system in Korea are summarized in Tables 2 and 3. Public assistant programs support the minimum standard of living for the poor who are not covered by the social insurance system and also the disabled, the aged, the homeless, single-parent families, and underprivileged juveniles.[2] Because the pension-related issues seem more controversial than issues related to other social insurance or public assistance programs, we shall limit our discussion to the pension-related issues.[3]

The nature of the challenge. All pensions are expected to experience an actuarial imbalance in the near future. Military Personnel Pensions have already faced serious deficits in 1975 that resulted in financial support from the general account of the central government. The Pri-

2. Those supports are presently inadequate and should be increased to a level high enough to guarantee at least the minimum standard. For those who are able to work, an effective self-help program needs to be developed and implemented in tandem with the public assistance program for the greatest possible benefit. In particular, education and self-support programs for the physically challenged should be expanded and there should be expanded government support to increase job opportunities for them.

3. The industrial accident insurance scheme is expected to be out of balance and to impose an increasing burden on the next generation. For example, if classified as a first-level disability, beneficiaries will receive a lump-sum disability benefit 4.5 times more than the annual pension benefit. This first-level disability annuity is paid for a longer period—from the time of the accident to death—than other pensions. Unlike pension schemes, however, we may eliminate or at least minimize the outlay for industrial accident insurance by accident-prevention safety measures. We recommend reducing the insurance premiums of companies that invest in safety facilities and increasing premiums charged to companies according to the frequency of accidents. Preventing accidents is certainly not simply economical; all safety schemes primarily protect employees against potential risks and play a part in maintaining a healthy labor force for Korea. Employment insurance was introduced in July 1995, and this fund has accumulated owing to its strict criteria for benefit payments. The balance of employment insurance will be very sensitive to economic conditions. The expenditures for unemployment benefits will increase payments, while the expenditures for job security and job training will help save costs. It is desirable to put more emphasis upon the latter in a boom and upon the former in a slump. For this purpose, we suggest dichotomizing those two kinds of tasks and assigning an independent fund for each task.

TABLE 2 Public Pension Plans in Korea

Scheme	*Starting year*	*Coverage*	*Contribution*	*Benefit*
National Pension	1988	Eligible age interval: 18–59 Compulsory: employees in companies with more than 5 workers Voluntary: self-employed in rural areas, farmers, and fisherman	Insured: 2% of earnings Employers: 4% of payroll Government: administration cost	Retirement pension[a] Lump-sum disability pension Survivor's pension
Civil Servants Pension	1960	Civil servants of central & local government	Insured: 6.5% of earnings Government: 6.5% of payroll + accident compensation	Retirement pension Lump-sum disability pension Survivor's pension (18 types)
Military Personnel Pension	1960[b]	Officers & noncommissioned with long-term service	Insured: 6.5% of earnings Government: 6.5% of payroll + operational cost, accident compensation, deficit financing	Retirement pension Disability pension Survivor pension (14 types)
Private School Teachers Pension	1973	Private school employees	Insured: 6.5% of earnings Employer: 4% (6.5%)[c] Government: 2.5% (0%)	Retirement pension Lump-sum disability pension Survivor's pension (18 types)

[a] Full retirement pension benefit $= 2.4(A+B)(1+0.05n)+S$ where A = average wage of total contributors in the preceding year, B = average wage of beneficiary himself during the whole contributory period, n = number of contributory years − 20, S = family supplements

[b] In 1963, it was separated from the Civil Servants Pension scheme.

[c] The Private School Teachers Pension has two different contribution schedules, one for teaching staff, another for nonteaching staff. The schedule for the latter is reported in parentheses.

vate School Teachers Pension program is projected to have a deficit in 2015.[4] The Civil Servants Pension, the first pension program in Korea, is also projected to begin recording a deficit from 2003. Even more serious is that the National Pension, which started in 1988 and currently only accumulates funds, is still projected to experience a deficit around 2023. In view of the growing aging population, it is likely that all these deficits will occur even earlier than projected.

Second, the segmented pension programs need to be integrated. The three different pension schemes (Table 2)—the National Pension, Civil Servants Pension, and Private School Teachers Pension—cover those with seemingly similar characteristics: probability of death and disability. Although military personnel are assumed to have very different pension designs from the other three categories, we do not see any logical reason for having different plans for the first three groups. Integrating the programs might improve administrative efficiency. The National Pension has a redistributive schedule, while the other two have income proportional schedules. If the three schemes were integrated, a consensus on the contribution-benefit schedule of the integrated pension would be a *sine qua non* for the implementation: whether redistributive or income proportional.

Third, attention must be paid to the efficient management of the pension funds. Particularly in the case of the National Pension program started in 1988, a huge reserve fund will accumulate because the program currently is based on a fully funded system. About half of the fund has been put into fiscal investments and financing special accounts. The rate of return for this deposit is around 10 percent as of 1996, which is lower than the return on bonds that the National Pension fund would otherwise use and much lower than that on private sector investments.[5] The other half of the fund is invested in deposit trusts, government bonds, beneficiary securities, and cash management accounts.

Fourth, Korean public pensions covered 8.8 million people as of November 1996: farmers, fishermen, the self-employed, and workers in companies with more than five employees. Workers in companies with fewer than five employees and full-time homemakers are so far not covered. The ultimate goal of the Korean public pension program is to cover the whole population.

4. See KDI Executive Brief (December 1996).

5. The average rate of return from the private sector was over 12 percent in 1996.

TABLE 3 Other Social Insurance in Korea

Scheme	*Starting year*	*Coverage*	*Contribution*	*Benefit*
Health Insurance				
Employees' Insurance	1977	Employees of companies with more than 5 workers	Insured: 2–8% of earnings Employer: 2–8% of payroll	Covered services: Outpatient & inpatient care provided by designated hospital or clinic including medical examination, medications, nursing service, and ambulance service Cost-sharing: 20–55% of medical expenses
Civil Servants & Private School Teachers Insurance	1979	Civil servants, private school employees, and dependents of military personnel	Insured: 2–8% of earnings Employer: 2–8% of payroll	Same as the above
Regional Insurance	1988	Employees of companies with fewer than 5 workers, self-employed, and pensioners	Insured: 2–8% of earnings by the standard wage class Employer: 2–8% of payroll by the standard wage class	Same as the above

Industrial Accident Insurance	1964	Employees of companies with more than 5 workers	1.94% of earnings, on average Differentiated rate applied by the types of incomes and business	Medical benefit Wage compensation: 70% of average wage Disability benefit Survivor's benefit Funeral benefit Extended benefit
Employment Insurance	1995	Unemployment benefit: employees of companies with more than 30 workers Job stability & vocational development benefit: employees of companies with more than 70 workers	0.6–1.3% Differentiated rate by the size of company applied	Unemployment benefit Job stability program Job development program

Proposals for a more effective system. Our proposals will address these four major issues. We discuss the first and the second issues—actuarial imbalance and integration of the public pension system—at the same time, since the solutions are in fact combined.

Actuarial imbalance is strikingly evident from the contribution-benefit schedules. Under the current schedules, the National Pension assures, on average, benefits worth more than twice the contributions including interest. An even greater imbalance is found in the Private School Teachers Pension and Civil Servant Pension programs, owing to the generous benefits compared to contributions, and also in the Military Personnel Pension plan, which accords benefits on average more than three times the amount of contributions. For additional reasons the Military Personnel Pension program is inherently even more seriously prone to an imbalance. First, military personnel retire early; currently, the average retirement age is forty-five. Second, those who are involved in combat receive triple benefits—that is, a soldier with one year of combat duty obtains credit for three years of regular peacetime service. Third, although the number of contributors is fixed, the number of beneficiaries keeps increasing at a rate of 7.4 percent per year.

Imbalances are generally attributed to the overambitious, indeed virtually impossible, effort to guarantee a sufficient after-retirement income for everyone at an affordable price. Theoretically, there may be two possible approaches to addressing such an imbalance: raising contributions and/or curtailing benefits. Keeping the present benefit level of the National Pension program demands that contributions be increased up to 25 percent from the current 6 percent of enrollees' earnings. For the same purpose, the other three public pensions need to raise their contributions up to 35 percent from the present 13 percent. It is clear that there must be either a sharp increase in contributions at every income level or drastic income redistribution if we are to maintain the current level of benefits. In either case, we are apt to provide disincentives to work.

The government's main role in formulating the desired income security policy would be to guarantee minimum requirements for income protection against various risks without distorting the incentive to work and thus impeding economic growth. Overgenerous benefits, we emphasize, are not overgenerous compared with the income necessary to sustain a living standard similar to the preretirement period. Middle-class or high-income groups in general would like to prepare for a comfortable retirement even at a considerable expense.

The public and private sectors should have balanced roles in postretirement welfare. The public sector provides basic income security guaranteeing a minimum living standard, and the private sector offers additional income security to protect consumer sovereignty. We propose integrating all public pensions except the Military Personnel Pension into a comprehensive scheme and dividing the current contribution-benefit schedule into the income invariant and income proportional parts, the former to serve as a basic pension program covering the whole population and the latter to serve as an additional pension program for voluntary enrollees. The government would take charge of managing the former; the private sector would manage the latter.

A three-part system of income support would suit the purpose. The three parts would consist of (1) minimum income security through a consolidated public pension with a flat structure, (2) additional income security through a corporate pension proportional to the income level, and (3) supplementary income security through private pensions or savings—the first to be compulsory, the other two completely voluntary. This three-part system would constitute the first-level safety net for income security.

Private pensions in Korea consist of the personal pension, corporate pension, and lump-sum severance payment called *toejik-kum*. The first two are not yet very popular. As a severance payment, companies with more than five workers should pay 8.3 percent of the average wage for every working year to an employee who has worked for the company for more than one year. One of the crucial problems of the lump-sum severance payment is that there is no guarantee that employees can collect the payment in case the company goes bankrupt. Currently, 36 percent of the *toejik-kum* fund is deposited in an outside financial institution in the name of employee retirement insurance. Only 15.9 percent of corporate firms choose outside financial institutions for the whole management of the fund; moreover, in the case of bankruptcy, the ownership of the fund belongs not to employees but to the firm under the current employee retirement insurance. This seriously undermines the income security of employees of small and medium-sized firms, which are the most likely to fail.

In addition, because the Labor Standard Act stipulates that the severance payment should be paid as a lump-sum payment, the payment actually functions as income compensation for unemployment rather than income security for old age for employees in long-term service. On the other hand, corporate pensions allow employees to collect monthly benefits even in the event of bankruptcy.

Some tax or financial incentives could encourage the conversion from the severance payment system to corporate pension system. Under the current system, up to 50 percent of the fund retained inside the firm is eligible for a corporate tax deduction. This tax incentive makes inside retainment more attractive, certainly for small and medium-sized firms that can use the funds as working capital. We propose to reduce or gradually eliminate such a corporate tax deduction and, instead, give tax credit to firms for whole contributions toward corporate pensions.

The market for personal pensions is still small but it keeps growing. The Korean government allows those who enroll in a personal pension plan an income tax deduction of up to 720,000 won per annum, or 40 percent of the annual contribution, whichever is less. As national income grows and the demand for income security of postretirement age increases, the personal pension market is expected to become more attractive to workers. Tax deduction incentives therefore need to be expanded to employees and their spouses in companies of all size.

We recommend that all adjustments for a more efficient pension system should proceed gradually to minimize the anticipated resistance from beneficiaries. It is expected to take a while for the changes to take root fully. Considering that the current pension system will suffer from a deficit soon, a conversion from a fully funded system into a pay-as-you-go system seems inevitable. Priority should be given to a careful balancing of intergenerational equity in contributions and benefits. In order to minimize potential intergenerational inequity created by the conversion, we suggest restructuring the benefit schedule by delaying the normal retirement age, reducing the amount of early retirement benefits, and offering monetary incentives for delayed retirement.

Currently, pension beneficiaries between ages 55 and 65 may decide when first to claim pension benefits. They will receive a reduced amount before 60 and a constant full amount after age 60. We propose that the normal retirement age should be advanced to age 65 from the current 60, and subsequently advanced even further. The current starting period for reduced benefits at age 55 should be adjusted upward correspondingly. To encourage delaying retirement, a modified discount schedule in which the pension reductions would begin when benefits were first collected and decrease with the approaching established retirement age would be effective. Along the same reasoning, pension increases at a marginal rate in line with delayed retirement would serve as good incentives for delaying collecting pension benefits. The present scheme not only fails to reward those who wait until after they are 60 to collect benefits, but indeed actually discourages them.

A third aspect of the pension program is the efficient management of the pension funds. There are opposing views on the National Pension fund. One is that the government, the manager of the fund, should maximize the return on the fund because it serves as the deferred wages to ensure the employee's future income stability. The other is that the fund should be used to improve public welfare. This is necessary not only because, should a deficit occur, it would be covered by government transfers from the general account, but also because pension beneficiaries would receive indirect benefits for the returns on their unclaimed pensions in the form of social overhead capital or education improvements. The most widespread argument against investing the fund in the private sector seems to be that a high return from the private sector is a premium for taking high risks that could undermine the stability of the pension fund.

A compromise solution would be to invest the fund partly in the public sector and partly in the private sector in the form of index funds. Index funds hold a fraction of the shares of all the firms that make up some index such as the Korean Stock Price Index 200, Maekyung Index, and Hankyung Dow Index. Index funding would reduce risk as well as produce higher returns by hedging against fluctuations in the stock market. Passive investment into indexes is considered to be both prudent fiduciary behavior for the trustees, as a manager of deferred wages, and for the government.

HEALTH SECURITY SYSTEM

Korea's national health security system consists of a health insurance scheme run on a beneficiary-pays-the-cost basis, covering 95.7 percent of the whole population, and a medical aid, noncontributory, program financed by the general revenue of the government and covering the rest of the population. The health insurance plan has been successful in the sense that it has taken only twelve years to cover the whole population, but there are still important related issues that should be dealt with soon. First, the financial status of health insurance providers varies to a great extent. Second, health care costs have increased rapidly. Third, medical personnel and facilities are unequally distributed across regions. We address these three issues and suggest some solutions.

There are very distinct financial differences among insurers—from severe deficits to great surpluses. In general, insurance societies for employees maintain reasonable surpluses, while insurance societies for the self-employed in rural areas suffer from severe deficits. In particular, *Kun* (or county) insurance societies make up only 66.3 percent of their expenses, on average, through self-financing. Reinsurance programs aiming to stabilize health insurance financing for societies that accumulate deficits and smooth out financial differences among insurers were begun in 1991. A huge transfer between insurers proved difficult and controversial: the share ratio of *Kun* area insurance societies, for example, was more than four times that of employees' insurance societies.[6]

Clearly there are limitations to resolving the financial differences among insurance societies by means of reinsurance programs. At present, such programs are limited to very expensive medical services and medical expenses for the elderly. It is likely that if the reinsurance project expands to cover other expenses as well, financial transfers and conflicts of interest among insurance societies will only increase, even to the extent of undermining the very social solidarity that the social welfare policy wants to achieve. But if the financial transfers smooth out the differences completely, then what would be the rationale for keeping the approximately 400 independent insurance societies? Integrating them into several bigger insurance societies would save administrative costs owing to economies of scale and efficient management.

Recently, the increasing demand for medical care and rising health care costs have required the extension of health insurance benefits in terms of expenses as well as covered items. With low premiums, it seems virtually impossible to provide comprehensive coverage that includes expensive medical care services.[7] One solution to this problem would be a two-tier health insurance system that offers basic coverage through public insurance and supplementary coverage through private insurance. The approximately 400 independent insurance societies

6. Share ratio is the share divided by the contribution, where the former is the money from the reinsurance program fund and the latter is the payment into the fund by each insurance society.

7. As an another related issue to financial status, the very low insurance premium, which enabled the unprecedent rapid expansion of national health insurance to the whole population, consequently results in high out-of-pocket expenditures for patients. Patient complaints about high out-of-pocket costs increase along with the demand for medical care in a society that enjoys higher wages and health insurance.

should be integrated into a unified public health insurance authority. Public health insurance would provide basic coverage, including preventive care and standard care that are necessary to lead a normal life. Private health insurance would supply more comprehensive coverage to the middle class or high-income groups so that consumers could opt for better in-patient care or high technology treatments at more affordable costs.

One of the most important questions relating to private health insurance is whether or not private insurance should be limited to a supplementary plan. There are two main arguments against private insurance as a comprehensive plan. First, public health insurance in Korea is now undergoing change, and it is possible that introducing private insurance could undermine the foundation of the public insurance system because the high-income group will opt for the private plans and thus upset the financial balance of the public system. Some economists argue that if the public health insurance system could be replaced completely by private plans, this situation would not be so harmful. In view of the incomplete information problem inherent in the medical care market, such arguments make little sense, for it is certain that only public health insurance can assure basic medical care for the whole population. Furthermore, it is highly probable that comprehensive private health insurance plans competing with the public plan will degrade medical care: medical institutions will avoid public plan enrollees and medical costs will become inflated, thus putting more financial stress on the public plan. The experience in the United States has shown that the private health insurance system lacking effective checking devices at the governmental level eventually loses its ability to curb inflating costs.

Under the current system in Korea, the government through the National Federation of Medical Insurance investigates medical bills and reimburses the suppliers accordingly. By and large, such government intervention works effectively as a checking device in a supplier-led market. It is practically impossible for private insurance companies to exercise such checking power against the providers. Medical providers have an incentive to submit higher bills to private insurance companies, from whom it is relatively less difficult to get reimbursements. It is nothing less than natural for medical institutions maximizing profits to avoid public plan enrollees. Actually, medical institutions in Korea discriminate against the beneficiaries of the Medical Aid program, and such a phenomenon is reported to be an inveterate problem of the program. In addition, higher medical bills charged to private plan enrollees will inevitably be reflected later on in medical costs to public plan enrollees.

We support the argument that private health insurance should be confined to a supplementary plan. There are no legal restrictions in the private health insurance market in Korea; nevertheless, the market for private health insurance is very small, and it is limited in coverage. Only a few cancer plans and geriatric disease plans, both of which are supplementary, exist in the market. The Korean Medical Association and the Korean Hospital Association contend that the government should provide tax and financial incentives to develop the market. A tax credit favoring private plan enrollees over public plan enrollees will raise an inequity issue among those two groups.

The optimal role of the government would be to intervene as little as possible even when the market fails. As the demand for medical care services increases and becomes high-quality oriented, the private health insurance market will develop without such incentives. Instead, the government should construct an environment under which enrollees for the private plans are effectively protected. All private health insurance in Korea operates on an indemnity payment system, not picking up the residual cost left by the public plan. Considering the enormous medical bills resulting from illnesses such as cancer and cardiac and cerebral diseases the benefit level is relatively low. The current private plans do not sufficiently protect the enrollees, while life insurance companies profit enormously owing to the very low incidence of mortality from such diseases. (Selling dread disease insurance has been prohibited in the U.S. since the 1980s.) Current disease-specific plans in Korea should be converted to more comprehensive supplementary plans paying for the out-of-pocket expenditures of patients or uncovered services.

The second major concern to the Korean medical care system is the rapid and continuing increase in the costs of medical care. According to the Korea Institute of Health Services Management, the propotion of national health care expenditure to GNP rose from less than 3 percent in 1975 to 5.4 percent in 1994. This increase is attributed mainly to increasing utilization owing to the universal coverage of health insurance, although part of the increase comes from high technology medical services. Many economists blame the inflation on the third-party-payment system combined with a fee-for-service scheme.

From the consumer side, moral hazard effects are observed significantly in many empirical studies.[8] The third-party payment system affects consumer behavior. Because the third-party insurer pays most of the cost, consumers are largely unaware of the costs of the services they receive. Thus, restraints on the demand for medical services are very weak for insured consumers. Being insured encourages consumers to demand more medical services than they otherwise would and reduces incentives to search for more efficient services. Resources are not being used in ways that bring maximum medical benefits for the money spent.

From the supplier side, physician-induced demand raises the utilization. In the medical care market, information seems to be asymmetric as well as incomplete. The doctor owns private information on the effectiveness and price of the medical service he provides and on which service is best for his patient's symptoms; that is asymmetric information in the sense that it is generally not revealed to his customer. Under a fee-for-service scheme, the more costly and excessive the medical care he provides, the more he is paid: a physician has incentive to prescribe overtreatment, and consumers, lacking full information, have no choice but to accept the physician-induced service.

We propose a diagnosis-related-group (DRG) pricing system instead of a fee-for-service system as a way of curbing the increasing utilization generated by the physician-driven demand. Regardless of the number of services, a DRG reimburses a standardized fee for the whole treatment of the same disease. The Ministry of Health and Welfare announced that it will adopt a DRG system tentatively in 1997 only for five cases, including normal deliveries, cesarean sections, and appendectomies at a maximum of sixty medical care institutions on a voluntary basis. The DRG system should be extended universally in terms of institutions and diseases.

As another measure to contain the increasing health care costs, we suggest the introduction of insurer-owned hospitals or managed care systems in tandem with private health insurance. An institution like the Health Management Organization may reduce overutilization, contain inflation in health care costs, and provide comprehensive and preventive care at a relatively lower cost.

Third, there is a serious regional imbalance in the distribution of medical personnel and facilities. Hospital beds per 1,000 people in rural areas are reported to be three times lower than in urban areas. Community clinics that are already established in each county need to expand

8. See H. H. Lee (1993), Manning et al. (1987), and Cameron and Trivedi (1986).

and diversify their functions into preventive care, nutrition counseling, and treatment for chronic diseases and mental health. Group clinic systems and open clinic systems will have comparative advantages in rural areas that lack sufficient capital to construct a general hospital. Other effective measures would be government investment in improving health facilities in poor areas and various fiscal and financial incentives to attract medical resources to those areas.

SOCIAL WELFARE SERVICES

So far, social welfare services, mainly provided as cash or in-kind benefits through social welfare institutions, have been insufficient to guarantee a minimum living standard for the disadvantaged. The target, provision, and place of social welfare services have undergone drastic changes. First, the target expands gradually to include the general public without being restricted to the underprivileged or disadvantaged. The needy person as well as his family need to become eligible for welfare services. Second, the provision converts monetary payments into actual nonmonetary care such as rehabilitation programs. Furthermore, preventive measures such as information provision, counseling, and various assistance for socialization and development become more important than ex post facto measures such as institutional care, medical care, or rehabilitation service. A third change is the trend away from large-scale institutions or public facilities toward homes or small home-like institutions where conditions are psychologically stable.

Reflecting all these changes, social welfare service should be general and comprehensive, preventive and productive, and home-based. Private provision is relatively adequate in social welfare service, and there is a big gap between the ideal and feasible levels of social investment under the current fiscal conditions. There does not seem to be much room for increased public expenditures in social services, taking into account other high government priorities such as social overhead capital, economic development, and national defense. Government subsidies, therefore, and tax or financial incentives inducing private investment in social welfare service provision are highly encouraged. Here, we focus on the three most controversial types of welfare—for the aged, women, and the disabled.

Welfare for the aged. The target of welfare policy for the elderly should serve more than the low-income elderly and should be expanded to the entire elderly population, with different programs designed to serve those distinct elderly populations: the low-income elderly who cannot work, the low-income elderly in good health, and the middle-class or wealthy elderly.

For the low-income elderly not healthy enough to work, income support and medical care should be supplied so that they may be assured a minimum standard of living. As an income security measure for the unhealthy elderly excluded from the current pension system, a noncontribution old-age pension plan needs to be introduced. This scheme may target those who are over age seventy, in poor health, and without pension benefits under the present system. For those who need medical service and daily support, a home-based care system should be established at the local level so that they may receive full support in homelike surroundings. Crucial conditions for a successful home-based care system would be active participation in volunteer activities and an efficient system matching the volunteers to the needy. We suggest establishing a home-based care management center at the small community level so that it may take charge of surveying the actual demand for home-based care, circulating information, and providing medical care, counseling, and nursing services for the elderly.

For the low-income elderly in good health, the best plan is to encourage them to be self-sufficient by providing job opportunities. As life expectancy increases, the proportion of the aged population willing and able to work even after retirement also increases, particularly now that the Korean economy has been experiencing sluggish economic growth and early retirement has become more popular. Demand by the elderly population for reemployment keeps increasing. It is essential to develop jobs appropriate for them and to diversify programs promoting their reemployment such as the Senior Corps of Retired Executives in the United States.

Over 60 percent of all companies in Korea have a mandatory retirement age of 55. Over 95 percent of all employees retire between ages 55 and 59 (Kim 1996). It is reported that in spite of the accumulated know-how from a lifetime of service of senior employees, employers encourage retirement because of their high wages. On average, the cost of employing those with more than twelve years of continuous service is at least twice the cost of hiring those with less than a year's service. The high wages are attributable to the seniority system, characteristic of Korea's labor market. But if an employer can rehire an experienced retired employee at a lower wage he can gain a lot of experience and knowledge at a relatively lower cost.

For the middle class or wealthy elderly, we suggest creating infrastructure to enhance the quality of their later years. As the trend toward nuclear families and female participation in social as well as economic activities intensifies, the elderly, even those who are well-to-do, can no longer count on remaining part of the traditional family structure. A variety of social and economic incentives to revitalize the traditional family-based care of the Korean society need to be devised and implemented. Retirement communities, a growing industry in the United States and elsewhere, are a logical response—developed to meet the demand of the wealthy and educated elderly for independent lifestyles.

Volunteer activities are an important way in which the well-to-do elderly can make a positive contribution to the social welfare program and at the same time enhance their own well-being. A program of information and networking could connect volunteers to the needy. For this purpose, we suggest building up a computer network and well-organized programs like the U.S. Retired Senior Volunteer Program.

Welfare for women. Ending discrimination against women is most essential for women's welfare, particularly in Korea, where there is evidently severe discrimination against women in every aspect of employment such as recruitment, placement, promotion, retirement, and wages. Women make up half of the rapidly aging population, and they are very important to the labor force. In addition, women's participation in the labor force will increase opportunities for self-realization. One of the prerequisites for encouraging the active participation of women in the labor market would be to give them equal opportunities to work in every sector of society based on their ability and to treat them accordingly.

A compulsory quota system mandating that female employees fill a certain percentage of positions seems dangerous if it is implemented without other conditions being satisfied, for it may create resistance or even deepen antipathy against women in the long run. Rigid quotas might mean that when there are not enough qualified female applicants for a certain area because of long-term modes of discrimination such as implicit entry barriers or inherent disadvantages for women in that area, less-qualified female applicants might be recruited over better-qualified male applicants. That may not only foster the groundless opinion that female workers are inferior on average compared with their male counterparts, but also cause another unfairness because of the recruitment of less qualified applicants.

Another form of discrimination against women lies in the under-evaluation of women's work in the home—childbearing, child care, supporting parents, and housekeeping. It is understood that such work supports the status quo and promotes social order, supplies a healthy labor force, and prevents potential social problems, but full-time homemakers are excluded from pension schemes, and women in the labor force are not always guaranteed leaves of absence for child delivery or infant care. Providing an appropriate reward for this work requires cooperation as well as a deep understanding within the society, not just at the company level. Compensation for the leave of absence for delivery or infant care would be better paid by social insurance than by a single employer. We propose introducing a social compensation scheme for women who care for the old, children, and handicapped so that they may be awarded pensions or other social benefits. In addition, we suggest expanding the child care system even to the small community level at a reasonable price and introducing an extensive school catering system to lessen the working female's burden of household affairs. A corporate tax or other financial incentives for companies that provide child care facilities will induce private investment to enhance the welfare of women.

Welfare for the disabled. For the severely disabled in need of assistance, we recommend that the government provide sufficient support to allow them to maintain at least a minimum standard of living. The current public assistance program provides assistance to the low-income disabled, but owing to its limitations in eligibility and benefits this assistance in general does not meet the basic requirements for minimum living standards. Rules and regulations regarding eligibility and benefits should be revised to reflect rapidly changing socioeconomic conditions and meet the practical needs of the disabled.

For the disabled who can work on a part-time basis with some educational or rehabilitative assistance, we propose providing employment opportunities and all other necessary support through education and rehabilitation programs, in addition to income support during the learning period. There is a tendency to avoid employing the disabled, partly because of social prejudice and partly because their physical limitations may result in real losses. In order to eliminate social prejudice, we suggest that the government conduct more effective campaigns to help the disabled develop their self-respect. The Vocational Promotion Law for Disabled People was enacted in January 1990, stipulating that a company with more than 300 employees must fill at least 2 percent of its positions with disabled workers. The law has not proved effective, however, because most companies prefer to pay the penalty rather than comply. We propose reinforcing the law either by raising the penalty or by providing other administrative or monetary incentives. More should be done to prevent the causes of disability. We need to enhance prenatal and child health care and promote early detection and treatment of diseases that could develop into serious illness or injury. A management system, including vaccination service for infants and adolescents on a periodic basis, has been developed but is not yet comprehensive. We propose placing more emphasis and financial support on the development of preventive and rehabilitative medicine at the policy-making level.

We also suggest creating a barrier-free environment for the disabled. Even though the Korean government has endeavored to improve infrastructure for the disabled, only 27 percent of public buildings are equipped with special facilities for the handicapped, and few general educational institutions are disabled-friendly and equipped with barrier-free facilities. Disabled persons do not have sufficient opportunities to receive even basic education. It is urgent not only to enact but also to reinforce related laws and regulations effectively on the installation of barrier-free facilities.

Finally, we propose some policy measures that will make all sorts of medical equipment affordable. Instruments such as wheelchairs, prostheses, crutches, and hearing aids are crucial for the disabled not only to maintain a normal life and but also to participate in social activities. Because these expensive instruments are excluded from health insurance coverage, we first propose extending health insurance coverage to include expenses for such instruments. Next, we suggest inducing investment into industries producing such instruments through tax and other financial incentives in order to make medical devices for the disabled more affordable.

Financing Social Welfare Policy

We have discussed a variety of necessary steps to enhance social welfare in Korea. Most of them involve government investments, financial as well as tax incentives, and transfer payments. How, then, should the necessary finances be raised? Policy suggestions without feasible financing are impractical, especially in Korea.

Table 4 compares the uses and sources of social welfare expenditures in various countries. Even though Korea does not seem to spend a significant amount of its national income on social welfare policy compared with other developed countries, there does not seem to be much room for raising social welfare expenditures substantially; investment in social overhead capital, economic development, and education still take higher priority among government expenditures. It has become apparent from the experience of Western European countries that excessive social welfare expenditures can accumulate fiscal deficits, which hinder economic growth and thus social welfare. Such experiences imply that social welfare expenditures should be financed very cautiously with the help of an in-depth analysis on various possible financing methods and their effects on the economy.

We offer a simple simulation model of the Korean economy and rank the order of various financing options for social welfare policy with respect to economic growth, price stability, external balance, and fiscal consolidation. Appendix Table A1 lists seventeen financing options for social welfare expenditures: fifteen "neutral" and two deficit financing options, money and bond financing. They are neutral in the sense that the same amount of taxes or expenditures other than transfer payments are adjusted in order to neutralize the budget balance. However, the neutralization is not complete because other items in revenues or expenditures eventually change as a result of financing. For example, higher wage tax rates will affect personal income, consumption, and even labor supply, which have a secondary influence on the consumption tax and wage tax revenue.

THE MODEL

The model is a macroeconomic simulation model in which behavioral relationships between key macroeconomic variables and policy instruments are explicitly specified within a consistent accounting framework. The model links major policy instruments with growth, inflation, balance of payments, and budget balance, all of which are determined endogenously as well as simultaneously. Thus the model enables a variety of analyses of fiscal, monetary, and external policies by varying exogenous or policy variables. The complete model, consisting of seven behavioral equations and fifty-one equations of identities and fixed proportions, is summarized in the Appendix in Table A2. A glossary of the variables is presented in the Appendix in Table A3.

The model is the Keynesian version based on income-expenditure

TABLE 4 Social Welfare Expenditures: An International Comparison (in percents)

	Social welfare expenditures (SWE)				*Out-of-pocket payments*			
Country	*Health insurance*	*Pensions*	*Others*	SWE / GDP	*Total*[a]	*Tax*	*Contributions to social insurance*	*Population*
Korea								
1994	32.5	40.4	27.1	3.7	22.9	20.1	2.9	5.5
1990	40.4	31.2	28.4	2.9	20.6	18.5	2.1	5.0
U.S.	29.5	49.4	21.1	14.8	38.1	29.4	8.7	12.5
Japan	38.7	51.8	10.2	11.1	40.6	31.4	9.2	12.0
U.K.	28.8	41.1	30.1	20.2	43.2	36.9	6.3	15.7
Germany	26.9	48.0	25.1	24.4	50.6	36.8	13.8	15.3
France	24.6	49.0	26.4	29.5	63.0	43.7	19.3	14.0
Sweden	26.7	36.3	37.0	45.1	70.1	55.6	15.1	17.8

SOURCES: *International Financial Statistics*, IMF, 1994; *The Cost of Social Security in Japan*, Social Development Research Institute, 1994.
[a]The ratio of total out-of-pocket expenditures including tax and contributions for social insurance to GDP.

theory. However, it also incorporates the supply side by estimating the potential GNP and making it affect the determination of income and prices. In the model, changes in the demand side such as consumption and investment are directly linked to the changes in income and prices, while changes in capital stock and labor supply determine the level of the potential GNP. The level simultaneously determines income and prices through the change in the capacity utilization ratio, which is defined by the ratio of actual GNP to potential GNP. Potential GNP is obtained by estimating the Cobb-Douglas production function using capital and labor as factors of production.

The GNP deflator plays a key role in the model, and is assumed to depend on both cost push factors and demand pull factors, such as the unit value index of imports, money supply, and the capacity utilization ratio. In the model, the consumption equation incorporates the permanent income hypothesis, life-cycle hypothesis, real balance effect, and intertemporal substitution effect by including variables of current disposable income, past period consumption, real money supply, and real interest rates, respectively. In the investment equation, the real interest rate is also added to capture opportunity costs in investment decisions.

The model is formulated in the context of a small open economy in that the Korean economy faces a completely price-elastic supply schedule for its imports. However, it is assumed that the prices of its exports are determined in the domestic market and that international capital flows are not perfectly mobile because of government controls. The exchange rate is treated as an exogenous variable.[9]

Since the model is designed primarily for fiscal policy simulations, the fiscal sector is specified in a rather flexible manner, which allows in-depth analysis of likely macroeconomic impacts of the various fiscal policy options listed in Table A1. In this model, different types of expenditures and taxes may have different macroeconomic impacts. In particular, macroeconomic impacts of raising social welfare expenditures may differ according to how they are financed.

In this model, the central bank may decide to increase or decrease money or bonds by changing foreign reserves. Furthermore, we have two important relationships derived from the model: (1) the gain or

9. In accordance with the expansion of the volume of external trade, Korea adopted a market-average exchange rate (MAR) system in 1990. But the new system still has certain limitations, particularly with respect to its inability to take full account of the supply and demand situation of the domestic foreign exchange market.

loss in net reserve is directly related to the expansion of monetary credit not backed by domestic or external saving; (2) increment in total asset, that is, the sum of money supply and government bonds in this model, is equal to the financial surplus in the household sector.

SIMULATION RESULTS

We estimated seven behavioral equations with annual data from 1972 to 1992, in which all real variables are measured in 1985 prices. We constructed a baseline scenario by solving fifty-eight simultaneous equations, including seven behavioral equations and fifty-one identities and fixed proportions. We performed simulations over a five-year period by changing each of the seventeen variables listed in Table A1 to increase social welfare expenditures. We examined temporary increases taking place in the first year only and permanent increases lasting all five years. The predicted impacts of the financing method are measured as the difference between the baseline scenario and the simulated path for the five years.

Even though a lot of simulations have been done for various macroeconomic variables, we report the simulation results only for the real GNP, the GNP deflator, the current account balance, and the budget balance for a more parsimonious discussion. We measured the impact with the net dynamic multiplier in the case of the real GNP and budget balance, as a percentage change in the case of the GNP deflator, and as the difference in millions of U.S. dollars in the case of current account balance. Table 5 reports the effects of policy mixes on those four macroeconomic variables. Tables 6 and 7 summarize the rank order of the seventeen financing options.

We elaborate on the more interesting cases only. Such cases are option 1 versus 2, i.e., wage tax increases via tax rate increases versus via tax relief reductions; options 6 versus 7, i.e., corporate tax increases via tax rate increases versus investment tax credit reductions; options 8 versus 9, i.e., consumption tax increases versus custom duties increases; options 11 versus 12, i.e., reductions in the government wage bill versus expenditures on other goods and services; options 16 versus 17, i.e., money versus bond financing.

For the first case, wage tax rate increases versus wage tax relief reductions, the rankings are consistent. In terms of the GNP deflator, current account balance, and budget balance, the former is better. On the other hand, the latter turns out to be a better financing method in

TABLE 5 Effect of Policy Mixes on Macroeconomic Variables

Option	*Real GNP*	*GNP deflator*	*Current account balance*	*Budget balance*
Increasing revenue				
+ Tax on Wages[a]				
Via tax rate	−/+	−	+	+
Via income tax relief	−/+	−	+	+
+ Tax on dividends	−/+	−	+	+
+ Tax on interest	−/+	−	+	+
+ Tax on operating surplus	−/+	−	+	+
+ Corporate income tax				
Via tax rate	+/−	+	−	+
Via investment tax credit	+/−	+	−	+
+ Consumption taxes	+/−	+	−	−
+ Custom duties	+/−	+	−	−
+ Non-tax revenue	+/−	+	−	−
Reducing expenditures				
− Wages	−	−	+	−/+
− Other goods and services	−	+	−	−/+
− Interest payment	+	+/−	−	+
− Transfer payments or investment	−	+	+/−	+
− Net lending	+/−	+	−	+
Deficit financing				
+ Money finance	+/−	+	−	−
+ Bond finance	+	+	−	−

[a]The plus sign before financing option indicates increases in corresponding taxes; the minus sign indicates decreases in government expenditures.

general for the real GNP. Elaborating on the transmission mechanism of the policy mixes starting with the case of a budget balance, the corporate wage bill falls as the transfer payment increases. The gross wage tax will, therefore, fall under the latter, so the wage tax will increase to a greater extent under the former option as will also the budget balance.

For the external sector, exports will rise but imports will fall; therefore the current balance will increase if transfer payments increase. When financing via the wage tax rate, the increase in export and de-

TABLE 6 Rank Order of Financing Options: Temporary Increase

Option	Fifth year				All years[a]			
	GNPR[b]	PGNP	CA	BB	GNPR	PGNP	CA	BB
Increasing revenue								
+Tax on wages								
Via tax rate	3	1	1	6	14	1	1	6
Via income tax relief	5	3	3	10	11	3	4	8
+Tax on dividends	4	2	2	8	13	2	3	7
+Tax on interest	5	3	3	10	11	3	4	8
+Tax on operating surplus	7	5	5	12	10	5	6	10
+Corporate income tax								
Via tax rate	12	14	14	4	5	14	14	4
Via investment tax credit	11	13	13	3	6	13	13	3
+Consumption taxes	9	11	11	14	8	10	11	14
+Custom duties	8	10	10	13	9	8	10	13
+Non-tax revenue	10	12	12	15	7	11	12	15
Reducing expenditures								
−Wages	14	6	6	7	17	6	2	12
−Other goods and services	15	9	9	9	16	9	9	11
−Interest/payment	1	7	17	1	1	15	17	1
−Transfer payments or investment	17	15	7	5	15	12	7	5
−Net lending	13	16	15	2	3	16	15	2
Deficit financing								
+Money finance	16	17	16	16	4	17	16	16
+Bond finance	2	8	8	17	2	7	8	17

[a] The effects of all five years are measured as a sum of discounted values for each year. The discounting factor, social rate of time preference, is set at 0.2.
[b] GNPR = real GNP, PGNP = GNP deflator, CA = current account balance, BB = budget balance

crease in import will be larger and therefore the current account balance will also increase.

With respect to the GNP deflator, ranking is determined by the relative size of changes in the capacity utilization ratio and in the money supply under two options. The money supply will fall, and the capacity utilization ratio will first fall and then rise. In both cases, the GNP deflator will fall. The change in the money supply and the ratio will be bigger under option 1 and also in the GNP deflator decrement.

TABLE 7 Rank Order of Financing Options: Permanent Increase

Option	Fifth year				All five years			
	GNPR	PGNP	CA	BB	GNPR	PGNP	CA	BB
Increasing revenue								
+ Tax on wages								
Via tax rate	13	1	1	6	14	1	2	6
Via income tax relief	10	3	5	8	11	3	5	8
+ Tax on dividends	12	2	3	7	13	2	4	7
+ Tax on interest	10	3	5	8	11	3	5	8
+ Tax on operating surplus	9	5	6	10	10	5	7	10
+ Corporate income tax								
Via tax rate	5	14	14	4	4	14	14	4
Via investment tax credit	4	13	13	3	5	13	13	3
+ Consumption taxes	7	10	11	14	8	10	11	14
+ Custom duties	8	8	10	13	9	9	10	13
+ Non-tax revenue	6	11	12	15	7	11	12	15
Reducing expenditures								
− Wages	17	6	2	12	17	6	1	11
− Other goods and services	16	9	8	11	16	8	8	12
− Interest payment	1	16	17	1	1	17	17	1
− Transfer payments or investment	15	12	7	5	15	12	3	5
− Net lending	3	15	15	2	3	15	15	2
Deficit financing								
+ Money finance	14	17	16	16	2	16	16	16
+ Bond finance	2	7	9	17	6	7	9	17

Regarding the real GNP, the relative magnitude of changes in the nominal GNP and the GNP deflator determines the rank order. When the transfer payment increases, the real GNP will first fall and then rise. Which option is better in terms of the real GNP depends on the degree to which the GNP deflator decrease outweighs the nominal GNP decrease.

For the corporate tax rate increase versus the investment tax credit reduction, the simulation results suggest that the latter is the better financing method in almost all cases. The former surpasses the latter only in terms of the fifth-year effect for the real GNP. The rank differences in these two cases are not so distinct, however. A similar explanation of the case under options 1 and 2 will apply here as well.

For the consumption tax increase versus the custom duties increase, the latter is generally superior to the former. Only in terms of the real GNP will the reverse hold true.

For the government wage bill reduction versus expenditures reduction on other goods and services, the former is reported to be better consistently with respect to the GNP deflator and current account balance. In terms of the real GNP and budget balance, the latter performs better with the exception of the fifth-year impact in the event of a temporary increase. The corporate wage bill and profit will rise under the former option, while the opposite will hold under the latter option. When the transfer payment increases, so does private consumption.

For bond versus money financing, the former turns out to be generally better. In all cases except the budget balance, bond financing is definitely superior to money financing. The former generates a slightly higher budget deficit. Money supply will rise under the latter option but will fall under the former option. The corporate wage bill, corporate profit, and private sector investment will increase under the latter while the reverse will occur under the former. In particular, the revenue increase will fall short of the expenditure increase under the latter as will also budget balance.

Concluding Remarks

We propose a Korean model of social welfare policy that combines the best of the lessons from other developed countries with the merits of traditional Korean culture. We suggest basic principles along which the Korean model of social welfare policy should be constructed and program-specific proposals necessary for giving shape to the model. The Korean model should be one that balances growth and welfare, induces private sector investment as much as possible and keeps the public sector providing necessary social services where markets fail, prevents the need for welfare, and makes the best of traditional Korean culture. Along these principles, we suggest specific policy measures for income security, health security, and social welfare services. We address the financing issue by analyzing the macroeconomic effects of various financing options to implement the proposed policy devices.

Mental, cultural, and environmental issues did not draw our full attention in this chapter. As the national income increases, the demand for social welfare in the mental and cultural dimension will rise remarkably. As working hours are shortened and working at home becomes more popular, the demand for leisure activities also increases. Reflecting such a changing context, the ultimate goal of social welfare should be shifted from a passive one such as "extrication from absolute poverty" to a more positive one such as "enhancement of the quality of life through self-realization in the mental dimension."

The mental dimension in social welfare is very crucial in constructing a more productive and preventive social welfare system. As shown in Western countries, a well-established social welfare system alone, if not supported by mental stability, cannot prevent a society from encountering various social problems such as juvenile delinquency, drugs, alienation of the elderly, and destruction of the family. Sound leisure and cultural activities that engage the whole family will do much to prevent such social problems. As urbanization and industrialization intensify, a comprehensive plan to preserve a pleasant environment will be essential for social well-being. In Korea, rapid industrialization has so far generated serious air, water, and other kinds of pollution. Urbanization has increased the density of population in cities, thereby causing deteriorating environmental conditions and aggravating shortages in housing. Enhancing the quality of life will not be achieved without a healthy and pleasant environment.

APPENDIX

TABLE A1 Financing Options for Social Welfare Policy

Neutral financing	
Increasing revenue	
Personal income tax	
Tax on wages: via tax rate	Option 1
via income tax relief	Option 2
Tax on dividends	Option 3
Tax on interest	Option 4
Tax on operating surplus	Option 5

(Table A1 continued)

Corporate income tax: via tax rate	Option 6
via investment tax credit	Option 7
Consumption taxes	Option 8
Custom duties	Option 9
Non-tax revenue	Option 10
Reducing expenditures	
Wages	Option 11
Other goods and services	Option 12
Interest payments	Option 13
Transfer payments or investment	Option 14
Net lending	Option 15
Deficit financing	
Money finance	Option 16
Bond finance	Option 17

TABLE A2 The Macroeconomic Model

Behavioral Equation

1. Private Consumption
   PCON = PCON(PCON − 1, YDR, MS/PGNP, rd − p)
   + + + −
2. Private Investment
   PINV = PINV($PINV_{-1}$, EX, exr, MS/PGNP, rl − p)
   + + − + −
3. Exports
   EX = EX(EX_{-1}, FGNP, PX/FWPI)
   + + −
4. Imports
   IN = IN (IM_{-1}, GNPR, I/GNP, PNW/PGNP)
   + + + −
5. GNP Deflator
   PGNP = PGNP(PMW, MS, GNPR/POTGNP)
   + + +
6. Export Price
   PX = PX($PGNP_{-1}$, exr, PNW, FWPI)
   + − + +
7. Potential GNP
   GNPR = GNPR(LE, KS)
   + +

Identities and Fixed Proportions

8. GNP = PGNP(PCON + PINV) + WG + CG + IG + PGNP(EX − IM)
9. NNP = GNP − A
10. NI = NNP − TCN − TN
11. PI = NI − TCI − RE + TR + INT + NTR
12. YD = PI − TPI
13. S = SH + SC + SG
14. I = IP + IG
15. IP = PGNP * PINV
16. IR = I/PGNP
17. KS = KS − 1 + IR
18. CP = PGNP * PCON
19. SH = YD − CP
20. IH = h * IP
21. OSH = s * PI
22. NIC = NI − OSH − WG − NTR = WC + PT
23. WC = w * NIC
24. PT = NIC − WC = TCI + D + RE
25. PTA = PT − TCI
26. D = d * PTA
27. SC = RE + A
28. A = a * + GNP
29. IC = IP − IH
30. FC = IC − SC = FDC + FFC
31. FDC = FDCI + FDC2 + FDC3
32. FDCI = SH − IH − BH
33. FDC3 = NL
34. CA = PGNP(EX − IN)
35. KA = FFC + FFG
36. OB = CA + KA
37. R = − OB
38. REV = TPI + TCI + TCN + TM + NTR
39. TPI = TW + TD + TI + TOS
40. TW = tw(WC + WG) − ITR
41. TD = td * D
42. TI = ti * INT
43. TOS = tos * OSH
44. TCI = tci * PT − ITC
45. ITC + t + b * IC
46. TCN = tcn * CP
47. TM = tm * PGNP * IM
48. NTR = n * REV

(Table A2 continued)

49. EXP = CEX + IG + NL
50. CEX = WG + CG + INT + TR
51. INT = rdl * GB − 1
52. rdl = (rd + rl)/2
53. NL = 1 * EXP
54. SG = REV − CEX
55. BB = REV − EXP
56. FG = − BB = FDG + FFG
57. FDG = MF + BF
58. GB = GN − 1 + BF − C * R
59. NFA = NFA − 1 − R
60. CRG = CRG − 1 + MF
61. CRP = CRG − 1 + FDCI + FDC2
62. MS = MS − 1 + MF + FDC1 + FDC2 − (1 − C)R = NFA + CRG + CRP − PIN
63. TA = MS + GN

TABLE A3 A Glossary for Variables

Endogenous Variables

A	Capital consumption allowance	N,B
BB	Budget balance	N,B
CA	Current account	N,B
CEX	Current expenditures	N,B
CP	Private consumption	N,B
CRG	Credit to government	N,B
CRP	Credit to private sector	N,B
D	Dividends	N,B
EX	Exports	R,B
EXP	Government expenditures	N,B
FC	Corporate sector financing	N,B
FDC1	Corporate financing from commercial bank	N,B
FDC3	Corporate financing from government lending	N,B
FFC	Corporate foreign financing	N,B
FFG	Government foreign financing	N,B
FG	Government sector financing	N,B
GB	Government bonds	N,B
GNP	Nominal GNP	N,B
GNPR	Real GNP	R,B
I	Total investment	N,B
IC	Corporate investment	N,B
IH	Household sector investment	N,B
IM	Imports	R,B
INT	Government interest payments	N,B

IP	Private investment	N,B
IR	Total investment	R,B
ITC	Investment tax credit	N,B
KA	Capital account	N,B
KS	Capital stock	N,B
MS	Money supply (=M2)	R,B
NFA	Net foreign assets	N,B
NI	National income	N,B
NIC	National income by corporations	N,B
NL	Net lending	N,B
NNP	Net national product	N,B
NTR	Nontax revenues	N,B
OB	Overall balance in external sector	N,B
OIN	Other items net	N,B
OSH	Operating surplus in household sector	N,B
P	Percent change of PGNP	%
PCON	Private consumption	R,B
PGNP	GNP deflator	1985=100
PI	Personal income	N,B
PINV	Private investment	R,B
POTGNP	Potential GNP	R,B
PT	Cooperated profits	N,B
PTA	After-tax corporate profits	1985=100
PX	Export price index	N,B
R	Change in external reserves	%
rdefc	Budget deficit/GNP	N,B
RE	Retained earnings	N,B
REV	Government revenues	N,B
S	Total saving	N,B
SC	Corporate saving	N,B
SG	Government saving	N,B
SH	Household saving	N,B
TA	Total assets	N,B
TCI	Corporate income tax	N,B
TCN	Consumption taxes	N,B
TD	Tax on dividends	N,B
TI	Tax on interests	N,B
TM	Custom duties	N,B
TOS	Tax on operating surplus	N,B
TPI	Personal income tax	N,B
TW	Tax on wages	N,B
WC	Corporate wage bill	N,B
YD	Nominal disposable personal income	N,B
YDR	Real disposable personal income	R,B

Exogenous Variables and Parameters

d	Dividend ratio to PTA	R,M$
FGNP	Foreign countries' GNP	1985 = 100
FWPI	Foreign countries' WPI	
h	Fraction of IH out of IP	
LE	Number of the employed	T
PM	Import price index	1985 = 100
PMW	PM in terms of won = PM*exr	
s	Fraction of OSH out of PI	
w	Fraction of WC out of NIC	

Policy Variables and Parameters

a	Depreciation allowance coefficient	
b	Fraction of IP qualified for ITC	
BF	Bond finance	N,B
c	Degree of sterilization	
CG	Other purchases of goods and services	N,B
exr	Exchange rate	
FDC2	Corporate financing from central bank	N,B
FDG	Government domestic financing	N,B
IG	Government investment	N,B
ITR	Income tax relief	N,B
l	Fraction of NL out of EXP	
MF	Money finance	N,B
n	Fraction of NTR out of REV	
rd	Deposit rate	%
rd1	"Quasi" market rate	%
rl	Lending rate	%
t	Investment tax credit rate	
tci	Corporate income tax rate	
tcn	Consumption tax rate	
td	Tax rate on dividends	
ti	Tax rate on interests	
tm	Custom duty rate	
tos	Tax rate on operating surplus	
TR	Government transfer payments	N,B
tw	Tax rate on wages	
WG	Government wage bill	N,B

*N = nominal, R = real (based on 1985), B = billion won, T = thousand, M$ = million U.S. dollars.

REFERENCES

Cameron, A. C., and P. K. Trivedi. 1986. "Econometric Models Based on Count Data." *Journal of Applied Econometrics*," no. 1: 29–53.

Diamond, P. A., D. C. Linderman, and H. Young. 1996. *Social Security: What Role for the Future?* Washington D.C.: National Academy of Social Insurance.

Heller, P. S., and J. Diamond. 1990. "International Comparisons of Government Expenditure Revisited: The Developing Countries, 1975–86." International Monetary Fund Occasional Paper.

International Monetary Fund. 1994. *International Financial Statistics*.

Kim, Jinsoo. 1996. "A Study of the Financial Solvency of the Korean National Pension System"(in Korean). Mimeo.

Korea Statistical Office. 1996a. *Annual Statistics of Korea for 1995* (in Korean).

———. 1996b. *A Projection of Future Demographic Trends* (in Korean).

Lee, H. H. 1993. "The Effect of Health Insurance on the Demand for Medical Care." Ph.D dissertation, University of California at Los Angeles.

Lee, K. S. 1991. "Financing Social Welfare in Korea." In S. Cho., ed., *Korea's Choice for the 21st Century* (in Korean). Seoul: Dong-A Daily Press.

———. 1994. "A New Role for Fiscal Policy and Tax Finance in Korea." In R. A. Musgrave et al., eds., *Taxation and Economic Development Among Pacific Asian Countries*. Boulder, Colo.: Westview Press.

———. 1995. "Korea's Fiscal Policy at the Crossroads: How to Finance Social Development." Mimeo.

Manning, W. G., I. P. Newhouse, N. Duan, E. B. Keeler, A. Leibowitz, and M. S. Marquis. 1987. "Health Insurance and the Demand for Medical Care: Evidence from a Randomized Experiment." *American Economic Review* 77, 4: 251–77.

Min, J. S., and I. H. Yoo. 1991. "Optimal Integration of Korea's Public Pension Schemes." In W. Puschra and J. S. Min, ed., *Policy Issues in National Pension Schemes: Korea and Germany*. Friedrich Ebert Stiftung.

Ministry of Finance and Economy, Republic of Korea. 1996. *Social Indices of Korea: 1995* (in Korean).

Ministry of Health and Welfare, Republic of Korea. 1996a. *Major Programs for Health and Welfare* (in Korean).

———. 1996b. *Yearbook of Health and Welfare Statistics* (in Korean).

Moon, H. P. 1996. "The Public Pension Reform: Motive and Direction" (in Korean). Korea Development Insistute Executive Brief, December.

Nam, S. W., et al. 1990. *Policy Issues for Financial Stabilization of the* NPP (in Korean). Korea Development Institute.

Yoo, I. H. 1993. "Pension Policy in Korea." In *Social Issues in Korea: Korean and American Perspectives*. Korea Development Institute, Conference Series no. 93-01.

What Programs Make Up the U.S. Welfare System?

In fiscal year 1994, over 12 percent of the U.S. federal budget went to income support and health services programs. However, only a small share was spent on programs that could be classified as welfare. The lion's share was spent on two programs for the elderly. Social Security, the primary income support for retirees (as well as the disabled and minor survivors), absorbed $318 billion in 1994. The associated health insurance program, Medicare, cost another $160 billion. In fact, after subtracting unemployment insurance for the short-term unemployed, the remaining $50 billion spent on welfare programs accounted for only 4 percent of spending on social programs and 8.5 percent of all federal spending.

Nevertheless, the rhetoric around welfare reform legislation in 1996 highlights Americans' dissatisfaction with the delivery of welfare in the United States. Much of this dissatisfaction arises from concerns over the best-known program, Aid to Families with Dependent Children or AFDC. It is worsened by the complexity of the U.S. welfare system, which not only makes the system difficult to understand but also produces unintended consequences owing to lack of coordination between programs.

The U.S. welfare system is a patchwork of different programs, operating mostly independently of one another and often in conflict.

This project was funded in part by NIH grant HD32055–02. Opinions stated herein do not necessarily represent the official position or policy of NIH. I owe special thanks to Sasha Afanasieff for her research assistance and review of the literature.

Responsibility for administering the various programs is spread throughout the executive branch of the federal government and across many committees of the U.S. Congress. Responsibilities are also shared with state, county, and city governments, not only because these agencies actually deliver the services but also because they contribute to the funding of certain programs. At the federal level alone, there were at least seventy means-tested programs in 1994.[1] Virtually every cabinet department of the executive branch administers at least one of these programs, and no single department manages more than half the total. Legislative responsibility is equally diffuse. No fewer than two committees create the legislation governing the functions and funding of each program, and almost every committee has jurisdiction over at least one welfare program. In addition, state and local governments create their own programs to modify features or cover deficiencies of the federal programs, thus further complicating the overall system and leading to inconsistencies in benefits and rules across the country.

This paper describes the essential programs making up the U.S. welfare system and how these public assistance programs work together to provide basic support for poor families. It summarizes not only how each program works individually but also how programs operate in conjunction when families participate in several simultaneously, as is typical. Finally, the discussion outlines the basic features of the welfare reform that became law in 1996 and how this reform is likely to alleviate shortcomings of the overall system. This paper begins by identifying those public assistance programs that form the backbone of the welfare system and describing for each the general purpose, the governmental entities responsible for the conduct of the program, the number of families that participate, how much is spent on the program, and how eligibility and benefits are determined for participants. The discussion then shows how the main public assistance programs combine to provide income support to low-income families, illustrating some of the adverse consequences of the lack of coordination across various programs in terms of their payout of benefits. This is followed by a brief outline of the features of recent welfare reform that alter the basic structure of the U.S. system. The concluding section speculates on how these changes will affect problems with the current system.

1. A means-tested program is one that determines eligibility solely or partially on the basis of low income.

The Primary Welfare Programs

The U.S. welfare system would be an unlikely model for anyone designing a welfare system from scratch. The programs that make up the "system" have different (sometimes competing) goals, inconsistent rules, and overlapping client populations. Nevertheless, the very complexity of the system suggests some important lessons in terms of alternative strategies for program design. This section looks at the public assistance programs individually; the next section looks at the programs in combination.

Public assistance or welfare programs are means-tested programs that provide basic support for low-income families. This support includes cash income as well as in-kind support for necessities such as food, housing, medical care, and home heating.[2] Families as a whole or individual members may qualify for and participate in a number of programs at the same time. Based on levels of participation and expenditures, one can naturally divide public assistance programs into two broad categories: major programs that offer the core of resource support for poor families, and minor programs that provide only modest support.

The six programs that are most expensive in terms of federal expenditures and most extensive in coverage are: Aid to Families with Dependent Children (AFDC), Food Stamp Program (FSP), Supplemental Security Income (SSI), Housing Assistance, Medicaid, and Earned Income Tax Credit (EITC). These make up the "major programs." All six are funded primarily through the federal government, although AFDC and Medicaid each require a 25 to 50 percent state funding match. The first five programs are those commonly associated with "welfare"; they are administered locally (by the states or counties). EITC operates as part of the regular federal tax system and is not considered as a welfare program. AFDC, SSI, and EITC pay cash assistance to low-income families. FSP provides food vouchers denominated in dollars to low-income households, regardless of family structure or disability. Housing assistance programs come in two varieties: rent subsidies for occupancy of private dwellings and low-income public housing, which is built, managed and maintained by government agencies. Finally, Medicaid is an in-kind benefits program providing medical assistance to poor persons.

2. This definition excludes means-tested programs that provide specific services such as job training, legal services, and child care.

Outside the six major programs, there exist many smaller public assistance programs, collectively referred to here as "minor programs." Examples of minor programs include: the Special Supplemental Food Program for Women, Infants, and Children (WIC), General Assistance (GA), school-based food programs, and energy assistance. The WIC program provides vouchers for specific food items such as milk and infant formula, and GA provides minimal cash assistance primarily to low-income individuals who do not qualify for AFDC or SSI. School lunch and breakfast programs offer subsidized meals at school for children of low-income families. Energy assistance is provided through the Low-Income Home Energy Assistance Program (LIHEAP), which subsidizes heating and electricity purchases by relatively low income households. Some of these programs have extensive numbers of participants, but because the benefit amounts paid per participant are quite modest these programs are not discussed here.

AID TO FAMILIES WITH DEPENDENT CHILDREN

The early version of AFDC, Aid to Dependent Children, was established by the Social Security Act of 1935 as a cash grant program to enable states to help single mothers who were widowed or abandoned by their husbands. It was originally designed to allow mothers to stay at home and take care of their children, providing the basic requirements of food, shelter, and clothing. The program was expanded in the 1950s and 1960s to provide cash assistance to needy children and to families who have been deprived of support or care because their father or mother is continuously absent from the home for any reason, in addition to these spouses being incapacitated or deceased. This expansion coincided with renaming the program Aid to Families with Dependent Children (AFDC).

Many governmental agencies have a hand in administering and funding AFDC. In the executive branch of the federal government, the Department of Health and Human Services manages the program. The Committee on Ways and Means of the U.S. House of Representatives is responsible for conduct of the program, and in the Senate the Finance Committee possesses the primary legislative authority. The federal government provides sweeping guidelines and program requirements, and states are responsible for administering and organizing the program, determining benefits, establishing income and resource limits, and setting actual benefit payments. States are required to submit any proposed modifications of their conduct of AFDC to the Department of Health and Human Services for approval.

All state governments share the cost of the program. The federal government supplements the states' contributions with matching funds for operating the AFDC program. The federal government matches administrative and training costs at a 50 percent rate. It matches AFDC benefit payment costs using a formula that accounts for a state's per capita income relative to the national value; this matching rate ranges from 50 percent for states with the highest per capita income to 83 percent for the state with the lowest.

Caseload and expenditures for AFDC. In 1993, almost 5 million families and over 14 million individuals received AFDC benefits, representing over 5 percent of the population. Total costs of AFDC were $22.5 billion in fiscal year 1993. The monthly benefits averaged $376.70 per family and $132.64 per recipient, although there was significant state-to-state variation.

Figure 1 shows the percentage of the population receiving benefits from AFDC during the last two decades. For comparison, this figure also presents the participation rates for the other major welfare programs: SSI, Medicaid, and food stamps. It further plots the percentage of persons living in families whose income placed them at or below the U.S. poverty level in each year. We see in the figure that the percentage of the population collecting AFDC benefits has remained steady at about 5 percent of the population throughout the period. Most people who apply for AFDC receive it for only a short period. Approximately 60 percent of applicants receive benefits for less than two years; however, the remaining 40 percent receive benefits for a much longer time, and thus make up the majority of the caseload at any given time.

Figure 2 graphs the percentage of the federal budget spent on the four major welfare programs since the mid-1970s. Between one and two percent of the budget was spent on SSI, food stamps, and AFDC throughout the past twenty years. Of these three, AFDC ranked as the highest in late 1970s at a little over 1.5 percent, but fell steadily to become the lowest ranked of the three at about 1 percent of the federal budget in 1993.

Figure 3 presents the spending in each of the four major welfare programs as a share of total federal spending on the four. AFDC, SSI, and food stamps each amounted to about 12 percent of total welfare spending in 1993. The funding for SSI and food stamps remained fairly constant during the period 1975–1993, staying between 10 percent and

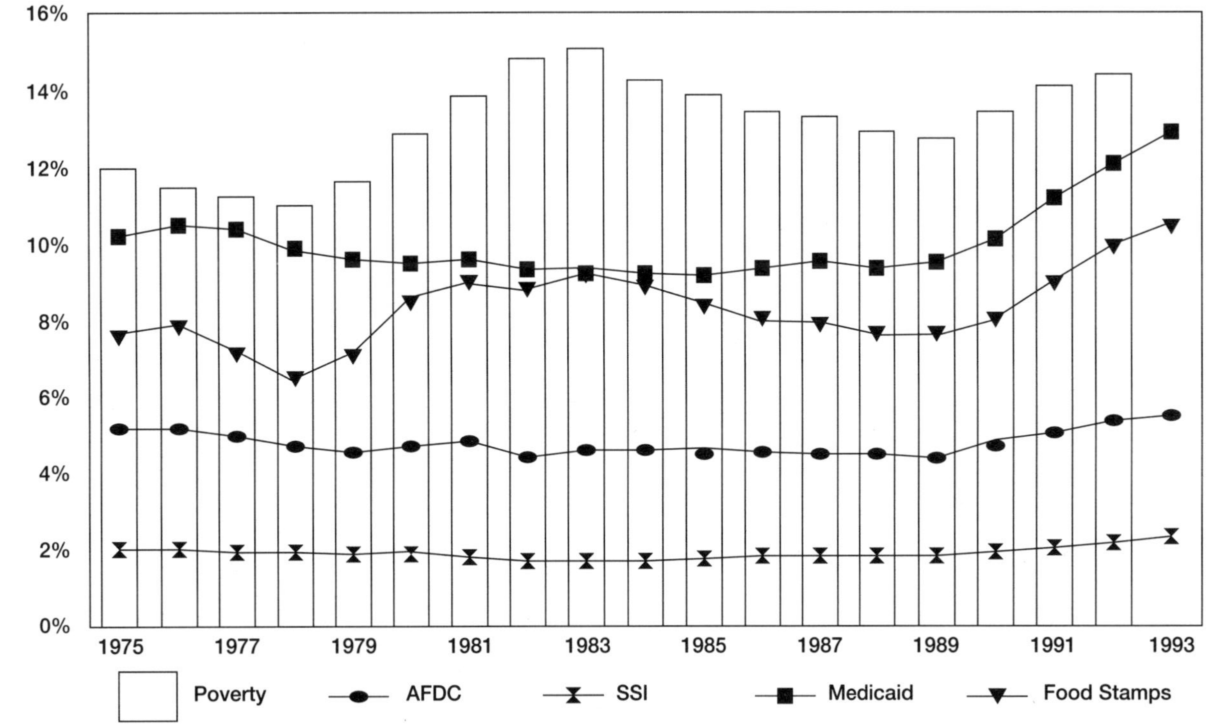

FIGURE 1 Percent of the population receiving benefits. Statistics from Green Book, AFDC, pp. 389, 399; SSI, pp. 262, 248; Medicaid, pp. 796, 798; Food Stamps, pp. 782, 777.

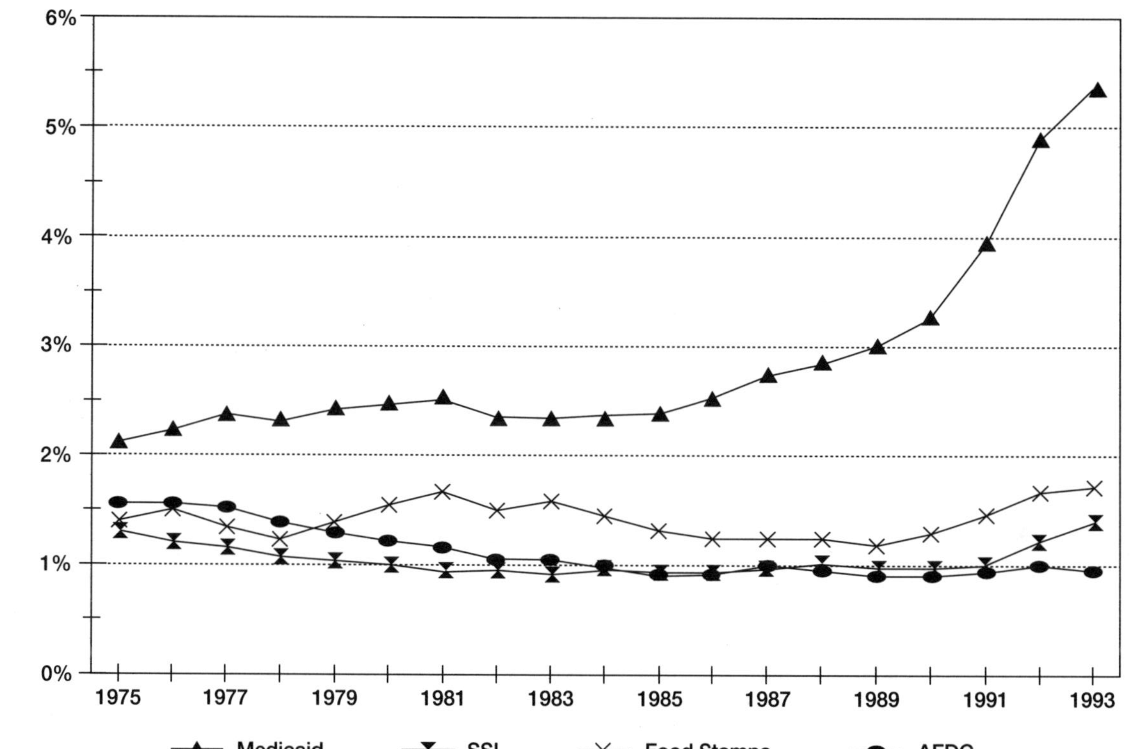

FIGURE 2 Individual welfare programs; percent of the federal budget. Statistics from Green Book, AFDC, p. 389; SSI, p. 262; Medicaid p. 798; Food Stamps, p. 782; 1996 Budget of the U.S. Government, Historical Tables, p. 14.

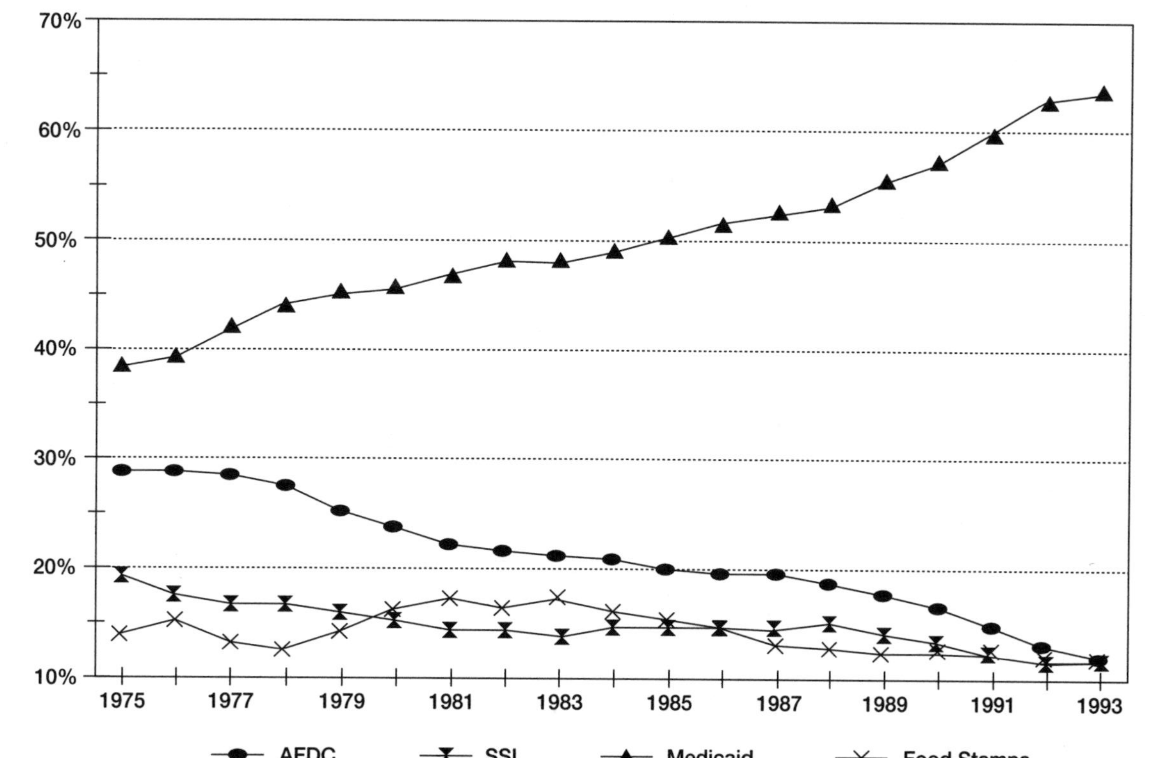

FIGURE 3 Percent of total spending of four major welfare programs.

20 percent. AFDC experienced the greatest reduction in funding, going from about 30 percent in 1975 to a low of around 12 percent in 1993.

Figure 4 shows the annual amounts spent per participant in the various welfare programs. We see that AFDC per recipient spending steadily decreased from around \$2,500 in 1975 to around \$1,700 in 1993, where all per capita numbers are in 1995 dollars. AFDC amounts started between those of Medicaid and the higher SSI value and fell below both by 1993. AFDC per recipient payments always exceeded those of food stamps even though the gap steadily closed after 1975.

Determination of AFDC benefits. To be eligible for AFDC in a given state, a family must have a dependent child who is: (1) under age eighteen; (2) deprived of parental support or care because of a parent's death, continued absence, incapacity, or unemployment; (3) living in the home of a parent or other specified, close relative; (4) a resident of the state; and (5) a U.S. citizen or permanent alien lawfully residing in the United States. To receive AFDC payments, a family's gross income may not exceed 185 percent of the state-determined needs standard (known as the MBSAC) for the relevant family size. This applies to applicants and enrollees alike. Each state sets its own needs standard specifying the level of income a family of a particular size "needs" to cover its most basic expenses. It also establishes its own payment standard (known as the MAP = maximum aid payment) to determine an assistance unit's benefit amount, which may be lower than the needs standard, and is the maximum amount the state actually pays to a family for assistance. The state determines the benefit amount by considering the countable income of all persons included in the assistance unit and applying it against the state's payment standard.

The formula for calculating AFDC benefits is: Grant = min (MAP, MBSAC − net income), where net income = other unearned income + (child support − 50) + α (earnings − 120). The values 50 and 120 in this formula have not been constant over time or across states. The value of α is the benefit reduction rate for AFDC, for it determines how much AFDC benefits fall as a family's earnings rise. (Note that the benefit reduction rate is 100 percent for income other than earnings, since AFDC benefits decline by \$1 for every \$1 increase in income.) The value of the parameter α in this formula has varied during the past thirty years: it began at the value of 2/3 in the 1960s and 1970s, was raised to 1 in the 1980s, and was dropped back to 2/3 in the 1990s.

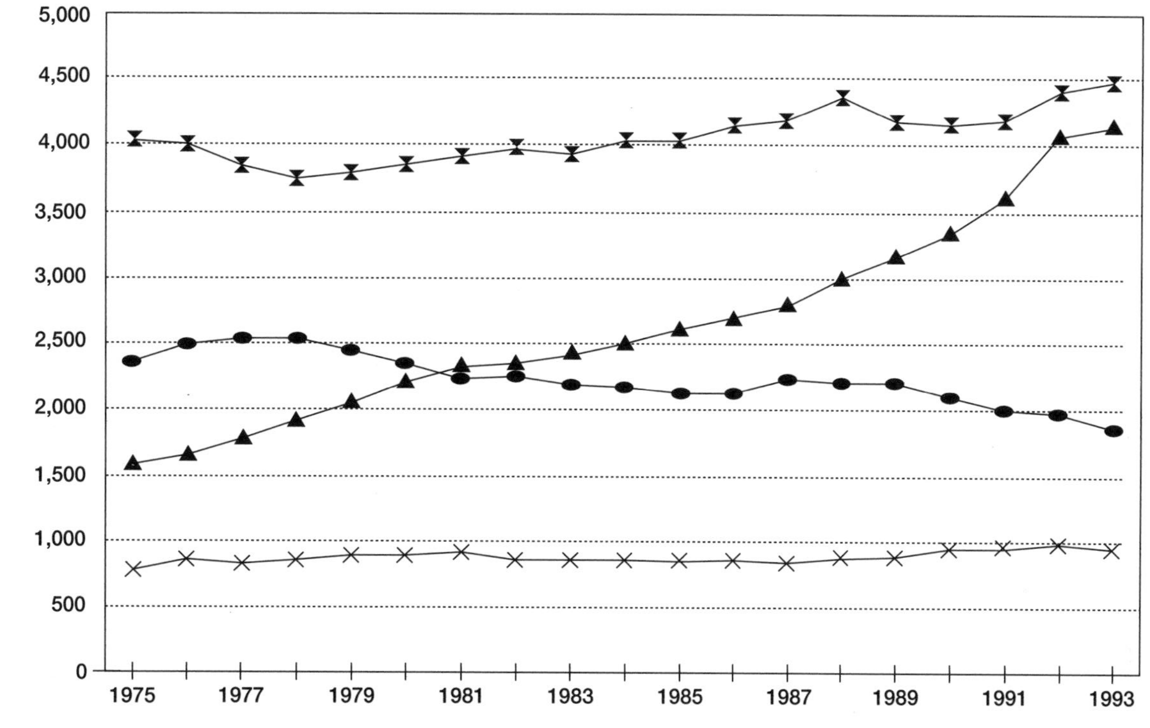

FIGURE 4 Per participant spending in welfare programs (in 1995 dollars). Statistics from Green Book, AFDC, pp. 389, 399; SSI pp. 262, 248; Medicaid, pp. 796, 798; Food Stamps, pp. 782, 777. Historical Tables, 1996 Budget of the U.S. Government, 1995 Composite Deflator, p. 17.

The policy of setting $\alpha = 2/3$ is known as adopting the "30 and a third rule."

In 1988, the Family Support Act established the Job Opportunities and Basic Skills Training (JOBS) program to promote self-sufficiency. The program provides training, work experience, and education opportunities for AFDC recipients. As a condition of eligibility, some AFDC recipients are required to participate in JOBS.

FOOD STAMPS

The Food Stamp Program (FSP), authorized as a permanent program in 1964, works through state agencies by issuing food stamp coupons to eligible recipients. After 1974, Congress required all states to offer the program to low-income households to enable them to buy more nutritional, low-cost food. Recipients use food stamps like cash to purchase food at retail stores authorized by Food and Nutrition Service (FNS). Retail stores deposit the food stamps at banks, which credit the store accounts for their value. The banks send the redeemed food stamps to a Federal Reserve Bank, which credits the bank's account, bills the U.S. Treasury for the value of the food stamps, and destroys them. There are limitations on what items can be purchased with food stamps (e.g., they cannot be used to purchase cigarettes or alcohol). Recipients pay no tax on items purchased with food stamps.

The federal government is entirely responsible for the rules and the complete funding of FSP benefits. All states offer the program and must comply with federal rules. The states are responsible for administrative costs and are liable for any inaccurate benefit determinations. States, through local welfare offices, have primary responsibility for administration of the Food Stamp Program. They determine eligibility, calculate benefits, and issue food stamp allotments. Usually the federal government covers half of the state welfare agency administrative costs. At the federal level, the program is administered by the Department of Agriculture's Food and Nutrition Service (FNS). Agricultural committees in the House and Senate of the U.S. Congress determine the legislation governing the operation of the FSP. The FNS helps state welfare agencies follow federal regulations. They print out the food stamp coupons and distribute them to the welfare agencies. The FNS also approves and oversees participation by retail food stores and other outlets. Several other federal agencies are involved in the Food Stamp Program: the Federal Reserve System redeems food stamps for cash; the Social Security Administration assigns required social security numbers, provides limited application "intake" services, and provides info to verify recipients' income; the Internal Revenue Service assists in verifying recipients' income and assets; and the Immigration and Naturalization Service confirms alien applicants' status.

Caseload and expenditures for FSP. An average of 27.5 million individuals received food stamp benefits in 1995. The total federal program expenditures amounted to $24.6 billion, with $22.8 billion spent in benefits. According to Figure 1, which shows the percent of the population receiving various welfare benefits, between 8 percent and 10 percent of the population participated in the FSP during the period 1975–1993 with a slight upturn occurring in the 1990s. Figure 2 indicates that almost 2 percent of the federal budget went toward the Food Stamp Program steadily throughout the last two decades. Figure 3 reports that FSP amounted to over 10 percent of all major welfare program spending. From Figure 4 we see that the average food stamp participant received around $1,000 annually. In fiscal year 1993, monthly benefits averaged $68 a person and about $170 a household.

Most FSP participants receive food stamps as a second or third form of government assistance. Fewer than 20 percent of food stamp households receive no governmental cash aid. About 41 percent of food stamp households receive AFDC, and some 19 percent receive SSI benefits. About 20 percent of food stamp households receive Social Security or veteran's benefits. Nearly 15 percent receive General Assistance, Unemployment Insurance, or Workers' Compensation Benefits. Eighty-one percent of those with income below half the federal poverty guidelines participate in the Food Stamp Program, and 17 percent of those with incomes above the poverty line participate.

Determination of food stamp benefits. Monthly cash income is the primary determinant of food stamp eligibility. A household's gross and net monthly cash incomes must be below the food stamp gross and net income maximums, which are based on the federal poverty guidelines. The household's gross income = earnings + AFDC + other unearned income + child support, and its net income = 80% of earnings + AFDC + other unearned income + child support − deductions − child care deductions, where deductions = $510 in 1994 and, if a member of the family works, child care deductions = $175 in 1994. Households without an elderly or disabled member must have a gross income below 130 percent of the federal poverty guidelines to receive food stamps. Households without an elderly member cannot have accessible savings above $2,000 to maintain its food stamp eligibility; households with an elderly member cannot have liquid assets above $3,000. Each unemployed adult must be looking or training for a job and must accept suitable job offers. Most AFDC, SSI, and General Assistance recipients are automatically eligible for food stamps. Eligibility for or benefits provided by other welfare programs are not affected by receipt of food stamps.

If deemed eligible, the formula for calculating food stamp benefits is: Grant = maximum allotment − 30% of net income. The maximum allotment value depends on household size and has varied over time. In 1994 the maximum allotment for a two-person household was $212, rising to $459 for a five-person family. The benefit reduction rate on earnings for the FSP is 24% (= 30% of 80%), meaning that benefits decline by $0.24 for every $1 increase in earnings. Other income experiences a higher benefit reduction rate, whether this other income comes from relatives or from another public assistance program.

SUPPLEMENTAL SECURITY INCOME (SSI)

Authorized by the Social Security Act in 1974, SSI replaced the former federal-state matching grant program for old-age assistance, aid to the blind, and aid to the permanently disabled. It provides monthly cash payments to needy individuals who are age sixty-five or older, blind, or disabled, including children. The Social Security Administration (SSA) manages SSI for the executive branch of the federal government. The Committee on Ways and Means of the U.S. House of Representatives is responsible for conduct of the program, and in the Senate the Finance Committee exerts the primary legislative authority.

SSI benefits are financed from the general funds of the United States Treasury. States may supplement the basic SSI benefits with state funds. In addition, any state may enter into an agreement to have SSA administer its supplementation program and pay the state supplementary amounts along with the basic SSI benefits. Each month SSA will charge the state an administration fee for every state supplementary payment issued during that month.

Caseload and expenditures for SSI. Over 5.9 million individuals, or over 2 percent of the population (Figure 1), received SSI benefits in 1993. Total SSI spending amounted to $23.9 million, or approximately 1.5 percent of the federal budget, as revealed in Figure 2. Figure 3 shows that the SSI program accounts for around 12 percent of all major welfare programs. The greatest amount of welfare spending per participant goes to individuals receiving SSI benefits. Figure 4 indicates that the average SSI participant received almost $4,500 in 1993, which is slightly above what it was in the late 1970s. Monthly federal benefits for individuals amounted to $434 in 1993, and $652 for couples.

Determination of SSI benefits. Either an individual or couples can qualify for SSI. Individuals must satisfy particular disability conditions to be eligible for SSI payments, where the disability can be a physical or mental impairment interfering with the person's ability to work. Both individuals and couples can also qualify for SSI by being over age sixty-five and low income. A child under age eighteen with an impairment comparable to that of an adult may be considered disabled. To be eligible for SSI, a person must have limited income and resources and be a U.S. citizen, a legal immigrant, a permanent resident residing in the United States, or a child of military personnel stationed outside the United States.

A person cannot receive SSI payments and AFDC payments concurrently. However, SSI recipients can also receive Social Security, if eligible. In 1993, 40.7 percent of all SSI recipients also received Social Security benefits (65 percent of aged SSI recipients). Social Security benefits are the single highest source of outside income for SSI recipients.

SSI benefits are determined by first calculating the countable income of the disabled individual or couple, and subtracting it from the SSI payment standards. The equation for countable income is calculated as: countable income = unearned income − 20 + 50% of (earned income − 65). The monthly SSI payment is equal to: SSI payment = payment standard − countable income, where the payment standard was $446 for one person and $669 for two persons in 1994. A state's contribution depends on a similar formula if it chooses to supplement SSI. This contribution, known as SSP (state supplemental payment), varies significantly across states; in 1994, monthly SSP for one person ranged from $5 in Hawaii to $374 in Alaska.

MEDICAID

Medicaid became law in 1965, under the Social Security Act, as a jointly funded program between the federal and state governments to assist states in providing adequate medical care to eligible needy persons. Medicaid provides health care services to over 36 million low-income individuals who are aged, blind, disabled, members of families with dependent children, and certain other children and pregnant women. Medicaid is the largest program providing medical and health-related services to the United States' poorest people and the largest single funding source for nursing homes and institutions for people with mental retardation. At the federal level, the Health Care Financing Administration (HCFA) of the Department of Health and Human Services oversees operations. Subcommittees of the Committee on Ways and Means of the U.S. House of Representatives have legislative responsibility for the program, and, similarly, subcommittees of the Finance Committee of the U.S. Senate have the principal authority for funding and organization of Medicaid.

Within federal guidelines, each state is responsible for designing and administering its own program. Individual states determine persons covered, types and scope of benefits offered, and amounts of payments for services. The federal law requires that a single state agency be responsible for the administration of the Medicaid program, generally the state welfare agency, state health agency, or human resources agency. The federal government covers 50 percent of state administrative costs. The federal government shares costs with states by means of an annually adjusted variable matching formula, with the matching rate inversely related to a state's per capita income ranging from 50 percent to 83 percent (highest current rate is 78.85 percent).

Caseload and expenditures for Medicaid. The Medicaid program has more participants than any other major welfare program. Figure 1 shows that slightly over 12 percent of the population received Medicaid benefits in 1993, up from about 10 percent in the 1970s and 1980s. Medicaid covers 47 percent of families whose incomes fall below the federal poverty level. According to Figures 2 and 3, spending on Medicaid rose steadily as a fraction of the federal budget during the past twenty years, increasing from approximately 2 percent in 1975 to 5.5 percent in 1993. Between 1975 and 1993, funding for Medicaid steadily increased from less than 40 percent to over 60 percent of total federal expenditures on the four major welfare programs. In fiscal year 1995, the federal government spent $96 billion in Medicaid outlays, and the states expended $72 billion. Given the relatively stable participation rates and the dramatic increase in expenditures, it is not surprising to find in Figure 4 that per capita expenditures on Medicaid beneficiaries rose significantly throughout the period 1970–1990s, almost reaching a value of $4,000 in 1995.

Determination of Medicaid eligibility. Medicaid eligibility is generally linked to eligibility for other welfare programs. States must provide Medicaid to all persons in the following categorical groups: all AFDC recipients, SSI recipients, qualified Medicare beneficiaries, pregnant women, families with children under age six whose incomes fall below 133 percent of the federal poverty level, and families with children under age eighteen whose incomes fall below the poverty level. Optionally, states can cover particular groups designated as "medically needy," which are persons with particular medical conditions whose income is somewhat above the poverty thresholds specified above. Because eligibility requirements for children are less restrictive than for adults, poor children are much more likely to receive coverage.

Since states design and administer their own programs, there exists substantial variation among states in terms of persons covered, types and scope of benefits offered, and amounts of payments for services. The scope of covered services that states must provide to the categorically needy is much broader than the minimum scope of services for the medically needy.

HOUSING ASSISTANCE PROGRAMS

The Department of Housing and Urban Development (HUD) and the Federal Housing Administration (FHA) administer several federal programs to aid the housing needs of lower-income households. These programs aim to improve housing quality and to reduce housing costs for lower-income households. This includes residential construction, helping disadvantaged individuals and groups with special housing needs attain affordable housing, promoting neighborhood preservation and revitalization, increasing home ownership, and empowering the poor to become self-sufficient. The U.S. House Energy Committee provides oversight for most federal housing programs, and in the U.S. Senate, the Committee on Banking, Housing, and Urban Affairs primarily deals with housing legislation.

There are principally two types of housing assistance for low-income families: subsidized rent, and the actual provision of dwellings (known as public housing). The federal government has provided rental and mortgage-interest subsidies to lower-income households since the mid-1930s. The Section 8 program provides rent subsidies to low-income families and single people. Local governments commonly provide for subsidized housing through their building authority in that they require a portion of new construction to be made available to low-income families at below market rental values as a condition of receiving permission to undertake the construction. Public housing is almost exclusively a federal program administered by local public housing agencies (PHAs), not private owner-managers. PHAs are governed by a board that is appointed by a city council or a county board of supervisors. In contrast to the mid-1960s, public housing is now a small fraction of overall housing assistance. In 1990, passage of the Housing Act established housing block grants to state and local governments, which may use these funds for various housing assistance activities specified in the law.

Caseload and expenditures for housing programs. Approximately 5.8 million low-income households obtained assistance in 1994, with 5.0 million receiving rental subsidies. The proportion of all assisted households receiving home ownership assistance declined from 34 percent in 1977 to 13 percent in 1994. In this same period, the proportion of renters receiving rental assistance increased from 13 percent to 40 percent, and the fraction of renters collecting household-based subsidies increased from 8 percent to 28 percent. Of the 3 million people in public housing, nearly 40 percent are elderly and live alone; the remainder are predominantly single-parent households with children. Each resident pays 30 percent of his or her income for rent, with the average rent payment at $169 per month in 1995.

Because of a continuing increase in the number of households served, total outlays for all HUD's housing assistance programs combined have steadily increased from $6.9 billion in 1977 to an estimated $21.8 billion in 1994, an increase of 215 percent. Average federal outlays per unit for all programs combined continually increased in real terms, from around $2,750 in 1977 to an estimated $4,540 in 1994—with both figures expressed in 1994$— an increase of 65 percent.

There are several reasons for the growth: rents in assisted housing probably rose faster than the income of assisted households, causing subsidies to rise faster than the inflation index; the number of households that occupy housing units has risen; recently constructed units require larger subsidies than older units; the share of households receiving less costly home ownership assistance has decreased; and housing aid is being targeted toward a poorer segment of the population, requiring larger subsidies per assisted household.

Determination of housing assistance benefits and eligibility. Most federal housing aid is given to very low income renters through the rental assistance programs administered by HUD and the FHA. Rental assistance is provided through two basic approaches: (1) project-based aid, which provides aid through new construction or substantial rehabilitation, and (2) household-based subsidies, which permit renters to choose standard housing units in the existing private housing stock. Some funding is also provided each year to modernize units built with federal aid. Each year, the federal government also assists some lower- and moderate-income households in becoming homeowners by making long-term commitments to reduce their mortgage interest.

To qualify for rent subsidies under the Section 8 program, families must have incomes at or below 80 percent of the area median (adjusted for family size) as determined by HUD. Countable annual income is defined as gross annual income (which excludes a few sources, such as earnings of children, foster care payments, educational scholarships) minus the following: $480 for each family member under eighteen, a student, or elderly (other than head and spouse): $400 for elderly family members; child care and handicap expenses; and medical expenses above certain thresholds. Countable income is discounted for families with assets greater than $5,000. Section 8 families pay rent equal to 30 percent of their countable income or 10 percent of gross income, whichever is higher, with the government making up the difference.

The low-rent public housing programs operate in the same manner as the Section 8 program, but the benefit is a rent subsidy for a unit in a public housing project rather than a rent subsidy for a unit of the recipient's choosing.

EARNED INCOME TAX CREDIT (EITC)

The Earned Income Tax Credit or EITC, enacted in 1975, was greatly enhanced in generosity in 1993 with full implementation in 1996. President Clinton described the expanded EITC as a commitment that full-time workers with children would not live in poverty. This completed the conversion of EITC from a rebate of payroll taxes for the poor to a large refundable credit, in many ways akin to a negative payroll tax. As the only refundable tax credit, the EITC is now intended to bridge the gap between low-wage work and the poverty level. In 1996 the maximum value of the credit reached $3,556 per year.

Unlike most taxes or public assistance programs, the value of the EITC depends not on wage rates or total income but on the combined earnings of both parents in a household. EITC is administered by the Internal Revenue Service. Because workers file for the credit along with their standard 1040 tax forms, receiving EITC is private, unremarkable, and without stigma. Although the EITC is generally paid all at once as an annual refund, a worker need not wait until the end of the year to receive EITC; it can be paid along with an employee's weekly, biweekly, or monthly paycheck.

In the U.S. Congress, EITC falls under the authority of those committees responsible for the federal income tax system. This includes the Committee on Ways and Means in the U.S. House of Representatives and the Finance Committee in the U.S. Senate. Local governments play no role in administering or funding EITC, although some states offer their own earned income credit.

Caseload and expenditures for EITC. When fully implemented in 1996, nearly 19 million families received the EITC. By the end of the decade, over $30 billion in credits a year will be paid to low-income families—several billion dollars more than the amounts projected to be spent on other primary programs such as AFDC and food stamps. At this level, the expanded EITC will provide as much support and can have as much effect on behavior as any welfare program. EITC has proven to be one of the few programs that effectively reaches the eligible population. In 1990, between 80 percent and 86 percent of eligible individuals received EITC. In contrast, only about 59 percent of eligible individuals received food stamp benefits. Welfare recipients who make the transition to work are still eligible for EITC, regardless of the amount of other forms of public assistance they received during the year.

Determination of EITC benefits. To be eligible for the credit, an individual must be working and must file the appropriate tax forms. The IRS computes the credit amounts for any filer who supplies minimum information. If an eligible individual does not claim the EITC, the IRS sends a letter to the person telling him about the credit.

The EITC applies differently in three distinct income ranges: a phase-in range where the credit is a percentage of earnings, a flat range where the maximum credit is paid to all qualifying families, and a phase-out range where the credit is reduced from its maximum at a given rate. Considering a family with two children in 1996, the EITC credit is 40 percent of earnings up to an earned income of $8,900. At this point, the credit reaches its maximum of $3,560 annually, available to families earning between $8,900 and $11,620. Above $11,620, the credit is reduced at a rate of 21 percent, completely phasing out at $28,524.

Families with two or more children are eligible for the maximum credit of $3,560, a 200 percent increase over the pre-1991 EITC amount. The 1996 EITC maximum payment works out to approximately $296 per month, which puts it clearly in the same range as major welfare programs. For comparison, the 1993–1994 maximum food stamps allotment for a mother and two children was $295 per month. The 1994 maximum AFDC (Aid for Families with Dependent Children) benefit for a mother of two was also below $297 in fifteen states. The 1996 EITC exceeds the average 1993 monthly AFDC payments made to all families in twenty states.[3] A family with one child can receive a maximum credit of $2,154, an increase of about 80 percent of the pre-1991 level.

Table 1 provides an overview of the six major federal programs in the U.S. welfare system. As this table shows, the programs are designed to provide different kinds of support to different, but overlapping, groups of families. Except for Supplemental Security Income, which is designed to support individuals who are unable to work, these programs support both the long-term and short-term poor. In general, these individual programs are not seen as encouraging long-term poverty, with the exception of the cash welfare program, AFDC. In the following section, we look at the programs in combination.

How the Programs Combine to Provide Income Support

In principle, developing different programs for different population groups may be a reasonable strategy for designing a welfare system. For the U.S. system, however, the flaws in this approach become apparent

3. AFDC and food stamps data come from the 1994 Green Book. Food stamps maximum allotment is $295 for the forty-eight contiguous states and the District of Columbia. It is somewhat higher in Hawaii, Alaska, and Guam.

TABLE 1 Characteristics of U.S. Welfare Programs

Program	*Type of assistance*	*Types of families*	*Families with earnings*
Aid to Families with Dependent Children	Cash	With children, single-parent, or unemployed two-parent families	9.5%
Food stamps	Vouchers for food	Any family	21%
Supplemental Security Income	Cash	Elderly, blind, or disabled	4.4%
Medicaid	Medical insurance	Children in poverty, medically needy	—[a]
Housing Assistance	Public housing, housing subsidies	Any family, plus a separate program for elderly and disabled	24%
Earned Income Tax Credit	Refundable tax credit	Working with children	100%

[a] An exact figure for the percentage of Medicaid cases is unavailable from government published sources, but auxiliary statistics suggest that this figure exceeds 45%.

when we examine the interaction between programs. It is common for families to participate in a number of welfare programs simultaneously. The combined effects of these programs have unintended consequences, in particular, the creation of extremely high tax rates on work.

As we saw in the preceding discussion, each program has its own benefit reduction rate that determines how much benefits decline as a family's earnings increase. These rates then act as tax rates on earnings, in that they dictate how much families get to keep out of any incremental earnings they receive while collecting benefits. Because programs typically do not recognize the existence of other programs, the combined benefit reduction rate that results when a family participates in several programs rises to staggeringly high levels, levels that no policy maker ever intended. This in turn produces significant disincentives for families to work or achieve self-sufficiency.

COMBINED EFFECTS OF PROGRAMS

Figure 5 shows how net governmental transfers change as a family's earnings rise when this family participates in various combinations of public assistance programs. The figure depicts three scenarios: the lower curve indicating transfers when the family receives benefits from just EITC, the middle curve giving the total benefits received when the family collects food stamps in conjunction with EITC, and the upper curve measuring the total transfers when the family also participates in the AFDC program. The curves are for a single-parent family with two children living in California—only the AFDC benefit schedule depends on California residency. Other than the Social Security tax (about 7.5 percent), families at the low-income levels figure pay no federal or state income taxes. As earnings increase, moving left to right in the figure, net transfers initially rise regardless of which particular combination of programs the family participates in, but eventually these transfers decline with higher levels of earnings. The reversal is fastest when the family collects AFDC, food stamps, and EITC simultaneously and slowest when collecting only EITC.

For a family participating in all three programs, the uncoordinated nature of the programs leads to some unintended and undesirable features. As this family's earnings rise within the first \$750 per month earned (= 30 hours per week at \$5.75) in 1996, the EITC provides a tax credit increasing the value of work by 40 percent. If this were the only program, the family would face an implicit tax rate of −32 percent (a negative tax), paying only Social Security taxes. However, since both

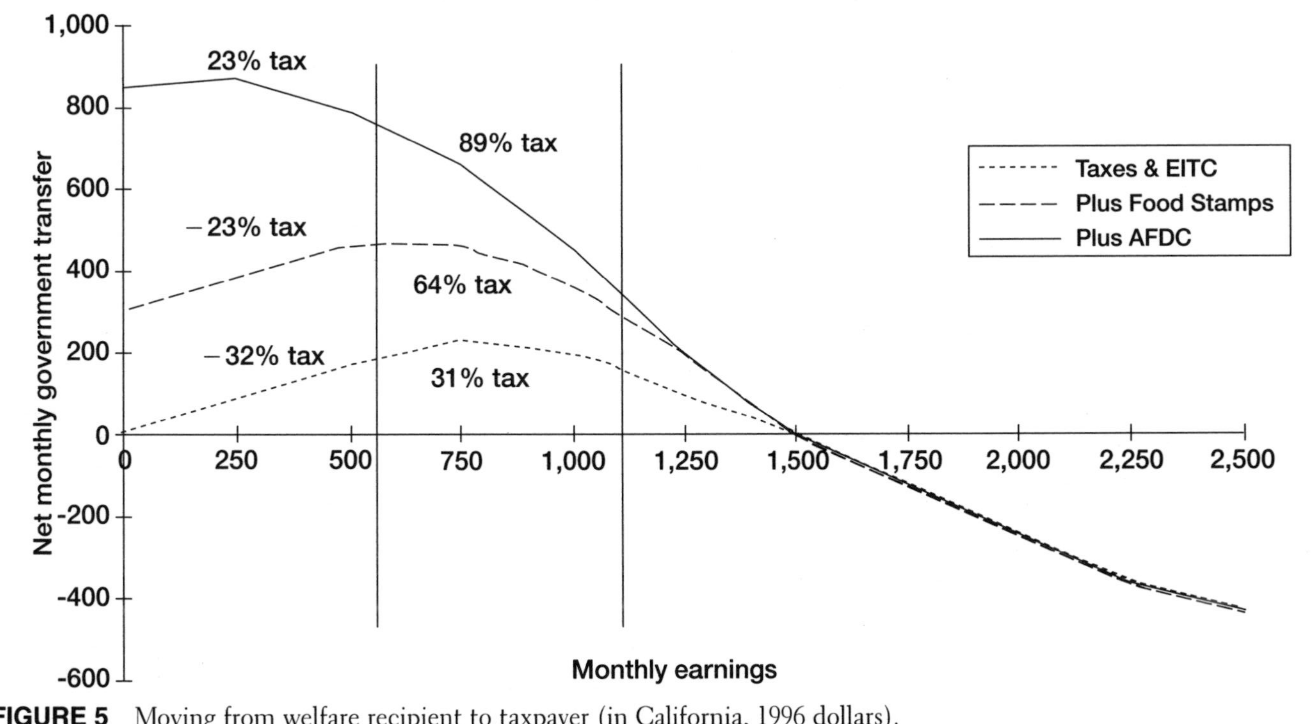

FIGURE 5 Moving from welfare recipient to taxpayer (in California, 1996 dollars).

food stamps and AFDC benefits decline more rapidly with earnings than EITC rises, a family who also participates in these programs ends up losing about 23 cents out of every $1 earned up to $750 a month. This translates into an effective positive tax rate of 23 percent on earnings. Earning $750 a month, this family still receives benefits from all three programs. Increasing family earnings from $750 to $1,500 a month would put it in an income range with effective tax rates of about 89 percent, meaning that it would retain only 11 cents out of every dollar earned.

Ironically, this high tax rate is the result of changes over the past five years that were designed to increase work incentives. Recent federal legislation increased the generosity of the EITC, and at about the same time California lowered the benefit reduction rates through the passage of "30 and a third" reforms in AFDC. Comparing the benefit structure and tax rates in 1996 with those in 1992 reveals that these federal and California state changes did, indeed, decrease the effective taxes for families in the lowest earnings range: the marginal tax rate for the first $750 of earnings fell from 71 percent to 23 percent. However, these changes simultaneously raised the marginal tax rate for the second $750 of earnings from 59 percent to 89 percent. Consequently, recent policies substantially increased the tax rate for families trying to reach self-sufficiency.

Knowing that AFDC participants do not work extensively under the current system says little about their motivation or prospects for working, because the existing benefit structure creates strong disincentives to working. It is quite rational for AFDC recipients to work little or not at all, since the current rules tax income highly as earnings increase. These work disincentives become more severe the more a recipient works and the closer she or he gets to self-sufficiency.

Under the system today, an AFDC recipient would need to work forty hours a week at $6.90 per hour to make enough to leave AFDC (= $1,104 per month). She would need to earn $7.88 an hour to lose food stamps as well (= $1,261 per month). Yet in moving from $750 per month to $1,500 per month, her net income would rise by only $82 owing to a combination of benefit reductions in both AFDC and food stamps and a reduction in the EITC as earnings enter a "phase out range" for EITC. Unfortunately, the resulting 89 percent tax rate falls precisely on the earnings range that makes the difference between welfare receipt and self-sufficiency.

DIFFERENCES ACROSS STATES

Figure 6 illustrates how different AFDC programs across states affect the benefit amounts received by a family participating in all three programs. The top curve is for our California family; the middle curve is for an identical family who lives in South Carolina. The lowest curve corresponds to the taxes a family would pay if they did not participate in any low-income transfer programs.

The AFDC program is less generous in South Carolina than in California. As a consequence, the net transfers received by the South Carolina family are everywhere below those from California until between $1,250 and $1,500 when both AFDC programs cease to pay benefits. The higher generosity of California's program has a serious downside: California's implicit tax rates on earnings are much higher. The benefit reduction rates are similar, but more is lost for every dollar earned in California because the reduction rate applies to a larger benefit amount. Whereas the tax rate faced by a South Carolina family increasing their earnings from $750 to $1,500 a month is almost 20 percentage points below the rate faced by a California family with the same earnings increase, this lower rate is still 70 percent. Such tax rates are still staggeringly high and surely greatly discourage work.

Summary. There have been two major complaints about the U.S. welfare system. First, it discourages self-sufficiency. Second, it is too expensive. In fact, the two complaints are related, because the expense of the programs (fairly small relative to the federal budget) is seen as money ill-spent if it encourages long-term dependency. Given the high effective tax rates on work for welfare recipients, it is no surprise that most families who receive these combined benefits do not work. Thus there was fairly broad consensus that welfare was a system that needed to be fixed, leading to the welfare reform legislation passed in August 1996.

How Welfare Reform Changes the System

On August 22, 1996, President Clinton signed into law H.R. 3734, the Personal Responsibility and Work Opportunity Reconciliation Act of 1996. This legislation makes significant changes in the already complex welfare landscape. The major programs of AFDC, SSI, and food stamps

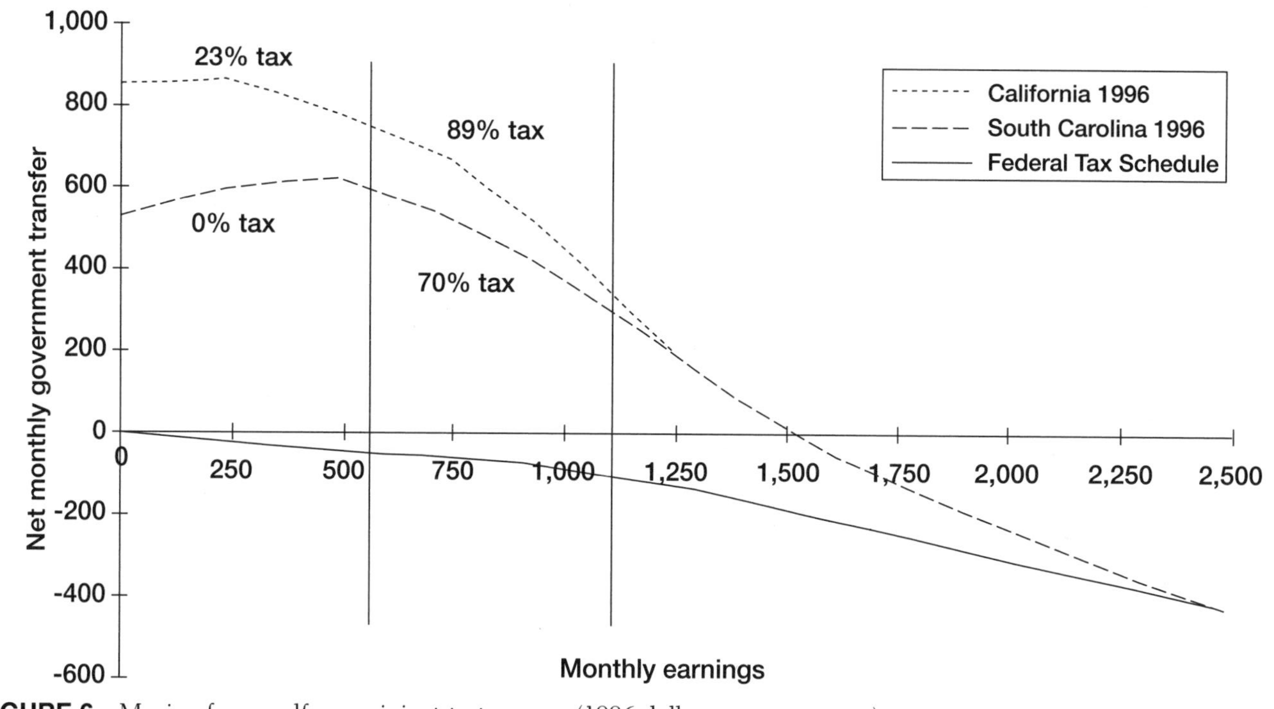

FIGURE 6 Moving from welfare recipient to taxpayer (1996 dollars, no state taxes).

are all affected, with the most radical changes affecting AFDC. In this section, we briefly review the major elements of the welfare reform legislation, identifying how the basic structure of the system has been modified to alter governmental responsibilities and the coordination of programs.

CASH WELFARE: TEMPORARY ASSISTANCE FOR NEEDY FAMILIES (TANF)

The most fundamental change in the reform legislation is the elimination of the AFDC program. In its place, states will provide Temporary Assistance for Needy Families (TANF) with block grants funded by the federal government. The block grant amount is equal to the federal AFDC expenditures for the relevant state in fiscal 1995. Since caseloads have fallen as a result of the economic recovery, the block grant amount is currently higher than the federal share would have been under AFDC, so most states are likely to gain over the next several years.

Cash welfare under the block grants will differ from AFDC in a number of ways.

No entitlement to cash welfare. By block granting TANF, the federal government eliminated the entitlement to cash welfare. An entitlement means that all eligible applicants to a program are funded, and the funding level depends on the number of recipients. In the absence of an entitlement, the budget for a program is fixed, and eligible applicants may be denied benefits if the funding runs out.[4]

Flexibility in use of funds, state maintenance of effort. The block grant gives each state much greater flexibility in its use of state and federal funds for public assistance. However, the reform legislation does require states to maintain nonfederal (state and local) spending on public assistance at 80 percent of fiscal year 1994 spending on AFDC and related programs.

TANF recipients are required to work within two years. To receive the entire block grant, states must ensure that TANF recipients participate

4. The elimination of the AFDC entitlement applies to federal funding but need not apply to state funding. Prior to this reform, AFDC benefit payments were funded 50-50 by state and federal dollars. This matching payment relationship is broken down under block grants. Therefore, although the federal funding is no longer an entitlement, the state could continue to treat cash welfare as an entitlement by funding benfits beyond the block grant entirely out of state funds.

in work activities. The state is sanctioned (loses part of its grant) unless 25 percent of federally funded cases are working in 1997 and 50 percent are working by 2002. Work requirements are particularly stringent for two-parent families: 75 percent of these families must work in 1997, and 90 percent must work by 1999.

A family is considered to be working if an adult is participating in employment, on-the-job training, vocational education, job search, or community service. A single parent must work at least 20 hours per week in 1997 and 1998. The required hours rise to 30 per week in 2000. From 1997 on, adults in two-parent families must work at least 35 hours per week.

While the state sanctions are based on the share of the total caseload working, an individual family cannot receive aid for more than twenty-four months without working. The state has the option to exempt families with children under the age of one. Recipients who refuse to participate in work activities must be sanctioned.

A family cannot receive TANF benefits for more than five years. In addition to the two-year time limit for receiving aid without working, TANF prohibits a family from receiving block grant funds for more than five years. This is a lifetime limit, cumulative across welfare spells. A state may exempt up to 20 percent of families from this time limit.

Other provisions. The welfare reform legislation also includes provisions to discourage teenage pregnancy and out-of-wedlock births. Under the block grants, teen parents cannot receive TANF unless they attend school and live with their parents or other supervisory adults. In addition, a family's grant must be reduced by 25 percent for failure to cooperate in establishing paternity.

Finally, the legislation gives the state the option to make two additional reforms. TANF rules permit states to deny additional benefits for children born to families on welfare. This is known as imposing a family cap on benefits. The legislation also permits states to set grant levels for people who move from another state to the grant level in the former state of residence.

Medicaid eligibility continues. In the shift from AFDC to TANF, states may not change the eligibility rules for Medicaid. In other words, all persons who would have been eligible for AFDC and thus for Medicaid must continue to receive Medicaid under the income-eligibility rules in place on July 16, 1996. However, states may deny Medicaid to capable adults who refuse to work.

FOOD STAMPS AND SUPPLEMENTAL SECURITY INCOME

The Personal Responsibility and Work Opportunity Reconciliation Act of 1996 addresses not only AFDC and TANF but also many other public assistance programs, including the two other major cash or near-cash programs: food stamps and Supplemental Security Income (SSI). The SSI and food stamps reforms include a variety of administrative changes intended to rationalize and streamline procedures. The two most substantial changes to benefits under food stamps and SSI are discussed below.

Food stamps: Benefit reductions, work requirements. The food stamp change that has prompted the greatest outcry is the imposition of work requirements. Childless recipients between the ages of eighteen and fifty will be denied food stamps if they receive benefits for more than three months while not working. H.R. 3734 also reduces food stamp benefits by 3 percent across the board and makes some changes that reduce benefits by increasing the income counted when determining benefits.

SSI: No payments to inmates, reduced eligibility of children. The SSI reforms are designed to address two areas of perceived abuse in the program. First, the legislation sets up procedures to help ensure that SSI payments are not made to prison inmates. Second, the legislation eliminates benefits to less disabled children, particularly children with behavioral problems rather than physical disorders.

LEGAL IMMIGRANTS: BARRED FROM SSI AND FOOD STAMPS

Deep reductions in immigrant eligibility for welfare constitutes one of the most dramatic elements of the welfare reform legislation. For the first time, citizenship or substantial U.S. work history will be required for welfare eligibility. Such states as California will be greatly affected by these restrictions, since 38 percent of all noncitizens in the U.S. reside in California.

Prior to H.R. 3734, legal permanent residents could qualify for participation in all major public assistance programs. Under the new law, all legal immigrants, including those already in the country, will be denied SSI and food stamps unless they have worked in the United

States for forty quarters (the Social Security qualification period) or become citizens.[5] States are also permitted to deny permanent residents cash welfare assistance and Medicaid. Newly arrived legal immigrants would be denied eligibility for all federal means-tested programs for five years after arrival.[6] After this period, new arrivals are treated like current resident immigrants. For example, if a state continues Medicaid eligibility for immigrants, new arrivals would be banned from the program for the first five years and then become eligible.

There are a few exceptions to these rules. Within the first five years after arrival, refugees and asylees remain eligible for means-tested public assistance. After this initial five-year period, however, they are treated like other legal permanent residents. In addition, immigrants who are veterans or active armed forces personnel or their dependents are eligible for benefits.

Concluding Remarks

The welfare reform was designed to promote self-sufficiency, decrease costs, and improve flexibility in the design of welfare programs. Will the reforms also improve coordination of programs making up the welfare system and clarify some of the diffusion of governmental responsibilities? The answer is yes, though improvements are likely to be quite modest without careful consideration of the relevant issues.

The fundamental structural change that clearly defines responsibility involves the replacement of the AFDC program by TANF. Under the new TANF program, states are fully responsible for the design and implementation of the core welfare program, a program that has served as the basic support of poor families with children during the last five decades in the United States. Each state now has the flexibility to create virtually any welfare system it desires. The TANF regulations explicitly leave many options for state policy makers, including decisions on benefit schedules and family caps, and on the treatment of new residents. In principle, the federal government relinquishes responsibilities

5. Under the new legislation, illegal immigrants are denied all federal, state, and local benefits, means-tested or otherwise.

6. Certain emergency services are excepted: emergency medical assistance, short-term non-cash disaster relief, public health assistance for immunization and serious communicable diseases, and community-level in-kind services such as soup kitchens.

and, more important, its onerous regulations on what states can and cannot do.

The various mandates contained in the federal legislation, particularly those concerning time limits and work requirements, might lead some to surmise that the federal government is not turning over welfare to the states without significant rules, but this interpretation fails to appreciate how easily these mandates are likely to be overcome. They apply only to the federal block grant funding under TANF, and, further limiting the restrictions, the definition of work is quite broad in assessing time limits and work requirements. Under AFDC, the state contributed up to half of the funding for benefits. This state funding is not subject to the TANF regulations. Theoretically, then, each state could establish almost any program and use its funding to support families that are denied benefits under the federal rules, and use the federal money just to fund those TANF participants who satisfy the regulations. The level of the federal funding will typically permit this option because substantially more than half of the AFDC participants met the new TANF regulations under the old system. For example, if a state wanted to keep the old AFDC program as its own, it could satisfy the work requirements by putting all working welfare families in the TANF-funded program and create an entirely state funded program to support nonworking families. Consequently, the federal TANF regulations impose few constraints on the state.

Although welfare reform offers considerable opportunities for progress, policy makers must understand the issues and meticulously craft programs to exploit these opportunities. Of the myriad of public assistance programs sponsored by the federal government, only one, albeit a critical one, has experienced any significant reform. The remaining programs (food stamps, SSI, housing assistance, Medicaid, and EITC) are as inflexible as ever and are generally ignorant of what is going on in the rest of the system. To mitigate the adverse effects of simultaneous participation in these programs, state authorities must design their versions of TANF fully recognizing how other programs operate individually and in combination, as well as taking full advantage of whatever flexibility they have to modify existing federal and state policies. Through a judicious design of a TANF program, states are now capable of creating a wide range of systems offering particular levels of support and incentives for their welfare participants. Accomplishing this task is indeed a challenge, but it is a challenge that represents a promising opportunity that has been unavailable during the past four decades.

REFERENCES

Holtzblatt, Janet, Janet McCubbin, and Robert Gillette. 1994. "Promoting Work through the EITC." *National Tax Journal* 47, no. 3 (September): 591–607.

Kosters, Marvin H. 1993. "The Earned Income Tax Credit and the Working Poor." *American Enterprise* 4 (May/June): 64–72.

U.S. House of Representatives, Committee on Ways and Means. "Overview of Entitlement Programs." *1994 Green Book.*

WEB SITES

Arizona Legislative Information System. "Food Stamp Definitions." Http://www.azleg.state.az.us:80/ars/42/1381. Accessed 1/8/97. Last updated 1/4/96.

Boulder Valley School District, Boulder, Colo.: Food Stamps. "Food Stamps, by Amy Herr-Ross." From Vocal Point 2/96. Http://bvsd.k12.co.us/schools/cent/Newspaper/feb95/FOOD_STAMPS.html. Accessed 1/6/97.

California Department of Finance: Governor's Budget Summary—Federal Block Grants. "Where We Are Going." Http://www.dof.ca.gov/html/budgt6–7/fedblk.htm. Accessed 1/6/97. Last revised 1/10/96.

General Assembly of the State of Ohio: Ohio Revised Code. "Section 4141.161." Http://38.223.23.20:80/stacks/orc/title-41/sec-4141/sec-4141.161.htm. Accessed 1/8/97. Last modified 8/1/96.

Health Care Financing Administration. "1996 HCFA Statistics at a Glance." Http://www.hcfa.gov/stats/stathili.htm. Accessed 1/5/97. Last updated 10/4/96.

National Housing Institute: Progressive Housing Plan. "National Housing Institute: A Progressive Housing Plan for America." Http://www.nhi.org/about/prog.html. Accessed 1/8/97. Last updated 11/27/96.

National Performance Review. "USDA07: Deliver Food Stamp Benefits Via Electronic Benefits Transfer to Improve Service to Customers While Remaining Cost-Effective." Http://www.npr.gov/cgi-bin/print_hi...brary/reports/ag07.html?food + stamps. Accessed 1/6/97.

New Hampshire Division of Public Health Services: WIC Nutrition Programs. "WIC Nutrition Services. New Hampshire WIC Program." Http://www.mednexus.com/nhdphs/wic.html. Accessed 1/2/97.

Social Security Online. "Supplemental Security Income." SSA Publication No. 05–11000, March 1996. Http://www.ssa.gov/pubs/11000.html#Part1. Accessed 1/2/97. Last updated 12/30/96.

Texas Health and Human Services Commission: Texas Medicaid reform FAQ. #1. "What Is Medicaid?" Http://www.hhsc.state.tx.us/medfaq.html. Accessed 1/6/97. Last updated 8/24/95.

Texas Low Income Housing Home Page: Public Housing Information. "Federal Housing Programs: Public Housing." Http://uts.cc.utexas.edu:80/~txlihis/phinfo.html. Accessed 1/8/97. Last updated 8/13/96.

Texas Low Income Housing Home Page: U.S. Housing Conditions. "Housing Conditions: The State of Housing in the U.S." Http://uts.cc.utexas.edu;80/~txlihis/ushcond.html#anchor118663. Accessed 1/8/97. Last updated 8/13/96.

U.S. Department of Agriculture. "USDA Agency Missions: Food, Nutrition, and Consumer Services." Http://www.usda.gov/mission/fncs.hhtm. Accessed 1/5/97. Last updated 12/17/96.

U.S. Department of Agriculture: Food and Consumer Service. "Introduction to the Food Stamp Program." Http://www.usda.gov/fcs/stamps/fsintro.htm. Accessed 1/2/97. Last updated 12/16/96.

U.S. Department of Agriculture: Food and Consumer Service. "Nutrition Program Facts—Food Stamp Program, November 1996." Http://www.usda.gov/fcs/library/961101–3.txt. Accessed 1/2/97. Last updated 12/16/96.

U.S. Department of Agriculture: Food and Consumer Service. "Nutrition Program Facts—National School Lunch Program, November 1996." Http://www.usda.gov/fcs/library/961101–1.txt. Accessed 1/7/97. Last updated 12/16/96.

U.S. Department of Agriculture: Food and Consumer Service. "Nutrition Program Facts—School Breakfast Program, November 1996 Fact Sheet." Http://www.usda.gov/fcs/library/961101–2.txt. Accessed 1/2/97. Last updated 12/16/96.

U.S. Department of Agriculture: Food and Consumer Service. "Nutrition Program Facts—WIC Program, November 1996." Http://www.usda.gov/fcs/library/961101–4.txt. Accessed 1/2/97. Last updated 12/16/96.

U.S. Department of Agriculture: Food and Consumer Service. "Some Food Stamp Facts." Http://www.usda.gov/fcs/stamps/fsfacts.htm. Accessed 1/3/97. Last updated 12/16/96.

U.S. Department of Health and Human Services. "10.553: School Breakfast Program." Http://aspe.os.dhhs.gov/96cfda/p10553.htm. Accessed 1/4/97. Last updated 12/3/96.

U.S. Department of Health and Human Services. "10.555: National School Lunch Program." Http://aspe.os.dhhs.gov/96cfda/p10555.htm. Accessed 1/2/97. Last updated 12/3/96.

U.S. Department of Health and Human Services. "10.557: Special Supplemental Nutrition Program for Women, Infants, and Children." Http://aspe.os.dhhs.gov/96cfda/p10557.htm. Accessed 1/3/97. Last updated 12/3/96.

U.S. Department of Health and Human Services, Administration for Children and Families, Office of Family Assistance: Fact Sheet. "Aid to Families With Dependent Children Program." Http://www.acf.dhhhs.gov/programs/afdc/afdc.txt. Accessed 1/6/97. Last modified 9/12/96.

U.S. Department of Health and Human Services, Administration for Children and Families. "Fact Sheet: Low Income Home Energy Assistance Program." Http://

www.acf.dhhs.gov/programs/LIHEAP/liheap.txt. Accessed 1/2/97. Last updated 9/28/96.

U.S. Senate: Committee on Finance. "Committee on Finance." Http://www.senate.gov/committee/finance.html. Accessed 1/897. Last modified 1/8/97.

Urban Institute. "Child Nutrition and Health, 2/95." Http://www.urban.org/period/prr25_2j.htm. Accessed 1/3/97. Last updated 12/16/96.

Washington State Legislature. "RCW 82.08.0297." Http://www.leg.wa.gov:80/pub/rcw/title_82/chapter_008/rcw_82_08_0297. Accessed 1/8/97. Last updated 3/15/96.

Part V

Distribution of Income

The Problems of Income Distribution and Related Policy Issues in Korea

In characterizing the nature and capitalist spirit of the Korean economic development model, one of the key issues we have to analyze and evaluate is that of income and wealth distribution. During the last thirty years, the Korean economy accomplished a so-called "compressed" growth, showing an unprecedented high economic growth rate. In terms of quantitative measures of economic development, the Korean model can surely offer excellent lessons for other developing countries. But to evaluate the Korean development model completely and to find suitable policy directions and lessons, we have to focus on more qualitative aspects of development, including problems of equity and fairness. It is very important to examine the distributive problem of the Korean economy in this context of complete evaluation and policy suggestions.

The lack of comprehensive data complicates any real evaluation of the current status of income and wealth distribution in Korea. Some findings suggest improvement in income distribution in recent times, but there are also counterarguments. The lack of data on wealth holding is even more serious. Since it is generally believed that there is severe inequality in wealth holding, the general public perception of distributive justice tends to be rather skeptical in spite of some official indicators showing a relatively equal distribution. The judgment on the distributive status itself would provide a crucial insight into the nature and future development of the Korean capitalist model.

This paper is another attempt to evaluate the current status of distribution in Korea, using the annual Urban Households Income and

Expenditure Survey and the Daewoo panel data for the period after the 1980s. The key question is whether, and to what extent, income distribution has improved or worsened in the 1980s and 1990s and what an appropriate policy stance for distributive justice should be. Following the analyses of income distribution, we attempt to measure the inequality of wealth distribution and find the absolute and relative size of poverty using the same data. In combining all the findings that are inevitably based on incomplete data, we have done our best to make an objective evaluation of the distributive accomplishment of the Korean economy and to provide policy suggestions.

The paper is organized as follows. In the next section, we summarize the debates on the current status of income distribution and present our new estimates on the inequality of income distribution in the 1980s and 1990s. This is followed by our estimates on wealth distribution, which show that inequality in the distribution of wealth is the core element of the inequality in distribution. We report the absolute and relative size of poverty for recent periods. Based on our new estimates and evaluations, we then suggest a policy stance and directions for distributive equity; this discussion will include some tax and chaebol policy issues from a distributive perspective. The last section summarizes our main conclusions.

Income Distribution in the 1980s

Several data and findings suggest that income distribution has improved in Korea in the last decade or so. The most important among these may be data from the Statistical Office and the research results of the late Dr. Hakchung Choo of the Korea Development Institute (KDI). Dr. Choo's studies on income distribution in Korea are known for their thorough examination of the underlying data, and these two pieces of evidence are consistent with each other in showing a decrease in income inequality at least in the period after 1980. As noted, the single most serious problem in estimating income distribution in Korea has been the scarcity of reliable and comprehensive data. So far, the best sources may be the annual Urban Households Income and Expenditure Survey (UHIES) and the Farm Households Economic Survey (FHES), but neither of these two reports investigates income distribution as such, and their data, while useful in other ways, cannot be of much help in analyses of income distribution. The standard way to overcome this difficulty has been to add assumptions, some of which are quite arbitrary.

IS INCOME DISTRIBUTION IMPROVING?

The two prominent researchers whose extraordinary efforts to solve the data problems for the analyses of income distribution in Korea were Dr. Surjit S. Bhalla (1979) of the World Bank and the late Dr. Hakchung Choo of KDI. The latter's research has been widely quoted by scholars both in Korea and abroad. His research results are summarized in Table 1.

According to Dr. Choo's figures, income inequality in all sectors, including urban and rural areas, decreased in the late 1960s, rose in the early 1970s, and has been decreasing since 1976. The current level of inequality in Korea is now comparable to that of advanced capitalist countries. The lower rate of income inequality in the rural area compared with the urban sector is to be expected considering the vast number of small farms in Korea. Income inequality in cities among both workers and nonworkers (employers and the self-employed) has followed essentially the same trend over time; inequality among the latter group is much higher than that of the former. Indeed, the overall income inequality in Korea may very well depend on the level of inequality among employers and the self-employed, a large group that includes wealthy owners of big firms and poor barbers and owners of small shops. Because, for some reason or other, government statistics do not include information on the income of this group, any analysis of income distribution has to make certain arbitrary assumptions, which of course can differ depending on who is doing the analyzing.

The Statistical Office has conducted four surveys to date since

TABLE 1 Income Inequalities in Korea, 1965–1990 (Gini Coefficients)

Year	*National*	*Farm*	*Nonfarm*	*Workers*	*Nonworkers*
1965	0.344	0.285	0.417	0.399	0.384
1970	0.332	0.295	0.346	0.304	0.353
1976	0.391	0.327	0.412	0.355	0.449
1982	0.357	0.306	0.371	0.309	0.445
1986	0.337	0.297	0.342	0.319	—
1990	0.323	0.299	0.324	0.305	—

NOTE: Nonworkers = employers and the self-employed.
SOURCES: Choo and Yoon (1984); Choo (1992).

1980. The results, shown in Table 2, are quite consistent with those of Dr. Choo: the data show that income inequality in Korea has rapidly and steadily declined, in both urban and rural areas. However, the magnitude of the Gini coefficient, 0.310 in 1993, is too low by international standards and so casts some doubt on the quality of the data.

Some additional evidence. Some additional evidence that suggests improvement in income distribution in Korea comes from the Savings Market Survey that has been conducted annually since 1967 by the Bank of Korea. The sample size is 2,500 households in urban areas. The purpose of this survey is to discover the motivation, size, and forms of household savings, but we can find some information on income as well. In the published version of the survey, households are classified by the size of income, and we can compute the approximate value of the Gini coefficient out of this grouped data by applying the method developed by Nanak Kakwani (1981). The results (Table 3) show that income inequality declined remarkably at least up to 1988 and then leveled into a fairly stable trend. Although the data are to some extent limited in both the representativeness and sample size, the magnitude of the changes in income distribution would seem to be strong further evidence supporting the improvement argument in the equality of income distribution.

Other sources of evidence suggesting improvement in income distribution are the numerous surveys of wages and earnings. The UHIES contains valuable data on incomes of worker households (Table 4). Though we do not know much about property income or unearned income, we can get a clear-cut picture of the distribution of labor income since the early 1960s. The level of income inequality among

TABLE 2 Income Inequality in the Social Statistical Survey, 1980–1993 (Gini Coefficients)

Year	*National*	*Urban*	*Rural*
1980	0.388	0.405	0.356
1985	0.363	0.385	0.320
	(0.344)[a]	(0.369)[a]	(0.297)[a]
1988	0.336	0.350	0.290
1993	0.310	0.306	0.310

SOURCE: Statistical Office, Social Indicators in Korea, 1987, 1990, 1993.
[a]Old estimates.

TABLE 3 Income Inequality According to Savings Market Survey, 1967–1995

Year	*Survey coverage*	*Sample size*	*Gini coefficient*
1967	40 cities	2,822	.444
1969	Nation	4,500	.395
	10 cities		.378
1978	Urban		.329
	3 cities	4,936	.326
	Rural		.317
1984	Urban	2,000	.305
1988	51 cities	2,500	.289
1990	67 cities	2,500	.297
1995	73 cities	2,500	.286

SOURCE: Bank of Korea, *Savings Market Survey*.

worker households showed some fluctuations until 1976. It should be noted that there was an income cap at that time so only households with income below that level were surveyed, hence it is hard for us to say anything about the true state of the distribution of income for this period. However, the trend of income inequality after 1976 looks clear enough. We no longer have an income cap in the survey, and the Gini coefficient has shifted continuously downward. This leads us to conclude that income distribution, at least among urban worker households, has improved since 1976.

Further evidence suggesting the decrease of income inequality among workers is to be found in the Occupational Wage Survey of the Ministry of Labor, which contains the wage data for individual workers on the payroll of firms in the private sector that employ ten or more

TABLE 4 Income Inequality Among Urban Worker Households, 1963–1994

Year	*Sample size*	*Income cap*	*Average income*	*Gini coefficient*
1963	955	500.0	6.0	.341
1965	998	500.0	8.5	.300
1970	890	2,000.0	28.2	.277
1976	981	4,200.0	88.3	.332
1980	2,458	—	234.1	.316
1985	2,667	—	431.2	.314
1990	2,820	—	943.3	.304
1994				.277

SOURCE: Statistical office, Urban Households Income and Expenditure Survey.

workers. As Table 5 shows, the overall trend in the Occupational Wage Survey is a decrease in wage differentials: the wage gap among different occupations shows a movement of an inverse U-shape with the year 1976 as its peak. The income premium of relatively high income occupations such as professional, technical, managerial, and clerical over the blue collar has decreased by a substantial margin over the last two decades. We can hardly imagine such a substantial narrowing of the wage gap in such a short period in any other country. Although this is not direct evidence of the improvement in the distribution of income itself among worker households, it strongly suggests that this is the situation.

IS INCOME DISTRIBUTION GETTING WORSE? NEW ESTIMATES

Though arguments that income distribution in Korea is improving have been accepted by the Korean government as well as academic circles, some new findings that indicate the opposite have appeared recently. The problem has been approached in two ways. One is the research conducted mainly by economists at Choong-Ang University, who, using essentially the same data as Dr. Choo, obtained completely different results. The other is research that focuses on distributive justice and/or the explosion of unearned income in Korea.

Results of research on income distribution in Korea conducted by economists at Choong-Ang University have been presented by Kim and Ahn (1987), Kang (1990), Ahn and Kang (1990), and Ahn (1995); Iwamoto (1989) showed similar results. (See Table 6.) Like Dr. Choo, they used data from the Urban Family Income and Expenditure Survey and the Farm Households Economic Survey, but they applied many different assumptions. These data sets are in many ways not suitable for the analyses of income distribution: single-person households are excluded from the survey; the ratios of people who are considered unemployed

TABLE 5 Changes in Occupational Wage Differentials, 1971–1994

Year	*Prof./tech.*	*Managerial*	*Clerical*	*Sales*	*Services*	*Blue collar*
1971	250	359	204	118	90	100
1976	292	474	222	112	103	100
1980	246	395	162	89	100	100
1985	234	340	153	136	99	100
1990	173	256	131	98	87	100
1994	150	218	114	87	87	100

SOURCE: Ministry of Labor, Occupational Wage Survey.

TABLE 6 Estimates of Income Equality in Korea, 1965–1993 (Gini Coefficients)

Year	*Choo (1992)*	*Kim-Ahn (1987)*	*Iwamoto (1989)*	*Ahn-Kang (1990)*	*Ahn (1995)*
1965	0.344	0.365	—	—	0.272
1970	0.332	0.346	—	0.314	0.288
1976	0.391	0.408	0.398	0.391	0.346
1982	0.357	0.406	0.394	0.385	0.377
1986	0.337	0.411[a]	0.413	0.393	0.377
1990	0.323	—	—	—	0.402
1993	—	—	—	—	0.380

[a] 1985.

are different from the figure in the macroeconomic statistics; there is no information on the income of employers and the self-employed. As a matter of fact, the distributive results would be quite different if we were to choose different assumptions on each of these problems. In other words, we obtain different Gini coefficients depending on how many unemployed people we add to the original data, how much we assume the income of the unemployed to be, how we treat single-person households, and so on.

However, even using different assumptions, we might reasonably expect to get similar results when we all use the same data. The results are, on the contrary, quite different. New estimates of income distribution generally show not only much higher Gini coefficients than those of Dr. Choo, but also rising coefficients in the 1980s. Professor Ahn concludes his recent paper (1995) this way: "Income distribution in Korea did not improve in the 1980s, but stayed at the same level up to the mid-1980s, and then worsened in the latter half of the 1980s. . . . The year of the worst income distribution in Korea was 1989, with income inequality improving in the 1990s."

These results, especially the argument that income inequality rose in the latter half of the 1980s, directly contradict the results of Dr. Choo and the Statistical Office, which concluded that income inequality had been declining throughout the 1980s. These two completely different views on the issue, one that income distribution is getting better, and the other that it is getting worse, cannot both be right. But how to determine which opinion is the more accurate? To arrive at an answer, we tried to access the two major data sets used by both groups of economists to estimate income distribution in Korea, the UHIES and the FHES. Unfortunately, we could not access the FHES. Only the tape data of UHIES after 1982 were available to us. We had no other choice but to limit our attention to urban income distribution.

As noted earlier, the main drawback to using the UHIES in income distribution analyses is that it has no data on the income of nonworker households (employers and the self-employed); it does, however, have consumption data for this group, which make it possible to estimate the income of these households by, first, estimating their consumption function, and, second, putting the consumption figure in the consumption function to arrive at the income level. We assumed the consumption function for nonworker households to be the same as that for worker households. The consumption function is specified as follows:

$$C = \alpha + \beta Y + \gamma W + \delta F + \eta DH + \epsilon \tag{1}$$

where C stands for consumption, Y is income, W is wealth (the sum of the cash balance at the end of the period, the imputed value of rent, and the imputed value of the owner-occupied housing), F is the size of the households, DH is a dummy variable for house owners, and is the error term. This is a seemingly crude formula, but we could not think of a better way to derive the incomes of the employers and the self-employed households. We assumed that the magnitudes of the parameters, α, β, γ, δ, η are the same for both worker and nonworker households. Because we have information on C, W, and F of nonworker households, we could derive their incomes. All four explanatory variables in the regression turned out to be significant at the level of one percent, and the adjusted-R^2 was between 0.22 and 0.45.

After calculating the incomes of the nonworker households, we could analyze the distribution of income in the urban areas. The results of analyses are summarized in Table 7. Since the inequality measures sometimes move in different directions, we adopted several measures to double-check. The measures are the Gini coefficients, coefficients of variation, log variances, and the decile distribution of income. The results show that all four measures indicate improvement in income distribution at least up to 1988. After that year the decile distribution of income and the Gini coefficient stopped moving downward, and the coefficient of variation and the log variance actually increased. Since the coefficient of variation is known to be very sensitive to the incomes of the upper class, this may be a sign of widening disparity in income. But since the Gini coefficient, and especially the decile distribution of

TABLE 7 Urban Income Distribution, 1982–1994

Deciles	*1982*	*1985*	*1988*	*1991*	*1994*
First	1.85	1.97	2.31	2.13	2.08
Second	3.73	3.95	4.25	4.36	4.25
Third	5.04	5.20	5.40	5.50	5.56
Fourth	6.13	6.25	6.39	6.53	6.59
Fifth	7.25	7.24	7.42	7.56	7.57
Sixth	8.48	8.46	8.58	8.58	8.62
Seventh	9.98	9.98	10.05	10.04	10.21
Eighth	12.14	12.10	12.07	11.89	12.05
Ninth	15.65	15.57	15.36	15.17	14.99
Tenth	29.76	29.29	28.16	28.57	28.09
Decile gaps[a]	2.711	2.611	2.372	2.362	2.331
Gini coefficient	0.393	0.384	0.365	0.365	0.363
Coeff. of var.	0.963	0.979	0.905	1.049	1.101
Log var.	0.871	0.876	0.685	0.747	0.759

SOURCE: Statistical office, UHIES (computer tapes).

[a] Decile gaps = the income shares of the top two deciles divided by those of the bottom four deciles.

income, has shown no signs of going up, we could safely conclude that income distribution did not worsen in this period. These findings lead us to conclude that urban income distribution improved during the 1980s and stayed essentially the same in the early 1990s.

Table 8 shows that income inequality among worker households has evidently declined. The Gini estimates for the worker households in this table almost match those reported by Dr. Choo. The Gini coefficients in the 1980s were in the neighborhood of 0.31, and slightly declining. The Gini coefficient for 1994 is remarkably lower than in the

TABLE 8 Income Inequalities Among Worker and Nonworker Households in Urban Areas, 1982–1994

	Worker households					*Nonworker households*				
	1982	*1985*	*1988*	*1991*	*1994*	*1982*	*1985*	*1988*	*1991*	*1994*
Gini	0.317	0.319	0.311	0.285	0.277	0.478	0.467	0.442	0.472	0.485
C.V.[a]	0.668	0.670	0.650	0.636	0.627	1.183	1.245	1.140	1.393	1.558
Log var.	0.731	0.803	0.602	0.578	0.499	1.087	1.000	0.842	1.049	1.165

NOTE: Nonworkers = employers and the self-employed.

SOURCE: Statistical Office, VHIES (computer tapes).

[a] C.V. = Coefficient of variation.

1980s. For nonworker households, however, we obtained different results. All three of the inequality measures decreased up to 1988, but reversed after that year. The Gini coefficient and the log variance rose slightly, and the coefficient of variation rose noticeably. Since the coefficient of variation is especially sensitive to the movement of income among the richest, a new development in the 1990s calls for caution, especially because nonworker households, which cover a wide range of occupations and classes, are very important in determining the overall distribution of income in the urban areas. We found the Gini coefficient of these households, 0.47–0.48, to be a little higher than that estimated by Dr. Choo. The overall movement of income inequality in all urban households seems to be a clear decline up to 1988 and a very slow decline since then. However, owing to our uncertainty about income inequality among nonworker households, the possibility of an actual increase in income inequality in the latter subperiod cannot be totally ruled out.

How does this finding compare with the earlier research results? It conforms to that of Dr. Choo in the sense that income inequality declined in the 1980s, though the magnitude of improvement in our finding is much less than in Dr. Choo's. Our results do not support the findings of the Choong-Ang University economists, who asserted that income distribution did worsen in the 1980s. On the contrary, it appears more likely that income distribution improved in the 1980s, and perhaps has not changed much in the 1990s. It is not implausible that it may have actually worsened in the 1990s. Viewed in this way, our finding differs from the existing two schools of the debate. The three points of view are summarized in Table 9 along with our findings. Dr. Choo and the Statistical Office say income inequality has continuously and substantially declined in the 1980s. The economists at Choong-Ang University say it has stayed constant or rose a little in the 1980s. We contend that neither is correct. We believe that income inequality decreased in the 1980s, but not by as much as Dr. Choo's estimates, and has been almost constant in the 1990s.

Still, because the data on rural income distribution are missing, our findings do not allow any definite conclusion on the overall distribution of income in Korea. To fill in the gap, we tried to get a rough measure of income distribution in the rural areas from the published version of the FHES. We found some grouped rural data for just two years, 1967 and 1988. By using the Kakwani method of approximation, we could compute a Gini coefficient of 0.324 for 1967 and 0.288 for 1988. This

TABLE 9 Comparisons of Urban Inequalities, 1976–1994 (Gini Coefficients)

Year	*Choo 1992*	*Statistical Office 1995*	*Ahn-Kang 1990*	*Whang-Lee 1996*
1976	0.412		0.461	
1980		0.405	0.416	
1982	0.371		0.442	0.393
1985		0.389	0.443	0.384
1986	0.342		0.443	
1988		0.350	0.447	0.365
1990	0.324			
1991				0.365
1993		0.306		
1994				0.363

NOTE: The units of analyses are a little different across the studies. Nonfarm households were used for Dr. Choo, nonfarm and nonfishery households were used for Ahn, Kang, and urban households were used for our study.

is, of course, very limited information, but it suggests a downward movement of income inequality in the rural area. Based on this, we find it hard to accept the Choong-Ang University economists' assertion that the equality of income distribution deteriorated in the 1980s. Using the same data, but with some different assumptions and methods, we reach a different conclusion. Owing to the limitations of the two data sets, we cannot completely rule out the possibility that income distribution actually worsened in the 1980s, but we do think it unlikely that data from the UHIES and the FHES tell us that income inequality actually rose in the 1980s.

It may be interesting to compare the distribution of income in Korea with that of Japan. Table 10 shows Japan's income distribution in 1988. The Gini coefficient of worker households in Japan was 0.310, almost the same as the Korean figure for the same year. But there is a

TABLE 10 Income Inequality in Japan, 1988

	Gini coefficients
Nation	.365
Employers, self-employed	.368
Employers	.315
Self-employed	.415
Worker households	.310

SOURCE: Department of Welfare (Japan), *Basic Survey of People's Living*, 1988.

big difference between the two countries for employers and the self-employed (nonworkers). The Gini coefficient is 0.368 in Japan, significantly lower than the Korean counterpart for 1988, 0.442. The difference in income distribution between the two countries is clearly traceable to the nonworker households.

THE INEQUALITY IN CONSUMPTION EXPENDITURES

Another aspect of the distribution of economic well-being worth examining is the distribution of consumption expenditures of households. Such an examination would be illuminating in several ways. Consumption expenditures are important measures of the economic welfare of households, and in some sense income and wealth are the means to achieve the objectives of maximizing consumption expenditures. Also, of course, consumption expenditures would be useful data in view of the paucity of data on income of employers and the self-employed in the UHIES. A third point has to do with the reluctance of respondents to a survey to state their income or wealth accurately; fearing that a frank response may increase their tax burdens in the future, many people understate income. Respondents are more likely to be truthful in answering questions about consumption expenditures. This often makes the reliability of consumption data higher than income or wealth data.

To analyze recent changes in the distribution of consumption expenditures, we computed the Gini coefficient of all households, worker households, and nonworker households. Table 11 shows that consumption inequality stayed constant for households as a whole during the 1982–1991 period and declined in 1994. Consumption inequality among worker households, however, rose in the 1980s, as it at the same time declined among nonworkers. For reasons yet to be determined, these findings contradict our analyses of income distribution in the same period. It would be very interesting to know the reasons behind

TABLE 11 Consumption Inequality in the Urban Sector (Gini Coefficients), 1982–1994

Households (HHs)	*1982*	*1985*	*1988*	*1991*	*1994*
All HHs	0.330	0.337	0.332	0.333	0.316
Worker HHs	0.311	0.325	0.322	0.327	0.312
Nonworker HHs	0.351	0.352	0.344	0.335	0.320

SOURCE: Statistical Office, UHIES (computer tapes).

these results, but it seems that the diverging movements of the distribution of consumption expenditures across the two groups brought about the almost constant degree of consumption inequality in the 1980s.

The Distribution of Wealth

Though we found some evidence to support the assertion that income distribution improved in the 1980s, it is hard to conclude definitely that it actually happened. The evidence of the UHIES and FHES data, which are most frequently used for analyses of income distribution in Korea, suggests that income distribution has not worsened. Obviously, we cannot assume that these data cover the vast amount of unearned income that seems to have accrued to the rich in the 1980s as a result of skyrocketing real estate prices and the stock market boom. Quite understandably, because the speed at which land prices rose far exceeded that of other commodities, people believe that a small number of landowners benefited.

According to a study by Toung-Woo Lee (1991), the amount of realized capital gains increased very rapidly in the 1980s, culminating around 1989. The booming stock market in the late 1980s further increased unearned income. For 1988, the realized capital gains from land seem to have reached around 20 percent of the GNP, and those from the stock market about 5 percent. The sum of all capital gains realized in 1988 was almost half of the total labor income in that year. When we add these kinds of unearned income to the normal income, the equality of income distribution must deteriorate significantly.

In 1988 the Gini coefficient was 0.336, as reported by the Statistical Office; adding capital gains from land as a part of income raises it to 0.388; adding also income from the stock market raises it to 0.412. Since a Gini coefficient of 0.336 looks too low to start with, it is likely that the overall distribution of income including capital gains exceeded 0.412 in 1988. Thus when we consider that capital gains are very unlikely to be caught in the households income survey, we cannot deny the possibility of worsening income distribution in the 1980s. In summary, we do not deny the possibility of rising income inequality in the 1980s, but we do not think the household survey data of UHIES and FHES suggest worsening income distribution.

The distribution of income in Korea may well compare favorably with that of other countries, yet many people believe that the core of inequality in Korea lies in the concentration of wealth, especially land, in a few hands. Korean land prices are so high that the total value of land in Korea, notwithstanding its small size, may rank third-highest in the world, after only Japan and the United States. The ratio of the total value of land to GNP in Korea is around five, which appears to be the highest in the world; usually this ratio is in the neighborhood of one in the advanced capitalist countries except for Japan, which has a notoriously high ratio of three. Undoubtedly, land ownership lies at the heart of household wealth distribution in Korea.

The lack of data on wealth distribution in Korea is not unusual in comparison with other countries. One of the best and first surveys of the distribution of wealth in Korea was the survey of 5,107 households conducted by the Korea Development Institute in 1988. This was the first major national survey to ask household heads about both income and wealth. According to this survey, the Gini coefficient of the distribution of income was 0.40, and that of the distribution of wealth was 0.58. Of the latter, the Gini coefficient of land turned out to be 0.60, and of financial assets 0.77. Economists at the World Bank who tried an international comparison of the distribution of wealth in Korea by utilizing this data concluded that wealth inequality in Korea was about the same as or a little lower than that of other advanced countries.

This does not agree with the popular perception in Korea that there has been a growing gap between wealthy landowners and the rest of the people. This notion may perhaps be due to the incomplete data on the most wealthy in the 1988 KDI survey. In another survey taken in 1990 covering 1,792 households—too small a number to ensure reliability—the Gini coefficients of the distribution of income and wealth were 0.42 and 0.66, respectively, higher than those of the KDI 1988 survey.

In this regard, it is worth mentioning the Daewoo panel data. This survey, conducted in the years 1993, 1994, and 1995, asked about financial assets but not about real assets such as land, houses, and buildings. However, it contains information about the amount of tax paid on land, houses, and buildings, from which we can make some estimates about real assets—always allowing, of course, for a certain degree of unreliability in people's responses to questions about financial assets and losses. In the absence of other sources of information, this survey may be very useful for the analyses of wealth holdings.

Table 12 summarizes the results of household wealth distribution revealed in the Daewoo survey. The Gini coefficients of the distribution

TABLE 12 Distribution of Household Wealth, 1993–1995 (Gini Coefficient)

Year	*Total*	*Buildings*	*Land*	*Real assets (Land + building)*	*Financial assets*
1993	0.788	0.704	0.901	0.837	0.767
1994	0.773	0.696	0.905	0.841	0.724
1995	0.762	0.664	0.900	0.836	0.656

SOURCE: Daewoo panel data, 1993–1995.

of financial assets, land, and buildings show much higher values than previous estimates. For financial assets and buildings, the Gini coefficients are around 0.70; and for land they are over 0.90. The inequality of land and buildings is higher than that of financial assets, contradicting the earlier research results. Which is correct? It seems that our findings match the widespread beliefs in Korea that wealth concentration is of an extraordinary degree.

Some characteristics of household wealth inequality can be found when we disaggregate the Daewoo data by region and by occupation (Table 13). Though the Daewoo panel data showed greater income inequality in rural rather than urban areas, which is hard to explain, wealth inequality was less in rural areas than in urban areas. Big cities show greater wealth inequality than small towns—findings that look quite plausible considering the extremely high price of land in the big cities. Wealth inequality among the self-employed and workers does not differ much.

If we accept these data, we may have to reconsider the results of the international comparisons of wealth inequality attempted by the World Bank economists. Based on the results of the KDI 1988 survey, they concluded that wealth inequality in Korea was comparable to or even lower than that of other advanced capitalist countries. The top

TABLE 13 Household Wealth Inequality, 1993–1995 (Gini Coefficients by Region and Occupation)

Year	*National*	*Rural*	*Urban*	*Big cities*	*Small towns*	*Self-employed*	*Workers*
1993	0.788	0.640	0.800	0.833	0.714	0.822	0.787
1994	0.773	0.752	0.775	0.799	0.730	0.767	0.749
1995	0.762	0.736	0.764	0.789	0.724	0.724	0.743

SOURCE: Daewoo panel data, 1993–1995.

line of Table 14 shows this. Our estimate based on Daewoo panel data, Korea (2), presents a totally different picture. The top 1 percent of households possess 30 percent of total wealth, and the top 5 percent has 53 percent. This degree of concentration cannot be found in advanced capitalist countries, though it may be the case in some less developed countries. Undoubtedly, wealth inequality in Korea is significantly higher than that of advanced countries.

Summing up the discussion so far, we may conclude that the inequality in distribution of household wealth in Korea, especially that of land, is extremely high by international standards. Although we have some evidence of moderate income inequality and some sign of improvement in income distribution, the core element of inequality in distribution of economic well-being in Korea may be found in the concentration of wealth. Policy makers and academicians would do well to pay more attention to this problem in the future.

The Problem of Poverty

The problem of poverty is closely related to income distribution. The best study so far on poverty in Korea is that by Suh and Yeon (1986),

TABLE 14 International Comparisons of Wealth Inequality

				Share of the most wealthy		
Country	*Unit*	*Data*	*Year*	*1%*	*5%*	*10%*
Korea (1)[a]	HH	survey	1988	14	31	43
Korea (2)[b]	HH	survey	1993	30	53	68
Australia	HH	survey	1966	9	25	36
France	HH	survey	1975	13	30	50
Canada	HH	survey	1970	20	43	58
Sweden	HH	survey	1975	21	44	60
New Zealand	ind'l	estate	1966	18	45	60
France	ind'l	estate	1977	19	47	65
Australia	ind'l	estate	1971	20	41	57
United States	ind'l	estate	1969	25	44	53
Britain	ind'l	estate	1980	23	43	58

NOTE: HH = households.

SOURCE: Leipziger et al. (1992, 37).

[a] Korea (1) is based on KDI 1988 survey.

[b] Korea (2) is based on Daewoo panel data, 1993.

which attempts to clarify the amount of both absolute and relative poverty. In this study, for absolute poverty, the authors define the minimum cost of living by adding up the cost for food, clothes, shelter, and miscellaneous items. Households whose income falls short of this minimum level are regarded as absolutely poor. The authors define relative poverty as households whose income is less than one-third the average income, rather than the usual definition of one-half the median income. The discrepancy is insignificant as long as one figure is used consistently. Table 15 summarizes the trends of both absolute and relative poverty over time in Korea as reported by Suh and Yeon. Two caveats are in order when reading the results. One is that the standard of the minimum cost of living taken by the authors is one of the lowest among a dozen estimates published in the last two or three decades; the low standard of poverty inevitably makes the number of absolutely poor people very low. Also, this study has the same limitations in both data and methodology as Dr. Choo's research.

Keeping these in mind, let us look at Table 15. Absolute poverty declined substantially during the two decades of rapid economic growth, dropping from 40.9 percent in 1965 to 4.5 percent in 1984. As a matter of fact, Korea, along with Taiwan, Hong Kong, Singapore, China, and the former Yugoslavia, is appraised by World Bank economists to be a country that has successfully combined economic growth and the reduction of poverty. Compared with such countries as Brazil, Mexico, Malaysia, and the Philippines, all of which had high economic growth rates but failed to reduce poverty, or countries like India, Pakistan, Bangladesh, and Indonesia, which could not reduce poverty sim-

TABLE 15 The Trend of Absolute and Relative Poverty, 1965–1984 (in percent)

	1965	*1970*	*1976*	*1980*	*1984*
Absolute poverty					
All	40.9	23.4	14.8	9.8	4.5
Urban	54.9	16.2	18.1	10.4	4.6
Rural	35.8	27.9	11.7	9.0	4.4
Relative poverty					
All	12.1	4.8	12.5	13.3	7.7
Urban	17.9	7.0	16.0	15.1	7.8
Rural	10.0	3.4	9.2	11.2	7.5

SOURCE: Suh and Yeon (1986).

ply because of their stagnant economies, Korea has alleviated poverty relatively well.

However, notwithstanding the rapid decline in absolute poverty, other poverty factors have changed very little: the number of households whose income falls short of one-third of the average has fluctuated over time with no indication of a clear trend in either direction.

A third point: although the ratio of absolute poverty in urban areas was higher than that in rural areas in the 1960s, by the mid-1980s, both were at 4.5 percent. Whereas in the past the bulk of poverty was in rural areas, by the 1980s, more than 60 percent of the poor lived in cities. This differs from the situation in third world countries, where the majority of the poor live in rural areas, and it is to be accounted for by the unusually high rate of urban migration since industrialization began in Korea in the 1960s.

One should, as noted, be somewhat skeptical of Sun and Yeon's results because of the low minimum cost of living they assumed. According to their findings, the rate of absolute poverty in Korea in the 1980s, 4.5 percent, is lower than that found in advanced capitalist countries.

To see what happens if we extend the analyses of Suh and Yeon into later periods, we used the UHIES and applied their poverty factors, adjusting for inflation. The results are shown in Table 16. Because Suh and Yeon's minimum cost of living was very low to begin with and society's general standard of living has risen substantially during the last quarter century, the poverty line seems too low even after the adjustment for price-level changes. Indeed, absolute poverty turns out to be as low as 1 percent, which is rare in any country. Relative poverty fluctuates around 10–11 percent with no clear trend over time.

Considering the current state of research on poverty in Korea, we feel the need for a new study. What we especially need to know is the extent of absolute poverty, and how it compares with other countries. The starting point for the research would be to determine a more reliable threshold of poverty or the poverty line. Fortunately, a new minimum cost of living was recently reported by the Korea Institute for

TABLE 16 Hypothetical State of Poverty, 1982–1994 (in percent)

	1982	*1985*	*1988*	*1991*	*1994*
Absolute poverty	6.4	3.6	1.5	1.1	1.0
Relative poverty	12.4	11.0	8.8	10.2	11.5

Health and Social Affairs (KIHASA). Based on a nationwide survey of households, this institute published new estimates of the minimum cost of living (Park et al. 1994), which are much more realistic than the earlier ones. We use their results as our poverty line to classify the poor and the non-poor. Since the UHIES covers only urban areas, we used Daewoo panel data to analyze poverty for the nation. The results are reported in Table 17.

Here the two most traditional measures of poverty are used, namely, the head count ratio (HCR) and the poverty gap. The head count ratio is defined as the number of poor households divided by the number of whole households, and the poverty gap is the size of income needed to raise the income of poor households to the poverty line divided by the total income. These measures are often criticized by economists for neglecting the Pigou-Dalton transfer principle. However, one

TABLE 17 Absolute and Relative Poverty and the Poverty Gap

		Absolute poverty		*Relative poverty (mean)*		*Relative poverty (median)*	
	Groups	*HCR*[a]	*Pov. gap*[b]	*HCR*[a]	*Pov. gap*[b]	*HCR*[a]	*Pov. gap*[b]
1993	National	19.02	2.94	12.71	3.13	8.69	1.53
	Rural	50.98	15.86	21.18	4.30	12.56	1.61
	Urban	15.89	2.27	10.79	2.65	7.17	1.31
	Big cities	13.04	1.62	12.95	2.36	5.65	0.83
	Small towns	25.77	5.39	14.17	3.49	12.30	2.26
1994	National	15.83	2.59	22.43	5.28	19.31	4.07
	Rural	40.67	9.86	38.04	7.68	22.97	2.46
	Urban	12.60	1.92	19.43	4.66	16.90	3.62
	Big cities	9.90	1.36	13.80	2.62	16.90	3.71
	Small towns	22.36	4.18	27.75	6.75	24.10	5.30
1995	National	12.95	1.39	26.72	5.92	18.10	3.56
	Rural	34.14	6.96	35.05	7.59	25.68	3.73
	Urban	10.32	1.01	24.16	5.26	16.23	3.13
	Big cities	7.82	0.73	14.64	4.45	14.64	2.39
	Small towns	18.13	2.19	28.23	7.28	23.08	4.99

SOURCE: Daewoo Economic Research Institute, *Korea Households Economic Survey*, 1993–1995.

[a] Head count ratio (HCR) = the number of poor households divided by the number of whole households.

[b] Poverty gap = the size of income needed to raise the income of poor households to the poverty line divided by the total income.

good thing about these two measures is that they are very easy to understand. They simply reveal the number of poor people and to what extent they are poor. The head count ratios show the number of poor, using the minimum cost of living as calculated by the KIHASA as the definition of poor. Because the minimum cost of living was reported only for 1994, we adjusted the consumer price indexes for the adjacent years. The head count ratios of the absolutely poor households turned out to be in the range of 10 to 20 percent. This is evidently higher than those of advanced capitalist countries and looks much more persuasive than the earlier results.

As mentioned above, these data seem to represent the rural area rather poorly. But comparisons of the rural and urban areas show that poverty in the former is much more pervasive than in the latter. This conforms to the casual observations about the destitution of poor peasant households frequently quoted in the press. Similarly, poverty in small towns is greater than in big cities. These findings cast some doubt on the validity and usefulness of previous surveys of impoverished areas, which have been conducted mainly in large cities, as if the core of poverty lay there. Since the extent of poverty turns out to be more severe in the countryside and small towns than in big cities, it seems to be desirable to direct poverty surveys and antipoverty policy measures more toward rural areas.

On the other hand, the poverty gap, which is the necessary amount of income to bring poor households' income at least up to the poverty line, is not great: in most cases it is in the neighborhood of 2 percent of the total income of all households. This suggests that the real cause of poverty lies more in income distribution than in the absolute scarcity of material well-being.

A little improvement in income distribution might contribute greatly to the reduction of poverty. Relative poverty is also higher than in Suh and Yeon's study because their poverty line is set at one-half instead of one-third of the mean income. If we define relative poverty as one-half of the median income, relative poverty goes down a little, which is quite natural considering the asymmetry in the distribution of income.

Policy Issues for Distributive Equity

Although several attempts have been made to measure the degree of income inequality in Korea, how to evaluate the right current distribution status is still an open question. With serious data problems, different assumptions on data manipulation have led to different estimates of income distribution. However, based on recent estimates, including ours, that were presented in the previous section, we can reach the following points on the distribution status in Korea.

1. Income distribution in the early stage of economic development in the 1970s worsened, showing the highest Gini coefficient in 1976.

2. There is no clear explanation of the changing pattern of distribution since the 1980s. Our survey of expenditures showed that income distribution in urban areas improved until 1988 but then began to deteriorate in self-employed and employer households while at the same time it improved in employee households. No steady trend is seen in income distribution in urban areas in the 1990s; however, in terms of the decile distribution ratio, we see a slight improvement in distribution since 1991.

3. There is a serious inequality in wealth distribution. According to our new estimates of the Gini coefficient for real and financial assets, the degree of inequality in wealth distribution in Korea is higher than that of some developed countries, contradicting the conclusion of the World Bank's report (Leipziger et al., 1992).

4. Public perception of income distribution in Korea tends to be rather skeptical, in spite of the measured income distribution. This phenomenon can be explained by some interrelated reasons such as inappropriate income concepts, a high level of expectation and a strong egalitarianism particular to Korea, and the Hirschmanite tunnel effect (see Choo 1992). We believe that the serious inequality problem in wealth distribution and the lack of justice in some resource allocation processes in the rapid development era led to this kind of skepticism.

Since we do not have any conclusive explanations of the recent trend in income distribution, we need to investigate some underlying factors of the distributive changes so that we can have some clues about Kuznet's hypothesis in the case of Korea. As major attributing factors that explain the inverse U-shaped hypothesis of Kuznets, one has to focus on the income difference between urban and rural areas on the one hand, and the allocation of income between capital and labor on the other.

According to the dual structural model of urban and rural sectors, the factor that leads to more equal income distribution is a rising rural-urban income ratio. This happens because the surplus labor force in the rural sector decreases sharply in the later part of development. How-

TABLE 18 The Rural-Urban Income Ratio, 1965–1994 (in percent)

Year	*Rural-urban income ratio*
1965	99.7
1970	75.6
1975	111.0
1980	95.9
1985	112.8
1990	97.4
1993	95.5
1994	99.52

SOURCE: *Social Indicators in Korea*, 1995.

ever, in Korea, we observe that the ratio was higher in the period 1975–1985 (Table 18). The argument for the second factor goes as follows: Since in the early stage of capital accumulation and industrialization, capital is owned by only a few, the degree of income inequality is very high. As the industrialization process continues, the size of the labor force and their income share as compared with the capitalists' share increases, resulting in a more equal income distribution. Table 19 shows a pattern of labor's rising income share over a period of forty years, but

TABLE 19 The Trend of Labor Income Share, 1953–1993 (in percent)

Year	*Labor income share*	*Year*	*Labor income share*
1953	25.8	1978	46.5
1955	30.1	1979	48.9
1960	37.4	1980	52.1
1965	31.8	1981	51.9
1966	33.0	1982	53.2
1967	36.7	1983	54.7
1968	37.5	1984	54.4
1969	38.7	1985	53.9
1970	41.4	1986	52.6
1971	41.5	1987	53.5
1972	40.8	1988	54.7
1973	41.2	1989	57.5
1974	39.5	1990	59.0
1975	40.6	1991	60.2
1976	42.0	1992	61.0
1977	44.2	1993	60.6

SOURCE: Bank of Korea, *National Income Account*, 1994.

with some cyclical movements, even into the 1990s, and, especially, no rising pattern in the middle of 1980s.

We do not detect any change in the 1980s and the 1990s either in fiscal policy or welfare and income distribution policy. Until now, the primary policy goal has been national competitiveness and growth potential. We are not aware of any changes in policy that will have profound effects on income distribution. For this reason, we do not see any underlying conditions that definitely support Kuznets's hypothesis. Even if there has been some recent improvement in income distribution, this tendency can be offset by an extraordinarily high level of inequality in wealth distribution and related unearned income. We believe that we have to pay attention to more qualitative measures and social aspects of distribution problems in Korea. The policy suggestions also should be based on this kind of observation and evaluation of the current status of income and wealth distribution.

POLICY DIRECTIONS FOR DISTRIBUTIVE EQUITY

The issue of the trade-off between efficiency and equity has always been a main concern in any economic decision-making process. In principle, economic efficiency is maximized when all agents in society pursue their utility and profit maximization without any distortional interruptions that could be caused by an equity criterion. It is generally true that there exists a certain degree of trade-off between efficiency and equity: progressive taxation, for instance, reduces saving and investment motivation and work efforts. However, it should be noted that government intervention to support equity and distributive justice do not always have harmful effects on economic efficiency. We can find some policy domains in which the policy makers can pursue harmonization of efficiency and equity in their policy goals. This concept of harmonization would be a key concept in setting policy goals for a future Korean capitalist model.

Following Okun (1975), we see that the removal of discrimination in the labor market would be compatible with our harmonization concept. Usually, discrimination in the labor market not only worsens equal chances of employment but also decreases labor productivity by distorting right employment decisions. Blinder (1987) indicated that the tax reduction policy for the rich in the Reagan administration could be an example of a policy that changed efficiency and equity in the same direction.

Furthermore, from a long-run perspective, we can obtain a complementary relationship between efficiency and equity. Thurow (1985) indicated that traditional economic theory has ignored some important aspects of economic development such as motivation, cooperation, and teamwork among agents in a society, and he also showed that these various factors worked fully for the society when the agents perceived that they were treated fairly and equally. A high degree of inequality in income and wealth distribution can cause low economic growth.

In the process of so-called "compressed" economic growth of the Korean economy, some of the discretionary policy decisions that have been made to promote growth are not supported even by the efficiency criterion. Political decisions have all too frequently dominated economic considerations, and a close relationship between government and big business has often been the persuasive key. This being so, some policy measures that rectify past decisions about resource allocations would be those to augment efficiency as well as equity and distributive justice.

Hence we can illustrate some main policy directions for both efficiency and equity in the Korean economy. First, regulations for irrational discrimination in the labor market such as sexual discrimination should be removed. Second, the role of the government in education and human capital accumulation should be enhanced. Both the removal of discrimination in the labor market and the enhancement of the government's role in education would result in the supply of more efficient workforces as well as more equal opportunities to work. Third, the "productivism" aspect in social welfare and fiscal policies should be emphasized more. For instance, the government investment for nursery schools is crucial not only for improving the welfare of mothers and children but also for increasing the labor supply by raising the female work participation rate. A higher female work participation rate as a result of this kind of government expenditure can often contribute to greater equality and efficiency in income distribution. Fourth, some resource allocation mechanisms that were adopted in the government-led compressed economic development era should be replaced or reformed. Some important examples can be found in the financial allocation mechanisms such as preferential policy loans and mutual loan guarantees, both of which have harmful effects on efficiency and economic equity.

These observations and concerns lead us to focus on two policy issues for distributive justice: tax and fiscal policy, and chaebol policy.

TAX AND FISCAL POLICY FOR EQUITY AND FAIRNESS

The general characteristics and problems of the Korean taxation system are summarized as follows (see Kwack 1993): (1) The public sector has depended heavily on indirect taxation to generate revenue; (2) the system has been heavily utilized as an industrial policy tool, resulting in complicated tax incentives; (3) the nominal statutory tax rates have been maintained at very high levels; (4) relatively low compliance on the part of the taxpayers and an inefficient tax administration are also features of the Korean tax system. These characteristics have contributed negatively to both horizontal and vertical equity. Table 20 shows the incidence of personal income tax by ten income classes. In the 1970s, we cannot find an increase in the progressiveness of income tax. If we focus on the tax/income ratio of the upper 20 percent, that ratio decreases from 15.24 percent in 1970 to 13.37 percent in 1976, to 10.18 percent in 1978, and to 8.99 percent in 1980. However, since the introduction of the global system in 1975, the progressiveness of income tax by income class within a year holds consistently.

The imbalance of the tax burden between employee households and the self-employed/employer households is a more serious problem in Korea. The estimates of Hyun and Na (1995) show that the average tax burden ratio of employee households is 3.35 percent while that of the self-employed/employer is just 2.67 percent. If we compare those

TABLE 20 Incidence of Personal Income Tax, 1970–1991
(unit: tax/income, %)

Decile	*1970*	*1976*	*1978*	*1980*	*1991*
1	2.24	0.00	0.00	0.00	0.91
2	2.06	0.00	0.00	0.06	1.58
3	2.40	0.19	0.59	0.74	2.14
4	2.07	0.71	0.84	1.21	2.44
5	2.17	1.20	1.25	1.56	2.86
6	5.29	1.73	1.62	1.90	3.85
7	6.18	2.40	2.07	2.32	4.87
8	5.71	3.42	2.69	2.89	5.77
9	7.50	6.07	3.89	3.79	7.14
10	7.74	7.30	6.29	5.20	10.26
Average	3.90	3.11	2.63	2.49	5.79

SOURCES: Han (1982), Hyun and Na (1995).

ratios for the highest 10 percent, the tax burden ratios are 12.98 percent and 3.14 percent, respectively. This kind of imbalance problem stems mainly from an inefficient tax administration.

As mentioned above, another important feature of the Korean tax system is a high dependence on indirect taxation, which, as is well known, results in a regressive tax incidence. For instance, the indirect tax burden ratio of the lowest 10 percent income class was 7.34 percent while that of the highest 10 percent was 2.85 percent in 1984 (Lee and Bae 1986). This imbalance was somewhat improved in 1991, showing a 4.39 percent burden ratio for the lowest 10 percent and 3.57 percent for the highest 10 percent. The trend of direct-indirect tax composition has been improved and the share of direct tax in 1995 is 53.8 percent (see Table 21).

Property-related taxes are another important issue in the context of wealth and wealth-related income distribution. It is widely accepted that property-related taxes in Korea are a weak and unsatisfactory way to accomplish distributive justice. For instance, the total tax revenue coming from landownership (aggregate land tax, city planning tax) in 1991 was 713 billion won, which is just 0.08 percent of the estimated total land value. Real estate–related taxes absorbed only 7.5 percent of the estimated capital gains from land price increases in 1991 (Hyun 1995).

A traditionally important property-related tax to prevent the excessive concentration of wealth, the inheritance and gift tax, has not contributed significantly to the redistribution of wealth in Korea; it has generated only small revenue and the tax base was assessed at very low levels. As Table 22 shows, the share of inheritance and gift tax in the total national tax revenue is less than 2 percent, though it has shown an increasing trend. It is worthwhile mentioning that the highest inheritance tax rate has been reduced from 70 percent in 1967 to 40 percent in 1996. The share of inheritance–gift tax is lower than that of Japan (4.7 percent) and Taiwan (2.6 percent). However, in the United States, Great Britain, Germany, and France, the share is in the range of 0.5–2.0

TABLE 21 The Share of Direct Taxes, 1970–1995 (in percent)

	1970	*1975*	*1980*	*1985*	*1990*	*1995*
National tax	38.5	33.9	28.7	31.8	43.7	45.7
Overall tax	43.5	39.5	36.9	39.3	49.5	53.8

SOURCE: Ministry of Finance and Economy.

TABLE 22 The Share of Inheritance/Gift Tax, 1985–1996 (in billions of won)

	1985	*1990*	*1995*	*1996*[a]
National tax (A)	11,876	26,847	56,736	64,509
Inheritance–gift tax (B)	47	295	1,029	1,275
B/A	0.39%	1.10%	1.81%	1.98%

[a] Estimate.

percent. The most recent change in the inheritance–gift tax law (December 1996) has the following features: simplification and unification of the tax system, alleviation of the burden on the middle class, and increase of the burden on the highest class. The highest tax rate was raised to 45 percent. We believe that this kind of change is desirable; with this simpler and unified tax system the efficiency of the tax administration in the collection of inheritance–gift tax should be greatly improved.

To sum up, the Korean tax system has failed to pursue distributive justice and fairness for all income brackets. To correct the problems of distribution, measures should be undertaken to increase the share of direct taxes, to strengthen the function of property-related tax including inheritance and gift tax, to balance the tax burden of employee-employer households, to obtain more consistent progressiveness of income tax, and to make tax administration more efficient. It should be noted, however, that it is not possible to redistribute significantly only through taxation. Also, the desirable direction for tax policy to achieve equity goals is not just to make the tax system more progressive; it should also simplify and clarify the horizontal inequality and tax administration by relaxing constraints on progressive taxes and broadening the income tax base. By broadening the income tax base, we can cure the notorious problem of unbalanced tax burdens among different groups (see Kwack 1993). We believe that the recent change in the inheritance–gift tax system reflects these concerns.

Finally, the most important outcome of these changes in the tax system will be higher revenues, which can be used for more public assistance programs and social welfare benefits. Since redistribution can be achieved much more effectively by some combination of taxation and income transfers, the charges we recommend would be compatible with the equity goal in that they would result in more revenues for social development programs—particularly important in Korea, which has traditionally neglected the fiscal role in social development. Even as recently as 1994, the share of social security and welfare expenditure was just 1.9 percent of the GNP.

We conclude that budgetary policy should be strengthened to cure vertical inequality while the tax system should be altered to solve mainly horizontal inequality; it should be made simple and clear, and the tax administration should be reformed. The income tax base should be broadened and property-related taxation should be strengthened, while the progressiveness requirement should be rather relaxed.

CHAEBOL POLICIES FROM A DISTRIBUTIVE PERSPECTIVE

The concentration of economic power in the chaebols has long been an intriguing feature of Korean wealth. The share of chaebols' production in the manufacturing and mining sector increased until the middle of the 1980s and then decreased. But a different estimate shows that the relative size of the thirty largest chaebols increased sharply in the period 1991–1993 (Lee and Yoo 1995). Although there exist various arguments on the values and evils of the chaebols and the chaebol-dominated economic system, it seems that a consensus can be formed on the negative aspects of chaebols from the point of view of inequality, fairness, and legitimacy. The so-called economic democracy has been hampered owing to the concentration of economic power in the hands of a small number of chaebols, and it is generally agreed that an economic system in which a small number of chaebols can exert substantial influence has created such issues as inequality of economic opportunities, inequality of income and wealth distribution, and lack of fairness and legitimacy.

Even from the point of view of efficiency and competitiveness, the role of the chaebols can be strongly criticized. As the size of chaebols increases, they more and more seek to use their economic power to influence political and social issues and even the policy-making processes. This power has had harmful effects on the national economy not only by distorting resource allocations but also, because of excessive and irrational diversification, by creating bureaucratic confusion and inefficiency, as well as, quite obviously, by severely restraining competition in the market. Some of the policy measures outlined above may be a key to lessening the chaebols' economic power and cultivating harmony between efficiency and equity.

Criticism of the chaebols in association with the issue of distributive equity generally focuses on the concentration of ownership as a solution, but any attempt to enhance distributive equity by ownership dispersion based on normal stock market operations has certain limits (Yoo 1996). As long as the government does not forcefully intervene on private property rights, the process of deconcentration basically means some changes in the portfolios of asset holders. We have to pay attention to some illegal and unfair transactions of the chaebols and their families, such as insider trading in the stock market and the private use of corporation funds. These abuses should be cured by a proper tax system or a surveillance system for transparent corporate management.

Discussions of the fairness and legitimacy of the chaebols usually follow a certain line of argument: the concentration of economic power is unfair and undesirable because it restricts competition. There have been these restrictions even in the factor markets, including the labor and financial markets, and the growth of chaebols was indeed made possible by preferential policy loans and the repression of the financial sector. The so-called mutual loan guarantees facilitated the utilization of limited financial resources. The real issue, then, is the establishment of fair rules of the game for the economy. Regulations that have restricted competition and equal opportunities should be removed or reformed, not only to instill fairness but to enhance efficiency.

Questions about legitimacy address the lack of fairness of past actions. In the process of the rapid development of the Korean economy, the government adopted a growth-oriented strategy that usually favored the chaebols and permitted them to grow at the expense of the relatively weak in society, partly by regulations that allowed property owners to raise rents. From the point of view of distributive justice, what would be the right policy stance toward chaebols? Here again we encounter the issue of a trade-off between efficiency and equity. It is generally accepted that chaebols have been a machine that made the rapid growth and modernization of the Korean economy possible. Therefore, those who favor the market principles and mechanism would assert that any antimarket interventions by the government cannot be justified by the standard of liberalism, by which they mean efficiency. This is an argument that needs to be reconsidered (see Jun-Koo Lee 1989). Nozick (1974), for example, proposes an entitlement formula of modern liberalism that includes justice principles in acquisition, justice principles in transfer, and principles of rectification of injustice. According to these principles of justice, we can obtain distributive justice when everybody in society owns what he is entitled to own.

The question we have to raise is whether, in the process of so-called compressed economic development of the Korean economy, chaebols have just what they are entitled to own. Our observations lead us to a negative answer to this question. We believe that the principle of rectification of injustice should be reflected more seriously in forming policy stance toward chaebols from a distributive perspective. The reinforcement of a property-related tax system that includes inheritance–gift taxes and a surveillance system to increase the transparency of corporate management is crucial in this context. We stress that this argument follows from the pure liberalist view that basically advocates the market mechanism and market forces.

Summary and Conclusions

Our findings on income and wealth distribution and policy directions in Korea can be summarized as follows.

1. Debates continue on the equality of income distribution status in the 1980s. While Dr. Choo and the Statistical Office show that income inequality has been continuously and substantially reduced in the 1980s, some economists at Choong-Ang University assert it has either stayed constant or has risen a little. Using UHIES data, we attempted to measure income inequality in the 1980s and 1990s. Our new estimates show that income inequality decreased in the 1980s, but not by as much as Dr. Choo's estimates, and has been almost constant in the 1990s. The Gini coefficients in urban areas in 1982, 1988, and 1994 are 0.393, 0.365, and 0.363, respectively. While income distribution in the urban sector improved until 1988, the distribution in self-employed and employer households has worsened until now. As a result, income distribution in the urban sector in the 1990s does not show any deterministic trend. With a serious data problem, our findings still do not allow any definite assertions on overall income distribution in Korea.

2. Even though the distribution of income in Korea may well compare favorably with that of other countries, many people believe that the core of inequality in Korea lies in the concentration of wealth, especially land, in a few hands. But the results of some earlier studies on wealth distribution, including those by KDI and the World Bank, do not coincide with the popular perception that there has been a growing gap between wealthy landowners and the rest of the people. Using the Daewoo panel data, we found that the Gini coefficients for financial

assets and buildings are around 0.70, and for land they are over 0.90. It is worth mentioning that the inequality of land and building ownership is higher than that of financial assets, contradicting earlier research results. Our results allow us to conclude that the inequality in the distribution of household wealth, especially that of land, is extremely high by international standards. Though we have some evidence of moderate income inequality and some signs of improvement in income distribution, the core element of inequality may be found in the concentration of wealth. Policy makers and academicians had better pay more attention to this problem in the future.

3. To extend the analyses of Suh and Yeon's study on poverty into later periods, we used the Daewoo data and applied updated poverty factors adjusting for inflation. Here the two most traditional measures of poverty are used, namely, the head count ratio (HCR) and the poverty gap. The head count ratios of the absolutely poor households turned out to be in the range of 10 to 20 percent. This is evidently higher than those of advanced capitalist countries and looks much more persuasive than the earlier results. The poverty gap, which is the necessary amount of income to bring incomes of poor households at least up to the poverty line, does not look as great; in most cases it is in the neighborhood of 2 percent of the total income of all households. This suggests that the real issue of poverty lies more in income distribution than in the absolute scarcity of material well-being. A little improvement in income distribution may contribute greatly to the reduction of poverty.

4. We believe that we have to pay attention to more qualitative measures and social aspects of distribution in Korea. It should be noted that government interventions for equity and distributive justice do not always have harmful effects on economic efficiency. We can find some policy domains in which the policy makers can pursue harmonization of efficiency and equity. This concept of harmonization should be at the center of policies for a long-term capitalist model for Korea.

The Korean tax system has been largely ineffectual in working out distributive justice and fairness. Much is still to be done: increasing the share of direct taxes, strengthening the function of property-related taxes including the inheritance and gift tax, balancing the tax burden of employee-employer households, obtaining more consistent progressiveness for income tax, and reforming the inefficient tax administration. It should be noted, however, that it is not possible to redistribute significantly by means of tax reforms alone. Also, a desirable direction for tax policy to achieve equity goals is not just to make the tax system more progressive. More emphasis on the horizontal inequality and inefficient tax administration would both clarify and simplify the tax system; reforms should relax the progressiveness constraint and broaden the base of income taxation. By broadening the income tax base, we can cure the notorious problem of unbalanced tax burdens among different groups.

It seems that a consensus can be formed on the negative aspects of chaebols from the point of view not only of inequality, fairness, and legitimacy, but, quite as much, of inefficiency and lack of competitiveness. Though many critics believe that the deconcentration of ownership can lessen the inequality of competition and wealth, we have to recognize certain limits to enhancing distributive equity by ownership dispersion based on normal stock market operations. These problems could, however, be solved by a modified tax system or a surveillance system for transparent corporate management. The important point is to establish fair rules of the game for the economy. We believe that the efficiency argument based on liberalism should be reconsidered in making out the chaebol institutes in Korea; that is, the principle of the rectification of injustice should be reflected more noticeably in policies aimed at controlling the chaebols. We stress that this argument is coming from a pure liberalist view, which advocates the market mechanism and market forces.

REFERENCES

Adelman, Irma. 1974. "South Korea." In Hollis Chenery et al., eds., *Redistribution with Growth*, pp. 280–85. London: Oxford University Press.

Ahn, Kook-Shin. 1995. "Economic Development and Income Distribution in Korea" (in Korean). *Economic Development Review*, vol. 1.

Ahn, Kook-Shin, and Sun-Dae Kang. 1990. "The Trend of Size Distribution of Income in Korea and Its Determinants" (in Korean). *Choong-Ang University Economic Review*, vol. 4.

Bhalla, Surjit S. 1979. "The Distribution of Income in Korea: A Critique and a Reassessment." Mimeo. World Bank.

Blinder, A. 1987. *Hard Heads, Soft Hearts*. Reading, Mass.: Addison-Wesley.

Brenner, Y. S., et al., eds. 1991. *Income Distribution in Historical Perspective*. Cambridge: Cambridge University Press.

Chenery, Hollis, and Moises Syrquin. 1975. *Patterns of Development: 1950–1970*. London: Oxford University Press.

Choo, Hakchung. 1979, 1982. *Income Distribution in Korea and Its Determinants* (in Korean). 2 vols. Seoul: Korea Development Institute.

———. 1992. "Income Distribution and Social Equity in Korea." KDI–CIER Joint Seminar, April.

Choo, Hakchung, and Juhyun Yoon. 1984. "Size Distribution of Income in 1982 and the Causes for Changes" (in Korean). *Korean Development Review*, March.

Daewoo Economic Research Institute. Korea Households Economic Activity Survey, 1993–95 (in Korean).

Fields, Gary S. 1985. "Industrialization and Employment in Hong Kong, Korea, Singapore, and Taiwan." in Walter Galenson, ed., *Foreign Trade and Investment: Economic Growth in the Newly Industrializing Asian Countries.* Madison: University of Wisconsin Press.

Han, Seung-Soo. 1982. "Studies on Tax Incidence and Optimal Burden" (in Korean). Korea Economic Research Institute, Seoul.

Hirschman, Albert O. 1973. "Changing Tolerance for Inequality in Economic Development." *Quarterly Journal of Economics* 87 (November): 544–66.

Hyun, Jin-Kwon. 1995. "Distribution of Land Ownership and Distributive Effect of Land Taxes" (in Korean). Korea Institute of Public Finance, Seoul.

Hyun, Jin-Kwon, and Seong-Lin Na. 1995. "Incidence of Indirect Taxes" (in Korean). *Review of Public Finance.*

Iwamoto, Takuya. 1989. "Analyses of Income and Assets Distribution in Korea" (in Korean). Master's thesis, Korea University.

Kakwani, Nanak. 1981. *Income Inequality and Poverty.* London: Oxford University Press.

Kang, Sun-Dae. 1990. "Size Distribution of Income in Korea and Its Determinants" (in Korean). Ph.D. diss., Choong-Ang University.

Kim, Daemo, and Kook-Shin Ahn. 1987. "Income Distribution in Korea: Estimates, the Determinants, and Popular Perceptions" (in Korean).

Kim, Whang-Joe. 1992. "The Determinants of Personal Income and Policy Issues" (in Korean). In *Inequality and Equality in Korea.* Nanam.

Koo, Hagen. 1984. "The Political Economy of Income Distribution in South Korea: The Impact of the State's Industrialization Policies." World Development Agency.

Kuznets, Simon. 1995. "Economic Growth and Income Inequality." *American Economic Review* 45 (March): 1–28.

Kwack, Tae-Won. 1993. "Tax Policy and Distributive Equality in Korea." In *Social Issues in Korea.* Seoul: Korea Development Institute.

Kwon, Soon-Won. 1991. "International Comparisons of Living Standards" (in Korean). *Korea Development Review*, fall.

Kwon, Soon-Won, et al. 1992. *The Reality of Distributive Inequality in Korea and the Policy Agenda* (in Korean). Seoul: Korea Development Institute.

Lee, Joung-Woo. 1991. "Wealth, Capital Gains, and Income Inequality in Korea" (in Korean). *Korea Economic Journal* (Seoul National University), September.

Lee, Jun-Koo. 1989. *The Theory and Realities of Income Distribution* (in Korean).

Lee, Kye-Sik, and Jun-Ho Bae. 1986. "Analysis of Indirect Tax Incidence in Korea" (in Korean). Korea Development Institute.

Lee, Seong-Soon, and Seung-Min Yoo. 1995. "Industrial Organization and Policy Issues in Korea" (in Korean). Korea Development Institute.

Leipziger, Danny M., David Dollar, Anthony F. Shorrocks, and Su-Yong Song. 1992. *The Distribution of Income and Wealth in Korea.* World Bank.

Nozick, R. "Anarchy." 1974. In *State and Utopia.* New York: Basic Books.

Okun, A. 1975. *Equality and Efficiency: The Big Trade-off.* Washington, D.C.: Brookings Institution.

Oshima, Harry. 1970. "Income Inequality and Economic Growth: The Postwar Experience of Asian Countries." *Malaysian Economic Review* 15, no. 2: 7–41.

Park, Soon-Il, et al. 1994. A Study on the Minimum Cost of Living (in Korean). KIHASA.

Park, Won-Am, and Jong-Ha Yoon. 1988. "Changes in the Pattern of Income Distribution and Their Sources in Korea." KDI Working Paper no. 8804.

Rao, D. C. 1978. "Economic Growth and Equity in the Republic of Korea." World Development Agency.

Renaud, Bertrand. 1976. "Economic Growth and Income Inequality in Korea." World Bank, Staff Working Paper no. 240.

Smeeding, Timothy. 1996. "America's Income Inequality: Where Do We Stand?" *Challenge*, Sept./Oct., pp. 45–53.

Suh, Sang-Mok. 1985. "Economic Growth and Change in Income Distribution: The Korean Case. KDI Working Paper no. 8508.

Suh, Sang-Mok, and Ha-Cheong Yeon. 1986. "Social Welfare During the Structural Adjustment Period in Korea." KDI Working Paper no. 8604.

Szal, Richard. 1981. "Emerging Trends in Income Distribution in Korea and Their Implications for Further Planning." *Labour and Society*, October.

Thurow, L. 1985. *The Zero-Sum Solution.* New York: Simon & Schuster.

Yoo, Seung-Min. 1996. "The Economy Grows as It Distributes" (in Korean). *Mirae Media.*

Kenneth L. Judd

Policy Challenges in Dynamic, Growing Economies

Economic growth is the main objective of economic policy since it will raise the living standards of a society. The two main ways in which governments pursue economic growth are by participating in international trade and encouraging the adoption of new and more productive technologies. Unfortunately, the benefits of economic growth and the costs of growth-enhancing policies will not be uniformly shared; in fact, some may be hurt by policies that help most individuals. Particularly troublesome are economic forces that widen the gap between the rich and the poor, a common occurrence in modern dynamic, growing economies. While the United States economy has grown over the past twenty years, there has also been a widening gap between the wages of low-skill and high-skill workers. This paper presents an overview of the relation between growth-enhancing policies and income distribution, the likely trends in economic growth and income distribution, and the policy challenges ahead.

First, while trade and technological progress unquestionably offer opportunities to improve overall economic health, it is not true that they help everybody; in fact, it is possible for an economic change to help the average person but hurt many others. This makes both trade and innovation continuing sources of political conflict between those who lose and those who gain. Many argue that trade developments have contributed to the increase in inequality in the United States in the past twenty years. Though the contribution of trade to this trend is unclear, this perception plays an important role in trade policy debates.

Second, much of the discussion of who benefits from economic growth is incorrectly focused on job creation and the industry in which one works, instead of on the standard of living. The long-run impact of economic change on the number of jobs is ambiguous, depending on job market institutions and the demand for jobs. In the long run, who gains and who loses from economic growth has less to do with the industry in which one works than with the skills one brings to the marketplace. This misplaced focus on jobs confuses the dialogue and is unlikely to lead to rational resolutions of the conflicts.

Third, we need to define the concept of inequality we care about and why. We often use the phrase "worsening income distribution" to refer to an increase in income inequality. This phrase unfortunately prejudges income inequality. I shall argue that some increases in income inequality are a natural outcome of otherwise desirable economic developments. The focus should be not on inequality of outcomes, such as wages or income, but on inequality of opportunity. Rather than using the word inequality in a literal sense, we should focus on providing floors, not ceilings, on economic opportunity and income.

Fourth, debating whether the reason for the widening wage gap between the skilled and the unskilled is trade or technology is interesting but not of central concern here: both are probably part of the story. Furthermore, likely trends in trade and technology will tend to widen this gap even more. As some very populous countries with low-wage workforces enter the world market, the low-wage American worker will face increasingly fierce competition. Also, the continuing revolution in computer technology is going to erode the relative position of lower skilled workers.

Finally, recognition of these possibilities has important implications for a variety of policies. The best way to deal with the problems of income inequality is to do so in a unified fashion, independent of the cause of inequality. A common objective of economic policy is to help persons who have experienced economic adversity. There is little reason to treat people differently depending on whether their problems are due to foreign competition, domestic competition, or technical progress. Furthermore, since education and training are the critical determinants of income inequality, economic policy makers must act today if they wish to prevent further long-run increases in income inequality. Recognition of this would help policy makers focus on improving the economic condition of all.

An Illustrative Tale

Before we begin our discussion of the economic issues, we consider an imaginary tale. Once upon a time, a firm named Trees2Cars announced that it had invented a new, far more efficient way to make cars. Their secret technology could take $8,000 worth of lumber and turn it into a fuel-efficient, reliable, quality automobile. This was a major improvement, for the cars from Trees2Cars were as good as $15,000 cars being produced by General Motors, Ford, and Chrysler. The company set up a factory on the harbor in Seattle. Trees floated into one end of the factory and cars came out the other and were shipped via rail and trucks to all parts of the United States.

Trees2Cars was hailed as an example of Yankee ingenuity and the superiority of American advanced technology. The new technology caused many changes in the American economy. The lumber industry in the state of Washington boomed, with rising wages for lumberjacks and thousands of new jobs in the lumber industry and in services for the new lumber industry workers. Real estate prices rose and the housing industry flourished in the state of Washington.

There were some that weren't so happy. General Motors, Ford, and Chrysler suffered sharp drops in sales and had to close some plants. Many workers in other plants were laid off. Fortunately, most of the workers found new jobs after several months, some close to home, and some elsewhere. Some found jobs as good as their old jobs, but many were not so lucky and had to settle for jobs with lower wages. Real estate prices in Detroit fell and the construction industry there collapsed. The competition from Trees2Cars forced the Big Three to reduce prices on their cars, reducing their profits. The UAW also had to reduce its wage demands in order to keep remaining jobs.

The impact in most of the country was not so dramatic. Millions of American auto buyers were very grateful for the lower-priced quality cars that were now available. Even those who did not buy cars from Trees2Cars were happy since Detroit had to reduce prices on their cars to compete. In spite of the fact that the business generated by Trees2-Cars hurt some individuals, the general feeling was that the country benefited. While many sympathized with the workers who lost their jobs, this was considered the price of progress. Those who lost jobs got unemployment insurance payments until they found new jobs. Those who were hurt were hurt only temporarily and social welfare programs helped them make the transition. Some workers argued for shutting down Trees2Cars, but they were ridiculed and called Luddites. Total employment was negligibly affected; in fact, some argued that the total number of jobs in the economy fell. Since cars were cheaper, some married women who were working part time to help save up for a car were able to stay home with their children. The stock market was also affected. GM, Ford, and Chrysler stock went down substantially, but the market values of lumber firms and their suppliers rose. Few investors complained because most of them had diversified portfolios with both auto and lumber firm stocks, and saw only negligible changes in the value of their portfolios.

There was great interest in this new technology. Many thought that it should be helpful in producing other goods. However, Trees2Cars refused to reveal anything about their invention.

Eventually, a reporter was able to sneak into the factory. He discovered that there was no machinery in this "factory." He found instead an underground submarine pen. Some submarines were loading up the logs and some submarines were unloading cars that were made in Asia. Instead of building cars from trees, Trees2Cars was selling lumber to Asian countries and buying cars made in Asia.

This revelation created an enormous scandal. Trees2Cars was pilloried for destroying an American industry, and for destroying the lives of thousands of workers. They were called traitors for conspiring with foreigners, assisting them in their invasion of the American economy. The American worker was being destroyed by the unfair competition from cheap foreign labor. Also, many of the foreign autoworkers did not receive good health insurance, and worked fifty hours a week in factories that lacked air conditioning. Buyers of these cars were criticized for helping to enslave foreign workers, condemning them to working in unacceptable conditions. The customers of Trees2Cars were criticized for their selfish decision to favor foreign cars over those made by their fellow Americans. Auto and union executives assured Congress that there was no need for foreign imports since the American firms were charging the same price for similar models.

Therefore, Trees2Cars was humiliated and driven out of business.

National Benefits of Trade

The tale of Trees2Cars is a moral economic tale that illustrates the effects of trade and its similarity to technical progress and illuminates the policy problems created by economic change. As the tale points out, trade presents new opportunities to an economy, just as innovation and technical progress do.

SPECIALIZATION

International trade allows individual countries to specialize in doing what they do best. This will generally improve the economic well-being of all nations involved in trade. First, by trading with other nations, a country can focus on doing what it does relatively well. Consider, for example, trade between the United States and Saudi Arabia. Both countries can produce food and oil. While the United States can do a good job at both, Saudi Arabia is poor at growing food but very good at producing oil. Through trade, the United States can focus on food and Saudi Arabia can focus on producing oil.

Second, by dividing up tasks the international economy can enjoy a greater variety of goods. Consider the luxury car industry. The United States produces Cadillacs, the English produce Jaguars, the Germans produce Porsches, the Italians produce Lamborghinis, and the Japanese produce Acura NSX's, and they all trade with each other. Without trade, Americans would have to produce Cadillacs, Jaguars, Porsches, Lamborghinis, and NSX's. But since U.S. demand alone would not be big enough to support a full factory for each, it is likely that there would be fewer models of luxury cars available to U.S. car buyers. Furthermore, smaller countries, such as Korea, would probably not get any luxury cars because Korean demand would not be great enough to support any luxury car factory. The luxury car example is not, of course, particularly important, but it is indicative of industries where there are large fixed costs of production and substantial increasing returns to scale, or where research and development or design costs are high.

These are just two examples of a very general principle: international trade presents opportunities that do not exist otherwise. No one forces a nation to pursue these opportunities. Trade also gives Americans the chance to buy shoes made in Russia, though I doubt that anyone would want to pursue that option given the reputation of Russian shoes. Trade presents a nation with many opportunities, some valuable, some worthless. It is up to the nation to chose among these opportunities. Since some of these opportunities will be profitable, a nation will generally be better off in an international free trade system than if it cut itself off from the rest of the world.

TECHNOLOGY TRANSFER

For many nations, the most significant aspect of international trade is that it brings in new, modern technologies. A nation could learn about state-of-the-art and new technologies without trade, but trade offers easy ways to secure this knowledge; and trade with technologically advanced nations also generally leads to investment by those nations; not only because wages in less-developed nations are usually lower but also because the workers are often well motivated and can be trained to use modern technology. This encourages firms from the advanced nations to build factories in lesser-developed countries and to bring in modern equipment and train local workers and managers to use the new technology. Once these workers have learned how to use the new machines and technology, other firms in the local economy can hire these workers and bring in the new technology for them to use. This further helps the local economy. Over time, some workers may even move up to supervisory and technical positions and acquire more knowledge and skills.

Sometimes this technology transfer is an explicit part of trade agreements. A foreign firm that wants to enter a local market may need a local partner, which in turn demands access to advanced technology. Sometimes this technology transfer is less formal, but it is no less important. Through employment relations and related interactions, the local residents become acquainted with advanced technologies; some may even become entrepreneurs and set up their own firms using their new skills. Less formal but also important are the personal contacts that accompany international trade. In many ways, commercial exchange facilitates intellectual exchanges of all kinds and helps a lesser-experienced and skilled society learn from other societies.

National Benefits of Technological Progress

The benefits of innovation and technology are even greater than those of trade. Technological advances make it cheaper to produce basic products such as grain, meat, fuel, and steel. Innovation brings to the market new products such as the telephone, television, automobiles, and airplanes. Many new products also reduce the costs to produce old goods and services. For example, when computers were first introduced into offices, they did old tasks such as typing. Over time, computers have so evolved that word-processing software can now check spelling and grammar, and even take dictation. Innovation and technical progress improve the efficiency of old activities and create new services. Trade and technological progress are in many ways similar: some new technologies turn out to be of no value, just as some trade opportunities are not valuable, but trade and innovation both present new opportunities, many of which will contribute to the economic health of a nation.

To a large extent, economic progress depends on technological progress. Increases in the stock of machinery and other types of physical investment and worker training in machine skills are, of course, contributing factors, but ultimately these depend on the technological innovations themselves.

INDIVIDUAL EFFECTS OF TRADE AND TECHNOLOGICAL CHANGE

Although we can argue that trade and technology can improve the economic well-being of a nation, it does not follow that all will benefit from free trade. There are several reasons why the benefits will not be distributed in such a way as to improve the lot of everybody. Trade and technological change can make the skills of some individuals obsolete. The invention of the automobile reduced the demand for blacksmiths and wagon producers. Some of them could transfer their skills to producing cars, but those who worked with horses found little demand for the care and feeding of horses. Trade can also hurt individuals. The introduction of small and relatively cheap Japanese automobiles into the American market reduced the number of automobile production jobs in the United States. Furthermore, even if no one is hurt by technological change, some may benefit disproportionately. Henry Ford benefited enormously from the invention of the automobile, as did Bill Gates from the invention of the personal computer. The presence of big winners is a common feature of new technology, and it will tend to increase income inequality.

Gains from economic change are seldom distributed evenly. The uneven distribution of benefits will generate political pressures on policy makers to undo the changes in income distribution. The difficulty lies in doing this without losing the benefits of economic change.

CONSUMER PRICES

One group that does clearly benefit in many ways from technological change is consumers. Inventions tend to reduce the price they pay for old goods, and innovation brings goods that were formerly unavailable. The impact of trade on consumer prices is less clear. To the extent that trade introduces new goods, consumers clearly benefit. By bringing new competition into a market, as, for example, in automobiles, international trade can spur beneficial change. Strong competition for the Big Three, General Motors, Ford, and Chrysler, forced them to respond.

For trade in existing goods, however, the picture for consumer prices can be less evident. For example, the United States imports cars and exports lumber. This reduces the price American consumers pay for cars, since these imports compete with domestic producers, forcing all car producers to lower their prices. But the export of lumber, bringing foreign consumers into competition with American consumers for that lumber, drives up the price of lumber for domestic consumers. There is an ambiguity here: consumers who don't need a car but want to buy a new, wood-frame house definitely lose from trade, but residents of skyscrapers who buy cars will gain from the importation of cars.

However, the average consumer does gain, since he is also the average producer in the economy. The average individual will gain from trade simply because trade offers up new opportunities; whether that gain comes from lower prices for the goods he buys or from an increase in his income is not of concern. When it comes to all economic policy questions, we must realize that individuals are not just consumers and not just workers or just investors. It is convenient to break down the effects of economic change into the impact on consumer prices, wages, and returns on investment, but we need to realize that the final result is the sum of these effects for any individual.

A simple way to proceed is to assume that, though all people are similar in their role as consumers, they differ in terms of their job skills and their wealth. Rich people still eat hamburgers, and many welfare recipients buy color TVs and stereos; but most seamstresses would be poor math professors and most math professors would be lousy seamstresses. This approach helps us understand the critical factors that determine income inequality and its relation to trade and innovation. With this in mind, we now focus on how economic growth may affect those incomes.

WORKERS' WAGES AND INVESTMENT RETURNS

Economic and technical change will affect the income of different groups in different ways. When the United States trades trees for cars, some workers and investors will gain and some will lose. Lumberjacks have skills that are special to the lumber industry. An increased demand for lumber will increase the demand for lumberjacks and they will find their wages increasing. But in the automobile industry workers on the assembly lines will suffer as the demand for U.S. cars slackens with more imports. Trade can affect other workers in related occupations. Consider, for example, truck drivers. While there will be fewer truck driving jobs associated with the U.S. auto industry, there will be more truck driving jobs associated with shipping the trees for export and delivering the imported cars.

Which workers benefit and which lose from economic change depends on the changes in the relative demand for their skills. One way to look at the workforce is by classifying skills. More precise measurements focus on the number of years of education. If a change causes the demand for low-skill workers to fall and the demand for higher-skill workers to rise, one expects the wages of low-skill workers to fall and the wages of high-skill workers to rise. It does not matter where they work, since all employers must pay, in the long run, the same wages for the same skill.

The impact on investors is also unclear. Stockholders in auto firms clearly lose from trade, whereas stockholders in lumber firms clearly gain. On the other hand, since most stockholders hold diversified portfolios wherein they own stock in both auto firms and lumber firms, gains and losses may come close to balancing.

Another way in which investors are affected differently from workers is the presence of a world capital market. There may be quotas on Japanese automobiles and tariffs on textiles imported from Hong Kong, but there are few limitations on the ability of Japanese and Chinese investors to invest in the American capital market. Americans also have increasing opportunities to invest in other economies. This means that interest rates and stock market returns must be roughly equal across economies. In the labor market there is no such equalizing force; the average worker has to contend with strong if unstated barriers to moving freely to where he can earn the most.

The effects of technological change are in many ways similar to those of trade on workers' wages and investment returns. If we invented a machine that could turn trees into cars, the impact on wages and investor profits would be the same. The critical factor is the effect of trade or innovation on the relative demand for various inputs. Here again we see that technology and trade are similar in their impact on income and economic welfare.

The Policy Dialogue on Trade and Technology

For all the similarities between technological progress and trade, there are substantial differences in how they are treated in discussions of economic policy and by the decisions of policy makers. Discussions of technology are generally open to weighing both the benefits and costs; trade policy discussions are much more contentious, with both sides overselling their case. The general attitude toward technological progress differs from that taken in trade policy discussions.

TECHNOLOGY POLICY

Economic policy makers are aware that technological progress can produce winners and losers and that it may even worsen income distribution. However, the general response is to allow technological progress but to help the losers. Unemployment insurance is available to those who lose their jobs as a result of new technology. Welfare programs are available to those who have serious problems finding a productive role in society, and retraining programs are sometimes available to help workers adjust to new conditions after their old skills become obsolete.

Critics of technological progress in the U.S. have often been successful in slowing down technological progress. Persistent opposition has shackled nuclear power. Irrational fears of gamma-irradiated food have slowed down this process. Recombinant DNA research has been attacked out of fear that experiments will create new devastating diseases. But these are exceptions, and they are somewhat understandable. Nuclear power plants are potentially dangerous; witness Chernobyl. Most people do not have the scientific literacy to understand the difference between radiated food and radiation from nuclear fallout, or why the dangers from recombinant DNA are infinitesimal.

By and large, however, society welcomes technology. Even many losers realize that, though they may lose from today's advances, they will benefit from future technology. Telephone operators may lose their jobs to computer switchboards, but they realize that automation in general makes most goods cheaper to produce and workers more productive.

THE CONFUSING TRADE DEBATE

Unfortunately, trade policy discussions are very different. Critics of free trade focus on the employment effects of imports, neglecting the benefits to consumers. They also focus on the impact of trade on wages. This is more relevant, but again it ignores the fact that the nation as a whole gains from trade. However, if the winners are not willing to pay off the losers, then the losers may use the political system to block trade. Protectionist arguments have always been with us, and they will continue to present challenges.

While protectionist arguments focus on the losers, the advocates of free trade often make errors in the opposite direction and oversell the benefits of trade. Free trade advocates often seem to be arguing that all will benefit from trade, and they downplay the possible uneven distribution of benefits. The major effect of trade is seen in the average standard of living. Under free trade, a country has more choices: products can be produced at home or can be imported. An increase in choices will never harm a competitive, free market economy, and it will generally improve the average standard of living. We must remember, however, that these arguments only apply to the average individual. They do not say that most individuals gain from trade. It may even be the case that most people lose from trade. I doubt that this applies in the United States, but keeping this possibility in mind will prevent us from overselling trade. For example, economists generally criticize politicians who claim that the country loses from trade, but one should remember that politicians running for office care about the majority and the median voter, not the average voter whom economists are implicitly speaking of.

Some try to sell free trade by arguing that it will increase the number of jobs. In contrast, economic analysis tells us that there is no interesting connection between trade and jobs in the long run. In the short run, trade shocks may affect unemployment rates as workers change jobs and move out of sectors competing with new imports and move into export sectors. In the long run, however if labor policies are flexible and rational, the number of jobs roughly equals the number of individuals looking for work. Since free trade will improve economic productivity, some may decide to use the higher economic productivity to justify working less and enjoying more leisure. The number of workers and jobs may even fall with trade.

International trade benefits the economy, but we must not oversell the benefits. Trade raises living standards and average productivity, and certain economic policies will help to spread the gains more evenly without sacrificing the benefits of trade.

Income Inequality

I have discussed the ways in which trade and technology can affect various groups in an economy. Turning to the implications for income inequality, we need to distinguish among several concepts and measures of inequality that determine how we view the critical issues. What kinds of inequality do we care about, and what are their causes? Which kinds are of little or no concern? We also need to be clear about what kind of "equality" we want.

CAUSES OF INEQUALITY

Presumably, when we speak of economic inequality we are referring to the economic well-being of individuals. However, many measures of inequality, by focusing on differences in income and wealth, do not accurately measure economic well-being. Young medical students, for example, have less income than middle-aged doctors do, and far less wealth. Is this income inequality, and should we try to eliminate it? Certainly the inequality is just a reflection of individuals at different stages in their life cycle of study and work: today's doctors were once poor medical students, and today's medical students have a bright future ahead of them. But even when we correct for age, there are still many natural differences among individuals. For example, some professionals, such as doctors and lawyers, earn more than other comparably trained individuals simply because they take on more cases and work more hours. Many people increase their income by taking on second jobs. As long as all have the opportunity to work more, these income differences do not reflect any injustice or "unfairness."

Other differences are related to career choices. For example, I believe (perhaps mistakenly) that I could double or triple my income by getting a "rocket scientist" job on Wall Street. However, I don't want such a job even at that income, preferring the flexibility, tasks, and responsibilities associated with being a Senior Fellow at the Hoover Institution.

Social change has also increased income inequality in the United States. In the 1950s, most families conformed to the ideal, with the husband working at a job to earn money and the wife making a comfortable home for the husband and caring for the children. In that society, income inequality is related only to the husband's income. In today's American society, that sterotype represents only a minority of homes. The growing acceptance of divorce has led to more broken homes, and marriage, too, is considered optional. The result is a large number of homes with a single mother, often poor, with some children. At the other end there are many households where both husband and wife have jobs. This greater variety in family situations increases the measured income inequality.

The key fact is that there is more to life than money, and measures of income inequality that focus on money and financial wealth alone are likely to overstate social tensions and problems that arise from income inequality. This is particularly true in societies where people are not restricted by custom to follow rigid norms and where the general level of affluence is great enough to offer many economically feasible ways for one to lead one's life.

Differences that arise owing to age and individual choices are of little concern to most economists. Most people will lead long lives and benefit from age advantages when they reach those ages. If we believe that individual tastes should be respected, then income inequality that results from taste and choice differences is natural and should not be frustrated. Of more relevance are differences that result from differences in ability and skill. Some skills are valued more highly by the economy than others. People are born with different skills. Those with the more valuable skills will have a higher income. In a free society where individuals decide which jobs they will take and employers are free to compete for the services of skilled individuals, those with highly valued skills will inevitably earn more. Even if the government tries to redistribute income, there will still be substantial income inequality because the only way to tax the rich to help the poor is to first let the rich be rich.

One current concern is the large differences in income between the college-educated and those with less education. Some of this difference is due to different abilities and skills; some who do not go to college lack the necessary skills and would get little value from attending college. However, some of this difference is due to poor educational opportunities, financial hardship, poor decisions made by individuals in their youth when they were planning their high school curriculum, and parental and student ignorance of the value of education. Some economic and educational policies try to avoid these mistakes by helping qualified students get the appropriate education. Other social factors, such as religious, ethnic, and racial prejudice, then result in an inequality that is generally considered illegitimate, particularly if discriminatory laws and government policies augment and implement these social factors.

These considerations show that we should not focus solely on simple indices of income inequality. Instead we should examine the sources of inequality and decide which ones should be the focus of policy.

WHAT CONCEPT "EQUALITY"?

In view of the many sources of inequality, we must decide what kind of equality we want: which causes of inequality are acceptable, and which can be adjusted by policies? In my discussion, I focus on age-adjusted wage inequality arising from differences in education and ability. This inequality is not related to size of family, how many hours one wants to work, or to one's age. Inequality due to prejudice is also of concern, but I shall not discuss it since it is best dealt with by legal and social reforms, not economic policies.

Another important distinction economists often make is that between equality of results versus equality of opportunity. If two individuals have access to the same education, but one does better in school than the other and ends up with a better career, this constitutes equality of opportunity but inequality of result. When individuals are offered similar opportunities, they are less likely to object to the outcome. Most understand the value of competition and agree that the more productive citizens should be able to keep the fruit of their labors. However, if individuals are not offered equal opportunities then they are less likely to accept the results.

We should take care when defining equality of opportunity. This is particularly clear in the case of education. Some have argued that equality of opportunity in education means that all children should receive the same education, with no differences in quality or extent. This is an ideal of questionable appeal. Does this mean that parents should not be permitted to help their children beyond what other parents do? Does this mean that schools in rich suburbs should be forbidden to spend more on education than is spent in poor rural schools? If the rich are required to spend a dollar to bring up the level of expenditure on the poor for each dollar they spend on their own children, the result will ultimately be less expenditure for all.

There is tension between the desire for equal opportunity and allowing individuals to use their resources as they see fit. The compromise that many subscribe to is to enact policies that provide a minimum level of opportunity to everyone, but allow individuals to spend resources beyond this as they please. The level of this minimum support will be debated, but any policies that effectively enact a ceiling are likely to be self-defeating.

Historical Experience and Future Possibilities

I conclude by discussing the recent experience in the United States and speculating on two future possibilities. In keeping with my theme that technology and trade are similar, I discuss one possible trade scenario and one anticipated development in technology.

RECENT U.S. EXPERIENCE

Wage inequality of individual workers is a more appropriate measure of equality than total household income. Household income inequality can arise because of differences in household labor supply. As I have pointed out, differences in household income due to individual decisions to work more hours or take on second jobs do not reflect inequality of opportunity; the true differences in the standard of living available to households are wage rate differences. During the past twenty years there has been a substantial increase in wage inequality in the United States.[1] In the 1980s, real weekly earnings of college-educated workers were roughly constant but the real weekly earnings of high school graduates declined by more than 15 percent.

There are many arguments as to the causes. One of the primary causes has been an increase in the demand for educated and experienced workers who can adapt to new technologies such as those related to computers. As new technologies proliferate, the demand for skilled workers increases and less-skilled workers find themselves at a competitive disadvantage.

International trade is also likely to have contributed to the increase in wage inequality. The growth in international trade has made it easier for products produced by less-skilled workers in foreign factories to compete with less-skilled American workers. American consumers enjoy buying the cheaper clothing and automobiles available from foreign firms, but American workers in the garment and automobile industries find fewer jobs. College-educated American workers do not face such

1. See Borjas and Ramey (1993), Katz and Murphy (1992), and Murphy and Welch (1992) for discussions of the extent and causes of increased wage inequality in the U.S.

problems. In fact, the products they produce, such as computer software, are in high demand in foreign markets and face little competition from foreign producers.

Thus, both trade and technology, the primary sources of economic growth, are also the prime suspects in the recent growth of inequality. There are heated arguments about the relative contributions of technological change and international trade, but most agree that these are contributing factors. Whatever the cause, it is tied to the level of education of a worker. Most agree that the return to education has turned out to be greater than was expected twenty years ago.

NEW PARTICIPANTS IN THE WORLD MARKET

The political changes of the past decade have created new economic possibilities. In China, economic changes have produced a dynamic new economy. The collapse of the Soviet Union has led to tremendous changes in the economies of Eastern Europe and Russia. Even the relatively closed economy of India has moved toward more participation in the world market. In total, these economies have about 2.5 billion people. If there were free trade between these countries and the developed world, the impact on income distribution could be massive, since the labor in these countries is of low to moderate skill and these countries have little physical capital. We are already seeing some conflict. For example, many nations in Central Europe want to join the European Union, but many in the richer nations of Western Europe oppose their entry because of the cheap labor problem.

The prospect of such developments makes previous debates in the United States concerning Korean shoes, Hong Kong sweaters, and Japanese autos pale in comparison. However, though the threat to low-skill labor presented by the lesser-developed nations is clear, it may be only temporary. Many so-called cheap labor economies have quickly evolved into middle-class economies—witness the evolution of the cheap-labor Japanese economy of the 1950s and 1960s into the high-wage, high-productivity economy of the 1990s. Other East Asia economies are following the same path. Still, as the world economy moves over the next decades to integrate poorer nations into the world marketplace, there will likely be deterioration in the distribution of income in developed countries. Again, a key factor is likely to be the relative level of education. It was relatively easy for the Japanese economy to grow rapidly after World War II since it had been a relatively productive economy with an experienced and educated workforce; the same was true of

West Germany. But most of today's poor nations do not begin with such a skilled workforce. It will take much more time for them to catch up with the rest of the world.

THE COMPUTER REVOLUTION

A far greater long-term threat to low-skill labor is the continuing computer revolution. The computer has already eliminated several lesser-skilled jobs in manufacturing. Even so-called white-collar labor is affected, since offices can now operate with fewer secretarial and clerical workers.

Some will argue that they have heard all this before, and that computer enthusiasts have been consistently wrong. Many computer scientists confidently predicted in the 1960s that computers would compete with the human brain by 1980; in particular, they predicted that the world chess champion in 1980 would be a computer. A central character in the 1968 movie *2001* was HAL, a highly intelligent computer; it was supposedly "activated" on January 12, 1997. When 1980 came, the best computer chess program was only a bit above average. More generally, most were skeptical that computers could ever challenge the human brain. Even a few years ago, Garry Kasparov, the world chess champion, declared that no computer would beat a grandmaster. And January 12, 1997, passed without the appearance of anything resembling HAL. It may be that the predictions of the 1960s did not come true on schedule, but now most agree that it is a question of timing. In fact, the time for chess came in 1997 when Big Blue beat Kasparov in a six-game match.

To see the trend clearly, we should understand some basic technological facts. The fastest computer in the mid-1970s was capable of only millions of operations per second. In 1996, a computer broke the teraflops barrier—a trillion arithmetic operations per second. In comparison, rough estimates say that the brain performs up to possibly 10,000 trillion operations per second. The general trend, which is expected to continue for at least ten to twenty years if not longer, is that computer processing speeds double every two years or less. Furthermore, software advances have also been substantial, exceeding hardware advances in many cases. The combination of hardware and software advances indicates that computing power will continue to increase rapidly well into the twenty-first century.

But if the optimism of the 1960s now seems excessive, we must recognize that we have only seen the beginning of the computer revolution. Though HAL is not with us yet and won't be at the beginning of the twenty-first century, it would be surprising if he were not with us by the end of the twenty-first century. Little HALs highly skilled in specific tasks will likely be with us by mid-century if not sooner.

Some might ask what these long-run technology developments have to do with anything of importance. The answer is not much—if you are over fifty years old. However, the children who began first grade this past fall will be middle-aged and at their peak earning ability in 2040. They will have to survive in a world full of 2040 technology, not 1996 technology, and do so with an education provided by the educational institutions we have today and the ones we are now planning for the next decade. The policies made today will be of enormous importance to these children.

Alternative Policies

What can we do about income inequality? This is a question that confronts policy makers of all political stripes. Most argue that we should do something: liberals typically want to reduce income inequality, and even many conservatives, though they may not care about income inequality on ethical principles, recognize that large income differences may generate political conflict and turmoil and argue for some equalization for the sake of social stability. I do not intend to argue these issues; their resolution depends on ethical and political judgments beyond the scope of this paper. My objective is to discuss how effective various policies are in reducing income inequality.

SHORT-RUN ASSISTANCE

Individuals who experience economic difficulties, as a consequence of trade, technology, recession, incompetent managers, or whatever, are eligible for short-run assistance—whereas unemployment insurance, which is paid to those who recently lost their job, or, if they have experienced more prolonged problems, a variety of welfare programs. Some workers may be eligible for retraining programs to help them get back into the job force. These policies are designed to help those who are temporarily at the bottom of the income distribution.

TAX POLICY AND INCOME DISTRIBUTION

A common way to deal with income inequality is to use a progressive tax system that taxes the poor lightly if at all, taxes the rich heavily, and uses some of the revenue to provide goods and services to the poor. In spite of its initial attraction, progressive taxation has high costs and is of limited value. It is at best a weak tool in addressing income inequality.

Taxing the rich has substantial economic costs. High taxes on the rich will discourage them from engaging in economically valuable activities and instead encourage them to engage in tax-avoidance activities and spend their time on leisure activities instead of productive work. Reducing the income of the rich means that there is less to tax. Furthermore, since the rich do most of the saving, taxing them will reduce investment, which in turn will reduce the productivity of workers, including the poor. Indeed, some economic analyses argue that imposing even a one-dollar tax on the investment income of the rich will hurt the wages of the poor by more than one dollar in the long run. Taxing the rich to give to the poor is a relatively ineffective tool.

SHORT-RUN VS. LONG-RUN PRIORITIES

Unemployment and welfare programs and income redistribution policies have limited effectiveness because they deal with the problem after it has arisen. A person's income is strongly tied to the extent and quality of his education, most of which occurs before he has a job. Conventional progressive taxation policies are therefore ineffective simply because by the time an individual is a poor taxpayer, it is too late to help him much. A more prudent route would be to focus on policy changes that prevent the problem. Just as with disease, prevention is often much more effective than any cure.

There are, however, ways in which income can be distributed through the distribution of education and training. Because they attack the problem at the source, good policies in this direction are much more likely to have the desired effects.

HUMAN CAPITAL INVESTMENT VS. PHYSICAL CAPITAL INVESTMENT

I have argued above that as trade and technology have their effects, low-skilled workers will fall even further behind skilled and better-educated workers. The way to prevent the income inequality problems that could arise is to encourage the necessary and valuable investments in education. To evaluate that strategy, we must first understand some basic facts about education.

Modern economies invest in the future in two distinct ways. They spend some money on machinery, equipment, buildings, and transportation systems; this is called physical capital investment. They also spend a comparable amount on educating and training their young people, which we call human capital investment. Before evaluating various policy changes and their impact on income inequality, we should note how well we are currently doing in allocating funds across these two basic categories of investment.

Economists have measured the return to educational investments and compared it to alternative investments for the United States. They find that investing in the bond market returns about 1 percent (after inflation) per year while investments in the stock markets yield 7 percent per year on average. The large difference is attributed to the fact that stock market investments are much riskier than bonds. The rate of return on education is harder to measure, but most studies argue that the average return to education is at least 6–8 percent; and some put it as high as 16 percent. Based on these observations, some have argued that there is a rough balance to the allocation between human and physical capital investments.

However, modern finance theory shows that such comparisons should take into account the riskiness of the alternative investments. For example, blue-collar workers, who typically have only a high school education, are the first ones to be laid off in a recession, whereas white-collar workers, particularly if they are college educated, are more secure during a recession. Also, education gives workers more flexibility, making them better able to take advantage of new opportunities and learn the skills necessary to stay ahead in a dynamic, growing economy. Certainly there is no reason to believe that workers are spending too much time in school. On this dimension, there is clearly no evidence of overinvestment in education; if anything, there may be underinvestment. This observation is important when evaluating the income distribution and economic effects of various policy alternatives. If the gap between low- and high-skill workers continues to grow and we want to avoid the resulting increase in income inequality, we should focus on education. If we do that now, we may be able to avoid problems that may arise from increasing income inequality. Arguments that we have not overinvested in education in the past also show that policies that focused on education had little chance of wasting resources. With these ideas in mind, we now consider various economic policies that are related to human capital investment.

EDUCATIONAL POLICIES AND INCOME INEQUALITY

Our concern for wage inequality and the critical role of education in wage determination tells us that educational policies are critical ingredients in any policy addressing income inequality concerns. There are many policies that can be used to increase educational attainment. First, general literacy programs have very high value in less-developed countries. Similarly, free general education up through high school is a common policy in developed countries. The very high rate of return to education tells us that there is no reason to reduce these educational programs and indicates that universal free education up to college is a policy that will be economically productive as well as a powerful tool to prevent excessive income inequality.

Second, there is also no evidence that there is excessive investment in college education in spite of the substantial subsidies that are available to many students. Maintaining and extending these programs also appears to be an effective way of addressing the problem of income inequality without substantial waste.

Third, extensive educational opportunities will blunt criticisms of income inequality even from those who forgo these opportunities and choose lower-income lifestyles. Restrictions in opportunities and unequal access to educational opportunities will generate much resentment and create political constituencies that demand other policies for income redistribution. Educational opportunities will address these concerns and prevent political demands for more damaging policies.

These considerations all bring to mind a famous homily about the value of education: Give a man a fish and you feed him for a day; teach a man to fish and you feed him for a lifetime.

Conclusions

I have discussed a wide variety of economic issues related to income inequality. Many economic policy issues revolve around helping the losers regain ground lost in the process of economic change. The challenge is to keep the engine of economic growth and progress running without being dragged down by unwise policy decisions on problems of income distribution. The twenty-first century will present advanced nations with many such challenges as the world market expands to include poorer nations and as technology progresses.

The trends in both trade and technology will likely expand the gap between college- and high school–educated workers. This gap is an important source of income inequality that will generate some political conflict and is a concern to many. I argue that we should avoid ex post measures such as redistributive taxation and instead focus on educational opportunity as a preventive measure.

REFERENCES

Borjas, George J., and Valerie A. Ramey. 1993. "Time-Series Evidence on the Sources of Trends in Wage Inequality." *American Economic Review* 84; no. 2: 10–16.

Katz, Lawrence F., and Kevin M. Murphy. 1992. "Changes in the Wage Structure, 1963–87: Supply and Demand Factors." *Quarterly Journal of Economics* 107; no. 1: 35–78.

Murphy, Kevin M., and Finis Welch. 1992. "The Structure of Wages." *Quarterly Journal of Economics* 107, no. 1: 215–326.

Part VI

Labor and Industrial Relations

Dae Il Kim and Ju-Ho Lee

Changes in the Korean Labor Market and Future Prospects

The "Korean Miracle" is probably one of the most frequently spoken phrases in recent economic development literature. The rapid economic growth of the four Asian tigers has been a popular research subject in academe as well as among the policy makers of other developing countries. The rapid economic growth of Korea in the 1970s and the first half of the 1980s centered around the well-publicized export drive. The export-oriented economic policy of the 1970s led to a boom in labor-intensive industries such as textile and apparel; this was followed in the late 1970s by the Big Push, the expansion of heavy manufacturing industries such as steel and chemical. During the 1970s, the real GDP grew at an annual rate of 7.6 percent and the per capita real GDP grew at 5.7 percent per year. As output and employment shifted to manufacturing, the process was fed by a steady urban migration of cheap young labor from rural sectors. With the exception of the economic slowdown in 1980, the early 1980s were a continuation of the 1970s. For the 1980–1985 period, the growth rates of real GDP and per capita real GDP were 7.8 percent and 6.2 percent, respectively.

The late 1980s and the early 1990s were a somewhat different picture. After the rapid expansion in the 1970s of manufacturing supported by an export-oriented economic policy and an elastic labor supply from the ever declining agricultural sector, the late 1980s and the early 1990s were a period of structural adjustment, mostly induced by the changing conditions in market supply and demand. Urban migration slowed: the number of young rural workers fell below 10 percent, and population growth also declined. Shifts in foreign demand as well as changes in the supply side caused adjustments in employment and output in various sectors. Also, the labor union activity that increased sharply in 1987 may have contributed to higher wages and accelerated the structural changes. Though the annual growth of real GDP was maintained at a level of 9.6 percent in the 1985–1990 period, in 1990–1993 it dropped to 6.4 percent.[1]

This paper attempts to document the structural changes in the Korean labor market in the late 1980s and the early 1990s, focusing on the recent changes in the supply side. In the following section we discuss changes in the structure of employment and market institution (mainly unionism), along with changes in real and relative wages as they relate to a simple supply and demand framework. We then discuss recent changes in labor market flexibility, focusing on the role of labor supply, union, and growth-driven factors such as increasingly specific skills. The final section discusses labor market deregulation and future prospects.

Korea's Labor Market, 1977–1994

As has been observed also in many other developing countries, the labor force in Korea has changed rapidly during the period of economic growth. The upgrading of a skilled labor force that began in the 1960s and continued into the 1970s and the 1980s has been even more intensified recently as a result of the expansion of college education in 1981, which effectively doubled the number of college entrants. This upgrading, along with the slowdown in urban migration, has made unskilled labor increasingly scarce. Meanwhile, female labor force participation and employment increased both quantitatively and qualitatively.

LABOR FORCE AND SECTORAL SHIFTS

The changes have not been limited to the labor supply. Shifts in demand and market incentives led to shifts in output and employment in various sectors. As a result, the growth of manufacturing finally slowed and the tertiary sectors continued to expand, the pattern being toward greater growth in highly skilled industries. One major institutional change in the labor market was an increase in union activity

1. An exceptional foreign demand shock in the late 1980s was partly responsible for Korea's high growth rate during that period.

following the Presidential Decree of June 29, 1987, that liberalized industrial relations. These changes led to restructuring in both employment and wages.

Labor force. The 1980s saw a striking decline of young workers in the Korean labor force, largely as a result of a decline in population growth. From an annual rate of 2.4 percent in the 1960s, population growth fell by half, to 1.2 percent in the 1980s, and fell again, to 0.9 percent in the first half of the 1990s. This decline mostly reflects the aging of the baby boomers (birth cohorts of the late 1950s and the early 1960s). Figure 1 plots the population share of various age groups where the shares are extended beyond 1996 using the projected age distribution. It shows that the share of 0–19-year-old population began to decline in the late 1970s, and it is expected to continue to decline into the twenty-first century. By 1996, the share had fallen to 30 percent; by 2020 it is projected to fall another 10 percent. The share of 20–29-year-old population started declining similarly in the early 1980s. In contrast, the share of the population 60 years old or older has steadily increased and will continue to do so as the cohort size of the younger population declines. Panel 1 of Table 1 shows that the share of 20–29-year-old workers de-

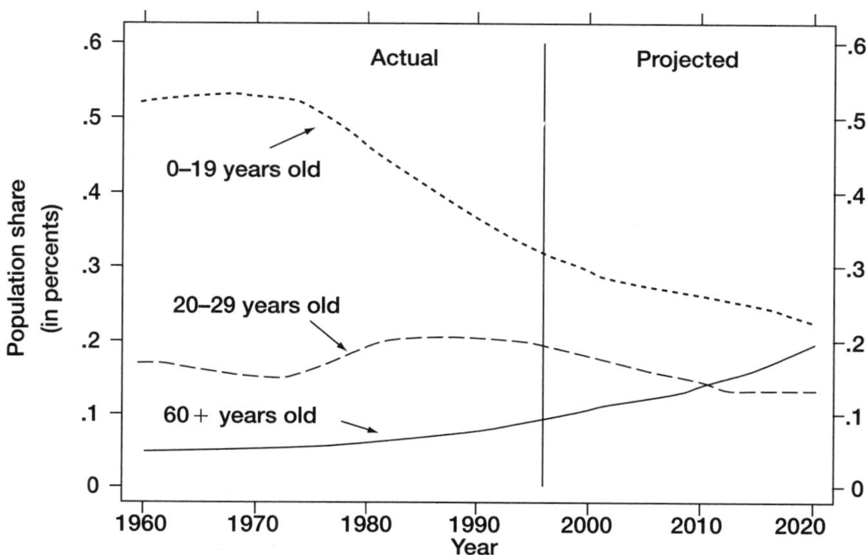

FIGURE 1 Actual and projected population share by age group, 1960–2020. Based on the projection by the National Statistical Office, Seoul, Korea.

TABLE 1 Changes in the Korean Labor Force, 1970–1993

1. Age Distribution in Employment (in percents)

	Male (ages)				*Female (ages)*			
Year	*20–29*	*39–39*	*40–49*	*50–59*	*20–29*	*39–39*	*40–49*	*50–59*
1970	24	35	26	14	30	30	26	14
1975	27	34	24	15	29	27	26	17
1980	28	31	26	14	31	25	28	16
1985	29	32	25	14	33	27	25	16
1990	25	34	24	17	31	27	24	18
1993	23	37	23	17	31	30	22	17

2. Education Distribution in Employment (in percents)

	Male—years of education				*Female—years of education*			
Year	*6*	*9*	*12*	*+*	*6*	*9*	*12*	*+*
1980	42	22	26	9	66	17	14	2
1985	29	22	35	14	52	20	24	5
1990	21	19	42	17	41	20	31	8
1993	17	16	45	21	34	18	37	11

NOTE: The employment share in panel 1 is the fraction of 20–59-year-old workers.
SOURCES: Authors' calculations from *Annual Report on the Economically Active Population Survey* (various issues) and *Population and Housing Census Report* (various issues), National Statistical Office, Republic of Korea.

clined in the 1980s from 28 percent to 25 percent, and declined further to 23 percent in 1993. The labor supply has become more inelastic also, a result of lowered urban migration. The rural share of young (20–24-year-old) population decreased from 23.6 percent in 1980 to 6.5 percent in 1994, and the rural share of young participants dropped from 27.1 percent to 7 percent during the same period (see Table 2).

At the same time, women have become an increasingly important part of the Korean labor force, although the employment rate of women is still far lower than that of other advanced countries. Figure 2 shows that the employment rate of women has been rising since the early 1960s while that of men has remained stable with some cyclical fluctuation. The aggregate employment rate has been rising from slightly above 50 percent in 1963 to 61 percent in 1993, most of which reflects increased female employment.

The reduction in the growth of the supply of young labor can potentially slow the growth of the Korean economy. Kim and Topel (1995)

TABLE 2 Decline of the Rural Workforce, 1980–1994

1. Rural Population Share by Age Cohort

	Year			
Age cohort	*1980*	*1985*	*1990*	*1994*
15–19	30.1	21.8	14.5	11.1
20–24	23.6	15.0	8.2	6.5
25–29	18.6	12.3	7.2	5.2
30–34	19.8	13.2	7.6	4.9
35–39	27.4	16.3	10.3	6.9
40+	47.2	32.6	26.5	20.2
All	33.5	22.3	16.5	12.3

2. Rural EAP Share by Age Cohort

	Year			
Age cohort	*1980*	*1985*	*1990*	*1994*
15–19	29.2	26.8	9.4	7.5
20–24	27.1	16.1	8.5	7.0
25–29	22.5	13.8	7.8	5.7
30–34	22.9	14.9	8.5	5.6
35–39	30.4	18.2	11.7	7.9
40+	53.6	37.6	31.2	24.9
All	37.7	24.7	18.7	14.4

NOTE: EAP = Economically Active Population.
SOURCE: Authors' calculations from *Annual Report on the Economically Active Population Survey* (various issues), National Statistical Office, Republic of Korea.

show that the rapid expansion of manufacturing in the 1970s and the 1980s was achieved by an ever increasing number of young workers entering manufacturing. Plentiful cheap young labor met the growing demand of manufacturing and also expanding service sectors during that period, but it may no longer be the case; nor does the increase in female labor participation appear to have compensated for the reduced cheap young labor supply to manufacturing sectors, since women are entering nonmanufacturing sectors at an even faster rate than men (see Figure 3). Also, married women newly entering the market are coming from relatively better endowed households.[2] When married women are classified by their husbands' employment status, the employment rate

2. This result is calculated from the Employment Structure Survey microdata files, 1986 and 1992, provided by National Statistical Office, Seoul, Korea.

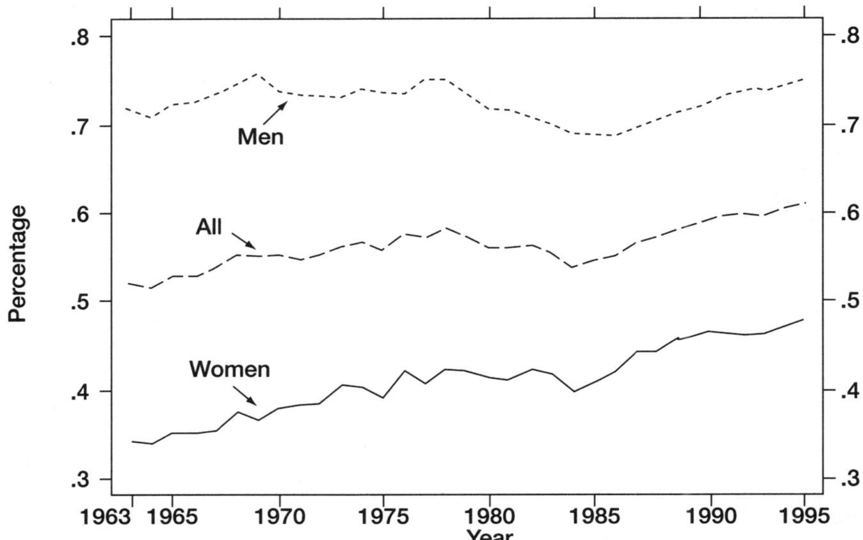

FIGURE 2 Employment rate of men and women 15 years old or older.

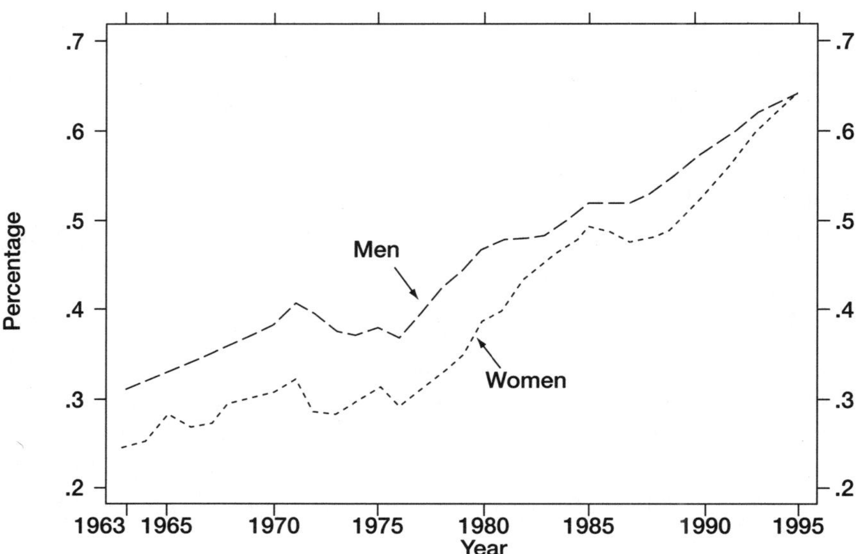

FIGURE 3 Employment share of tertiary sector by men and women.

of wives of employed men increased from 40 percent to 43 percent between 1986 and 1992 while that of others remained stable or slightly declined. The employment rate of wives of high school (or college)–educated men increased from 27.4 percent (17.9 percent) to 35.2 percent (24.2 percent) during the same period while that of wives of high school dropouts increased from 52.4 percent only to 57.4 percent.[3] The increased participation of married women in Korea also appears to result from increased demand for highly skilled women in nonmanufacturing sectors rather than from the need to substitute for young labor in manufacturing.

The Korean labor force also achieved an enormous upgrading of skills during the 1980s and the 1990s: the share of male workers with high school diploma or above increased from 35 percent in 1980 to 66 percent in 1993 (Table 1, panel 2). The upgrading is even more dramatic in terms of college education: the employment share of workers with two or more years of college increased from 9 percent in 1980 to 21 percent in 1993 among male workers. During the same period, the female labor force experienced a similar upgrading, from 16 percent to 48 percent for those with high school education or above.

Although most of the educational upgrading of male workers took place through increased educational achievement of young cohorts, the increased participation of women has helped the overall educational upgrading of the working population as better-educated women have increasingly entered the workforce. Between 1980 and 1990, women's employment rate rose from 38 percent to 46 percent among high-school graduate women and from 33 percent to 48 percent among two-year-college or better educated women. In contrast, the employment rate increased from 66 percent to only 55 percent among women with six or fewer years of schooling during the same period.

Sectoral employment and output. Sectoral shifts of employment and output in the 1970s in Korea are characterized as a rapid shift from agriculture to manufacturing and other sectors.[4] Figure 4 shows that the employment share of the agricultural sector has declined steadily

3. This pattern is quite comparable to the results of Juhn and Murphy (1997), who found that in the U.S. in the 1980s the employment of wives of high-income men rose relatively more than that of wives of lower-income men.

4. The results in this section are mostly based on Korea Statistical Yearbook, various issues, National Statistical Office, Seoul, Korea.

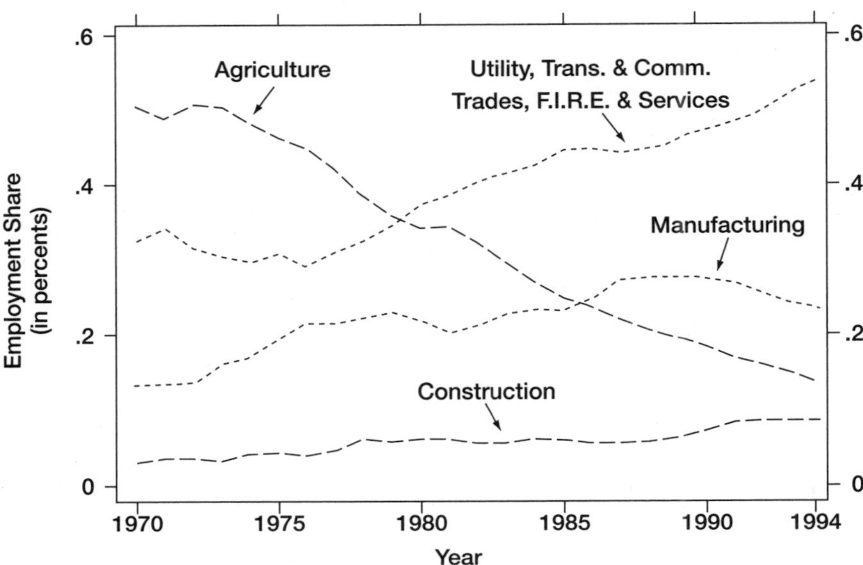

FIGURE 4 Sectoral distribution of employment, private sectors, 1970–1994.

since 1970 while manufacturing and service sectors have expanded. As Kim and Topel (1995) note, a growing demand for labor in manufacturing has been met by an ever increasing entry of young workers: during the 1970–1990 period the share of 20–25-year-old workers entering manufacturing rose from 23.7 percent to 44.6 percent, while the share of those entering agriculture fell from 40.4 percent to 6.0 percent. This is partly to be explained by the massive entry of young cohorts into manufacturing, leaving fewer young workers in rural areas. The effects of the decline in the population share of young workers and the consequent scarcity of cheap young labor are evident in the slowdown of manufacturing in the late 1980s.

The slowdown of manufacturing also appears to reflect shifts in demand: income growth has increased the demand for service goods more than that for manufactured goods, and an increasing number of young workers and women have chosen to enter service industries rather than manufacturing. By 1995, the share of 20–24-year-old workers entering manufacturing had dropped to 29 percent. Moreover, of the younger workers employed in manufacturing jobs between 1990 and 1995, a good many left manufacturing industries for jobs in construction, trades, and service.[5] The share of the 1961–1965 birth cohort (25–29 years old in 1990) in manufacturing dropped by more than 10 percentage points between 1990 and 1995. Kim and Topel (1995), however, found almost no strong mobility out of or into manufacturing along worker careers in the 1980s.

Sectoral distribution of output shows a similar pattern as employment. As Figure 5 shows, the share of manufacturing increased steadily in the 1980s until 1988 when it began to decline. In the tertiary sector, financial and service sectors have grown steadily. Construction sectors experienced a sudden spurt in the late 1980s as a result of the government housing drive and continued to climb until 1991 when it stabilized.

Within manufacturing itself there has also occurred an important shift toward skill-intensive sectors. This began to occur in the mid-1980s; the hours-weighted employment share of skill-intensive sectors grew from 37 percent in 1987 to 50 percent in 1994.[6] This pattern

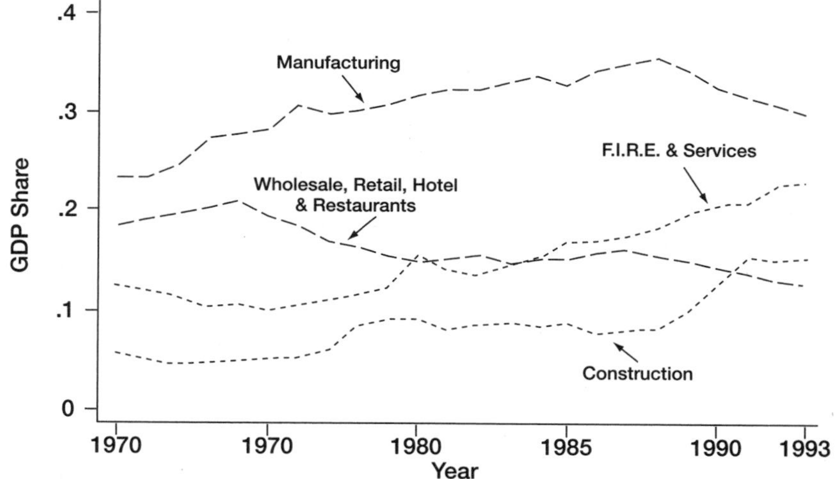

FIGURE 5 Sectoral distribution of GDP (private sectors), 1970–1993.

5. President Roh initiated the construction drive in 1989 by building 2 million new housing units over the next few years and emphasizing stable housing prices.

6. Skill intensity is defined as the average efficiency units of workers in each sector. For each gender × education × age cell, we calculated the average wages during the entire period (1977–1994) and normalized them to their weighted mean. Using these normalized indices as the efficiency units and also using the composition of workers in each sector, we calculated per-worker skills in each sector to rank industries.

appears to be the result of changes in both demand and supply. The relative increase in skilled labor in the economy led to expansion of skill-intensive sectors, but at the same time, the emergence of other developing countries such as China and Malaysia has affected the pattern of comparative advantages of Korean manufacturing in the world market; thus output patterns have shifted away from low-skill industries such as apparel and shoes.

EMERGENCE OF UNIONISM

Labor unions in Korea have a relatively short history. Although the Korean labor law has allowed the freedom to organize and bargain and labor unions have existed since 1960s, the military governments in the 1970s and 1980s kept unionism strictly under control by suppressing collective bargaining. A so-called wage guideline discouraged firms from raising wages beyond a recommended level. As a result, labor unions were virtually ineffective during the period.

In 1987, President-elect Roh's June 29 Declaration effectively liberalized unionism in the Korean labor market. Following the declaration, union membership rose sharply and since then labor unions have become a major player in the Korean labor market. As Figure 6 shows, the

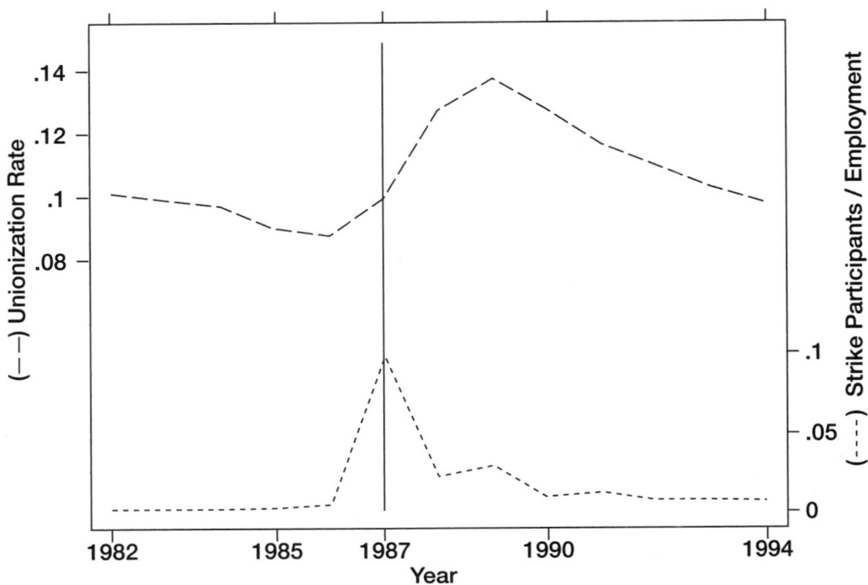

FIGURE 6 Unionization rate and strike activity, 1982–1994.

unionization rate jumped from 9 percent in 1986 to 10 percent in 1987, and in the next year rose another 2.5 percent. Unionization reached a peak at a level of 14 percent in 1989, when it started declining. The increase in strike activity was even more dramatic. Until 1986, strikes were virtually nonexistent: there were only 267 strikes in that year. In 1987, however, the number of strikes skyrocketed to 3,749. Whereas in 1986, only 46,941 workers participated in strikes, one year later over 1.2 million, or almost one-tenth of the workforce, went on strike. This was only a temporary phenomenon, a direct result of the new liberalization; since then, strikes have stabilized at pre-1987 levels. The reduced frequency of strikes did not, however, imply weaker unions in the post-1987 period. Figure 7 shows that, although the number of strikes declined, their duration increased. At its peak, an average strike participant was out of work for a month. The average duration of strikes has stabilized in the 1990s but at a permanently higher level than that of the pre-1987 period.

One of the notable features of Korean labor unionism is that the unionization rate is highly correlated with firm size, and also with the presence of chaebols. Panel 1 of Table 3 shows that in manufacturing larger firms are significantly more likely to be organized. Among firms

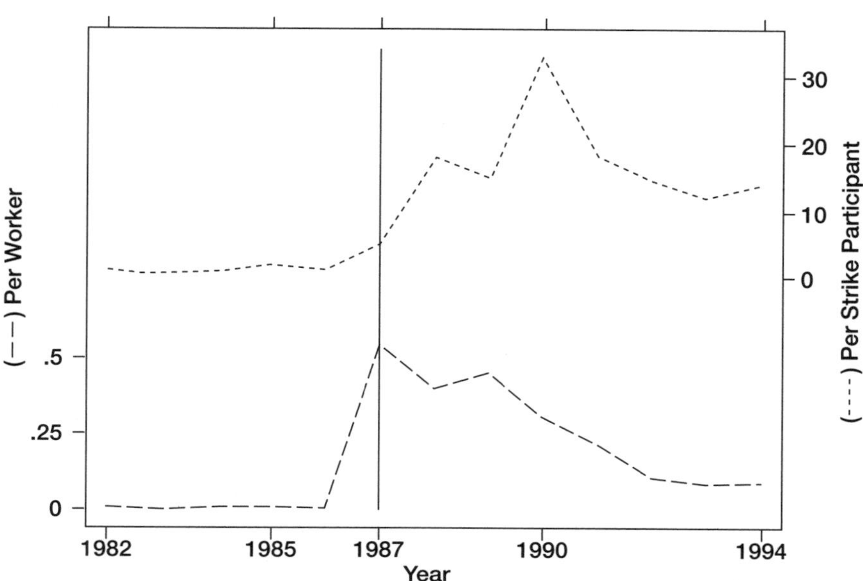

FIGURE 7 Work days lost due to strikes, 1982–1994.

TABLE 3 Extent of Unionization in Korean Manufacturing

1. Unionization by Firm Size

Firm size	*Unionization rate (%)*	*Firm size*	*Unionization rate (%)*
10–29 employees	0.9	500–999 employees	37.5
30–99 employees	5.4	1,000–4,999 employees	59.6
100–299 employees	26.3	5,000–15,000 employees	62.1
300–499 employees	36.4	15,000 or more employees	76.0

2. Sectoral Unionization Rate

Sector	*Unionization rate (%)*	*Sector*	*Unionization rate (%)*
Food	29.9	Primary metal	28.3
Textiles	32.0	Fabricated metal	39.0
Apparel and fur	16.4	Machinery	15.1
Leather and shoes	29.3	Office equip.	1.6
Wood projects	31.3	Electrical equip.	16.4
Pulp and paper	21.3	Communication equip.	34.3
Printing	18.9	Precision equip.	25.1
Petroleum refining	67.9	Automobiles	62.3
Chemical	23.6	Other trans. equip.	56.1
Rubber products	23.2	Furniture	26.3
Stone and glass	24.8		

NOTE: The Database of Labor Unions surveys all firms with labor unions and the number of union members in manufacturing is calculated from the data. In calculating the unionization rates, the number of workers in each industry is estimated from the Occupational Wage Survey.

SOURCES: Authors' calculations from the Database of Labor Unions (No-Dong-Jo-Hap Gi-Cho-Ja-Ryo), 1992, and Occupational Wage Survey microdata file, 1993, Ministry of Labor, Republic of Korea.

with 10–99 employees, the rate is below 10 percent, whereas it is 60 percent or higher among firms with 1,000 or more employees. Workers tend to be more organized in the sectors where chaebol is present: in an industry where the employment share of chaebol is higher by 10 percentage points, the unionization rate is higher by 5 percentage points. Sectoral variation in unionization rates within manufacturing is shown in Table 3, panel 2.[7] The unionization rate is highest, 68 percent,

7. Sectoral variation in the unionization rate is not easy to estimate owing to insufficient data. The primary source of data for labor unions is No-Dong-Jo-Hap Gi-

in petroleum refining and lowest, 1.6 percent, in office equipment manufacture. The correlation between firm size and unionization rates is even more noticeable: approximately 50 percent of the sectoral variation is explained by differences in firm size, a correlation that may be linked to the fact that unions in Korea are mostly enterprise-level. Larger firms, especially the chaebols, generate more rents through market imperfection and also government protection. This means that larger firms tend to be more organized as unions pursue a greater share of the rents.[8]

WAGE STRUCTURE

Real wages. Real wages have been rising during most of the 1980s and the 1990s for both male and female workers.[9] Figure 8 shows that monthly real wages rose by 70 percent for male workers, from below 500,000 won in 1980 to over 850,000 won in 1994, with a slight setback in 1980 and 1981.[10] Female workers have seen an even more rapid increase in real wages: they doubled between 1980 and 1994, from below 250,000 won to 500,000 won.

The long-run real wage growth in Korea appears to have kept pace with the growth in labor productivity. Figure 9 plots nominal GDP per worker and nominal wages, both of which are normalized to the averages during the period for comparability. The two indices have developed in somewhat different paths from period to period: nominal wages grew somewhat faster until the early 1980s, the period of the Big Push when Korean heavy manufacturing was highly subsidized to attract workers from other sectors. Wage growth slowed in the early 1980s,

---

Cho-Ja-Ryo (Database of Labor Unions) administered by the Ministry of Labor, which surveys all firms with labor unions. To calculate the sectoral unionization rate, we have to match these data to the estimates of sectoral employment from other sources; the resulting unionization rates are subject to errors because the industry code of each observation is variable in the union data.

8. Many economists argue that imperfection in market structure and consequently less-disciplined unions result in higher output price and that consumers are the main victims of the process (Pencavel 1996). There is plentiful supporting evidence for this argument: deregulation of trucking and airline industries in the U.S. led to expansion of the industries and (eventually) to lower wages and output prices (e.g., Hirsch and MacPherson 1996).

9. Most of the results on wages are based on the Occupational Wage Survey microdata files provided by the Ministry of Labor, Seoul, Korea.

10. In calculating average wages, we fix gender-age-education distribution to control for compositional changes. See Katz and Murphy (1992).

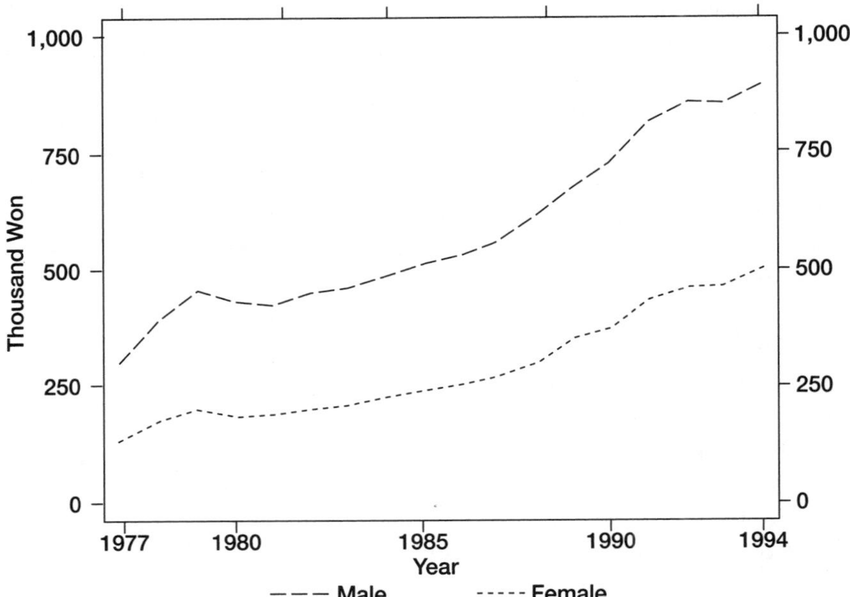

FIGURE 8 Real monthly wages, 1977–1994 (in 1990 won).

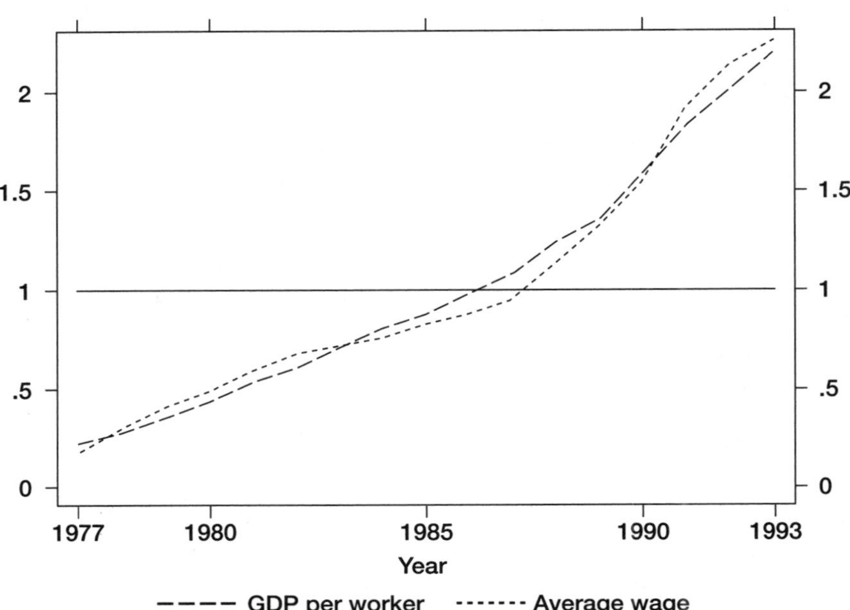

FIGURE 9 Indices of nominal wage and labor productivity, 1977–1993.

probably owing to the government's wage suppression, and by 1987 the average wage had fallen relatively below the level of labor productivity. After 1987 wage growth increased for a time until it finally slowed down again in the early 1990s. In spite of these temporary divergences, the two indices started and ended at almost the same points.[11]

The argument that the rapid wage growth in the late 1980s resulted from the increased labor union activity that began in 1987 is convincingly supported by the sharp increase in strikes. There is no doubt that workers obtained a stronger bargaining position and many employers made wage concessions during the period. It is not clear, however, that the resulting wage growth has exceeded the level tolerable in the market without an upward pressure on unemployment. Indeed, the Korean economy enjoyed an exceptional economic upswing in the late 1980s, which provided the room for a large wage increase. A strong Japanese yen made Korean manufactured goods relatively cheaper in the world market, and the low price of crude oil helped reduce production costs. Futher, even with wage growth, the unemployment rate has continued to decline in the post-1987 period. This consideration implies that the level of wage growth has been determined in the market, although the labor unions are quite likely to have prompted the growth. This conclusion is supported by the finding of Lee and Kim (1996) that during the period 1987–1990, manufacturing wages rose relative to the rest of the economy among workers of all skill types, even among those who were least likely to be union members.[12] Further, manufacturing wage growth finally slowed in the early 1990s when the economic upswing leveled off but unions still remained very powerful.

Relative wages. Throughout the 1980s and the early 1990s, various relative wages have shrunk in the Korean labor market except for employer size differentials. Gender premium, age premium, and college premium declined in the latter half of the 1980s, and the pattern continued well into the 1990s. The changes in relative wages for age and college can be explained mostly by the rapid changes in relative supply; changes in

11. Wage growth is quite likely to be overestimated because the wage series is based on the survey of firms with no less than ten employees: as will be seen in Figure 13, wages in smaller firms grew at a slower rate. Thus, nominal wages in the entire labor market are likely to have grown at a slower pace than the GDP per worker.

12. We consider four skill types among men: young workers with high school or less education, young workers with college education, old workers with high school or less education, and old workers with college education.

the gender premium appear to have resulted from an increasing demand for female workers in the economy. Although there is not much evidence that union activity pushed the aggregate wages above the level implied in the market, there appears to be plenty of evidence showing that increased union activity had a strong effect on relative wages.

Gender premium. Female labor participation has traditionally been low in Korea, especially among educated and married women, female education having traditionally been more valued in the marriage market than in the labor market in Korea. Even among women who entered the market, careers were often interrupted, voluntarily or involuntarily, by marriage or childbirth. Although the Labor Standard Law forbids different wages based on gender on the same type of jobs, the law per se has not been considered to have a significant effect in reducing gender gaps in wage and employment, not only because the law has not been strictly enforced but also because employers tend to place male and female workers into distinct jobs so that the wage gaps would not violate the law. As a result, an average male worker earned 130 percent (85 log points) more than an average female worker in the late 1970s, but the situation appears to have improved since the 1980s.

Figure 10 shows that the premium dropped to 70 log points by

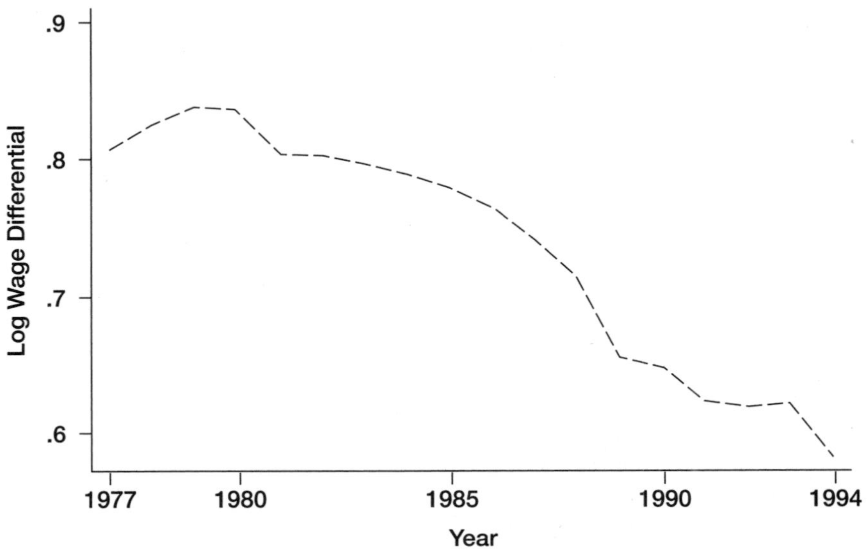

FIGURE 10 Gender wage premium 1977–1994.

1988, and dropped by another 10 log points in 1989. Since then, the decline has been moderate and stabilized. As we have seen, female employment has increased relative to male workers. The relative gains in both wages and employment among female workers imply that the demand has shifted toward female workers in the Korean labor market as retail trade and service sectors, both female-intensive, have expanded.

Age premium. As in most Asian countries, it is a social norm in Korea that elders should be respected, and this norm often extends to compensation in the labor market. Many employers adopt a compensation schedule that ties a major part of wages to worker age independently of productivity. It is also argued that the same norm also gives promotion priority to elders ahead of younger and more able workers, the notion being that worker discipline is more effective when the hierarchy is based on age rather than on worker ability or productivity.

Nevertheless, the age premium, too, appears to have been subject to market forces. As we have seen, young workers have become increasingly scarce in the Korean labor market, and the age premium has declined among male workers in the 1980s in line with the changes in relative supply. In the late 1970s the male age premium was as high as 48 log points for those 35 years old or older compared with younger workers (Figure 11), but more recently the premium has been on a decreasing trend. The figure shows also that the female age premium, always relatively small (below 10 log points), has been fluctuating with no apparent trend.

Changes in the male age premium are well explained by the relative supply. We estimated the elasticity of complementarity (Hamermesh 1993) by regressing the premiums on the relative supply (measured in efficiency unit man-hours) and report the results in the top panel of Table 4. We did not use any demand control except for time trend variable. Among male workers, the elasticities are -0.35 among all workers and -0.18 among less-educated workers where adjusted R^2s are higher than 0.6. The implied elasticity of substitution is 2.9, and it is larger among less-educated workers, at a level of 5.6. For female workers, the estimated elasticity is often wrong, probably because of incomplete controls of demand shifts.

One notable change in the age premium took place between 1988 and 1989 when the premium sharply declined for both genders. As we argue in Lee and Kim (1996), this one-time decline appears to have

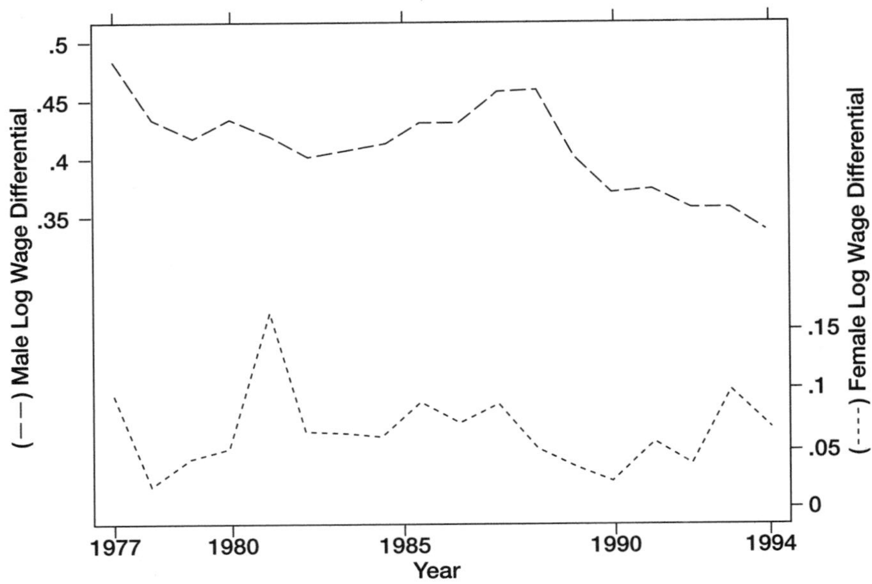

FIGURE 11 Age premium: 35+ years old vs. under 35 years old, 1977–1994.

resulted from the increase in union activity rather than from market forces such as the foreign-demand shocks. The economic upswing in the late 1980s would have resulted in a decline in the premium, since manufacturing is more intensive in young employment than the rest of the economy, but such an effect would have shown up in 1986 and 1987 after the upswing began. Also, as we show in Lee and Kim (1996), the sudden decline in the premium is concentrated only among larger firms that are highly unionized.

College premium. The supply of highly educated workers has been steadily increasing at the market-entry level in Korea, and the trend made a sharp upward turn in the mid-1980s as a result of the expansion of college education in 1981, which within a few years effectively doubled the number of college graduates. Reflecting the supply changes, the college premiums as shown in Figure 12 follow a decreasing trend in most of the 1980s and the 1990s. The male college premium was on a decreasing trend until the mid-1980s, and the decline accelerated in the late 1980s. Among female workers, premiums were relatively stable in the early 1980s but began to decline in 1985, reflecting the sudden

TABLE 4 Relative Wages and Relative Supply (Elasticity of Complementarity)

1. Old-Young Premium (35+ years old vs. less than 35 years old)

	All workers		*High school or less*	
	Male	*Female*	*Male*	*Female*
Relative supply	−.348	−.058	−.177	.041
	(1.22)	(.105)	(.067)	(.055)
Trend	.003	.007	.001	.002
	(.003)	(.010)	(.003)	(.006)
Adjusted R^2	.606	.080	.738	.334

2. College/High School Premium

	All workers		*35 years old or younger*	
	Male	*Female*	*Male*	*Female*
Relative supply	−.458	−.320	−.231	−.433
	(.153)	(.260)	(.080)	(.179)
Trend	−.021	−.016	−.021	−.014
	(.002)	(.006)	(.002)	(.005)
Adjusted R^2	.866	.515	.900	.645

NOTE: The sample contains 15–65-year-old workers working in private sector firms with no fewer than 10 employees. The relative supply measures are the ratio of efficiency unit weighted hours worked of each group of workers. The number of observation is 18 (time series over the 1977–1994 period); standard errors are in parentheses.
SOURCE: Authors' calculations from Occupational Wage Survey microdata files, Ministry of Labor, Republic of Korea.

increase in the number of female college graduates.[13] The biggest decline in college premiums, however, occurred between 1987 and 1989 among both genders, partly, it seems, owing to increased union activity in 1987, since no such decline occurred in smaller, mostly nonunion firms (Lee and Kim 1996).

The estimated elasticity of complementarity between college and high school graduates is reported in panel 2 of Table 4. The elasticity is −0.46 among male workers and −0.32 among female workers, imply-

13. Previous studies (Kwark and Rhee 1993; Kim and Topel 1995) did not find an inverse relationship between college premiums and the supply of college-educated workers among women. It appears that it took a sufficiently large increase in relative supply, such as the college expansion in 1981, to cause female college premiums to decline as the demand for educated female workers increased.

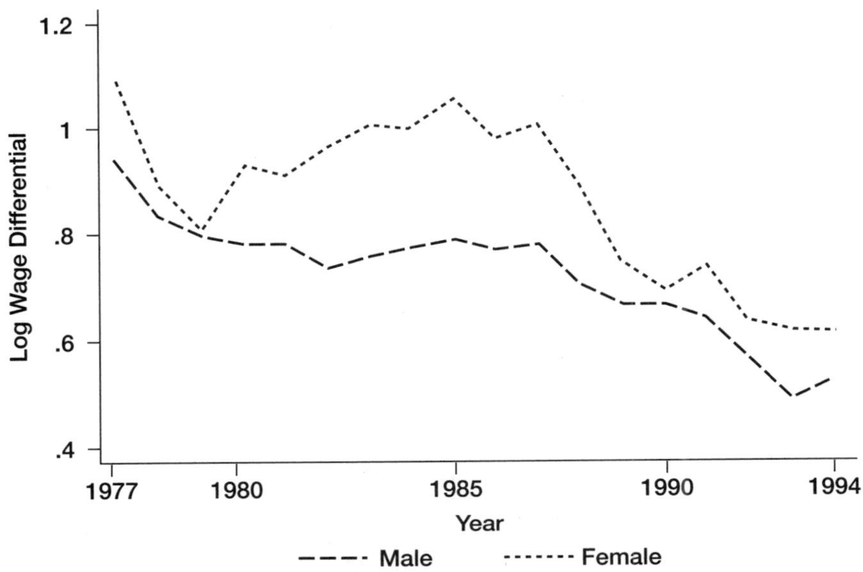

FIGURE 12 College/high school premium, 1977–1994.

ing that the elasticity of substitution is 2.2 and 3.1, respectively. Again, the relative supply and the trend variables explain the premiums quite well: the adjusted R^2s are high, as high as 0.9. Among young workers (less than 35 years old), the elasticity of substitution increases to 4.3 among male workers, implying that workers of differing education levels are better substitutes when they are young; among young female workers, however, the elasticity of substitution declines to 2.3.

Employer size premium. Employer size differential is an exception: it has been on an increasing trend throughout the 1980s and the 1990s with a sharp fluctuation in the late 1980s. Figure 13 plots the logarithm of size differentials relative to medium-size employers (100–299 employees) in manufacturing. It shows that the size differentials were on an increasing trend in the early 1980s and then increased dramatically in 1987, after which they gradually returned to the original upward trend. This temporary widening of the size differentials between 1987 and 1988 appears to have been the result of union activity, since larger firms are highly organized and more vulnerable to hostile unions. Strikes were frequent among these firms and many of them had to make wage concessions under pressure from unions or political forces.

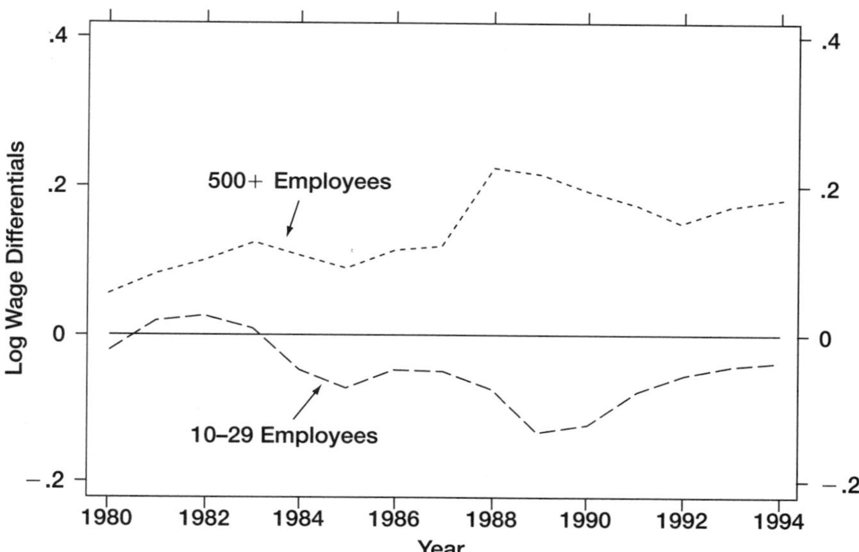

FIGURE 13 Employer size wage differentials, manufacturing, relative to medium size (100–299 employees), 1980–1994.

The economic upswing during the period may also have contributed to the temporary widening of the differentials, though the possibility is not so strong. In order for an economic upswing to have such an effect on firm size differentials, it has to favor large firms far more than small firms. Jeffrey Nugent (1996), however, shows that the share of large firms decreased in manufacturing during this period, which indicates that the demand shocks did not necessarily favor larger firms. Further, the widening of the differentials was very abrupt and the differentials had already started to decline in 1988 while the economic upswing continued until 1989.

How, then, did the wages in small firms catch up following the surge in 1987? Two hypotheses are possible: one is that there was an increased demand for the products of smaller firms as a consequence of union activity concentrated among larger firms. Another hypothesis is that workers in small firms used the labor-management agreement in larger firms as their benchmark position in collective bargaining. Nugent (1996) favors the first hypothesis because the labor demand among small firms would have declined under the second hypothesis. Thus we may conclude that higher (union) wages in larger firms promoted outsourcing and subcontracting and the demand for the intermediate goods and services produced by smaller firms increased in the process. In the market for consumer goods, higher wages in larger firms implied higher relative prices of their products, with a corresponding increase in demand for the products of smaller firms also. As a result, both the labor demand and wages of smaller firms increased.

Union premium. The wage data (Occupational Wage Survey) are far from ideal for any sound estimates of union premiums. Though the data provide information on the unionization of firms, they say nothing about union membership of the individual worker. We are obliged to estimate the union premium by guessing who are union members in unionized establishments. We can assume with some confidence (though it is only an assumption) that only the production workers in unionized establishments are union members. The regressors in the equation include four education dummies, seven five-year age interval dummies, quadratic tenure profiles, employer size, and industry dummies.[14] The estimated union premiums are reported in the first two columns of Table 5 for the years 1987–1994.[15]

The estimated premiums are not large and are often negative for both male and female workers. For both genders, the premiums reached a peak in 1989, 4.4 percent for male, and 2.2 percent for female. The premiums then declined for both genders, but the female union premiums started increasing again in 1991, to reach 4.1 percent in 1994. One possible explanation for the gender difference in the post-1991 period links the finding to the construction drive that was completed by 1992. With the end of the construction drive, a male worker–intensive enterprise, the demand for unskilled male labor decreased relatively more than the demand for unskilled female labor. The market for unskilled labor consequently became thin, and, to the extent that male and female workers are incomplete substitutes, it is likely to have reduced the bargaining position for male union members relatively more.

Another question is, why are the premiums so low? We can make

14. We limit the sample to workers age 21 to 60 in manufacturing and estimate the premiums for male and female workers separately each year.

15. The standard errors in Table 5 are somewhat misleading because we estimate the premiums in employment weighted regression using the cell average data. The cells are defined over two genders, ten age groups, five education groups, twenty-three industries, two occupations (production and nonproduction), and five establishment size groups.

TABLE 5 Estimated Union Premiums in Korean Manufacturing, 1987–1994

(Male) Year union	Union premium		Log real wage growth		
			Unionized		
	Male	Female	Prod.	Nonprod.	Nonunionized
1987	−.034 (.006)	−.040 (.006)	.171	.060	.061
1988	.034 (.006)	−.006 (.006)	.109	.114	.111
1989	.044 (.006)	.022 (.006)	.088	.084	.145
1990	.010 (.006)	.016 (.007)	.102	.166	.081
1991	.012 (.007)	−.007 (.007)	−.004	.036	.090
1992	−.005 (.006)	.004 (.006)	.050	.029	.071
1993	−018 (.007)	.018 (.008)	.045	.024	.034
1994	−.023 (.007)	.041 (.009)			

NOTE: The wage equation for columns 1 and 2 is the following:

$$\log(W_{ct}) = \alpha_t + X_{ct}\,\beta_t + \delta_t{}^*UP_{ct} + \varepsilon_{ct}$$

X_{ct} : Education, age, tenure, occupation, employer size, and industry for cell c at time t

UP_{ct} : Union*Production worker interaction dummy for cell c at time t

ε_{ct} : Normal error term

Cells (unit of observation) are defined as gender × education × age × employer size × industry × occupation × union.

SOURCE: Authors' calculations from the Occupational Wage Survey microdata files, Ministry of Labor, Republic of Korea.

two conjectures (other than the possibility of a false assumption): first, labor union activity raises the wages of nonunion members as well as those of union members through the threat effect, and second, the macrodemand shocks provided sufficiently large upward pressure on wages of nonunion members. Both conjectures are consistent with data. Columns 3–5 of Table 5 show the annual growth of real wages for production workers in unionized establishments, nonproduction workers in unionized establishments, and workers in nonunionized establishments. The growth rates move quite closely between these groups, especially between production and nonproduction workers in unionized sectors. That is, wages in unionized sectors move together regardless of union membership status, and so also, though to a lesser extent, do the wages of unionized and nonunionized sectors. The strong correlation among wages of all workers indicates that marketwide forces are dominant. The somewhat stronger correlation among wages of workers in unionized establishments appears to reflect the threat effect.[16]

Labor Market Flexibility

Employment adjustment at the firm and/or industry level in response to demand shocks is an important market feature that must not be sacrificed in order to maintain efficient labor allocation in a dynamic economy. It has been argued, however, that the Korean labor market has increasingly suffered from employment rigidity, owing primarily to union pressures. Another issue that affects flexibility is the transition between employment and unemployment status. In many OECD countries, longer and longer unemployment spells and the continuous decline in demands for unskilled labor have become a growing concern. In this section we document the changes in labor market flexibility in Korea and investigate the causes for reduced flexibility.

OUTPUT ELASTICITY OF EMPLOYMENT

The output elasticity of employment in manufacturing declined significantly in the late 1980s. Using monthly output and employment data in manufacturing, Lee and Moh (1996) show that the short-term (one-month lag) output elasticity of employment was 0.283 in the period preceding 1987, but dropped to 0.065 in the post-1987 period. When the adjustment periods of three months and six months were considered, the elasticity declined from 0.386 to 0.137 in the three-month case and from 0.405 to 0.180 in the six-month case. The long-run (one-year) elasticity declined as well, but only slightly, from 0.376 in the pre-1987 period and 0.333 in the post-1987 period.

We interpret this finding as reflecting the reduced labor supply

16. An alternative explanation is possible: workers have a greater incentive to organize when there are sustained (long-term) demand shocks, and consequently growing industries tend to be more organized. In that case, in unionized sectors wages move together between production and nonproduction workers, while wages may move differently between unionized and nonunionized sectors.

elasticity at the entry level, not necessarily the harmful effects of unionization. This interpretation is based on the observation that the decline in the long-run output elasticity of employment in the post-1987 period was concentrated among smaller firms with scarce unionism and remained stable among larger firms (Lee and Moh 1996). Lee and Moh (1996) also show that the short-run output elasticity of employment declined in *all* firm size groups, including the largest firms as well as those with 10–29 employees where the unionization rate is only .9 percent. Since larger firms are highly organized, the decline in the output elasticity of employment is hardly linked to unions but must instead have a specific connection to smaller firms. The explanation would appear to be the fact that small firms have been the main employers of unskilled labor migrating from rural areas during the period of the quantitative expansion of manufacturing, hence the reduced labor supply and decline in rural young population.[17]

LABOR MOBILITY

In a dynamic economy where there are frequent shocks in different sectors, economic growth and/or stability relies on a high labor mobility to respond to shortages and demands. Kim and Topel (1995) argue that because labor mobility was high in the period of rapid growth, sectoral shocks were quickly arbitraged by employment adjustment. The situation appears to have changed as a consequence of a smaller young workforce, both rural and urban, which has made it difficult to respond quickly to demand shocks at the entry level without placing upward pressure on wages; further, as skills become more sector-specific, it has become more costly to attract workers from other sectors.

To measure the extent of labor mobility, we followed Kim and Topel (1995). First, we regressed the log labor productivity (industry GDP per worker), log wages, and log employment shares on industry and year dummies. The residuals from these equations are sectoral deviations from aggregate demand shocks and aggregate wages and employment. We regressed the wage and employment residuals on the productivity residuals to gauge the responsiveness of wage and employment to the sectoral changes in labor productivity. The results of this second-stage regression are reported in Table 6.

17. This conclusion does not necessarily imply that unions had no distortionary effect at all in the Korean labor market. The union effect may have arisen in the form of a decline in the manufacturing sector, which was more unionized.

TABLE 6 Wage and Employment Responsiveness to Productivity Shocks

	1977–1990	*1977–1986*	*1987–1990*
Log wage residuals	.045	.003	.082
	(.022)	(.028)	(.038)
Log employment residuals	.522	.381	.679
	(.069)	(.077)	(.140)

NOTE: We first regress log wages, log employment share, and log labor productivity on year and industry dummy variables.

$$\log (W_{it}) = \lambda_i + \mu_t + RW_{it}$$
$$\log (E_{it}) = \pi_i + \gamma_t + RE_{it}$$
$$\log (LP_{it}) = \varrho_i + \sigma_t + RP_{it}$$

where RW, RE, and RP are the residuals from each equation. Then we regress the wage and the employment residuals on the productivity residuals.

Row 1 in the top panel: $RW_{it} = \alpha + \beta^*RP_{it}$
Row 2 in the top panel: $RE_{it} = \alpha + \beta^*RP_{it}$

SOURCES: Authors' calculations from Occupational Wage Survey microdata files, Ministry of Labor, and the Census of Mining and Manufacturing, various issues, Ministry of Commerce, Republic of Korea.

The table indicates that sectoral wages responded to the labor productivity growth only to a limited extent while employment response was quite large. The coefficient on productivity in the wage equation is 0.045; in the employment equation it is 0.522. This finding is consistent with Kim and Topel (1995): sectoral productivity shocks are arbitraged mostly by labor reallocation, not by wages. There is evidence, however, that the wage responsiveness increased somewhat in the post-1987 period. When the sample is grouped into the pre- and post-1987 periods, the patterns are quite similar, but the coefficient in the wage equation is somewhat larger in the post-1987 period at a level of 0.082, compared with the pre-1987 period in which wages were not responsive at all. The higher wage responsiveness to productivity suggests that labor mobility has declined in the post-1987 period.[18] If the trend continues, sectoral reallocation of labor will be increasingly costly in the coming years.

One interesting result is that employment responsiveness, too, increased in the post-1987 period. We do not consider this finding incon-

18. Alternatively it can be said that unions capture part of higher productivity by limiting employment in growing industries. Such an effect does not appear strong; however, when the unionization rate is added to the regression rate, the wage coefficient does not change and the unionization rate has an insignificant coefficient.

sistent with the decline in labor mobility; on the contrary, it seems to reflect the changing nature of sectoral shocks. A significant shift within manufacturing began in the mid-1980s; the hours-weighted employment share of skill-intensive sectors grew from 37 percent in 1987 to 50 percent in 1994, indicating that the sectoral shocks in that period were more permanent than those in earlier periods. The magnitude of sectoral shocks also was greater in the late 1980s. Compared with the pre-1987 period, sectoral shocks were 38 percent greater in the post-1987 period in terms of standard deviation of the labor productivity residuals. As sectoral shocks become greater and more permanent, firms have a stronger incentive to adjust employment, especially in firms in declining industries.

UNEMPLOYMENT

The unemployment rate in Korea has been exceptionally low in recent periods at around 2 percent.[19] The rate was as high as 8 percent in the early 1960s, but it declined throughout the 1960s and the 1970s (see Figure 14). The rate rose briefly in 1980 when the Korean economy

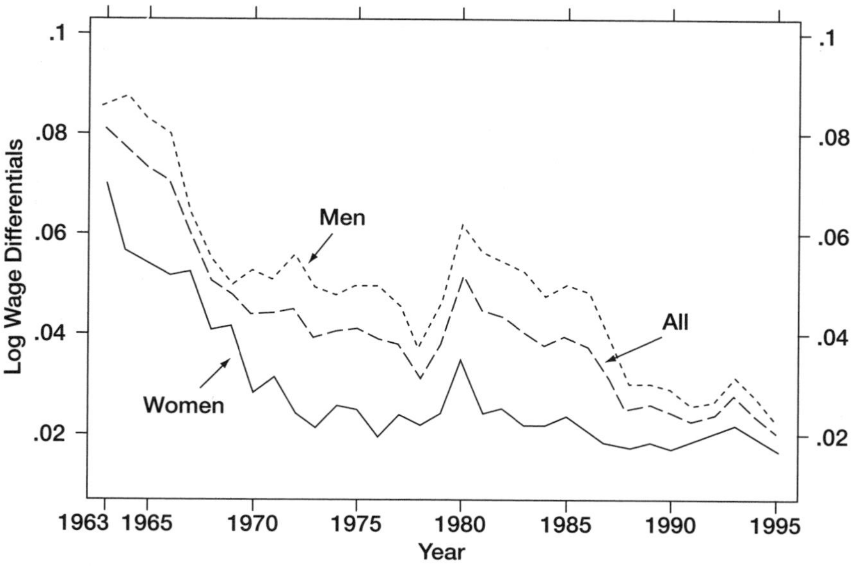

FIGURE 14 Unemployment rate, age 15 or older, 1963–1995.

19. Annual Report on Economically Active Population, various issues, National Statistical Office, Seoul, Korea.

experienced a rare setback, but the decline resumed again in the 1980s. The unemployment rate is somewhat higher among men than among women, mostly reflecting that the former are more strongly attached to the labor market than the latter.

The low unemployment rate is strikingly lower than rates not only of advanced countries but of other developing countries: for example, the unemployment rate has been recently no lower than 5 percent in the United States, and many European countries have suffered from two-digit unemployment rates. The main reason for the difference appears to be the low participation of women. The employment rate among prime age men exceeds 90 percent in Korea, which is higher than that of most advanced countries. The opposite pattern is true for women: the employment rate is below 50 percent, and most nonworking women declare themselves as nonparticipants.[20]

A more important issue in unemployment is the exit rate from unemployment and the duration of unemployment. Frequent but short unemployment spells are rather innocuous, but many OECD countries report an increase in the number of long unemployment spells. The unemployment trap is burdensome both to the unemployed and to the employed, who may have to endure higher tax rates to finance welfare programs. The OECD countries recently initiated a reduction in welfare programs and promoted a welfare reform that tied mandatory work to welfare receipts.

In spite of Korea's low unemployment rate, the unemployment trap appears to be on the increase in the Korean labor market. In a hazard analysis using the matched Economically Active Population Survey, Kim (1998) shows that the average unemployment duration has been increasing in the 1990s. The share of (completed) unemployment spells longer than one year rose from 9 percent in 1990 to 13 percent in 1996, and during the same period the share of (completed) unemployment spells longer than six months also rose from 19 percent to 28 percent. Kim suggests that both the stronger labor market attachment of female workers and declining job opportunity for the unemployed are responsible for the result.

20. Until unemployment insurance was introduced in 1995, the unemployed had less incentive to declare themselves as unemployed. Lee and Kim (1996) attempt to correct for the difference by investigating whether each nonparticipant searched for jobs within the previous six months and had an intention to work. A liberal estimate of unemployment then increases to 4.8 percent in 1992, which is much larger than the reported 2.5 percent but still far lower than those of advanced countries.

Labor Market Regulation and Future Prospects

We have seen that there have been a few signs of increased rigidity in the Korean labor market since the late 1980s. Slower growth in the labor supply has made sectoral employment more costly, and labor mobility has also declined, the result, it appears, of labor union activity in larger firms. In the large firms the effects were mostly income transfer between union members and nonunion employees, necessarily compromising the overall employment. We found little empirical evidence to support the frequent charge that unions have pushed wages above the market level but unions do appear to have affected various wage differentials.

DEREGULATION IN THE MARKET

Even though the rigidity has become more serious owing to the diminishing labor supply, the legal framework governing the Korean labor market has remained highly restrictive. Its distortionary effect may have been negligible in the past when the labor supply was fairly elastic, but the previously innocuous regulation is now a binding constraint on the current market. The labor reform bill passed in 1997 was far from a full-scale reform in two senses: it was limited to the labor market, and it left unresolved several controversial but crucial items. We shall attempt to define the principles that should be kept in the minds of labor market policy makers and shall suggest the direction of further reforms.[21]

On the Labor Standard Law: more deregulation. The following is a list, obviously not comprehensive, of the proposed but still unresolved legal framework for a revised Labor Standard Law. First, employers have been discouraged from laying off workers without "right cause." The court has determined the rightness of a layoff, and until very recently, the decision has been favorable to workers, and redundancy layoffs have been quite rare. Second, employer-financed severance pay is mandatory: a worker with more than one year of tenure is entitled to at least a month's salary per year of service, the salary being the three-month average prior to separation; the minimum severance pay schedule rises more than linearly with the worker's tenure. Third, fixed-term

21. For a discussion of the reform bill, see Kim and Lee (1997).

labor contracts exceeding one year are illegal, and so is labor outsourcing.

It has been argued that these regulations have reduced flexibility in employment adjustment and will continue to do so. It does not immediately follow, however, that they should be banned by another legal framework to enhance labor market flexibility. For example, there is plentiful literature on the back-loaded payment schedule such as severance pay that can enhance worker productivity (e.g., Becker 1983; Lazear 1979); also some of the regulations are intended to enhance worker welfare and induce labor supply. The most desirable policy therefore is to minimize the statutory regulation that stipulates the *decentralized* contracts between employers and employees. Redundancy layoff, for example, can be internalized in labor contracts between employer and employee if both parties understand the risk of separation. Some risk premiums may be added to wages in firms with higher risks of redundancy layoff, and/or severance pay may work as the compensation for such risk. Direct regulations through a legal framework would be efficient only if all contingencies can be identified and listed in the law.

On unionism: product market deregulation. As we have shown, there is no strong evidence that increased union activity resulted in a significant bottleneck in long-run resource allocation in the Korean labor market. The effects of unions appear to have occurred in the form of income transfers between young and old, between the skilled and the unskilled, and between small and large firms, and probably also in the form of reduced short-term employment flexibility among larger firms, but not in the form of reduced long-run employment flexibility. This finding is not surprising, for the entry and birth of small firms is still an effective tool for sectoral adjustment under enterprise-level unionism.[22]

This consideration does not imply that the Korean unionism is market-friendly. Industrial relations in Korea are often pictured as hostile confrontations between labor and management, and the unions in many cases have been militant, as is partly reflected in the permanent increase in strike duration per strike participants in the 1990s. Current labor reform efforts in Korea are intended to discipline industrial relations and facilitate employment adjustment by providing the amended

22. It can be argued that the entry and birth of firms is a more costly tool of employment adjustment than adjustment at firm levels when demand shocks are temporary.

legal framework for redundancy layoff, flexible work hours, and more flexible management of severance pay.

These measures are designed to enhance labor market flexibility, and eventually they will bring about some efficiency gains. But because they still allow the law to dictate dos and don'ts, they will not prove to be the best measures to enhance labor market economic efficiency. The court will again be the one judging each case of redundancy layoff, and the amount of time and effort spent in such cases is known to be large. Such costs come almost always with direct regulation, and we should like to focus on the argument that the best way to discipline industrial relations is product market deregulation, not direct intervention in the labor market by governments (e.g., Pencavel 1996). The importance of product market deregulation cannot be understated, especially with respect to Korean unionism. As previously shown, the unionization rate is highly correlated with firm size, and also with the presence of chaebols. Lack of competition in the product market creates rents, a greater share of which unions pursue. Market imperfection (limited entry) gives employers some buffer from market forces, and consequently employers will excessively hold back. At the same time, knowing that excessive requests and/or strikes will not drive a firm into bankruptcy, unions also have the incentive to become more militant. The bargaining power of unions is reinforced by the ban on replacement workers during strikes, which violates one of the most basic economic principles—substitution. Neither bargaining side has been effectively disciplined by the market force, competition, under these environments. Many disputes have ended with higher product prices, leaving the Korean consumers, not the employer or the union workers, the chief victims.

FUTURE PROSPECTS

Blank and Freeman (1993) analyzed the effect of reduced social protection programs in OECD countries and found no evidence of large tradeoffs between such programs and labor market flexibility. They interpret their (and others') findings:

> Why has research failed to turn up the large tradeoff that the 1980s conventional wisdom posited? One possible reason is that there is in fact no sizeable tradeoff between *specific* programs, flexibility, and efficiency. . . . This may be because the programs are embedded in a larger system of employment and family relations, so that changes in one program do not change incentives as much. . . .

> Another possibility is that the program changes are too modest. . . . Only major changes, abolishing whole sets of programs, may produce the degree of market flexibility.

Although these authors' findings point to the ineffectiveness of partial deregulations, we cannot dismiss the current deregulation efforts in Korea. Deregulation, though partial, is expected to enhance labor market flexibility to some extent. The message the findings of Blank and Freeman suggest as applied to the current situation in Korea is that further systematic and comprehensive measures are needed to minimize the costs of the future sectoral adjustment. They also suggest that the future successful reform must be carried out with proper understanding of the very decentralized mechanism in the economy: the division of labor within households, labor supply decisions by workers, and the firm's incentive in hiring and firing decisions.

We emphasize the need for product market deregulation and a restoration of the mechanism by which market forces squeeze the economic margins, but we also see a need for an active labor market policy in some areas, notably labor upgrading. The emergence of China and South Asia as market forces has put pressure on unskilled labor-intensive industries in Korea which have declined because of relatively high costs of production and as a result of shifting employment toward skill-intensive sectors. The skill premiums have declined in recent years, reflecting the rapidly increasing supply of skilled labor, but as the young population declines, so also will the supply of skilled labor. It is to be expected that as industries in Korea become more skilled and specific, higher unemployment and lengthy unemployment will emerge as new problems. In order for the economy to continue to grow, more efficient educational and vocational-training investment seems essential.

REFERENCES

Becker, Gary S. 1983. *Human Capital.* 2d ed. Chicago: University of Chicago Press.

Blank, Rebecca M., and Richard B. Freeman. 1993. "Evaluating the Connection Between Social Protection and Economic Flexibility." NBER Working Paper no. 4338.

Hamermesh, Daniel S. 1993. *Labor Demand.* Princeton, N.J.: Princeton University Press.

Hirsch, Barry T., and David A. MacPherson. 1996. "Earnings, Rents, and Competition in the Airline Labor Market." Unpublished ms., Florida State University.

Juhn, Chinhui, and Kevin M. Murphy. 1997. "Wage Inequality and Family Labor Supply." *Journal of Labor Economics* 15: 72–97.

Katz, Lawrence F., and Kevin M. Murphy. 1992. "Changes in Relative Wages, 1963–87: Supply and Demand Factors." *Quarterly Journal of Economics* 107: 35–78.

Kim, Dae Il. 1998. "Increase in Unemployment Spells and Policy Implication (in Korean)." Mimeo. Korea Development Institute.

Kim, Dae Il, and Ju-Ho Lee. 1997. "Labor Reforms in Korea." Paper presented at the East-West Center–Korea Development Institute Joint Seminar on Restructuring the National Economy, Honolulu, Hawaii.

Kim, Dae Il, and Robert H. Topel. 1995. "Labor Markets and Economic Growth: Lessons from Korea's Industrialization, 1970–1990." In *Differences and Changes in Wage Structure,* pp. 22–64. Richard B. Freeman and Lawrence F. Katz, eds., Chicago: University of Chicago Press.

Kwark, Noh-Seon, and Chang-Yong Rhee. 1993. "Educational Wage Differentials in Korea." *Seoul Journal of Economics* 6: 1–35.

Lazear, Edward P. 1979. "Why Is There Mandatory Retirement?" *Journal of Political Economy* 87: 126–84.

Lee, Ju-Ho, and Dae Il Kim. 1996. "Labor Market Development and Reforms in Korea." Mimeo. KDI–World Bank joint project.

Lee, Ju-Ho, and Yeong-Kyu Moh. 1996. "An Empirical Study of the Changes in Employment Adjustment in Manufacturing" (in Korean). *Kyeong-Je-Hak Yeon-Ku.*

Ministry of Commerce, Korea. *Census of Mining and Manufacturing,* various issues (in Korean), Seoul.

Ministry of Labor, Korea: 1977–1994. *Occupational Wage Survey.*

National Statistical Office, Korea. *Annual Report on Economically Active Population.* Micro Data Files.

———. *Korean Statistical Yearbook.*

Nugent, Jeffrey B. 1996. "What Explains the Trend Reversal in the Size Distribution of Korean Manufacturing Establishments?" *Journal of Development Economics* 48: 225–51.

Pencavel, John. 1996. "The Legal Framework for Collective Bargaining in Developing Economies." Policy Paper, Center for Economic Policy Research, Stanford University.

Edward P. Lazear and Sherwin Rosen 12

Labor in a Global Economy

In this essay we outline a number of issues that affect international labor markets. After a discussion of some general trends and their potential causes and effects, we describe the roles of different governments in labor markets.

There are many ways in which governments can and do affect labor markets. Though most are well intentioned or at least packaged to convey the good-spirited aspects of a proposal, some have unintended effects. Indeed, it has been argued that the so-called secondary effects are, in fact, the desired effects fostered by the special-interest groups that pursued the legislation. The selfish motives that may lie behind particular aspects of government intervention are generally disguised by language that seems to further the general good of society. It is important to examine whether specific policies have beneficial consequences or whether they merely transfer income from one group to another.

Trends

Before engaging in policy analysis, it is useful to consider various trends in the labor market: the roles of women and men, income inequality, the growth in jobs over time, and unemployment.

Edward Lazear's research was supported in part by the National Science Foundation.

WOMEN

By far the most important trend in labor markets during the latter half of the twentieth century has been the increased labor force participation of women. The trend has been experienced, though not necessarily in the same ways, in virtually all Western countries. The typical pattern is that shown by Figure 1 displaying three patterns of labor participation over the life cycle. The first pattern, labeled I, reflects an essentially agrarian economy, here representing the situation in the United States around 1900. Labor force participation rates for females are very low at all ages, and the curve is very flat as it relates to age. Few women are in the formal labor market, although many are working at home and perhaps even performing market jobs that do not show up in the statistics. Women who are in the labor market are career women, most of them single and childless; as such their labor force participation behavior is similar to that of men at the corresponding ages. Curve II reflects an economy in transition—here, the United States around 1960. Women are becoming an important part of the labor market but still take time out for child rearing. The two humps in the curve reflect the fact that women's labor force participation is very similar to that of men at given ages—young, and middle age. As women reach childbearing ages they drop out of the labor market to have and raise children; many, but not all, reenter after those children have gone off to school, and participation rates reach another local peak around age forty-five.

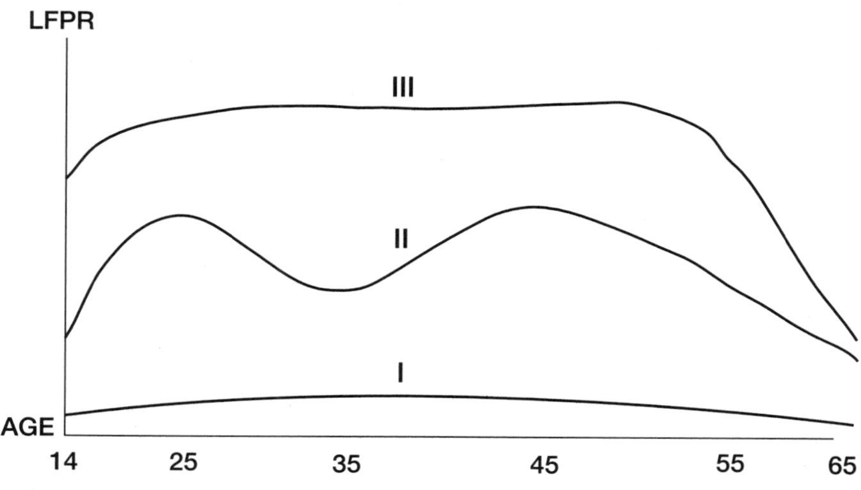

FIGURE 1 Female labor force participation rates, by age.

At that point labor force participation rates taper off as they move into retirement. Curve III reflects a mature labor market that has very high rates of female labor force participation with virtually no noticeable reduction in participation at childbearing ages. Labor force participation rates for females are close to those for males and remain so throughout the life cycle. This curve shows labor force participation rates as they relate to age in the U.S. and European economies today.

The changing role of women in the labor market is probably the most important phenomenon in the twentieth-century labor market behavior in Western countries primarily. Asia is not at the Curve III stage of labor participation, nor is the pattern quite the same: in Japan, for example, one observes high rates of labor force participation among young women, but the second hump that reflects reentry into the labor market is not very pronounced. In order to understand why Asia might be different it is useful to try to understand why female labor force participation behavior in the West has changed. There are a number of contributing factors. One cause, at least chronologically, was an exogenous change in home technology, which reduced the demands for female time at home. The invention of processed foods and mechanical housekeeping devices made time at home much more productive. To the extent that home-produced goods are necessities, rising income did not increase the demand for home-produced goods at the same rate as it did the demand for other goods. Since women were the primary producers of home-produced goods, the natural consequence was that women had more time for other activities such as joining the labor force. This was a gradual change that continued throughout the twentieth century, with the most rapid advances in home technology occurring during the 1940s and 1950s.

A second contributing cause was the significant drop in fertility rates over the second half of the century. Since the double-humped structure of labor force participation was primarily related to childbearing, the reduction in the fertility naturally reduced the dip in labor force participation at childbearing ages. At the same time, reductions in fertility or planned fertility increased female attachment to the labor market and their career orientation.

One can, of course, question which is the cause and which the effect. If the value of women's time in the labor market goes up exogenously, then the cost of staying home to care for a child also goes up. Children become more expensive (Becker et al., 1990), and the number of children desired will fall. Conversely, changes in technology that make it either tougher to have children or less costly to avoid them reduce the number of children exogenously and therefore push women into the labor market. A number of authors have explored the effects of contraceptive technology during the 1960s on female labor force participation behavior and find that improved contraception increases female labor force participation.

A final factor that changed female labor force participation, particularly in more recent years, is an increased demand for skilled labor, particularly for the kind of labor for which women have a comparative advantage. When the West was engaged in heavy manufacturing, construction, and agriculture—jobs in which physical strength had positive value—women were at a disadvantage relative to their male counterparts. Over time, jobs have become less physically demanding particularly among skilled workers, and any comparative disadvantage that women had disappeared. Consequently, the demand for female labor relative to the demand for male labor has gone up. This tends to pull women into the labor market, other factors constant.

All these trends show up in college enrollment rates. During the early part of the century college was primarily a male institution. There was a significant break with that pattern in the 1970s. Today's college enrollment in the United States is more than 50 percent female. Both supply and demand factors are relevant, but this clearly reflects an increased attachment to the labor market and careers by females.

MEN

The story for men complements that for women. Whereas labor force participation rates among females have risen, participation rates for males have fallen. There are two primary reasons for this drop. One is earlier retirement; another is increased school enrollment. Earlier retirement means that older men are significantly less likely to work today than they were at the beginning of the century, although that trend seems to have leveled off very recently. Similarly, men who are eighteen and twenty-five years old are significantly more likely to be in school today than they were fifty years ago. The resulting slack in the overall labor market has almost exactly been taken up by women. According to Kevin Murphy et al. (1993), approximately as many women have entered the labor market as men have left over the period.

INCOME INEQUALITY

Western countries have for the most part experienced increasing inequality of income over the past twenty years. The United States has seen the largest increase but other Western countries have followed. It has not always been this way; indeed the post–World War II period saw a shrinking inequality in the United States. Rising levels of per capita income generally are associated with greater equality due to urbanization and rising equality of education.

One of the few rapidly growing economies to experience reduced inequality in recent years is Korea. Wages of less skilled workers have risen relative to those of more skilled workers (Davis 1992). On the face of it, the coupling of reduced inequality and increased U.S. inequality suggests trade as a possible explanation for the Korean phenomenon—that is, increased globalization and more trade between countries is consistent with the view that the United States has a comparative advantage in skilled labor and Korea has comparative advantages in unskilled labor. As trade increases, the premium earned by Korean skilled labor goes down, and the premium earned by American unskilled labor also goes down. Trade creates expanded opportunities for less skilled Korean workers, because the products produced were able to find additional markets. At the same time, trade creates additional opportunities for American managers and skilled technicians to export their services to other countries.

But the evidence on this point is not strong. Although a number of papers have attempted to ascertain the effects of trade, wages, and inequality (e.g., Katz et al. 1992; Freeman 1995), they are at best inconclusive. If trade were important, one would expect industries that have been most affected by trade to be the ones with the largest changes in wages or employment. Yet it is difficult to find evidence to support this view. Trade probably accounts for too small a share of the U.S. output to be significant determinant of overall labor market conditions.

THE GROWTH OF JOBS

Political parties like to take credit for the growth in the number of jobs "created" in a particular economy. The truth is that the most important variable in any regression in jobs is the size of the population. A country's employment moves directly with its working population. This is clearly true when one examines differences between the current situation and the beginning of the century, but it is apparent even over a ten-to-fifteen-year horizon. As the size of the U.S. population grows, so does the size of the American labor force. The only intervening factors are increases in labor force participation of females and, to a lesser extent, reductions in labor participation rates among males.

The number of jobs in an economy is largely supply driven. It is folly for political leaders to take credit or blame the opposition for changes in the number of jobs in the economy over any significant period of time because those factors are beyond government control. Government policy does, of course, affect the environment in which jobs are created or destroyed—that is, it affects the efficiency with which labor resources are used.

UNEMPLOYMENT

During most of the post–World War II period, unemployment rates in the United States were above those in Europe and Japan, but the past fifteen years have seen a change: unemployment in Europe now seems to hover at rates consistently above those for the United States. A number of observers have labeled the phenomenon Euro-sclerosis and indeed there is evidence that specific government policies may be involved. Still, policies do not account for more than a small part of aggregate changes in employment over time. In our discussion of government policies, we try to focus on the conditions that may influence short-term disruptions to employment and the process by which labor moves to its highest-valued contributions.

Government Policies and Labor Markets

Before beginning this section on specific government policies, it is worth making one general observation: it is impossible to write laws that are sufficiently specific to every particular situation. Laws tend to be like "one size fits all" garments, more suitable in some situations than in others. This is true to large extent in laws pertaining to labor: for example, a minimum wage of $5 an hour may seem ridiculously low in New York City, but it may be reasonably high in rural Alabama. Furthermore, any attempt to tailor legislation to specific situations leaves the process open to rent-seeking by various interest groups that would like to insert their own special provisions into the law. Often this is an attempt by the group to protect itself; in other cases, it simply reflects the desire to transfer income from other groups to themselves. This point will reappear in a number of specific contexts below.

The following discussion concerns three areas of government policy: government action that affects employment directly, government action that is intended to affect the compensation for employment, and government action that is intended to affect the conditions of employment.

THE ROLE OF GOVERNMENT IN LABOR MARKETS

We start by offering three criteria against which government policies can be judged: (1) labor should be encouraged to move to its highest valued use; (2) workers should be encouraged to invest in themselves so that the marginal social return to skills equals its social costs; (3) firms should be able to employ labor in a way that makes the best use of their human resources and technology.

Why should governments intervene in labor markets at all? There are two potential economic explanations for specific government policies. One is that government policies improve economic efficiency; the other is that the policy serves the interest of a particular group and is instituted for political reasons rather than for economic efficiency. Most policies can serve both ends. Some examples may be instructive.

It has often been argued that unemployment compensation must be provided by the government because no company can bear the diversification risk associated with business cycle downturns. When a recession strikes, so many individuals are out of work that any private insurance company would face bankruptcy. Only the government is sufficiently large to be able to buffer such risk. This is the efficiency argument for government provision of unemployment compensation. The efficiency argument is less clear-cut for other government policies. Consider the minimum wage, for example: the economic efficiency rationale of the minimum wage relies on a significant amount of monopsony power and is not suitable in modern competitive labor markets. Instead, the minimum wage is best interpreted as an attempt to transfer income from one group to another and to restrict competition.

The legal system plays an important role in these processes. The United States is often said to be an overly litigious society, but the United States is also an extremely open society; U.S. law allows individuals to exercise a great deal of freedom ex ante, but it relies on the courts ex post to determine whether their actions were acceptable. In other societies, particularly in Asia, individuals are more constrained ex ante in their choices and adjudication through the court system is less prevalent. There seem to be fewer infractions, or at least fewer that seem to be litigated in Asian economies. Tradition is more important.

POLICIES THAT AFFECT EMPLOYMENT

In most Western countries, governments impose explicit limitations on an employers' freedom to hire or fire as he sees fit. Hiring in the United States is constrained by laws that affect the power of unions to direct employment decisions and prohibit employers from discriminating against protected workers in hiring and compensation. Many European countries, too, also impose severe penalties on termination of workers. Even in the United States increased litigation for wrongful discharge has reduced the freedom with which employers may terminate their workforce. Throughout Europe, one of the pervasive restrictions placed on employers is severance pay, which means that if a firm terminates a worker it must pay in some measure according to years of prior service. These payments are getting larger and larger; in France, separation payments are now so high that termination by an employer is very rare because the cost is prohibitive.

The logic behind severance pay requirements is, of course, to deter employers from capricious firings. A desired by-product is higher levels of employment in the economy. Since employers cannot capriciously terminate their workers, they are forced to maintain larger labor forces than they perhaps need—or so goes the argument. However, the policy also affects the employer's choices in hiring. Since the size of the labor force is altered both by rates of termination and by rates of hiring, it is possible that the workforce falls below the level that would have prevailed in the absence of severance pay. Indeed, there are theoretical reasons to believe that reduced hiring effects induced by such policies will dominate reductions in terminations.

The efficiency argument in favor of severance pay is that workers make investments that are specific to a particular firm. At any given point, a firm may have incentives to terminate a worker in order to avoid paying him his return on the specific investment. This, of course allows the firm to capture too large a share of the rents, but it results in an inefficient termination when the firm is required to make severance payments, and thus can restore efficiency in such an environment. There are two problems, however, with this explanation. First, there is no obvious reason why government action is necessary. Firms and workers would negotiate private severance pay contracts when these investments are significant and labor markets are competitive. In fact, such contracts do evolve in managerial circumstances where investments specific to the firm are large.

A parallel argument suggests that workers should themselves make severance payments to the firm if they quit at inappropriate times. To the extent that a specific investment has been made in a worker, the firm bears a cost that the worker does not take into account when opting to leave. In the same way that firms may be required to make severance payments to workers, workers might be required to make separation payments to firms for voluntary but premature separation. Contracts of this sort exist but are unusual. For example, the state of Alaska, which does not have a well-developed university system, gives its residents scholarship money to attend schools in other states, on condition that they return to Alaska for a specified period of time. The student cannot be required to return, of course, but if the student does not return the loan must be repaid. The loan is forgiven if the student returns for the specified time.

Criticism of government severance pay requirements is that the government does not have the information to tailor the severance contract to a specific situation. Even if greater efficiency were possible through government-imposed severance pay, the appropriate amount of severance pay would not be the same across firms and workers. It is almost impossible for the government to gather an appropriate amount of information to set up an efficient severance pay schedule in all cases.

European-style severance pay programs can actually be offset as long as experience earning profiles can be adjusted to extract the value of the severance pay from workers in their first years on the job. A theoretical analysis is presented in Lazear (1990). Summarized, it states that a firm can offset severance pay rules by paying higher wages to experienced workers and lower wages to inexperienced workers. The way it works is as follows: Because of the government-mandated severance pay system, firms are reluctant to lay off workers. However, their reluctance would be tempered had the firm contracted to pay very high wages to experienced workers. The high wages offset the firm's unwillingness to lay workers off, and if set just right, they can restore the proper amount of turnover.

Of course, firms do not want to pay high wages simply to ensure a certain freedom to fire a worker without making a severance payment. There must be some compensation: it comes as lower initial wages. Because workers know that they will either receive high wages when they have gained experience and are retained, or be given severance pay if they are laid off, they are eager to get the job in the first place. Their initial enthusiasm for the job pushes wages lower initially. The firm makes the money that it will later spend on workers by getting them to work for relatively lower wages initially.

In fact, any severance pay arrangement can be offset by an optimal contract that should evolve in a competitive labor market. In order for the mandatory severance pay to be undone, the worker must be willing to accept lower initial wages, but as long as there are no constraints on borrowing and lending, all is well; any inability or apprehension by workers on this score causes problems. Without the ability to extract a payment from workers before the job even begins, it is impossible to maintain profit and achieve efficient employment. But for a number of reasons listed below, workers may have cause to resist making up-front payments to the firm. If a payment is not made, then firms cannot offer a sufficiently high wage in subsequent periods to achieve efficiency. Thus, the effects of severance pay are offset completely only if there are no limitations on buying the job. It is also true that the effects of severance pay are neutral only when the payment made by the firm is received by the worker. No third-party intermediary can receive the payment. If this occurs, then incentives are necessarily distorted. Thus, an unemployment insurance system that does not have a perfect experience rating will induce inefficiencies. This is shown rigorously in Lazear (1990).

All these arguments are somewhat surprising when put in the context of international comparisons. Consider a country that has strict severance pay laws but no system of state unemployment compensation. Payments are made directly from firms to workers at termination. Under this system, as long as up-front payments can be made, there are no inefficiencies from employment at will. Neither underemployment in good times nor overemployment in bad times results because wages adjust to offset any detrimental effects. Contrast this situation to the situation in the United States, where severance pay is not very important but state-run unemployment compensation is pervasive. As Topel (1984) has shown, experience rating is far from perfect for many firms in many states. This results in overemployment in good times and underemployment in bad times. If these are the facts, and if impediments to perfect offsets are ignored, then the conclusion is not that Europe has too few layoffs during downturns but that the United States has too many. The European system is equivalent to an unfunded mandate: it has the virtue that in the absence of experience rating, forcing firms to make severance payments induces them to take account of the costs that they levy on society through unemployment compensation. The

American system is an alternative but inefficient way of accomplishing the same thing. The inefficiency results from incomplete experience rating.

Still, it may be that European employment constraints are tighter than those that bind American firms. This is likely because of the inability to undo completely what the government has done. The usual arguments against such up-front payments are the ones that apply here. Imperfections in capital markets that prevent complete smoothing of consumption limit the amount that workers will pay up front. Workers trust of the firm may be incomplete and they may fear that the firm may "take the money and run," say, by declaring bankruptcy. Other strategic considerations may apply.

To the extent that restrictions on severance pay are not undone by the market, empirical effects are ambiguous. In the short run it is possible that reductions in rates of termination increase employment, but one would expect that, over the longer run, the greater costs of labor and reduction in hiring rates would have a more significant impact. In order to get at this, a data set was used that examined twenty-two countries over a twenty-nine-year period from 1956 to 1984. These countries came primarily from Europe but also included the United States, Canada, Israel, Japan, Australia, and New Zealand. The rules regarding severance pay varied across countries and also changed over time. By estimating fixed-effects models, it was possible to use the changes in severance pay laws to estimate the effects of in-country changes on employment. The signs were clear: increases in severance pay have depressing effects on employment and increase the unemployment rate. According to the estimates in Lazear (1990), if the United States were to go from zero to three months of required severance pay at ten years of service, there would be a reduction in the number of jobs of approximately 1.5 million. This would raise the unemployment rate by one point or by about 18 percent of the unemployment rate. It is difficult to believe that such a change would further the goals of efficient labor mobility or use of best technology, though there might be some increase in firm-specific human capital investments because workers would feel less susceptible to firm-initiated layoffs.

UNEMPLOYMENT INSURANCE

Unemployment insurance differs across countries. The Europeans have adopted the attitude that most incentives should be placed on the side of the employer; thus, severance pay and restrictions on employment policies create strong incentives for employers to behave in certain ways. In the United States, the incentives are shared between employers and workers. Partial experience rating in the unemployment system makes it costly for an employer to lay off a worker because some of that payment to the worker is passed along to the firm. But there are also incentives for the worker in that unemployment insurance is of limited duration (usually 26 weeks, or in times of recession 52 weeks).[1]

The two different methods of unemployment compensation have different consequences. The duration of unemployment in Europe is longer than it is in the United States, and rates are also higher. One reason for longer duration of unemployment is that European employers are reluctant to hire new workers because severance pay and other restrictions on termination make mobility expensive. Employers must be fairly certain that they are going to keep the worker for a long period of time before they hire the worker in the first place. This reduces the rate of absorption of workers from the unemployment pool, thereby increasing unemployment duration.

There is evidence on this point. John Kennan et al. (1989) found spikes in the hazard rate of returning to work from a state of unemployment in the American data. Such spikes occur when unemployment compensation runs out. Thus, across states, when unemployment compensation runs out at the twenty-sixth week, the probability goes up that the worker will find another job in that very same week. This suggests that there is a substantial amount of choice associated with unemployment duration and that the choice is exercised by the worker. Thus, the American system that puts some of the burden on the worker rather than on the firm may result in a more efficient job search.

NOTICE REQUIREMENTS

Most European countries, and recently the United States, require large employers to give advance notice before terminating a worker. In the United States, employers who are going to close a plant must inform the workforce three months before the closing date. Notice requirements are a mild version of severance pay because, at worst, an

1. Unemployment insurance periods are extended during times of recession partly because it is assumed to be more difficult to find a job and therefore a long period of insurance is necessary, and also because it is assumed that in a recession workers are less responsible for their being unemployed. In this circumstance, the government chooses to soften the incentives to return to work.

employer could simply terminate the worker immediately, without notice, and pay three months' salary as severance to avoid giving any advance notice at all. The employer is aware that workers will not produce much during this three-month period, but retaining the worker is no worse than the extreme alternative.

As such, the finding on notice restrictions should be similar but weaker than those on severance pay. The empirical literature on notice requirements is somewhat mixed. Ronald Ehrenberg et al. (1993) find no adverse effects of notice requirements whereas some OECD European studies do find adverse consequences on employment. Because they are a form of severence pay, notice requirements fail to meet our policy criteria on the same grounds. Notice is generally given by firms, and if it were desirable to write notice requirements into the labor contract, there is no reason why this could not be done voluntarily.

WORK SHARING

In response to high unemployment rates encountered in recent years, a number of European countries, notably Germany, have instituted shorter work weeks in order to share the work and reduce unemployment rates. The notion behind work sharing is that there is a fixed amount of work to be done and that the work must be spread around evenly in order to accommodate goals of income equality. Such a notion defies simple economic reasoning, which takes as a basic postulate that demand curves slope downward.

Let us consider the theoretical effects of work sharing. Work sharing is generally implemented by raising the overtime wage. The overtime premium can easily be undone by a combination of changing the straight time wage and coupling it with a stated number of hours of overtime (see Figure 2). Suppose that the straight time rate had initially been $12.50 per hour and that employees were working eight hours a day. Total take home pay per day was $100. Now the government reduces the length of the standard work week from a forty-hour week to a thirty-hour week by reducing the daily hours from eight to six. The government effects such a reduction by requiring that overtime (in this case 150 percent of straight-time pay) be paid after six hours of work. If eight hours and a wage of $12.50 per hour was the initial equilibrium, the new equilibrium wage-and-hour structure will be $11.11 for the first six hours with an additional two hours of overtime offered each day at a wage of $16.67. By doing this the employer is paying exactly $100 per day for eight hours, just as he did before the change

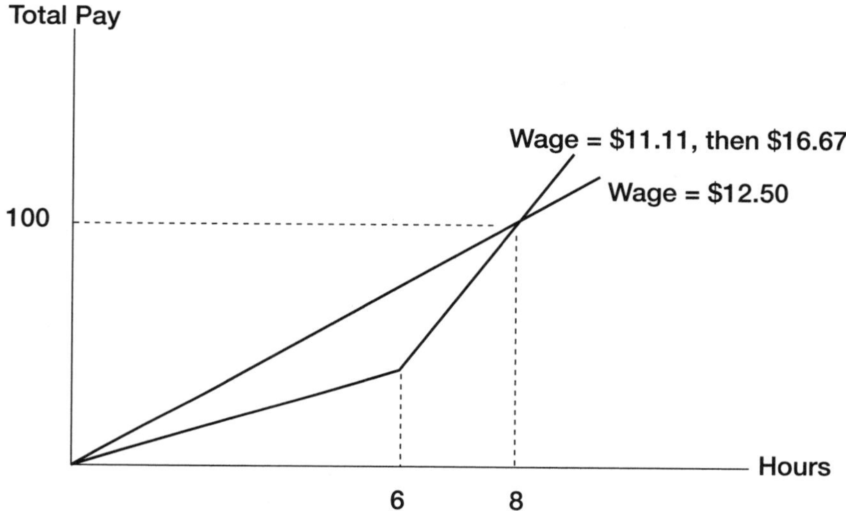

FIGURE 2 Changes in overtime schedule. From Trejo et al. (1991).

in the length of the work week. Thus, it is possible to completely undo the change in the length of the work week simply by altering the straight-time wage.

Of course, Europeans were aware of some of these possibilities and prevented employers from reducing wages at the time shortened work weeks were implemented. Thus, one would expect some real effects of policy. In two papers Jennifer Hunt (1996a, 1996b) estimates the effects of the changes in German industry. She finds that earnings did not fall after the work week was reduced, implying either that the straight-time wage was increased just enough to offset the reduction in hours of work, or that there was no reduction in hours of work at all. In fact, she finds that there was a reduction in hours of work per worker and that the total number of hours worked fell, although the work was shared more evenly across people.

This is consistent with standard theory of supply and demand (see Figure 3). Initially the equilibrium is at point B with wage W and labor quantity L. The change in standard hours of work has the effect of raising the straight time wage from W to W^1 and cutting employment from L to L^1. But the total wage bill could be the same in both cases, depending on the elasticity of demand. In fact, the wage bill goes up if the demand elasticity is less than one at point B. Since earnings per worker remained stable and employment fell in Germany, the demand

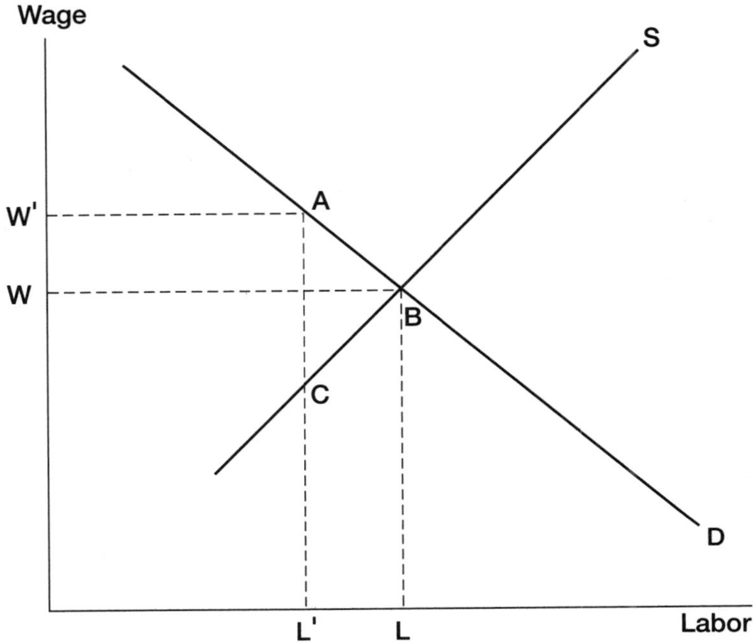

FIGURE 3 Wage and labor equilibrium: the German example (from Hunt 1996a, 1996b).

elasticity was less than one. The total wage bill increased, but the amount of earnings per worker remained the same. But though individual workers benefited, there is a social loss associated with this effect, measured by the welfare triangle ABC, which reflects a reduction in the consumer and producer surplus.

MANDATORY RETIREMENT

The United States has all but abolished mandatory retirement as a legal practice. The Age Discrimination in Employment Act was amended in 1979 to prohibit mandatory retirement at any age for most workers. This means that an employer is not free to write a contract with termination at a fixed age for highly paid managerial employees. The elimination of mandatory retirement is unusual and specific to the United States, and somewhat surprising given the relatively noninterventionist role of the American government in labor markets. The statutes against mandatory retirement were an outgrowth of antidiscrimination law that was extended to cover age discrimination in the 1970s.

As a practical matter, the prohibition on mandatory retirement has not had significant effects on much of the labor force. The modal age of retirement for American males is sixty-two, which is the age for entitlement for Social Security benefits. Retirement ages, if anything, have gone down since the elimination of mandatory retirement. Changes in Social Security law, which will soon raise the normal age of eligibility from sixty-five to sixty-eight, affect retirement ages much more significantly than did changes in mandatory retirement legislation.

Policies Designed to Affect Compensation

A number of policies have been designed to affect compensation. These relate to unions, minimum wages, licensure, and include various laws against discrimination.

UNIONS

The major difference between unionism in the United States and Europe centers on business unionism in the United States versus political unionism in Europe. The American labor movement adopted goals of working directly at the level of the industry or enterprise to determine wages and working conditions. Although American unions do get involved in politics and support particular candidates, most of their activity centers on relations with management.

Unions in Europe operate differently. French syndicalism and British unions have regarded the state as an important part of their economic strategy, though union power declined significantly in Britain in the 1980s. Unions in Europe are much more centralized than they are in the United States. Wages and work policies are often negotiated in tripartite settings with representatives from labor, management, and government; policies and wage levels are set nationally. As a result, exceptions must be made to accommodate individual circumstances.

In the United States, wages, working conditions, and employment restrictions are sometimes negotiated at the level of the industry, but more generally wages are negotiated firm-by-firm. Firms are sometimes linked to one another through practices such as pattern bargaining, where a union negotiates with one firm and other firms in the same industry follow, but for the most part, unions and employers negotiate on an individual basis even when workers at different firms are represented by the same union. The flexibility provided by decentralized negotiation probably enhances economic efficiency because parties can take into account idiosyncratic circumstances.

An additional feature of American union-management is that when wages are negotiated centrally and all parties must comply, it is easier to enforce monopoly power than it is when individual unions negotiate separately with individual employers. Under those circumstances, individual union-employer pairs have incentives to deviate from the nationally set standard in order to benefit from high-wage competitors. Competition is an important factor in the American union structure. On the whole, however, American unions have not been as powerful or as effective as European unions, particularly during the last thirty years. Union membership reached a peak in the late 1950s of about 35 percent of the labor force; today union membership is down to approximately 13 percent. The only growth sector for unions is government service, where managers are not so closely tied to profitability and to competitive market constraints as are managers in the private sector.

The strongest unions historically in the United States have been craft unions, which are organized on the basis of occupation: in construction, medicine (the American Medical Association), and airline pilots (Airline Pilots Association). There is evidence that unions have been more effective in regulated industries such as public utilites (Pergamit 1983). Airline pilots have lost power since deregulation of the U.S. airline industry, and after trucking was deregulated at the end of the 1970s, the union premium associated with driving trucks over similarly skilled workers declined markedly.

Organized labor in the United States is granted exemption from antitrust laws, the rationale being that workers are at a bargaining disadvantage relative to firms. A job, it is argued, is more important to a single worker than is any single worker to a large company. This argument must be qualified for a variety of reasons. First, to the extent that workers' skills are general, workers can move easily from one firm to another, a worker with general skills does not command much of a wage premium at a given firm, so moving to another firm does not involve large costs. A worker who has firm-specific skills does lose by switching to another firm, but the same can also be said of the employer. The amount of rent that is lost by the worker relative to the amount of rent lost by the employer depends on the nature of the employment contract. It is by no means clear that workers suffer the majority of rent loss. Exceptions come to mind: lawyers who are tied to a particular client often take those clients with them when they spin off and form their own firms. Thus, the point that workers are at disadvantage relative to a firm is not always true.

Public sector unionism works somewhat differently. In private firms, competition and the profit motive put constraints on union demands, but in the public sector, the money comes from general revenue pools that depend on taxes and are only indirectly linked to the actions taken by the public sector manager. Furthermore, public sector agencies do not face the risks of bankruptcy that private sector firms do. A manager in the private sector who increases the wages of his workforce is constrained by competition from lower-cost firms, which can drive an overgenerous manager out of business, but a local fire department can hardly be driven out of business by competition from another city. Nonetheless, most public sector unions have not been particularly effective in raising the wages of their members. A notable example is the American Federation of Teachers; teachers still receive relatively low wages given their skills. However, though unionism has not significantly helped teachers receive higher salaries, it may have affected employment and teaching practices. Indeed, unions are as important in negotiating working conditions as they are in negotiating wages. Union workers receive a larger proportion of their total compensation in the form of benefits than do nonunion workers at similar skill levels, and unions have led the way in obtaining pension, vacation, and health benefits for their members (Freeman et al. 1993).

One of the chief roles of unions in American industrial relations is settling work disputes. Unions and management set up procedures and committees to deal with a variety of issues. These grievance procedures are highly structured and replace formal courts as a way of resolving union-management disputes. In Europe work councils play a similar role, but they are less likely to be involved in worker-manager interactions. This may actually be an efficient substitute for a government-run court structure. The union and firm may be able to take advantage of some of the benefits of decentralization and competition. In addition, these methods are less formal and less bureaucratic than the state or federal court structure.

MINIMUM WAGES

Virtually all countries have minimum wage constraints. In the United States, minimum wages are passed at both federal and state level; the largest one binds. Minimum wages have not had much effect on employment or wages in the United States, because the minimum wage is too low to apply to many workers. It is a different story in the other countries. Perhaps the study that observes the largest effect is that by Castillo-Freeman and Freeman (1992), who examine changes in Puerto Rico that occurred about thirty years ago. Up to that time, Puerto Rico, though it is a territory of the United States, did not comply with American minimum wage law; all at once, it was required to comply, and unemployment rates shot up to about 25 percent. They returned to normal when exemptions were once more enacted.

The general conclusion from this literature is that minimum wages decrease employment when they become a significant constraint. For the most part, political factors have ensured that they do not distort labor allocations by too much in the United States. However, in other countries where minimum wages have been much higher and affect a larger proportion of the workforce, they have caused serious distortions. An example is Sweden, where minimum wages are so high that they have virtually eliminated the personal service sector. A large variety of low-skilled work that is prevalent in other countries is absent in Sweden; there are few Swedish service workers who bag groceries, carry baggage, sell newspapers, or perform similar sorts of productive tasks at below minimum wage. France, too, has experienced significant effects of the minimum wage, some of which have affected income inequality among low-wage workers (Card, Kramarz, and Lemieux 1996).

One effect of the minimum wage is to assist incumbents, perhaps at the expense of new entrants into the labor market. Minimum wages make it difficult to replace high-wage labor with lower-wage labor. Also, it is less likely that incumbents will suffer job loss from an increase in the minimum wage than it is that new hiring rates will decline, particularly in manufacturing, where turnover rates are somewhere on the order of 20 percent per year. It is very easy to bring about an employment adjustment by reducing the rate of hiring. As a result, new entrants to the market tend to be at a disadvantage relative to the current stock of workers.

It is possible also to evade the minimum wage law by changing the structure of the compensation package. Since minimum wage compensation legislation pertains to the monetary wage and not to benefits, a firm can maintain increasing labor costs by the proportion of compensation of pecuniary payments and by reducing nonmonetary but otherwise valuable benefits.

LICENSURE

A number of professions have secured government licensure to obtain monopoly rents. Licensure is usually sold as a way to protect the public from danger and incompetence. Proponents of information arguments claim that in the absence of licensure, consumers would be at the mercy of unscrupulous or incompetent sellers. Government licensure can reduce the number of low-quality providers and make it easier for consumers to buy a product without fear of getting cheated. The main effect, however, is probably to prohibit entry and to raise the price of the goods in question. In a famous article, Reuben Kessel (1970) argued that licensing physicians may actually reduce the quality of medical care provided. Instead of having a larger number of somewhat lower quality physicians, patients may move away from physicians altogether and toward pharmacists, home remedies, and nonlicensed personnel as substitutes. A lower price of medical services might provide better public health than a small stock of very high quality doctors.

The efficiency case for government regulation rests on economies of scale. It is inefficient for each consumer to collect all the information on every firm that provides services in the economy. It is more efficient to have a limited number of centralized agencies do this and to distribute it widely throughout the economy. An agency like Consumer Reports, which is private, could function as a certifying group. But this need not be government run. Private provision of the information has the advantage of allowing for competition; the firm that provides the most reliable data survives in the market. By any of the criteria listed at the beginning of this essay, it is difficult to argue that licensure enhances efficiency.

DISCRIMINATION

A number of countries have laws prohibiting discrimination. The United States and Australia are perhaps the most celebrated and studied examples. In the United States, Title VII of the Civil Rights Act of 1964 made it illegal for employers to discriminate on the basis of race, gender, or religious belief. In addition, the Equal Pay Act of 1972 extended the law to cover certain jobs that were not necessarily equal in name: for example, a maid and a janitor, both of whom do the same work, are required by the Equal Pay Act to be paid the same wage.

There have been attempts to extend the Equal Pay Act into the area of comparable worth, where jobs that are not the same are compared to one another. The argument goes that female jobs are as valuable as jobs dominated by male workers, but because of discrimination, female jobs command lower salaries. For the most part, the courts have rejected these claims and comparable worth has been on the decline in recent years.

It is quite easy to argue that Title VII of the Civil Right Act is efficiency-enhancing whereas comparable-worth policies are efficiency-decreasing. In the United States, average wages of women are much lower than those of men. Further, women tend to be segregated into different jobs from men, and many are low-paying. Some have argued that "female" jobs pay lower wages than "male" jobs of comparable worth, and they have used various indices to determine the "right" wages. However, even if an acceptable index were available and it revealed inequities, regulation of wages based on those indices would not alleviate the problem. If women earn lower wages than men because they are in different jobs, this can perhaps be accounted for in two ways. First, if women chose those jobs, then lower wages reflect compensating differentials for nonpecuniary attributes. For example, professors earn less than similarly skilled physicians because the professor's workload is less arduous. If women earn lower wages than men because their jobs have better nonpecuniary benefits, and if men in those jobs also earn low wages because they have opted for a softer job, then no adjustment is warranted. On the contrary, raising the wages of women's jobs would result in a surplus of workers wanting those jobs and would cause unemployment.

Second, women may be in low-wage, female jobs not because they want to be, but because they are excluded from higher-paying male jobs. In this case, an inefficiency needs to be remedied, but not by an adjustment in wages. Consider Figure 4, which shows demand and supply for two occupations, electricians and nurses. The current supply curves for the two occupations are given by S and Σ for electricians and nurses, respectively. The market wage is W for electricians and ω for nurses. As the figure shows, nurses receive lower wages than electricians, because women are (usually) excluded from electrical work. Suppose that women were not excluded from electrical work and were therefore not forced into nursing; the supply of electricians would be then S^* and supply of nurses would be Σ^*. The resulting wages would then be W^* and ω^*. What would be the effect of forcing nurses' wages up to those of electricians? If nothing else changed, unemployment of women would result. Wages would be above their equilibrium amount and labor supply would exceed demand.

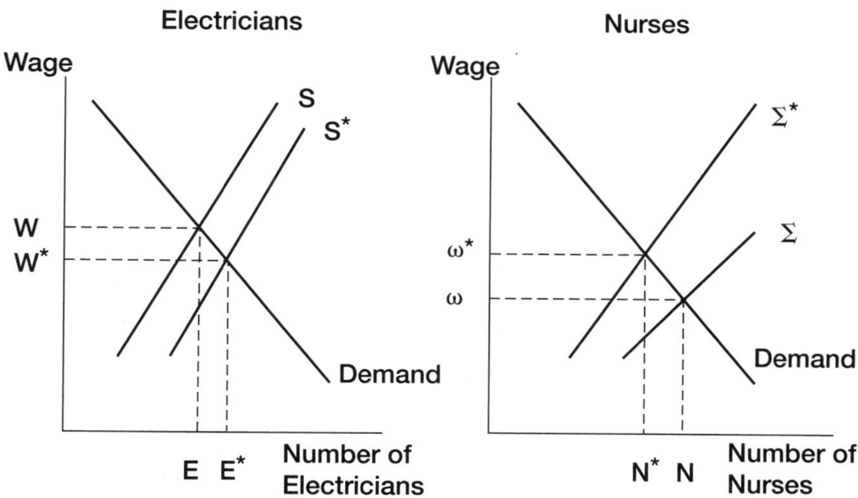

FIGURE 4 Demand and supply correlations for two occupations: electricians (male) and nurses (female).

The appropriate solution is simply to enforce Title VII of the Civil Rights Act of 1964. It is illegal to prevent women from being electricians. If that barrier were removed, efficiency is ensured. Title VII is an efficient law because it allows labor to move to its most productive use. The excess supply of women in female-dominated jobs and the shortage of females in male-dominated jobs would be eliminated by enforcement of Title VII. This argument holds without recourse to fairness arguments, which may be tougher to defend and depend on individual perspective. The efficiency argument for Title VII is valid, regardless of personal views of fairness.

Because Title VII eliminates any monopolistic behavior by electricians who wish to keep nurses out, it is efficiency-enhancing. By contrast, raising nurses' wages to the distorted level of electricians' wages may actually worsen things significantly by creating unemployment in the nursing market without bringing about any increase in the number of electricians.

Government Action Designed to Affect Working Conditions

The argument in favor of government action that affects working conditions hinges on some weaknesses in market information. The idea is that it is simply too costly for workers or labor market intermediaries to gather enough information about any given firm because the market for such information is prohibitively small. The government therefore legislates minimum standards that are acceptable in the market. But this has the undesired consequence of eliminating some possible trades that both parties would view as beneficial if fully informed. A discrete standard is selected in order to minimize the cost of implementation. The claim is that it is cheaper to monitor the same standard than to monitor different standards across many firms. It is possible that some workers would prefer to work in firms with less desirable working conditions for higher wages; it might even be possible to provide firms with a label certifying their average level of compliance with the standard. Few, if any, governments have chosen to go that route.

The same kinds of information arguments for licensing can be applied to labor markets in general. It is difficult to believe that regulation or a government agency is superior to the private market when it comes to providing information about jobs or employers. It is more likely that such regulation is used to further the monoply interests of labor or monopsony interests of certain employers in driving others out of business or limiting substitution. In sum, we believe that it is unlikely that government regulation of working conditions can enhance economic efficiency of human capital acquisition or efficient mobility under most circumstances.

Conclusion

This essay has attempted to provide a discussion of a wide variety of topics as they relate to international labor markets, primarily from the point of view of efficiency. Most regulations of the labor market work to reduce rather than enhance economic efficiency. It is reasonable to conclude that regulation is primarily the outcome of a political process that attempts to transfer resources from some groups to others.

REFERENCES

Becker, Gary, et al. 1990. "Human Capital, Fertility, and Economic Growth." *Journal of Political Economy* 98, part 2 (October): S12–37.

Card, David, Francis Kramarz, and Thomas Lemieux. 1996. "Changes in the Relative Structure of Wages and Employment: A Comparison of United States, Canada, and France." NBER Working Paper no. 5487.

Castillo-Freeman, Alida, and Richard B. Freeman. 1992. "When the Minimum Wage Reality Bites: The Effect of the U.S. Level Minimum on Puerto Rico." In *Immigration and the Work Force: Economic Consequences for the United States and Source Areas*, pp. 177–211. NBER Project Report. Chicago: University of Chicago Press.

Davis, Steven J. 1992. "Cross Country Patterns of Change in Relative Wages." In Jean Oliver and Stanley Fischer, eds., *NBER Macroeconomics Annual*, pp. 239–92. Cambridge, Mass.: MIT Press.

Ehrenberg, Ronald G., et al. 1993. "Why WARN? The Impact of Recent Plant Closing and Layoff Prenotification Legislation in the United States." In Christoph F. Buechtemann, ed., *Employment Security and Labor Market Behavior: Interdisciplinary Approaches and International Evidence*, Report no. 23, pp. 200–214. Ithaca, N.Y.: ILR Press.

Freeman, Richard B. 1995. "Are U.S. Wages Set in Beijing?" *Journal of Economic Perspectives*, summer: 15–32.

Freeman, Richard B., et al. 1993. "How Much Has De-Unionization Contributed to the Rise of Male Earnings Inequity?" In Sheldon Danziger and Peter Gottschalk, eds., *Uneven Tides: Rising Inequity in America*, pp. 133–63. New York: Russell Sage Foundation.

Hunt, Jennifer. 1996a. "Has Work-Sharing Worked in Germany?" NBER Working Paper no. 5724.

———. 1996b. "The Response of Wages and Actual Hours Worked to the Reduction of Standard Hours in Germany." NBER Working Paper no. 5716.

Katz, Lawrence, et al. 1992. "Changes in Relative Wages and Demand Factors." *Quarterly Journal of Economics* 107 (February): 35–78.

Kennan, John, et al. 1989. "Strategic Bargaining Models and Interpretation of Strike Data." *Journal of Applied Econometrics* 4 (Suppl. September): S87–130.

Kessel, Reuben. 1970. "The AMA and the Supply of Physicians." *Law and Contemporary Problems* 35 (spring): 267–83.

Lazear, Edward P. 1990. "Job Security Provisions and Employment." *Quarterly of Economics* 105 (August): 699–726.

Murphy, Kevin M., et al. 1993. "Industrial Change and the Rising Importance of Skill." In Sheldon Danziger and Peter Gottschalk, eds., *Uneven Tides: Rising Inequality in America*, pp. 101–32. New York: Russell Sage Foundation.

Pergamit, Michael R. 1983. "Wages and Employment in Regulated Industries." Ph.D. diss. University of Chicago.

Topel, Robert H. 1984. "Experience Rating of Unemployment Insurance and the Incidence of Unemployment." *Journal of Law and Economics*, April: 61–90.

Trejo, Stephen J., et al. 1991. "The Effects of Overtime Pay Regulations on Worker Compensation." *American Economic Review* 81 (September): 719–40.

Part VII

Property Rights and Economic Development

Sung Hee Jwa

Property Rights and Economic Behavior

Lessons for Korea's Economic Reform

This paper seeks to apply the neoinstitutional economic approach to the Korean economy in order to determine what institutional requirements are needed for the economy to become a successful capitalistic market economy—that is, an economic system in which the market order evolves endogenously for efficient resource allocation under given sets of economic institutions. One of the most important economic institutions in the market economy is the property rights system.

Recently, neoinstitutionalism, led by North (1990, 1992) and Eggertsson (1990) and inspired by Coase (1937, 1960), Alchian (1961), Alchian and Demsetz (1972), Demsetz (1967), and others, began to emphasize the existence of non-zero transaction costs in the real world economy and the importance of economic institutions in determining economic behaviors and performance. Neoinstitutional economics thus returned the economic institution, which had been treated as given in neoclassical economics, to the forefront of economic analysis. In the non-zero transaction cost world, the economic institution becomes the ultimate determinant of the size of the transaction costs the economy should bear and thereby influences the structure of economic organization and economic performance. The type of economic institution built into the economy becomes the crucial factor in determining economic performance. More than any other, the property rights system has been emphasized as the most crucial economic institution.

The author appreciates valuable comments and criticisms by various participants in the seminars held at the Hoover Institution and the Economic Research Institute of Economic Planning Agency, Japan.

After summarizing the analytical framework of neoinstitutional economics in the form of testable hypotheses that can easily be put into empirical analysis, this paper discusses the neoinstitutional framework, analyzing the relationship between the degree of property rights protection and the structure of economic organization in Korea as well as in other nations. It then presents a historical overview of the anecdotal evidence of property rights protection in Korea, which has so far lacked a well-defined property rights system and is a high transaction cost economy. This is followed by an effort to rationalize the organizational behaviors of large business firms in Korea and resolve some conflicting observations of the Korean economy that seem contradictory to the prediction of neoinstitutional economics. This leads to the concluding section, which suggests that the establishment of well-defined and fairly enforced economic institutions, including a property rights system, that reduces economic uncertainties and transaction costs, may be the most important prerequisite for a successful capitalistic market economy in Korea.

Some Testable Hypotheses of Neoinstitutional Economics

With the advent of neoinstitutionalism, the neoclassical assumption of zero transaction costs and exogenously given economic institutions appears an even greater contrast to the neoinstitutional treatment of transaction costs and economic institutions.

TRANSACTION COSTS AND ECONOMIC INSTITUTIONS

Transaction costs are all the costs involved in operating an economic system—the costs incurred in the negotiation, monitoring, coordination, and execution of transactions. In contrast to the neoclassical assumption of zero transaction costs, non-zero transaction costs arise from the fact that information is not a free good and is shared asymmetrically among agents involved in transactions. On the other hand, an economic institution embodies the rules that regulate economic activities, including both formal rules such as law, order, and regulations, and informal constraints such as customs and consciousness and the degree to which formal rules are enforced. Enforcement is an important part of economic institutions, since an unenforced formal rule is not really a rule. Here, the property rights system has been regarded as the most important economic institution in any free market economy, the core of the rules of the game in economic life.

In neoclassical economics, which assumes zero transaction costs, there is no concern for the economic institution as such; the optimal resource allocation problem could be treated as institution-free. As shown by R. H. Coase (1937, 1960), when we assume zero transaction costs, the difference in economic institutions, especially the property rights system, does not affect the outcome of resource allocation. Therefore, in this case, an economic institution could be treated as exogenously given without affecting the substance of relevant economic analysis. However, once non-zero transaction costs are introduced, as is the case of any real economy, the size of transaction costs is inherently and systematically affected by the differences in economic institutions, and thereby also resource allocation and economic performance are inevitably affected. Therefore, in the real world economy, the character of the economic institution adopted becomes important in determining the size of transaction costs and the overall performance of the economy.

Neoinstitutionalism has as its base introduced non-zero transaction costs in economic analysis and the recognition of the systematic causal relationship between the economic institution and the size of transaction costs and general economic performances. It recognizes the system of property rights as the most important feature in the structure of economic organization, optimal resource allocation, and, ultimately, economic performance. Neoinstitutionalism has further introduced the concept of treating the economic institution as endogenously evolving. To see this aspect more clearly, it is useful to distinguish three different levels of an economic system (Eggertsson 1990). An economic system can be described as consisting of individual economic agents, economic organizations that organize individual agents, and economic institutions that regulate the agents and organizations (see Figure 1).

According to this classification, one can characterize three different levels of economic analysis of an economic system. The first and simplest level would be the analysis of the effects on the economic behavior of individual agents and the resulting effects on the performance of the given structure of economic organizations and the given type of economic institutions. The second, intermediate, level would be an analysis of the effects on the structure of economic organizations and the resulting effects on the performance of the given types of economic institutions. The last and most comprehensive level of analysis would

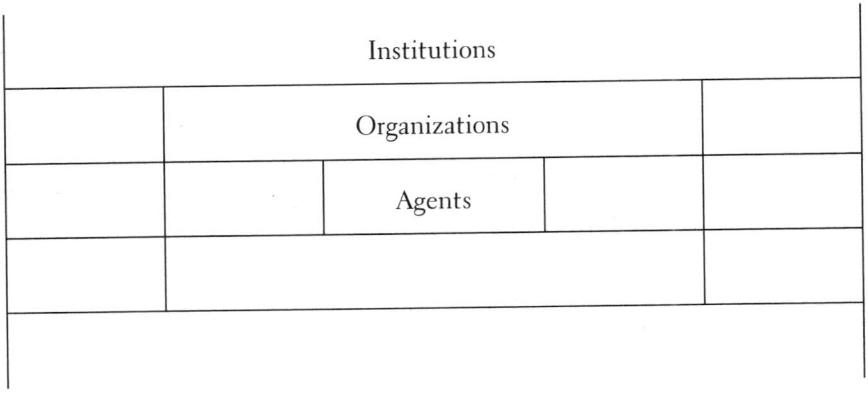

Institutions

Organizations

Agents

FIGURE 1 Structure of an economic system.

be to treat the economic institutions as endogenously formed and to explain how the institution evolves through various political processes and how the different types of economic institutions affect the economic behavior of individual agents and economic organizations, and, in turn, the economic performance of a society. At this level of analysis, economic agents and organizations are treated as the players who take the initiative to change existing institutions for their own advantage. If necessary, they exert pressure on and lobby politicians and the government to make institutional changes. At this stage, the neoinstitutional approach sounds very much like a public choice approach or a positive theory of political economy (Buchannan and Tollison 1972).

PROPERTY RIGHTS AND TRANSACTION COSTS

How clearly and securely the property rights system is established is considered to be the main determinant of the size of transaction costs that an economy should incur for optimal resource allocation. The property rights system is a criterion for defining interrelationships among economic agents concerning the use of scarce economic resources, that is, who has the exclusive rights to particular economic resources so that possible conflicts among agents that may be resolved in advance. The system seeks to define who has the right to use and dispose of certain resources, and, in turn, to help determine the realm of an individual agent's free economic decision. A property rights system is in essence a social behavioral norm concerning the utilization of scarce economic resources.

In this context, it is interesting to note Irving Fisher's remarks: "A property right is the liberty or permit (under the sanction and protection of custom and law) *to enjoy benefits* of wealth (in its broader sense) while assuming the costs which those benefits entail. . . . Property rights, unlike wealth or benefits, are not physical objects or events, but are abstract social relations. A property right is not a *thing*" (Fisher 1920, 27). Svetozar Pejovich defines the term in a similar way: "Property rights specify the norms of behavior with respect to economic goods that all persons must observe in their interactions with other people or bear the penalty cost of non-observance" (Pejovich 1990, 27).

To determine the implications of property rights on economic behavior and performance, one has to identify three aspects of the right of ownership: (1) the exclusivity of ownership, which means that the owner has the right to choose what to do with his assets; (2) the transferability of ownership, which means that the owner has the right to transfer his assets to others at mutually agreed upon terms; (3) a constitutional guarantee of ownership that separates economic wealth from political power. Exclusivity provides incentives for those who own assets to put them into the highest-valued uses, transferability provides incentives for resources to move from less-productive to more-productive owners, and the constitutional guarantee of ownership separates the accumulation of economic wealth from the accumulation of political power (Pejovich 1990, 28).

On the other hand, in relation to the neoinstitutional approach emphasizing non-zero transaction costs, alternative property rights systems, for example, could have different effects on the size of transaction costs that the society should bear in resource allocation, and consequently also different effects on economic behavior and performance. The lack of a clear and secure system of property rights under the real world of non-zero transaction costs implies high transaction costs. If a secure and well-defined system of property rights does not exist, only physical power could be used to resolve conflicts over rights to economic resources, and therefore there would be no room for voluntary economic transactions to take place. In the absence of a well-defined system of property rights, transaction costs may be prohibitive, and will in turn inhibit voluntary transactions for optimal resource allocation.

PROPERTY RIGHTS AND ECONOMIC ORGANIZATION

The relationship between the system of property rights and the structure of the economic organization in the neoinstitutional approach can be deduced from the following remarks by North (1990, 67):

> Firms come into existence to take advantage of profitable opportunities, which will be defined by the existing set of constraints. With insecure property rights, poorly enforced laws, barriers to entry, and monopolistic restrictions, the profit-maximizing firms will tend to have short time horizons and little fixed capital, and will tend to be small scale. The most profitable businesses may be in trade, re-distributive activities, or the black market. Large firms with substantial fixed capital will exist only under the umbrella of government protection with subsidies, tariff protection, and payoffs to the polity—a mixture hardly conducive to productive efficiency.

Inadequate protection of property rights implies a lower probability that all market contracts made with other agents will be fully honored and faithfully observed. If a formal system of property rights protection is not clearly established or, even if it is clearly defined, is not fully enforced, and, at the same time, if there are no well-established informal customs of mutually respecting each others' property rights, transaction costs for large business firms will tend to become excessive. Forming a large business organization will inevitably require complicated informal as well as formal economic relationships, all involving separate agents that lead to high transaction costs. It tell us that, unless there is secure protection of property rights, it will be very difficult for large fixed investments and large business organizations to be formed smoothly out of natural economic forces.

However, potentially high transaction costs resulting from an insecure system of property rights will encourage economic agents to minimize costs by means of a less expensive economic organization—for example, as a natural alternative to large business organization, the small-sized business organization, the formation of which would involve relatively low transaction costs. Smaller organizations, especially in nonmanufacturing trading and distribution sectors, can reduce transaction costs by simple interactions among family members, relatives, or a small number of people.

Recently, Francis Fukuyama (1995, 1996) introduced the concept of social capital as a part of human capital in a broad sense. Social capital induces social members to trust each other and cooperate in forming solidarity, so that as social capital accumulates, mutual trust among social members becomes deeper and formal economic organizations become more active relative to informal ones. In terms of neoinstitutionalism, Fukuyama's social capital can be interpreted as a kind of informal constraint, and therefore it can be argued that the accumulation of social capital informally helps to protect each other's property rights and thereby lowers transaction costs. According to this view, a strong family-oriented social tradition as a particular form of social capital tends to create a social environment in which social members are likely to mistrust nonfamily members and to discourage the formation of large economic organization, and can, in an extreme cases, lead to social and economic stagnation. Fukuyama argues that China and Korea with their strong family orientation tend to have economies based on small-sized firms, whereas Japan, with a group-oriented tradition, tends to create strong mutual trust among social members, thereby promoting the growth of large economic organizations. This argument supports the argument of neoinstitutionalism, that informal constraints such as customs and tradition can affect the amount of transaction costs that a society should pay for economic organization and therefore can systematically influence the structure of economic organization—that is, the extent of mutual trust among social members can be an important part of informal constraints.

In sum, economic activities that require complicated formal contracts among various economic agents, with which not all are familiar, may not be favored in an economic environment of high transaction costs. Yet in the same environment, relatively simple economic activities that do not require formal contracts may be able to survive. Therefore, the attenuation of property rights protection, which tends to increase transaction costs, creates an environment favorable for small-sized firms over large business organizations and for short-term liquid assets over long-term fixed investment activities. One can further extend this reasoning to argue that the attenuation of property ownership tends to create an environment that is favorable to business management with strong family orientation, closed to outsiders and having unified ownership and control, and is unfavorable to modern business management having specialized managers and separation of ownership and control. These points are summarized in Table 1.

PROPERTY RIGHTS AND ECONOMIC PERFORMANCE

The relationship between the extent of property rights protection and the economic performance of a society can easily be deduced from

TABLE 1 Extent of Protection of Property Rights and Economic Behavior

Extent of property rights protection	*Economic organization*				*Economic performance*
	Transaction costs	*Type of organization*	*Types of management*	*Economic activities favored*	
Attenuated property rights	High	Small-sized firms Self-employed business	Family management Closed management Unified ownership and control	Trade and distribution Small and liquid investment Black market	Low
Secure property rights	Low	Large business	Specialized manager Open management Separation of ownership and control	Manufacturing Large and fixed investment	High

the discussion made so far. The point is that, unless a society has a system that compensates for high transaction costs, such costs stemming from insecure property rights protection will be realized and built into the society and will tend to retard economic development by preventing the best allocation of resources. The establishment of a secure and transparent property rights system thus seems a necessary prerequisite for high economic performance of any society.

On the other hand, the exclusivity of private property rights creates an incentive structure favorable to a strong will to economize. The owner decides what to do with his property, captures the benefits of his decision, and bears its cost. Therefore, the secure private property rights creates strong incentives for the owner to seek the highest-valued use of resources, that is, to maximize "the willingness to economize," in the words of Lewis (1955). The fall of socialist economic systems is a vivid example that supports this proposition.

According to the neoinstitutional approach (North 1981; Wallis and North 1986), the secure establishment of a property rights system has been the most crucial factor in determining the long-term trend of economic development. North (1992) has argued that, compared with the decentralized feudalistic political system, centralized bureaucracy in the monarchy system tended to allow only a very limited realm of private activity, including the protection of property rights as well as individual freedom. Clague et al. (1996) have also shown that a democratic political regime tends to have a relatively secure property rights system, whereas unstable and insecure autocracy tends to have weak protection for private property rights. Of course, an unstable democracy can be much worse for property rights protection than a secure and stable autocracy, but this situation would only be a transient phenomenon because a permanent state of autocracy could not be a normal situation in the modern world.

In sum, the centralized bureaucracy under monarchism and autocracy in the modern world tend to be unfavorable to property rights protection, in comparison both with decentralized feudalism and with modern democratic systems. North (1990) has further observed that countries that follow the tradition of Spanish centralized bureaucratic monarchism exhibit lower economic performance than do countries that follow the English tradition of decentralized feudalistic monarchism; he attributes this phenomenon to differences in property rights protection. In this context, Fukuyama's argument that Japan is a high-trust society could imply that Japan under the tradition of feudalism has succeeded in establishing informal constraints to respect each others' property rights and has thus achieved a higher economic performance than China and Korea.

The Impact of Transaction Costs on Economic Behavior

In order to conduct an empirical investigation of the relationship between transaction costs and economic behavior summarized in Table 1, I decided to measure transaction costs by some proxy.

MEASUREMENT OF TRANSACTION COSTS

I adopted the cash ratio in a broadly defined money (M2) as a proxy for transaction costs. Clague et al. (1996) utilized contract-intensive money in M2, (M2 – C)/M2 where M2 is a broad definition of money and C is currency outside banks as a proxy for a measure of security of property rights. Their logic is as follows:

> In environments in which third-party enforcement of contracts is reliable and where property rights facilitate pledging of assets as security for loans, banks and other financial intermediaries will profit from providing retail banking services at low cost, and sometimes even from paying interest on bank deposits, in order to obtain money that they can lend at higher rates. If the public can rely on institutional stability and third-party enforcement of contracts, they can be confident that the banks or government will not confiscate their deposits. Thus the rationale for this measure is that those forms of money, such as currency, that rely least on the fulfillment of contractual obligations by others will be preferred when property and contractual rights are insecure, whereas other forms of money are more advantageous for most purposes in environments with secure contract-enforcement and property rights. (Clague et al. 1996, 254)

This concept of contract-intensive money is directly opposite to the cash ratio, C/M2. Therefore, following the same logic, the cash ratio can be taken as a measure of the degree of property rights attenuation and also as an index for the extent of transaction costs incurred owing to the attenuated property rights system, not only in the financial sector but also in the overall economy in a broad sense.

Table 2 compares the cash ratios in M2 for selected countries from 1970 to 1994. It is interesting to observe that the cash ratio tends to

TABLE 2 Cash Ratio in M2 for Selected Countries as a Proxy for Transaction Costs (period average)

	Period			
Nation	*1970–79*	*1980–89*	*1990–94*	*1970–94*
Australia	8.65	8.69	6.77	8.29
Canada	9.33	6.77	5.85	7.61
France	14.09	4.52	4.37[a]	8.48[b]
Germany	10.12	10.12	10.41	10.18
Italy	10.15	8.16	9.14	9.15
Japan	9.16	7.91	7.67	8.36
Korea	15.92	12.01	9.84	13.14
Norway	14.44	9.32	7.05[a]	11.07[b]
Portugal	19.12	11.75	8.00	13.95
Spain	10.77	10.42	13.06	11.09
Sweden	11.70	10.30	9.53	10.70
Taiwan	12.48	8.30	4.96	9.30
United Kingdom	15.45	7.68	3.14[a]	10.16[b]
United States	7.19	6.48	7.72	7.02

SOURCE: International Monetary Fund: International Financial Statistics Yearbook, 1995.
[a] Average, 1990–1993.
[b] Average, 1970–1993.

be high in countries such as Portugal and Spain that North (1990) characterizes as high transaction cost countries under the Spanish tradition of centralized bureaucracy, and in countries such as France, Italy, and Korea that Fukuyama (1996) describes as low-trust countries. The cash ratio tends to be low in England (especially in recent years), the United States, Canada, and Japan, which North (1990) describes as low transaction cost countries under the English tradition of liberal, decentralized feudalism, and Fukuyama (1996) describes as high-trust countries. Korea has been ranked among the highest transaction cost countries in the sample of OECD countries during the 1970–1990 period.

In sum, the cash ratio in a broad concept of money can be a useful proxy for transaction costs incurred as a result of uncertain property rights protection. According to this criterion, Korea turns out to be a country with high transaction costs.

TRANSACTION COSTS AND SMALL AND MEDIUM-SIZED FIRMS

One of the interesting hypotheses of neoinstitutionalism is the positive relationship between transaction costs and the weight of small-sized firms in the economy. In this section, this hypothesis will be tested utilizing Korean data as well as cross-country data.

The structure of Korea's industrial organization has been criticized as dominated by the large business groups called chaebols. Based on this perception, there has been a continuing argument that Korea has to promote small and medium-sized firms to have a balanced industrial structure. Careful study of the structure of Korea's industrial organization reveals some interesting facts that are somewhat contrary to the common perception. Table 3 shows the international comparison of firm size distribution. In this comparison, Korea exhibits an extremely high ratio of small-sized firms, especially those employing fewer than ten persons. Japan, too, carries a similarly high weight of small-sized firms relative to other developed countries—a finding that is, however, inconsistent with the expectation based on Fukuyama's argument that Japan is a high-trust country.

Similarly, looking at Table 4, which shows the weight of the self-employed to the total employed persons in the nonagricultural sector for fourteen selected countries, we find Korea ranks highest—even higher than Italy and Taiwan, which have characteristically been dominated by small and medium-sized firms. These findings again belie the common perception of Korea as dominated by large firms. It is also interesting to observe that Italy, Taiwan, and France, which Fukuyama

TABLE 3 International Comparison of Firm Size Distribution in Manufacturing Sector (in percents)

<table>
<tr><th>Number of employees</th><th>Korea (1993)</th><th>Japan (1993)</th><th>U.S. (1985)</th><th>U.K. (1989)</th><th>West Germany (1986)[a]</th></tr>
<tr><td>Below 10</td><td>79.7</td><td>73.5</td><td>48.2</td><td rowspan="3">96.1[b]</td><td>—</td></tr>
<tr><td>10–19</td><td>9.7</td><td>11.8</td><td>16.5</td><td>—</td></tr>
<tr><td>20–99</td><td>9.1</td><td>12.4</td><td>24.8</td><td>69.9</td></tr>
<tr><td>100–299</td><td>1.1</td><td>1.8</td><td>6.5[c]</td><td rowspan="2">3.0[d]</td><td rowspan="2">20.4[d]</td></tr>
<tr><td>300–499</td><td>0.16</td><td>0.27</td><td rowspan="2">3.4[e]</td></tr>
<tr><td>500–999</td><td>0.13</td><td>0.18</td><td>0.04</td><td>3.1</td></tr>
<tr><td>Above 1,000</td><td>0.07</td><td>0.10</td><td>0.01</td><td>0.04</td><td>2.5</td></tr>
</table>

SOURCES: Korea, Report on Industrial Survey; Japan, Industrial Statistics; U.S., Census of Manufactures; U.K., Census of Production; Germany, Produzierendes Gewerbe.

[a] Only above 20 employees.

[b] Average for first three categories.

[c] 100–249 employees.

[d] 100–499 employees.

[e] 250–500 employees.

TABLE 4 International Comparison of the Weight of Self-Employed to Total Employed Persons

	Period			
Nation	*1970–79*	*1980–89*	*1990–93*	*1970–93*
Australia	10.51	12.38	10.91	11.60
Canada	6.47	7.06	7.91	6.96
France	11.27	10.54	9.08	10.60
Germany	9.02	7.46	7.66	8.14
Italy	21.91	21.01	22.79	21.68
Japan	13.86	12.97	10.91	13.00
Korea	29.96	25.50	22.59	26.87
Norway	7.20[a]	6.54	6.14	6.71[b]
Portugal	12.31	16.31	17.65	14.87
Spain	15.78	17.46	17.83	16.82
Sweden	4.73	5.26	7.77	5.46
Taiwan	24.17	20.20	18.27	21.54
United Kingdom	7.02	9.43	11.82	8.82
United States	6.87	7.49	7.66	7.26

NOTE: Period average for nonagriculture, forestry, or fishery sectors.
SOURCES: ILO, Yearbook of Labor Statistics, 1988, 1990, 1993; Korea, Ministry of Labor, Yearbook of Labor Statistics, 1982, 1988, 1994.
[a] Sample period, 1972–79.
[b] Sample period, 1972–93.

describe as low-trust countries, and Spain and Portugal, which North describes as high transaction cost countries, exhibit a relatively high weight of self-employed persons. Canada, England, and the United States, which North describes as low transaction cost countries, exhibit a relatively low weight, as expected. However, Japan, a country characterized as a high-trust country, shows a relatively high weight, which again seems inconsistent with Fukuyama's expectation.

In sum, the data seem consistent with the neoinstitutional perspective: Korea exhibits a high cash ratio (implying high transaction costs) as well as a high weight of small-sized firms. Also, broadly speaking, the positive relationship between the cash ratio and the weight of small firms seems to be easily observable, with some exceptions, even if this is a cursory comparison using cross-country data.

Korean evidence. To analyze the relationship between the number of small and medium-sized firms and the index of transaction costs in the

Korean economy more systematically, I regressed the weight of the self-employed in the total employment (as a proxy for the weight of the small and medium-sized firms) on the index of transaction costs (CR), and the logarithm of per capita income. Here, the per capita income variable enters to take into account the possible impact of economic growth on the number of small and medium-sized firms. This income variable may have two opposing effects: one is the negative impact, because the scale of production and the average size of the firm are expected to become larger as the extent of market increases and thereby the economies of scale become more fully utilized in the process of economic development; another is the positive impact, because economic growth could accompany new entries of small firms. Therefore, it will be difficult to judge which impact will dominate a priori.

It should be noted, however, that because GNP (income variable) and CR should show strong and negative correlation theoretically as well as empirically (−0.84 in this case), per capita GNP is regressed on CR and the series of the residuals (RESGNP) is actually utilized as the per capita income variable. The empirical results (Table 5) seem to support the a priori expectation that the transaction costs variable will have a positive impact. On the other hand, the GNP effect turns out to be significantly negative, which seems to imply that economic development tends to relate more closely to growth in firm size than to growth in the number of firms.

TABLE 5 Regression Result of the Weight of Small and Medium-Sized Firms on Transaction Costs in Korea

	Independent variable					
Dependent variable	*Constant*	*Transaction costs (CR)*	*RESGNP*[a]	*D−W*	*Adj. R2*	*Estimate period (D.F)*
Weight of the self-employed to the total employed	16.10 (14.76)	0.75 (9.23)	−1.42 (−4.24)	0.96	0.82	1971–93 (20)

NOTE: The data set for the regression is reported in appendix Table A1.

[a]The series is obtained with the following relationship:

log (per capita GNP) = 19.25 − 0.41 CR + RESGNP: R2 = 0.73, D − W = 0.34
(27.16)(−7.72)

Estimate period: 1971–93

: (   ) is t-value.

Cross-country empirical evidence. In the cross-country analysis, the weight of self-employed workers to total workers (again as a proxy for the weight of small and medium-sized firms in the economy) is also regressed on the variables of transaction costs (CR) and per capita income. As already discussed, the per capita income variable enters to take account of the effect of economic development, and the income variable actually utilized in the regression is obtained as a series of residuals of the regression of the per capita income on the CR variable. I used three data sets: data set 1, in which all the individual country data are averaged over a twenty-year period, 1972–1991; data set 2, in which the same individual country data are averaged over a ten-year period and pooled over two periods; and data set 3, which is constructed in the same way as data set 2 but with a five-year average. The data are averaged over a long-term period in order to take account of the long-term nature of the impacts of institutional change on the organizational structure; for Korea, however, long-term averages were not possible owing to insufficient data. The regression results are reported in Table 6.

The results seem to support the prior expectation of a positive impact of high transaction costs but a negative impact of economic development on the number of small and medium-sized firms in the economy. One interesting point to be noted concerning the effect of GNP is that economic development has accompanied the growth of firm size more strongly than the growth of the number of small firms via new entry, as observed in the case of Korea.

Property Rights and the Evolution of Large Business Firms in Korea

Our cross-country comparison of cash ratio in M2 as a proxy for transaction costs and the weight of the self-employed in the economy seems to suggest that Korea is a relatively high transaction cost economy. This observation is quite intriguing for two reasons: (1) Korea is acknowledged to be a country that has achieved a remarkably high growth rate during the last thirty years, though this seems contradictory to its also being a high transaction cost economy; (2) Korea is also recognized as a country that has been dominated by large manufacturing business firms—another apparent contradiction. In this section I shall try to resolve these apparent contradictions by reviewing the factors influ-

TABLE 6 Regression Result of the Weight of Self-Employed on Transaction Costs in Cross-Country Comparison

	Independent variable					
Data set	*Constant*	*Transaction costs (CR)*	*RESGNP*	*D − W*	*Adj. R2*	*D.F*
1	2.17 (0.47)	1.07 (2.32)	−11.36[a] (−4.96)	1.64	0.68	11
2	7.92 (2.71)	0.49 (1.72)	−7.74[b] (−5.18)	1.84	0.51	25
3	8.36 (4.01)	0.44 (2.21)	−6.04[c] (−6.28)	1.22	0.44	53

NOTE: The data sets for the regressions are reported in Appendix Table A2.
[a]RESGNP is obtained with the following relationship:
LPGNP = 10.80 − 0.18 CR + RESGNP
(18.57) (−3.11)
R2 = 0.40, D-W = 3.11, D.F. = 12.
where LPGNP is log (per capita GNP) and CR is cash ratio.
[b]LPGNP = 10.59 − 0.17 CR + RESGNP
(27.56) (−4.62)
R2 = 0.43, D-W = 2.10, D.F. = 26
[c]LPGNP = 10.60 − 0.18 CR + RESGNP
(35.91) (−6.23)
R2 = 0.41, D-W = 1.42. D.F. = 54
: ( ) is the t-value.

encing informal customs as well as formal systems of property rights protection and investigating their implications on the industrial structure and the organizational behaviors of large business firms.

In this analysis, I shall first look at the effectiveness of the third party (especially government) enforcement of property rights protection in Korea by documenting some important but anecdotal observations of historical events that are considered to have influenced the Korean systems of private property rights, both formal and informal. In recent years, the formal system has been under a continuous siege by the government in the name of expediting economic development. Informal customs formed gradually under the general perception of property rights attenuation have themselves been unfavorable to the establishment of secure ownership protection, and the level of mutual trust has become very low, especially among people from different family, school, and regional backgrounds.

Korea was under very strong centralized bureaucratic monarchism during the Yi dynasty that lasted from the fourteenth century through the nineteenth century, then under Japanese colonial rule until the mid-twentieth century, and until recently, under a strong prodevelopment authoritarian government. This history implies that Korea has had little opportunity to establish a transparent and secure rule-based property rights system.

PROPERTY RIGHTS: A HISTORICAL SUMMARY

Some historical details of particular events of property rights attenuation in Korea will illuminate the way in which the informal as well as formal system of Korea's property rights protection developed.

Disorder in the tax system of the Yi dynasty. The Yi dynasty was a strong centralized monarchy with an extremely disorderly tax system, especially during the last century of the dynasty. In this period, government bureaucrats became corrupt and local officials in particular exacted heavy and unjust taxes, *Garyum Junoo,* by using an extremely arbitrary interpretation and application of tax laws. Since the mid-eighteenth century, the tax system had been a tripartite system, consisting of a land tax, a military tax, and a system of grain exchange, all operating in increasingly oppressive ways.

First, taxes were levied on the basis of the provincial unit collectively regardless of the number of taxpayers and/or the size of lands in each individual province. This standard tax made it possible for the provincial head and bureaucrats to exercise whatever power they chose in order to meet the tax burden, including, in the case of poorer provinces, downright extortion.

Second, land taxes were often levied even on wasteland and fallow land, and public funds unlawfully appropriated by public officials were made up for by additional land taxes.[1]

Third, the military tax imposed a given quantity of cotton fabric for military use per adult male unless he volunteered for military service. This tax was often levied even on men who were deceased, and also on children. If a taxpayer was unable to pay the specified duty, his relatives and even neighbors were forced to pay for him.

Fourth, the system of grain exchange, which was supposed to allevi-

1. Land tax in those days was not a property tax but rather a tax on the harvests on the relevant land. Therefore, the taxes on wasteland and fallow land were simply unjust confiscation.

ate grain shortages during the sowing season by lending old grain during that time and collecting new grain during the harvest season, was manipulated to favor the public authority; this included not only notorious price fixing but also extortionary changes in the kind of grain exchanged, such as the arbitrary one-to-one exchange of high-grade grain (rice) for a low-grade grain (barley) and confiscation of grain that was in fact not lent out.

The tax system in the Yi dynasty could altogether be characterized as an official system to extort wealth. It was far from being a tax system in the normal sense that delineates the tax duty in a transparent manner and delimits the government power of arbitrary infringement on private property. Almost all property was subject to arbitrary appropriation by the government, and the property rights system, for all its formal code, was the victim of continuous government attack, which in turn generated the informal perception that the system of property rights protection was practically nonexistent.

Land reform of 1950 and the fall of the landlord class. It is well understood that agricultural capitalists in Korea failed to transform themselves into industrial capitalists because the compensation method used for land reform in 1950 was so unfair that property rights to land were, in fact, made void. Landlords were forced to surrender their lands at specified compensation terms that favored the government, not the owner.

A bond was issued for the land given up, the face value being set in kind in terms of a specific grain and according to a given formula that reduced the value of grain land in excess of a specified amount of grain at an increasing rate of reduction. The monetary value of this bond was determined by applying the government's set grain price, usually less than half the market price, and the bond was redeemed annually at the same value for five years. This application of an increasing rate of reduction in the value of grain land in excess of the arbitrary set limit, and of extremely low prices in evaluating the monetary value of the grain land, amounted to a systematic undercutting of agricultural capitalists.

Privatization of banks, and confiscation of private banks. In the 1950s, following liberation from Japanese rule, the new Korean government privatized banks that were under Japanese ownership. A decade later, the military government reconfiscated the stocks of banks held by big businesses under the official justification of punishing unfair accumulation of wealth. Neither of these interventions was fair. The privatization of the 1950s allocated stocks not to the highest bidder at public auction but instead to the low bidder in a system probably involving personal favoritism.

The military government of the 1960s not only confiscated bank stocks held by the so-called "unfair wealth accumulators," it also established the upper limit of bank stock that could be held by private concerns, and it regained a majority stock holding, in order to control bank management to finance economic development. This maneuver set a precedent for many similar measures thereafter that infringed on private property rights in the name of promoting economic development.

Emergency measures of August 3, 1972. In 1972, in an effort to improve the economic conditions for business, the Korean government took emergency measures through a presidential decree that allowed the deferment of a firm's curb market liabilities, stipulated drastic cuts in interest rates for firms borrowing in the official financial market, as well as comprehensive tax cuts for business firms, and set up special government lending at preferential rates.

Probably the most important of these measures was the deferred payment of unofficial market borrowings, which included loans from relatives, friends, and neighbors as well as from professional curb market lenders.[2] This measure amounted to an infringement of individual property rights of nearly all citizens on a broad scale. In addition, the interest rate cuts across the board on loans in the official financial market, another serious infringement of financial property rights, became a precedent that the Korean government invoked repeatedly thereafter in the name of reactivating business activities whenever business firms complained about hardships in foreign competition.

Structural adjustment policies during the 1980s. Between 1986 and 1988, the government enacted various structural adjustment policies, again to form big business—specifically, to address the insolvency problems that resulted from overinvestment induced by the heavy and chemical industry promotion policies of the 1970s. However, the crite-

2. The deferment measure included cutting the curb market rate from an average 3.84 percent monthly market rate to a 1.35 percent monthly rate and a three-year deferment with installment payment for five years thereafter.

ria to select the troubled firms for structural adjustment policies were set so broadly that there was wide room left for government discretion to play a bigger role than the transparent rules, and this in turn generated far-reaching negative implications on property rights protection. The target firms were selected not only for their financial solvency but also for their suitability under industrial policy concerns such as upgrading industrial structure and promoting specialization of the chaebols. It was evident to the general public that the choice of firms for government-forced ownership transfer was not transparent: for example, the government forced dissolution of Kukjae, one of the large chaebols.

The real name financial system. The real name system for financial transactions introduced by the Korean government as a part of the reform of the income tax system in August 1993—scheduled to be fully effective from 1997—was intended to improve equity in the tax system. It introduced a comprehensive income tax system that included financial income, which had formerly been treated separately, and thereby applied an equal tax system to all income regardless of its source. To achieve this purpose, it was necessary to have every financial transaction carried out only under real names.

Though the intentions were good, the real name system actually opened up the possibility that the newly available information on financial transactions could be used not only for tax purposes or criminal investigation but also for general investigation of financial sources or political purposes. The government requires information on all financial transactions above a certain amount to be made available not only to tax authorities but also in investigations of the sources of financial funds, regardless of whether or not the concerned asset holder is suspected of being involved in illegal activities. In effect, this requirement puts almost all major financial asset holders at risk of government confiscation of private financial property. It is true that some major financial asset holders have been associated with illegal activities, particularly bribery, which was widespread under the past authoritarian rule. Also, almost all financial asset holders are likely to have violated the tax law in some way or another simply because of the complexities of the law and its often arbitrary application.

Thus, though it is sincerely hoped that the new system will improve the equity of the tax system, at the same time it has created uncertainty about financial property rights. That being so, it may be desirable to minimize the risks by the open commitment of the government to use the information not for political purposes but only for tax purposes and criminal investigations. In this context, however, it is important to understand that although bribery was made easier, it was not caused by the use of pseudo names, and we ought not to expect the real name system to eliminate bribery altogether. Bribery is the by-product of a nontransparent and rent-seeking political and/or government regulation system, and its solution lies in institutional reforms in these areas.

The weakness of formal protection of property rights. Law enforcement has been emphasized as an important part of the economic institution together with formal as well as informal institutional constraints (North, 1992). Even if a formal institution of ideal economic incentive structure is legalized, that institution will be of no use if it is not fully and fairly enforced. Korea has been notorious for introducing many important economic institutions no less ideal than those in some advanced countries, but failing to pay attention to how these institutions are enforced. From the National Assembly, the nation's lawmaker, to the law enforcement authority of the government and to administrative officials at the lowest level, the importance of transparent and fair legal enforcement does not seem to be well understood. It seems that concerns for political and administrative conveniences in law enforcement have been dominating the concerns of fairness so that even ordinary citizens have become very insensitive to abuses. Yet because the government can always enforce the law if it is seen to be convenient and beneficial to its goals, the situation tends to create many uncertainties about the formal economic institution. The tax law can be regarded as a typical example.

Hardly anyone really understands Korea's tax system. The system, consisting of tax law and related orders and regulations, is revised so often (regularly on an annual basis) and is so complicated that the enforcement by the tax authority and certainly the understanding by ordinary citizens of how the system works are unclear. As a result, the system tends to have been enforced to a large extent through the arbitrary judgment of authorities. Taxpayers have been violating the system not only because of a general lack of knowledge of tax laws but also because the authorities' arbitrary application and enforcement of the laws create opportunities for tax evasion.

The Korean public is quite aware that this society is not governed under a fully enforced formal economic institution, especially not under a well-defined property rights system. As a result, Korea's economic institutions, including the property rights system, have carried on under a pattern of informal constraints rather than formal rules, which in turn has increased uncertainties about the property rights system.

THE PROPERTY RIGHTS SYSTEM AND LARGE BUSINESS FIRMS

In this section, I discuss the implications of the attenuated property rights system in Korea as they apply to large business firms and their successful growth, even under high transaction costs. If we understand that Korea's property rights protection has been relatively attenuated throughout its economic history, we can infer the possible pattern of economic behavior of large business firms.

According to Table 1, we would expect Korea's industrial structure to be dominated by small firms and self-employed entrepreneurs in a pattern of closed family-owned management, operating mostly in the trade and distribution sectors. This expectation is a result of Korea's high transaction cost economy under a weak system of property rights protection. The evidence presented in the earlier sections seems to confirm this expectation. In light of this evidence, it will be reasonable to assume that in this economy, large-scale business firms in the manufacturing sector, where large long-term fixed investment commitments are required, can survive only with the strong protection of private property rights for those investments by some outside power, such as the government, that is exogenous to formal and informal institutional constraints.

Table 7 gives the business concentration ratios for the one hundred largest firms of the five selected countries. The table is constructed to

TABLE 7 International Comparison of Business Concentration for 100 Largest Firms

Size in terms of number of employees	*Korea (1990)*	*Japan (1984)*	*United States (1985)*	*West Germany (1984)*	*Canada (1983)*
Shipment	37.7	27.3[a]	—	39.5	—
Value added	35.1	—	33.0[b]	24.8	47.1
Fixed assets	40.8	33.0	49.1	—	52.2

SOURCES: Korea Fair Trade Commission; Mafels (1988).
[a] 1980.
[b] 1982.

control the level of economic development between Korea and other developed countries by selecting a different year of comparison for the developed countries. The evidence suggests that the business concentration in Korea is indeed high but not extraordinary compared with that of other developed countries. This confirms the earlier finding that Korea has a very high weight of small-sized firms but also a relatively high weight of large businesses in terms of sales volume, value added, and the size of assets held by firms.

How can we rationalize this conflicting evidence? First, as already suggested, the possible explanation of the healthy state of large businesses, even in a high transaction cost environment, may lie in the role of the government. The Korean government has promoted large-scale heavy and chemical industries with subsidies, entry barriers, preferential bank loans, and so on, under a strong protective umbrella, so that any businessman selected by the government could feel safe about the property rights protection—at least until the relationship turned sour. Once the relationship soured, there could of course be no sure guarantee of his fortune. Therefore, it can be argued that strong government support for and protection of property rights on long-term fixed investments, which contributed to the reduction of economic uncertainty on property rights, have been the necessary prerequisite for the rapid growth of large-scale business firms and also for rapid economic growth generally in Korea.

On the other hand, from this perspective, one can see that many behavioral patterns of large business firms that have been criticized as abnormal could indeed be rationalized by the fact that large firms have been operating under the possibility of property rights attenuation by a strong interventionist government and in an atmosphere of strong antichaebol sentiment among the general public.

Since Korea had for years been controlled by an authoritarian government with strong interventionistic economic policies, large business firms were aware that property rights could be revoked by government discretion even though these firms were receiving various kinds of preferential treatment during the rapid growth period. The government was, in other words, the promoter of the big business firms but also the prime source of uncertainties over property rights protection. In some sense, the government had the power to hire and fire: it could choose the individual businessman as a manager for a specific corporation and provide the necessary resources for the rapid growth of that corporation, but if the choice was found to be a poor one, it could install a new owner, or at least adversely affect the growth of the corporation with various measures. Therefore, it can be said that the big corporation was under government protection but the incumbent owner had very uncertain property rights protection.

Another source of property rights attenuation as far as big business firms are concerned has been the anti-chaebol sentiment of the general public. Ever since the groups of big business firms were formed and given the popular name chaebol, the public has continuously questioned the fairness of the birth and growth of these large corporations. The popular notion is that chaebols have grown as a result of unfair government protection and ought now to be penalized in some way, or even dissolved.

The government of Korea has long been sensitive to and constrained in economic policy making by this public sentiment. Occasionally it has been obliged to make a politically oriented economic policy decision against large business groups, such as setting restrictions on bank borrowing and business diversification. It is evident that once public sentiment becomes a constraint on government policies relating to big businesses, it will turn into an informal economic institution and become an important real constraint, no less powerful than a formal legal institution.

Therefore, it may be reasonable to assume that, constrained by the high uncertainty about property rights protection as such, big corporations have been looking for various strategies to avoid the actual occurrence of property rights nullification. These have taken the form of seeking political power, and the seemingly excessive business diversification or expansion even into the areas of banking and mass-media industries. Whatever the strategy, it can be argued that they all originate from the concerns of how to reduce the economic uncertainty about property rights, and thereby also the likelihood of failure, resulting from arbitrary governmental decisions.

It can be assumed that the owner's attaining political power will reduce the probability of his corporation's being under political threat. Aggressive expansion by diversification can also help reduce the probability of failure due to a nonmarket decision or a market mechanism, because the government as well as the general public may not easily accept the economic impact of the big firms' failure even if the facts prove insolvency. Big corporations may understandably take advantage of the so-called general public's sentiment of "too big to fail." More to the point, however, are chaebols' diversification efforts to enter into the banking sector. Banks have traditionally been regarded as special in providing transaction accounts because of the possibility of a bank run and therefore have been least likely to be allowed to fail, since the government usually steps in to bail them out of trouble. Since banks are treated as a sort of public institution, business groups that diversify into the banking sector are unlikely to be treated heedlessly by the government. Therefore, entering into the banking sector would not only provide easy access to ever insufficient financial resources but also help to reduce the possibility of failure. Owning banks appears, in this context, to be a very good investment to defend oneself from the threat to one's private property rights. Finally, owning firms in the mass media industry appears no less attractive, because mass media can become a powerful instrument for the business group's public purposes. The influence of the mass media on public opinion and politics implies that owning such firms can lend a significant degree of power to protect oneself from arbitrary governmental intervention into private property rights and business activities.

The diversification behavior of Korean chaebols has been systematically analyzed in Sung Hee Jwa (1996). This work emphasizes the causes for diversification as follows: the small size of the domestic market for each line of businesses under the relatively high accessibility to financial as well as real resources, the technological innovation creating economies of scope among various economic activities, and the business environment created by government policy where the government took the responsibility for a firm's survival once the firm entered the designated and regulated areas. Here one can add the institutional aspect as a fourth factor: diversified expansion could be a self-protective measure against the high probability of property rights attenuation.

Concluding Remarks

What should be the purpose of economic reforms, especially institutional reforms, in the effort to search for the model for Korean capitalism? I think the prime goal of economic reforms should be to reduce economic uncertainties and thereby transaction costs in the economy.

Transaction costs arise basically from economic uncertainty in the world of imperfect information, and the extent of transaction costs incurred by any economy is affected by the extent of economic uncertainty dictated by the institutional environment that surrounds the economy. The existence of ill-defined institutions or the nonexistence of necessary institutions indicate the absence of well-defined game rules that will become a source of uncertainties on how economic activities (transactions) are guided, and in consequence, a source of increasing transaction costs. Economic reforms should therefore, try to establish well-defined rules. Without such rules, government regulations based mainly on discretion will continue to foster uncertainties, not just for individual terms but for the economy on a whole. Nontransparent enforcement of formal institutions such as the tax codes will again become a source of uncertainty regardless of the completeness of formal institutions.

This paper has tried to confirm empirically the importance of economic institutions, especially the property rights system, in determining the extent of transaction costs and thereby economic behavior. It has shown that countries with relatively insecure property rights systems tend to incur relatively high transaction costs, which in turn generate a systematic behavioral pattern of industrial organization of individual economies, with consequent implications for neoinstitutional economics. Korea, as a country with relatively high transaction costs and a relatively insecure property rights system, especially in terms of informal institutions as well as comprehensive fairness in the enforcement of the formal institution, must face these problems by establishing new institutions and streamlining or repealing existing institutions as necessary. Furthermore, these reforms should be carefully designed and implemented in order not to create additional uncertainties, for otherwise they will not truly be economic reforms.

I have also suggested that formal institutions are very important in setting up the general framework of the rules of the game, though informal constraints as well as strict enforcement may be as important as formal institutions. The legal system of private property rights in Korea is perhaps no less complete than in other developed countries, but it is hampered by often inadequate enforcement as well as by the way in which the public perceives the system. Such an informal constraint as the people's perception, developed over a long period, seems to have been critical in determining economic organizational behavior.

In this context, it may be useful to note the point emphasized by Andrzej Rapaczynski (1996), that the property rights system is endogenous and tends to be formed in a gradual, incremental, and evolutionary manner. Though a formal institution may easily be set in place following an advanced model, the whole system of any institution, consisting of informal constraint and enforcement as well as a formal structure, cannot simply be implanted and made effective overnight. An institution tends to evolve out of a long history of experiences with the system as it operates over a long period of time. An informal system of property rights that evolves from what people see and experience in their interrelationship with the government power as well as among themselves tends to dominate the formal system. Korea's experience with a relative attenuation of its property rights system seems to confirm this process.

How well an institution is formally built, how firmly and fairly the institution is enforced, and how people perceive the effectiveness of the institution—all these come into play to form an overall system of economic institution. It seems that the role of the government as a fair third-party referee as well as an introducer of formal institutions turns out to be paramount in determining the characteristics of an institution. But the Korean experience also suggests that it will be even more important for the government to take special care not to override and infringe on the formal system of private property rights and not to be a prime source of economic uncertainties. The government should keep this point in mind when considering economic reforms so that the reform itself does not become another source of economic uncertainty.

APPENDIX

TABLE A1 Data Set for the Regression for Korea

Year	*SEP*	*CR*	*PGNP*
1971	29.576	14.930	102645.985
1972	28.352	15.013	123962.996
1973	29.156	15.707	157741.935
1974	28.435	16.727	216287.114
1975	29.227	16.095	285289.115
1976	27.419	16.099	385439.330
1977	27.126	16.224	489068.937
1978	26.260	17.202	649229.104
1979	26.740	16.238	820730.082
1980	27.058	14.807	964060.860
1981	26.718	12.921	1175826.446
1982	28.053	12.932	1326773.455
1983	27.131	12.529	1555650.212

(Table A1 continued)

Year	*SEP*	*CR*	*PGNP*
1984	24.954	12.583	1758104.429
1985	24.864	11.503	1943175.692
1986	25.230	10.873	2254525.600
1987	24.463	11.030	2636400.768
1988	24.105	10.488	3125648.346
1989	22.371	10.471	3485088.339
1990	21.852	10.204	4158199.206
1991	22.329	9.448	4951236.422
1992	23.024	8.914	5467361.429
1993	23.167	10.790	6026282.342

NOTE: (1) SEP = weight of the self-employed persons in total employment; (2) CR = cash ratio in M2; (3) PGNP = per capita GNP in Korean won.

TABLE A2 Data Sets for Cross-Country Regressions

		Data Set						
		1	*2*		*3*			
Country	*Period*	*1972–91*	*1972–81*	*1982–91*	*1972–76*	*1977–81*	*1982–86*	*1987–91*
Australia	SEP(%)	11.71	11.13	12.28	10.03	12.22	12.44	12.13
	CR(%)	8.49	8.77	8.20	8.36	9.18	9.04	7.37
	PGNP	11634.85	5167.85	20614.31	3427.10	7029.21	15960.24	25133.53
Canada	SEP(%)	6.83	6.38	7.27	6.19	6.57	7.19	7.36
	CR(%)	7.61	8.53	6.68	9.72	7.34	6.84	6.53
	PGNP	12796.40	8434.52	16089.99	6646.87	9848.75	13037.48	19306.88
France	SEP(%)	10.60	10.92	10.28	11.24	10.61	10.52	10.04
	CR(%)	7.68	10.94	4.32	15.27	6.61	4.55	4.29
	PGNP	11596.99	7721.29	14136.36	5311.32	10134.25	10205.05	19603.30
Germany	SEP(%)	7.99	8.43	7.56	9.06	7.81	7.49	7.62
	CR(%)	10.06	10.00	10.12	9.97	10.03	9.78	10.47
	PGNP	11680.50	8242.11	1543.90	5935.62	11356.36	11363.03	21698.52
Italy	SEP(%)	21.28	20.98	21.57	22.91	19.05	21.05	22.09
	CR(%)	8.80	9.38	8.22	10.44	8.32	8.02	8.42
	PGNP	9444.97	5009.28	11863.89	3268.43	6244.78	7881.82	17125.43
Japan	SEP(%)	13.14	13.78	12.51	13.80	13.76	13.06	11.95
	CR(%)	8.37	8.99	7.75	9.31	8.68	7.82	7.68
	PGNP	10450.74	6053.82	16719.73	4008.80	8729.66	11679.23	24977.19
Korea	SEP(%)	26.09	27.65	24.54	28.52	26.78	26.05	23.02
	CR(%)	13.46	15.70	11.21	15.93	15.48	12.08	10.33
	PGNP	2687.33	1071.24	3547.94	524.68	1466.67	2149.75	5067.64
Norway	SEP(%)	6.77	7.06	6.47	7.51	6.62	6.66	6.27
	CR(%)	11.05	13.74	8.35	14.50	12.97	9.40	7.31
	PGNP	13840.69	8508.61	17769.21	5759.83	11439.79	13514.70	22988.77

(Table A2 continued)

		Data Set						
		1	*2*		*3*			
Country	*Period*	*1972–91*	*1972–81*	*1982–91*	*1972–76*	*1977–81*	*1982–86*	*1987–91*
Portugal	SEP(%)	14.71	12.69	16.74	12.13	13.25	16.36	17.13
	CR(%)	14.63	18.47	10.80	20.12	16.82	11.35	10.26
	PGNP	3330.14	1717.37	3689.77	1356.26	2026.99	2065.03	5314.08
Spain	SEP(%)	16.68	15.73	17.64	15.70	15.76	17.49	17.79
	CR(%)	10.58	10.11	11.06	10.26	9.96	10.40	11.71
	PGNP	6007.23	3603.35	7166.53	2407.30	4462.68	4426.78	11004.22
Sweden	SEP(%)	5.18	4.55	5.81	4.62	4.47	4.60	7.01
	CR(%)	10.80	11.53	10.08	11.56	11.49	10.45	9.71
	PGNP	14350.52	9931.83	17129.90	7433.23	12273.26	11937.06	23836.73
Taiwan	SEP(%)	21.45	23.09	19.80	24.74	21.45	20.78	18.83
	CR(%)	9.52	11.93	7.10	12.59	11.27	8.13	6.08
	PGNP	3174.47	1408.35	4918.36	841.41	1949.10	3190.87	7320.66
United	SEP(%)	8.71	7.12	10.30	7.19	7.04	9.25	11.36
Kingdom	CR(%)	10.06	14.32	5.81	14.43	14.20	8.07	3.5+6
	PGNP	9077.86	5475.27	11737.41	3480.80	7425.99	8319.99	16080.91
United	SEP(%)	7.25	6.93	7.57	6.79	7.08	7.55	7.59
States	CR(%)	6.77	7.04	6.50	7.16	6.91	6.35	6.66
	PGNP	14203.35	9114.55	18476.65	6948.78	11172.72	15860.44	20974.96

NOTE: (1) SEP = weight of self-employed persons in total employment; (2) CR = cash ratio in M2; (3) PGNP = per capita GNP in U.S. $.

REFERENCES

Alchian, Armen A. 1961. *Some Economics of Property*. RAND P-2316. Santa Monica, Calif., RAND Corporation. Reprinted in Armen A. Alchian, *Economic Forces at Work*, Indianapolis: Liberty Press, 1977.

Alchian, Armen A., and H. Demsetz. 1972. "Production, Information, Costs, and Economic Organization." *American Economic Review* 62: 777–95.

Arthur, W. Lewis. 1955. *The Theory of Economic Growth*. London: Allen & Unwin.

Buchanan, J. M., and R. D. Tollison, eds. 1972. *The Theory of Public Choice*. Ann Arbor: University of Michigan Press.

Clague, Christopher, Philip Keefer, Stephen Knack and Mancur Olson. 1996. "Property and Contract Rights in Autocracies and Democracies." *Journal of Economic Growth*, June: 243–76.

Coase, R. H. 1937. "The Nature of the Firm." *Economica* 4: 368–405.

———. 1960. "The Problem of Social Cost." *Journal of Law and Economics* 3 (October): 1–44.

———. 1984. "The New Institutional Economics." *Journal of Institutional and Theoretical Economics* 140: 229–31.

Demsetz, Harold. 1967. "Toward a Theory of Property Rights." *American Economic Review* 5: 347–59.

Eggertsson, Thrainn. 1990. *Economic Behavior and Institutions*. Cambridge: Cambridge University Press.

Fisher, Irving. 1920. *Elementary Principles of Economics*. New York: Macmillan.

Fukuyama, Francis. 1995. "Social Capital and the Global Economy." *Foreign Affairs* 74, no. 5: 89–103.

———. 1996. "Social Capital and Future of Asia." Seminar Paper, Seoul: Samsung Economic Institute.

Jwa, Sung Hee. 1997. "Globalization and Industrial Organization: Implications for Structural Adjustment Policies." In Ito and Krueger, eds., *Regionalism vs. Multilateral Trade Arrangement*. NBER–East Asia Seminar on Economics, vol. 6. Chicago: University of Chicago Press.

Marfels, Christian. 1988. "Aggregate Concentration in International Perspective." R. S. Khemani et al., eds., *Mergers, Corporate Concentration, and Power in Canada*. Institute for Research on Public Policy, pp. 53–88.

North, Douglass C. 1981. *Structure and Change in Economic History*. New York: W. W. Norton.

———. 1990. *Institutions, Institutional Change, and Economic Performance*. Cambridge: Cambridge University Press.

———. 1992. *Transaction Costs, Institutions, and Economic Performance*. International Center for Economic Growth, San Francisco, Occasional Papers, no. 30.

Pejovich, Svetozar. 1990. *The Economics of Property Rights: Towards a Theory of Comparative Systems*. Dordrecht: Kluwer Academic.

Rapaczynski, Andrzej. 1996. "The Roles of the State and the Market in Establishing Property Rights." *Journal of Economic Perspectives* 10, no. 2: 87–103.

Wallis, John Joseph, and Douglass C., North. 1986. "Measuring the Transaction Sector in the American Economy, 1870–1970." In Stanley L. Engerman and Robert E. Gallman, eds., *Long-term Factors in American Economic Growth*, Income and Wealth Series, vol. 51, pp. 95–161. Chicago: University of Chicago Press.

John V. C. Nye

Economic Growth and Institutions

What We Think We Know vs. What We Pretend to Measure

Both our natural intuition and reams of scholarly publications suggest but do not prove that the structures of our legal, social, and political institutions are critical for economic development. I use the term institutions here as Douglass North (1990) defines it—namely, the rules that order social and economic activity and the attendant set of formal and informal norms that structure our daily lives.

Despite the sense that institutions must matter, it is difficult for us to get a very precise handle on just how and when institutions matter, particularly when the subject is long-term economic growth. This then results in the unfortunate tension between what we learn inductively from historical and comparative case studies and the needs of a social scientific profession that places a high value on formal models and precise quantification.

I shall explore these tensions by discussing some of our received wisdom in the literature on institutions and contrasting that with the findings derived from the empirical growth literature.

Qualitative Aspects of Our Understanding

Perhaps the two most important questions that we need to answer when considering economic growth are: (1) What are the known or claimed variables that affect economic growth in a qualitative sense? (2) What is known about the precise relationships between these variables and economic growth or at least about the precise quantitative effect of these variables? A secondary and subsidiary set of questions, which sometimes get mixed in with the two above, asks: What are the variables that policy makers can manipulate successfully for the purposes of fostering economic development?

From an institutional perspective many economists and economic historians believe that the most important necessary conditions for growth include the development of a stable property rights regime for both goods and services, which includes intangibles like ideas. Many further feel that this was critical for the long-term development of the most successful industrial nations. As Ronald Coase observed in a world of positive transactions costs, the precise structure of a given set of rules may have radically different consequences for the efficiency of contractual relations.[1] While stable and well-articulated property rights may emerge spontaneously through repeat play or other private arrangements, a well-ordered government is a sensible response to the problem of developing a coherent set of rules for society as a whole.

Unfortunately, the problem throughout the ages has been that most governments have not managed to produce progressive regimes for the purposes of promoting economic growth. Indeed, rapid economic growth has occurred in such a limited time span that for all intents and purposes we can view the last two hundred years as a one-time event in human history. For the most part this is because property rights enforcement requires a state or agency with the power to coerce. But the nature of the market for coercion and its attendant transactions costs, which subsumes the entire realm of politics and negotiation, has imperfections that often lead to situations in which one cannot credibly create a regime with both the will and the power to promote efficient allocation of resources. Often the very same arrangements that give authorities the power to carry out necessary measures also give them the power to engage in arbitrary taxation, theft, or confiscation of property. The very guarantees that are needed to restrain the power of the state to the most significant managerial functions may rob rulers of their ability to expand, enforce, and develop the necessary legal structures conducive to a growing economy—hence the present-day tension between the costs and benefits of large government.

To some extent, the classical economists like Adam Smith and the statesmen who wrote the American constitution believed in small gov-

1. This is, of course, the oft-ignored flip side to the well-known Coase theorem, and was the central point of Coase's path-breaking work.

ernment not because they were unaware of the beneficial activities states may engage in but because they feared that big government would rapidly abuse its authority. However, the problem ever since has been to devise a government that is sufficiently limited to deter abuse while remaining sufficiently powerful to preserve order, establish the appropriate rules of conduct, and withstand the threat of outside conquest. Thus, the modern-day debate about the proper role of the state in the economy is not just about which facets of the economy should be regulated or left alone by the state in isolation; we also argue about the extent to which any given intrusion or lack thereof contributes to the unnecessary strengthening or untoward weakening of the coercive capacities of the state. These remarks take as a benchmark the classical liberal ideal of limited government restrained by constitutional checks and balances. The argument holds a fortiriori for more expansive conceptions of the role of the state providing social insurance and the like.

A further confusion arises because of the association but not equivalence between political and economic liberalism. The two are often associated but may have different functions. On the one hand there are those who note that market societies usually have at least semidemocratic institutions and therefore point approvingly to the link between democracy and economic performance. Conversely there is a tradition that dates back to Marx but may have been most eloquently articulated by Schumpeter, who believed that big government is a normal, even a supernormal good, in that wealthy nations will demand more interference with the economy for purposes other than wealth creation as the people become richer, which will then undermine the effects of past economic successes and precipitate crises or stagnation. In modern-day work this emerges in debates about the costs of democracy and in frequent claims that authoritarian rule is a necessary although insufficient condition for market reform and successful emergence from poverty. In this version of the story, an authoritarian regime has more temptations to plunder the nation's wealth and can less credibly guarantee the safety and long-term enforcement of its promises, but such regimes can, if so motivated, also put into place the legal infrastructure for growth more easily than democratic regimes that must overcome the problems of obtaining coherent collective action. Again, strong rulers and states can do good more easily than weaker regimes if properly motivated, but are just as likely to do grievous harm.

There is a further problem that economists are reluctant to explore in their own research but are surprisingly quick to cite in more applied public-policy contexts and that is the rule of culture and cultural norms. Anthropologists have found themselves faced with great difficulty in establishing the limits to culture and the extent to which it is exogenous or endogenous. Conversely, the economist tends to treat culture as either irrelevant at one level, or decisive and fully exogenous at another. Indeed, models of the economy that ignore culture either presume cultural irrelevance and/or malleability or else extreme cultural fixity (cf. Jones 1995). Yet as the examples of the Far East have shown, cultural coherence has a lot to do both with the form that economic organizations take and with the capacity of a nation to work within the constraints of the system and to overcome the imperfections that all nations face in their chosen political and economic systems. Consideration of the role of culture and informal norms in economic analysis is in its infancy, but I would guess that we will eventually come to view much culture in social capital terms with relatively fixed effects in the short run but quite a good deal of endogenous variability in the very long run. Thus groups endowed with different cultural and social characteristics will exhibit different comparative advantages. Cohesive family ties and self-policing social norms will facilitate self-enforcing trade but will also limit the capacity of outsiders to compete successfully in such a society. A nation that places a high value on formal rules and anonymous exchange will benefit from greater diversity and adaptability but will be hampered by a greater amount of friction in social and political interactions among groups. These differences will not only mean that nations will tend to specialize in different types of managerial and productive arrangements, but they will also result in the advantages of a given type of society being highly dependent on the state of world trade and the long-term character of changing production technology, so that characteristics that seem beneficial in one period may seem to radically hinder growth in another.

In addition to these large-scale observations we have various bits of partial knowledge about how a few particular institutional arrangements work. Public-choice theory and the rational-choice literature in political science have given us some specific insights into the mechanics of different bureaucratic and political arrangements. Work in the theory of contracts deriving both from the legal empiric and the partial equilibrium traditions in economics as well as from more formal principal-agent models and the exploding game theoretic literature provide us with some of the equivalent knowledge for private organizations. Comparative work in history and in regulatory studies seeks to enlighten us as to the evolution as well as the costs and benefits of a variety of rules affecting the marketplace.

Unfortunately, in none of this work is there much talk of how to gauge the importance of such arrangements for the precise workings of the economy. At best, we can say that some reforms can promote greater output. But we cannot say which ones are necessary, let alone which ones are sufficient—other than to observe that some nations have many imperfections but still seem to function reasonably well. Hence we need to ask, how should we go about acquiring quantitative information about the balance of institutional effects on the macroeconomy?

Sadly, I am not optimistic about the possibilities inherent in the mainstream empirical literature.

The Empirical Literature on Economic Growth

I hope I will be forgiven if I remark that the empirical work that has been undertaken on the proximate causes of modern economic growth is more to be admired for its suggestiveness than for either its precision or its rigor. I say this not because the statistical analysis of macroeconomic data is an uninteresting or unworthy exercise. To the contrary, its insights are at the heart of much long-term analysis of particular interest to economic historians such as myself. However, in spite of the many caveats and warnings that hem any careful presentation of the analysis, it is all too easy to make more of an impressive mass of statistics than is warranted by the data quality.

To paraphrase one of the more important contributors to the literature: "Even if I run a million regressions, should you believe what I get?" It is a cliché to note that the precision of our estimates is unrelated to the accuracy of the underlying data, but it needs especial emphasis when dealing with statistical fishing expeditions designed to test hypotheses with masses of cross-country data. To begin with, no one has any clear idea of how comparable national product data is across nations, even when one leaves out the always vexing problem of correcting for differences in purchasing power. Reuven Brenner (1994, 1) has made light of the fact that in 1987—known as the year of *il sorpasso*—Italy overtook Britain in total output. But that adjustment was heavily dependent on the judgment that the Italian national product needed to be adjusted to take account of the underground economy. Unfortunately, the suspicion remains that the estimate of the size of the underground economy—18 percent—was chosen for no better reason than that is what it would take for Italy to exceed Britain in the rankings of the world's richest nations. Or who can forget the adjustments in national income made by the World Bank for China in the 1980s, when a sudden recalculation led to the Chinese receiving four times as high an income per capita as previously assumed with little comment of what such monumental error suggests for the usefulness of other national data, even when such data are substantially superior to those of the Chinese.

I shall advance a further speculation that I have not seen discussed in the literature. The creation of measures of national income between the two world wars meant that backward-looking aggregates could be constructed that were imperfect but to a large extent independent of the policy process itself. The same cannot be said of the postwar period. When governments both socialist and capitalist undertook specific policy programs designed to improve the economy and were then judged and chose to judge on the basis of certain standard measures that were routinely collected, we must wonder whether the underlying basis for some of these numbers is greatly weakened. For the most part, governments have an incentive to make the numbers look good. There are limits to what they can manipulate, but given a choice between a policy that may have benefits but does not seem to affect the relevant aggregates and those that may have unmeasurable costs but measurable benefits for the standard indices, policy makers will invariably choose the latter. It is patently obvious that if politicians are judged by the public measures of economic growth and welfare, they will work on policies that improve those figures even if the reliability of those measures is in question. Worse yet, the relationship between measured components of welfare and the unmeasurables would not remain constant across time periods, endogenizing what are presumed to be exogenous relationships. I conjecture that this would certainly add an upward bias to all government-mandated measures of well-being for the period after World War II. Furthermore, to the extent that governments gave in to the temptations of tampering with the data in various degrees, it will severely restrict our capacity to make good cross-country comparisons.

Some readers may be growing impatient with this line of criticism, noting that all serious scholars are aware of these problems and have tried to take them into account. But trying is one thing, obtaining success and taking *seriously* our lack of success, another. I recall my irritation that until the early 1990s, many if not most development textbooks continued to maintain that East Germany's growth rate for the forty years after World War II was superior to that of West Germany even though the data were extremely flawed. This is one instance where a confused mass of calculations seems to have overcome the overwhelming evidence of anecdotal data. And at least in this case, sensible observers should agree that informal, common-sense observation beats weak statistical analysis. When one is dealing with very bad figures and highly variable qualitative changes, the experts are not to be trusted.

If that is too extreme an example, let us take a more recent problem. We are all aware of the reexamination of the U.S. consumer price index that has been under way for the last decade, and most knowledgeable scholars felt the CPI to have been a problem for many years before that. Nonetheless, many of these same scholars thought nothing of pondering the puzzle of slow growth in the 1980s while acknowledging that the inflation numbers, hence measures of real income growth, were inaccurate. Perhaps the CPI was biased upward and we still had low real growth, but I knew of no one who convincingly argued that the weight of evidence (of which there was little at the time) favored both hypotheses simultaneously. It is not enough to observe casually that data set X is the best there is. For some calculations, data set X's problems may not matter. For others, we might be better off ignoring this data set altogether, but I think we still need more investigation into the probable robustness of any stylized facts to reasonable variation due to probable identification errors.

Furthermore, casual empiricism suggests that this self-same problem bedevils the last decade's PPI corrections for U.S. growth vis-à-vis its European allies. While PPI corrections do take some account of higher European prices, I have seen no systematic corrections that note the impact of more frequent sales, less regulated retail stores, easier shopping, and wider quality and price variation, and consequently, more difficult price measurements in the United States vs. the Continent. Again, conversation with professionals who work in both countries suggest that our current PPI measures do not go far enough to capture the gap between U.S. and European prices. A serious consideration of the problem of the overestimation of American inflation would indicate that the bias was less severe in Europe, and therefore suggest that current PPI comparisons understate the gap between American and European incomes.

Of course, some of the more diligent scholars of macroeconomic empiricism have sounded a warning:

> Growth accounting may be able to provide a mechanical decomposition of the growth of output into growth of an array of inputs and growth of total factor productivity. Successful accounting of this sort is likely to be useful and may stimulate the development of useful economic theories of growth. Growth accounting does not, however, constitute a theory of growth because it does not attempt to explain how the changes in inputs and the improvements in total factor productivity relate to elements—such as aspects of preferences, technology, and government policies—that can reasonably be viewed as fundamentals. (Barro and Sala-I-Martin 1995a, 352).

Nonetheless, many speak as if such accounting were theoretically cogent explanations of growth rather than weak indicators that often do little more than indicate other manifestations of growth. This is a particularly easy trap to fall into when discussing policy aided by accounting rules that treat government investment as akin to private investment and government-financed consumption similarly to privately chosen consumption, even ignoring the known problems of measuring technological improvement. Indeed, the residuals on various measures of technology are often so great that even historians are apt to see technology as causing economic growth.

One of the greatest insights contained in North and Thomas's 1973 monograph, *The Rise of the Western World,* was a criticism of their fellow cliometricians for their overemphasis on technology and the Industrial Revolution in causing modern growth. As North and Thomas rightly noted, investment in new technology was rarely an independent cause of growth; rather, it was itself a manifestation of the overall process of economic growth. For North and Thomas, saying that the Industrial Revolution explains Western economic success is to beg the question entirely.

There is one other set of problems that are not so much empirical as conceptual and that involve the treatment of population, or demographic trends. While it makes sense to think of the welfare of the country in per capita terms, comparisons between nations or in one nation across time must be dogged by the problem of how to treat growing or shrinking populations. Is country X with a high standard of living but no population growth really doing better than country Y with slow per capita economic growth but very rapid population growth? Economic historians are especially familiar with this problem because of the case of France in the nineteenth century. While all her major rivals, Britain, the United States and Germany, experienced economic growth and rapid population growth, France's population growth slowed to a crawl. How should we treat this case and how do we make the comparison?

Or take productivity measures. How does one compare country A with high productivity and high unemployment, with country B with somewhat lower productivity and low unemployment? What if labor market restrictions in country A make it difficult to hire cheaper workers who would lower average measured productivity but actually raise profitability and GNP per capita? How much weight should be attached to the differences in minimum wage laws as well as regulations restricting the hiring and firing of workers? Should population growth be treated as an exogenous or endogenous variable in growth comparisons? The problems are increased when one takes immigration into account where a low-income worker might enter the country and raise both his wages and the wages of his neighbors, but actually lower the overall average of measured productivity.

The problem of demography bedevils not only simple comparison but also the long-term problem of analyzing modern economic growth. As Richard Easterlin has more recently noted, the period of modern economic growth in the West that characterized the late eighteenth and early nineteenth centuries was also unique in that populations worldwide expanded at a dramatic pace throughout the globe in countries both rich and poor, both with and without industrialization. No discussion of the problems of growth or the role of institutions can be complete without considering this puzzling and important upward shift.

But let us presume away these large and ungainly criticisms as unwarranted, or at least unseemly. What do we learn from the million or so regressions that economists have run? And what about the many attempts to use cross-country macrodata to test such big questions as the role of property rights, market forces, or human capital in economic success? Since we are now talking about combining poor data with unreliable measures, any relationships that are revealed are a triumph of scholarly love over numerical adversity. Like the proverbial dog walking upright on its hind legs, it is amazing to see it done at all.

Again, I emphasize that this work is extremely useful, if we use it to help us ferret out relationships whose existence we might not have heretofore suspected. I do not believe it is of much use as a means of explicit hypothesis testing. The controls are so weak, and the universe of growth events so far removed from independence, that any rejections should be viewed with skepticism, and it is relevant that such refutations do not dissuade economists from pursuing their pet theories. It is said that when Linus Pauling taught chemistry for decades at Caltech, he would brusquely observe that when a well-established theory was contradicted by a laboratory experiment, you were well advised to rerun the experiment.

In a more positive vein, let us focus on the successes of this research and some of the more useful findings on the institutional prerequisites of growth.

For instance, simply looking over the work of Barro and Sala-I-Martin, I am surprised and somewhat pleased to find that use of variables from the Knack and Keefer ranking of nations by the rule of law produces a positive and significant correlation with economic growth. The authors would like "to interpret the coefficient on the rule-of-law variable as an estimate of the effect of the legal and political framework on the growth rate" (p. 440) and this is certainly a reasonable interpretation, but I am still troubled by this. How many would change their minds about the rule-of-law's importance in economic growth if such a relationship had *not* been found? Moreover, does one place any credence in the quantitative measure of the rule-of-law variable? I would believe it to be positive, but I would not bet much on the likelihood that the measured relationship actually gives me an accurate parametrization of the relationships involved.

Other measures tried by various authors have even more problems when it comes to characterizing the economic and political systems of nations. The finding that democracy is correlated with economic growth is significant but apparently weak. Moreover, it is difficult to disentangle from considerations of economic liberty. There is no uniquely acceptable index of which nations are more or less economically liberal and the complication of calling some nations capitalist and others totalitarian socialist, which inherently conflate economic and political questions and have led to some indexes where China is ranged at the farthest end away from market capitalism simply because of its political controls (see, for example, some of the indexes used by Hall and Jones 1996). This in spite of the fact that China in the 1980s is probably more market-oriented than all socialist countries in the world before the mid-1970s.

Another interesting result that seems to occur is the openness of a country to trade. This either suggests that somewhat free trade—again, virtually no large country has ever been completely open in its trade policies—has obvious benefits or that wider trade is another manifestation of the overall phenomenon of successful economic performance. Though it is difficult to be closed to trade and perform well, isolating the independent effect of trade policy is enormously complicated, but it is gratifying to see that the standard intuitions of neoclassical theory have some relevance to policy discussions.

In other work on productivity levels cross-nationally, Hall and Jones (1996) also pick up the effects of openness to international trade and institutions that favor production over diversion, as well as the importance of private ownership. However, I do not feel that their institutional measures are particularly robust—particularly in their classification of economic organizations. Most important of all, I confess I am at a loss as to how to treat their latitude effect where countries farther from the equator do better than those near the equator, except to note that this probably indicates a sort of cultural proxy, with the English-influenced and Germanic-Scandinavian nations predominantly to the north (few countries are far from the equator in the southern hemisphere).[2]

Again, it is gratifying to see that property rights and open trade seem to matter, but to get beyond this to more precise, reliable relationships is, I feel, to ask too much of cross-country data, hence the need for case studies and, especially, comparative historical analysis.

Reform and the Problem of Policy Advice

It has been the contention of this essay that the measures of the economy are not the economy itself. That is a truism that will strike most

2. A somewhat different thesis might emerge if we take a Boserupian view of equatorial regions as having been relatively favorable to agriculture and early settlement. Boserup has argued that the fertility of the land in ancient Africa made life sufficiently easy to discourage technological innovation. We might extend this to other near-tropical regions, many of which have not only the benefits of good agricultural land but also abundant natural resources such as oil or minerals. The argument would then run to the effect that the opportunities for rent-seeking and redistribution overwhelmed the possibilities for investment and development.

readers as being a trivial matter not worthy of discussion. But allied to this obvious but oft-ignored claim is a more profound set of claims about the nature of economic growth and the appropriate attitude of policy makers toward its promotion.

Within the mainstream of the economics profession the last half-century has seen a constant tug-of-war between those who see the economy as a machine capable of manipulation by skilled engineers and those who see the economy in more organic terms, as a living entity that can be nurtured but not controlled. In this latter view, the human impulses toward economic growth and market competition are pervasive and it is the primary duty of the state seeking to encourage that growth to create an environment in which human welfare can increase without in any way being subject to easy analysis, prediction, or forecasting.

In contrast, the view of the economy as a gigantic and easily manipulated machine was encouraged and made viable by the rise of commonly available economic aggregates collected for the purposes of the compiling national income accounts. Vulgar Keynesianism, the impulse toward collectivization, social planning, and the rise of the welfare state, all conspired to encourage analysts and government policy makers to see the economy as a comprehensible and manageable device. Correspondingly, the disillusionment with central planning, the collapse of the Keynesian-neoclassical paradigm, the search for microfoundations of macroeconomics, and the increasing evidence of the law of unintended consequences have led to a greater awareness that the economy is not what the state makes of it but what the individuals within the state make of it subject to the constraints established by law, time, and circumstance. Initially, this advice often took the form of the need "to get the prices right." This led to two dangerous simplifications. On the one hand is the pure laissez-faire view that nothing is to be done, the market will assert itself. This impulse, while a necessary corrective to the notion that the government knows best, ignores the tradition that goes back to Adam Smith that stresses that even a minimalist government bears a great deal of the responsibility for establishing order and laying down and enforcing sensible rules of the game. The other less common simplification is simply to transfer the central-planning ethos while relabeling it as some version of strategic trade policy or market development. In this version of the economy as machine, the goal is to promote competitive markets, but once again, the state is capable of identifying industries, products, and outcomes that need promotion else they will be ignored by the market.

All this is the inevitable outcome of the systematic misuse of the highly valuable statistical indicators that serve as the barometers of the economy's health. If one takes seriously the problems inherent in measuring economic performance, it should not be surprising that there is a less than perfect fit between ideal policy and observed outcome. Of course policy is often mistaken, and it is necessary to have objective measures of our performance. But such measures are hard to come by. It is therefore important to stress that even if we had a perfect policy that would produce the optimal environment for economic growth, our measures might not reflect that improvement. Consequently, a policy that is judged solely by its ability to show improvements on the indexes we use will be biased toward distortions that are otherwise harmful.

This is especially the case when one considers that the professional politician comes to be judged by the economic measures that we take and therefore has an interest in promoting outcomes favorable to reelection and political stability, even when state policies may actually lower the welfare of the public at large.

We thus come to a further class of problems that falls under the heading of institutions, although it certainly fits into classical traditions of political economy. Even if we agreed that a particular set of institutions were unambiguously beneficial for the economy, its political feasibility comes into question. We are thus faced not just with the standard political obstacles to growth and growth-enhancing institutions but with the more general problem: What is the stable and sustainable mix of political and economic regimes that promote cumulative economic development?

Our answers here are weakest of all. We have a variety of intuitions, aided by work in political science and public choice theory, that the costs of political organization and the attendant difficulties in overcoming the free-rider problem make systematic reform difficult even when a majority sees such improvements as desirable. When the costs of any reform are clear but the potential benefits and the distribution of those benefits are unknown or poorly understood, then such change is even more difficult.

Second, the theory of rent-seeking has contributed greatly to our understanding of how interest in preserving inefficient arrangements comes about. Any set of rules, no matter how constraining, becomes embedded in the system because rational actors will take such imperfections into account. Indeed, some will try to profit from imperfections to the point where all rents are dissipated. Thus, any move to reorder the institutions so as to favor global efficiency gains will almost surely run up against the problem of disenfranchising not just those who benefited from the original imperfections but also those who quite honestly tried to make the best of a poor situation. Here the variety of studies of tariffs and quotas around the world is especially revealing, as is the literature on regulation and the welter of state interventions that are rarely at the center of political attention but often constitute the lion's share of the microeconomic costs imposed on an economy.

In general, though, we are still left with the problem that, for all our research, we have never observed any countries that are anywhere close to being paradigmatic economic liberals. For all the claims to the contrary, no country has ever practiced unbridled free trade and market capitalism. All nations, both the rich and the poor, have interfered with their economies in ways that we would recognize as being disruptive of continued economic improvement. Some have occasionally done so purposefully, constraining market forces or imposing regulations for some perceived social gain. But for the most part, one would be hard pressed to explain away the variety of rules that seem to provide little social gain while imposing large costs on the populace at large in both explicit and foregone economic output. Can a nation be too good at promoting growth, is the modern variant of the Schumpeter question regarding the self-destructiveness of successful capitalist societies. Are there ways for policy makers to encourage substantial improvement without endangering the very life of existing societies?

Using the language of revealed preference, humanity—or its political aggregates—has obviously shown a historical unwillingness to promote growth, in spite of the fact that subsistence was barely within reach of most people throughout history. Is the current period a once-and-for-all turning point? Should we assume that some long-term growth is foreordained? We need to determine how to do better, but we also need to be concerned with preventing a return to a period of long-term stagnation and decline. Hence the challenge before us: to decompose the elements of growth and the institutions that promote them, to understand the interactions between human competition in the economic and political sphere, and finally to understand in a more general, social-scientific sense, how the evolution of attitudes toward the economy (as expressed in real world policy) functions as part of general human evolution. Ultimately, we want to do more than simply understand these processes and be able to point to situations when careful intervention provides the maximum capacity for keeping us on the right path to continued improvement.

REFERENCES

Barro, Robert J. 1991. "Economic Growth in a Cross Section of Countries." *Quarterly Journal of Economics* 106 (May): 407–43.

Barro, Robert J., and Xavier Sala-I-Martin. 1995a. *Economic Growth.* New York: McGraw-Hill.

———. 1995b. "Technological Diffusion, Convergence, and Growth." NBER Working Paper no. 5151.

Brenner, Reuven. 1994. *Labyrinths of Prosperity.* Ann Arbor: University of Michigan Press.

Feige, Edward L., ed. 1989. *The Underground Economy.* Cambridge: Cambridge University Press.

Hall, Robert E., and Charles I. Jones. 1996. "The Productivity of Nations." Stanford Working Paper.

Jones, Eric. 1995. "Culture and Its Relationship to Economic Change." *Journal of Institutional and Theoretical Economics* 151, no. 2: 269–85.

Knack, Stephen, and Philip Keefer. 1995. "Institutions and Economic Performance: Cross-Country Tests Using Alternative Institutional Measures." *Economics and Politics* 7 (November): 207–27.

North, Douglass C. 1981. *Structure and Change in Economic History.* New York: W. W. Norton.

———. 1990. *Institutions, Institutional Change, and Economic Performance.* Cambridge: Cambridge University Press.

North, Douglass C., and Robert P. Thomas. 1973. *The Rise of the Western World.* New York: W. W. Norton.

Olson, Mancur. 1982. *The Rise and Decline of Nations.* New Haven, Conn.: Yale University Press.

Part VIII

Culture and Economic Development

In Search of a New Capitalist Spirit for the Korean Economy

For more than thirty years, the Republic of Korea has recorded one of the highest economic growth rates in the world. In fact, between 1960 and 1990, Korea had the highest growth rate of real per capita GDP in a sample of 114 countries, and Korea's annual growth rate of 6.7 percent was more than three times the sample average of 1.8 percent per annum.[1] Only a few other countries in world history have managed to sustain such a high growth rate for more than a few decades.

Given this spectacular record of economic achievement, a foreign observer might expect that Koreans would take much pride in their economic system and have a great deal of respect for the firms that have spearheaded Korea's march toward prosperity. Korean culture *must* be favorably disposed toward moneymaking and the rich *must* command a high degree of social respectability, he or she might presume.

Surveys of public economic opinion in Korea, however, typically produce results quite contrary to these expectations. For example, in a 1990 opinion survey, only 35.2 percent of respondents felt that the rich had become economically successful through their own legitimate efforts; 22.6 percent cited speculative profit and unearned income as the reason for their success; 21.8 percent pointed to special political favors; and 14.9 percent mentioned inherited wealth.[2] This generally

1. Robert Barro and Xavier Sala-I-Martin, *Economic Growth* (New York: McGraw-Hill, 1995), p. 3.

2. In-sik Oh, Myung-ho Park, and Jong-kil Ahn, "A National Opinion Survey on the Market Economy and Policy Choice" (in Korean; Seoul: National Institute for Economic System and Information, 1990), p. 4. The rich might not receive the credit that

negative attitude toward the rich extends to Korea's giant conglomerates (chaebols) as well. In poll after poll, respondents cite chaebols as one of the most corrupt and least credible groups in Korean society.[3] Thus, at least in popular perception, the economically influential are identified with the morally reprehensible, and the Korean economy is seen as a morally bankrupt system.[4] This popular concern about the ethical dimension of the Korean capitalist system is shared by economic commentators who lament that the spirit of "pariah-capitalism" dominates the Korean economy.[5] They argue that without a new ethical foundation, Korea's economic growth cannot be sustained.

In short, for a people with an exceptionally dynamic and successful economy, Koreans seem to have remarkably critical and negative views of their economic system. What exactly is wrong with the Korean version of capitalism? What is the spirit of Korean capitalism that has served as a driving force behind Korea's economic development and alleged moral degradation? How can something as intangible as "a new spirit or ethos of capitalism" take root in Korean society?

In addressing these questions, this paper makes two general observations. First, although the Korean version of capitalism has serious shortcomings in its ethical dimension, other countries also have had similar problems with their versions of capitalism. As giant corporations came to dominate the economy and industrial relations became a source of social conflict, advanced industrial countries, much like Korea today, also had to wrestle with the problem of defining "social responsi-

they deserve in other countries as well; still, the combined total of 44.4 percent for speculative profit and political favors in the Korean case seems rather high.

3. See, e.g., Kyung-dong Kim, *The Value System and Social Consciousness of the Korean People* (in Korean; Seoul: Pakyoungsa, 1992).

4. In a 1996 survey, for instance, more than 60 percent of respondents thought that the norms of economic behavior and "the rules of the game" were usually not observed in Korean society. See Center for Economic Education, "A Survey of Public Economic Opinion in the Era of $10,000 Per Capita Income," March 26, 1996 (Seoul: Korea Development Institute, 1996), p. 5. The Hanbo Steel scandal of January 1997, involving a great deal of influence-peddling and an astronomical amount of questionable bank loans, has only reinforced such a popular perception.

5. In his seminal work on the spirit of capitalism (1905), Max Weber used the term pariah-capitalism to characterize "the politically and speculatively oriented adventurous capitalism" of the Jews. He noted that this type of capitalism was involved in "war, Government contracts, State monopolies, speculative promotions, and the construction and financial projects of princes." See Max Weber, *The Protestant Ethic and the Spirit of Capitalism*, trans. by Talcott Parsons, with a new introduction by Anthony Giddens (London: Allen & Unwin, 1976), pp. 166, 271.

bility" within the context of "the pursuit of self-interest" in a capitalist economy. Second, it is pointless to try to find a solution to this problem solely in the form of a new capitalist spirit or ethos. A new capitalist ethos may provide "a creative minority" with an intellectual and moral basis for institutional reform, but without concrete structural changes in institutions, even the most ethically commendable variety of capitalist spirit would accomplish very little in the way of changing people's behavior. Ideas certainly can have a powerful impact on society, but a purely moral campaign, detached from institutional reform, is not an effective way of tapping the full potential of ideas.

This paper is organized as follows: the first section defines the concept of "capitalist spirit" and traces its origin and development from the precapitalist age to modern times. This section argues that although the individualistic orientation of capitalism had played a critical role in the abolition of arbitrary authority, it became a threat to social cohesion when it lost its moral anchor in transcendental values and began to be guided solely by the logic of competition and self-interest. This section then briefly reviews the cultural aspects of Japanese capitalism and examines how a non-Western society managed to adapt both the spirit and the institutions of capitalism to its traditional culture.

Following this, we examine the origin and development of the capitalist spirit in Korea. After reviewing Korea's traditional values and indigenous sources of capitalist development, this section notes that once the economic institutions of capitalism were put into place, the traditional values of loyalty to the nation and devotion to the family could be remolded as Korea's equivalent to the Protestant ethic in the West.

We then review the attitude of the Korean people toward the acquisition and disposal of wealth as well as toward competition and work. This section then outlines a program of economic reform for Korea, taking into account both institutional and ethical dimensions.

The final section reflects on the relationship between wealth and honor and concludes that for wealth to be positively connected to honor and respect, *enlightened* self-interest should be an integral part of the capitalist ethos.

The Origin and Development of the Capitalist Spirit

When economic commentators concerned with "the moral decay of Korean capitalism" speak of a need to establish a new capitalist ethos for the Korean economy, what they usually have in mind is the spirit of puritanical capitalism as described by Max Weber—namely, the belief in one's economic activity as a God-ordained mission, a calling, in this world, which leads to the kind of worldly asceticism and commitment to work rarely seen in precapitalist societies. What they tend to overlook, however, is that this particular type of capitalist ethos was shaped under rather special precapitalist conditions that may not be reproducible in a mature capitalist economy.[6]

Certainly, by Weber's time, it had become clear that the spirit of puritanical capitalism was not the dominant economic ethos in capitalist societies, and Weber himself made no particular attempt to revive it, apparently feeling that it was pointless to appeal to old morality. In his view, "victorious capitalism" no longer needed the moral support of religious asceticism, and the pursuit of wealth, stripped of its religious and ethical meaning, became associated with "purely mundane passions."[7]

In order to have an understanding of this historical process, it is perhaps necessary to examine in some detail the distinguishing features of the spirit and the institutions of capitalism. Interaction between cultural-motivational factors and institutional-structural conditions constitutes a critical element of this evolution, and is consequently accorded a careful consideration.

THE ORIGIN OF THE SPIRIT AND INSTITUTIONS OF CAPITALISM

In almost every world culture, the merchant class was traditionally accorded a low social status. The ruling class—be it scholar-officials, priests, or warriors—typically condemned trading and moneymaking as a socially nonproductive and spiritually corrupting activity. Philosophers and theologians often drew a rigid dichotomy between what was

6. Moreover, as Werner Sombart among others pointed out, the Protestant ethic might not have been the dominant motivational force in the subsequent development of capitalism. Sombart wrote: "Puritanism hardly encouraged farsighted and adventurous enterprises; shopkeeping was the most it could achieve. Your Scotchman is a Puritan. But to regard as Puritans men like Cecil Rhodes and the really great undertakers who came to the fore in England and America in the 19th century, that is hardly warranted by facts." See Werner Sombart, *The Quintessence of Capitalism*, translation of *Der Bourgeois* (1913) by M. Epstein (London: T. F. Unwin, 1915), pp. 261–62.

7. While the Puritan *wanted* to work in a calling, people in modern societies are *forced* to do so because they cannot escape from the "iron cage" of mature capitalism. See Weber (1976), pp. 181–82.

right and what was profitable and never tired of warning against the pursuit of wealth for its own sake. As a result of this "spiritual indoctrination," merchants felt a profound sense of reservation and uncertainty about the spiritual merits of their work. In medieval Europe, some merchants on their deathbed went so far as to donate their wealth to the Church and instruct their sons to pursue an occupation less detrimental to their spiritual well-being.[8]

In these precapitalist societies, a person's material needs were defined by his or her social station, and these limited needs, in turn, defined the amount of work to be performed.[9] In those days, a constant striving to satisfy ever increasing material needs must have been a foreign *and* dangerous idea, which had the potential of disrupting the status quo.

Precapitalist societies, in short, were characterized by a high degree of social stratification and preoccupation with spiritual values. The predominant cultural values of precapitalist societies supported the institutional structure of these societies, since spiritual authority and classical learning, rather than material wealth, constituted the source of power and social respectability. Whether intended or not, the prescription of spiritual values by the ruling class had the effect of checking the rise of the merchant class and preserving the status quo.

It was in Western Europe that the merchant class was first able to break free from the customs of precapitalist societies and establish new economic institutions and norms of behavior—and rise to the top of the social strata. This breakthrough is the subject of Max Weber's famous work, *The Protestant Ethic and the Spirit of Capitalism*. According to Weber, a critical institutional innovation and a new economic ethos distinguish modern capitalism from the previous forms of economic organization: the rational organization of formally free labor (that is, wage labor) and the idea of pursuing profit as a God-ordained mission in this world.[10]

8. See Richard Henry Tawney, *Religion and the Rise of Capitalism* (London: J. Murray, 1926), particularly a section entitled "The Sin of Avarice," pp. 36–55.

9. Starting out with "the conception of limited and well-defined wants to be satisfied," both peasants and craftsmen directed their attention to "a sufficiency for existence." See Sombart (1915), p. 16.

10. For various attempts to define capitalism, see Michael Novak, *The Spirit of Democratic Capitalism* (New York: Simon & Schuster, 1982), pp. 431–32. Novak notes that the usually cited triad of "private property, markets, and profits" does not sufficiently characterize modern capitalism, since economies around the world for thou-

While many of his contemporaries emphasized the secular nature of the capitalist spirit, Weber argued that this new ethos had a fundamentally Christian origin.[11] He held that the doctrine of Protestantism, particularly that of predestination in its logically extreme form, and the remote and unknowable God created intense anxieties in the individual regarding personal salvation. Practical means of reducing these anxieties took the form of worldly asceticism, a systematic commitment to a calling based on the principle of hard work, discipline, and thrift.[12] Because these qualities were conducive to success in the modern capitalist economy, Protestants became the nucleus of the new capitalist class. Furthermore, success in the secular world came to be regarded as a sign of God's grace and promise of eventual salvation: those who overcame the weaknesses and temptations of the flesh and devoted themselves to a sober and industrious life *had to* succeed in this world and *had to* be the ones chosen by God.

Although this line of reasoning was rather suspect from a purely logical point of view, Weber noted that it constituted the essential link between the Protestant faith and the spirit of capitalism and liberated the merchant class from their previous doubt about the spiritual merits of their work. Moneymaking could now become an *honorable* profession, and the merchant could serve as "wisdom for the foolish, strength for the weak, warning to the wicked, and a blessing to all."[13] Adopting

---

sands of years contained these three institutional features. Novak's own candidate for the unique element of capitalism is "invention and discovery and innovation." It is, however, easy to point out that Ancient Greece, Medieval Europe, and China, among others, also had this element. What they lacked was the institutional setting to promote individual initiative and competition on a continuous basis.

11. Sombart, for instance, argued that the capitalist spirit was dominated by "acquisition, competition, and rationality" and emphasized its "rat race" aspect: man had been the measure of all things in the Middle Ages, but the modern capitalist seemed to be engaged in what might be termed "a rational pursuit of an irrational goal." See Werner Sombart, "Capitalism," in *The Encyclopedia of the Social Sciences*, vol. 3 (New York: Macmillan, 1930), reprinted in *Source Readings in Economic Thought*, ed. Philip C. Newman et al. (New York: W. W. Norton), pp. 492–99.

12. Weber emphasized that a sense of calling was a crucial element in the rise of the spirit of capitalism in the West. On this point, see his discussion of Martin Luther's concept of the calling; Weber (1976), pp. 79–92. Weber, however, did not adequately explain how the previously despised occupation of moneymaking had been able to attain the status of "a calling."

13. Thus spoke a distinguished New England priest in the 1850s. In addition, he praised the merchant as "a moral educator, a church of Christ gone into business—a saint in Trade." Re-cited from Louis M. Hacker, *The World of Andrew Carnegie: 1865–1901* (Philadelphia: J. B. Lippincott, 1968), p. 74.

a predominantly religious-motivational approach throughout his work, Weber thus found in the Protestant conception of calling and worldly asceticism the origin of the capitalist drive for accumulation.

As Weber's critics later made clear, however, institutional-structural conditions, such as the legal guarantee of individual autonomy and loosening of central control, were no less important than religious-motivational factors in the rise of capitalism. In the case of Calvin's Geneva, for instance, the first impact of Protestantism on capitalist development was largely negative; only after the downfall of "the totalistic-religious regime"—namely, the Calvinist theocracy—could capitalism prosper there.[14] No matter how deeply they were imbued with the Protestant ethic, capitalists first had to be freed from government control.

In this regard, it may be argued that the most important legacy left by Protestantism on the spirit of capitalism was its general individualistic orientation rather than any of its particular codes of conduct and discipline such as hard work and frugality. Indeed, the common practice of equating the Protestant ethic with the Protestant *work* ethic might be a serious mistake. The Protestant doctrine stipulates that one does not need the assistance or intervention of intermediary authorities to attain salvation. Moreover, Protestantism rejects the notion that one can be saved by good works or material contributions to religious institutions, the most notorious example of which might be the purchase of indulgences. Only through God's grace can one be saved.[15]

Of these two aspects of the Protestant doctrine, challenge to arbitrary authority implicit in the former seems to have had the greater impact on the development of capitalism. Indeed, the development of both Protestantism and capitalism was centered around the idea of individual autonomy, and the direction of causality seems to have run both ways. Precursors to the Reformation, such as the religious movement by Jan Hus in the fifteenth century, failed primarily because institutional and structural conditions were not in place. By Martin Luther's time, however, the Holy Roman Empire had been considerably weakened by its struggle with the papacy and the growth of virtually inde-

14. See S. N. Eisenstadt, "The Protestant Ethic Thesis in an Analytical and Comparative Framework," in S. N. Eisenstadt, ed., *The Protestant Ethic and Modernization* (New York: Basic Books, 1968), pp. 6–7.

15. Clearly, Weber placed a great emphasis on this latter aspect of the Protestant doctrine, focusing on the worldly resolution of the intense religious anxieties created by the unknowable design of God.

pendent princedoms from within and nation-states from without. Economically, the rise of commerce and development of urban centers had created a stronger middle class.[16]

It was only natural that the legitimation of wealth and challenge to authority implicit in the Protestant doctrine be welcomed by the newly emerging class of capitalists as they sought to break free from medieval restrictions, and it is this individualistic orientation and freedom from central control that defines the general contours of modern capitalism.[17] On the whole, the work ethic element of Protestantism has been less important for the development of capitalism than its individualistic orientation.

THE TAMING OF UNBRIDLED CAPITALISM

Although the individualistic orientation and work ethic of capitalism played a critical role in the abolition of arbitrary authority and the growth of the European economy, modern capitalism began to create problems of its own when it lost its moral anchor in the transcendental values of Protestantism. First, the individualistic orientation of capitalism could, and did, easily degenerate into preoccupation with individual self-interest and denial of all notions of "social responsibility." Reflecting on the development of capitalism in its relation to religion, Richard Tawney noted that this potential for perversion had already materialized:

> To insist that the individual is responsible, that no man can save his brother, that the essence of religion is the contact of the soul with its Maker, how true and indispensable! But how easy to slip from that truth into the suggestion that society is without responsibility, that no man can help his brother, that the social order and its consequences are not even the scaffolding by which men may climb to greater heights, but something external, alien and irrelevant.[18]

Second, the combination of hard work and frugality by the capitalist class led to the accumulation of riches, which only intensified the

16. On the background of the Reformation, see E. H. Harbison, *The Age of Reformation* (Ithaca, N.Y.: Cornell University Press, 1963).

17. To the new capitalist class, "a creed which transformed the acquisition of wealth from a drudgery or a temptation into a moral duty was the milk of lions." See Tawney, p. 253.

18. Ibid., p. 254.

fundamental contradiction between spiritual values and the spiritually corrupting influence of wealth. Some church leaders clearly recognized the self-defeating nature of hard work and frugality for spiritual purposes and acknowledged that a continual struggle with the spiritually corrupting influence of wealth was inevitable. For instance, John Wesley, leader of the Methodist movement, lamented:

> I fear, wherever riches have increased, the essence of religion has decreased in the same proportion. Therefore I do not see how it is possible, in the nature of things, for any revival of true religion to continue long. For religion must necessarily produce both industry and frugality, and these cannot but produce riches. But as riches increase, so will pride, anger, and love of the world in all its branches. So, although the form of religion remains, the spirit is swiftly vanishing away. Is there no way to prevent this—this continual decay of pure religion?[19]

In the end, Wesley exhorted all Christians to gain all they could, save all they could, and give all they could so that they could grow in grace. He thus found in philanthropy at least a partial solution to the problem of conflict between spiritual values and the spiritually corrupting influence of wealth.

With secular success beginning to be accepted as a sign of election by God, however, it was only a matter of time before the idea of "brotherly love" began to lose its importance.[20] It took only a small logical step to carry the Protestant conception of secular success to its limit and argue that the haves owed nothing whatsoever to the have-nots. In its most extreme form, unbridled capitalism denied the value of anything other than individual self-interest and the survival of the fittest—be it faith in God, obedience to authority, loyalty to the nation, or belief in social responsibility. An advocate of such a view, William Graham Sumner, declared: "In general . . . it may be said that those whom humanitarians and philanthropists call the weak are the ones through whom the productive and conservative forces of society are wasted. They constantly neutralize and destroy the finest efforts of the wise and industrious, and are a dead-weight on the society in all its struggles to better things."[21]

19. Re-cited from Weber (1976), p. 175.

20. For instance, the Right Reverend William Lawrence, Episcopal Bishop of Massachusetts, declared in 1901, "It is only to the man of morality that wealth comes." Re-cited from Hacker, p. 74.

21. Sumner was a proponent of Social Darwinism. See William Graham Sumner, *What Classes Owe to Each Other* (New York: Harper & Brothers, 1883), esp. pp. 13–24.

As Lester Frank Ward was to point out in an article titled "The Laissez Faire Doctrine Is Suicidal," however, Sumner's assumption that material success was a perfect measure of personal worth contained a fundamental error, for the rich could and often did use their political influence to limit competition and exploit the poor. Moreover, although Sumner assumed that "a society of free and independent men [would] co-operate without cringing or intrigue," it was not at all clear why the have-nots, who might have to suffer through a life of indignity and (relative) deprivation, would willingly cooperate with the haves, who kept the spoils of the pseudo-Darwinian competition to themselves. In order to preserve social order and guarantee the equality of opportunity for the next generation, capitalism had to be transformed so as to balance the objectives of efficiency and equity.

In fact, this was what the Progressives set out to do in the United States in the early part of the twentieth century. Imbued with a sense of personal responsibility for widespread corruption in society, the Progressives attempted to enact various reforms that would eliminate social evils ranging from monopolies to liquor traffic.[22] Pressed by the threat of labor union organization and condemned by middle-class reformers, thoughtful businessmen, in turn, began to address themselves to restructuring the existing capitalist order and checking the rise of socialism.[23] Replacing Social Darwinism with an ideal of a responsible social order, the business leaders recognized labor unions as legitimate institutions in America and supported moderate union leaders, most notably Samuel Gompers.[24] As a result of these concessions, everyone would share in the benefits of an ever expanding economy.

22. There are various interpretations of the Progressive movement. For a comprehensive review, see, e.g., Gerald N. Grob and George A. Billias, "The Progressive Movement: Liberal or Conservative? in *Interpretations of American History* (New York: Free Press, 1982), pp. 163–79. It seems reasonably clear that the Progressive movement was a broadly based movement, drawing support from middle-class and underprivileged reformers and sophisticated business leaders as well as from WASP types filled with a sense of "status anxiety."

23. See Gabriel Kolko, *The Triumph of Conservatism* (New York: Free Press, 1963), and James Weinstein, *The Corporate Ideal in the Liberal State* (Boston: Beacon Press, 1968). At the forefront of "corporate liberalism" in the United States was the National Civic Federation (NCF), which was founded in 1900 with a view to stabilizing the economic system in the interests of big business.

24. More radical labor leaders were actively persecuted. See Nick Salvatore, *Eugene V. Debs* (Urbana: University of Illinois Press, 1982). On the evolution of the legal status of labor unions in the American cultural context, see William E. Forbath, *Law*

Some of the sophisticated business leaders went even further and wholeheartedly embraced the notion that wealth was a *stewardship*. For example, Peter Cooper wrote: "I do not recognize myself as owner in fee of one dollar of the wealth which has come into my hands. I am simply responsible for the management of an estate which belongs to humanity."[25] Similarly, in his *Gospel of Wealth* (1889), Andrew Carnegie argued that it was the duty of a wealthy man to live unostentatiously, "to provide moderately for the legitimate wants of those dependent upon him, and, after doing so, to consider all surplus revenues which come to him simply as trust funds . . . to administer in the manner . . . best calculated to produce the most beneficial results for the community." In addition, Carnegie expressed misgivings about the institution of inheritance and felt that of all forms of taxation the estate tax was "the wisest."[26]

Reforms such as the institution of the estate tax and federal income tax, enactment of antitrust laws, and recognition of labor unions might not have seemed far-reaching enough to radical critics of modern capitalism, but these measures did manage to check the excesses of unbridled capitalism and respond to the threat posed by the twin challenges of socialism and Social Darwinism.[27] As Edouard Bernstein among others noted, capitalism was capable of transforming itself, and only those countries that managed to inject a new sense of social responsibility into the capitalist ethos were able to overcome social and economic crises.

---

and the Shaping of the American Labor Movement (Cambridge, Mass.: Harvard University Press, 1991), esp. pp. 10–36.

25. Re-cited from Hacker, p. 75. Peter Cooper created the Cooper Union, an evening technical school at the collegiate level, where instruction in engineering and architecture was free.

26. Re-cited from Joseph A. Pechman, *Federal Tax Policy*, 5th ed. (Washington, D.C.: Brookings Institution, 1987), p. 235. Carnegie wrote: "the parent who leaves his son enormous wealth generally deadens the talents and energies of the son, and tempts him to lead a less useful and less worthy life than he otherwise could."

27. The income tax law was designed to address the problem of income inequality. Historian John D. Buenker notes: "By 1912, when the average worker rarely sported an annual income of $1,000, the income of John D. Rockefeller soared to an unbelievable $50 million and that of his son William to a scarcely more modest $35 million. The first income tax law in 1913 exempted all incomes under $4,000 per year, an estimated 95 percent of the population." John D. Buenker, "The Progressive Era: A Search for a Synthesis," *Mid-America* 51 (1969): 175–93, reprinted in Grob and Billias (1982), p. 198.

THE CAPITALIST SPIRIT IN A NON-WESTERN CULTURE: THE CASE OF JAPAN

The historiography of modern Japan presents an interesting problem to those who want to trace the cultural roots of Japan's economic success: appraisals of Japanese culture have undergone a radical change with Japan's rise to economic prominence. Although many culturalist explanations have appeared since Japan achieved its economic success, no major social scientist seems to have predicted that Japan's traditional customs and institutions would have a positive effect in facilitating modernization. In fact, in the 1870s, even the Japanese leaders themselves thought that Japanese culture was a hindrance to modernization.[28]

With the benefit of hindsight, however, Japan does seem to have been more favorably disposed toward capitalism by the mid-nineteenth century than Korea and China. Various institutional and cultural factors seem to have accounted for this development. First, the Japanese feudal system, characterized by the lack of a strong central government with arbitrary powers, allowed some room for Japanese merchants to establish their autonomy and mobilize ideological resources in their support. Second, strongly influenced by both Buddhist and Confucian teachings, the Japanese had a particularly strong sense of professional commitment and dedication.

A Zen monk named Suzuki Shosan (1579–1655), called "the father of Japanese capitalism" by an influential writer, preached that *all* occupations were Buddhist practice—hence *equally honorable*. When a peasant complained that his farm work spared him no time to practice Buddhism and prepare for life after death, Shosan replied: "Torture yourself—plow, reap—work with all your heart. . . . When one is unoccupied, the thicket of desire grows, but when one toils, subjecting one's mind and body to pain, one's heart is at peace. In this way one is engaged in Buddhist practice all the time. Why should a peasant long for another road to Buddhahood?"[29] Just as Protestants used hard work,

28. In the face of threats posed by the Western powers, many Japanese leaders shared the following sentiment: "No matter how good the old morality was, we cannot follow any such moral law and preserve our national independence and achieve any progress. . . . We must forsake our past." Kenneth B. Pyle, *The New Generation in Meiji Japan: Problems of Cultural Identity, 1885–1895* (Stanford, Calif.: Stanford University Press, 1969), p. 17.

29. Re-cited from Yamamoto Shichihei, *The Spirit of Japanese Capitalism and Selected Essays*, trans. by Lynne E. Riggs and Takechi Manabu (New York: Madison Books, 1992), p. 80.

discipline, and thrift as practical means of reducing their anxieties about the state of grace, Shosan pointed to the spiritual value of professional commitment and emphasized that anyone could attain Buddhahood through work. Combined with the ascetic ethos of Buddhism, this strong sense of commitment created in Japan what may be called "Protestantism without God."[30]

Nevertheless, in spite of these elements of the Japanese equivalent to the Protestant ethic, it is important to remember that Japan was well behind the Western powers in capitalist development when Commodore Matthew Perry's black ships arrived on Japanese shores in 1853.[31] In fact, had it not been for the threat posed by the Western powers and the effective response generated by the Japanese ruling class, the development of Japanese capitalism might well have been further delayed. Unlike the ruling classes in Korea and China, most of whom sought to protect their vested interests from foreign as well as domestic threats, a core of the ruling class in Japan strongly felt that the modernization of the nation had to come before the protection of their private interests. They believed that a Japan internally torn apart would be an easy prey to the Western powers.

Under the slogan "Rich Nation, Strong Army," the Japanese elite abolished class distinctions and replaced the vertically divided feudal structure (*ie*) of Tokugawa Japan with a strong centralized state.[32] Here, *ie* (which literally means "house," as in "the House of Tokugawa") refers to the tightly knit group structure of Japanese organizations based on mutual obligations and devotion to a common goal. Forming a society of its own, each *ie*, or each autonomous group, demands personal loyalties from its members and guards their well-being in return. The principle of *vertical* reciprocity evident within each group, however, may not extend to the *horizontal* relationship between groups. In fact, unless there is a broad consensus at the national level, each autono-

30. For this and other interesting observations on the Meiji period (1868–1912) in Japan, see Ryotaro Shiba, *A Nation Called Meiji* (in Japanese; Tokyo: Nihon Hoso Shuppan Kyokai, 1989). See also Michio Morishima, *Why Has Japan Succeeded?: Western Technology and the Japanese Ethos* (Cambridge: Cambridge University Press, 1982).

31. On the state of capitalist development in Japan, see Thomas C. Smith, *Native Sources of Japanese Industrialization, 1750–1920* (Berkeley: University of California Press, 1988).

32. To understand how this slogan has driven Japanese policy for more than a century, see Richard J. Samuels, *"Rich Nation Strong Army": National Security and the Technological Transformation of Japan* (Ithaca, N.Y.: Cornell University Press, 1994).

mous group might well pursue mutually conflicting agenda. Military adventurism by the Japanese army in the 1930s, which completely ran against the principle of civilian control, may be understood in this broad cultural context.[33]

After Japan's defeat in World War II, a single-minded pursuit of economic success replaced the disunity of purpose that plagued the vertically divided society of prewar Japan. Nevertheless, the principle of subjugating the interests of individual members to those of their group remains a basic tenet of social organization in Japan. In contrast to the prominence of various autonomous groups in Japanese society, the state remains somewhat elusive, and the individual is all but invisible. In particular, the Japanese employment system in the postwar period has reinforced the *ie* principle by reducing interclass conflict and increasing interfirm competition, where each firm consists of workers with a lifetime membership.[34] The individualistic orientation of Western capitalism is, in effect, replaced by a strong group orientation in Japan.

In short, Japanese capitalism seems to contain two somewhat conflicting strands. Combined with a strong sense of professional commitment, group orientation, based on Japan's feudal past, is the dominant element, but the historical experience of state-led development under the slogan "Rich Nation, Strong Army" has also left its imprint. Japanese capitalism has, in effect, fused these two elements and created a plan-rational economic system, centered around those industries where incremental quality improvement is important.

It is this plan-rational, group-oriented system of capitalism that has been coming under severe criticism both in Japan and abroad since the

33. On *ie* as a defining feature of Japanese culture, see Murakami Yasusuke, "*Ie* as a Pattern of Civilization," *Journal of Japanese Studies* 10(1984): 281–363.

34. Those who regard the Japanese system of employment as a natural product of group-oriented Japanese culture may be surprised to find that the Japanese system based on lifetime employment, seniority wages, and enterprise unions became firmly established only after World War II. In fact, numerous Japanese businessmen in the 1920s, led by their German and American counterparts, joined a so-called rationalization movement, which dictated "policies that increased the insecurity of the worker's place in the company, in the belief that insecurity, not paternal care, would promote labor efficiency." Andrew Gordon, *The Evolution of Labor Relations in Japan: Heavy Industry, 1853–1955* (Cambridge, Mass.: Harvard East Asian Monographs, 1988), p. 428. Managers and workers typically appealed to a similar set of cultural values to pursue diametrically opposite ends. World War II mobilization and gains made by labor unions after the war proved decisive in shaping the Japanese system of employment.

serious economic downturn of the early 1990s. Although it will be easy enough to pronounce that Japanese capitalism will have to take on "a more individualistic and freer style," it remains to be seen whether "allocation problems that had once been resolved at the corporate level" can be effectively taken up by the state.[35] Although the postwar democratic reform has effectively dealt with the excesses of unbridled capitalism in Japan, the strongly group-oriented version of capitalism has produced its own set of challenges.

The Evolution of the Capitalist Spirit in Korea

Although the economic development of Korea is often compared to that of Japan, the development of capitalism in Korea took a rather different course. On an institutional-structural level, the most crucial difference is the absence of decentralized power centers and the lack of European- or Japanese-style feudal experience. A vertical division of the society never really took place in Korea. Instead, a pyramid-like structure, with the central government at the apex, has characterized the social organization of Korea for more than a thousand years. The central government in Korea allowed little room for merchants to pursue moneymaking ventures on their own. Thus, in the Korean context, both economic stagnation *and* economic development had to be state-led.

On a cultural-motivational level, the most crucial element of Korean capitalism is the centuries-long dominance of Confucianism and the upsurge of egalitarianism following the collapse of the Confucian order in this century. The authoritarian legacy of Confucianism and the populist appeal of egalitarianism have given Korean capitalism its unique flavor.

TRADITIONAL CULTURAL VALUES AND SOCIAL ORGANIZATION OF KOREA

The traditional value system of Korea was based on life-affirming humanism. According to the foundation myth of Korea, Hwan Ung, Son of Heaven, envied the human world and descended upon Mount Taebaek to establish a holy city. A bear and a tiger, symbolizing the Earth, pleaded with Hwan Ung to make them human, but only the

35. See Yasuo Takeuchi, "The Ethics of Japanese-Style Capitalism," *Japanese Economic Studies* 22(1994): 73.

bear who persevered through a weeks-long test of darkness and hunger was born again as a human being, a woman. Hwan Ung took this woman to be his wife, and she gave birth to Tan Kun, the legendary founder of Korea. Thus, the Heaven and the Earth were symbolically united in the human figure of Tan Kun.

A confident affirmation of the human world is unmistakable in this myth. Unlike Jesus, Son of God who came to this world to save humanity, the Son of Heaven in Korea's foundation myth came simply to join humanity. He spoke of neither original sin nor eternal salvation. Under the principle of *Hongik Ingan* ("widely benefit humanity"), Korea's legendary founder sought to reach all people and improve their lot in this world. In this secular cultural context, the Protestant notion of using anxiety about the state of one's grace as a motivational tool would have seemed rather foreign indeed.[36]

Instead, what motivated the Korean people from ancient times was a strong sense of patriotism and commitment to the principle of justice rather than expediency. As a motivating force, material gain and profit had a relatively limited appeal; a grandiose "just cause" proved to be much more effective. Whenever Korea was in danger of being overrun by a foreign power, common people volunteered to organize "Righteous Armies" and fought an uphill battle against foreign invaders in defense of their country, well after the regular armies had been defeated. Even Buddhism, which is typically noted for its otherworldly orientation, was transformed into a secular, patriotic religion in Korea. For example, the Five Commandments for the Secular World, issued by a Buddhist monk, emphasized loyalty to the king, filial devotion to parents, trust between friends, courage in battle, and discretion in killing.

It is in this traditional cultural context that Confucianism found its way to Korea. Confucianism, with its emphasis on secular humanism and moral righteousness, was readily incorporated into the Korean culture, and it replaced Patriotic Buddhism as the state ideology during the Yi dynasty (1392–1910). Because Confucianism had such a dominant influence on the lives of the Korean people for centuries before

36. As a matter of fact, separation of the sacred realm from the secular world seems to be a rather foreign concept to the Korean mind. Praying to God, Buddha, or other divine figures for security and comfort in the secular world is the dominant form of religious worship in Korea.

the modernization of Korea, the spirit of Korean capitalism cannot be discussed in sufficient depth without a prior understanding of the economic aspects of Confucianism. Although it has become fashionable to speak of "Confucian capitalism" following the recent economic success of Asian countries, Confucianism is not inherently conducive to economic development, and it indeed contains many elements that are hostile to capitalism.[37] To understand the evolution of the capitalist spirit in Korea, it is necessary to analyze the Confucian value system in some detail.

The ideal society of Confucius is based on moral government and harmonious yet rigidly defined human relations. The essential good in this society is emotional bonds that enable people to locate their proper place in their community. According to Confucius, the sense of proper place in relation to other people leads to social harmony; in relation to Heaven, it imparts a sense of purpose to life. The individual, in effect, is not allowed to become marginalized or atomized in a Confucian society.

Giving priority to the moral and emotional needs of the individual throughout his teachings, Confucius believed that anyone could, and should, cultivate virtue and strive to become as benevolent as possible.[38] Confucius also felt that cultivation of moral character should start at home. Being good as a son and obedient as a young man laid the foundation of a man's moral character, and the genuine feeling of love between family members—not contractual obligation between individuals—was to form the basis of all social bonds. Confucius

37. The experience of these Asian tigers again suggests that religious-motivational factors alone cannot account for economic development. Peasants in these developing countries typically endured backbreaking labor; they were at least as hard working and frugal as workers in advanced industrial countries. If these societies escape from poverty and exhibit impressive economic growth, is this economic transformation due to a belated discovery and application of the Protestant ethic or its equivalent, such as "Confucian values"?

38. At the same time, Confucius promised neither material benefit nor eternal salvation for moral striving. To Confucius, pursuing the Way (*Tao*) was a moral imperative, whereas fame and fortune were a matter of fate. As for afterlife, he had little to say. He did not even offer a sense of ultimate triumph to those who pursued what is right. Confucians were later to criticize the Christian religion because they felt that it seemed to offer salvation, a reward, for one's faith. Under the Confucian ethic of virtues, one does something because it is right, not because it offers a material or spiritual reward.

thought that it was natural to love one's own family members more than others,[39] and he believed that benevolence should be the guiding principle in any social interaction: adhering to rigid moral standards (*chung*), yet sympathizing with the situation of others (*shu*), one must not impose on others what one oneself does not desire.[40] According to Confucius, these rigid moral standards were to be discovered in the ancient rites, a body of strict rules governing action in every aspect of life.[41] Guided by moral government and regulated by the rites, people would find their proper place in an ideal society where virtue and benevolence, rather than force and power, define human relations.

As anti-Confucians were quick to point out, however, the emphasis on emotional bonds and ancient rites in the Confucian scheme could easily degenerate into a kind of smug elitism that neglects the material basis of emotional bonds and confuses formality with propriety. Confucius himself was not free from such pitfalls, and, in fact, the founder of Confucianism at times exhibited an unmistakably elitist attitude toward all nonruling classes.[42] He once said: "The gentleman devotes his mind to attaining the Way and not to securing food. Go and till the land and you will end up by being hungry . . . study, and you will end up with the salary of an official. . . . The gentleman worries about the Way, not poverty."[43] In a polemical writing entitled "Against Confucians," Mo Tzu, for one, pointed out: "[Confucians] propound fatalism and ignore poverty, and behave with the greatest arrogance. . . . They are greedy for food and drink and too lazy to work, but though they

39. Though it seems to be grounded in common sense, this Confucian doctrine of "graded benevolence" creates a tension between loyalty to the family and obligation to the community, and could lead to partiality, nepotism, and conflict of interests.

40. See Confucius (5th c. B.C.), *The Analects*, trans. with an introduction by D. C. Lau (London: Penguin Classics, 1979), Book XII: 2, p. 112.

41. Confucius believed that the foundation of benevolence lay in "the observance of the rites through overcoming the self." Ibid., Book XII: 1, p. 112.

42. For instance, when a man named Fan Hsu asked about growing crops, Confucius commented: "How petty Fan Hsu is! When those above love the rites, none of the common people will dare be irreverent. . . . What need is there to talk about growing crops?" It is not clear how an orthodox version of "Confucian capitalism" could accommodate this kind of remark. Ibid., Book XIII: 4, p. 119.

43. Ibid., Book XV: 32, p. 136. Under the division of labor and the hierarchy of social relations envisioned by Confucius, it was quite possible that a scholar-official, while living off the common people, would do nothing productive for the society other than prescribing what *he* believed was the Way.

find themselves threatened by hunger and cold, they refuse to change their ways."[44]

On balance, it seems fair to say that Confucianism has a greater potential of becoming a hindrance to economic development than a conducive force. First, authoritarian and elitist in mentality, Confucianism is preoccupied with the idea of *control*, not just self-control and discipline; whereas, capitalism requires autonomy, diversity, and experiment.[45] Second, Confucianism gives priority to emotional goods over material goods, and generally looks down on moneymaking activities. Unless the focus of the Confucian emphasis on moral-intellectual development is shifted from classical philosophical texts to more practical subjects, Confucianism is not likely to contribute to economically useful human capital development. Third, Confucianism prescribes different obligations depending on the degree of closeness of personal relations, and this doctrine of "graded benevolence" can lead to a confusion of private and public spheres.[46]

Imported into Korea in 372, Confucianism was not a major force in Korean society for a long time, but when it became the state ideology upon the foundation of the Yi dynasty (Chosun) in 1392, it was to dominate the lives of the Korean people for the next five centuries.[47] Although Confucianism was conducive to maintaining social order and insuring the survival of the Yi dynasty, it was to have a stifling effect on capitalist development. In accordance with the Confucian social scheme, the social hierarchy of the Yi dynasty, from top to bottom,

44. Mo Tzu (5th c. B.C.), *Mo Tzu: Basic Writings*, trans. by Burton Watson (New York: Columbia University Press, 1963), p. 127.

45. These three guiding principles, when guaranteed by secure legal institutions, foster competition and innovation and give market economy its characteristic dynamism. See Nathan Rosenberg and L. E. Birdzell, Jr., *How the West Grew Rich: The Economic Transformation of the Industrial World* (New York: Basic Books, 1986).

46. Certainly, Confucianism, with its emphasis on learning and self-control, can contribute to human capital development. Moreover, as the experience of the Asian tigers has demonstrated to a certain extent, Confucianism can provide support for economic development under an authoritarian regime if the rulers are economically minded enough to appreciate the material basis of emotional goods and mobilize resources for the production of wealth. Such rulers, however, can hardly be called Confucian in the orthodox sense.

47. The type of Confucianism that became predominant in Chosun was an abstract variety developed by Chu Hsi (1130–1200), a type that was to generate much philosophical speculation detached from material reality.

consisted of neo-Confucian literati, peasants, craftsmen, and merchants. The sole legitimate route to the top of the social hierarchy was to pass state examinations and join the ranks of scholar-officials. Under the growing influence of Confucianism, craftsmen dropped in social status, and as a result, few, if any, peasants wanted to become craftsmen of their own will.[48] Merchants were even more despised than craftsmen for being engaged in "nonproductive, parasitic activities." Except for a limited amount of trade carried out by a small group of licensed merchants with exclusive privileges, commercial activities were discouraged.

INDIGENOUS SOURCES OF CAPITALISM IN KOREA AND THEIR LIMITATIONS

Even under the stifling Confucian rule of the Yi dynasty, however, some changes conducive to economic development began to make their appearance in Korea by the mid-sixteenth century. Combined with a dramatic increase in agricultural productivity in the fifteenth century, a significant expansion of arable land due to reclamation efforts had raised income and encouraged domestic and foreign trade in luxury goods and gold- and silver-mining activities. Seeking better opportunities in cities, a number of peasants began to leave rural areas and engage in commercial and manufacturing activities.[49] In addition to these economic changes, two great wars within a span of a half-century further destabilized the existing social system. A seven-year war with Japan at the end of the sixteenth century not only devastated the Korean economy but also raised doubts about the effectiveness of the existing system. An invasion by the Ching army of China in 1636 resulted in national humiliation and confirmed that the system was due for an overhaul.

Influenced by these changes in society, a group of reform-minded scholars began to promote *Shilhak*, or pragmatic studies, in the mid-seventeenth century and urge others to pay a closer attention to the subject of material production and economic incentive. Yu Hyung Won (1622–1673), for instance, advocated a mass distribution of land, and Park Ji Won (1737–1805) urged the government to build up national

48. The social position of craftsmen had not always been so low in Korea. Throughout the Three Kingdoms period, which lasted until 668, many craftsmen seem to have come from the ruling class and vice versa. At least one king during this period is recorded to have been a former blacksmith.

49. See Tae-jin Lee, *A Study of Korean Social History: Development of Agricultural Technology and Social Change* (in Korean, Seoul: Chisik Sanupsa, 1986).

power by importing advanced technologies and promoting industry and trade. These pragmatic scholars condemned Confucian elitism and called for a new economic ethos. Chung Yak Yong (1762–1836), the most prominent of the *Shilhak* scholars, once wrote:

> What in the world are the Confucian literati? Why do they swallow up other people's land and live on other people's effort without moving their own hands and legs? Agricultural production is not increasing because the Confucian literati are not working. Once they realize that they can't eat if they don't work, they will become farmers. When they become farmers, agricultural production will increase . . . and there will be no popular uprisings.

Chung Yak Yong clearly understood that effective social reform could not be carried out without a sound economic ethos, and, in fact, this kind of economic ethos, potentially a functional equivalent to the Protestant ethic, was present in pockets of Korean society. Merchants from the Kaesung area, for instance, were known for their hard work, savings, thrift, and mutual aid.[50] Kaesung merchants also used an advanced bookkeeping system and often pooled their financial resources to open a new shop in an unfamiliar territory. While a majority of merchants in other areas relied on political connections to earn monopoly rights, Kaesung merchants actively sought new market opportunities in domestic and foreign trade. Instead of seeking protection from imports or electing to serve as a local outlet for foreign firms, Kaesung merchants were not afraid to compete against foreign capital.[51]

Unlike in the West, however, the merchant class in Korea was unable to break free from traditional rules and regulations and spread a new economic ethos throughout society. Although there were some major capitalistic developments by the end of the eighteenth century,[52]

50. Located sixty kilometers north of Seoul, Kaesung was the capital of Koryo (918–1392). A large number of Kaesung citizens refused to cooperate with the new dynasty of Chosun and chose to use their talent in trade instead.

51. See Man-kil Kang, "The Development of Commercial Capital in the Late Yi Dynasty" (in Korean; Ph.D. diss. Korea University, Seoul, 1974).

52. In 1791, for instance, King Chungjo, a reform-minded monarch who ruled from 1776 to 1800, adopted a measure known as the Liberalization of Commerce Act (*Shinhae Tonggong*), and abolished special privileges granted to licensed merchants with the exception of the owners of the original Six Licensed Stores in Seoul. As a result, private merchants, not sanctioned by the government, could compete on equal terms with licensed merchants.

the reform program of the *Shilhak* scholars was abandoned upon the death of King Chungjo in 1800, and was followed by a corrupt rule of regents over the next sixty years. In the end, full-fledged capitalistic development did not take root in Korea until the Yi dynasty was on the verge of collapse.

THE COLLAPSE OF THE CONFUCIAN ORDER AND THE SPREAD OF EGALITARIANISM

The subsequent occupation by the Japanese and mobilization of Korea's resources for colonial purposes ushered in a new stage in the development of capitalism in Korea.[53] Under the Japanese colonial occupation, the use of factory labor became commonplace and the capitalist mode of production greatly expanded. Unlike in the West, however, the new Korean capitalist class failed to secure legitimacy and win social respectability. Although there were several notable exceptions,[54] successful enterprises during the colonial period were often run by businessmen who actively collaborated with the Japanese.[55] The collaboration of the comprador capital with the Japanese colonial government tarnished the image of capitalists in Korean society. Needless to say, their material wealth and secular success could not be regarded as a sign of election by God or outstanding personal merit. In its ethical dimension at least, Korean capitalism was tainted from the start.

Unlike in most other developing countries with colonial experience, however, the comprador capital in Korea failed to dominate the economy after independence. The predominantly Japanese ownership of capital in the colonial period could partly explain this peculiar development, but the post-1945 land reform and the Korean War (1950–1953) should be accorded greater weight.

After the liberation and division of Korea, the de facto government in the North confiscated large landholdings without giving compensation to landowners and distributed land free of charge to peasants according to "the land to the tiller" principle. In addition, the communist

53. See Sang-chul Suh, *Growth and Structural Changes in the Korean Economy, 1910–1940* (Cambridge, Mass.: Harvard University Press, 1978).

54. Dr. Il-han Yu, the founder of Yuhan Co., was one of the several prominent businessmen whose patriotism was beyond doubt.

55. For example, Heung-sik Park, the owner of the Hwashin Department Store, actively supported the Japanese colonial government and contributed to Japan's war efforts during World War II. After Korea's liberation in 1945, Park became the first to be arrested by the Special Commission on Anti-National Activities.

government nationalized large industrial enterprises, which had been built primarily in the northern half of the country during the Japanese occupation. In the South, the government adhered to capitalist principles and allowed private enterprise. When it did carry out its own land reform in 1949, it was careful to compensate landowners for their land. The subsequent inflation and war, however, greatly reduced the real value of this compensation, and, as a result, most landowners failed to transform themselves into industrial capitalists.[56]

If the post-1945 land reform had a serious impact on the fortune of agricultural capitalists, the Korean War played a similar role for industrial capitalists. As a result of the three-year conflict, approximately 43 percent of manufacturing facilities, 41 percent of electrical generating capacity, and 50 percent of the coal mines in the South were destroyed or damaged.[57] After the war, old entrepreneurs basically had to compete on equal terms with new entrants into the market. Few of Korea's largest enterprises today had a significant presence in the market prior to the Korean War.

The leveling effect of the land reform and the Korean War also had a significant impact on Korean society in general. Although the Japanese colonial occupation had led to the collapse of the traditional social hierarchy in Korea, the corresponding change in the pattern of wealth distribution had been relatively insignificant. Even after the collapse of the Yi dynasty, the landowning class, traditionally associated with the neo-Confucian literati, still held on to their land. The only notable change in the pattern of wealth distribution was caused by the emergence of the new capitalist class, whose conduct often ran counter to the nationalistic sentiment of the Korean people. The two post-1945 events had the effect of wiping out the existing pattern of wealth distribution. Practically everyone was placed at ground zero. The Korean people were now liberated from the traditional pattern of wealth distribution as well as from the Confucian system of social hierarchy, and anyone could now, in principle, entertain the hope of climbing up the social ladder through hard work and individual initiative. Combined with an awareness of potential for social mobility, this strong sense of

56. Je-uk Kong, *A Study of the Korean Capitalists of the 1950s* (in Korean; Seoul: Paeksan Sodang, 1993), pp. 187–90.

57. Ki-baik Lee, *A New History of Korea*, trans. by Edward W. Wagner and Edward J. Shultz (Cambridge, Mass.: Harvard University Press, 1984), pp. 380–81.

equality was to have a profound effect on the development of capitalism in Korea.[58]

THE SHAPING OF THE KOREAN MODEL OF CAPITALISM

The new ethic of hard work and individual initiative, however, did not materialize in the 1950s. Instead of providing an appropriate institutional setting to support the new ethic, the Syngman Rhee government encouraged rent-seeking activities by limiting competition and distributing special favors. The government gave special treatment to a few favored industrialists in the distribution of imported raw materials and bank loans as well as the allocation of U.S. dollars at favorable exchange rates.[59]

The April 1960 Revolution eventually brought an end to the corrupt regime of Syngman Rhee, but the new democratic government lacked the political leadership and cohesion to implement a comprehensive program of economic development. In the end, it took the May 1961 coup d'état by General Park Chung Hee for Korea to move on to the next stage of capitalist development. General Park was determined to channel national energy into economic development; other policy issues, such as national unification and democratization, were placed on the back burner.[60] Making a break from the import substitution policy of the Syngman Rhee regime, he adopted an outward-oriented export promotion policy centered around light manufacturing industries.[61] He also encouraged agricultural production and sought to reduce the income gap between urban and rural residents. In addition, he redirected the traditional Confucian zeal for education to more productive and practical subjects.

The development dictatorship model adopted by President Park

58. If this sense of equality is too strong and becomes identified with the equality of outcome rather than opportunity, it will generate a great amount of jealousy and have a negative effect on capitalist development. On the whole, however, a strong sense of equality, combined with an acute awareness of potential for social mobility, should encourage hard work and individual initiative.

59. Kong, pp. 201–18.

60. See Park Chung Hee, *Country, Revolution, and I* (in Korean; Seoul: Hyangmunsa, 1963).

61. After much deliberation and discussion, this decisive policy shift took place around 1964. For a thorough overview of Korea's development model, see Chung-yum Kim, *Policymaking on the Front Lines: Memoirs of a Korean Practitioner, 1945–79* (Washington, D.C.: Economic Development Institute of the World Bank, 1994). Mr. Kim was one of the main architects of the Korean model.

Chung Hee heavily relied on state intervention, but it was very different from the command economy in socialist countries. Although the Korean government pre-announced macroeconomic targets and relied on indicative planning, it never assigned production quotas at the firm level. Prices, on the whole, reflected supply and demand conditions and served as useful signals for firms. Most importantly, although it often promoted specific policy objectives, the Korean government respected the individual initiative of industrialists. The developmental state under the leadership of Park Chung Hee thus provided institutional-structural conditions conducive to the flowering of the ethic of hard work and individual initiative.

In addition to building up the economic institutions of capitalism, the government took direct measures to promote the spirit of capitalism. It recognized that the Korean people, already driven by a strong sense of equality and awareness of potential for social mobility, were ready to put their best efforts into the new economic environment; they only needed confidence and some encouragement from the government. Although government officials themselves initially had doubts as to whether Korea really had anything to sell on the international market, they adopted a strategy of growth through export expansion and effectively exploited Korea's comparative advantage. A series of early successes boosted the confidence of government and business leaders and helped to give rise to Korea's famous "Can do!" spirit. As a leading industrialist later reflected, "A pioneering spirit and unshakable faith—that was the key to the miracle."[62]

Now convinced that a life of poverty need not be their fate, people began to work harder to improve their living standards. The best-known example of such a change in attitude was the *Saemaul* ("New Community") Movement, a rural development program that emphasized the values of self-help, cooperation, and hard work. The program had a rather interesting course of development: In 1970, bags of cement were distributed free of charge to each of 34,665 rural villages on the condition that they be used for communal projects. According to a thorough government evaluation in 1971, about 45 percent of the rural villages had done something worthwhile with the government support, often contributing their own money as well as labor. In 1972, President Park decided to provide more construction materials to only these "self-

62. Ju-young Chung, *There May Be Ordeals, But There Are No Failures* (in Korean; Seoul, 1991), foreword.

help" villages. From the outset, President Park thus made it clear that the government was willing to help only those who helped themselves. Those villages that had squandered the initial government support became aware of their mistake as they increasingly, and noticeably, fell behind their neighboring "self-help" villages. Belatedly, many of these villages made their own efforts to participate in the *Saemaul* Movement, seeking a second chance.[63] Finally liberated from the curse of fatalism and self-resignation, farmers now believed that their hard work would be meaningfully rewarded. "Let us live well, let us live well for a change," a line from the *Saemaul* anthem, became a rallying cry. For the first time in Korean history, people now seriously entertained the hope that their lives could be thoroughly transformed within a few years.

In promoting the spirit of capitalism, the government also tried its best to establish a link between economic activities and honor. President Park helped Korean entrepreneurs to take pride in their work by providing moral as well as material support. Awarding the Order of Industrial Service Merit to outstanding entrepreneurs on National Export Day might be the most symbolic of his efforts to make business a respectable occupation in Korea.[64] Much like Protestant capitalists who viewed their endeavors as service to God, Korean capitalists could now justify their activities in terms of accepted cultural norms, presenting themselves as patriotic entrepreneurs in service of the nation. For instance, Ju-young Chung, chairman of Hyundai Group, declared in his memoirs: "Since its establishment, Hyundai has been growing together with our country. I take pride in the fact that our country truly appreciates a company like Hyundai Construction, which I think has been supplying an unbounded amount of energy and potential into our national economy and industries."[65]

Workers, for their part, were motivated by the traditional value of devotion to the family as well as loyalty to the nation. During the hey-

63. See Kim, pp. 91–92. Each village was free to choose from a variety of improvement projects such as expanding the road leading to the village, building a small bridge, reinforcing a river bank, etc.

64. Similarly, President Park honored outstanding *Saemaul* leaders by awarding the Order of *Saemaul* Service Merit each year. He thus diversified channels of attaining honor in Korean society. Becoming a scholar-official was no longer the only route to social respectability.

65. Chung, p. 134. *Sanup Boguk* (serving the nation through industry) became a slogan among Korean entrepreneurs.

day of Korea's economic development, it was not uncommon to hear about young female textile workers putting in extra hours to provide for their families while spending a minimum amount of money on themselves. Traditional values above and beyond the pursuit of individual self-interest thus played a critical role in the rise of the Korean spirit of capitalism, which was in many ways as effective as the Protestant ethic in promoting capitalist development.

The authoritarian nature of Korea's development model has, however, created serious side-effects that threaten to limit future growth. First, active government intervention in the economy has produced a complex web of regulations and has created a huge potential for corruption. Second, although the development dictatorship of the military regimes from the 1960s to the mid-1980s provided the capitalists with an opportunity to present themselves as patriotic entrepreneurs, the involvement of the Korean capitalists in political scandals and speculative investment and their support of oppressive labor policies have limited the effectiveness of their legitimacy-building efforts. In particular, the souring of labor-management relations under the previous military regimes remains a serious problem. These legacies of the development dictatorship by previous military regimes present additional challenges as Korea now faces the general problem of defining social responsibility in maturing capitalist societies.

A New Capitalist Spirit for Korea

Most economic experts now agree that the Korean economy must undergo a thorough reform if it is to make a qualitative leap to the next stage of development. They feel that the Korean economy not only has serious structural problems but also suffers from a much deeper crisis of spirit. In their view, in spite of all its apparent success, the Korean economy is a totally corrupt system in which no economic agent seems to care much for ethical principles: bending every rule in the book, entrepreneurs pursue profit with no sense of higher duty or public purpose in mind. Government officials all too readily take bribes and compromise public health and safety. The rich derive a great amount of unearned income from speculative investment in real estate and flaunt their wealth through conspicuous consumption. Employers complain of high wages and low work discipline but make little effort of their own to improve the R&D capacity and productive efficiency of their firms. Workers, for their part, complain of not getting their fair share, but they too do not show the kind of commitment and dedication that could help raise productivity. In the eyes of the concerned economic commentators, the real miracle of the Korean economy is that it has been able to grow for so long in spite of the moral bankruptcy of the system.

Before despairing over the future of the Korean economy, however, it would be worthwhile to put the present crisis in perspective. Consider the following quotation:

> Capitalists, workingmen, politicians, citizens—all breaking the law, or letting it be broken. Who is left to uphold it? The lawyers? Some of the best lawyers in this country are hired, not to get into court to defend cases, but to advise corporations and business firms how they can get around the law without too great a risk of punishment. The judges?. . . . The colleges?. . . . There is no one left; none but all of us.[66]

Where is this quotation from? A Korean newspaper in the 1990s? A polemical writing by a Korean economist? No. It is actually taken from a popular U.S. magazine at the beginning of the Progressive Era. This comment made by S. S. McClure in 1903 seems to be just as applicable to Korea today as it was to the United States then. Perhaps, a crisis of capitalist spirit is not unique to present-day Korea.

By now, a general pattern in the development of the capitalist ethos should be clear: While a sense of calling and worldly asceticism might be essential elements of the capitalist spirit in the early stages of capitalist development, a relentless pursuit of self-interest in the Darwinian struggle for survival soon becomes the dominant value, and this potentially destructive ethos has to be moderated by a newly defined sense of social responsibility.

In addition to this general problem, a new capitalist ethos for the Korean economy should address the following issues: (1) lack of legitimacy for the Korean capitalist class, (2) unnecessarily large government presence in the economy, and (3) adversarial relationship between labor and management. Korea's present task is to formulate a new social contract and carry out institutional reforms based on this new understanding of social responsibility.

66. "S. S. McClure Discovers a Trend of the Times," in Richard Hofstadter, *Great Issues in American History: A Documentary Record* (New York: Vintage Books, 1958).

AN ECONOMIC ANALYSIS OF THE KOREAN MIND

Before proceeding to search for a new capitalist ethos for the Korean economy, it may be worthwhile to examine in some detail the economic attitude of the Korean people. How favorably disposed is Korean culture to capitalist development?

In its social dimension, "culture" may be viewed as a system of values that define the role of the individual in a society and provide the context within which the "worth" of an individual is evaluated. As a comprehensive system of values, culture certainly plays a critical role in determining the course of economic development; however, in using culture as an explanatory variable, it is important to keep in mind that culture contains many contradictory and malleable elements. In the end, it is up to the people to decide *which* aspect of culture should receive priority in order to achieve a particular objective. Culture may restrict the range of effective future alternatives for a particular people, but it does not determine the future path of a society, and it is itself influenced by institutional-structural changes. In discussing the future evolution of the capitalist spirit in Korea, this interaction between cultural-motivational factors and institutional-structural conditions should be accorded careful consideration.

As has been suggested in the historical survey of Korean capitalism in the previous section, the most economically significant feature of the Korean culture is the tension between the old Confucian legacy and the new egalitarian mentality. The centuries-long dominance of Confucianism encouraged authoritarian and antimaterialistic tendencies, and combined with the traditional clan mentality of Korean culture, the Confucian doctrine of graded benevolence also contributed to the tendency to emphasize hometown and school ties and to confuse public and private matters. Although Confucian values such as self-control, loyalty, commitment, and education could potentially be molded into something conducive to economic development, these values remained tied to an existing order that was generally hostile to capitalism.

The Japanese colonial occupation and the Korean War shattered the Confucian social hierarchy, discredited the traditional elite, and led to an upsurge of egalitarianism. The Western values of individualism, rationalism, and materialism partly filled the void created by the collapse of the Confucian order, but these values were imported into Korea without a deeper understanding of their ethical foundations. As a result, a coherent set of moral values for economic and social development has yet to take root, and a search for a new capitalist spirit continues in Korea.

Attitude toward the acquisition and disposal of wealth. Society's attitude toward material accumulation is the most critical element of culture for capitalist development. The experience of precapitalist societies clearly demonstrates that capitalism cannot flourish in a society where the worth of an individual is measured in strictly nonmaterial terms, where the acquisition of wealth itself is condemned.

Influenced by the Confucian thought and examples of pariah-capitalism throughout the development era, Koreans harbor an ambivalent attitude toward material accumulation. Certainly, Confucianism does not necessarily condemn legitimately acquired wealth. In fact, the Confucian literati themselves felt that their work as scholar-officials entitled them to wealth and social respectability, and though they criticized the pursuit of profit per se, they did not shun material comfort. Yet, material success in and of itself was not honorable. To become a scholar-official was glorious; to become rich was *not*. The idea that an individual could make a positive social contribution by accumulating and utilizing material capital never took hold in traditional Korean society. In this regard, it is interesting to note that traditionally the Korean people have spoken highly of "honest poverty" or "honorable poverty" (*chungbin*). The corresponding word for "honorable wealth," however, does not exist in Korean vocabulary.

This reluctant acceptance of wealth forms the basis of Koreans' basic attitude toward material accumulation. In Korean society, even legitimately acquired wealth does not seem to bring a sufficient degree of honor to the acquirer; it has to be combined with the traditionally accepted measure of social respectability which had been reserved for scholar-officials. This weak link between wealth and honor may in part explain Korean business leaders' preoccupation with collecting honorary degrees from prestigious universities and running for political office.

The questionable channels through which a new class of capitalists acquired and disposed of wealth further damaged the traditionally weak connection between wealth and honor in Korean society. The Korean capitalists might have acquired only a fraction of their wealth through political connections and land speculation, but their involvement in these scandalous cases called into question the legitimacy of wealth in general. The way they tended to dispose of their wealth raised even more concern. Since the beginning of the capitalist era in Korea, only a handful of business leaders have expressed and put into practice the idea that wealth carries its share of social obligations.[67] Instead, the primary concern of Korean business leaders seems to be the establishment of a family dynasty that will prosper on the strength of a business enterprise whose fortunes affect an increasing number of people. Family interests come before those of stakeholders or shareholders, and when a chairman retires, the ownership and management rights of the firm are typically transferred to one of his sons in spite of his lack of business experience and, quite possibly, competence. The wholesale inheritance of wealth, so deplored by Andrew Carnegie, is a sacred institution among Korean capitalists. Compared with this feudalistic inheritance practice, conspicuous consumption by the rich is a minor problem.

Unless wealth acquisition and disposal channels become more transparent and legitimate, Koreans' fundamentally ambivalent attitude toward material accumulation will become increasingly negative. The government will first have to eliminate illegitimate sources of material accumulation if Koreans are to view wealth as a well-deserved reward for hard work, good judgment, and courageous risk-taking in a market economy. The wealthy, for their part, should be mindful of their negative image in Korean society and use at least a fraction of their fortunes for social purposes if only to support the socioeconomic system that has helped to make their success possible. If the transparency of the process of acquiring wealth is established and the use of wealth for social purposes becomes a common practice, the general attitude toward material accumulation will turn positive without the rich having to demand that their legitimate efforts be acknowledged. Until then, no collection of honorary degrees will bring true social respectability to the wealthy in Korean society.

Attitude toward competition. Fair competition and acceptance of its result form one of the most important operational principles of market

67. Dr. Il-han Yu's family was one of these exceptional cases. Dr. Yu believed that the wealthy should live frugally and return their remaining wealth to society. In his will, Dr. Yu left his estate to the Yuhan Foundation, a nonprofit charity organization that he had established in 1970, the year before he died. His daughter followed his example in 1991, and when his sister donated her estate in 1995, the founding family's share in Yuhan Corporation was reduced to zero. See "Estate of 1 Billion Won Returned to Society," *Dong-A Ilbo*, May 18, 1995.

economy. Korea's precapitalist heritage and egalitarian mentality, however, have proved to be an obstacle for the establishment of this principle. Deeply influenced by the control ideology of Confucianism, the Yi dynasty regulated economic activities through the use of exclusive government licenses and monopoly grants. A tacit agreement to divide the market under government sanction rather than free competition was the norm for centuries. Although Korean capitalists began to be exposed to domestic and international competition once Korea's modernization drive got under way, the precapitalist tradition of limiting competition in the domestic market has not disappeared, and the selection process for "winners" in government-sponsored projects has not always been transparent. The lack of fair competition and consequent reluctance on the part of "losers" to accept defeat thus remain a serious problem. In fact, producing clear winners and losers through merciless competition in any field is a relatively new phenomenon in Korea.[68]

It is imperative, however, if the Korean economy is to make a leap to the next stage of development, that fair and merciless competition be the basic operational principle at all levels. The "live and let live" spirit of collusion stifles innovation and economic progress. A safety net for those who fail in competition may be provided, but the prospect of producing "losers" should not be used as an excuse to eliminate competition itself. The government, in particular, should remove various entry and exit barriers and let the fittest thrive and the worst-fit die away. Only then will winners gain full legitimacy and losers learn to accept defeat graciously.

Attitude toward work. According to Max Weber, a strong sense of commitment to one's work and worldly asceticism constitute two of the main elements of the Protestant ethic that served as a motivating force in the West. Although Koreans were often noted for hard work and thrift during the heyday of economic development, Koreans now seem to display a depressingly casual attitude toward work and consumption.

This attitude is actually understandable in many ways. The kind of professional commitment and pride in one's work displayed by Japanese

68. Although it could be argued that the traditional state examinations separated the outstanding from mediocre talents through competition, "losers" in this competition maintained their preexamination status—they did not go bankrupt. The upsurge of egalitarianism after the Korean War has exacerbated the situation, as the members of the same cohort who all started at ground zero now find themselves in very different social positions. They do not feel that the increase in inequality is all that justifiable.

and German technicians, for instance, was largely forgotten during the long Confucian rule of the Yi dynasty. Handicraft and manufacture were not considered socially respectable occupations during this period, and this prejudiced view survives to this day. Most technicians themselves want their children to become today's equivalent of scholar-officials rather than inherit their occupation. Moreover, stories of the rich getting richer through speculation and unearned income further depress the morale of these workers as they struggle to make ends meet. Unless these fundamental problems are addressed, a talk of making professional commitment to one's work and taking pride in it is likely to fall on cynical ears. At the least, employers should reward good craftsmanship and make these workers feel that their work is important.

INSTITUTIONAL REFORM

After tracing the evolution of the spirit of capitalism, Werner Sombart coolly observed:

> Those who believe that the giant Capitalism is destroying both nature and man cannot but hope that he will be captured and put within the bounds that restrained him of old. Some people, indeed, expected to overcome him by appealing to ethical principles; I, for my part, can see that such attempts are doomed to utter failure. When we remember that capitalism has snapped the iron chains of the oldest religions, it seems to me hardly likely that it will allow itself to be bound by the silken threads of the wisdom that hails from Weimar and Königsberg.[69]

Sombart might have been too cynical to appreciate the power of ideas, but there seems to be little doubt that a purely moral campaign cannot accomplish very much in the way of changing people's economic behavior. Institutional reform must accompany moral reformation. After all, it is important to remember that institutional-structural factors, such as the legal guarantee of individual autonomy and loosening of central control, were as crucial as religious-motivational factors in the development of capitalism.[70]

69. Sombart, *The Quintessence of Capitalism*, pp. 357–58.

70. In explaining the origin of "the European miracle," some economic historians have emphasized these institutional innovations. On this point, see E. L. Jones, ed., *The European Miracle: Environments, Economies, and Geopolitics in the History of Europe and Asia* (Cambridge: Cambridge University Press, 1987); Douglass C. North, "Institutions," *Journal of Economic Perspectives* 5(1991): 97–112; Nathan Rosenberg and L. E. Birdzell, Jr., *How the West Grew Rich: The Economic Transformation of the Industrial World* (New York: Basic Books, 1986).

As the economic analysis of the Korean culture makes clear, one of the most serious problems for the Korean economy is the lack of legitimacy for the Korean capitalist class. This problem is primarily connected with two sources: speculative profit and special political favors. Accordingly, a heavy taxation on gains from speculative investment in real estate will go a long way toward enhancing the legitimacy of wealth in Korea and forcing capitalists to focus on investment in real productive capacity.

More generally, since the legitimacy of the Korean economic system depends on the extent to which it ensures the equality of opportunity, the government should adopt various measures to enhance social mobility. The wholesale inheritance of wealth by an incompetent heir may be as detrimental to society as the feudalistic inheritance of title in premodern times, and ability rather than ascription should be the guiding principle in allocating resources. In this regard, both "the carrot" to encourage the use of wealth for social purposes and "the stick" to discourage the wholesale inheritance of wealth should be considered.

For instance, a heavier estate and gift tax, combined with an effective enforcement mechanism to close loopholes, can be used to enhance the equality of opportunity while minimizing disincentive effects associated with redistributive taxes imposed on a generation of cohorts. In general, wealth creation, rather than redistribution, should be accorded policy priority when the government adopts measures to enhance social mobility. Giving talented young people more opportunities through transgenerational tax and transfer measures can improve efficiency and increase the size of the overall pie, whereas giving untalented old people more wealth through redistributive measures within the cohort may well result in an efficiency loss. Presently, the rate structure for Korea's estate tax consists of only five brackets, compared with nine for Japan and seventeen for the United States. The top rate of 45 percent applies to an amount in excess of 5 billion won (approximately $5.6 million). In contrast, the U.S. top rate of 55 percent kicks in at $3 million, and the Japanese top rate of 70 percent begins to apply at 2 billion yen (approximately $16 million).[71] To limit the wholesale inheritance of wealth and promote efficiency-enhancing redistribution, Korea's estate and gift tax system should be restructured to allow for a greater number of brackets and higher top rates.

71. See Sang-kuk Han, Joon-ho Bae, and Kwang-jae Lee, *A Proposal to Rationalize the Estate and Gift Tax System* (in Korean; Seoul: KiPf, 1996), pp. 299–301.

At the same time, a greater tax incentive should be provided to encourage the wealthy to use their fortunes for social purposes.[72] Under the present tax system, political donations and contributions to government-designated nonprofit organizations are fully deductible, whereas gifts to other nonprofit organizations of the donor's choice can be only partially written off. From a public interest point of view, it is not at all evident why political donations and contributions to such government-designated organizations as the Fund for the Promotion of Culture and Arts should receive a more favorable tax treatment than gifts to schools and charity organizations. In order to encourage private initiative in selecting and carrying out projects for public interest, the present system of tax discrimination should be abolished.[73]

In addition to taking tax reform measures to address the concentration of wealth problem, the government should also stop acting as the implicit insurer of bank loans taken by large firms and encourage them to rely more on the equity market for raising capital. Often combined with influence-peddling practices in the loan-issuing stage, government-insured loans not only perpetuate the "too big to fail" myth but also block the dispersion of ownership.

Finally, the government can promote social mobility by reducing the heavy burden of private tutoring cost on households and making publicly funded schools more effective. Koreans typically cite education as the item for which the greatest degree of "excessive consumption" occurs; it accounts for more than 20 percent of household expenditure. The tradition of placing a heavy emphasis on education, combined with the present social hierarchy overwhelmingly dominated by graduates from top universities, has driven up the share of private tutoring costs in total household consumption. According to a 1995 report by Korea Education Development Institute, private tutoring costs now account for 51 percent of direct educational costs. Although education expenditure may be viewed as investment rather than consumption, the fact still remains that Korean schools have been failing to respond effectively to this demand for education. As a result, students from poor

72. For an interesting empirical study of the impact of taxation on donations, see Charles T. Clotfelter, "The Impact of Tax Reform on Charitable Giving: A 1989 Perspective," NBER Working Paper no. 3273 (Cambridge, Mass.: National Bureau of Economic Research, 1990).

73. See Won-ik Son, A *Proposal to Improve Taxation on Nonprofit Organizations* (in Korean; Seoul: KiPf, 1995), esp. pp. 77–78.

families are being increasingly placed at a disadvantage in the competition for top schools.

Compared with modest reform measures connected with tax and education policy, the elimination of special political favors requires a fundamental restructuring of the Korean economy, for it ultimately depends on reducing government intervention in the economy. In that sense, the elimination of special political favors is closely connected to the problem of unnecessarily large government presence in the economy. There are primarily two ways to address the problem of corruption: elimination of rent created by excessive government regulation and imposition of a heavy penalty on those government officials who betray public trust. According to a document submitted to the Budget Committee of the National Assembly in 1996, a prospective factory owner in Korea must go through 58 stages, prepare 336 document forms, and wait 925 days to secure a government approval for building a new factory. The rent created by this kind of cumbersome administrative procedure is all too readily cashed in by government officials. Even if government officials had a strong moral sense, the problem of corruption would remain latent unless extensive deregulation eliminates this rent.

But because government oversight is to a certain extent necessary, there is a limit to how far deregulation can be carried out. Only the imposition of a heavy penalty on corruption will ultimately deter government officials from taking bribes. Korea's record has not been good in this regard. For example, although lack of oversight by bribe-taking city officials contributed to the collapse of the Sampoong Department Store and led to the death of more than 600 people in 1995, only two of the fifteen city officials originally convicted of corruption charges remained behind the bars after a year. The expectation of a large gain combined with a minimum penalty clearly encourages government officials to take a chance and compromise public health and safety.

Although the elimination of speculative profit and corruption will go a long way toward addressing the ethical shortcomings of Korean capitalism, the restructuring of the Korean economy will not be complete until institutions designed to reduce class conflict and promote interfirm competition are established. The experience of advanced industrial countries makes it clear that such an institutional reform calls for the determined efforts of a de facto coalition joining sophisticated business and labor union leaders as well as reform-minded citizens. Though preceded by a serious policy misstep and an outbreak of labor strife, the eventual passage of a new Labor Relations Law through the National Assembly in March 1997 is a step in the right direction for the future of labor-management relations in Korea.[74]

MORAL REFORMATION

In order for these institutional reforms to be effective, a corresponding set of ethical values for policy makers, entrepreneurs, workers, and consumers should be firmly established. A sound economic way of thinking should underpin these ethical values.

Government. A reorientation in values is most crucial for the government because it is the body that sets the rules of the game. First and foremost, policy makers should abandon the urge to micromanage the economy. Still endowed with considerable powers after having guided Korea's rapid economic development with some intelligence, government officials all too naturally wish to control and redirect market mechanism. Many of them seem to have a fundamental distrust of market mechanism and behave as if they were still living in the 1960s when the government did have a reason to assume the role of the market and allocate resources directly.[75]

There are now few, if any, missing markets in Korea, and it is about time that the government left the market to itself. Autonomy, diversity, and experiment should be the guiding principles. Policy makers should use state intervention primarily for the purpose of promoting competi-

74. The railroading of a new labor bill by the ruling party in a secret predawn session in December 1996 precipitated the biggest general strike in Korean history and eventually led to the overhauling of this bill. A compromise reached through negotiation between the ruling and opposition parties, the new Labor Relations Law guarantees the right of association by legalizing the establishment of multiple unions and improves labor market flexibility by defining the circumstances under which employees can be laid off. Prior to the passage of this law, employees in Korea could not be laid off without "a just cause," which was not statutorily defined. The new law also firmly establishes the "no work, no pay" principle.

75. In this context, the recent controversy over the "high-cost, low-efficiency" structure of the Korean economy only betrays a general lack of appreciation for market mechanism that plagues economic discussions in Korea. Unless there are serious market distortions, the price of goods exposed to competition should reflect their efficiency. It is rather strange to compare the nominal interest rates in Korea (around 13 percent) and Japan (around 2 percent) and pronounce that Korea suffers from a high cost of raising capital when Korea's real economic growth rate and inflation rate far exceed Japan's.

tion and guarding public interest against unscrupulous business practices that threaten public health and safety. Rent-creating powers should be taken away from government officials.

Entrepreneurs and workers. Entrepreneurs and workers, for their part, should understand that they are on the same team, and they should exercise self-control in demanding their "fair share." They should work together to increase the size of the total pie, and accept their share in accordance with their contribution. A sense of professional commitment should guide their endeavors.

Their past behavior in this regard, however, has been less than exemplary. During the recent controversy over "high wages," for instance, employers complained that wage increase had outpaced labor productivity improvement over the past decade, and suggested that something as drastic as a wage freeze was necessary to help the Korean economy survive the current downturn. What they neglected to mention was that the phenomenon of wage escalation was concentrated in the late-1980s and that the trend has weakened since 1990. In fact, the wage escalation of the late 1980s was primarily a reaction to the wage suppression of the early 1980s, when wage increases failed to keep pace with improvement in labor productivity. Moreover, when the belated wage hikes were effected, the unemployment rate actually dropped.

Employers were, however, not alone in using faulty logic. Instead of using economic logic, workers also employed a strange argument of their own to defend the wage increase. Observing that most households in advanced industrial economies are double-income households whereas a majority of Korean households are single-income families, some workers argued that Korean workers would have to receive higher wages if Korean households are to enjoy comparable living standards as their double-income counterparts in other countries. Instead of reducing consumption expenditure or having their spouse look for a job, these workers are in effect asking their employers to give them wages beyond the level justified by their marginal product of labor.

This kind of economic nonsense on both sides does not bode well for the future of labor-management relations in Korea. The determination of wages certainly contains some elements of bargaining, but both sides should understand that economic logic sets some bounds on the appropriate level of wages. A systematic economic education program may help to reduce the labor-management conflict. As both sides begin to receive their "fair share," the problem of legitimacy for the capitalist class will subside.

Returning at least a fraction of wealth to the community is another way for Korean entrepreneurs to solve the problem of legitimacy. It may be naïve to expect Korean business leaders to subscribe to the view that wealth is a stewardship. Unless business leaders learn to overcome their preoccupation with family interests and think seriously about such notions as stewardship and noblesse oblige, however, a strong link between wealth and honor will never be established.

Certainly, the absence of tradition for volunteering time and money to help others outside the immediate family and neighborhood has retarded the development of corporate philanthropy in Korea. It is, however, important to note that Korea does not suffer from the lack of traditional ideas about helping others. The national ideal of *Hongik Ingan*, the Buddhist notion of compassion, and the Confucian notion of benevolence can all be readily tapped to justify using one's wealth for social purposes—much like the Christian notion of loving one's neighbor in Western countries.

Much like their Japanese counterparts, Korean business leaders are now only beginning to think about their social responsibilities.[76] Again, much as in Japan, corporate philanthropy is becoming synonymous with *mécénat*, a French term for corporate support of the arts. Business leaders may feel that they can more readily enhance the corporate image by sponsoring a concert than by, for instance, giving money to an orphanage. But corporate support of the arts can make only a limited contribution to legitimating wealth. Promoting the equality of opportunity through intergenerational transfer and wealth redistribution should be the focus of corporate as well as individual philanthropy.

Consumers. As for consumption, Korea's problem is not the American-style "reckless spending." After all, the household savings rate in Korea is still around 30 percent. Rather, the problem is what may be called "imitative consumption," or "keeping up with the Kims"—to use the most common surname in Korea. Preoccupied with outward appearance and sensitive to other people's assessment, a typical Korean is not reluctant to spend money in order to *look* respectable. In the egalitarian atmosphere of Korean society, he or she should follow the socially re-

76. For an overview of philanthropy in Japan, see Osamu Fujiwara, "*Philanthropy: Learning from America*" (in Japanese; Tokyo: IIGP, 1992).

spectable mode of consumption or risk being looked down upon. Conspicuous consumption quickly gives rise to imitative conspicuous consumption, and the existence of rich people who have all too easily accumulated their wealth and are all too willing to spend it aggravates this problem. Until Koreans learn to value individuality and place less emphasis on outward appearance, this kind of consumption behavior is unlikely to disappear.

Consumers should think twice before engaging in imitative conspicuous consumption. Given the human desire to stand out in a crowd, conspicuous consumption may be an important element of any human society, and the suppression of economic freedom for the sake of maintaining "the solidarity of the community" may do more harm than good. But consumers should understand that a high price does not necessarily correspond to high quality and that the emulation of the rich through imitative conspicuous consumption does little to improve their personal worth while doing much damage to their economic conditions.

Conclusion

The changing relationship between wealth and honor and the tension between the pursuit of self-interest and social responsibility are the two central elements in the evolution of the capitalist spirit. In precapitalist societies, moneymaking was condemned as a spiritually corrupting and socially dangerous activity. With the weakening of central control and the loss of moral authority by the Church, however, the individualistically oriented ethos of capitalism and Protestantism began to spread in Europe. A positive link was established between wealth and honor, and the pursuit of self-interest was rationalized in the name of God. But as the capitalist spirit lost its moral anchor in transcendental values and began to be guided solely by the logic of the survival of the fittest, the link between wealth and honor was considerably weakened. In order to make capitalism socially acceptable, a new sense of social responsibility had to be integrated into the capitalist ethos.

Korea is now at that critical stage of capitalist development when a new social contract needs to be drawn, when the pursuit of self-interest should be moderated by a newly defined sense of social responsibility. In particular, the acquisition and disposal of wealth must take place through transparent and legitimate channels in order for a positive connection to be established between wealth and honor. Each economic actor has a role to play in this reform. In addition to promoting fair competition, the government should stop handing out favors in return for business contributions. Business leaders, for their part, should go beyond the narrow confines of family interests and make positive efforts to support and improve the economic system that has helped to make their success possible. Only then will workers come to accept the notion of "honorable wealth." For a capitalist system to operate smoothly, enlightened self-interest should be an integral part of the capitalist ethos.

Henry S. Rowen

Societies, Politics, and the Rise of East Asia

Why have so many East Asian countries had remarkably strong and sustained economic growth in recent decades? The conventional, and clearly correct, answer is that they adopted unusually good policies. But why did they do so? Their record is exceptional, not only in comparison to other developing regions but in world history.

The current interest in what can be called the new Asian exceptionalism is juxtaposed against a long-standing puzzle of why China, after creating the world's earliest mechanized industry from the tenth to the fourteenth century, was unable to sustain that progress. Although Japan was the first non-European culture country to begin rapid modernization, in the mid-nineteenth century, almost another century passed before other East Asian nations followed suit. In spite of this lag, they were still ahead of the rest of the developing world.

The fact that their policies have been superior only pushes the inquiry one stage further: why was this? Were favorable social (including political) factors responsible for their adoption, and might such factors independently have helped to produce exceptional results?

Such success was not predicted. Newly independent South Korea inherited little industry and suffered great damage from war. Given the record of the Kuomintang, there was no strong basis for optimism in 1949 about Taiwan's economic prospects. Hong Kong was the destination for many poor and unskilled refugees and there was uncertainty about Beijing's behavior toward it after 1949. Singapore's prospect

This chapter is an adaptation of the author's chapter in *Behind East Asian Growth.*

under a socialist-oriented party in a region dominated by less than friendly Malaysia and Indonesia was problematical. The Indonesian economy under Sukarno was thoroughly mismanaged. China's Great Leap Forward and the Cultural Revolution were disruptive and its overall performance through the end of the 1970s was unimpressive. Japan aside, the Philippines in 1950 seemed to have the brightest prospect, an assessment that turned out to be spectacularly wrong.

Their performances need little recording here. The region's six fastest-growing economies (Japan, South Korea, Taiwan, Hong Kong, Singapore, and China) experienced about 5 percent a year per capita growth (in international purchasing power units) from 1965 to 1995, while three Southeast Asian countries (Thailand, Malaysia, and Indonesia) averaged about 3.5 percent a year. The rest of the developing world averaged only 1.5 percent per year. Eight of the twelve best-performing developing countries, *all* of the large population, high performers, were in East Asia; the other four are tiny. Seven East Asian countries—North Korea, Mongolia, Vietnam, Cambodia, Laos, the Philippines, and Myanmar—performed poorly. (Vietnam has been doing well since 1986 but that is too short a record to warrant inclusion among the sustained high growth economies.)

There has been no comparable performance in history. Japan's annual per capita growth from the Meiji Restoration to 1940 was respectable at 1.5 percent but that was no better than that of the United States and Sweden over the period. In the rest of the world, Egypt was the only large country whose performance was close to that of the Southeast Asians over the period 1965 on but it stagnated after 1980.

Explanations

It has been argued that the Asian Newly Industrial Economies (NIEs) were lucky in their timing. The international environment was favorable after World War II: the Bretton Woods agreement provided a stable financial system; the industrial countries were booming; the United States provided a large, relatively open market; development assistance was available; and American military protection was supplied. Not everyone was accorded equal opportunity or help, but the environment favored development-oriented and competent governments everywhere, those that avoided the off-ramp of socialism and were not crippled by domestic or foreign conflicts. Although world growth slowed at a lesser pace after the early 1970s, world trade continued to grow strongly and multinational companies were transferring technology to countries offering good opportunities. The NIEs exploited these potentials. The Southeast Asians began to grow rapidly about then as did China after 1979 and Vietnam after 1986.

This seems to leave some combination of three major explanations: (1) better policies were adopted, (2) their social capabilities are greater, and (3) external influences favored them.

Policies. There is a wide consensus on economic policies that are good for development, albeit with some disputes at the margin, those that affect physical investment, the formation of human capital, and the acquisition of technology. There is, however, no developed theory that enables one to predict which countries will adopt good policies (other than continuity with the past).

Social capabilities. Successful countries also have favorable social attributes. This category encompasses institutions that affect the key growth requisites. The character of the politics and laws is crucial; this cluster is addressed below under the heading of effective governance. Another is the distribution of income, especially the distribution of opportunities. Still another is the value people put on achievement through learning.

External influences. These are influences from outside individual countries, including from outside the region. Europe's extension of power from the sixteenth century on had huge effects wherever it impinged, including in Asia. So did Japan's colonial activities from the late nineteenth century on. More recently, competition between the communist and noncommunist powers was played out in the region with varying degrees of intensity. And the United States was important as a market, as an occupying and reforming power, and as a protector.

METHODOLOGICAL DIFFICULTIES

There are problems with some aspects of the literature on East Asia's rise. Some scholar identifies a possible explanatory factor such as a pattern of initially authoritarian regimes or government micromanagement of the economy and asserts its singular importance. Such claims need to be validated by comparisons among the largest feasible set of countries; this is not always done, and when it is, the claims sometimes fail to stand up. For instance, the governments of all the recently successful countries in the region (Japan being an earlier one) were authoritarian forty years ago. But there have been many such regimes in the world and the data show no growth advantage to them. Also, the pattern of governments favoring some industries over others through preferential access to credit, subsidies, and trade protection is nearly universal; moreover, such interventions are judged to have contributed much to the poverty of nations. Either the parameters at issue actually differed (e.g., Asian "authoritarianism" or "industrial policies" were not the same as Latin American or South Asian ones) or other influences were at work—or both. A finer-grained description and analysis is needed. In any case, single factor explanations do not take us very far; it is the interaction of several, perhaps many—which ones is an open question—that accounts for the outcomes we observe.

A similar problem arises with cultural explanations. The successes of the Chinese cultural sphere states (China, Japan, Korea, Vietnam, Taiwan, Hong Kong, and Singapore) are sometimes attributed to a quality called Confucianism. There are several difficulties here. Most obviously, forty years ago all these countries except Japan were poor and some still are. Has Confucianism basically changed in that short interval? If it is a contributor to success, it clearly works along with other conditions. More importantly, how can one distinguish a potential positive factor without examining countries that do not have it? Since Confucianism consists of a bundle of attributes that are not precisely defined, there are serious difficulties with this kind of explanation. Nevertheless, there does seem to be much in the view that attributes derived from history, that is, "culture," can affect behavior in ways important for development.

In the absence of an accepted theory encompassing all these varied factors, the best we can do is to present them, argue their plausibility, make comparisons with other countries and regions, and await the reaction of the audience. With further research, some of these factors—and perhaps others neglected here—will doubtless be seen as much more important than others.

Their Economic Policies

Economic possibilities, too, are addressed briefly. Consider several basic policy categories:

Macroeconomic stability. East Asia has the best record of any developing region on inflation and exchange rate stability.

Openness. The East Asians are distinguished by their engagement with the world economy, in particular their pushing of exports. The resource-poor NIEs had little choice but to export manufactured goods to pay for raw materials; the Southeast Asians had more resources and therefore more options, but by 1990 manufacturing's contribution was 27 percent of GDP for Malaysia, 25 percent for Thailand, and 19 percent for Indonesia. Their trade policies varied. Korea strenuously promoted exports and Taiwan also subsidized them while both constrained imports to certain channels. Hong Kong was laissez-faire, and the others were in between. Openness to foreign direct investment, a major source of technology, also varied. Hong Kong had virtually no restrictions while Korea had many; but Korea worked hard to acquire foreign technology, including licensing it on a large scale.

The allocation of resources. The share of national resources consumed by these governments has been low, tax administration variable in efficiency and honesty but relatively good in the NIEs, and investment in infrastructure high. There has been some financial repression (implying rationing of credit), but highly negative real interest rates have been avoided. Although many state enterprises were created early and few have been privatized, their shares of national output sharply declined. Damaging regulations and obstacles to new enterprises were few, nor was agriculture drained of resources to support urban areas.

Property and other economic rights. According to one analysis, "without exception, countries with either a *high level* or a *substantial increase* in economic freedom achieved positive growth . . . the overwhelming majority of countries with *low* and/or *contracting* levels of economic freedom experienced declines in per capita GDP."[1] These freedoms include protecting the value of money, the ability to move it abroad, free exchange of property, low taxes, a fair judiciary, few trade restrictions, labor market freedom, ability to start a business, absence of economic coercion by political opponents, and no large-scale corruption.

1. James Gwartney, Robert Lawson, and Walter Block, *Economic Freedom of the World: 1975–1995* (Vancouver, B.C.: Fraser Institute, 1996), pp. 4–16 (emphasis in original).

Several East Asian countries rate among the highest in the world on these freedoms. In the mid-1990s, Hong Kong (a colony!), Singapore, and Malaysia received high scores. From 1975 to 1995, only two non-OECD countries, Hong Kong and Singapore, had consistently high ratings. In 1993–1995, five other East Asian countries were in the top twenty (out of 102 that were rated).

Certain policies along with other influences affected the proximate causes of growth.

Physical capital. The fast-growing East Asian countries had low savings rates several decades ago, inevitably given their poverty, but their savings grew to being the world's highest at 30–40 percent of GDP. For some countries, this might reflect a Confucian propensity to save, although the earlier widespread destruction and redistribution of wealth might have led to increased savings as people restored their ratio of wealth to income.[2] All their governments encouraged savings and Singapore introduced a forced savings system (the Provident Fund). In any case, a cultural explanation is unnecessary: when countries grow fast for whatever reasons, good investment opportunities provide a high payoff from deferring consumption; moreover, consumption tends to lag behind income growth

Human capital. According to Jeffrey Williamson, "a good share of the differences in growth performance along the Asia-Pacific Rim, or between it and Latin America, can also be explained by human capital and demographic forces."[3] (This topic is discussed further below.)

Technology. Firms in developing countries have two main disadvantages in technology: (1) they are behind, have poorly developed industrial and academic infrastructures, and are far from the centers of science and innovation; (2) they are out of mainstream international markets, having small markets themselves and unsophisticated users. They need strategies to overcome these technological and market barriers: engaging in trade, allowing foreign firms to invest directly, emphasizing li-

2. Jeffrey G. Williamson, "Human Capital Deepening, Inequality, and Demographic Events Along the Asia-Pacific Rim," in Naohiro Ogawa, Gavin W. Jones, and Jeffrey G. Williamson, eds., *Human Resource Development Along the Asia-Pacific Rim* (Singapore: Oxford University Press, 1993), p. 146.

3. Ibid., p. 131.

censing and indigenous development.[4] All these methods entail building domestic competencies. The Northeast Asians, especially Japan and Korea, chose the path of licensing and indigenous development; the others chose to acquire technology mainly via foreign direct investment.

WHAT WAS THE MIRACLE?

The World Bank's *East Asian Miracle* report of 1993 credited success mainly to getting the fundamentals right.[5] It also identified important roles for various institutions, including intermediaries between government and the private sector, as well as relatively equal income distributions. In accordance with the near-universal pattern, most of these governments intervened extensively in favor of particular industries and firms, including owning banks, varying degrees of import protection, subsidies, restrictions on foreign investment, controls over trade unions, and spending on applied research. *Miracle* graded these activities positively in Northeast Asia and negatively in Southeast Asia (as elsewhere in the world), attributing the difference to the competency of bureaucrats and their insulation from rent-seeking politics.

These findings have proved to be very controversial. Some critics hold that *Miracle* did not adequately make the case on the role of the fundamentals or, alternatively, on the merits of the state microinterventions in Northeast Asia.[6] Ian Little criticizes both *Miracle* and some of its critics. He faults *Miracle* for using shaky data in estimating significant gains in total factor productivity as well as for claimed industrial policy successes; a fortiori, analysts who give even more credit to industrial policies than did *Miracle* are in still greater error. He finds that rapid growth was mainly based on labor-intensive manufacturing that employed well-educated, hard-working, docile labor forces. In short, these achievements are fully explicable in conventional terms: high rates of material and human investment plus avoiding macroeconomic disasters and not to governments favoring shipbuilding, steel, autos, and the like.

4. Michael Hobday, *Innovation in East Asia* (Brookfield, Vt.: Edward Elgar, 1995).

5. World Bank, *The East Asian Miracle: Economic Growth and Public Policy* (New York: Oxford University Press, 1993).

6. See: Dani Rodrik, "King Kong Meets Godzilla: The World Bank and the East Asian Miracle," in "Miracle or Design," Overseas Development Council Policy Essay no. 11 (1994); Ian Little, "Picking Winners: The East Asian Experience," Social Market Foundation, London, 1996.

A related line of investigation asserts that high levels of accumulation of both physical and human capital account for almost all the growth (excepting Japan).[7] But there remains the question of how these countries managed such large capital accumulations. As Lawrence Lau says, "the miracle lies . . . in the ability to mobilize the savings and use them efficiently."[8]

Their Social Capabilities

According to Ohkawa and Rosovsky, Tokugawa Japan (1603–1868) was backward economically but advanced socially.[9] Crafts were well developed and services were sophisticated. Nearly half of all males had some formal schooling. It was a vigorous, advanced, and effective traditional society, "in many ways more advanced than many countries in Africa or Latin America today." Edo, Kyoto, and Osaka were among the largest cities in the world. There were good roads, inns, and restaurants. Housing was usually well designed and made, dress was beautiful and functional, and the cuisine was nutritional and attractive. Japan lacked one essential for wealth: the technology being created in Europe and North America. Its effective institutions enabled it to reduce this technological gap rapidly once it made the decision to do so.

Simon Kuznets in his pioneering work on modern economic growth identified three social requisites for development: "Secularism," defined as a concentration of life on earth with a high priority toward economic progress; "Equalitarianism," as the denial of inborn differences among human beings except insofar as they manifest themselves in human activities; and "Nationalism," based on the claim of a community of feeling grounded in the past, which overrides particularist

7. See: Alwyn Young, "A Tale of Two Cities: Factor Accumulation and Technical Change in Hong Kong and Singapore," *National Bureau of Economic Research Macro-Economic Annual* (1992); Jong-Il Kim and Lawrence J. Lau, "The Sources of Economic Growth of the East Asian Newly Developing Countries," *Journal of the Japanese and International Economies* 8 (September 1994): 235–71; Paul Krugman, "The Myth of Asia's Miracle," *Foreign Affairs* 73 (Nov./Dec. 1994): 62–78.

8. Lawrence J. Lau, "How the East Grew Rich," paper prepared for the Salzburg Seminar, December 1994.

9. Kazushi Ohkawa and Henry Rosovsky, *Japanese Economic Growth: Trend Acceleration in the Twentieth Century* (Stanford Calif.: Stanford University Press, 1973).

attitudes and ideologies.[10] These attributes are found in greater abundance in East Asia than in other developing regions. The Confucian countries clearly warrant the label Secular and the Islamic ones of this region have not displayed the damaging radicalism of those in the Middle East. On Equalitarianism, this region is famous for having narrow income differences. And internal divisions, along lines of clan, language groups, or religion, a common source of political instability and poor policies, are muted, especially in Northeast Asia—that is, Nationalism tends to override particular interests.

Social capabilities are expressed in institutions that reduce uncertainty by providing a structure to everyday life; once established, many activities can then be carried out more predictably and at a low marginal cost. The costs of doing business are increased if there are uncertain or poorly structured property rights, if contracts are weakly protected, information is scarce and access to it highly skewed, and corruption is endemic. These conditions lead to transactions being kept smaller than optimal out of people's aversion to risk, to capital being kept in liquid form, and to the avoidance of long-term agreements.

One set of institutions and norms in which the region is remarkably strong, those involving economic rights, has been noted. Other valuable ones are discussed below under these headings: Effective Governance, Achieving and Learning Societies, Growth with Equality, and External Influences.

EFFECTIVE GOVERNANCE

The high-growth countries have development-focused governments. Such an observation might be a tautology: governments that have good results can, ex post, be called "developmental." As we have seen, also unhelpful is the observation that thirty years ago most of these countries were authoritarian. It is more useful to distinguish among the motivations of leaders to produce better economic results, their scope for doing so, and their understanding of how best to proceed.

MOTIVATIONS

Aims. One might assume that all leaders wanted their countries to develop rapidly. At some level of abstraction no doubt that was true, but

10. Simon Kuznets, *Modern Economic Growth* (New Haven, Conn.: Yale University Press, 1966), p. 13.

they also had other things in mind, including surviving in power and building a national identity. Many were struggling to create new states, and surviving in power often entailed distributing rents on a scale that hurt productive investment. Decisions that did not have early payoffs but did have short-term costs were unappealing.

Many postindependence leaders were charismatic founders of their countries or at least leaders of political and social revolutions, usually populist and some communist in ideology, ignorant of economics, and hostile to the West. They are legendary figures: Castro, Ho Chi Minh, Kenyatta, Kim Il-Sung, Mao, Nasser, Nehru, Nkrumah, Qaddafi, and Sukarno. As Edward Mason et al. said of South Korea's first president: "President Rhee was more interested in other things than in economic development. As in so many of the new states, the leader who fought for independence proved not to be a man capable of effective administration. Like others with similar careers—Sukarno, Nkrumah, Sheik Mujib—Rhee was more adept at bringing a new nation into being than directing its development."[11] Although Latin America's independence had come a century earlier, it continued to throw up populist leaders such as Peron in Argentina, Allende in Chile, and Garcia in Peru. Lee Kuan Yew stands out as a rare, economically rational, exception among the founders.

Legitimacy. Political legitimacy is not an acute problem in democracies, the system many newly independent countries inherited from their metropoles; but many were weak and were soon succeeded by authoritarian regimes that had such problems. Having played a central role in achieving independence provided enough legitimacy for most first-generation leaders, but in time the aura wore off and some of them ran into difficulties as their economies languished. Some, such as Nasser in Egypt, offered socialist ideology, but this did not put bread or rice on the table. Among Latin American intellectuals and politicians a common line was to blame the "core" industrial, imperialist countries and their multinational corporations, but eventually that argument lost credibility. As Mario Vargas Llosa said of his Peruvian countrymen, "one of our worst defects—our best fictions—is to believe that our miseries have been imposed upon us from abroad."[12] Some Arabs have

11. Edward S. Mason et al., *The Economic and Social Modernization of the Republic of Korea*, Council on East Asian Studies, Harvard University, 1980, p. 253.

12. Mario Vargas Llosa, quoted in James Como, "Hero Storyteller," *National Review*, April 17, 1995, 54.

had a similar tendency, but, as Bent Hansen put it, "Egypt's main enemy has been Egypt."[13]

In East Asia, regimes that came to power through the use of force also had legitimacy problems: in South Korea, Indonesia, Taiwan, and, periodically, Thailand. Their leaders perceived that a cure was raising the people out of poverty—and found strategies for doing so. It helped that they saw to spreading the benefits of growth widely; and, not least, their regimes became politically more inclusive over time.[14]

External threats. Several countries faced serious threats to their security, including domestic insurgencies supported from outside. Taiwan and South Korea had such powerful enemies that survival required becoming economically strong. They were at war. Beijing could survive doing a mediocre economic job (up to a point) but Taipei could not. Singapore, a predominantly Chinese outcast in a sea of Malays, also had to prosper. Malaysia, while still Malaya, had suppressed an internal insurgency as well as hostility from Indonesia and for some years there was worry about a revival of these troubles; Thailand had externally supported communists in the countryside and faced direct threats from Vietnam and Cambodia; and Indonesia worried about the revival of the communists—supported by China.

These threats created an incentive for leaders to recruit all possible sources of support. In Thailand, they caused the regime for the first time in its history to pay attention to the condition of the peasants. There and elsewhere they provided an incentive to invest in rural infrastructure and education. Although countries elsewhere were also seriously threatened, including Turkey, Israel, Egypt, and Pakistan, the threat of hanging, as Samuel Johnson observed, was not always sufficient to motivate rational policies. This is another illustration of the proposition that single-factor explanations are inadequate. In any case, as Campos and Root put it, "Nowhere else in the developing world has there been a confrontation between communist and Western forces on such a large scale involving so many countries."[15]

13. Bent Hansen, *The Political Economy of Poverty, Equity, and Growth* (Oxford: Oxford University Press, 1991), p. 254.

14. Pei Minxin, "Constructing the Political Foundations of an Economic Miracle," in *Behind East Asian Growth: The Political and Social Foundations of Prosperity*, ed. H. S. Rowen (London: Routledge, 1997).

15. Jose Edgardo Campos and Hilton Root, *The Key to the Asian Miracle* (Washington, D.C.: Brookings Institution, 1996), p. 31.

One result was to stimulate military spending. Daniel Landau finds, but not statistically robustly, that military spending below 9 percent of GDP—a larger share than the NIEs spent—is associated with a positive effect on growth and above that a negative one.[16] Positive mechanisms might be the above-mentioned motivations to succeed, the modernizing influence of the military, and the sharing of benefits of growth for reasons of political solidarity. A clear negative mechanism is diverting resources from civil investment.

Forestalling competing power centers. Economically destructive behavior can be motivated by the aim of destroying obstacles to power or potential competing ones. Thus, with the aim of weakening opposition to his rule, Stalin destroyed the kulaks, thereby greatly damaging Soviet agriculture, and in Egypt, Nasser systematically undermined the efficacy of the many state-owned enterprises out of fear that they might challenge his power. In India, Nehru's view was that the state had to keep basic industries out of the private sector. The contrast with Park Chung Hee's view is striking: Park controlled these industries, but he understood that having efficient industries entailed their being in private hands. The Kuomintang in Taiwan arranged matters so that very large private firms did not develop but the many small firms became highly productive.[17] In general, potential dangers from competing power centers were forestalled by various combinations of repression and sharing of benefits.

Positive models in the neighborhood. East Asia had a superb role model nearby in Japan. That was true of no other developing region with the possible exceptions of Turkey, the Maghreb countries and Mexico vis-a-vis Western Europe and the United States; but cultural distances were large in these cases. In East Asia, one, and then successively more, countries geographically close and of similar culture were succeeding. This must have served both as an embarrassment to the leaders of those that were still doing poorly and as models to emulate. Words written on Beijing's Democracy Wall in 1979 expressed the point concisely: "East Germany is not doing as well as West Germany, North Korea as well as South Korea, or China's mainland as well as Taiwan."

16. Daniel Landau, "The Economic Impact of Military Expenditures," World Bank Policy Research Working Paper no. 1138 (1993).

17. Campos and Root, p. 110.

SCOPE FOR ACTION

Leaders need political support to survive and even more to carry out policies that, at least initially, inevitably hurt some interests. Being a founding father, having been elected, or having support of the military help to some extent, but these are sometimes inadequate. Dysfunctional institutions pose obstacles, including class structures that support privileges, block advances on the basis of merit, and cause public funds to be wasted. Some countries have rooted systems of privilege—the Philippines and Latin American and Arab ones, for example. When they are dysfunctional enough, people fall back on informal, largely family and clan-based activities that limit the scope of business activities. Some countries have such sharp differences among groups, usually ethnically based, that governance is ineffective. Most East Asian countries, through varying mixes of historical legacies, political skills, and a capacity to learn and adapt, were not severely afflicted by these ills or managed to overcome them.

The destruction of old orders. Large systemic changes that undermine existing distributional coalitions, such as wars and revolutions or entry into radically new trading arrangements, weaken or destroy growth-inhibiting institutions and have a liberating effect.This happened widely in East Asia. There was destruction as a result of Japanese occupation, wars, decolonization, and revolutions in Japan, Korea, Taiwan, China (twice, in 1949 and during the Cultural Revolution), Singapore, Malaysia, and Indonesia. Indonesia had a terrible bloodletting in 1965–1966. Singapore was removed from Malaysia. Land reforms in Japan, Korea, and Taiwan reduced the potential blocking power of landholders. And in Japan the Americans weakened the power of the *zaibatsu*. These events removed potential obstacles to regimes motivated to produce results. With a few exceptions, there were no dominant economic classes to protect and seek rents. These events—some of them grave crises—opened the way for changes in leaders and new policies.

Bureaucratic competencies. Aside from, in some cases, finance ministries and central banks, most newly independent countries had few competent civil servants to manage their ambitious programs. And since these deplorable situations were worsened by poor systems of recruiting talent and low pay, administrations were incompetent, often corrupt.

In contrast, Japan has a long tradition of excellence in its administration. The British left a legacy of competent and honest administration in Singapore, Hong Kong, and Malaysia, and Thailand has a history of more than a century as a bureaucratically run state, although the quality of its civil service has been hurt by low pay. In the Chinese cultural sphere countries, a bureaucratic career—becoming a mandarin—was long the main path for success and attracted the most able young men. Singapore created an exemplary civil service (one with the world's highest pay). In Korea, Park Chung Hee promptly appointed able technocrats and began to revitalize the civil service. The KMT in Taiwan had talented people from the mainland. Under Deng Xiaoping, the former balance in favor of Reds was tipped in favor of Experts and the ancient tradition of the examination system was revived. And in Indonesia, Suharto brought in the Berkeley mafia economic technocrats to manage macroeconomic policy. However, it would certainly be an error to assume that bureaucrats and politicians have been highly competent and honest everywhere, especially in the industry-focused departments. For example, an authoritative account of Thailand's bureaucracy describes it as being "marked often by patronage and rent-seeking"[18]

Corruption is damaging because it is highly correlated; with bureaucratic inefficiency, one can make money out of red tape.[19] Unlike taxes, bribes must be kept secret and this leads to greater distortions of resources. A lack of established property rights by corrupt officials in the benefits they bestow sometimes means that many of them need to be bribed. In the Philippines under Marcos, corruption flowed to the top, but after his demise the reported number of independent bribe takers increased and social efficiency probably declined even further.

Recent public revelations in Korea raise questions about the honesty not only of politicians but also of some bureaucrats. There have been disturbing charges in Taiwan. And, according to President Jiang Zemin, China is rife with corruption at all levels of government. In 1996, Transparency International reported Thailand to be the 37th, In-

18. Scott R. Christiansen, David Dollar, Ammar Siamwalla, and Pakorn Vichyanond, "Institutional and Political Bases of Growth-Inducing Policies in Thailand," draft paper prepared for the World Bank project on the East Asian Development Experience, October 1992.

19. See: Andrei Shleifer and Robert W. Vishny, "Corruption," *Quarterly Journal of Economics* 43 (August 1993): 599–617; Paulo Mauro, "Corruption and Growth," *Quarterly Journal of Economics* 110 (August 1995): 681–712.

donesia the 45th, and China the 50th most corrupt countries out of 54 surveyed, yet these have been some of the most rapidly growing nations.[20] Evidently, if countries have enough other social positive factors and have adopted good policies, as all these countries have, they can overcome this negative factor. However, Singapore (rated no. 7 in honesty) and Hong Kong (no. 18, ahead of France) probably would not have become so rich without high standards of probity.

Shared growth. The propensity of these regimes to spread the benefits of growth widely not only helped their legitimacy, it also reduced obstacles to adopting policies that entailed short-term costs for long-term benefits. (Recall that one of Kuznets's attributes for success is Equalitarianism.) This theme is expanded upon below.

Weakness, suicide, or destruction of the political left. In many developing countries, the radical left, often supported by Moscow or Beijing, created political instabilities and supported growth-retarding policies. It was different in East Asia. The basic conservatism of the Japanese kept the left parties marginal throughout. The Korean War wiped out the radical left in the South, and the KMT assured a non-left for Taiwan. Lee Kuan Yew saw to its emasculation in Singapore. The massive killings in Indonesia destroyed it there. Several of these events amounted to self-destruction, including China's Cultural Revolution and the abortive move by Indonesia's Communist Party in 1965. In both Indonesia and China the victorious right adopted equity-enhancing policies that both helped development and undermined the political left.

Again, external threats. These not only supplied an urgent motivation for development, they supplied a political basis for removing obstacles to that end.

Governments' relations with business. In most developing countries, government-business relations have had a rent-seeking, sometimes even predatory, character. That characteristic has not been absent in East Asia, most notably in the Philippines and elsewhere in Southeast Asia; however, on the whole it seems to have been positive, with bu-

20. *Financial Times,* June 3, 1996.

reaucracies becoming partners with business in promoting growth.[21] The reasons included tight governmental fiscal controls that limited available funds, merit-based bureaucracies, and their firm political foundations. Campos and Root highlight the important role of functional intermediaries between government and business, industrial associations and consultative bodies. These were vehicles for sharing information and reducing uncertainty and political risks.

The political character of relations between government and business has varied. In Taiwan and Korea, strong state institutions gave government elites scope for reforms. In Taiwan, the arm's-length relation between the KMT and largely native Taiwanese businesses caused the government initially to build state enterprises, while in Korea the government's greater dependence on the private sector led to more support to private business and to a concentrated industrial structure. In both countries, the power of business expanded over time, and the autonomy of technocrats declined. In Southeast Asia, the bureaucracies were less competent and governments were less insulated from political pressures. Particularly striking there are the close personal links between Chinese capitalists and governments; these entail extensive networks of rent-seeking, but also much productive investment

Why did favorable institutions emerge in some settings and not in others? Stephan Haggard argues that they are affected by broad political relations, especially the reliance of government elites on business for political support.[22] He proposes the idea of an optimum distance between them: where it is too great, antigrowth policies are likely but if the government-business nexus is too close the result is capture and rent-seeking. The larger political structures limited business influence in Korea, Taiwan, and Thailand, provided scope for ethnic rent-seeking in Malaysia, fostered personalistic ties in Indonesia, and provided opportunities for nearly unchecked plunder in the Philippines.

Nationalism versus ethnic diversity and conflict. Differences along lines of class or ethnicity (that is, racial, tribal, linguistic, or religious) are often an obstacle to effective governance. Most East Asian countries have few such differences. The countries of Northeast Asia and China are ethnically highly homogeneous. Indonesia, which has many distinct

21. Campos and Root, p. 110.

22. Stephan Haggard, "Business, Politics, and Policy in East and Southeast Asia," in Rowen, ed., *Behind East Asian Growth.*

language groups, has had troubles in Sumatra, Timor, and Irian Jaya, but such tensions have not been disabling. There is also hostility (largely latent) there to the role of the Chinese. In Malaysia, the division between the Malays and the Chinese erupted in violence in 1969 but has been managed adequately since. Singapore, with a large minority of ethnic Malays and Indians, has adopted policies of decent housing for all, and universal education and other policies supportive of its minorities. For the region, overall, nationalisms have overcome particularisms.

The transformation of political institutions. Pei Minxin describes how most of these countries went through transformations in which political order was restored by autocratic regimes from conditions of instability, a monopoly of power by the military or a party was allowed to be gradually eroded, the treatment of dissidents gradually became less harsh, and some political opposition gradually was permitted.[23] All this involved the slow building of institutions, formal and informal. Alternative groups were allowed to participate in politics, usually first at the local level, and not in great numbers. Minxin poses two puzzles: why did strong development occur under weak rules of law? And what forces restrained predation of these autocratic regimes? (A partial answer is supplied above: the existence of grave external threats.)

Eventually, South Korea, Taiwan, Thailand, and the Philippines joined Japan among the "Free" nations (Singapore among the "Partly Free" ones) as rated by Freedom House.[24] In spite of assertions that Asian democracy is different from the Western sort, there is in Asian democracies the same positive correlation between incomes and democracy (of the Western sort) as there is in the rest of the world (which is not to argue that there are no differences between them). This evolution of political institutions—parties, bureaucracies, semi-open electoral procedures, some rule of law—promoted political stability and property rights. These political transitions paralleled market-opening events with the arrival of a second generation of leaders committed to development and with adequate scope to act.

UNDERSTANDING HOW TO PROCEED

The third main attribute of governance effective for development is knowing the right things to do—"right" in this context depending

23. Pei Minxin, in Rowen, ed.

24. *Freedom in the World: The Annual Survey of Political Rights and Civil Liberties, 1995–96* (New York: Freedom House, 1996).

on leaders' goals. For development, understanding means understanding the importance of the economic policies described above.

For several decades after World War II, "good" policies were widely understood in the developing countries to mean something quite different: pervasive state involvement. This usually resulted in insecurity of property rights, government ownership of industry, heavy regulation, and autarky. The communist countries were the worst, but there were many statist countries such as India and Mexico. Mexico's experience is illustrative. Its GDP per capita before the 1910 revolution was about equal to that of Japan. It had a high level of foreign investment and free trade; in 1900 its export/GDP ratio was about 20 percent. After the revolution it restricted foreign trade and investment, and by the 1970s it had an inefficient, corrupt system with a small wealthy class and a huge poor one. Even after nearly a decade of opening its economy from the mid-1980s, its export/GDP ratio in 1991 was only 7 percent. By then its per capita GDP was about one-third that of Japan.

The two most damaging ideas for development have been economic autarky, and collectivism, which in extreme form requires autarky. The power of the collectivist ethos is shown by the fact that in the mid-1980s over 80 percent of the world population lived in socialist countries (about one-third of the total) or in highly state-controlled ones (about one-half), almost all of which had performed poorly.

How did most of the East Asian countries either avoid these errors or, having committed them, manage to escape? History played a large role. Perhaps Japanese society is too intelligent and conservative ever to have accepted socialism, but occupation by U.S. forces ruled out that possibility. The United States also saw to the survival of South Korea as a capitalist society and, less directly, to that of Taiwan, which under the KMT, although Leninist in original style, became strongly anticommunist. The defeat of communist insurgents in most of Southeast Asia left that region capitalist. As for China's escape, the self-destruction of its radical left in the Cultural Revolution helped greatly, as did the examples of nearby successes.

ACHIEVING AND LEARNING SOCIETIES

Systematic and large differences in values, both within the region and outside, are revealed in surveys and behavior. The Japanese by comparison with Americans, and to a lesser extent the Europeans, are much less individualistic, more attuned to duties than rights, more hierarchical and deferential to authority, have more elaborated institutions of social control, place more value on loyalty and stability, and are much less religious.[25]

One might expect such cultural differences to be expressed in economic institutions. It is probably no accident that a Japanese firm invented the just-in-time system of manufacturing that depends on close cooperation and trust among workers and firms. Masahiko Aoki describes a model of the Japanese firm with wide sharing of information at low levels and broad job specifications, all embedded in a main bank (*keiretsu*) system in which the bank takes charge when things go badly.[26] He holds that neither the U.S. nor the Japanese model may be superior in all dimensions and for every industry, but the Japanese is distinctive.

Another prominent, and productive, institution is the Chinese family firm and its networks, though few of these have professional managers or have institutionalized themselves. Redding and Fukuyama emphasize the Chinese limitation of trust to the family as a major explanation of this phenomenon, which largely grew out of the insecurity of property in traditional domestic China; in a country with no history of feudal responsibilities, the family becomes doubly important.[27] In contrast, the Japanese firm long ago made a transition from being wholly within the family, first through the custom of adopting sons, then by bringing in professional managers, and eventually by moving to public ownership, which allowed firms to grow large and live indefinitely. The evolution of the Korean chaebols is following the Japanese pattern. In short, even among the Sinitic countries there is no single model, but there is a pattern of more reliance on personal relations than an arm's-length dealing (one also found more in continental Europe than in the Anglo-Saxon countries).

Another important, distinctive, and rapidly growing institution in China is the town and village enterprise. These are predominantly local government-owned or collective firms, mostly in manufacturing. They express Chinese entrepreneurship and are also a by-product of the rapid increase in agricultural productivity after the partial privatization be-

25. Seymour Martin Lipset, *American Exceptionalism* (New York: W. W. Norton, 1996).

26. Masahiko Aoki, "Evolutionary Organizational Diversity and Its Implications for Reform in Transitional Economies." Mimeo. Stanford University, 1995.

27. See: Gordon S. Redding, *The Spirit of Chinese Capitilism* (Berlin: De Gruyter, 1990); Francis Fukuyama, *Trust: The Social Virtues and the Creation of Prosperity* (New York: Free Press, 1995).

ginning in 1979, which made available many more workers and new market opportunities.

Confucianism. It is often asserted that Confucianism has been an important element in East Asia's successes. The first question to ask about Confucianism is, "What is it?" The answer is not obvious because its values are numerous: benevolence, moral-oughtness, conscientiousness, filial piety, respect for authority, brotherly respect, propriety, sincerity, self-cultivation, human knowledge, uprightness, and more. At bottom, it is a creed that extols merit and concern for the welfare of others. It is often observed that Confucianism consists of a set of moral norms that center primarily on relations among humans and not those between man and God or spirits, primarily a personal ethic, centered on relations within the family. Its secular focus (again, corresponding to one of Kuznets's precepts for development) has averted clashes of the kind that marked medieval Christianity and affect Islam to this day. East Asian governments have not had to deal with serious religious strife.

Confucianism in Japan acquired a different character from that of its place of origin; one more overtly nationalistic, paternalistic, and group oriented and without the role for "benevolence" in the Chinese original.[28] Indeed, Japan is often held to have several cultural attributes that are quite different from those of China. Whereas the primary unit of affiliation or loyalty in China is the family, in Japan it extends beyond the family to the "village"—under modern conditions represented by the company and the political faction. Max Weber attributed China's poverty to the inhibiting influence of traditional Confucianism, having at its core rigid social and family hierarchies that were "opposite to the development of rational economic corporate enterprise"; moreover, "the poise and harmony of the [Confucian] soul are shaken by the risks of acquisitiveness." To Weber, the family piety and strong cohesion of the system prevented impersonal economic rationalization:

> It is very striking that out of this unceasing and intensive economic ado and the much bewailed crass "materialism" of the Chinese, there failed to originate on the economic plane those great and methodical business conceptions which are rational in nature and are presup-

28. Michio Morishima, *Why Has Japan Succeeded? Western Technology and the Japanese Ethos* (Cambridge: Cambridge University Press, 1982).

> posed by modern capitalism. . . . [China is] a typical land of profiteering. . . . Confucianism has not favored the rise of modern capitalism.[29]

Overall, the Confucians lacked what Weber termed the "mighty enthusiasms" of the Puritans. Nor did Confucianism provide protection for property. Local officials could exploit merchants and peasants for increased taxes and bribes without their having any recourse to the law.

To the extent that there is a plausible answer to Confucianism's long-delayed—but in hindsight arguably positive—role in development, it lies in the path taken by history. China had been the world's most technologically advanced country for hundreds of years through about the fifteenth century, at which time it stagnated—at about the time Europe began to advance. Political events had led to an inward focus that became stultifying. Traditional Confucian society had never esteemed the merchant, and even the tradition of respect for scholar-officials eroded in the Ming Dynasty (1368–1644). It was not until countries in the Confucian tradition acquired political centers oriented toward development that economics began to expand, first in Japan, then in others through colonialism, communist rule in China, and the other processes described here.[30]

Under the heading, "Industrial Neo-Confucianism," Ezra Vogel identifies four clusters of institutions and attitudes common to the four NIEs: Meritocratic Elites, Entrance Exam System, Importance of the Group, and Self-Cultivation, that is, the drive for self-improvement reflected in hard work and other achievement-focused activities.[31] Of these four clusters, those other than Importance of the Group can be subsumed under the heading of a high value attached to achievement through education and other forms of learning.

There are also negatives in Confucian tradition: family loyalty can justify nepotism, for example, and respect for authority implies a passivity that allows scope for political leaders that can result in larger and more persistent mistakes—as in China under Mao's rule. Reliance on

29. Max Weber, *The Religion of China: Confucianism and Taoism* (New York: Free Press, 1962).

30. Thomas A. Metzger, "Confucian Culture and Economic Modernization: An Historical Approach," in Tzong-shian Yu and Joseph S. Lee, eds., *Confucianism and Economic Development* (Taipei: Chung-Hua Institution for Economic Research, 1995).

31. Ezra F. Vogel, *The Four Little Dragons* (Cambridge, Mass.: Harvard University Press, 1991).

personal networks, though it has important benefits, also constrains the growth of firms, especially in technologically advanced industries. And reliance on relationships rather than rules fosters corruption, a phenomenon not limited to Confucian countries but apparent in them. Is "shared growth" an expression of Confucian values? It is consistent with them, but other influences were events that destroyed established interests, the motivation of leaders to exclude alternative power centers, and the need for social cohesion in the face of serious external threats.

Learning. Growth accounting estimates attribute varying proportions (20–60 percent) of the increased output between 1960 and 1985 in eight of East Asian high-performing countries to increased human capital. Countries that had primary- and secondary-school enrollment rates above the worldwide norm for their incomes at an earlier date grew faster later than those with lower initial levels; the high-growth East Asian countries had done just that, and they also spent smaller shares of their education budgets on higher education and larger ones on primary and secondary schooling.

Williamson asks: "What attributes of earlier economic and social history explain the above average commitment of some countries to human resource development, like schooling, and the below average commitment in others?"[32] Is it simply a cultural value or are there other explanations, such as the aim of achieving a more equal income distribution? Japan, Thailand, Korea (then a colony of Japan), and the Philippines increased their primary-school enrollment rates more rapidly after 1900 than almost all the developing nations in the twentieth century. Williamson reports that the East Asian countries have always invested more (South Korea, Japan, and Taiwan far more) and Latin America less in secondary education than other countries for which data are available. For example, South Korea had a far higher secondary-school enrollment rate than Brazil in the early 1970s when Brazil's income was higher and its teachers less well paid than Korea's (implying a lower cost of schooling). The difference seems to stem from much greater income inequality in Brazil and an unexplained factor that can be called a "cultural bias" *against* education in Brazil larger than a bias *favoring* education in Korea.[33]

32. Williamson, p. 131.
33. Ibid., p. 157.

The attitude toward basic education reflects deeply held values. Basic education was available through temple schools in the Tokugawa era and Japan had one of the world's highest levels of literacy in 1868. Education thereafter received high national priority so that by 1950, the average farm worker had seven years of schooling and the average manufacturing worker had ten years; the high quality of manpower contributed greatly to Japan's postwar success. When the Chinese moved to the Straits Settlements they promptly created schools. In colonized Korea, more than 50 percent of primary-age children were attending school by the mid-1940s, and by the 1950s South Korea had a literacy rate equal to that of Japan. China, the source of the Confucian ethic, was an exception; in spite of the traditional high standing of education, China's schooling level at the beginning of the postwar era was among the lowest in Asia—a result in part of the traditional attitude toward schooling for children of the elite to ready them for the civil service examinations.

Literacy in the Philippines (influenced by the American push for education) at the beginning of World War II at 60 percent was probably the highest in Asia after Japan. Malaysia was not far behind (at 58 percent in 1960), owing largely to Chinese private education. Thailand's literacy was at about the same level as Malaysia's (58 percent), in this case because of the efforts of Buddhist priests and government public schools beginning in the 1880s; there, "in the 1930s the Japanese system of moral and vocational education was brought in to inculcate the duties and responsibilities of citizenship—patriotism and national solidarity."[34] By 1940, Thailand had rapidly rising primary enrollments although it lagged later in secondary education. In contrast, the Dutch in Indonesia, like the British in Malaysia, did little for public education.

After World War II, unlike many nations elsewhere, all Asian countries emphasized primary and secondary education over tertiary education until development was well advanced. There is also much private spending on schooling, quite significantly in Korea, and Korea too, unlike many developing countries, invested in schooling in rural areas, a policy that helped equalize incomes, and in the education of girls as well as boys.

Women's education is especially beneficial in several ways: in the labor market, in helping to reduce birthrates, and in the development

34. Harry T. Oshima, *Strategic Processes in Monsoon Asia's Economic Development* (Baltimore: Johns Hopkins University Press, 1993).

of children. In 1960, females in the eight East Asia countries had one-half as many years of education as males (far behind Latin America's 80 percent, but far ahead of South Asia's 30 percent). The female-male ratio had narrowed by 1985 to 70 percent, a larger change than in any other region.

Table 1 shows that the educational attainments of the Confucian nations in 1960 were in the middle range of all regions/civilizations, a high level given their low incomes at that time. They then increased these attainments by more than any other group of countries defined broadly by culture, by nearly three years, between 1960 and 1985. Such results, together with the observation that non-wealthy Japanese, Korean, and Chinese families often pay for extra schooling for their children and in many other ways encourage their children's education, suggest systemic differences among cultures. This shows up at home. Mothers' estimates of the time spent on homework by first-graders in Sendai, Japan, were three times as high and for Taipei children seven times as high as for children in Minneapolis. At the fifth grade, the discrepancies were equally dramatic.[35]

Learning goes on at all levels of these societies. Japan from at least the mid-nineteenth century became an avid learning society and the Koreans display a similar capacity. Much knowledge is acquired both

TABLE 1 Average Years of Schooling (Age 25+) in Populations in Seven Regions/"Civilizations," 1960 and 1985

Region/"Civilizations"	*1960*	*1985*
Western European and offshoots	6.5	8.7
Latin American	3.0	4.9
Eastern Orthodox	5.0	7.6
Sub-Saharan Africa	1.3	2.8
Confucian	4.3	7.1
Buddhist	2.6	4.2
Islamic	1.1	3.1
Developing regions' average:	2.9	5.0
Average increase: 2.1 years		

SOURCE: Based on information in Robert J. Barro and Jong-Wha Lee, "International Comparisons of Educational Attainment," *Journal of Monetary Economics* (North Holland) 32 (1993): 383–84.

35. Harold W. Stevenson and James W. Stigler, *The Learning Gap* (New York: Simon & Schuster, 1992), p. 55.

from outside the region and within it: Japanese learning from Americans and Europeans, Koreans learning from Japanese and Americans, Chinese on the mainland learning from many sources, Southeast Asians learning from the Northeast Asians, and so on. In South Korea and Taiwan the proportion of the government elite with advanced degrees from American universities is striking; Indonesia has the famous Berkeley mafia; and Lee Kuan Yew, then called Harry Lee, received a double first at Cambridge.

There is further evidence of East Asia's human capital advantages from tests of achievement and of cognitive skills. Students from this region excel in international comparisons. Mathematics tests of thirteen-year-old children from OECD countries plus South Korea ranked the Korean students ahead of the others. Another comparison ranked Japanese children at the top in mathematics, Hong Kong's in the top half of the distribution, and Thai and Nigerian children near the bottom. Yet another comparison of mathematics achievements put in rank order Chinese, Japanese, Asian-Americans, and Caucasian-Americans.[36] In the United States, Asian-Americans are far overrepresented in many measures of intellectual and professional achievement. These accomplishments are also displayed by the ethnic Chinese in Southeast Asia.

The argument has been advanced that the Confucian peoples are more intelligent, at least as measured in nonverbal tests, notably those that measure visiospatial abilities.[37] However, Chen and Stevenson report finding no significant difference in the intellectual abilities of children in Japan, Taiwan, and the United States, and a comparison of Chinese-Americans and Japanese-Americans with Caucasians shows no significant difference in mean IQs but does show large differences in academic achievements and career choices. One estimate of the degree of overachievement relative to their IQs from these two factors is about 21 points for the Chinese and 10 points for the Japanese; that is, their achievements equal what one would expect if their IQs were higher.[38]

What explains this impetus to achieve? James Flynn conjectures that the Pearl River Delta, the origin of most of his sample of Chinese

36. Chuansheng Chen and Harold W. Stevenson, "Motivation and Mathematics Achievement: A Comparative Study of Asian American, Caucasian American, and East Asian High School Students," *Child Development* 64 (1995): 1215–34.

37. Richard Lynn, "Race Differences in Intelligence: A Global Perspective," *Mankind Quarterly* 31 (1991): 254–96.

38. James R. Flynn, *Asian Americans: Achievement Beyond IQ* (Hillsdale, N.J.: Lawrence Erlbaum, 1991).

in America, was for thousands of years perhaps the most work-intensive environment in the world and traditional China made education the "foundation on which rested the entire political, social, economic, and cultural life of the Chinese people. . . . The traditional Chinese examination system was the only way a village youth could rise to the Mandarin class."[39]

There was a rapid demographic transition in these countries with education playing an important role in it. Between the early 1960s and the 1990s, population growth rates declined from about 2.7 percent annually (aside from Japan) to 0–1 percent for Northeast Asia plus Singapore and in Southeast Asia from 2–3 percent earlier to 1–2.5 percent. "Virtuous circles" were at work.[40] Early high educational levels, including education of females, caused desired family size to decrease; higher incomes enabled more money to be spent on schools; reduced numbers of children enabled more money to be spent per child and allowed more mothers' time per child. All this increased the quality of education, and more equal distribution of income meant that more children, especially in rural areas, could be enrolled. More women entered the market labor force. And given their rapidly growing savings, the demographic transition meant that more physical capital became available per worker.

The ethnic Chinese in Southeast Asia. The role of the ethnic Chinese is similar to that of many outsiders elsewhere, with the one difference that they are much more numerous than others; there are about 30 million ethnic Chinese in Southeast Asia (not including Taiwan and Hong Kong). In Malaysia, the Chinese constitute 35 percent of the population; in Thailand, where they are more assimilated, the standard estimate is 10 percent, and it is 3–4 percent in Indonesia. They dominate commerce and industry; their business acumen, ability to mobilize capital, and networks are highly productive.

Their importance for national performance is difficult to judge given the understandably limited information about their activities in a climate of latent hostility to them—and, as well, the implausibility of any guess at how well the region would have done without their presence. Some facts that help put their contributions into perspective:

39. Ibid.

40. Nancy Birdsall, David Ross, and Richard Sabot, "Inequality and Growth Reconsidered," paper prepared for the annual meeting of the American Economic Association, May 1995.

much of the credit should be given to policies on macroeconomics, agriculture, and education made by leaders who were paying attention to their economic technocrats. This is not to deny the doubtless large contribution of the Chinese. When the international product cycle caused first Japanese businessmen then Koreans and Taiwanese to look for cheaper labor elsewhere, they found it mainly in Southeast Asia, and with the help of Chinese entrepreneurs working in their favor and against labor markets in Brazil, Mexico, and Egypt.

In sum, countries that are providing education universally are laying the basis for more equal incomes, and this will pay off in faster productivity growth and, probably, greater political stability. The growth-negative way, common elsewhere, is to spend much of the nation's educational budget on schooling for a small elite, to tax agriculture, or to adopt policies that (usually unsuccessfully) attempt to tax the rich to give to the poor (which is not an argument against a safety net for the very poor).

GROWTH WITH EQUALITY

All the countries that combined high growth and high income equality from 1965 to 1989 are in East Asia. (Only Malaysia had relatively high inequality.) In Indonesia, the share of the population below a postulated poverty line fell from 60 percent in 1970 to 14 percent in 1993. Taiwan in the 1970s became known for "growth with equity," and the concept of "shared growth" is familiar throughout the region. We have discussed the role of the wide availability of schooling and the relatively favorable treatment accorded agriculture. Hong Kong and Singapore saw to the provision of decent housing. Singapore has been sensitive to ethnic politics from the beginning and helps less productive peoples.

Inequality in outcomes might be the product of several influences: (1) a historically derived distribution of wealth perpetuated in a system of privilege, (2) differences in the distribution of talents as a consequence of class or ethnic discrimination, (3) the product (perhaps unintended) of economic policies.[41] The high concentration of wealth, initially mainly in the form of land, in Latin America and the Philippines contributed to inequalitarian norms, and the pattern of subsidizing higher education, in Latin America as well as in Africa, while neglecting primary schooling reflects the imbalance of wealth. The bias

41. Williamson, p. 144.

against the poor, many of whom are far from the centers of power, carries over from education to income. Landholdings in the rice-growing parts of Asia, by contrast, are typically small; only Malaysia and parts of Indonesia had much plantation agriculture, and even these are diminished owing to wartime devastations and large-scale land redistribution. And redistribution, admittedly a violation of economic freedoms, is often credited with contributing to later successes, and various justifications can be offered. Some of the land had been owned by the dispossessed Japanese. In Taiwan, compensation in the form of equity in state enterprises rose in value, thereby diminishing the scope for grievances. In Malaysia, wealth reallocation worked tolerably well because much of it involved British holdings and because rapid growth was sustained.

Differences in the distribution of talents are familiar—witness the varying tastes for and talents in education. The Chinese throughout Southeast Asia are more enterprising and successful than the non-Chinese, just as the Indians in East Africa do better than the Africans, the Coptic Christians of Egypt better than the Muslims, and Jews better than non-Jews. The Chinese are the commercial capitalists of the region, and their successes, not surprisingly, arouse envy on the part of others. Such differences are not necessarily growth-limiting but they can inspire resentment and violence that is bad for business, although the social consequences in Southeast Asia do not seem to have been great.

The third explanation, economic policies, has particular application in Argentina, Peru, and Chile where populist governments adopted redistributive policies that created distortions and tensions, as opposed to East Asian governments, which took advantage of their abundant production factor in the form of cheap, hard-working, usually docile, labor. Pushing exports increased the demand for workers and helped to narrow income differences. New skills were being learned and worker productivity increased.[42] Such a policy is equalitarian but not redistributive. Countries that, consciously or not, more or less isolated themselves from the world economy perpetuated inequalities.

Evidence has been accumulating that income inequality is bad for growth. In 1960, not only were the countries that were to grow fast well ahead of others in human capital, their inequalities of land and income were much lower than those for a set of comparison countries. One of

42. Birdsall, Ross, and Sabot.

the costs of extreme inequality is the political instability that can spiral into an economic-social seesaw.

> [It] leads to social pressures that governments have attempted to relieve through populist policies. After one or two years of economic expansion inflation soars, real wages fall, unemployment starts to increase, and output declines. The policies prove unsustainable, and the government has to switch to another set of policies. Many countries in the [Latin American] region have suffered this populist cycle, some of them more than once. In East Asia, the situation has been the opposite. A very equitable income distribution has facilitated macroeconomic stability.[43]

Extreme inequality is associated with the absence of a substantial middle class, arguably necessary for sustained progress; and greater equality usually generates less political pressure for wasteful redistribution. In contrast to the view that income differences inexorably widen during early stages of development, Birdsall, Ross, and Sabot have proposed a mechanism by which policies that increase the earning capacity of the poor also increased their productivity and savings and their demand for domestic goods.[44] Moreover, the ownership of land by many smallholders in Korea helped them finance the education of their children and lessened hostility to nearly universally authoritarian regimes.

One of the key distinctions is how greater equality of incomes is achieved, whether through the more even distribution of *opportunity* (for example, to schools or to the judicial system) or through government redistribution of *outcomes* (for example, money incomes). Achieving greater equality by equalizing opportunity is likely to increase the national income and foster social harmony, whereas the latter risks lowering the national income and encouraging social disharmony.

EXTERNAL INFLUENCES

External influences that is, influences from outside—in this context including from outside the region—have been felt for centuries:

43. Felipe Larrain and Rodrigo Vergara, "Investment and Macro-Economic Adjustment: The Case of East Asia," in Luis Serven and Andres Solimano, eds., *Striving for Growth After Adjustment: The Role of Capital Formation* (Washington, D.C.: World Bank, 1993), pp. 259–60; see also Rodrik, "King Kong Meets Godzilla."

44. In "Inequality and Growth Reconsidered" they estimate that the net effect of broadly based educational expansion is to narrow income inequalities, whereas lower inequalities, controlling for the direct effects of education, have a significant effect on growth.

ancient ones from China, those from Spain and America on the Philippines, those of capitalism and democracy from Europe and America, socialism from Europe. Military threats, too, as we have seen, have both motivated governments to develop and increased their political scope for doing so.

The case of Japan. Japan is a notable case of absorbing external influences and, in time, influencing others. The important early influence on Japan was China, mostly via Korea with significant modifications en route, including a written language and the Confucianist ethic. Later, Japan acquired a thin link to modern technology via the Dutch in Nagasaki. This was followed by a reaction against the perceived threat from Europe and America and followed in turn by the adoption, and modification, of many of the institutions of the Western nations.

After World War II, the United States helped during the occupation with economic aid, sound fiscal and monetary policies, land reform, and, inadvertently, through procurements in the Korean War. Nevertheless, Japan's achievements were largely homegrown. Although it continued to acquire much technology from abroad, it demonstrated organizational creativity, including inventing the main bank-*keiretsu* system and just-in-time manufacturing.

Before World War II, Japan had a strong impact on East Asia through its colonial activities. Although those on the receiving end suffered greatly, Korea and Taiwan also benefited from infrastructure, schools, and some (relatively low level) industrial and government experiences. Korea, especially, acquired institutions useful for development, and from 1920 to 1940 Korea was one of the world's most rapidly growing nations; between 1912 and 1945 the number of factory workers rose from 12,000 to 300,000. Park Chung Hee was thoroughly exposed to Japanese ways of doing things and Korea's development strategy became modeled largely on Japan's.[45] Park also became familiar with the American management style while working with the U.S. military.

Though less direct, Japan's influence has been important also in Southeast Asia. Being an occupying power gave the Japanese familiarity with these countries, and their increasing direct investments have had a large impact. A familiar image is that of "flying geese," with Japan in

45. Atul Kohli, "Where Do High Growth Political Economies Come From? The Japanese Lineage of Korea's 'Developmental State,'" *World Development* 22, no. 9 (1994): 1269–93.

the lead; perhaps a more apposite one is of "waves" of development that have moved from northeast to southwest.

Neighborhood effects. Although any developing nation could, in principle, learn from the success of Japan and Korea and Taiwan also, neighboring countries seem to have benefited most. The good performers got on the growth track in sequence, starting in the north and moving south. This process involved nearby countries with many cultural similarities and past interactions (albeit often unwilling ones).

The level of trade within the region is exceptionally high. Any given pair of countries there in 1990 tended to trade over four times more with each other than with otherwise similar countries (allowing for their proximity).[46] This could reflect the fact that manufactured goods are traded mainly through networks rather than mainly through impersonal markets. Networks are most easily formed where trust exists, that is, within families and ethnic groups such as the ethnic Chinese, and they also involve organizations that specialize in bringing buyers and sellers together.

Conclusions

The rise of East Asia can be attributed to the interaction of influences from the distant past with more recent ones. Ancient influences left some legacies, notably a taste for education in the Confucian countries, the movement of millions of ethnic Chinese through Southeast Asia, and perhaps a taste for equality of opportunity, that were good for development later on. Japan entered the modern era with an array of growth-positive institutions. More recent events then provided both motivation and scope for growth-positive policies. External factors of the modern period, including colonialism and the playing out of the rivalry between communist and non-communist powers, have been significant in shaping motivations and directions.

In short, cultures in various forms seem to have had much to do with recent economic success, but their interaction with other factors seems to have been necessary for them to be expressed in a highly positive way.

46. James E. Rauch, "Trade and Search: Social Capital, Sogos Shosa, and Spillovers," National Bureau of Economic Research Working Paper no. 5618, June 1996.

Index